THE BEST OF COUNTRY COOKING

Editor: Linda Piepenbrink
Assistant Editors: Patricia Kishpaugh, Sandy Trzesniewski
Art Directors: Ellen Lloyd, Linda Dzik
Art Associates: Michelle Paul, Julie Wagner
Cover Design: Linda Dzik
Food Editor: Mary Beth Jung
Test Kitchen Assistant: Denise Simeth
Food Photography: Mike Huibregtse; page 29 by Gilo Photography;
page 200 by Photography Unlimited

© 1993, Reiman Publications, L.P.
5400 S. 60th St., Greendale WI 53129
International Standard Book Number: 0-89821-179-4
Library of Congress Catalog Card Number: 93-83133
All rights reserved.
Printed in U.S.A.

TO ORDER additional copies of this book, specify code 11742 and send $24.98 each plus $2.50 postage and handling to: Country Store, Suite 3168, 5925 Country Lane, P.O. Box 990, Greendale WI 53129.

Here's Why It's the *Best* of Country Cooking!

Over the years, we've received many requests to create a cookbook that "combines the very *best* of all the country recipes ever published in your magazines and cookbooks". Talk about a tough task!

After sifting through the thousands of delicious recipes that have appeared in *Country, Country Woman, Reminisce,* and in our popular *A Taste of the Country* cookbooks, we were convinced that this cookbook would have to be *big* to hold the best! The result? Inside *The Best of Country Cooking,* you'll enjoy:

- More than 750 tried-and-true family favorites, with two-thirds of the recipes shown in full color, so you can see exactly what the dish will look like!

- Full chapters for every season, including the "holiday season"!

- Weeks' worth of "Meals in Minutes" menus that can be prepared fast—in half an hour or less!

- Specialties and family favorites of the "Best Cooks in the Country".

- Dozens of proven tips and shortcuts gathered from great country cooks to save you time, money and work in the kitchen!

- Recipes marked with this check ✓ that use less salt, sugar and fat—and include *Diabetic Exchanges.*

- All recipes complete on a page—you never have to stop to turn a page to finish a dish.

- Sturdy hard cover and spiral binding, so this convenient cookbook lies flat on your countertop.

With all those features, you'll be cooking up great country classics in no time! So turn the page and make your next meal your *best*—with *The Best of Country Cooking!*

CONTENTS

*Inside, help yourself to family favorites
for every season and every appetite*

🍂🍂🍂🍂🍂🍂🍂🍂🍂🍂🍂🍂🍂🍂🍂🍂🍂🍂🍂🍂🍂🍂

Pictured on the cover: Clockwise from bottom—Raspberry Glazed Ham (Pg. 77);
Potato Onion Supreme (Pg. 195); Rhubarb Strawberry Pie (Pg. 13); Oatmeal Rolls (Pg. 261).

Spring

SPRING SENSATIONS: Clockwise from lower left—**Wild Asparagus Quiche** (Pg. 11); **Stir-Fried Chicken Fajitas** (Pg. 11); **Spring Rhubarb Salad** (Pg. 11); **Dilly Casserole Bread** (Pg. 12);

Tickle your taste buds with the unique flavors and textures of the fresh foods of the budding season—spinach, asparagus, rhubarb, radishes and early peas.

Capture the tart taste of rhubarb in a molded salad, a creamy layered dessert for a special occasion or a fresh-baked pudding cake served with vanilla sauce.

Savor spring vegetables in an asparagus quiche, zippy spinach appetizer or dressed-up side dish of garden peas and scallions accompanied by dill-flavored bread.

Then, complete this taste-bud sensation with chicken stir-fried in a quick-and-easy main dish.

Rhubarb Pudding Cake (Pg. 12);
Party Spinach Spread (Pg. 12); **Rhubarb Cream Delight Dessert** (Pg. 12);
French Peas (Pg. 12).

Spring has sprung—and here's a four-star feast to prove it! Each delectable dish features healthy, garden-fresh fruits and vegetables.

Ladle out cups of Cream of Asparagus Soup, a delicate bisque of asparagus and green onion...serve a lovely Layered Spinach Salad... taste a hint of mint in Lamb Chops with Mint Stuffing...and sample Rhubarb/Strawberry Pie for a sweet-tart finish to a fabulous feast.

GLORIOUS GREENS: Clockwise from top—**Layered Spinach Salad** (Pg. 13); **Cream of Asparagus Soup** (Pg. 13); **Lamb Chops with Mint Stuffing** (Pg. 13); **Rhubarb/ Strawberry Pie** (Pg. 13).

MEALS IN MINUTES

IF Barianne Wilson of Falfurrias, Texas had a "theme song", it would likely be *On the Road Again*! Three days a week, this busy young wife of a ranch manager and mother of a 2-year-old drives 120 miles round-trip to teach at her church's preschool.

Sandwiched in between are 40-mile trips to the nearest market. "By the time I get home most days, it's late afternoon," Barianne says. "And that leaves me only about 30 minutes to get a meal on the table."

Making good use of those minutes means using quick-cooking standbys like ground beef and chicken...and reliable recipes like the ones featured here! Barianne shares one of her family's favorite fast menus—Saucy Chicken Strips with Rice Pilaf—along with some time-cutting tips.

"I begin with the flavored rice, since that takes the longest to cook. Then, while the Saucy Chicken Strips simmer, I get the apple topping for the dessert ready to cook."

Next comes a nice green vegetable —often steamed fresh broccoli or zucchini, or canned or frozen whole green beans.

Just before mealtime, Barianne microwaves the dessert topping so that it can cool slightly during the meal. "You can substitute plain yogurt for half the sour cream," she notes. "Either way, it's a tasty finale for a fast meal."

SAUCY CHICKEN STRIPS

    4 skinless chicken breast
      halves
    2 tablespoons butter *or*
      margarine
  1/2 cup chopped onion
  1/2 cup chopped green pepper
    1 can (4 ounces) sliced
      mushrooms, drained
    1 package (1-1/4 ounces)
      onion soup mix
1-1/4 cups water
    1 tablespoon Worcestershire
      sauce
    1 tablespoon cornstarch
    3 tablespoons water

Cut chicken breasts in 2-in. x 1/2-in. diagonal strips. Melt butter in a large skillet; add chicken and brown on all sides. Remove chicken from skillet, reserving drippings. Add onion, green pepper and mushrooms; saute until crisp-tender. Return chicken to skillet. In a small bowl, combine soup mix, water and Worcestershire sauce; mix well and pour over chicken. Cover. Reduce heat; simmer for 10 minutes. Remove chicken to a warm platter. Combine cornstarch and water; add to sauce. Boil 1 minute or until thick. Pour sauce over chicken. **Yield:** 4 servings.

RICE PILAF

2-1/2 cups chicken broth
    1 teaspoon dried parsley
      flakes *or* fresh minced
      parsley
    2 tablespoons butter *or*
      margarine
    1 cup uncooked long-grain rice

Combine broth, parsley and butter in a saucepan; bring to boil. Stir in rice; cover. Reduce heat; simmer 20 minutes. **Yield:** 4 servings.

APPLE CREAM CUPS

Vanilla ice cream
Chopped peanuts, optional
TOPPING:
  3/4 cup chopped peeled apple
    1 tablespoon water
    1 cup packed brown sugar
    1 cup (8 ounces) sour cream *or*
      1/2 cup sour cream plus 1/2
      cup plain yogurt
  1/4 teaspoon ground cinnamon

Combine apple and water in a small saucepan or glass bowl. Cover; cook on stove-top or microwave until water boils. Stir in remaining topping ingredients; cook until sugar melts, stirring once. Let cool slightly; serve warm over ice cream. Top with peanuts, if desired. **Yield:** 4 servings.

REAL "SOFTIES": Soften brown sugar by placing a piece of bread or an apple slice in the bag and closing it tightly. The sugar will draw moisture from the bread or fruit and become soft again.

● To soften cookies that have gotten too crisp for your liking, put them in a plastic bag with a piece of bread. The next morning you'll have soft cookies again!

Flavorful pork is the perfect palate-pleaser, whether you're planning a family picnic in the park or cooking dinner for Sunday company. These four dishes are sure to be winners with everyone who tastes them.

Who could resist a juicy slab of Indonesian-Style Pork Roast, a hot Ham and Vegetable Roll-Up, a mouth-watering Marinated Pork Tenderloin Sandwich or a hearty scoop of Hamslaw Salad? Again and again, pork proves to be a versatile meat that's delicious to eat!

PRIME PORK: Clockwise from top— **Marinated Pork Tenderloin Sandwich** (Pg. 14); **Ham and Vegetable Roll-Ups** (Pg. 14); **Hamslaw Salad** (Pg. 14); **Indonesian-Style Pork Roast** (Pg. 15).

TOMATO/SAUSAGE POLENTA

Carol Mead, Los Alamos, New Mexico

- 1 medium onion, chopped
- 1 garlic clove, minced
- 1/2 pound bulk pork sausage
- 1 can (16 ounces) tomatoes with juice, cut up
- 1 can (8 ounces) tomato sauce
- 1/2 teaspoon oregano
- 1/4 teaspoon salt
- 1/2 cup grated Parmesan cheese
- 1/2 cup all-purpose flour
- 1/2 cup cornmeal
- 2 tablespoons sugar
- 2 teaspoons baking powder
- 1/4 teaspoon salt
- 1 egg
- 1/2 cup milk
- 2 tablespoons vegetable oil
- 1 cup (4 ounces) shredded cheddar cheese

Brown onion, garlic and sausage together until sausage shows no pink; drain off grease. Add tomatoes, tomato sauce, oregano and salt; simmer, uncovered, for 5 minutes. Set aside. In a small bowl, stir together the Parmesan cheese, flour, cornmeal, sugar, baking powder and salt. Mix together egg, milk and oil; stir into dry ingredients just until mixed. Pour batter into greased 9-in.-square pan. Carefully pour tomato mixture over batter. Bake at 400° for 20-25 minutes until golden. Sprinkle with the cheddar cheese. **Yield:** 6 servings.

SUPER NACHO APPETIZER

Connie Bolton, San Antonio, Texas

- 1/2 pound ground beef
- 1/2 pound chorizo (Mexican sausage)
- 1 can (31 ounces) refried beans
- 1 can (4 ounces) diced green chilies, drained
- 3 cups (12 ounces) shredded cheddar cheese
- 3/4 cup bottled taco sauce
- 1 cup (8 ounces) sour cream
- 1 medium tomato, chopped
- 1/2 cup pimiento-stuffed green olives, sliced
- Additional cheese for garnish
- **GUACAMOLE:**
- 3 large ripe avocados
- 1 tablespoon fresh lemon juice
- 1/4 teaspoon garlic salt

Brown meats together; drain well. Layer the meat mixture, beans, chilies, cheese and taco sauce in 13-in. x 9-in. x 2-in. greased baking pan. Bake at 400° for 20 minutes. For guacamole, peel and pit avocados and mash with lemon juice and garlic salt. Remove nacho mixture from oven; let cool about 5 minutes. Top with layers of guacamole, sour cream, tomato, olives and cheese. Serve with tortilla chips. **Yield:** 30 appetizer servings.

SPRING RHUBARB SALAD

Joy Hansmeier, Waukon, Iowa

(PICTURED ON PAGE 6)

- 4 cups diced fresh rhubarb
- 1-1/2 cups water
- 1/2 cup sugar
- 1 package (6 ounces) strawberry-flavored gelatin
- 1 cup orange juice
- 1 teaspoon grated orange rind
- 1 cup sliced fresh strawberries

Combine rhubarb, water and sugar in saucepan. Cook and stir over medium heat until rhubarb is tender. Remove from heat; add gelatin and stir until dissolved. Add orange juice and rind. Chill until syrupy. Add strawberries. Pour into 6-cup mold; chill until set. **Yield:** 8-10 servings.

STIR-FRIED CHICKEN FAJITAS

Arlyn Kramer, El Campo, Texas

(PICTURED ON PAGE 6)

 This tasty dish uses less sugar, salt and fat. Recipe includes *Diabetic Exchanges.*

- 4 boneless skinless chicken breast halves, cut in thin strips
- 3/4 cup bottled Italian dressing
- 1 small mild onion, sliced and separated into rings
- 1 small green pepper, sliced in strips
- 1 small sweet red pepper, sliced in strips
- 1 small yellow pepper, sliced in strips
- 1 cup sliced fresh mushrooms
- 1/2 teaspoon garlic salt
- 2 tablespoons fresh lemon *or* lime juice
- Salt and pepper to taste
- Flour tortillas
- Picante sauce
- Sour cream

In a heavy plastic bag, combine chicken strips and dressing; refrigerate for several hours or overnight, turning bag occasionally. Drain juice. Heat a 12-in. non-stick skillet over medium-high; stir-fry chicken strips and onion for 2 minutes. Add pepper strips and mushrooms; stir-fry until chicken is done and peppers are crisp-tender. Season with garlic salt, lemon juice and salt and pepper. Serve in warm tortillas. Top with picante sauce and sour cream. **Yield:** 4 servings. **Diabetic Exchanges:** One serving equals 3 protein, 1 vegetable, 1 bread; also, 326 calories, 694 mg sodium, 78 mg cholesterol, 21 gm carbohydrate, 29 gm protein, 14 gm fat.

WILD ASPARAGUS QUICHE

Mary Weaver, Glenwood Springs, Colorado

(PICTURED ON PAGE 6)

CRUST:
- 1 cup all-purpose flour
- 1/2 cup vegetable shortening
- 1 teaspoon salt
- 1/4 cup ice water
FILLING:
- 1-1/2 cups low-fat small curd cottage cheese
- 2 tablespoons all-purpose flour
- 4 eggs
- 2 cups low-fat milk
- 1 teaspoon Dijon mustard
- Dash hot pepper sauce
- 2 cups sliced fresh wild asparagus (cut in 1/2-inch pieces)
- 2/3 cup shredded Swiss cheese
- Paprika

For crust, combine flour, shortening and salt; mix to a "crumb" consistency. Add ice water; mix well and form dough into ball. On floured board, roll out dough to fit 10-inch quiche pan. Place dough in pan; prick bottom with fork. Bake at 350° for 15 minutes. Cool. For filling, combine in blender cottage cheese, flour, eggs, milk, mustard and hot pepper sauce; blend until smooth. Pour into crust. Arrange asparagus evenly over filling. Sprinkle with Swiss cheese and paprika. Bake at 375° for 25 minutes or until knife comes out clean when inserted near center. **Yield:** 6 servings.

ODOR EATER: Eliminate cooking odors by boiling a tablespoon of vinegar mixed with a cup of water. That's it!

FRENCH PEAS

Ann Nace, Perkasie, Pennsylvania

(PICTURED ON PAGE 7)

✓ This tasty dish uses less sugar, salt and fat. Recipe includes *Diabetic Exchanges*.

2 green onions, diced
1 cup finely shredded lettuce
1 tablespoon vegetable oil
1 teaspoon all-purpose flour
1/4 cup water
1 package (10 ounces) frozen *or* fresh peas, cooked
1 can (8 ounces) sliced water chestnuts, drained
Dash black pepper

In a saucepan, cook onions and lettuce in oil over low heat for 5 minutes. Set aside. Combine flour with water; add to onion mixture and cook, stirring, until thickened. Add peas, water chestnuts and pepper. Heat through and serve. **Yield:** 8 servings. **Diabetic Exchanges:** One serving equals 1 vegetable, 1/2 fat; also, 54 calories, 48 mg sodium, 0 cholesterol, 8 gm carbohydrate, 2 gm protein, 2 gm fat.

RHUBARB CREAM DELIGHT DESSERT

Eleanor Timmerman, River Falls, Wisconsin

(PICTURED ON PAGE 7)

CRUST:
1 cup all-purpose flour
1/4 cup sugar
1/2 cup butter *or* margarine
RHUBARB LAYER:
3 cups sliced fresh rhubarb (cut in 1/2-inch pieces)
1/2 cup sugar
1 tablespoon all-purpose flour
CREAM LAYER:
12 ounces cream cheese, softened
1/2 cup sugar
2 eggs
TOPPING:
1 cup (8 ounces) sour cream
2 tablespoons sugar
1 teaspoon vanilla extract

For crust, mix flour, sugar and butter; pat into 10-in. pie plate. Set aside. For rhubarb layer, combine rhubarb, sugar and flour; toss lightly and pour into crust. Bake at 375° for about 15 minutes. Meanwhile, prepare cream layer by beating together cream cheese and sugar until fluffy. Beat in eggs one at a time, then pour over hot rhubarb layer. Bake at 350° for about 30 minutes or until al-

most set. Combine topping ingredients; spread over hot layers. Chill. **Yield:** 12-16 servings.

PARTY SPINACH SPREAD

Marie Macy, Fort Collins, Colorado

(PICTURED ON PAGE 7)

1 package (10 ounces) frozen chopped spinach
1/3 cup fresh parsley, stems trimmed and discarded
2 tablespoons chopped onion
1 teaspoon salt
1 teaspoon ground black pepper
1/2 cup mayonnaise

Thaw spinach and drain thoroughly, squeezing out extra liquid. Wash parsley; pat dry on paper towel. In a food processor, chop the parsley using steel blade. Add spinach and remaining ingredients; pulse until combined. Store in airtight container in refrigerator. Serve with thin wheat crackers, buttery crackers or celery and cheese sticks. **Yield:** 1-1/2 cups.

RHUBARB PUDDING CAKE

Sharon Merchant, Ithaca, Michigan

(PICTURED ON PAGE 7)

CAKE:
1 cup sugar
1 egg
2 tablespoons butter *or* margarine, melted
1 cup buttermilk *or* sour milk
1/2 teaspoon salt
1/2 teaspoon baking soda
1 teaspoon baking powder
2 cups all-purpose flour
1 cup diced fresh rhubarb
TOPPING:
2 tablespoons margarine, melted
1/2 cup sugar
VANILLA SAUCE:
1/2 to 1 cup sugar
1/2 cup margarine
1/2 cup evaporated milk
1 teaspoon vanilla extract

Blend together sugar, egg and butter. Beat in buttermilk until smooth. Stir together salt, baking soda, baking powder and flour. Stir dry ingredients into buttermilk mixture; mix well. Stir in rhubarb. Pour into a greased 9-in. square baking pan. Combine topping ingredi-

ents; sprinkle on top of batter. Bake at 350° for 45 minutes or until cake tests done. For sauce, mix sugar, margarine and milk; bring to boil and cook 1 minute, stirring constantly. Remove from heat; stir in vanilla. Serve sauce over cake. **Yield:** 12 servings.

DILLY CASSEROLE BREAD

Mrs. Delbert Hull, Spokane, Washington

(PICTURED ON PAGE 7)

✓ This tasty dish uses less sugar, salt and fat. Recipe includes *Diabetic Exchanges*.

1 packet active dry yeast
1/4 cup warm water (110°-115°)
1 cup cottage cheese, lukewarm
2 tablespoons sugar
1 tablespoon instant minced onion
1 tablespoon butter
2 tablespoons dill seed
1 teaspoon salt
1/4 teaspoon baking soda
1 unbeaten egg
2-1/4 to 2-1/2 cups all-purpose flour

Soften yeast in water; set aside. In mixing bowl combine cottage cheese, sugar, onion, butter, dill seed, salt, soda and egg. Mix until blended. Stir in softened yeast. Gradually add flour to form stiff dough. Cover; let rise in warm place for about 1 hour. Stir down dough. Turn into well-greased 8-in. round casserole, about 1- to 1-1/2-qt. size. Let rise 30-40 minutes. Bake at 350° for 35-45 minutes. Brush with additional butter. Cut in wedges to serve. **Yield:** 10 servings. **Diabetic Exchanges:** One serving equals 2 bread, 1/2 fat; also, 181 calories, 319 mg sodium, 34 mg cholesterol, 30 gm carbohydrate, 7 gm protein, 3 gm fat.

BAKING WITH BISCUITS: Inexpensive canned biscuits can be used in a variety of ways:
- Cut a hole in the middle and deep-fry them in fat for doughnuts.
- Flatten them for mini pizza crusts.
- Stretch and wrap them around wieners and bake.
- Make cheesy snack crackers by adding 1/2 cup shredded sharp cheese to one can of biscuits, rolling the dough thin, cutting it into small squares, and baking them until crisp.
- For delicious tea biscuits, flatten them, spread with butter, then sprinkle with sugar and cinnamon and bake.

LAYERED SPINACH SALAD

Connie Blommers, Pella, Iowa

(PICTURED ON PAGE 8)

1/2 to 3/4 pound fresh spinach
1/2 medium cucumber, thinly sliced
1/2 cup thinly sliced radishes
1/4 cup thinly sliced green onions
2 hard-cooked eggs, sliced
3/4 cup ranch-style salad dressing
5 slices bacon, crisply fried and crumbled
1/2 cup Spanish peanuts

Remove and discard spinach stems. Rinse leaves well; drain and pat dry. Tear into bite-size pieces and arrange in a salad bowl. Evenly layer cucumber slices, radishes, green onions and eggs on top of spinach. Spread dressing over top; do not mix. Cover; chill up to 24 hours. Just before serving, sprinkle with bacon and peanuts. **Yield:** 6 servings.

RHUBARB/ STRAWBERRY PIE

Sandy Brown, Lake Worth, Florida

(PICTURED ON PAGE 8)

1 unbaked deep-dish pie shell
Enough pie dough for a lattice crust
FILLING:
3 cups sliced fresh rhubarb (cut in 1/4-inch pieces)
3 cups sliced fresh strawberries
1/2 to 3/4 cup sugar
1-1/2 tablespoons instant tapioca
1/3 cup fresh orange juice
1-1/2 tablespoons orange marmalade, optional
1/4 teaspoon orange peel

Combine filling ingredients in large mixing bowl; let stand for 15 minutes while tapioca softens. Pour filling into pie shell. Prepare lattice strips for top crust. Bake at 400° for 20 minutes; reduce heat to 375° and bake 30 minutes more or until rhubarb is tender. **Yield:** 6-8 servings.

RHUBARB BREAD

Grace Capen, Sacramento, California

1-1/3 cups packed brown sugar
2/3 cup vegetable oil
1 egg, beaten
1 teaspoon vanilla extract
1 cup buttermilk or soured milk
2-1/2 cups all-purpose flour
3/4 teaspoon salt
1/2 teaspoon cinnamon
1 teaspoon baking soda
1-1/2 to 2 cups finely diced rhubarb (1/4-inch cuts)
1/2 cup nuts, chopped

Mix together sugar and oil; blend in egg, vanilla and milk. In separate bowl, combine flour, salt, cinnamon and baking soda; add to moist ingredients. Stir in rhubarb and nuts. Divide batter between two well-greased 8-in. x 4-in. loaf pans. Bake at 350° for about 45 minutes or until bread tests done with wooden pick. Turn out onto rack to cool. **Yield:** 2 loaves.

LAMB CHOPS WITH MINT STUFFING

Ione Banks, Jefferson, Oregon

(PICTURED ON PAGE 8)

1/4 cup chopped onion
1/4 cup chopped celery
1/2 cup butter or margarine
2/3 cup chopped and packed fresh mint leaves
4 cups torn white or brown bread (3/4-inch pieces)
Salt and pepper to taste
1 egg, beaten
8 shoulder lamb chops
4 teaspoons creme de menthe, optional

Saute onion and celery in butter. Stir together with mint and bread pieces. Season with salt and pepper. Add egg; mix lightly. Place lamb in a shallow baking dish; brush with creme de menthe, if desired. Pile stuffing on top of chops. Bake at 350° for 1 hour. **Yield:** 8 servings.

CREAM OF ASPARAGUS SOUP

Westelle Griswa, Monroe, Connecticut

(PICTURED ON PAGE 8)

4 cups sliced fresh asparagus (cut in 1/2-inch pieces)
2 cups water, divided
5 tablespoons butter
1/4 cup very finely diced green onion or 1 teaspoon onion powder
5 tablespoons all-purpose flour
1/2 to 1 teaspoon salt
1/4 teaspoon white pepper
4 cups milk
1 tablespoon chicken bouillon granules

Cook asparagus in 1 cup water until crisp-tender. Drain, reserving liquid. Saute onion in butter until transparent. Stir in flour, salt and pepper; cook over medium heat, stirring constantly, for 1 minute. Gradually stir in milk, 1 cup water, reserved liquid and bouillon granules. Cook, stirring with wire whisk, until mixture is thickened and hot. Stir in asparagus. Heat through and serve. **Yield:** 6 servings.

GRANDMA'S PEA SOUP

Carole Talcott, Dahinda, Illinois

1/2 pound dried whole peas
1/2 pound dried split peas
1 ham bone
3 quarts water
1 large onion, chopped
1 carrot, chopped
2 celery stalks, chopped
Leaves from 6 celery stalks, chopped
1 teaspoon bouquet garni (mixed herbs)
1 tablespoon minced fresh parsley
1 bay leaf
1 teaspoon salt
1/4 teaspoon pepper
1/2 pound smoked cooked Thuringer, chopped, optional
SPAETZLE DUMPLINGS:
1 cup all-purpose flour
1 egg, beaten
1/3 cup water

Cover peas with water and soak overnight. Drain, rinse and place in a Dutch oven or soup kettle. Add ham bone, water and all remaining ingredients except Thuringer and dumplings. Cover and simmer over low heat 2 to 2-1/2 hours. Remove ham bone, skim any fat, and cut and dice remaining meat from bone. Add ham and Thuringer, if desired, to kettle. To prepare dumplings, put flour in a small bowl; make a depression in the center of the flour; add egg and water. Mix until smooth. Place a colander with 3/16-in.-diameter holes over simmering soup; pour batter into the colander and press through with a wooden spoon. Cook, uncovered, 10-15 minutes. Remove bay leaf. **Yield:** 4 quarts. **If Cooking for Two:** Prepare soup without dumplings and freeze in serving-size portions to enjoy for months to come.

13

HAMSLAW SALAD

Marian Tammany, Sparks, Nevada

(PICTURED ON PAGE 10)

1 cup cooked diced ham
2 cups shredded cabbage
DRESSING:
1/2 cup sour cream
2 tablespoons honey
1 to 2 tablespoons Dijon
   mustard
1/4 cup finely chopped green
   onion, *divided*
1/2 cup toasted broken pecans

In a small bowl, combine dressing ingredients except for 1 tablespoon of green onion and the pecans. Mix well; cover; chill. Toss together ham and cabbage; add dressing, stirring gently to coat. Just before serving, sprinkle with reserved green onion and pecans. **Yield:** 4-6 servings.

HAM AND VEGETABLE ROLL-UPS

Jody Steinke, Nekoosa, Wisconsin

(PICTURED ON PAGE 10)

2 cups seasoned croutons
1/4 cup melted butter *or* margarine
1 can (10-3/4 ounces) cream of
   chicken soup, undiluted
1 cup mayonnaise
2 tablespoons lemon juice
1 package (10 ounces) frozen
   chopped spinach, thawed and
   drained
1/3 cup plain yogurt *or* sour cream
1 teaspoon instant minced
   onion
1 teaspoon Worcestershire
   sauce
8 thin slices boiled ham
8 spears fresh asparagus
1/2 pound fresh mushrooms,
   sliced crosswise
2 tablespoons butter *or*
   margarine

Mix the croutons with melted butter; spread in bottom of 9-in. baking dish. Combine soup, mayonnaise and lemon juice. Spoon half of mixture over croutons; set remainder aside. Mix together spinach, yogurt or sour cream, onion and Worcestershire. Spread spinach mixture on each ham slice. Place an asparagus spear on top; roll up. Place rolls seam side down in baking dish; spoon remaining sauce over top. Saute mushrooms in 2 tablespoons butter; spoon on top. Bake at

350° for 25 minutes or until bubbly. **Yield:** 4-6 servings.

MARINATED PORK TENDERLOIN SANDWICH

Alice Gregory, Overland Park, Kansas

(PICTURED ON PAGE 10)

✓ This tasty dish uses less sugar, salt and fat. Recipe includes *Diabetic Exchanges.*

1 whole pork tenderloin (1 pound)
24 small dinner *or* Parkerhouse
   rolls, warmed
MARINADE:
1/2 cup soy sauce
1/4 cup packed brown sugar
2 tablespoons vegetable oil
1 teaspoon ground ginger
1/2 teaspoon dry mustard
2 garlic cloves, minced

In a shallow 1-1/2-qt. glass baking dish, mix marinade ingredients. Place tenderloin in dish; turn to coat surface. Cover and refrigerate for 12 hours or overnight, turning several times. Drain, reserving marinade for grilling. Grill tenderloin over hot coals or gas grill on medium-high, brushing occasionally with marinade. Grill *each side* about 6 minutes for medium-well, or 7 to 8 minutes per side for well-done. Let stand for 10 minutes; carve in thin slices and serve on rolls. (Alternate cooking method: Bake tenderloin in 375° oven until meat thermometer registers 160°. Let stand for 10 minutes; carve in thin slices. Combine 1/4 cup reserved marinade and 1 cup water. Heat in chafing dish; add pork slices.) **Yield:** About 24 small sandwiches. **Diabetic Exchanges:** One serving equals 1 protein, 1 fruit; also, 112 calories, 435 mg sodium, 22 mg cholesterol, 13 gm carbohydrate, 7 gm protein, 4 gm fat.

BLUEBERRY/ORANGE MUFFINS

Irene Parry, Kenosha, Wisconsin

1 cup quick-cooking rolled oats
1 cup orange juice
1 teaspoon grated orange zest
1 cup vegetable oil
3 eggs, beaten
3 cups all-purpose flour
1 cup sugar
4 teaspoons baking powder
1 teaspoon salt
1/2 teaspoon baking soda

3 to 4 cups fresh blueberries
TOPPING:
1/2 cup finely chopped nuts
3 tablespoons sugar
1/2 teaspoon cinnamon

Mix oats, orange juice and zest; blend in oil and eggs; set aside. Stir together flour, sugar, baking powder, salt and baking soda. Add oat mixture; mix lightly. Fold in blueberries. Spoon batter into paper-lined muffin tins, filling two-thirds full. Combine topping ingredients; sprinkle over batter. Bake at 400° for about 15-18 minutes or until lightly browned. **Yield:** 24 large muffins.

BROADWAY BROWNIE BARS

Anne Frederick, New Hartford, New York

1 package (8 ounces) cream
   cheese, *divided*
1-1/2 cups sugar, *divided*
1 cup plus 2 tablespoons
   all-purpose flour, *divided*
1 cup butter *or* margarine,
   softened, *divided*
3 eggs, *divided*
2-1/2 teaspoons vanilla extract,
   divided
2 squares (1 ounce *each*)
   unsweetened chocolate,
   divided
1-1/4 cups chopped walnuts,
   divided
1 teaspoon baking powder
1 cup semisweet chocolate chips
2 cups miniature marshmallows
1/4 cup milk
3 cups confectioners' sugar

In a small mixing bowl, blend 6 ounces cream cheese, 1/2 cup sugar, 2 tablespoons flour, 1/4 cup butter, 1 egg and 1/2 teaspoon vanilla; set aside. In medium saucepan, over medium heat, melt 1 square chocolate and 1/2 cup butter. Remove from heat; add 1 cup sugar, 1 cup flour, 1 cup nuts, baking powder, 1 teaspoon vanilla and 2 eggs; blend well. Spray 13-in. x 9-in. x 2-in. pan with no-stick cooking spray; spread batter in pan. Spread cheese mixture over batter. In small bowl, combine 1/4 cup nuts and the chocolate chips; sprinkle over cheese layer. Bake at 350° for about 28 minutes or until almost done. Sprinkle marshmallows over all; return to oven for 2 minutes. In medium saucepan, melt 1/4 cup butter, 1 square chocolate, 2 ounces cream cheese and milk. Remove from heat; stir in confectioners' sugar and 1 teaspoon vanilla. Immediately drizzle over marshmallows. Chill well; cut into bars. **Yield:** 30 bars.

DIRT CAKE

Flo Burtnett, Gage, Oklahoma

- 1 package (16 ounces) Oreo cookies
- 1 package (8 ounces) cream cheese
- 1/2 cup margarine
- 1 cup confectioners' sugar
- 1 teaspoon vanilla extract
- 2 packages (3-1/2 ounces *each*) instant vanilla pudding
- 3 cups milk
- 1 container (12 ounces) nondairy whipped topping
- 2 new clay flowerpots, about 6 inches in diameter
- Heavy-duty aluminum foil
- Silk flowers
- Plastic garden utensils, optional

Line flower pots completely with foil; set aside. Crush cookies until they resemble potting soil. Place 1 cup crumbs (or more) in each flowerpot; set aside. Cream the cheese, margarine, sugar and vanilla together until blended; set aside. Combine pudding mix and milk fold in whipped topping. Gently fold cheese and pudding mixtures together. Pour half the mixture into each flowerpot. Top with remaining cookie crumbs. Cover with foil; refrigerate. When ready to serve, remove foil; top with silk or plastic flowers whose stems have been wrapped in foil. Display with plastic gardening tools, if desired. **Yield:** 12 servings.

LEMON RICOTTA CHEESECAKE SQUARES

Mrs. Glenn Holcomb, Tarrington, Connecticut

- 2 pounds ricotta cheese
- 3/4 cup sugar
- 3 eggs, slightly beaten
- Grated rind of 1 to 2 lemons
- 1 package (18-1/4 ounces) lemon cake mix with pudding
- 1/4 cup fresh lemon Juice
- Confectioners' sugar

Combine ricotta, sugar, eggs and lemon rind; set aside. In another bowl, mix cake mix according to package directions, *substituting lemon juice* for 1/4 cup of the water called for. Pour batter into greased and floured 13-in. x 9-in. x 2-in. baking pan; spoon ricotta mixture carefully on top. Bake at 350° for 60-65 minutes or until lightly browned. Cool cake. Store in refrigerator 4 hours before serving. Sift confectioners' sugar over top before cutting into squares. Serve chilled; refrigerate leftovers. **Yield:** 16-20 servings.

APPLE CAKE WITH LEMON SAUCE

Jean Camp, North Olmsted, Ohio

CAKE:
- 3 eggs
- 1-3/4 cups sugar
- 1 cup vegetable oil
- 1 teaspoon vanilla extract
- 2 cups all-purpose flour
- 1 teaspoon baking soda
- 1 teaspoon cinnamon
- 1 teaspoon salt
- 2 cups sliced peeled apples (cut in 1/2-inch pieces)
- 1 cup pecans, chopped
- 1 cup seedless raisins

LEMON SAUCE:
- 1 large lemon
- 2 egg yolks
- 1 cup sugar
- 2-1/2 tablespoons cornstarch
- 1/2 teaspoon salt
- 1-1/2 cups water
- 4 teaspoons butter *or* margarine

For cake, beat eggs; add sugar, oil and vanilla. In separate bowl, mix flour, soda, cinnamon and salt. Add flour mixture to egg mixture all at once; blend and stir. Add apples, nuts and raisins to mixture; blend well. Pour batter into a well-greased 11-in. x 7-in. x 2-in. pan (13-in. x 9-in. x 2-in. pan may be used; decrease baking time by 15-20 minutes). Bake at 375° for 55 minutes, or until cake tests done when wooden pick is inserted in center. For sauce, grate peel from lemon; measure out 1-1/2 teaspoons rind. Squeeze lemon; measure 3 tablespoons juice. Set aside. Beat egg yolks lightly; set aside. In a separate bowl, blend sugar, cornstarch and salt. Measure water into saucepan; gradually stir in sugar mixture. Cook, stirring, until mixture boils clear and thickens. Remove from heat. Beat small amount of hot mixture into egg yolks. Return yolk mixture to saucepan; cook and stir about 2 minutes. Remove from heat; add lemon rind, juice and butter. Pour sauce over cake. **Yield:** 20-24 servings.

INDONESIAN-STYLE PORK ROAST

Alice Vidovich, Walnut Creek, California

(PICTURED ON PAGE 10)

- 1 boneless pork loin roast (2 pounds)

COATING:
- 1/4 cup creamy peanut butter
- 3 tablespoons soy sauce
- 2 tablespoons ground coriander
- 1-1/2 teaspoons ground cumin
- 1/2 teaspoon chili powder
- 1 large garlic clove, minced
- 1 tablespoon lemon juice

PEANUT SAUCE:
- 1 cup soy sauce
- 2 tablespoons pineapple juice
- 1 garlic clove, minced
- 1/4 cup dry sherry, optional
- 1/2 teaspoon minced fresh gingerroot
- 1/2 cup chopped unsalted peanuts

Combine coating ingredients in a bowl; mix until smooth. Rub coating over all exposed surfaces of the roast; let stand for 30 minutes. Place roast in greased baking dish; bake at 325° until meat thermometer inserted in center registers 160° (about 75 to 90 minutes). To make sauce, combine all ingredients except peanuts in saucepan; bring to boil. Let cool; add peanuts. Set aside. Remove roast from oven; let rest 15 minutes. Slice into serving portions and serve with sauce. **Yield:** 6 servings.

MORNING GLORY MUFFINS

Paddy Webber, Exeter, Ontario

- 2 cups all-purpose flour
- 1-1/4 cups sugar
- 2 teaspoons baking soda
- 2 teaspoons cinnamon
- 1/2 teaspoon salt
- 2 cups grated carrots
- 1/2 cup raisins
- 1/2 cup shredded coconut
- 1/2 cup chopped pecans
- 3 eggs
- 1 cup vegetable oil
- 1 apple, cored and shredded
- 2 teaspoons vanilla extract

In a large mixing bowl, combine flour, sugar, baking soda, cinnamon and salt. Stir in carrot, raisins, coconut and pecans. In a separate bowl, combine eggs, oil, apple and vanilla. Add to flour mixture. Stir only until combined. Spoon into greased or lined muffin tins. Bake at 350° for 15-18 minutes. **Yield:** about 18 muffins.

Pussy willows, daffodils and the first robin are all harbingers of spring, but country cooks look for more savory signs —such as the first red strawberries, leafy spinach, spring "fryer" chickens and garden-fresh asparagus.

Build a springtime celebration around these brunch recipes—the handsome Country Brunch dish... colorful Asparagus Au Gratin... add crunch and color with two unusual fresh spinach salads...try the oven-fried chicken breasts or fruit-based chicken salad...and for a tasty accompaniment, serve hearty oat-orange muffins or truly flaky country biscuits.

SAVORY SPRINGTIME FAVORITES: Clockwise from lower left—**Spinach Orange Salad** (Pg. 23); **Colonel Muncy's Oven-Fried Chicken** (Pg. 23); **Flaky Biscuits** (Pg. 23); **Country Brunch** (Pg. 23); **Oatmeal Orange Bread/Muffins** (Pg. 24); **Asparagus Au Gratin** (Pg. 24); **Spring Strawberry Spinach Salad** (Pg. 24); **Pineapple Chicken Salad** (Pg. 23).

For a tart taste of spring, try rhubarb! Known as "pie plant" in grandmother's day, thanks to frequent appearances in pie fillings, rhubarb is still an all-time country favorite. Rhubarb finds its way into a host of desserts, since the piquant taste of this vegetable-masquerading-as-a-fruit is a delightful contrast for a sweet, crunchy topping...custard filling...melt-in-your-mouth meringue...or moist cake. Give these pie plant favorites a try!

PIE PLANT DESSERTS: Clockwise from lower right—**Rhubarb Crunch** (Pg. 24); **Rhubarb Cream Delight** (Pg. 25); **Rhubarb Custard Pie** (Pg. 25); **Rhubarb Cake** (Pg. 24).

BEST COOK

Debra Dennis
Convent, Louisiana

Food means more than just nourishment for Debra Dennis of Convent, Louisiana—it's part of what keeps her big family so close!

Debra learned to cook as a teenager when her mother became ill. She first cooked for their family of nine, but soon was making meals for workers on the family sugarcane farm, too.

These days, Debra's still a double-duty chef. She cooks every day at her father's house, whips up Cajun feasts for her own family of five...and cooks for big family gatherings each Sunday!

"When Mama died, I wanted to make sure everybody kept coming to Daddy's place on Sundays. So I always made sure they had something to eat," Debra explained.

Her sister, Lisa Rouillier, says Debra's recipes—particularly her original seafood dishes—are always a big hit.

"She has Cajun cooking down pat," Lisa says. "She's a natural cook—she never measures or writes down anything.

"And even though she's cooking and cleaning for two households, this fantastic woman always can whip up a feast for anyone who drops by."

Since Debra's *also* attending school 4 hours a day to become a medical assistant, we wondered whether she ever tires of cooking for a crowd.

"Never," she answered. "This is my hobby—it's what I do for relaxation."

🦐🦐🦐🦐🦐🦐🦐🦐🦐🦐🦐🦐🦐🦐🦐

CAJUN CORN SOUP WITH SHRIMP

   1/2 cup vegetable oil
   1/2 cup all-purpose flour
   1 small onion, chopped
   1/3 cup chopped green onions
   2 quarts hot water *or* heated chicken broth
   2 cans (14-1/2 ounces *each*) stewed tomatoes, cut up
   8 cups cut corn *or* 4 cans (16 ounces *each*) whole-kernel corn, drained
   2 pounds uncooked shrimp, peeled and deveined
Salt and pepper to taste

In a heavy 8-qt. pot, combine oil and flour until smooth. Cook over medium-high heat for 5 minutes, stirring constantly. Reduce heat to medium. Cook and stir about 5 minutes more or until mixture is reddish-brown (the color of a penny). Add onions; cook for 5 minutes, stirring often. Turn heat to high. Add hot water or broth, tomatoes and corn. Bring to boil; reduce heat. Cover and simmer 15 minutes. Add shrimp; simmer about 5 minutes more, until shrimp are done. Season to taste. **Yield:** 12 servings.

🦐🦐🦐🦐🦐🦐🦐🦐🦐🦐🦐🦐🦐🦐🦐

NEW ORLEANS BREAD PUDDING

   5 slices stale white bread
   1 can (12 ounces) evaporated milk
   1/2 cup margarine, softened
1-1/4 cups sugar, *divided*
   3 eggs, *separated*
   1 can (8 ounces) crushed pineapple in juice
   3/4 cup dark raisins
   3/4 cup golden raisins
   1 tablespoon vanilla extract

Tear bread into small pieces; soak in milk for 2 minutes. In a medium mixing bowl, combine margarine, 1 cup sugar and egg yolks. Add bread and milk mixture; stir well. Drain pineapple; reserve juice and set aside 2 tablespoons for the meringue. Add remaining pineapple juice, pineapple, raisins and vanilla to bread mixture; mix gently. Place in 2-qt. casserole dish; bake at 400° for about 40 minutes or until light brown. Meanwhile, prepare meringue by whipping egg whites until soft peaks form; gradually blend in remaining sugar, then reserved pineapple juice. After pudding is baked; spread meringue on top. Return to oven until topping is lightly browned, about 5-7 minutes. **Yield:** 8-10 servings.

🦐🦐🦐🦐🦐🦐🦐🦐🦐🦐🦐🦐🦐🦐🦐

EGGPLANT AND SHRIMP CASSEROLE

   3 medium eggplants (about 2 pounds)
Salt water, optional
   2 tablespoons vegetable oil
   1 large onion, chopped
   1/2 cup chicken broth, optional
   1 pound uncooked shrimp, peeled and deveined
Salt and pepper to taste
Cayenne pepper to taste
   1/2 cup seasoned bread crumbs *or* 1 cup seasoned croutons

Peel eggplants; cut into small cubes. If desired, soak cubes in salt water for 15 minutes; turn under several times. Drain and discard water. In large saucepan or a medium Dutch oven, heat oil over medium-high; add onion. Cook and stir until onion is tender. Add eggplant and chicken broth, if desired; bring to a boil. Reduce heat; cover and simmer for 20 minutes, stirring occasionally. Add shrimp; cook and stir about 10 minutes or until shrimp turns pink. Season to taste. Place in a 2-qt. casserole dish; sprinkle with bread crumbs or croutons. Bake at 350° for 20 minutes. **Yield:** 8 side-dish servings.

🦐🦐🦐🦐🦐🦐🦐🦐🦐🦐🦐🦐🦐🦐🦐

PORK CHOPS AND GRAVY

   8 pork chops (1 inch thick)
Salt and pepper to taste
   1/3 cup vegetable oil, *divided*
   1/2 cup all-purpose flour
   1/2 cup water
   1 large onion, chopped
   1 cup chopped green onions

Trim excess fat from chops; season with salt and pepper. In a large heavy skillet, brown chops in 2 tablespoons oil over medium heat, about 4 minutes per side. Remove. To drippings, add remaining oil and flour; mix until smooth. Cook over medium-high heat 5 minutes, stirring constantly. Reduce heat to medium; cook and stir 5 minutes. Return chops to skillet; add water and onions. Reduce heat to low; simmer 20 minutes or until meat is tender. **Yield:** 8 servings.

Casserloes and *country cooking* are almost interchangeable—what could be heartier fare than a fresh-from-the-oven dish deliciously deep in meat or poultry, cheese, vegetables and sauce?

The dishes featured here provide a full-flavored response to that question! Any of these "classic casseroles" would make a lasting impression at an Easter brunch, as a "dish to pass" at a potluck, or around your table all year!

FOR EASTER...OR ANYTIME: Clockwise from lower left—**Shrimp and Asparagus Casserole** (Pg. 26); **Western Beef and Corn Casserole** (Pg. 26); **Egg Foo Yung Casserole** (Pg. 26); **Chicken Crescent Almondine** (Pg. 27); **Sausage and Rice Casserole** (Pg. 27); **Zippy Baked Carrots** (Pg. 26); **Scalloped Potatoes Etc.** (Pg. 27); **Squash Casserole** (Pg. 26).

eed hearty food in a hurry? Nothing's quicker or easier to prepare than a casserole. These main dishes make marvelous meals for family gatherings, picnics, potlucks or any occasion that calls for flavorful "fast food".

Ham and Asparagus Casserole is a guaranteed crowd-pleaser, and pizza-loving kids go crazy over zesty Zucchini Pizza Casserole. For an international flair, put Chicken Normandy or Italian Heritage Casserole on the table. Prepare any one of these the night before—or freeze it for future use. Either way, you'll be pleased with the results.

DIG IN! Clockwise from top—**Italian Heritage Casserole** (Pg. 27); **Zucchini Pizza Casserole** (Pg. 27); **Chicken Normandy** (Pg. 28); **Ham and Asparagus Casserole** (Pg. 28).

SPINACH ORANGE SALAD

LeMae Weiland, Verona, Wisconsin

(PICTURED ON PAGE 16)

DRESSING:
- 1/4 cup vegetable oil
- 2 tablespoons white sugar
- 2 tablespoons white vinegar
- 1 tablespoon snipped parsley
- 1/2 teaspoon salt
- 1/4 teaspoon black pepper
- Dash Tabasco sauce

SALAD:
- 1/4 cup sliced almonds
- 4 teaspoons white sugar
- Fresh spinach, washed, dried and chilled (enough for 6-8 people)
- 1 cup thin bias-cut celery
- 2 tablespoons chopped green onion tops
- 1 can (11 ounces) mandarin oranges, drained

Combine dressing ingredients; cover. Shake well and refrigerate. Place almonds and sugar in small skillet. Stir over medium heat watching closely until almonds are golden brown. Remove to small bowl; cool. Place spinach in large salad bowl. Add celery, green onion and oranges. At serving time, add dressing and almonds; toss lightly. **Yield:** 6-8 servings.

COLONEL MUNCY'S OVEN-FRIED CHICKEN

Estle Muncy, Jefferson City, Tennessee

(PICTURED ON PAGE 16)

- 10 (24 ounces) chicken breasts
- 2 cups dairy sour cream *or* plain yogurt
- 1/4 cup lemon juice
- 4 teaspoons Worcestershire sauce
- 2 teaspoons celery salt *or* ground celery seed
- 2 teaspoons paprika
- 4 garlic cloves, chopped fine *or* 1/2 teaspoon garlic powder
- 2 teaspoons salt
- 1/2 teaspoon pepper
- 2 teaspoons poultry seasoning
- 2 teaspoons parsley
- 1/2 cup melted margarine
- Corn flake crumbs

Cut chicken breasts in half. Wipe dry; remove skin and excess fat. In large bowl, combine all ingredients except margarine and corn flakes; stir well. Add chicken, making sure each piece is cov-

ered well. Let stand overnight in refrigerator. Remove chicken pieces from mixture; blot off excess with dry towel. Dip each piece in melted margarine, then roll in corn flake crumbs. Place chicken in single layer on shallow baking pan. Sprinkle with additional parsley. Bake at 375° for 25-30 minutes or until chicken tests done. **Yield:** 10 servings.

COUNTRY BRUNCH

Katherine Clauson, Perham, Minnesota

(PICTURED ON PAGE 16)

- 16 slices firm white bread
- 2-1/2 cups cooked, cubed ham, about 1 pound
- 16 ounces cheddar cheese, shredded
- 16 ounces mozzarella cheese, shredded
- 6 eggs
- 3 cups whole milk
- 1/2 teaspoon dry mustard
- 1/8 to 1/4 teaspoon onion powder

TOPPING:
- 3 cups *uncrushed* corn flakes
- 1/2 cup butter, melted

Trim crusts from bread; cut slices in half. Grease a 13-in. x 9-in. x 2-in. baking pan and layer as follows: Cover bottom of pan with one-half of bread, one-half of ham and one-half of each of the cheeses. Repeat layers. Combine eggs, milk and seasonings. Pour over layers; refrigerate overnight. Remove from refrigerator 30 minutes before baking. Combine topping ingredients; sprinkle over casserole. Bake at 375° for 45 minutes (cover loosely with foil to prevent top from over-browning). Let stand 10-15 minutes before cutting into squares. **Yield:** 12-15 servings.

PINEAPPLE CHICKEN SALAD

Maxine Williams, Coulee Dam, Washington

(PICTURED ON PAGE 16)

- 1/2 cup mayonnaise *or* salad dressing
- 2 teaspoons prepared mustard
- 2 cups (12 ounces) cooked chicken, shredded
- 1/2 cup thinly sliced celery
- 1 tablespoon *finely* chopped onion
- 1/2 cup sliced fresh mushrooms
- 1/4 cup chopped green pepper
- 1/4 cup sliced pitted ripe olives
- 1 can (20 ounces) pineapple

chunks *or* tidbits*, drained
- 1 can (11 ounces) mandarin orange sections*, drained
- Lettuce leaves
- Croutons, optional

*Refrigerate drained fruits the night before for a well-chilled salad. In medium mixing bowl, stir together mayonnaise and prepared mustard. Stir in chicken, celery, onion, mushrooms, pepper and olives. Cover; refrigerate for several hours. Just before serving, add drained fruit. Serve on lettuce-lined plates; top with croutons, if desired. **Yield:** 6 servings.

FLAKY BISCUITS

Marie Hattrup, The Dalles, Oregon

(PICTURED ON PAGE 17)

- 2 cups sifted unbleached flour
- 4 teaspoons baking powder
- 3 tablespoons sugar
- 1/2 teaspoon salt
- 1/2 teaspoon cream of tartar
- 1/2 cup butter, chilled
- 3/4 cup milk, room temperature

Sift together into large mixing bowl—flour, baking powder, sugar, salt and cream of tartar. Cut in butter until bits of butter are the size of medium peas. Mix in milk, only until ingredients are blended. *Do not overmix.* Form into a ball; pat out on floured board to 3/4-in. thickness. Cut into biscuits using a 2-1/2-in. biscuit cutter. Place on ungreased cookie sheet or in 13-in. x 9-in. x 2-in. pan. Bake at 475° for 10 minutes or until golden brown. **Yield:** 10 biscuits.

BROCCOLI/CHEESE SOUP

Mrs. Roy Hochstetler West Salem, Ohio

- 2 cups *cooked* noodles
- 1 package (10 ounces) frozen chopped broccoli, thawed
- 3 tablespoons chopped onion
- 2 tablespoons butter
- 1 tablespoon flour
- 2 cups cubed processed cheese
- Salt to taste
- 5-1/2 cups milk

Combine all ingredients in slow cooker; stir to blend. Cook on low for 4 hours. **Yield:** 8 servings.

> **CUTTING ONION:** When slicing, tuck your fingertips under and use your knuckles to guide the knife blade.

23

FAVORITE PIZZA CRUST

Kathleen Miller, Battle Ground, Indiana

1 package (1/4 ounce)
  quick-rise yeast
2 cups warm water
  (110°-115°), *divided*
2 teaspoons salt
2 tablespoons sugar
1/4 cup vegetable oil
1 cup cornmeal
5 cups all-purpose flour,
  divided
**Pizza toppings of choice (sauce,
  meat, vegetables, cheese)**

Dissolve the yeast in 1/4 cup of warm water. In a large mixing bowl, combine yeast mixture with remaining water, salt, sugar, oil, cornmeal and 2 cups flour; mix well. Add enough remaining flour to form a soft dough. Turn out onto a floured surface and knead until smooth and elastic, about 5-6 minutes. Place dough in a greased bowl, turning once to grease top. Cover and let rise in a warm place until doubled, about 30 minutes. Punch the dough down and divide in half. Roll dough into two 16-in. circles; place on greased pizza pans. Top with desired pizza ingredients. Bake at 400° until crust is lightly golden brown, about 15-20 minutes. **Yield:** 2 16-inch pizzas.

ASPARAGUS
AU GRATIN

Deanna House, Portage, Michigan

(PICTURED ON PAGE 17)

1-1/4 pounds fresh asparagus *or* 1
  (10 ounces) package frozen
  asparagus
2 tablespoons butter *or*
  margarine
2 tablespoons chopped onion
2 tablespoons all-purpose flour
1/2 teaspoon salt
1/8 teaspoon ground white pepper
Dash of ground nutmeg *or* mace
2/3 cup chicken broth
1/3 cup half-and-half coffee
  cream
**Toast points, rusks *or* Texas toast
Butter *or* margarine**
1/2 cup (2 ounces) shredded
  cheddar cheese

Clean and cook asparagus in small amount of boiling water (or microwave) until tender crisp, about 3-4 minutes. Drain; set aside. In medium saucepan, melt butter; stir in onion; cook until transparent. Stir in flour, salt, pepper and nutmeg/mace over low heat until

smooth. Stir in broth and cream; cook until thickened, stirring constantly. Set aside. Butter Texas toast, rusks or toast points; place under preheated broiler until golden brown. Remove to 13-in. x 9-in. x 2-in. baking dish. Place asparagus over bread; pour sauce over all. Sprinkle with cheese. Bake at 400° for 8-10 minutes until cheese melts. **Yield:** 4 servings.

SPRING STRAWBERRY
SPINACH SALAD

Marilyn Hency, Tualatin, Oregon

(PICTURED ON PAGE 17)

10 large firm strawberries
1 large bunch spinach
DRESSING:
1/2 cup sugar
1 teaspoon salt
1 teaspoon dry mustard
1/3 cup white wine *or* white
  vinegar
1 cup vegetable oil
1 tablespoon (rounded) poppy
  seeds

Wash, drain and tear spinach into serving-size pieces. Place in large salad bowl; chill. Slice strawberries in half (may also leave whole, if desired). Set aside. Mix dressing ingredients (except poppy seeds) together in blender. Stir in poppy seeds. Just before serving, mix dressing with spinach and strawberries. **Yield:** 4-5 servings.

OATMEAL ORANGE
BREAD/MUFFINS

Julianne Johnson, Grove City, Minnesota

(PICTURED ON PAGE 17)

2 cups all-purpose flour
3/4 cup sugar
4-1/2 teaspoons baking powder
1/2 teaspoon baking soda
1/2 teaspoon salt
1-1/2 cups rolled oats
1 orange, rind and sections
2 eggs, beaten
2 tablespoons butter, melted
1 cup water

Stir together flour, sugar, baking powder, soda, salt and oats; set aside. Mix in 1 tablespoon of additional sugar with grated orange rind and diced sections; set aside. Combine beaten eggs with butter, orange mixture and water. Combine with dry ingredients; stir to blend. Pour into a 1-1/2-qt. greased casserole, 9-in. greased loaf pan or greased muffin tins. Bake casserole or loaf at 350° for

45-55 minutes; muffins for 30 minutes. **Yield:** about 10 servings

RHUBARB CRUNCH

Florence Rasmussen, Amboy, Illinois

(PICTURED ON PAGE 18)

3 cups diced rhubarb
1 cup sugar
3 tablespoons all-purpose flour
TOPPING:
1 cup brown sugar
1 cup old-fashioned rolled oats
1-1/2 cups flour
1/2 cup butter
1/2 cup vegetable shortening

Combine rhubarb, sugar and flour; place in greased 13-in. x 9-in. x 2-in. pan. Combine brown sugar, oats and flour; cut in butter and shortening until crumbly. Sprinkle over rhubarb mixture. Bake at 375° for 40 minutes. Serve warm with ice cream, whipped cream or milk. **Yield:** 10-12 servings.

RHUBARB CAKE

Nancy Moyer, DeRuyter, New York

(PICTURED ON PAGE 18)

1/2 cup softened butter
1-1/2 cups sugar
1 egg
1 cup buttermilk
2 cups flour, unsifted (reserve 2
  tablespoons to mix with
  rhubarb)
1 teaspoon baking soda
1/2 teaspoon salt
1 teaspoon cinnamon
1 teaspoon vanilla extract
2 cups diced rhubarb, fresh *or*
  frozen

Cream together butter, sugar and egg; add buttermilk alternately with combined flour, soda, salt and cinnamon. Mix until smooth. Add vanilla. Toss rhubarb with reserved flour, add to mixture; spread in greased and floured 13-in. x 9-in. x 2-in. cake pan. Bake at 350° for 35 minutes. Serve plain or with whipped cream. **Yield:** 10-12 servings.

SLOW-COOKING TIPS: If there's too much liquid in your cooker, stick a toothpick under the edge of the lid to allow steam to escape.

• Put vegetables into the pot first to form a rack for the meat.

• Add liquids and sauces last in order to moisten the surfaces of vegetables and meat.

RHUBARB CUSTARD PIE

Veronica Nuehalfen, St. Marys, Kansas

(PICTURED ON PAGE 18)

3 cups rhubarb, partially peeled, cut in 1/4-inch pieces
3 tablespoons all-purpose flour, well-rounded
1 cup sugar
1 9-inch unbaked pie shell
3 eggs, *separated*
1 tablespoon thick dairy sour cream

TOPPING:
1-1/2 cups old-fashioned *or* quick-cooking oats
1 cup brown sugar
1/2 teaspoon cinnamon
1/4 cup butter *or* margarine

Place cut rhubarb in large mixing bowl; combine flour and sugar. Add to rhubarb, mix and let stand while preparing the crust. Using your favorite pastry recipe for a single crust pie, make a pie shell with a high fluted edge in order to hold all of the topping. Brush the bottom and sides of crust with egg white from separated egg (prevents crust from becoming soggy). Beat egg yolks and sour cream until thick; add to rhubarb mixture. Pour into pie shell. Combine topping ingredients; spread evenly over pie. Bake at 400° for 10 minutes; reduce heat to 350°; bake 50 minutes more. **Yield:** 8 servings.

RHUBARB CREAM DELIGHT

Judy Jungwirth, Athol, South Dakota

(PICTURED ON PAGE 18)

CRUST:
1-1/2 cups all-purpose flour
3 tablespoons sugar
3/4 cup butter *or* margarine

CREAM FILLING:
2 cups sugar
4 egg yolks, beaten
2/3 cup cream *or* evaporated milk
3 tablespoons flour
1/2 teaspoon nutmeg
4 cups chopped rhubarb

MERINGUE:
4 egg whites
1/4 cup sugar

Combine crust ingredients until crumbly; press into a 13-in. x 9-in. x 2-in. baking pan. Bake at 350° for 20 minutes. While crust is baking, combine all filling ingredients and cook in heavy saucepan over medium heat. Stir constantly until thick-ened—watch carefully because mixture will scorch easily (Mixture may also be cooked in microwave.) Pour hot filling into crust; top with meringue made by beating egg whites with sugar until thick and satiny. Bake at 325° for 15-20 minutes or until golden brown. Refrigerate any leftovers. **Yield:** 10-12 servings.

BAKED EGGPLANT CASSEROLE

Rowena Champagne, New Iberia, Louisiana

2 medium eggplants, peeled, cut in 1-inch cubes
1 stick butter, *divided*
1/2 pound chopped ham
1 pound peeled and deveined uncooked shrimp
2 cups chopped onions
1 cup chopped green peppers
1 cup chopped green onions
1 cup seasoned Italian bread crumbs

Parmesan cheese

Steam eggplant in water until tender (approximately 15 minutes). Drain and set aside. Melt 3 tablespoons butter in large skillet; add ham and shrimp. Cook over medium heat for about 7 minutes or until shrimp turns pink. Remove from skillet; set aside. Saute onions, peppers and green onions in remaining butter until vegetables are tender; stir in eggplant, ham and shrimp. Pour into buttered 2-qt. casserole; sprinkle with mixture of bread crumbs and cheese. Bake, uncovered, at 325° for about 20 minutes. **Yield:** 8 servings.

BUTTERMILK PECAN PIE

Laura Julian, Littleton, New Hampshire

1/2 cup margarine, softened
2 cups sugar
2 teaspoons vanilla
3 eggs
1/4 cup all-purpose flour
1/4 teaspoon salt
1 cup buttermilk
3/4 cup chopped pecans
One 9 or 10-inch unbaked pie shell

Cream margarine and sugar. Blend in vanilla, then eggs, one at a time, beating after each addition. Gradually beat in flour and salt; add buttermilk,. Set aside. Sprinkle pecans in pie shell; pour in filling. Bake at 300° for 1-1/2 hours. Cool before cutting. May be served warm or cold. Refrigerate leftovers. **Yield:** 8 servings.

AMISH SUGAR COOKIES

Sylvia Ford, Kennett, Missouri

1 cup margarine, softened
1 cup corn oil
1 cup granulated sugar
1 cup confectioners' sugar
2 eggs
1 teaspoon vanilla
4-1/2 cups all-purpose flour
1 teaspoon baking soda
1 teaspoon cream of tartar

Combine margarine, oil and sugars in large mixing bowl; mix well. Add eggs; beat 1 minute. Add vanilla; mix well. Add flour, baking soda and cream of tartar; combine until smooth. Drop by small teaspoons on ungreased cookie sheet. Bake at 375° for 8-10 minutes. Cool on wire rack. **Yield:** 4 dozen cookies.

CHICKEN BROCCOLI CASSEROLE

Irene Conrad, Marion, Indiana

3 chicken breasts, skinned and boned
1 teaspoon salt
2 teaspoons leaf marjoram, crumbled
1/2 cup chopped celery
1 package (8 ounces) frozen chopped broccoli, thawed
2 teaspoons butter
1 can (4 ounces) sliced mushrooms
1 small can water chestnuts, drained

SAUCE:
1 cup creamy salad dressing
2 teaspoons prepared mustard
1 can (10-3/4 ounces) cream of mushroom soup
1/2 teaspoon lemon juice
1/2 teaspoon curry powder

TOPPING:
1 cup grated cheddar cheese
1/4 cup Parmesan cheese
1/2 cup fine buttered bread crumbs

Place chicken, salt, marjoram and celery in a skillet. Cover with water and cook until chicken is tender. Remove chicken; discard cooking liquid. Cool; cut or tear chicken into strips. Place in bottom of 2-1/2 quart casserole. Cover with broccoli, dot with butter. Add drained mushrooms and water chestnuts; set aside. Combine sauce ingredients in small bowl; pour over chicken/broccoli. Sprinkle top with cheddar cheese; combine bread crumbs and Parmesan cheese; sprinkle evenly over top. Bake at 350° for about 30 minutes. **Yield:** 10 servings.

SQUASH CASSEROLE

Angie Monk, Quitman, Texas

(PICTURED ON PAGE 20)

4 eggs, beaten
1/2 cup vegetable oil
1 cup biscuit mix
1 can (4 ounces) chopped
   green chilies with juice
1 medium onion, chopped
1 garlic clove, minced
2 cups (8 ounces) shredded
   cheddar cheese, *divided*
4 cups coarsely chopped
   summer squash *or* zucchini
   or yellow summer squash

Combine eggs, oil and biscuit mix. Stir in chilies, onion, garlic and half of the cheese. Stir in squash. Pour into a greased 13-in. x 9-in. x 2-in. baking dish. Bake at 350° for 40 minutes; sprinkle with remaining cheese and bake 5 minutes more. **Yield:** 8-10 servings.

WESTERN BEEF AND CORN CASSEROLE

Deb Poitz, Fort Morgan, Colorado

(PICTURED ON PAGE 20)

FILLING:
   1 pound ground beef
1/2 teaspoon salt
1/2 teaspoon chili powder
   1 cup (4 ounces) shredded
      cheddar *or* American cheese
1/2 cup hickory-flavored *or*
      regular barbecue sauce
1-1/2 cups (12 ounces) canned
      Mexicorn whole kernel corn,
      drained
   1 can (8 ounces) tomato sauce
CRUST:
   1 cup all-purpose flour
1/2 cup yellow cornmeal
   2 tablespoons sugar
   1 teaspoon salt
   1 teaspoon baking powder
1/4 cup butter *or* margarine
   1 cup (4 ounces) shredded
      cheddar *or* American cheese,
      divided
1/2 cup milk
   1 egg, beaten

Brown ground beef; drain. Stir in the remaining filling ingredients and set aside. To make the crust, stir together flour, cornmeal, sugar, salt and baking powder; cut in butter. Blend in remaining crust ingredients except 1/2 cup of cheese. Spread crust mixture over the bottom and sides of a greased (not

oiled) 9-in.-square baking pan. Pour filling into crust. Bake at 400° for 25-30 minutes; sprinkle with reserved cheese during last few minutes of baking. **Yield:** 6-8 servings.

EGG FOO YUNG CASSEROLE

Barb Fore, Mason, Michigan

(PICTURED ON PAGE 20)

CASSEROLE:
   8 eggs, beaten
1-1/2 cups thinly sliced celery
   1 can (16 ounces) bean
      sprouts, drained
1/2 cup nonfat dry milk powder
   2 tablespoons chopped onion
   1 tablespoon chopped parsley
1/2 teaspoon salt
1/8 teaspoon ground pepper
MUSHROOM SAUCE:
2-1/2 tablespoons cornstarch
1-1/2 cups chicken broth, *divided*
   1 tablespoon soy sauce
   1 can (4 ounces) sliced
      mushrooms, drained
   2 tablespoons sliced green
      onions

Stir together all casserole ingredients; pour into a greased 12-in. x 8-in. x 2-in. baking dish. Bake at 350° for 30-35 minutes or until knife inserted in center comes out clean. To make the sauce, combine cornstarch with 1/4 cup broth. Heat remaining broth to boiling in a saucepan; gradually whisk in cornstarch-broth mixture and soy sauce. Cook, stirring, until thickened and smooth; add mushrooms and green onions. To serve, cut casserole into squares and top with mushroom sauce. **Yield:** 6 servings.

SHRIMP AND ASPARAGUS CASSEROLE

Joan Vallem, Arroyo Grande, California

(PICTURED ON PAGE 20)

2 packages (10 ounces *each*)
   frozen asparagus cuts, *divided*
1/4 cup butter *or* margarine
1/4 cup all-purpose flour
   1 cup milk

3/4 cup light cream
1/4 cup dry white wine *or* 1/4 cup
      more cream *or* 1/4 cup
      chicken broth
1/2 teaspoon salt
1/8 teaspoon pepper
   1 egg yolk, slightly beaten
1/2 cup grated Parmesan cheese
   1 pound cooked small shrimp
1/2 cup buttered soft bread
      crumbs

On stovetop or in a microwave oven, blanch all of the asparagus for 3 minutes. Drain well; set aside. In a small saucepan, melt butter. Stir in the flour; cook, stirring constantly, for 1 minute. Gradually whisk in milk and cream; cook until thickened. Stir in wine or substitute. Season with salt and pepper. Stir in egg yolk, cheese and shrimp. In a buttered 2-1/2-qt. casserole, arrange half the asparagus; pour on half the sauce. Repeat layers. Top with crumbs. Bake at 350° for 30 minutes. **Yield:** 6 servings.

ZIPPY BAKED CARROTS

Jean Muldoon, Cincinnati, Ohio

(PICTURED ON PAGE 21)

5 to 6 cups sliced carrots
   (about 2 pounds), cut 1/4 inch
   thick, *divided*
6 slices Swiss cheese, *divided*
SAUCE:
   1 small onion, minced
   4 tablespoons butter *or*
      margarine
   3 tablespoons all-purpose flour
   1 teaspoon salt
   1 teaspoon chili powder
   2 cups milk
TOPPING:
   1 cup soft bread crumbs
   2 tablespoons butter *or*
      margarine, melted
   5 slices bacon, cooked and
      crumbled

On stovetop or in a microwave oven, blanch the carrots in a covered dish until crisp-tender. Layer half of the carrots in shallow 2-qt. baking pan; cover with half of the cheese. Repeat layers. To make sauce, saute onion in butter for 2 minutes; blend in flour and seasonings. Cook, stirring, for 1 minute. Add milk all at once; stir until thickened. Pour sauce over carrot-cheese layers. Combine bread crumbs and butter; sprinkle over all. Top with bacon. Bake at 350° for 25 minutes. **Yield:** 8 servings.

SCALLOPED POTATOES ETC.

Arlene Oliver, Waterloo, Iowa

(PICTURED ON PAGE 21)

 This tasty dish uses less sugar, salt and fat. Recipe includes *Diabetic Exchanges*.

SAUCE:
- 2 tablespoons butter
- 2 tablespoons all-purpose flour
- 3/4 teaspoon salt
- 1/4 teaspoon black pepper
- 2 cups milk

CASSEROLE:
- 4 cups peeled 1/8-inch thick potato slices, *divided*
- 1 cup 1/8-inch thick carrot chunks, *divided*
- 1/4 cup chopped onion, *divided*
- 1/4 cup chopped green pepper, *divided*
- 1 cup cooked cubed ham, *divided*
- 1 cup (4 ounces) shredded sharp cheddar cheese

For sauce, melt butter in small saucepan; stir in the flour, salt and pepper. Cook, stirring constantly, for 1 minute. Gradually whisk in the milk; cook until thickened. Set aside. In a buttered 2-qt. casserole, layer half of all vegetables and ham; cover with half of sauce. Repeat layers. Sprinkle cheese over all. Bake, covered, at 350° for 1 hour. Uncover; bake 10 minutes more. **Yield:** 4-6 servings. **Diabetic Exchanges:** One serving equals 1 protein, 1 bread, 1 vegetable, 2 fat; also, 233 calories, 387 mg sodium, 43 mg cholesterol, 20 gm carbohydrate, 13 gm protein, 12 gm fat.

SAUSAGE AND RICE CASSEROLE

Joyce Green, Bettendorf, Iowa

(PICTURED ON PAGE 21)

- 1 pound sage-flavored pork sausage
- 1 cup sliced celery
- 1/2 cup chopped onion
- 1/4 cup chopped sweet red pepper
- 1/4 cup chopped green pepper
- 1/2 cup sliced fresh mushrooms
- 1 can (8 ounces) sliced water chestnuts, drained
- 1 cup uncooked converted rice
- 2 cups chicken broth
- 1/2 teaspoon salt
- 1/8 teaspoon ground pepper

Brown sausage in a heavy skillet over medium heat; transfer to a 2-1/2-qt. greased casserole dish. In the drippings, saute celery, onion, peppers and mushrooms until lightly browned; transfer to the casserole. To casserole add water chestnuts, rice, broth and seasonings; mix well. Cover tightly and bake at 350° for 1 to 1-1/2 hours or until rice is fluffy and tender. **Yield:** 6 servings.

CHICKEN CRESCENT ALMONDINE

Nancy Reichert, Thomasville, Georgia

(PICTURED ON PAGE 21)

- 1 can (10-3/4 ounces) cream of chicken soup, undiluted
- 2/3 cup mayonnaise *or* salad dressing
- 1/2 cup sour cream
- 2 tablespoons instant minced onion
- 3 cups cooked cubed chicken
- 1 can (8 ounces) sliced water chestnuts, drained
- 1 can (4 ounces) mushroom stems and pieces, drained
- 1/2 cup chopped celery
- 1 tube (8 ounces) crescent dinner rolls
- 2/3 cup shredded Swiss *or* American cheese
- 1/2 cup slivered almonds
- 2 tablespoons butter *or* margarine, melted

In a large saucepan, combine soup, mayonnaise, sour cream and onion. Stir in chicken, water chestnuts, mushrooms and celery; cook over medium heat until mixture is hot and bubbly. Pour into ungreased 13-in. x 9-in. x 2-in. baking dish. Unroll the crescent roll dough and separate into two rectangles, trimming to fit dish. Place dough rectangles over hot chicken mixture. Combine cheese and almonds; sprinkle over the dough. Drizzle with butter. Bake at 375° for 20-25 minutes or until crust is a deep golden brown. Serve immediately. **Yield:** 8 servings.

ITALIAN HERITAGE CASSEROLE

Anne Frederick, New Hartford, New York

(PICTURED ON PAGE 22)

- 6 potatoes, peeled and quartered
- 1 sweet red pepper, cut in lengthwise strips
- 1 green pepper, cut in lengthwise strips
- 1 teaspoon oregano
- 1 teaspoon paprika
- 1/2 teaspoon garlic powder
- 1/2 teaspoon salt
- 1/2 teaspoon black pepper
- 1 frying chicken (3 pounds), skinned and cut in pieces *or* 6 chicken breast halves, cut in chunks
- 1 pound sweet *or* mild Italian sausage, cut in 1-inch to 2-inch chunks

Spray a 13-in. x 9-in. x 2-in. baking dish with no-stick cooking oil; arrange potatoes and peppers in bottom of the dish. Combine the seasonings; sprinkle a third of the seasoning mixture over vegetables. Layer chicken pieces and sausage over vegetables; sprinkle remaining seasoning mixture on top. Cover tightly with foil; bake at 425° for 30 minutes. Reduce oven temperature to 375°; bake 30 to 40 minutes more. **Yield:** 6 servings.

ZUCCHINI PIZZA CASSEROLE

Lynn Bernstetter, White Bear Lake, Minnesota

(PICTURED ON PAGE 22)

- 4 cups unpeeled, shredded zucchini
- 1/2 teaspoon salt
- 2 eggs
- 1/2 cup grated Parmesan cheese
- 1 cup (4 ounces) shredded cheddar cheese, *divided*
- 2 cups (8 ounces) shredded mozzarella cheese, *divided*
- 1 pound ground beef
- 1/2 cup chopped onion
- 1 can (15 ounces) Italian-flavored tomato sauce *or* 15 ounces tomato sauce with 1/4 teaspoon *each* oregano and basil
- 1 medium green pepper, chopped

Place zucchini in strainer; sprinkle with salt. Let drain for 10 minutes. Squeeze out moisture. Combine zucchini with eggs, Parmesan cheese and half of the cheddar and mozzarella cheeses. Press into greased 13-in. x 9-in. x 2-in. baking pan; bake at 400° for 20 minutes. Meanwhile, brown ground beef with onions. Drain and add the tomato sauce; spoon over baked zucchini mixture. Top with remaining cheeses and sprinkle with green pepper. Bake for 20 minutes more. **Yield:** 6-8 servings.

HAM AND ASPARAGUS CASSEROLE

Donetta Brunner, Savanna, Illinois

(PICTURED ON PAGE 22)

1 package (10 ounces) frozen cut asparagus *or* 1 pound fresh asparagus, 1/2-inch cuts
4 hard-cooked eggs, peeled and chopped
1 cup cooked cubed ham
2 tablespoons tapioca
1/4 cup shredded American cheese
2 tablespoons chopped green pepper
2 tablespoons chopped onion
1 tablespoon chopped fresh parsley
1 tablespoon lemon juice
1/2 cup light cream *or* evaporated milk
1 cup undiluted cream of mushroom soup

TOPPING:
1 cup soft bread crumbs
2 tablespoons butter *or* margarine, melted

On stovetop or in a microwave oven, blanch asparagus cuts in covered dish for 3 minutes; drain thoroughly. In a 2-1/2-qt. baking dish, combine asparagus, eggs and ham; sprinkle tapioca evenly over all. Add the cheese, green pepper, onion and parsley; mix gently. In a small bowl, blend the lemon juice, cream and soup; add to casserole and mix thoroughly. Mix topping ingredients; sprinkle over top of casserole. Bake at 375° for 25-30 minutes. Let stand a few minutes before serving. **Yield:** 6 servings.

CHICKEN NORMANDY

Mary Jane Cantrell, Turlock, California

(PICTURED ON PAGE 22)

CRUST:
1 package (8 ounces) seasoned bread stuffing mix
1/2 cup butter *or* margarine, melted
1 cup water

FILLING:
2-1/2 cups cooked diced chicken
1/2 cup chopped onion
1/2 cup chopped celery

1/2 cup mayonnaise *or* salad dressing
1 teaspoon salt
2 eggs
1-1/2 cups milk

TOPPING:
1 can (10-3/4 ounces) cream of mushroom soup, undiluted
1 cup (4 ounces) shredded cheddar cheese

The day before serving, combine crust ingredients; mix lightly. Spread half of crust mixture in buttered 13-in. x 9-in. x 2-in. baking pan. In a bowl, combine chicken, onion, celery, mayonnaise and salt. Spread chicken mixture over bottom crust; top with reserved crust mixture. Beat together eggs and milk; pour over all. Cover with foil and refrigerate overnight (or freeze for future use). An hour before cooking, remove casserole from refrigerator (or let thaw, if frozen); spread mushroom soup over top. Bake uncovered at 325° for 40 minutes. Sprinkle with cheese; bake 10 minutes more. **Yield:** 12 servings.

PILLOW POTATO BISCUITS

Jacqueline Thuma, Orange Park, Florida

1/2 cup instant mashed potato flakes
1 teaspoon sugar
2 tablespoons butter *or* margarine, softened
1/2 cup hot water
1/3 cup cold water
3 cups prepared biscuit mix
Milk, optional

Combine potato flakes, sugar, butter and hot water; mix well. Add cold water and biscuit mix, stirring until well blended. Add a little more cold water if necessary to make a soft dough. Turn out on a lightly floured surface; knead about 10 times. Roll dough to 1/2- to 3/4-in. thickness; cut with 2-in. biscuit cutter or jar lid. Place on ungreased baking sheet; brush with milk, if desired. Bake at 450° for about 13 minutes or until lightly browned. **Yield:** 12-18 biscuits, depending on thickness and size.

JIFFY CINNAMON ROLLS

Eula Colle, Marion, Kansas

4 to 5 cups all-purpose flour, *divided*
1 box (9 ounces) one-layer white cake mix

2 packages (1/4 ounce *each*) quick-rise yeast
1 teaspoon salt
2 cups warm water (120°-130°)
2 tablespoons butter *or* margarine
1/2 cup sugar
1 tablespoon cinnamon

In a large mixing bowl, combine 3 cups flour, cake mix, yeast, salt and warm water; mix until smooth. Add enough remaining flour to form a soft dough. Turn out onto a lightly floured surface; knead until smooth, about 6-8 minutes. Roll dough into a 9-in. x 18-in. rectangle. Spread with butter and sprinkle with sugar and cinnamon. Roll dough jellyroll style, starting with the long end. Slice the roll into 1-in. circles; place on greased cookie sheets. Cover and let rise in a warm place until doubled, about 15 minutes. Bake at 350° for 15-18 minutes. Frost, if desired. **Yield:** 18 rolls.

NO-KNEAD WHOLE WHEAT BREAD

Barbara Ann Gross, APO, New York

1 package (1/4 ounce) quick-rise yeast
1-1/4 cups warm water (110°-115°)
2 tablespoons honey
2 tablespoon butter *or* margarine
1 teaspoon salt
1-1/2 cups whole wheat flour
1-1/2 cups all-purpose flour

In a large mixing bowl, dissolve yeast in warm water. Stir in honey; add butter, salt and whole wheat flour. Beat on low speed until well blended. Stir in all-purpose flour. Cover and let rise in a warm place until doubled, about 30 minutes. Stir 30 strokes with a spoon; pour batter into a greased 8-1/2-in. x 4-1/2-in. bread pan. Cover and let rise in a warm place until batter reaches edge of pan, about 30 minutes. Bake at 375° for 30-40 minutes. Cool on wire rack. **Yield:** 1 loaf.

CLEVER CASSEROLE TIP: Store unbaked frozen casseroles in foil for quick, easy meals—and to keep your casserole dishes available for other uses. First, line casserole dish with foil, fill and freeze. Once ingredients are frozen solid, lift (foil and all) from dish; wrap well and return to freezer. To heat, simply pop the frozen block of ingredients back into casserole dish and bake. The foil lining also makes for easy cleanup!

Entertain a houseful of hungry friends or family with these reliably delicious recipes; they're elegant yet easy to make. Let them help themselves to the eye-appealing ham rolls, munch on mouthwatering muffins and pour the poppy seed dressing over a medley of fruits or greens.

BEST BRUNCH: Honey Poppy Seed Dressing; Orange Cream Cheese Muffins; Best-Ever Asparagus/Ham Rolls. All recipes on page 34.

O ur old-time stove is chockful of breakfast treats—from muffins to strata and French toast to pizza! Tried and true, or trendy and new, this breakfast bonanza will really open your eyes!

BOUNTIFUL BREAKFASTS: Clockwise from lower left—**Coffee Cake Wheels** (Pg. 35); **Oven French Toast with Nut Topping** (Pg. 35); **Hot Fruit Compote** (Pg. 35); **Spinach Quiche** (Pg. 36); **Lemon Yogurt Muffins** (Pg. 36); **Chili Cheese Strata** (Pg. 36); **Oatmeal Waffles** (Pg. 36); **Breakfast Pizza** (Pg. 35).

Y ou don't have to be a "Southern Belle" to bake up some scrumptious Southern desserts! Just try one of these family favorites… and count on serving seconds.

No Southern supper would be complete without a sweet, simple dessert of Banana Pudding, Texas Pecan Pie, Fresh Blackberry Cobbler or moist Banana Spice Cake. Top off your Southern "taste tour" in style—with one or more of these delicious Dixie desserts!

SWEET SOMETHINGS: Top to bottom —Banana Pudding; Banana Spice Cake; Texas Pecan Pie; Blackberry Cobbler. (All recipes can be found on Page 38.)

MEALS IN MINUTES

MENTION Colorado and most folks think of cowboys. Lois Enger of Colorado Springs thinks of cadets—she's the wife of a career officer at the Air Force Academy there.

With hundreds of hungry young men on hand, Lois is often called upon to serve up satisfying meals on a few moments' notice. That's when she turns to menus that can be made in *30 minutes or less.*

This time, Lois lends us her own timely taste treat—a quick, crunchy French toast that's perfect for an informal brunch or speedy supper. "I use 'Texas toast' to make it, but any thick-sliced fresh bread will do," she says.

"Originally, I topped the toast with ordinary syrup. Then a friend shared her recipe for homemade Cinnamon Syrup, and I've used it ever since. That along with the corn flake crumbs makes this French toast deliciously different."

Lois adds Canadian bacon or sausage on the side, and fresh or canned fruit or a fruit "smoothie" to fill out the menu. In less than half an hour, she's ready to fill any hungry cadet her husband might round up!

CRUMB-TOPPED BAKED FRENCH TOAST

- 2 eggs, well beaten
- 1/2 cup milk
- 1/2 teaspoon salt
- 1/2 teaspoon vanilla
- 6 slices "Texas toast" or other thick-sliced bread
- 1 cup corn flake crumbs
- 1/4 cup butter, melted

CINNAMON SYRUP:
- 1-1/3 cups sugar
- 1/3 cup water
- 2/3 cup white corn syrup
- 1 teaspoon ground cinnamon
- 1 can (5 ounces) evaporated milk
- 1/2 teaspoon almond extract
- 1 tablespoon butter

Combine eggs, milk, salt and vanilla; mix well. Dip bread slices into egg mixture; coat both sides with crumbs. Place on well-greased cookie sheet. Drizzle melted butter over crumb-coated bread. Bake at 450° for 10 minutes. To make syrup, combine sugar, water, corn syrup and cinnamon in saucepan. Bring to boil; cook 2 minutes. Remove from heat; add milk, almond extract and butter. Serve syrup warm with toast. **Yield:** 4 servings.

TASTY TOAST: Add more flavor to French toast by using raisin/cinnamon bread instead of white bread.

FRESH FRUIT CUPS

- 2 bananas, peeled and sliced
- 1 orange, peeled and cut in small pieces
- 2 red apples, washed, cored and cut in bite-size pieces
- 1 kiwi fruit, peeled and cut in bite-size pieces

Combine all ingredients and fold together gently. **Yield:** 4 servings.

For another fruity recipe on the run, try this refreshing "smoothie":

STRAWBERRY BANANA COOLER

- 2 cups unsweetened orange juice
- 1/2 cup whole frozen strawberries
- 1 large banana, sliced
- 2 to 4 ice cubes

Combine all ingredients in a blender container. Cover tightly; blend until smooth and serve immediately. **Yield:** 3 to 4 servings.

BEST-EVER ASPARAGUS/HAM ROLLS

Aida Babbel, Bowen Island, British Columbia

(PICTURED ON PAGE 29)

1-1/2 pounds fresh asparagus, trimmed
16 slices sandwich-type ham
Prepared mustard
6 tablespoons butter *or* margarine
6 tablespoons all-purpose flour
2 cups milk
Salt and pepper to taste
1-1/2 cups (6 ounces) shredded cheddar cheese
6 green onions, thinly sliced, optional

Cook asparagus to crisp-tender. Spread one side of each ham slice with mustard. Roll ham around 2-3 asparagus spears. Layer rolls, seam side down, in a 7-in. x 11-in. baking pan. Set aside. In a saucepan, melt butter over medium heat. Blend in flour to form a paste. Slowly stir in milk, salt and pepper. Cook and stir until sauce is thickened. Stir in cheese and add onions, if desired. Pour hot sauce over ham rolls. Cover and bake at 350° for 20 minutes. **Yield:** 8 servings.

HONEY POPPY SEED DRESSING

Abigail Stauffer, Port Trevorton, Pennsylvania

(PICTURED ON PAGE 29)

1/3 cup salad oil
1/4 cup honey
2 tablespoons cider vinegar
2 teaspoons poppy seeds
1/2 teaspoon salt
Fruit sections *or* mixed greens

In a screw-top jar, combine all ingredients except last one. Cover and shake well. Store in the refrigerator until ready to use. Serve over fresh fruit or mixed greens. **Yield:** 3/4 cup.

ORANGE CREAM CHEESE MUFFINS

Ed Toner, Howell, New Jersey

(PICTURED ON PAGE 29)

1 package (3 ounces) cream cheese, softened
1/4 cup sugar

1 egg, beaten
1/2 cup orange juice
1-3/4 cups buttermilk biscuit mix
1/4 cup chopped pecans
6 teaspoons orange marmalade

In a mixing bowl, beat cream cheese and sugar. Add the egg and juice. Beat well. Stir in the biscuit mix only until dry ingredients are moistened. Fold in pecans. Grease six Texas-size or jumbo muffin pans generously. Spoon 1/4 cup batter into each cup. Spoon 1 teaspoon marmalade into the center of each muffin. Divide remaining batter over marmalade. Bake at 400° for 20 minutes or until golden brown. Let stand 5 minutes before removing to a cooling rack. **Yield:** 6 jumbo muffins.

DUTCH SPINACH SALAD

Frances Miller, Baltimore, Maryland

3 to 4 bacon slices, diced
1 egg, slightly beaten
3 tablespoons sugar
1 tablespoon vinegar
Water
4 cups torn spinach greens
1/2 small onion, chopped
Salt and pepper to taste
Hard-cooked eggs, sliced

In a small frying pan, cook bacon until crisp. Do not drain. In a 1-cup measure, place egg, sugar, vinegar and enough water to make 3/4 cup; pour over bacon and grease. Cook, stirring constantly, until dressing thickens. Season to taste. Pour the hot dressing over greens and onion. Toss; garnish with egg slices. Serve immediately. **Yield:** 4 servings.

BROILED LIME SHRIMP

Mrs. Fayne Lutz, Taos, New Mexico

6 tablespoons lime juice
2 green onions, thinly sliced
1 serrano chili, stemmed, seeded and minced, optional
2 teaspoons olive oil
1 teaspoon minced garlic
1/4 teaspoon salt
36 extra-large uncooked shrimp, peeled and deveined
Shredded lettuce *or* sliced cucumbers, optional
2 tablespoons minced sweet red pepper, optional

Combine first 6 ingredients. Thread shrimp on metal or wooden skewers that have been soaked in water. Place in a large glass baking dish and pour marinade over shrimp. Cover and refrigerate several hours. Preheat broiler or grill. Cook shrimp, turning once, until pink, about 2-3 minutes per side. Brush frequently with the marinade. Do not overcook. Serve shrimp hot or at room temperature over a bed of shredded lettuce or sliced cucumbers. Sprinkle with red pepper, if desired. **Yield:** 6 servings.

ZESTY GRILLED CHOPS

Blanche Babinski, Minto, North Dakota

3/4 cup soy sauce
1/4 cup lemon juice
1 tablespoon chili sauce
1 tablespoon brown sugar
1 garlic clove, minced
6 rib *or* loin pork chops (about 1-1/2 inches thick)

Combine the first five ingredients. Place chops in a glass baking dish and pour marinade over. Cover and refrigerate 3-6 hours or overnight. To cook, remove chops from marinade and grill or broil 4 inches from the heat to desired doneness. Brush occasionally with the marinade. **Yield:** 6 servings.

RED BEAN TOSS

LuRicka L. Kough, Littleton, Colorado

1 can (15-1/2 ounces) red kidney beans, drained and rinsed
1 can (15-3/4 ounces) chili beans in chili sauce
1 cup thinly sliced celery
1/3 cup chopped sweet pickle
1/4 cup chopped onion
1 cup (4 ounces) shredded sharp cheddar cheese
1/2 teaspoon salt
1/2 teaspoon Worcestershire sauce
1/2 cup mayonnaise
1 cup coarsely crushed corn chips

In bowl, combine kidney beans, chili beans, celery, pickle, onion and cheese. In smaller bowl, blend salt and Worcestershire sauce with mayonnaise; toss with bean mixture. Place in 1-1/2-qt. casserole dish. Sprinkle with corn chips. Bake at 375° for about 25 minutes or until bubbly. **Yield:** 8 servings.

OVEN FRENCH TOAST WITH NUT TOPPING

Donna Justin, Sparta, Wisconsin

(PICTURED ON PAGE 30)

- 1 loaf (12 ounces) French bread, cut in 1-inch slices
- 8 eggs
- 1 cup milk
- 1 cup half-and-half
- 2 teaspoons vanilla
- 1/2 teaspoon nutmeg
- 1/2 teaspoon cinnamon
- 1/2 teaspoon mace

TOPPING:
- 3/4 cup butter, softened
- 1-1/3 cups brown sugar
- 3 tablespoons dark corn syrup
- 1-1/3 cups coarsely chopped pecans *or* walnuts *or* hickory nuts

Heavily butter 13-in. x 9-in. x 2-in. baking pan. Fill pan with bread slices to within 1/2 in. of top. Set aside. In blender, mix eggs, milk, half-and-half, vanilla, nutmeg, cinnamon and mace. Pour mixture over bread slices. Refrigerate, covered, overnight. Make topping by combining all ingredients; set aside until time to bake toast. Spread topping over toast; bake at 350° for 50 minutes until puffed and golden. (Shield top with foil if top browns too quickly.) **Yield:** 8-10 servings.

COFFEE CAKE WHEELS

Sue Pipkin, Baxter Springs, Kansas

(PICTURED ON PAGE 30)

- 1 cup butter
- 1/2 cup sugar
- 1/2 teaspoon salt
- 2 tablespoons grated lemon rind
- 2 eggs, well beaten
- 1 package active dry yeast
- 1/4 cup warm water (110°-115°)
- 1 cup dairy sour cream
- 4-1/2 cups sifted all-purpose flour
- 1/4 cup melted butter, *divided*
- 1/4 cup brown sugar
- 6 tablespoons sugar
- 1-1/2 teaspoons cinnamon
- 3/4 cup chopped nuts
- 3/4 cup raisins

Cream together butter and sugar until fluffy. Add salt, lemon rind, eggs and yeast which has been dissolved in warm water. Blend in sour cream. Add flour; mix thoroughly. Chill, covered, in refrigerator for 3 hours. Remove from refrigerator; let rise for 1-1/2 hours. Cover bottom of 13-in. x 9-in. x 2-in.

baking pan with 3 tablespoon melted butter; sprinkle on brown sugar. Roll dough on lightly floured board into 22-in. x 16-in. x 1/4-in.-thick rectangle. Brush dough with remaining butter. Combine sugar and cinnamon; sprinkle evenly over dough. Sprinkle nuts and raisins evenly over dough. Roll up long edge like jelly roll; seal edges. Cut crosswise into 3/4-in. thick slices. Arrange slices on top of brown sugar-butter mixture in pan. Cover; let rise in warm place until double. (Can refrigerate and bake next day—allow up to 1-1/2 hours rising time before baking.) Bake at 375° for 35 minutes. **Yield:** 16 servings.

HOT FRUIT COMPOTE

Jean Saveraid, Huxley, Iowa

(PICTURED ON PAGE 30)

- 1 can (20 ounces) pineapple chunks
- 1 can (16 ounces) peach halves
- 1 can (16 ounces) pear halves
- 1 can (16 ounces) apricot halves
- 1 jar maraschino cherries

ORANGE SAUCE:
- 1/3 cup sugar
- 2 tablespoons cornstarch
- 1/4 teaspoon salt
- 1/2 cup light corn syrup
- 1 cup orange juice
- 2 tablespoons orange rind

Drain fruit; arrange in a 13-in. x 9-in. x 2-in. baking dish with cherries in hollows. Set aside. To make sauce, combine sugar, cornstarch, salt, corn syrup, orange juice and rind in pan; heat to a boil. Remove; pour sauce over fruit compote. Bake at 350° for 30 minutes. **Yield:** 12 servings.

DUTCH HONEY SYRUP

Mary Grob, Tucson, Arizona

- 1 cup dark corn syrup
- 1 cup granulated sugar
- 1 teaspoon salt
- 2 tablespoons butter
- 1/2 cup evaporated milk
- 1/2 teaspoon coconut extract

Combine syrup, sugar, salt, butter and milk. Cook over medium heat, stirring constantly, until mixture *begins* to boil—do not allow to boil. Gently simmer 3 minutes, stirring occasionally. Remove from heat; add coconut extract. **Yield:** about 1-1/2 cups.

BREAKFAST PIZZA

Wilma Richey, Lead Hill, Arkansas

(PICTURED ON PAGE 31)

- 1 pound bulk pork sausage, crumbled
- 1 package (8 ounces) refrigerated crescent rolls
- 1 cup frozen loose-pack hash brown potatoes, thawed
- 1 cup (4 ounces) shredded sharp cheddar cheese
- 5 eggs
- 1/4 cup milk
- 1/2 teaspoon salt
- 1/4 teaspoon pepper
- 2 tablespoon grated Parmesan cheese

In skillet cook sausage until browned. Drain; set aside. Separate dough into eight triangles. Arrange on ungreased 12-in. pizza pan with points toward center. Press over bottom and up sides to form crust, sealing perforations completely. Spoon sausage over crust. Sprinkle with potatoes. Top with cheddar cheese; set aside. Beat together eggs, milk, salt and pepper in mixing bowl; pour over filling. Sprinkle Parmesan cheese over all. Bake at 375° for 25-30 minutes. **Yield:** 6-8 servings.

OVEN-BAKED SAUSAGE CASSEROLE

Patricia Crawley, Sunrise, Florida

- 1 pound bulk hot sausage
- 1 diced red pepper
- 1 diced green pepper
- 1 medium onion, chopped
- 6 eggs
- 1/4 cup milk
- 1/2 teaspoon garlic salt
- 1/2 teaspoon white pepper
- 1-1/2 cups grated sharp cheddar cheese

Crumble sausage; brown and drain. Saute the vegetables; drain. Set aside. Beat the eggs, milk, garlic salt and pepper until frothy. Layer sausage, vegetables and cheese in greased 1-1/2-qt. casserole. Top with egg mixture; bake at 350° until set, about 35 minutes. **Yield:** 6 servings.

> **CHANGE OF PACE:** Instead of your usual bacon and eggs, try some homemade granola served with canned peaches …"fruit soup" sprinkled with granola and topped with yogurt…zucchini and oat bran muffins…or homemade pancakes served with hot spiced applesauce.

OATMEAL WAFFLES

Marna Heitz, Farley, Iowa

(PICTURED ON PAGE 31)

✓ This tasty dish uses less sugar, salt and fat. Recipe includes *Diabetic Exchanges*.

1-1/2 cups all-purpose flour
1 cup quick-cooking rolled oats
1 tablespoon baking powder
1/2 teaspoon cinnamon
1/4 teaspoon salt, optional
2 eggs, slightly beaten
1-1/2 cup milk
6 tablespoons butter, melted
2 tablespoons brown sugar

In large mixing bowl, stir together flour, oats, baking powder, cinnamon and salt; set aside. In small mixing bowl, stir together eggs, milk, butter and brown sugar. Add to flour mixture; stir until blended. Pour batter onto grids of preheated, lightly greased waffle iron (amount will vary with size of waffle iron). Close lid quickly; do not open during baking. Use fork to remove baked waffle. Top with fresh fruit and yogurt. **Yield:** 12 waffles (4 inches square each), about 6 servings. **Diabetic Exchanges:** One serving equals 1 bread, 2 fats; also, 176 calories, 223 mg sodium, 65 mg cholesterol, 21 gm carbohydrate, 5 gm protein, 8 gm fat.

SPINACH QUICHE

Lois Dethloff, Amboy, Minnesota

(PICTURED ON PAGE 31)

1 package (10 ounces) frozen, chopped spinach
1 package (8 ounces) refrigerated crescent rolls
1-1/4 cups shredded Swiss cheese
1/4 cup finely minced onion
5 eggs
3/4 cup milk
2 teaspoons Worcestershire sauce
1/2 teaspoon salt
1/8 teaspoon pepper
8 slices bacon—fried crisp, drained and crumbled
Fresh chopped parsley
Parmesan cheese

Cook spinach according to package directions. Drain well; squeeze out excess moisture. Chop into smaller pieces; set aside. Unroll dough; press onto greased 10-in. glass pie plate, covering bottom and sides. Sprinkle cheese and onion over crust. Beat eggs; add milk, seasonings and spinach. Pour into crust. Sprinkle with bacon, parsley and Parmesan cheese. Bake at 350° for 40-45 minutes or until a knife inserted near center comes out clean. Let stand a minimum of 5 minutes before serving. **Yield:** 6-8 servings.

HELPFUL HINTS: For extra-light pancakes, turn as soon as pancakes puff up and fill with bubbles. If you wait until the bubbles break, pancakes will be tough.

● Leftover French toast freezes well. Reheat in oven, microwave or toaster.

● When the grocery has "very ripe" bananas on sale, buy a bunch. Peel, bag and freeze them. Then, when you make banana muffins or bread, remove as many bananas as the recipe calls for, thaw, mash and use as usual.

LEMON YOGURT MUFFINS

Bev Neuenschwander, Dalton, Ohio

(PICTURED ON PAGE 31)

✓ This tasty dish uses less sugar, salt and fat. Recipe includes *Diabetic Exchanges*.

2 cups all-purpose flour
1 teaspoon baking powder
1 teaspoon baking soda
1/4 teaspoon salt
1/4 cup sugar
2 tablespoons honey
2 eggs
1-1/4 cups (14 ounces) plain yogurt, room temperature
1/4 cup melted butter
1 tablespoon grated lemon peel
LEMON SYRUP:
1/3 cup lemon juice
1/3 cup sugar
3 tablespoons water

Combine flour, baking powder, soda and salt; set aside. In another bowl, combine sugar, honey, eggs, yogurt, butter and rind. Add dry ingredients; mix. Spoon into greased muffin tins. Bake at 375° for 15 minutes or until wooden pick in center tests done. To make syrup, combine ingredients in a saucepan; boil 1 minute. Drizzle syrup over warm muffins. **Yield:** 12 muffins. **Diabetic Exchanges:** One serving equals 2 breads, 1 fat; also, 188 calories, 213 mg sodium, 57 mg cholesterol, 31 gm carbohydrate, 5 gm protein, 5 gm fat.

CHILI CHEESE STRATA

Shirley Smith, Anaheim, California

(PICTURED ON PAGE 31)

1 loaf (12 ounces) French bread, cut in 1-inch cubes
2 cups shredded cheddar or Monterey Jack cheese, *divided*
1 jar (8 ounces) mild green chili salsa or 4 ounces chopped green chilies and 4 ounces salsa, combined
4 eggs
1 can (11 ounces) condensed cheddar cheese soup
2 cups milk or half-and-half
2 tablespoons minced onion
1 teaspoon Worcestershire sauce
Paprika

In buttered 2-qt. shallow dish, arrange bread cubes evenly. Sprinkle 1 cup cheese evenly over cubes. Pour chili salsa to cover evenly; set aside. In blender, combine eggs, soup, milk, onion, Worcestershire sauce; pour over bread mixture. Top with remaining cheese. Cover; refrigerate 6 hours or overnight. Uncover; dust top with paprika. Bake at 350° for 30 minutes or until lightly browned and bubbly. **Yield:** 8 servings.

MOM'S ONION CUSTARD

Patricia Tollis, Newark, Delaware

1 pound white onions
1/4 cup butter
3 eggs
1/4 cup heavy cream
1/2 teaspoon nutmeg
1/4 teaspoon salt
Pinch of pepper
1 strip of lean bacon

Peel onions; let stand in cold salted water for 1 hour. Drain onions; slice and saute in butter in large heavy skillet. Cook onions until soft, but do not brown. Cool. Beat eggs; add cream, nutmeg, salt and pepper. Mix with onions. Pour into buttered 1-1/2-qt. casserole or 10-in. quiche pan. Slice bacon into tiny strips (pre-cook for 10 seconds on high in microwave, if desired) and sprinkle on top of custard. Bake at 350° for 20 minutes. **Yield:** 6 servings.

May's 'Blackberry Drizzle' Makes Sweet Remembrance

For those who grew up in the country, the sweetest childhood memories often are the simplest.

By Janey Ashlene, Miami, Florida

Every time I see pretty rows of jams and jellies in the grocery, I think of the month of May, kerosene rags and my grandmother's wonderful blackberry preserves.

When I was growing up in Kentucky, there was always one week in May when the newly warmed air got a damp chill, and a fine, misty drizzle would fall for several days. Old-timers called it the "blackberry drizzle" or "blackberry winter", because that was the week that the wild blackberry bushes would bloom.

Our anticipation began to build that week as the briars changed from dark green vines with stickers into thorny greenery, covered with sweet-smelling white sprays of flowers. We knew that blackberry picking time was only weeks away!

Later, when the berries ripened, the women and girls would prepare for our "blackberry outing". And it took plenty of preparation!

We started by tearing an old sheet into strips, which we soaked in kerosene and tied around our wrists and ankles to keep out the chiggers (mite-sized insects). Then we'd don long-sleeved pants and shirts, and tie the pant legs with twine. After completing our costumes with straw hats or sunbonnets, we were ready to head out to the pastures.

The wild blackberry bushes were lovely when the fruit ripened. The berries at the end of each drooping branch ripened first, into clusters of soft, shiny, purple-black fruit, just waiting for your hand to catch them as they fell. Farther back on the branch, the berries ripened more slowly and turned a luscious red that matched the color of the leaves' edges.

I always knew I'd picked a good berry by the sound it made when it hit my small quart pail. If it landed with a soft *thunk* that sounded as if it might have squashed, it was a good one. The berries that made a *plink* would have a sharp, bitter taste.

Often I was accused of eating more than I put in my pail, but that wasn't always the case. It just seemed that the largest, shiniest, ripest berry on the end of each thorny green branch needed to be tested to see if it tasted as good as it looked!

There were hazards, though. The kerosene rags didn't do much to head off chiggers. We always counted our bites afterward, and anyone with fewer than 25 was considered lucky! "Sweat bees" always seemed to find me out there, too. And I often had to stop to pluck the blackberry thorns out of my legs.

We also had to watch for "cow pats", although Grandma always laughed at that and said it was nicer to call them "cow roses". Still, no matter what you called them, you had to watch where you stepped!

All those hazards were forgotten by afternoon, when the smell of blackberries filled our homes as the fruit was preserved and baked into pies. Grandma's preserves always tasted better than anyone's.

Each time I visited her house later on, Grandma would fetch me a jar of preserves from her fruit cellar. I always ate a spoonful straight from the jar, just to see if it was as good as I'd remembered. It was.

Those pretty pots of jam and jellies I see in the grocery these days never taste as sweet. But they always take me back to those simpler days that started each May with "blackberry drizzle".

BLACKBERRY COBBLER

Trudy Cinque Waynesville, North Carolina

(PICTURED ON PAGE 32)

1/2 cup butter *or* margarine
SYRUP:
  1 cup sugar
  1 cup water
COBBLER:
  1-1/2 cups of *self-rising* flour*
  1/2 cup butter *or* margarine
  1/3 cup milk, room temperature
  2 cups blackberries, fresh
    or frozen
  1/2 to 1 teaspoon cinnamon
  2 tablespoons sugar

(*If self-rising flour is not available, substitute 1-1/2 cups all-purpose flour plus 1/4 teaspoon salt and 2-1/4 teaspoons baking powder.) Melt 1/2 cup butter in 10-in. round or oval baking dish; set aside. Heat sugar and water until sugar melts; set aside. Make cobbler dough by cutting butter/margarine into flour until particles are like fine crumbs. Add milk and stir with a fork until dough leaves sides of bowl. Turn out on floured board; knead 3 or 4 times. Roll out to 11-in. x 9-in. x 1/4-in. thick rectangle. Spread berries over dough; sprinkle with cinnamon and roll up like jelly roll. Cut into 1-1/4-in.-thick slices. Carefully place in pan over melted butter. Pour sugar syrup carefully around slices (crust will absorb liquid). Bake at 350° for 1 hour. (Fifteen minutes before removing from oven, sprinkle 2 tablespoons sugar over crust.) Serve warm or cold. **Yield:** 8 servings.

BANANA SPICE CAKE

Meredith Barrett, Dalton, Georgia

(PICTURED ON PAGE 32)

CAKE:
  2-1/2 cups sifted cake flour
  1-2/3 cups sugar
  1-1/4 teaspoons baking powder
  1-1/4 teaspoons baking soda
  1 teaspoon salt
  1-1/2 teaspoons cinnamon
  3/4 teaspoon nutmeg
  1/2 teaspoon ground cloves
  2/3 cup solid vegetable
    shortening
  2/3 cup buttermilk
  1-1/4 cups mashed ripe bananas
    (3 medium)
  2 eggs, unbeaten
SEA FOAM FROSTING:
  2 egg whites

1-1/2 cups brown sugar
  5 tablespoons water
Dash salt
  1 teaspoon vanilla
  1 banana, sliced
CHOCOLATE GARNISH:
  2 squares sweet baking
    chocolate
  1 tablespoon butter

To make cake, sift together flour, sugar, baking powder, soda, salt, cinnamon, nutmeg and cloves. Add shortening, buttermilk and mashed bananas; mix until flour is dampened. Beat at low speed for 2 minutes. Add eggs; beat 1 minute. Bake in two 9-in. greased and floured layer pans at 350° for about 40 minutes or until cake tests done. Remove from pans; cool on wire racks. To make frosting, combine egg whites, sugar, water and salt in top of 6-cup double boiler; beat slightly to mix. Place over rapidly boiling water; beat with mixer at high speed until frosting stands in peaks, about 7 minutes. Remove from heat. Add vanilla; beat 1 to 2 minutes or until thick enough to spread. Spread frosting between cooled layers; top with banana slices; put layers together. Frost cake, drizzling melted chocolate/butter mixture in pattern of choice over frosting. **Yield:** 12-14 servings.

BANANA PUDDING

Doris Clayton, Germantown, Tennessee

(PICTURED ON PAGE 32)

  3 packages (3-1/2 ounces each)
    instant vanilla pudding/pie
    filling mix
  5 cups milk
  1 carton (8 ounces) dairy
    sour cream
  1 carton (12 ounces) frozen
    nondairy topping, thawed
    and divided *or* 8 ounces
    whipping cream, whipped to
    stiff peaks
  2 boxes (8 ounces each)
    vanilla wafers
  12 to 15 bananas, sliced

In large mixing bowl, blend pudding mix in milk with wire whisk. Add sour cream and *one-half* whipped topping, mixing well. Set aside. In large, deep glass bowl, alternate cookies, bananas and pudding mixture in layers. Top with reserved whipped topping and additional banana slices, if desired. Refrigerate overnight. **Yield:** 16 servings.

TEXAS PECAN PIE

Helen Suter, Rosenberg, Texas

(PICTURED ON PAGE 32)

  5 eggs
  3 tablespoons butter, soft
    or melted
  1/2 cup white sugar
  1-1/4 cups white corn syrup
  1 teaspoon vanilla
  1/4 teaspoon salt
  3 tablespoons flour
  2 cups pecan halves
  1 unbaked 9- *or* 10-inch pie
    shell*

Beat eggs lightly. Add butter, sugar, syrup, vanilla, salt, flour and pecans. Pour into pie shell (*9-in. pie will be full). Bake at 350° for about 40 minutes or until center is soft but not quite set. **Yield:** about 8 servings.

SPICY COCHILLA CHOWDER

Gloria Piantek, Skillman, New Jersey

  1 can (1 pound, 12 ounces)
    pork and beans
  2 jars (12 ounces *each*) medium
    hot chunky salsa
  1 pound cooked smoked
    sausage, cut in 1/2-inch
    rounds
  2 cups nacho cheese-flavored
    corn chips, broken
  1 cup shredded cheddar
    cheese

Combine pork and beans, salsa and sausage in 2-1/2-qt. casserole dish. Cover; cook 6 minutes on high in microwave; stir and continue cooking for 6 more minutes until mixture is hot. Sprinkle with chips, then cheese and microwave on high for 2 minutes or until cheese is melted. **Yield:** 6-8 servings.

VEGGIE HOW-TOS: To keep cauliflower white while cooking, add a little milk to the water.
  • When boiling corn, add sugar to the water instead of salt. Salt toughens the corn.
  • To ripen tomatoes, put them in a paper bag in a dark pantry, and they will ripen overnight.
  • Do not use baking soda to keep vegetables green—it destroys vitamin C.
  • When cooking cabbage, place a small cup or can half full of vinegar on the stove near the cabbage. It will absorb all the cabbage odor.

ORANGE BLUEBERRY MUFFINS

Irene Parry, Kenosha, Wisconsin

1 cup uncooked oatmeal
1 cup orange juice
3 cups all-purpose flour
4 teaspoons baking powder
1 teaspoon salt
1/2 teaspoon baking soda
1 cup sugar
1 cup vegetable oil
3 eggs, beaten
1-1/2 cups fresh *or* frozen
    blueberries
1 tablespoon grated orange peel
TOPPING:
1/2 cup finely chopped walnuts
1/3 cup sugar
1 teaspoon ground cinnamon

Combine the oatmeal and orange juice. Set aside. In a large mixing bowl, combine flour, baking powder, salt, soda and sugar. Make a well in the center of the dry ingredients and add oatmeal mixture, oil and eggs. Stir only until ingredients are moistened. Carefully fold in berries and orange peel. Spoon batter into greased muffin tins, filling about 3/4 full. Combine walnuts, sugar and cinnamon. Sprinkle over muffins and bake at 400° for 15 minutes or until muffins test done. Remove from tins and serve warm, if desired. **Yield:** 24 muffins.

TANGY CITRUS DRESSING

Kay Snead, Friona, Texas

Juice and grated peel of 1 lemon
Juice and grated peel of 1 lime
Juice and grated peel of 1 orange
1 cup sugar
1 egg, well beaten

In a small saucepan, combine all ingredients. Over medium heat, bring mixture to a boil and boil for 1 minute. Remove from the heat and cool. Serve with assorted fresh fruit. **Yield:** about 1-1/2 cups.

SHRIMP AND PASTA SUPPER

Mildred Sherrer, Bay City, Texas

3 tablespoons butter *or*
    margarine
1 pound fresh uncooked
    shrimp, peeled
    and deveined
1 cup diagonally sliced celery

1 jar (28 ounces) chunky
    spaghetti sauce
Hot pepper sauce to taste
12 ounces dried linguine,
    cooked and well drained
1 cup frozen peas, defrosted
1 tablespoon finely chopped
    fresh parsley
1 cup (4 ounces) shredded
    mozzarella cheese

In a large skillet, melt butter over medium heat. Saute shrimp and celery until shrimp turns pink. Stir in the spaghetti sauce and hot pepper sauce. Simmer, covered, 15 minutes. Add linguine and peas; toss well. Top with parsley and cheese. Heat until the cheese melts. Serve immediately. **Yield:** 4-6 servings.

GRILLED SALMON SANDWICHES

June Formanek, Belle Plaine, Iowa

1 can (8 ounces) red *or* pink
    salmon, well drained
1/3 cup finely chopped celery
2 tablespoons sweet pickle
    relish, well drained
1/8 teaspoon ground pepper
1/4 cup mayonnaise
8 slices white *or* Italian bread
1 egg, beaten
2/3 cup milk

In a small bowl, combine first five ingredients. Divide and spread over 4 slices of bread. Top with remaining bread slices and dip each sandwich into combined egg and milk mixture. Brown on a well-greased griddle or skillet on both sides. Serve immediately. **Yield:** 4 sandwiches.

OLD-FASHIONED RHUBARB TORTE

Katherine Kalmbach, Selby, South Dakota

1 cup all-purpose flour, *divided*
5 tablespoons confectioners'
    sugar
Pinch salt
1/2 cup butter
2 eggs
1-1/2 cups sugar
3/4 teaspoon baking powder
3 cups sliced fresh *or* frozen
    rhubarb
Whipped cream

In a mixing bowl, combine 3/4 cup flour, confectioners' sugar and salt. Cut in butter as for pastry. Pat into a 6-in. x 10-in. baking pan. Bake crust at 375° for 10 minutes. Meanwhile, beat the eggs, sugar, remaining flour and baking powder. Fold in rhubarb and spread over baked crust. Return to the oven and bake for 35-40 minutes. Cool. Serve with a dollop of whipped cream. **Yield:** 8 servings.

GRANDMOTHER'S BREAD PUDDING

Sherrie Hill, St. Louis, Missouri

PUDDING:
1 cup sugar
2 eggs, beaten
2 cups milk
2 teaspoons pumpkin pie spice
2 teaspoons vanilla extract
4 cups day-old torn white *or*
    French bread
1 cup raisins
CUSTARD SAUCE:
3 egg yolks
3/4 cup sugar
1/4 cup cornstarch
3 cups milk
2 teaspoons vanilla extract

For pudding, combine first five ingredients in a large bowl. Add bread and raisins; mix well. Turn into a greased 9-in. x 9-in. baking pan. Bake at 350° for 50 minutes. Meanwhile, for sauce, combine yolks, sugar and cornstarch in the top of a double boiler. Gradually add milk, stirring until smooth. Cook over boiling water, stirring constantly, until the mixture thickens and coats a metal spoon. Remove from the heat and stir in vanilla. Serve pudding and sauce warm or chilled. **Yield:** 9 servings.

BROWN SUGAR OATMEAL PANCAKES

Sharon Bickett, Chester, South Carolina

1 egg, beaten
2 tablespoons vegetable oil
1 cup buttermilk
1/2 cup whole wheat flour
1/2 cup all-purpose flour
1/2 teaspoon baking soda
1/2 teaspoon salt
1/3 cup packed brown sugar
1/2 cup plus 2 tablespoons
    quick-cooking oats

In a mixing bowl, combine egg, oil and buttermilk. Combine flours, baking soda, salt and sugar; add to egg mixture. Stir in oats. Pour by 1/3 cupfuls onto a lightly greased hot griddle; turn when bubbles form on tops of pancakes. **Yield:** about 10 pancakes.

ITALIAN RICE CASEROLE

Karen Witty, Bowmanville, Ontario

- 1 tablespoon cooking oil
- 1 pound Italian sausage, sliced
- 1 onion, chopped
- 1 cup uncooked brown rice
- 1 sweet red pepper, sliced thin
- 2 carrots, diced
- 3 beef bouillon cubes
- 3 cups boiling water
- 1 cup frozen peas, defrosted
- 2 cans (4 ounces *each*) sliced mushrooms, drained
- 3 fresh tomatoes, skinned and diced
- 1/2 cup sliced green olives
- 3 hard-cooked eggs, sliced
- 1/4 cup grated Parmesan cheese

In a large skillet, heat oil over medium-high. Brown sausage. Drain excess fat. Add onion and rice. Lightly brown. Stir in red pepper, carrots, bouillon and water. Bring to a boil. Cover and simmer for 30 minutes, stirring occasionally, until the liquid is almost absorbed. Add peas, mushrooms and tomatoes. Heat 5 minutes. Remove half the mixture to a serving bowl. Top with half the olives, eggs and cheese. Layer remaining rice mixture and topping ingredients. Serve immediately. **Yield:** 6-8 servings.

BEEF/MUSHROOM POCKETS

Mary Kay Morris, Cokato, Minnesota

- 1 box (16 ounces) hot roll mix
- 1 pound ground beef
- 1 can (10-3/4 ounces) cream of mushroom soup
- 1 can (4 ounces) mushroom pieces, drained
- 1 small onion, chopped
- 1 tablespoon Worcestershire sauce
- 1 cup (4 ounces) shredded cheddar cheese
- 1 egg
- 2 tablespoons water

Prepare roll mix according to package directions for pizza crust. While dough rises, brown meat in a skillet. Drain excess fat. Stir in the soup, mushrooms, onion and Worcestershire sauce. Remove from heat. Divide the dough into eight pieces. Form each piece into a ball. On a lightly floured surface, roll each ball into an 8-in. circle. Place circles on two lightly greased cookie sheets. Divide meat mixture over eight circles. Top with cheese. Moisten

edges of dough and fold in half. Press edges firmly together with a fork. Prick top of dough. Beat egg and water; brush over each pocket. Bake at 400° for about 20 minutes. **Yield:** 8 servings.

ZESTY ZUCCHINI SKILLET

Barbara Winders, Spencer, Indiana

✓ This tasty dish uses less sugar, salt and fat. Recipe includes *Diabetic Exchanges*.

- 2 tablespoons cooking oil
- 4 cups diced zucchini
- 1 cup chopped onion
- 1 cup chopped carrots
- 1/2 green pepper, sliced thin
- 3/4 cup chopped celery
- 1/2 teaspoon garlic powder
- 2 teaspoons dried basil
- 2 teaspoons dried oregano
- 1/4 teaspoon salt
- Pepper to taste
- 1/3 cup picante sauce
- 2 teaspoons prepared mustard
- 1 medium tomato, diced
- 1/2 cup shredded Monterey Jack cheese

In a skillet, heat oil over medium. Cook and stir the next six ingredients until vegetables are crisp-tender. Combine basil, oregano, salt, pepper, picante sauce and mustard; pour into skillet. Cook and stir for 3 minutes. Gently stir in tomatoes; heat through. Sprinkle with cheese and serve immediately. **Yield:** 8 side-dish servings. **Diabetic Exchanges:** One serving equals 1-1/2 vegetable, 1 fat; also 83 calories, 162 mg sodium, 8 mg cholesterol, 6 gm carbohydrate, 3 gm protein, 6 gm fat.

GRITS CASSEROLE

Georgia Johnston, Auburndale, Florida

- 4 cups water
- 1 teaspoon salt
- 1 cup quick-cooking grits
- 4 eggs, lightly beaten
- 1 pound pork sausage, browned and drained
- 1-1/2 cups (6 ounces) shredded sharp cheddar cheese, *divided*
- 1/2 cup milk
- 1/4 cup butter *or* margarine, softened

In a saucepan, bring water and salt to a boil. Slowly stir in grits. Reduce heat and cook 4-5 minutes, stirring occasionally. Remove grits from heat and add a small amount of hot grits into the

eggs; return to saucepan. Stir in sausage, 1 cup cheese, milk and butter; stir until the butter melts. Pour into a greased 13-in. x 9-in. x 2-in. baking pan. Sprinkle with remaining cheese. Bake at 350° for 50-55 minutes or until the top begins to brown. **Yield:** 10-12 servings.

CHILIES RELLENOS

Irene Martin, Portales, New Mexico

- 1 can (7 ounces) whole green chilies
- 2 cups (8 ounces) shredded Monterey Jack cheese
- 2 cups (8 ounces) shredded cheddar cheese
- 3 eggs
- 3 cups milk
- 1 cup biscuit mix
- Seasoned salt to taste
- Salsa

Split chilies; rinse and remove seeds. Dry on paper towels. Arrange chilies on the bottom of an 11-in. x 7-in. x 1-1/2-in. baking dish. Top with cheeses. In a bowl, beat eggs; add milk and biscuit mix. Blend well; pour over cheese. Sprinkle with salt. Bake at 325° for 50-55 minutes or until golden brown. Serve with salsa. **Yield:** 8 servings.

HONEY CRUNCH COOKIES

Germaine Stank, Pound, Wisconsin

- 2 cups all-purpose flour
- 2 teaspoons baking powder
- 1/2 teaspoon salt
- 1 cup butter *or* margarine
- 1 cup honey
- 2 eggs
- 1 cup shredded coconut
- 1 cup butterscotch chips
- 4 cups crisp rice cereal

Sift together first three ingredients; set aside. In a large mixing bowl, cream butter. Add honey a little at a time; mix well. Add eggs, one at a time, beating well after each addition. Mixture will appear to separate. Gradually add dry ingredients; mix until moistened. Fold in coconut, chips and cereal. Drop by teaspoonfuls onto greased cookie sheets. Bake at 350° for about 12 minutes or until golden brown. Remove cookies to cooling rack. **Yield:** about 5 dozen.

OIL SPILLS: Add 1/2 teaspoon salt to oil before frying to prevent splatters. Then omit salt from the recipe.

Best Cook

Sylvia Teague
Eureka Springs, Arkansas

When it comes to pleasing many palates, Sylvia Teague of Eureka Springs, Arkansas, has the knack.

"Everyone raves about Sylvia's cooking," her husband Raymond wrote in his nominating letter, "including family members, friends and guests. The Entertainment Editor of the Fort Worth, Texas, newspaper described her as a 'Renaissance Woman'.

"People who eat at our home often tell Sylvia she should start a restaurant in town. But she'd rather cook just for pleasure in her own kitchen.

"And what a pleasure it is to taste her treats! Sylvia turns our blackberries, raspberries, persimmons, wild grapes and strawberries into delicious pies, cakes, cobblers, jams and jellies. She grows her own basil for pesto, and lots of tomatoes for sauces.

"She doesn't need fancy, expensive ingredients…Sylvia makes the most of what's on hand. She bakes her own rolls, and serves an English-style breakfast every Sunday with scones or Irish soda bread."

Sylvia has loved to cook ever since she baked a batch of cookies at age 6.

"My mother was sick, and I decided to make cookies to cheer her up," she recalls. "I had to disturb her to find out the difference between 't.' and 'T.' in the recipe and what 1/2 and 1/3 were.

"I don't remember how the cookies turned out, but I know I learned the basics of reading recipes from the experience. Mom was always great about letting me make my own mistakes and discoveries.

"Nowadays I know my efforts will be rewarded by the pleasure of the people for whom I cook. The more love I put in my cooking, the more I get back!"

ALEXANDRA'S ORANGE COCONUT CAKE

2-1/4 cups whole wheat pastry flour*
1 tablespoon baking powder
1 teaspoon salt
5 egg yolks
1/2 cup honey
1/2 cup vegetable oil
1/2 cup orange juice
1 tablespoon grated orange rind
1/2 teaspoon cream of tartar
1 cup egg whites
1/4 cup honey
1 cup flaked coconut

FILLING:
1 pint vanilla ice cream swirled with orange sorbet

FROSTING:
1 pint whipping cream
2 tablespoons honey
1 teaspoon vanilla
1/2 cup shredded coconut
Fresh orange slices, garnish

*Whole wheat pastry flour is available at co-ops and health food stores. Combine flour, baking powder and salt. Add egg yolks, honey, oil, orange juice and orange rind. Beat well; set aside. Beat egg whites with cream of tartar until soft peaks form. Gradually add 1/4 cup honey; beat until mixture will stand in stiff peaks. Fold coconut into egg whites. Stir small amount of egg white mixture into flour mixture; then gently fold remaining egg whites into flour mixture. Divide among three 8-inch layer cake pans which have been lined with parchment or wax paper. *Do not grease sides of pans.* Bake at 350° for 20-25 minutes or until cake tests done with wooden pick inserted in center. Cool in pans on rack for 10 minutes. Remove from pans; cool thoroughly. Soften ice cream/sorbet. Spread between cooled cake layers. Place cake in freezer. Whip cream with honey and vanilla until it holds its shape. Spread on top and sides of cake. Sprinkle liberally with coconut. Decorate with orange slices cut in one-half. Keep in freezer until ready to serve. **Yield:** 16-20 servings.

PIZZALADA

CRUST:
1 cup masa harina
1/2 teaspoon salt
About 2/3 cup boiling water
SAUCE:
1 cup water
1-1/2 tablespoons chili powder or more to taste
3 ounces tomato paste
1/2 teaspoon salt
TOPPING:
1 cup cooked pinto beans, rinsed and drained
2 cups grated Monterey Jack cheese
Sliced black olives
Chopped green onions
Sliced chilies *or* other peppers of choice

Mix together crust ingredients to make a stiff dough, adding more water as necessary. Knead several times; roll out to fit a 12-in. greased pizza pan. Bake at 350° for 10 minutes. (Substitute prepared corn tortillas, if desired.) To prepare the sauce, combine sauce ingredients in small saucepan; bring to boil. Spread sauce evenly over baked crust. Cover with topping ingredients and bake for 10-15 minutes more. **Yield:** 6-8 servings.

REFRIGERATOR ROLLS

5 cups all-purpose flour
4 teaspoons baking powder
1/2 teaspoon baking soda
2 teaspoons salt
2 packages active dry yeast
1 cup warm water (110-115°)
1/4 cup honey
2 cups buttermilk
1/2 cup vegetable oil

Mix flour, baking powder, soda and salt together. Dissolve yeast in water. Add yeast mixture, buttermilk and honey to dry ingredients. Beat well. Add oil; mix thoroughly. Cover; set in refrigerator for at least 12 hours. Spoon into well-greased muffin cups, about 3/4 full. Let stand at room temperature for about 20 minutes before baking. Bake at 400° for about 20 minutes or until light brown. (Batter will keep, covered, in refrigerator for 2-3 days.) **Yield:** 2-1/2 dozen.

Summer

Hot sultry weather goes well with the guaranteed-to-please regional summer fare that's featured on these pages.

Get ready to cool off with hearty shredded beef sandwiches, robust salads, fruit-filled desserts and more. Now this is country cooking at its best!

REGIONAL FAVORITES: Clockwise from lower left—**German Potato Salad** (Pg. 49); **Stuffed Zucchini** (Pg. 50); **Black-Eyed Pea Salad** (Pg. 49); **West Virginia Blackberry Cake** (Pg. 49); **Wyoming Whopper Cookies** (Pg. 49); **Mile-High Shredded Beef** (Pg. 50); **Door County Sour Cherry Torte** (Pg. 50); **Peach Blueberry Cobbler** (Pg. 49).

For flavorful summer fare, seafood and fish are worth serving —and savoring! Whether it's an impromptu cookout or a family reunion where good cooks have a chance to "show their stuff", these recipes are bound to be repeated.

We gathered an ensemble of fish and seafood specialties here— each is a regional favorite in its part of the country.

These coastal treats let you capture the flavor of old-time Scandinavian fishermen's feasts with a Door County Fish Boil or the spiciness of a Gulf Shrimp Salad. Or, you can savor the simplicity of moist Pacific fish poached in lemon and fresh herbs...or the sweetness of Atlantic coast crab in a light souffle.

Taste the *bounty* of this country's rich fresh and saltwater food sources as you enjoy these regional heritage favorites!

OUTDOOR EATING! Clockwise from lower left—**Texas Shrimp/Rice Salad** (Pg. 51); **Maryland Crab Casserole** (Pg. 50); **Door County Fish Boil** (Pg. 51); **Steamed Pacific Salmon** (Pg. 51).

MEALS IN MINUTES

DELICIOUS...nutritious...and *fast*. That's the beauty of this ready-in-less-than-30-minutes meal from the kitchen of Grace Howaniec of Waukesha, Wisconsin. Enjoy the savory flavor of lime/dill marinade on the boneless chicken breast and the palate-pleasing tang of the vinaigrette dressing that highlights the spinach/orange salad. And for dessert, the simple-but-satisfying combination of fresh strawberries and shortbread cookies is sure to be a hit!

"You can save time by using a purchased salad dressing," Grace adds. "I make my own so I can control the amount of salt, sugar and oil...that's important if you're limiting those ingredients in your family's diet."

GRILLED CHICKEN BREASTS WITH LIME/ DILL SAUCE

4 chicken breast *halves*, deboned and skinned
MARINADE:
1/4 cup lime juice (may use lemon juice)
1/4 teaspoon salt
1/8 teaspoon pepper
1/2 teaspoon dried dill weed
1/2 teaspoon dried minced onion
2 tablespoons melted butter

Combine all marinade ingredients in heavy zip-lock plastic bag; mix. Add chicken breasts; seal bag. Turn to coat chicken with marinade; let stand at room temperature for 10-15 minutes. Meanwhile, pre-heat charcoal grill. Place chicken breasts over medium coals or low setting on gas grill. Cover grill; grill for 5 minutes on each side. (Chicken can also be oven-broiled.) Baste with butter after turning. Serve hot with buttered noodles. **Yield:** 4 servings.

SPINACH/ORANGE SALAD WITH VINAIGRETTE DRESSING

Fresh spinach leaves, washed, drained on paper towels and chilled

2 oranges, peeled and sliced into 1/2-inch slices
VINAIGRETTE DRESSING:
3 tablespoons vegetable oil
1 tablespoon white vinegar *or* white wine
1/2 teaspoon sugar
1 teaspoon lemon juice
1/4 teaspoon dry mustard
1/4 teaspoon salt
1/8 teaspoon pepper

Place spinach leaves on individual plates (or in one large salad bowl to save time). Garnish with orange slices. Immediately before serving, top with dressing made by combining all ingredients together in covered container and mixing well. **Yield:** 4 servings.

FRESH STRAWBERRY CUP

1 quart fresh strawberries, rinsed, drained and sliced
Confectioners' sugar, optional
Shortbread cookies

Arrange strawberry slices in dessert bowls; sprinkle with sugar, if desired. Mix gently. Serve with cookies. **Yield:** 4 servings.

PREPARE POULTRY PROPERLY:
Always rinse raw poultry thoroughly inside and out under cold running water. Then blot the skin with a dry paper towel to absorb moisture.

● When cutting raw poultry, use a plastic or ceramic surface (one that can be washed in the dishwasher or else scrubbed in hot, soapy water and chlorine bleach).

● Always wash your hands thoroughly before and after handling raw poultry.

● Wash chopping boards, knives and other kitchen items that come in contact with raw poultry with a bleach-based detergent. These measures work to destroy salmonella bacteria that could contaminate other foods.

● A frozen bird should be cooked within 12 hours of thawing.

ig, bountiful, beautiful strawberries! Before you head for
the patch to gather yourself a
basket, check out these pick-of-
the-crop recipes for some new and
wonderful ways to savor summer's
berry best.

Make the most of a special occasion with a spectacular chocolate-
dipped strawberry pie, or brighten a

luncheon with a colorful, garden-fresh strawberry/rhubarb salad. Tickle your taste buds with a brightly sparkling berry punch.

And when it's time to celebrate the season with family and friends, you'll find new variations for old-fashioned favorites such as home-made strawberry ice cream, sherbet and shortcake.

SENSATIONAL STRAWBERRIES: Clockwise from lower left—**The Ultimate Strawberry Pie** (Pg. 52); **Strawberry/Rhubarb Salad** (Pg. 52); **Strawberry Devonshire Tart** (Pg. 52); **Miniature Strawberry Muffins** (Pg. 53); **Strawberry Sparkle Punch** (Pg. 52); **Strawberry/Rhubarb Coffee Cake** (Pg. 53); **Rich Strawberry Shortcake** (Pg. 53); **Strawberry Ice Cream** (Pg. 52).

ucculent strawberries—they're the sweetest sign of summer. Start the season in style by serving up the tempting treats pictured below—from satisfying salads to delectable desserts.

THE BERRY BEST. Clockwise from upper left—**Strawberry Cheesecake Trifle** (Pg. 53); **Pavlova** (Pg. 54); **Super Easy Strawberry Sherbet** (Pg. 54); **Strawberry/Spinach Salad** (Pg. 53).

WEST VIRGINIA BLACKBERRY CAKE

Dorothy McComas, Branchland, West Virginia

(PICTURED ON PAGE 42)

CAKE:
- 2 cups sugar
- 1 cup butter
- 4 eggs
- 3 cups all-purpose flour
- 1 teaspoon cloves
- 1 teaspoon nutmeg
- 1 teaspoon cinnamon
- 1 teaspoon baking soda
- 1 teaspoon baking powder
- 1 cup buttermilk
- 1-1/2 cups fresh *or* frozen, drained blackberries *or* black raspberries

ICING:
- 1 cup butter
- 1 box (1 pound) confectioners' sugar
- 1 teaspoon vanilla
- 3 tablespoons *cold* coffee

To make cake, cream sugar and butter together; beat eggs and add to creamed mixture. Combine flour, spices, baking soda and powder; stir into creamed mixture alternately with buttermilk. Carefully fold in berries. Bake at 350° in three greased-and-floured 8-in. layer pans for 30 minutes. Cool on wire rack. Frost with icing made by beating all ingredients together until fluffy. (Add more coffee, if necessary.) Spread frosting between cake layers and on sides and top. **Yield:** 16-20 servings.

GERMAN POTATO SALAD

Gerlyn Gloe, Hermann, Missouri

(PICTURED ON PAGE 42)

- 3 pounds (12 medium) red salad potatoes, scrubbed, boiled, sliced 1/4-in. thick
- 1/4 cup finely diced bacon (2 strips)
- 1/4 cup chopped onion
- 1 tablespoon all-purpose flour
- 2 teaspoons salt
- 1-1/4 tablespoons sugar
- 1/4 teaspoon pepper
- 2/3 cup cider vinegar
- 1/3 cup water
- 1/2 teaspoon celery seed
- 1/2 cup finely chopped celery
- 3 tablespoons chopped fresh parsley

Cook unpeeled potatoes in enough water to cover until tender. Drain; cool slightly. Slice. Fry bacon in skillet until crisp. Saute onion in bacon fat for 1 minute. Blend in flour, salt, sugar and pepper. Stir in vinegar and water until mixture is smooth. Cook over low heat for 10 minutes, stirring well. Pour over sliced potatoes; add celery seed, celery and parsley. Mix; serve warm. **Yield:** 6 servings.

BLACK-EYED PEA SALAD

Mrs. Douglas Price, Morgan, Texas

(PICTURED ON PAGE 42)

- 1 can (16 ounces) black-eyed peas, drained
- 1 cup finely chopped celery
- 1/4 cup sweet *or* green onion, chopped
- 1/2 cup sweet green pepper, chopped
- 1 medium-sized tomato, chopped
- 2 cups lettuce, cut in long, thin strips
- 1 cup commercial coleslaw dressing

Mix all ingredients together; toss lightly. Serve immediately. **Yield:** 6 servings.

PEACH BLUEBERRY COBBLER

Ramona Banfield, Harrison, Arkansas

(PICTURED ON PAGE 42)

FILLING:
- 2 cups fresh *or* frozen peaches, sliced in 1/4-inch slices*
- 1/3 to 1/2 cup sugar
- 4 teaspoons quick-cooking tapioca
- 2 teaspoons fresh lemon juice
- 1 cup fresh *or* frozen blueberries

Nutmeg

COBBLER:
- 1 rounded cup all-purpose flour
- 2 tablespoons sugar
- 1-1/2 teaspoons baking powder
- 1/8 teaspoon salt, optional
- 1 teaspoon fresh grated lemon rind
- 1/4 cup butter *or* margarine
- 1/2 cup cream *or* evaporated milk

*(Can substitute nectarines.) Combine peaches, sugar, tapioca and lemon juice in 1-1/2-qt. baking dish. Sprinkle blueberries over top. Cook in micro-wave on high for 4-5 minutes (stirring after 3 minutes) or until mixture bubbles and is hot throughout. Sprinkle with nutmeg. Meanwhile, prepare cobbler by mixing flour, sugar, baking powder, salt, if desired, and lemon rind. Add butter/margarine, cutting in with pastry blender until mixture resembles cornmeal. Add cream/milk; stir until dough is moistened and mixed. Drop by tablespoons over hot filling. Dust cobbler with nutmeg. Bake at 400° for 25-30 minutes or until top is golden brown. Serve warm with ice cream. **Yield:** 8 servings.

WYOMING WHOPPER COOKIES

Jamie Hirsh, Powell, Wyoming

(PICTURED ON PAGE 42)

- 2/3 cup butter
- 1-1/4 cups brown sugar
- 3/4 cup granulated sugar
- 3 beaten eggs
- 1-1/2 cups chunky-style peanut butter*
- 6 cups old-fashioned oats, *not quick-cooking*
- 2 teaspoons baking soda
- 1-1/2 cups raisins
- 1 package (12 ounces) chocolate chips

(*I use Jif brand peanut butter. If unavailable, use another brand, but add several tablespoons water to mixture.) Melt butter over low heat. Blend in sugars, eggs and peanut butter; mix until smooth. Add oats, soda, raisins and chocolate chips (mixture will be sticky). Drop on greased baking sheet with No. 20 ice cream scoop or large spoon. Flatten slightly. Bake at 350° for about 15 minutes for large cookies, 3-in. diameter. Remove to cooling rack. **Yield:** 2 dozen cookies.

FROSTING FINESSE: Before frosting a cake, place strips of waxed paper on the serving plate under the bottom cake layer. Use quick, light strokes with a knife to frost cake, and after frosting, carefully remove the waxed paper—you'll have a clean plate.

● Unfrosted cake layers can be frozen on a cookie sheet until firm, wrapped separately with plastic wrap and kept in the freezer. When they're ready for use, just thaw, frost and serve.

STUFFED ZUCCHINI

Jeanette Mortenson, Albert Lea, Minnesota

(PICTURED ON PAGE 42)

      7 fresh zucchini, 4-6 inches long
    1/2 cup chopped onion
    1/4 cup vegetable oil
    1/2 cup coarsely chopped
          fresh mushrooms
      1 clove garlic, minced
      1 package (3 ounces)
          cream cheese
      1 beaten egg
    1/2 cup Parmesan cheese
    3/4 cup finely chopped
          fresh parsley
    1/4 teaspoon salt
    1/8 teaspoon pepper
Additional Parmesan cheese

Scoop out insides of zucchini (melon baller works great), leaving about 1/4-in. shell. Reserve pulp. Finely chop zucchini pulp; set aside. Saute onion in oil in large heavy skillet. Add mushrooms, garlic and reserved chopped zucchini; cook over medium heat until most of moisture evaporates. Add cream cheese, eggs, Parmesan cheese, parsley, salt and pepper. Mix well; cook for 10 minutes. Cool filling slightly and fill zucchini shells. Sprinkle with additional Parmesan cheese. Place in jelly roll pans; bake for 30 minutes at 350° until bubbly and golden brown on top. **Yield:** 7 servings.

DOOR COUNTY SOUR CHERRY TORTE

Irene Poehler, Sturgeon Bay, Wisconsin

(PICTURED ON PAGE 43)

CAKE:
      1 cup sugar
      2 tablespoons butter
      1 egg, beaten
      1 cup all-purpose flour
    1/4 teaspoon salt
      1 teaspoon baking soda
      2 cups sour cherries, drained
          (reserve juice for
          sauce below)
    1/2 cup chopped walnuts
CREAM LAYER:
      1 pint whipping cream
      2 tablespoons sugar
      2 teaspoons vanilla
SAUCE:
      1 cup cherry juice
    1/2 cup sugar
      2 tablespoons butter
      1 tablespoon cornstarch

Make cake by creaming sugar, butter and egg together. Add flour, salt and soda; mix. (Batter will be very stiff.) Add cherries and nuts to batter. Spread batter in greased 13- x 9-in. baking pan or large springform pan. Bake at 350° for 30 minutes (13- x 9-in. pan) *or* 1 hour in springform. Cool. Prepare cream layer by whipping cream, sugar and vanilla until thick. Spread over cool cake; refrigerate. Cook sauce by combining all ingredients in small pan over medium heat. Cook until thick; cool thoroughly. Spoon over cream layer in decorative pattern. Refrigerate until serving time. **Yield:** 16-20 servings.

MILE HIGH SHREDDED BEEF

Betty Sitzman, Wray, Colorado

(PICTURED ON PAGE 43)

      3 pounds chuck roast *or*
          round steak
Vegetable oil
      1 cup chopped onion
    1/2 cup chopped celery
      2 cups beef broth *or* bouillon
SAUCE:
Beef broth (1-1/2 cups, reserved from
      cooking beef mixture above)
      1 clove garlic, minced
      1 teaspoon salt
    3/4 cup catsup
      4 tablespoons brown sugar
      2 tablespoons vinegar
      1 teaspoon dry mustard
    1/2 teaspoon chili powder
      3 drops Tabasco
      1 bay leaf
    1/4 teaspoon paprika
    1/4 teaspoon garlic powder
      1 teaspoon Worcestershire
          sauce

Brown beef in hot oil on both sides, adding onion and celery at last minute. Combine beef, vegetables and broth in covered Dutch oven or crock pot. Simmer, covered, 3-4 hours, or until tender. Cool; shred beef, separating into strands. Drain vegetables; combine with beef. Reserve broth; skim off any fat. To make sauce, mix beef, vegetables, reserved 1-1/2 cups beef broth, garlic, salt, catsup, brown sugar, vinegar, mustard, chili powder, Tabasco, bay leaf, paprika, garlic powder and Worcestershire sauce. Simmer all ingredients together until heated thoroughly. *Remove bay leaf.* (This mixture keeps well in crock pot on low heat.) Serve with potato rolls or buns. **Yield:** 8 servings.

CAULIFLOWER/BROCCOLI SALAD WITH DRESSING

Marcia Hempfling, Hebron, Kentucky

      1 head cauliflower, broken
          into florets
      1 bunch broccoli, cut into
          bite-size pieces
    1/4 cup onion, chopped
      1 ounce pimiento, drained
      1 can (8 ounces) water
          chestnuts, sliced and drained
      1 can (16 ounces) kidney
          beans, drained
DRESSING:
    1/3 cup vinegar
    1/4 cup sugar
    1/2 cup creamy salad dressing
    1/3 cup vegetable oil
TOPPING:
      1 cup sharp cheddar cheese,
          grated
    1/2 cup crumbled bacon bits

Combine cauliflower, broccoli, onion, pimiento, chestnuts and beans in large bowl. Set aside. Dissolve sugar in vinegar; mix well. Add salad dressing and oil; mix. Drizzle dressing over vegetables; chill. Before serving, sprinkle topping of cheese and bacon over vegetables. **Yield:** 8 servings.

COOL CLOVES: Store garlic cloves refrigerated in a little olive oil, and they'll keep indefinitely.

MARYLAND CRAB CASSEROLE

Nancy Mahoney, Ellicott City, Maryland

(PICTURED ON PAGE 44)

      1 pound well-picked
          crab meat
      3 beaten eggs
      1 tablespoon fresh parsley
    1/3 cup butter, melted, *divided*
      1 teaspoon salt
Dash black pepper
    1/2 teaspoon Worcestershire
          sauce

1/2 teaspoon prepared mustard
1 cup evaporated milk
1 tablespoon minced
   green pepper
1/2 cup soft bread crumbs (mix
   with 1 to 2 tablespoons of
   reserved butter)

Butter sides and bottom of 2-qt. baking dish. Combine crab, eggs, parsley and *all but 2 tablespoons of melted butter,* salt, pepper, Worcestershire sauce, mustard, milk and green pepper. Gently pat into dish. Combine bread crumbs with reserved butter; sprinkle on top. Bake at 350° until brown, about 20 minutes. **Yield:** 4 servings.

STRAWBERRY SALAD

1 pint frozen strawberries,
   (reserve juice)
1 package (3 ounces) vanilla
   pudding, *not* instant
1 package (3-1/4 ounces)
   tapioca pudding, *not* instant
1 package (3 ounces)
   strawberry gelatin
2 bananas
2 cups whipped cream *or*
   topping

Pour strawberry juice and/or water into 2-qt. glass measure to make 2 cups liquid. Add puddings and gelatin. Microwave on high for 5-6 minutes or until mixture thickens and boils. Stir once or twice while cooking; cool. Add strawberries, bananas and whipped cream. **Yield:** 8 servings.

HAM, SWISS CHEESE POTATO SALAD

Ruth Swift, Portland, Oregon

1-1/2 pounds red salad potatoes
4-1/2 tablespoons white wine *or*
   3-1/2 teaspoons water plus 1
   tablespoon more vinegar
3 tablespoons white wine
   vinegar *or* white vinegar
1/4 cup green onion, chopped
3 tablespoons Dijon mustard
3/4 teaspoon salt
1 teaspoon pepper
1/2 cup vegetable oil
1/4 cup fresh parsley, chopped
3/4 cup cooked ham, finely
   chopped
1 cup Swiss cheese, finely
   shredded

Scrub potatoes, rinse and boil in jackets until tender. Drain; cool and peel. Cut into 1/2-in. cubes; set aside. Combine wine or water, vinegar, onion, mustard, salt, pepper, oil and parsley in jar. Shake well. Add ham and cheese to the potatoes; pour 2/3 of dressing over potato mixture. Mix until blended. Cover; chill thoroughly. Before serving, stir remaining dressing and add more, if desired. **Yield:** 4 servings.

DOOR COUNTY FISH BOIL

Linda Anderson, Sister Bay, Wisconsin

(PICTURED ON PAGE 44)

Large kettle with colander (canning
   kettle works fine)
Water
   1/2 cup salt
   16 small red potatoes
      (1-1/2-inch diameter),
      ends trimmed off
   16 small white onions, peeled
      (1-inch-diameter)
   16 chunks (2-inch) whitefish *or*
      lake trout
Butter
Lemons
   1/2 cup kerosene for boil-over

Bring water (fill kettle 1/2 full) and salt to boil in large kettle suspended over outdoor fire. *Be sure area surrounding fire is raked clear of burnable material—have water bucket nearby.* Add potatoes; boil for 15 minutes. Add onions; boil for 5 more minutes. Add fish; allow water to return to boil; boil for 5 minutes. Using fireproof gloves, *carefully* dash 1/2 cup kerosene on base of open flame. **Caution:** *Stand back immediately as fire will blaze in order to boil-over water and remove fish residue.* When flames subside, carefully remove colander from kettle. Ladle fish, onions and potatoes on platters with slotted spoon. Serve with melted butter and fresh lemon juice. (Traditional fish boil includes coleslaw, rye bread and cherry pie.) **Yield:** 8 servings.

TEXAS SHRIMP/ RICE SALAD

Pam Scales Crew, Oregon, Texas

(PICTURED ON PAGE 44)

4-1/2 cups water
1-1/2 pounds unpeeled *small*
   shrimp, uncooked
1-1/2 to 2 cups cooked rice
1 can (16 ounces) cut green
   beans, drained, *or* frozen
   beans, cooked and drained
1/2 cup pitted ripe olives, sliced
1/3 cup chopped green onions
1/2 cup commercial Italian
   salad dressing
3 tablespoons chili sauce
1/2 teaspoon dried basil leaves
1/4 teaspoon pepper
1/8 teaspoon garlic powder
Curly salad greens

Bring water to boil in large pot; add shrimp and return to boil. Reduce heat; simmer 3-5 minutes. Drain shrimp well; rinse with cold water. Cool shrimp; peel and devein. Combine shrimp, rice, beans, olives and onions; toss well. Combine salad dressing, chili sauce, basil, pepper and garlic powder; mix well. Pour over rice mixture; chill. Serve over salad greens. **Yield:** 6-8 servings.

STEAMED PACIFIC SALMON

Jutta Doening, Kelowna, British Columbia

(PICTURED ON PAGE 44)

1 piece (2 pounds) Pacific
   salmon *or* halibut (can use
   steaks, if desired)
2 tablespoons chopped
   fresh basil
1 teaspoon dried *or*
   fresh rosemary
1 teaspoon fresh parsley
3 tablespoons butter
3 to 4 tablespoons fresh lemon
   juice (1 large lemon)
Salt
Pepper
Heavy aluminum foil

Place fish on large double sheet of heavy foil. Sprinkle basil, rosemary and parsley over fish. Add butter, dotted evenly over fish. Season with lemon juice, salt and pepper. Seal foil tightly to retain juices. Bake at 375° for 25-30 minutes. Fish is done when flakes easily with fork. Garnish with additional fresh herbs, if desired. **Yield:** 4-6 servings.

FOOLPROOF POTATOES: For scalloped potatoes, layer sliced potatoes, sliced onions, ham pieces, flour, milk and *undiluted* cream of celery soup in a baking dish. Top with bread crumbs and Parmesan cheese; bake at 350° until sauce is bubbly and potatoes are tender. Enjoy!

STRAWBERRY/ RHUBARB SALAD

Joan Truax, Pittsboro, Indiana

(PICTURED ON PAGE 46)

 This tasty dish uses less sugar, salt and fat. Recipe includes *Diabetic Exchanges*.

    4 cups diced raw rhubarb
1-1/2 cups water
  1/2 cup sugar
    2 packages (3 ounces each)
      strawberry gelatin
    1 cup orange juice
    1 tablespoon grated orange rind
    2 cups fresh strawberries,
      sliced
Strawberries for garnish

Combine rhubarb, water and sugar in saucepan; cook until tender. Pour hot rhubarb mixture over gelatin and stir until completely dissolved. Add orange juice and rind. Chill until syrupy; fold in strawberries. Pour into a 1-qt. mold; chill until set. Garnish with whole strawberries with hulls. **Yield:** 8 servings. **Diabetic Exchanges:** One serving equals 3 fruit; also, 167 calories, 69 mg sodium, 0 cholesterol, 41 gm carbohydrate, 23 gm protein, .3 gm fat.

STRAWBERRY DEVONSHIRE TART

Carol Ziemann, Chesterfield, Missouri

(PICTURED ON PAGE 46)

TART SHELL:
    1 cup all-purpose flour
    2 tablespoons sugar
  1/4 teaspoon salt
    6 tablespoons butter, room
      temperature
    1 egg yolk
    2 tablespoons ice water
FILLING:
    2 packages (3 ounces each)
      cream cheese, softened)
  1/3 cup dairy sour cream *or*
      yogurt
    2 tablespoons sugar
    1 quart fresh strawberries,
      washed, dried and hulled
GLAZE:
    1 package (10 ounces) frozen
      raspberries in syrup, thawed
Water
  1/4 cup sugar
    1 tablespoon cornstarch

Combine flour, sugar and salt; cut in butter until crumbly. Combine egg yolk and water; stir into flour until dough forms a ball. Press dough onto bottom and up sides of 9-in. tart pan. Prick bottom and sides to prevent excess shrinkage. Bake at 400° for 12-15 minutes until light brown. Cool; set aside. Beat cream cheese until fluffy; beat in sour cream/yogurt and sugar. Spread over bottom of cooled shell. Arrange strawberries, tips up, over cheese. Puree raspberries in blender or processor; pour through sieve to remove seeds. Combine puree with enough water to make 1 cup liquid. In small saucepan, combine sugar and cornstarch. Gradually stir in puree; cook until thick and clear. Cool slightly; pour over strawberries. Chill at least an hour. **Yield:** 6-8 servings.

STRAWBERRY ICE CREAM

Jeri Dobrowski, Beach, North Dakota

(PICTURED ON PAGE 46)

    4 tablespoons all-purpose flour
    1 cup sugar
  1/4 teaspoon salt
2-1/2 cups milk
    3 eggs, beaten
    1 pint fresh hulled strawberries
      or 1-1/2 cups frozen berries,
      thawed
    1 teaspoon lemon juice
  1/2 cup sugar
    1 cup milk
    1 cup heavy cream
    1 to 2 tablespoons vanilla

In large glass bowl, blend first 5 ingredients with a wire whisk. Cook in microwave (or in heavy, 2-qt. saucepan on stove) until mixture coats spoon. Cover with plastic wrap; cool for 2 hours in refrigerator. Mash strawberries, lemon juice and sugar in large bowl or in food processor bowl. (*Don't* add whole berries—they will freeze and be impossible to eat.) Allow fruit to stand about an hour or until juicy. Add strawberry mixture, milk, cream and vanilla to chilled egg mixture; pour into 2-qt. ice cream maker. Follow the manufacturer's instructions for freezing. **Yield:** 2 qts. *or* 10-12 hearty servings.

THE ULTIMATE STRAWBERRY PIE

Judy Page, Edenville, Michigan

(PICTURED ON PAGE 46)

PAT-IN-PAN PIE CRUST:
1-1/2 cups all-purpose flour
  1/2 teaspoon salt
    2 tablespoons sugar
  1/2 cup vegetable oil
    2 tablespoons cold milk
FILLING:
   11 ounces cream cheese (one
      8-ounce plus one 3-ounce
      package), room temperature
    4 tablespoons sugar
    1 quart fresh strawberries,
      divided
    2 ounces semisweet chocolate,
      melted
    1 tablespoon finely chopped
      pistachios, pecans or walnuts

Combine all crust ingredients in 9-in. pie plate; mix and press onto bottom and sides of plate. *Do not prick.* Bake at 400° for 12-15 minutes until golden brown. Cool. Beat together cream cheese and sugar with mixer until smooth. Add about 3/4 cup of the strawberries; beat until just bits of berry remain. Spread mixture into cooled pie shell. Melt chocolate over low heat; dip tips of remaining strawberries into chocolate. Arrange, tips up over cream cheese layer. Sprinkle with nuts for garnish. Chill thoroughly. Cut with sharp knife. **Yield:** 8 servings.

STRAWBERRY SPARKLE PUNCH

Ida Wester, Shelbina, Missouri

(PICTURED ON PAGE 47)

 This tasty dish uses less sugar, salt and fat. Recipe includes *Diabetic Exchanges*.

    4 cups fresh unsweetened
      strawberries
    1 package (3 ounces)
      strawberry-flavored gelatin
    1 cup boiling water
    1 can (6 ounces) frozen
      lemonade concentrate
    1 bottle (32 ounces) cranberry
      juice cocktail, chilled
    2 cups *cold* water
    1 bottle (28 ounces) ginger ale,
      chilled
Strawberries for garnish, if desired

Puree strawberries in blender; place puree in large punch bowl. (Strain; if desired, to remove seeds.) Dissolve gelatin in boiling water; stir in lemonade concentrate. Add mixture to punch bowl. Add cranberry cocktail and *cold* water. Slowly add ginger ale. if desired, serve with fresh strawberry garnish or an ice ring with whole berries frozen in it. **Yield:** 28 (4 oz.) servings. **Diabetic Exchanges:** One serving equals 1 fruit; also, 65 calories, 10 mg sodium 17 gm carbohydrate, .5 gm protein, .1 gm fat.

RICH STRAWBERRY SHORTCAKE

Caryn Wiggins, Columbus, Indiana

(PICTURED ON PAGE 47)

2 cups all-purpose flour
2 tablespoons sugar
4 teaspoons baking powder
1/2 teaspoon salt
1/2 cup butter, softened
1 egg, beaten
About 1/2 cup light cream *or* milk
  (half-and-half preferred)
Soft butter
4 cups sweetened, sliced
  strawberries
Whipped cream *or* ice cream

Sift together flour, sugar, baking powder and salt. Cut in butter until coarse and crumbly. Combine egg and cream/milk; add to flour mixture, stirring just until dough follows fork around bowl. On lightly floured surface, pat or roll to 1/2-in. thickness. (You may need to work in a little additional flour if the dough is too sticky.) Cut with a 2-1/2-in. round cutter. Bake on ungreased baking sheet in very hot oven, 450° for 8-10 minutes or until biscuits are done. Split biscuits and spread each half with butter. Spoon berries between halves and over top. Serve warm with whipped cream or ice cream. **Yield:** 8 servings.

MINIATURE STRAWBERRY MUFFINS

Lois Black, San Antonio, Texas

(PICTURED ON PAGE 47)

 This tasty dish uses less sugar, salt and fat. Recipe includes *Diabetic Exchanges.*

1-1/2 cups *mashed* strawberries,
  3/4 cup sugar *divided*
1-3/4 cups all-purpose flour
1/4 teaspoon nutmeg
1/4 teaspoon salt
1/2 teaspoon baking soda
2 eggs, beaten
1/4 cup butter
1 teaspoon vanilla

Combine strawberries and 1/4 cup sugar; set aside. After 30 minutes, drain strawberries; reserve liquid. Combine flour, nutmeg, salt and soda; set aside. In a medium bowl, mix eggs, butter, vanilla, remaining 1/2 cup sugar and reserved juice from berries. Add to flour mixture; stir until combined. Fold in berries. Spoon into greased miniature muffin tins. Bake at 425° for about 15 minutes for mini-muffins, 20 min-

utes if baking larger muffins. **Yield:** about 32 mini-muffins or 12 large muffins. **Diabetic Exchanges:** One serving (mini) muffin equals 1/2 bread, 1/2 fruit; also 65 calories, 51 mg sodium, 25 mg cholesterol, 11 gm carbohydrate, 1 gm protein, 2 gm fat. One serving (large) muffin equals 1 bread, 1 fruit, 1 fat; also, 174 calories, 136 mg sodium, 67 mg cholesterol, 29 gm carbohydrate, 3 gm protein, 5 gm fat.

STRAWBERRY CHEESECAKE TRIFLE

Diane Evens, George, Wahington

(PICTURED ON PAGE 48)

2 packages (8 ounces *each*)
  cream cheese
2 cups confectioners' sugar
1 cup dairy sour cream
1-1/2 teaspoons vanilla extract,
  divided
1/4 teaspoon almond extract
1/2 pint whipping cream
1 tablespoon sugar
1 angel food cake, torn into
  bite-size pieces
2 quarts fresh strawberries,
  thinly sliced
3 tablespoons sugar
3 tablespoons almond-flavored
  liqueur *or* almond extract to
  taste

In a large bowl, cream together cream cheese and sugar; add sour cream, 1/2 teaspoon vanilla and almond extract. Set aside. In a small, deep bowl, whip the cream, remaining vanilla and sugar. Fold whipped cream into cream cheese mixture. Add cake pieces; set aside. Combine strawberries, sugar and almond liqueur/extract. Layer together in large glass bowl, starting with strawberries, then adding cake mixture. Continue layering; finish with strawberries. Cover with plastic wrap; chill well. **Yield:** 24 servings.

STRAWBERRY/RHUBARB COFFEE CAKE

Pat Walter, Pine Island, Minnesota

(PICTURED ON PAGE 47)

FILLING:
4-1/2 cups rhubarb, chopped
24 ounces frozen sliced
  strawberries, thawed
3 tablespoons lemon juice
1-1/2 cups sugar
1/2 cup cornstarch

CAKE:
3 cups all-purpose flour
1 cup sugar
1 teaspoon baking powder
1 teaspoon salt
1 cup butter, softened
1 cup buttermilk
2 eggs, slightly beaten
1 teaspoon vanilla
TOPPING:
3/4 cup sugar
1/2 cup all-purpose flour
1/4 cup soft butter

To make filling, combine fruits in saucepan and cook, covered, over medium heat for 5 minutes, stirring occasionally. Add lemon juice, sugar and cornstarch. Cook, stirring, for 5 minutes or until thickened. Cool. To make cake, combine flour, sugar, baking powder and salt in large bowl; cut in butter until mixture is crumbly. Beat together buttermilk, eggs and vanilla; add to the flour mixture. Spread one-half of batter in greased 13-in. x 9-in. x 2-in. baking pan. Spread fruit over batter. Spoon remaining batter in small mounds on top of filling. Mix topping ingredients until crumbly; sprinkle over all. Bake at 375° for 45 minutes. Serve slightly warm. **Yield:** 12-16 servings.

STRAWBERRY/ SPINACH SALAD

Perlene Hoekema, Lynden, Washington

(PICTURED ON PAGE 48)

 This tasty dish uses less sugar, salt and fat. Recipe includes *Diabetic Exchanges.*

2 tablespoons sesame seeds
1-1/2 pounds fresh spinach
1/3 cup vegetable oil
1/3 cup red wine vinegar
1 tablespoon sugar
2 teaspoons minced green onion
1/2 teaspoon paprika
1/4 teaspoon Worcestershire
  sauce
2 cups fresh strawberries,
  washed, hulled and halved

In a 7-in. skillet over medium heat, stir sesame seed until golden; set aside. Wash spinach thoroughly; dry on paper towels and tear into bite-size pieces. Wrap and chill. Blend oil, vinegar, sugar, onion, paprika and Worcestershire sauce. In large glass bowl, mix together spinach, strawberries, dressing and seeds. **Yield:** 8 servings. **Diabetic Exchanges:** One serving equals 1-1/2 vegetable, 2 fat; also, 133 calories, 66 mg sodium, 0 cholesterol, 9 gm carbohydrate, 4 gm protein, 11 gm fat.

SUPER EASY STRAWBERRY SHERBET

Jane Kennedy, Mayville, Michigan

(PICTURED ON PAGE 48)

2 cups buttermilk
1-1/2 cups strawberry freezer jam*
Fresh strawberries for garnish
Fresh mint leaves for garnish

Stir buttermilk into jam; pour into refrigerator tray and freeze until firm. Cut up frozen mixture; place in chilled mixer bowl. Whip until fluffy. Return to tray; cover and freeze until firm. (Can also freeze in ice cream freezer according to manufacturer's instructions.) Spoon into sherbet dishes. Garnish with fresh strawberries and mint leaves, if desired. **Yield:** about 1 quart.

***STRAWBERRY FREEZER JAM**
2 cups fresh mashed strawberries
4 cups granulated sugar
3/4 cup water
1 package (1-3/4 ounces) powdered pectin

Mash strawberries very fine; add sugar; let stand 10 minutes. Place water and pectin in small saucepan; bring to boil. Boil for 1 minute, stirring constantly. Remove from stove; add to strawberries. Stir for 3 minutes. Spoon into clean, sterilized jars, leaving 1/2-in. space at top. Seal; let stand at room temperature for 24 hours. Store jam in freezer. **Yield:** about 5 cups.

PAVLOVA

Gail Payne, Clive, Alberta

(PICTURED ON PAGE 48)

MERINGUE:
4 egg whites, room temperature
1 cup granulated sugar
1 teaspoon cornstarch
1 teaspoon vinegar
1 teaspoon vanilla
CREAM LAYER:
1 cup whipping cream
2 tablespoons granulated sugar
1 teaspoon vanilla
1 pint fresh strawberries
2 kiwi fruits
GLAZE:
1/4 cup granulated sugar
1/4 cup water
1-1/2 teaspoons cornstarch

(**NOTE:** This recipe works best on cool, dry days.) Beat egg whites until soft peaks form. Gradually add sugar

and cornstarch, beating until stiff and glossy. Beat in vinegar and vanilla. (Test meringue by rubbing between thumb and finger—it should not be grainy.) Spread meringue on a foil or parchment paper-lined 12-in. pizza pan (or form in any shape desired). Bake at 275° for 50-60 minutes; turn off heat and allow to stand in oven for at least 1 hour. Make cream layer by whipping cream, sugar and vanilla until stiff. Spread over top of cooled meringue. Arrange fruit in attractive pattern over top of cream layer. Set aside. Combine glaze ingredients in small saucepan. Bring to boil to thicken. Cool. Brush glaze over fruit to seal with small, soft brush. Chill until serving time. **Yield:** 12-16 servings.

STRAWBERRY SAUCE SUPREME

Helen Regan, Carle Place, New York

1-1/2 quarts strawberries, sliced
1/3 cup sugar
1 package (10 ounces) frozen raspberries, thawed
2 tablespoons sugar
2 tablespoons orange liqueur *or* 2 teaspoons grated orange rind
1 teaspoon fresh lemon juice

Combine strawberries and sugar; stir to blend. Add raspberries, sugar, liqueur or rind and lemon juice. Refrigerate at least 4 hours. Serve over ice cream, pound cake or angel food cake. **Yield:** about 2 quarts.

FRESH STRAWBERRY POUND CAKE

Frances Amundson, Gilby, North Dakota

CAKE:
1 box white cake mix (18-1/4 ounces)
1 cup crushed fresh strawberries
1 package (3 ounces) strawberry-flavored gelatin
1/2 cup vegetable oil
4 eggs, room temperature
GLAZE:
1/4 cup butter *or* margarine
3-1/2 cups confectioners' sugar
1/4 cup mashed strawberries

Combine cake ingredients together in large mixing bowl; mix for 3 minutes. Pour in well-greased-and-floured tube pan. Bake at 325° for 45-55 minutes or

until cake tests done. Cool in pan on rack for 10 minutes; remove to serving plate. Combine glaze ingredients until smooth and spread over cake. (May be frozen with or without glaze.) **Yield:** 12-16 servings.

STRAWBERRIES AND ALMOND CREME

Gail Yeskis, Bridgewater, New Hampshire

1 quart large strawberries
1 package (3-1/2 ounces) vanilla instant pudding and pie filling
3/4 cup milk
1 cup heavy whipped cream *or* nondairy whipped topping
1 to 2 teaspoons almond extract

Carefully wash berries; drain on paper towels. Cut a deep "X" from pointed end of each berry to 1/4 in. from stem end. Gently spread apart to make "petals". Set aside on pretty serving plate. Prepare pudding according to package instructions *except use only 3/4 cup of milk.* Gently fold whipped cream/topping and extract into pudding. Pipe cream into strawberries from a decorating bag with large tip. Serve immediately. **Yield:** 8 servings.

GERMAN CHOCOLATE ICE CREAM

Cynthia Kolberg, Syracuse, Indiana

1 cup sugar
1/4 cup all-purpose flour
1/4 teaspoon salt
1/4 teaspoon cinnamon
1 quart milk
2 bars (4 ounces *each*) German sweet chocolate, melted
3 eggs, beaten
1 cup shredded coconut
1 quart light cream *or* half-and-half
1 cup chopped pecans

Combine sugar, flour, salt and cinnamon in heavy 3-qt. saucepan. Gradually add milk. Cook over medium heat, stirring constantly until thickened. Cook 2 more minutes. Remove from heat. Blend in melted chocolate. Blend small amount of cooked mixture into eggs, stirring constantly. Return mixture to pan. Cook 1 minute. *Do not boil.* Remove from heat; add coconut. Blend in cream. Chill mixture 1-2 hours. Stir in nuts just before freezing. Freeze following ice cream maker's instructions. **Yield:** 1 gallon.

CARROT/WALNUT SALAD

Donna Thompson, Sweet Springs, Missouri

- 2 cups finely shredded raw carrots
- 1/2 cup walnuts, coarsely chopped
- 1/2 cup raisins
- 1/2 cup coconut

DRESSING:
- 1 egg, beaten
- 1/3 cup sugar
- 3 tablespoons light cream, half-and-half *or* evaporated milk
- 2 tablespoons vinegar
- 1/4 teaspoon salt

Shred carrots with fine shredder in food processor or grind (as Donna does) with a hand-turned food grinder. Add walnuts, raisins and coconut. Set aside. Combine in heavy small saucepan, beaten egg, sugar, cream, vinegar and salt. Cook, stirring constantly over medium heat until thickened. Cool to room temperature. Pour over carrot mixture; stir to blend. Let stand, covered, in refrigerator for 2-3 hours. **Yield:** 6-8 servings.

CALIFORNIA CLUB SALAD

Alex Michaels, Claremont, California

- 4 stalks celery, washed and drained
- 2 chicken breasts, skinned, boned, cooked and cooled
- 4 ounces Monterey Jack cheese
- 4 medium green onions
- 2 large tomatoes
- 1 cup loose, long-stemmed cilantro
- 2 slices sourdough bread
- 2 tablespoons soft butter
- 4 tablespoons grated Parmesan cheese
- 8 ounces lean bacon, cooked until crisp

DRESSING:
- 1-1/2 tablespoons mayonnaise
- 3 tablespoons dairy sour cream
- 1 teaspoon Dijon mustard
- 1-1/2 tablespoons honey

Leaf lettuce, washed, drained and chilled

Cut celery, chicken, cheese, onions and tomato in short, thin sticks, about 3-in. x 1/8-in. x 1/4-in. julienne cuts. Keep ingredients separate; set aside. Cut cilantro in similar lengths. Toast slices of bread in toaster oven or broiler until light golden brown on both sides. Remove and butter one side only. Sprinkle with Parmesan cheese; return to toaster oven or broiler and toast until Parmesan cheese bubbles. Remove; slice in similar sizes to other salad ingredients. Set aside. Cook bacon in microwave until crisp; break into pieces 1/2-inch long; set aside. Combine salad dressing ingredients thoroughly. Right before serving, blend all salad ingredients with dressing. Serve immediately from glass lettuce-lined bowl. **Yield:** 8 servings.

FAVORITE NICOISE SALAD

Mrs. Eddie Paulson, Stanley, North Dakota

 This tasty dish uses less sugar, salt and fat. Recipe includes *Diabetic Exchanges*.

- 3 cups boiled potatoes, sliced 1/4 inch thick
- 1 pound fresh green beans, cooked, drained
- 1 can (7-ounce) albacore (white) tuna
- 3 ounces olive oil
- 3 ounces vinegar
- 1 teaspoon salt
- 1/4 teaspoon white pepper
- 2 teaspoons Dijon mustard

Romaine lettuce leaves
- 2 tomatoes, quartered
- 12 pitted black olives

Capers (optional)

Gently mix cooked potatoes, green beans and drained tuna in large bowl. Set aside. Make dressing by mixing olive oil, vinegar, salt, pepper and mustard together. Pour over potato mixture; toss lightly. Arrange lettuce on plates; mound with salad. Decorate with tomatoes, olives and capers, if desired. Serve immediately; refrigerate leftovers. **Yield:** 6 servings. **Diabetic Exchanges:** One servings equals 1 protein, 1 bread, 1 vegetable, 2 fats; also 480 mg sodium, 21 mg cholesterol, 261 calories, 20 gm carbohydrate.

SOUR MILK DOUGHNUTS

Ada Urie, Glover, Vermont

- 3-1/2 cups sifted all-purpose flour
- 1 teaspoon baking soda
- 1/4 teaspoon baking powder
- 1 teaspoon salt
- 1 teaspoon nutmeg
- 1/2 teaspoon ginger
- 3/4 cup sugar
- 2 tablespoons lard *or*
- shortening
- 2 eggs
- 1 cup sour milk*

Lard *or* vegetable oil for deep frying

*Try to use freshly soured milk that is a thick clabber; otherwise dough will be too soft. Sift flour, baking soda, powder, salt, nutmeg and ginger 3 times. Set aside. Cream sugar and lard well. Add eggs, beating well with electric beater. Add sour milk; beat well. Stir in dry ingredients all at once; stir well. *Do not beat.* Chill dough overnight. Divide dough in half; roll out on floured board about 1/4-in. thick. Cut with doughnut cutter. Deep fry in fresh lard or vegetable oil at 400°. **Yield:** 2 dozen.

SOUR CREAM SCALLOPED POTATOES

Estelle Blasel, Orange, California

- 2 large baking potatoes
- 1 medium-size onion, diced
- 2 tablespoons butter
- 1 cup cultured sour cream
- 4 hard-cooked eggs, sliced

Salt
Ground pepper
Paprika

Pare and slice potatoes 1/8-in. thick. Parcook in boiling, salted water 5 minutes; drain. Set aside. Saute onion in butter until glossy, but not brown. Stir in sour cream and let heat thoroughly. *Do not boil.* In buttered 2-qt. casserole, layer 1/2 of potatoes, egg slices and sour cream mixture. Sprinkle salt, pepper and paprika lightly over sour cream mixture. Repeat layers with rest of ingredients. Bake, uncovered, at 350° for 45 minutes or until potatoes are tender. Do not overbake. **Yield:** 4 servings.

THE BERRY BEST: Garnish each piece of fresh strawberry pie with a dollop of whipped cream, a mint leaf and one perfect strawberry.

● Dip fresh strawberries into sour cream or yogurt and roll in strawberry-flavored gelatin granules for a tasty summer treat.

● Stir homemade strawberry jams and jellies occasionally while they cool to prevent berries from floating to the top of the jars.

● Strawberries stored with stems stay firm and fresh longer than those without stems.

Enjoy the special occasions of summer with a beautiful backyard buffet—country-style! These recipes from great country cooks will add a delicious difference to weddings, bridal or baby showers and graduation parties.

Sweeten the moment with glorious seasonal desserts such as fresh raspberry cake or pie, light-as-a-cloud cherry roll or irresistible strawberry and kiwi tarts.

Please your guests with pretty, portable treats, such as luscious lemon squares, butter-rich butterfly pastries and creamy handmade mints.

For a fine finale, serve a sparkling fruit-based punch decorated with fresh herbs and seasonal fruits. It tastes as refreshing as it looks!

SWEET STARS: Clockwise on our dessert table from lower left—**Cherries 'n' Cream Roll** (Pg. 63); **Raspberry Glace Pie/Tart** (Pg. 63); **Fresh Raspberry Cake** (Pg. 63); **Mom's Cream Cheese Mints** (Pg. 64); **Strawberry/Kiwi Tarts** (Pg. 64); **Wedding Punch** (Pg. 64); **Butterflies** (Pg. 63); **Delicate Lemon Squares** (Pg. 63).

Main dish salads just make sense for special-occasion buffets—and for cool summer suppers, as well.

These fix-ahead salads range from spicy pepperoni flavors to zesty artichoke/rice combinations, from chicken and spinach to creamy bean/cheese/ham blends. All are pretty as a picture...and pretty easy to prepare, too. Try one today!

SAVORY SALADS: Clockwise from bottom—**Pasta Picnic Salad** (Pg. 65); **Artichoke Rice Salad** (Pg. 65); **Spinach Chicken Salad** (Pg. 64); **Idaho Chef's Salad** (Pg. 64).

MEALS IN MINUTES

Ah, summertime. It's a time for rest and relaxation...for that respite you've been waiting for. Truth is, you're probably more rushed this time of year than any other, with family fun...yard work...and yes, some leisure time.

But this time of year is also when it's easier than ever to make quick meals visually appealing and attractive. Fresh garden produce—whether from your backyard or a stand—does the trick.

Corn on the cob just can't be beat, and you can make the most delicious of desserts from soft summer fruit.

One of the best things about this "Meals in Minutes" menu from Alice Ellison of Plymouth, Minnesota, is that it can be prepared either indoors or out. In good weather, turn to the grill. On rainy days, broil the kabobs in the oven in just minutes.

SUMMER SAUSAGE KABOB

- 1 pound sweet Italian link sausage, cut in 1-inch pieces
- 1 cup water
- 6 large mushrooms
- 1 tablespoon butter
- 1 red and 1 green sweet pepper, cut in chunks

Simmer sausage in water for 5-10 minutes; set aside. Simmer mushrooms in butter and enough water to cover for 3-4 minutes to soften. Alternate the sausage, mushrooms and pepper on skewers; grill 7-8 minutes on each side. (Can also be broiled in oven 3-4 in. from heat source for the same time.) **Yield:** 2-3 servings.

CORN ON THE COB

As many ears of husked sweet corn as desired

Wrap individual ears in plain paper towel. Microwave on high 6-7 minutes per pound (one medium ear weighs 7 to 8 oz.), rotating the ears halfway through cooking time. Serve with plain or flavored butters (chives and chili powder are this cook's choice).

YOGURT/BERRY PARFAITS

- 1 pint frozen vanilla yogurt
- 1 cup fresh blueberries
- 1 cup fresh red raspberries

Scoop yogurt into footed glasses; surround with the combination of berries. **Yield:** 2-3 servings.

When you have a little more time to barbecue, here's a recipe to try:

PLUM-SAUCED BARBECUED RIBS

Lee Gallahue, Piper City, Illinois

8 to 10 pounds pork spareribs
SAUCE:
- 1/2 cup chopped onion
- 2 tablespoons butter
- 1 can (17 ounces) purple plums
- 1 can (6 ounces) lemonade concentrate, thawed
- 1/4 cup chili sauce
- 1/4 cup reduced-sodium soy sauce
- 2 teaspoons prepared mustard
- 1 teaspoon ground ginger
- 1 teaspoon Worcestershire sauce

Cut ribs into 3- to 4-rib portions. Place in large kettle with lightly salted water and simmer, covered, for 45 minutes. Drain; set aside. Prepare sauce by cooking onion in butter in pan until clear. Drain plums, reserving liquid. *Remove and discard pits.* Puree plums and reserved liquid until smooth. Add puree to onion/butter mixture; stir in remaining sauce ingredients. Simmer, uncovered, 10-15 minutes, stirring occasionally. Grill ribs over *slow* coals about 25 minutes, turning 3-4 times and brushing with sauce. Serve with remaining sauce. **Yield:** 8-10 servings.

QUICK 'N' EASY APPETIZERS:
Combine catsup and brown sugar to taste; add cocktail sausages or slices of hot dogs. Heat and serve in a slow cooker or a fondue pot.

● Spread 1 8-oz. package of cream cheese on a large plate. Top with cocktail sauce; sprinkle with drained canned or frozen shrimp. Serve with crackers.

Bring on the blueberries...and discover the generous goodness of this versatile fruit in a variety of summer recipes!

Because they can be grown from Minnesota to Florida, fresh blueberries are in season from May to September—what a blessing for good cooks everywhere!

Toss a handful of blueberries into the Sunday supper pancakes...try blueberries in your favorite homemade ice cream recipe or fold the bright beauties into a gelatin salad.

Bake with blueberries for a good-taste bonus—they add color and flavor to muffins, cobblers, crisps, biscuits, cakes and pies.

No matter how you use them, blueberries are bound to please.

PICK OF THE CROP: Clockwise from lower left—**Blueberry Almond Crunch** (Pg. 66); **Blueberry Cheesecake** (Pg. 66); **Blueberry Bran Muffins** (Pg. 66); **Blueberry Orange Salad** (Pg. 66); **Baked Blueberry Pudding Cake with Lemon Sauce** (Pg. 67); **Fresh Blueberry Cream Pie** (Pg. 67); **Blueberry Sauce** (Pg. 67); **Blueberry Scones** (Pg. 66).

Beautiful, bountiful blueberries —they've been called "nature's convenience fruit". They need no pitting, peeling or coring to be enjoyed in a variety of ways.

Use blueberries to top a fancy-filled tart such as our Blueberry/ Kiwi Flan...or layer them in an old-fashioned dessert made of custard, cake and fruit called Trifle.

Blueberries also add texture and color to company-best coffee cakes... and make tasty toppings for crepes.

There are so many ways to enjoy this native North American berry—delicious blueberries make summer a real taste treat!

BEST BLUEBERRIES: Clockwise from lower left—**Blueberry Streusel Coffee Cake** (Pg. 68); **Blueberry Peach Trifle** (Pg. 68); **Blueberry/Kiwi Flan** (Pg. 67); **Blueberry/Lemon Crepes** (Pg. 67).

FRESH RASPBERRY CAKE

Margery Peterson, Nyssa, Oregon

(PICTURED ON PAGE 56)

1 white cake mix (18-1/4 ounces)
FILLING:
  1 package (8 ounces) cream cheese
  1 cup confectioners' sugar
  1 cup whipping cream, whipped
  1/2 cup confectioners' sugar
  1 package (3-3/4 ounces) Raspberry Danish Dessert*
  2 to 3 cups fresh raspberries

Prepare cake mix according to package directions and remove 2 cups batter before baking. Bake in greased and floured 13-in. x 9-in. x 2-in. pan at 350° until done. (Use remaining batter for cupcakes.) Set aside to cool. Mix cream cheese and 1 cup confectioners' sugar; fold in whipped cream combined with 1/2 cup of confectioners' sugar. Spread filling on cool cake and chill in refrigerator. Mix Danish Dessert with 1-1/2 cups cold water; cook as directed. Cool. Add fresh raspberries to cooled Danish Dessert; spread over filling layer on cake. Refrigerate overnight. *If Danish Dessert is unavailable, make sauce from 2 packages (10 oz. each) frozen raspberries, undrained. Crush raspberries in juice; strain through sieve to remove seeds. Place juice in saucepan and combine with 1/2 cup sugar and 2 tablespoons cornstarch; cook until clear. Chill. Proceed with recipe. **Yield:** 16 servings.

RASPBERRY GLACE PIE/TART

Elizabeth Karr, Tacoma, Washington

(PICTURED ON PAGE 56)

CRUST:
  1/2 cup butter, softened
  1/4 cup confectioners' sugar
  1/2 teaspoon vanilla
  1 cup flour
  1/8 teaspoon salt
  1/2 cup ground nuts
FILLING:
  1 quart fresh raspberries, rinsed gently and drained, *divided*
  1 cup water, *divided*
  3 tablespoons cornstarch
  1 cup sugar

For crust, cream together butter, sugar and vanilla; add flour, salt and nuts (I prefer walnuts). Chill in bowl 30-40 minutes. Press into *deep* 9-in. pie plate or 8-in. tart pan. Bake at 400° for 10-12 minutes or until golden brown. Cool. For filling, simmer 1 cup berries with 2/3 cup water for 3 minutes or until berries are soft. Strain out seeds and pulp. Blend remaining water, cornstarch and sugar; stir into berry mixture and continue cooking until thickened. Cool. Place remaining berries in baked crust; pour cooled glaze over all. Chill 2 hours or until set. Garnish with whipped cream, if desired. **Yield:** 8 servings.

CHERRIES 'N' CREAM ROLL

Mrs. John Nolt, Lititz, Pennsylvania

(PICTURED ON PAGE 56)

SPONGE CAKE:
  1 cup cake flour
  1 teaspoon baking powder
  1/4 teaspoon salt
  3 eggs
  3/4 cup sugar
  1 tablespoon frozen orange juice concentrate
  2 tablespoons water
FILLING:
  2 cups heavy cream, whipped
  1/2 cup confectioners' sugar
  1/2 teaspoon almond extract
  1 can (21 ounces) cherry pie filling *or* other fruit filling

Grease a 15-in. x 10-in. x 1-in. jelly roll pan and line with waxed paper or parchment. Sift together flour, baking powder and salt; set aside. Beat eggs at high speed until thick; add sugar and beat until smooth and lemon-colored. Blend in orange concentrate and water at low speed; add dry ingredients slowly. *Do not overbeat.* Pour batter in pan and bake at 375° for 12 minutes. Invert cake onto a clean towel that has been liberally sprinkled with confectioners' sugar. Whip cream; add sugar and almond extract. Spread cooled cake with half of whipped cream and three-fourths of cherry filling. Roll up carefully. Frost with remaining whipped cream and if desired, garnish with remaining cherry filling. Chill before serving. **Yield:** 10-12 servings.

FAST FROZEN FRUIT: In a hurry? Keep grated orange and lemon peels handy for baking by preparing them ahead and freezing in small containers. This saves time and extra work!

DELICATE LEMON SQUARES

Ruby Nelson, Mountain Home, Arkansas

(PICTURED ON PAGE 56)

CRUST:
  1 cup all-purpose flour
  1/4 cup confectioners' sugar
  1/2 cup butter
FILLING:
  2 eggs
  3/4 cup granulated sugar
  3 tablespoons fresh lemon juice
  2 tablespoons all-purpose flour
  1/2 teaspoon baking powder
Confectioners' sugar

Stir together flour and confectioners' sugar; cut in butter until mixture clings together. Pat into an ungreased 8-in. x 8-in. x 2-in. baking pan; bake at 350° for 10-12 minutes. Meanwhile, beat eggs in mixing bowl; add granulated sugar and lemon juice and beat until thick and smooth, 8-10 minutes. Stir together flour and baking powder; add to egg mixture, blending until all ingredients are moistened. Pour egg mixture gently over baked crust layer. Bake at 350° for 20-25 minutes. Cool slightly. Sift confectioners' sugar over top. Cool completely; cut cookies into 1-1/2-in. squares. **Yield:** about 3 dozen bars.

BUTTERFLIES

Marianne Robinson, Valencia, Pennsylvania

(PICTURED ON PAGE 56)

1 cup butter, chilled
1-1/2 cups all-purpose flour
1/2 cup dairy sour cream
1 teaspoon grated lemon peel
About 3/4 cup granulated sugar

Cut butter and flour together; stir in sour cream and lemon peel. Shape into a 4-1/2-in. square; place on waxed paper and refrigerate 2 hours. Cut dough into four pieces; work with *one piece of dough at a time*. Sprinkle 2 tablespoons sugar on wax paper surface; coat dough in sugar. Roll dough into a 12-in. x 5-in. rectangle, flipping often. (Do not re-roll dough scraps.) On 12-in. edge, mark center. From each short end, roll dough to center mark. Wrap rolls and refrigerate 2 hours. Cut chilled rolls into 3/8-in. slices. Dip each slice into sugar on both sides. Bake on foil-lined baking sheets at 375° for 12-15 minutes or until golden brown. Turn over; bake 3 minutes more. Cool on wire rack. **Yield:** 40 cookies.

STRAWBERRY/KIWI TARTS

Becky Duncan, Leming, Texas

(PICTURED ON PAGE 57)

CRUST:
- 1 cup flour
- 1/2 cup confectioners' sugar
- 1/2 cup butter

CREAM FILLING:
- 1 package (8 ounces) cream cheese
- 1/2 cup sugar
- 1/4 teaspoon fresh lemon juice

TOPPING:
- 1 pint fresh strawberries, washed, stemmed and mashed
- 4 tablespoons sugar
- 1 tablespoon cornstarch
- 2 kiwis, peeled and sliced crosswise
- 1 pint fresh strawberries, washed, drained, sliced

For crust, combine flour and sugar; cut in butter until mixture clings together. Pat dough into single-serving tart forms (2 tablespoons each in about 19 shallow forms) *or* 12-in. pizza pan. Bake at 325° for about 10-15 minutes or until golden brown. Cool. For filling, combine cream cheese, sugar and lemon juice; beat until smooth and spread over pastry. Refrigerate. For topping, cook mashed strawberries over medium heat until juice is bright red; strain to remove pulp. Add sugar and cornstarch to strawberry juice; cook, stirring constantly, until thick. Cool. Spread thickened juice over cream cheese mixture; top with sliced strawberries and kiwis. Chill for 1-2 hours before serving. **Yield:** 10 servings *or* about 19 individual tarts.

MOM'S CREAM CHEESE MINTS

Alice Sunseri, St. Louis Park, Minnesota

(PICTURED ON PAGE 57)

- 4 ounces cream cheese, softened
- Confectioners' sugar
- Peppermint extract, about 1/4 teaspoon *or* to taste
- Wintergreen extract, about 1/4 teaspoon *or* to taste
- Green food coloring
- Red food coloring
- Granulated sugar

Mix cream cheese and confectioners' sugar by hand until smooth and doughy. Divide mixture in half; add a few drops of peppermint extract to one half and a few drops of wintergreen extract to other half. Taste and adjust flavor. Blend green food coloring (several drops at a time) into wintergreen mixture until soft green; blend red food coloring (several drops at a time) into peppermint mixture until pastel pink. Pinch off small pieces of dough; roll into balls and dip into granulated sugar. (Mints pictured have been pressed in various candy molds.) Refrigerate, covered. **Yield:** about 7 dozen mints.

WEDDING PUNCH

Marybeth Curran, Waukesha, Wisconsin

(PICTURED ON PAGE 57)

- 2 cans (12 ounces *each*) frozen lemonade concentrate
- 2 cans (12 ounces *each*) frozen pineapple juice concentrate
- 1 quart water
- 1 liter bottle ginger ale
- 1 liter bottle sparkling water
- 1 large bottle sparkling white grape juice *or* champagne
- Fresh strawberries
- Mint leaves

Combine juices and water in a large punch bowl; mix well. Right before serving, add ginger ale, sparkling water and juice/champagne. Stir to blend. Garnish glasses with fresh strawberries and a sprig of mint. (Freeze some of juice mixture in a pretty mold to keep punch cool without diluting flavors.) **Yield:** About 50 half-cup servings (4 ounces each).

IDAHO CHEF'S SALAD

Gladys DeBoer, Castleford, Idaho

(PICTURED ON PAGE 58)

CHIVE DRESSING:
- 1/2 cup evaporated milk
- 1/2 cup vegetable oil
- 3 tablespoons cider vinegar
- 2 tablespoons chopped chives, fresh *or* freeze-dried
- 1 teaspoon salt
- 1 teaspoon white sugar
- 1/2 teaspoon dry mustard
- 1/4 teaspoon ground pepper

SALAD:
- 2 cups Great Northern beans, cooked and drained
- 1 cup thin-sliced celery
- Freshly ground black pepper
- Chilled salad greens
- 4 ounces ham, slivered *or* julienne cuts
- 4 ounces Swiss cheese, slivered *or* julienne cuts
- 4 ounces cheddar cheese, slivered *or* julienne cuts
- 4 ounces cooked chicken *or* turkey, slivered *or* julienne cuts
- 3 hard-boiled eggs, sliced

Combine dressing ingredients. Set aside. Place beans in a large salad bowl; stir in celery and fresh ground pepper. Pour dressing over beans until coated. Chill. Just before serving, tuck crisp salad greens around edges of bowl; arrange ham, cheeses and chicken on top of bean/celery mixture. Garnish with egg slices. **Yield:** 8 servings.

SPINACH CHICKEN SALAD

Kim Roe, Ventura, California

(PICTURED ON PAGE 58)

- 6 cups fresh spinach, stemmed, washed, drained and torn in bite-size pieces
- 3 chicken breasts, boned and skinned
- 1 avocado, pitted and sliced
- 1 can (8 ounces) crushed pineapple, drained
- 1 small bunch green onions, cut into 1/4-inch slices
- 1 red *or* green pepper, chopped
- 2 cups alfalfa sprouts, rinsed, drained and chilled
- 1/2 cup toasted sunflower seeds
- Buttermilk dressing

Place prepared spinach in a deep glass bowl; chill. Season chicken breasts as desired and cook in microwave or broiler until done; cool and cut into bite-size pieces. Toss together spinach, chicken, avocado, pineapple, onions and pepper. Garnish with sprouts and sprinkle with sunflower seeds. Serve with buttermilk dressing. **Yield:** 6 servings.

CASSEROLE HINTS: Cooking for only a couple? Divide casserole ingredients into two smaller dishes and freeze one for later. Casseroles that don't freeze well can be shared immediately with a friend or a neighbor.

● For fast, budget-stretching casseroles, keep canned cream-style soups on hand to mix with leftover meats, seafoods, frozen vegetables, rice, macaroni or potatoes.

● To avoid oven spills, place aluminum pizza pans sprayed with cooking oil under casseroles when baking.

STA PICNIC SALAD

amsey, Wymore, Nebraska

(CTURED ON PAGE 58)

- s rotini pasta, uncooked
- age (3-1/2 ounces) sliced
  peroni
- cados, peeled, sliced into
  ll chunks, sprinkled with
  on juice
- os sliced fresh mushrooms
- s cherry tomatoes, halved
- o sliced green onions
- spoon lemon pepper
- p bottled Italian salad
  ssing

ta according to package di-
Rinse with cold water; drain
combine with remaining ingredients, mixing gently but thoroughly.
Cover; chill 4 hours or overnight. **Yield:**
6 servings.

ARTICHOKE RICE SALAD

Virginia Shaw, Modesto, California

(PICTURED ON PAGE 58)

- 3 cups long grain rice, cooked and drained
- 1 jar (14-3/4 ounces) marinated artichokes, undrained and chopped
- 1/2 cup coarsely chopped red bell pepper
- 1/4 cup sliced ripe olives
- 3 tablespoons minced fresh basil, optional
- 2 tablespoons minced red onion
- 2 tablespoons minced fresh parsley

DRESSING:
- 1/2 cup olive oil
- 3 tablespoons white wine vinegar
- 1/2 teaspoon Dijon mustard
- 1 clove garlic, minced
- 1/4 teaspoon salt
- 1/4 teaspoon pepper
- 1/3 cup toasted pine nuts *or* unsalted sunflower seeds

In large bowl, combine rice, artichokes, pepper, olives, basil, onion and parsley; toss gently until well blended. Combine dressing ingredients; mix well. Blend thoroughly into rice mixture. Right before serving, stir in nuts/seeds. Salad may be served immediately or chilled overnight. **Yield:** 10 servings.

DON'T WASTE A BIT OF BROCCOLI: Make the most of all parts of broccoli—peel the stalks of tougher stems and slice inner parts into bias cuts...then cook along with florets.
- Fresh broccoli will keep well for up to 5 days in refrigerator. Cut off stems and halve them lengthwise, then store florets and stems in plastic bags.

CRUNCHY BROCCOLI/ BEAN CASSEROLE

Connie Bolton, San Antonio, Texas

- 2 packages (10 ounces *each*) chopped frozen broccoli
- 1 package (10 ounces) frozen baby lima beans

SAUCE:
- 1 can (10-3/4 ounces) cream of mushroom soup, undiluted
- 8 ounces dairy sour cream
- 1 package dry onion soup mix
- 1 can (6-1/2 ounces) water chestnuts, chopped

TOPPING:
- 1/2 cup butter, melted
- 3 cups crisp rice cereal

Cook broccoli and beans separately, following package directions; drain. Line 2-qt. or 3-qt. casserole dish with mixture of broccoli and beans. Combine sauce ingredients; spread over vegetable layer. Mix together butter and cereal; sprinkle over all. Bake at 325° for 30 minutes. **Yield:** 8-10 servings.

SIDEWINDERS SUCCOTASH SALAD

Gloria Piantek, Skillman, New Jersey

- 4 green onions, sliced, about 1/3 cup
- 1-1/2 cups canned *or* cooked whole kernel corn, drained
- 1 can (16 ounces) garbanzo beans, drained
- 1 cup coarsely chopped zucchini
- 1 can (4 ounces) mild *or* medium chopped green chilies
- 1/2 cup chopped seeded tomatoes
- 1/2 cup mayonnaise *or* salad dressing
- 1 clove garlic, minced
- 1 tablespoon brown sugar
- 1/2 teaspoon dry mustard
- 1/4 teaspoon salt *or* as desired
- 1/8 teaspoon pepper *or* as desired

Garnish of Bibb lettuce leaves

In large bowl, combine onions, corn, garbanzo beans, zucchini, chilies and tomatoes. Set aside. In small bowl, combine mayonnaise/salad dressing, garlic, brown sugar, dry mustard, salt and pepper. Stir together until well mixed. Toss the dressing with vegetables until well coated. Chill in refrigerator at least 1 hour or until serving time. Garnish bowl with fresh lettuce leaves. **Yield:** 6-8 servings.

BROCCOLI AND SWEET PEPPER STIR-FRY

Karen Collin, Lethbridge, Alberta

- 1 pound fresh broccoli, washed and drained
- 1 sweet red pepper
- 1 sweet yellow pepper
- 1 tablespoon vegetable oil plus more as needed
- 1 onion, chopped
- 1 teaspoon grated fresh gingerroot *or* 1/4 teaspoon ground ginger
- 1/4 cup chicken stock
- 2 teaspoons soy sauce

Cut broccoli stems into crosswise slices 1/4 in. thick and florets into 1-in. pieces. Seed peppers; cut into thin strips. In large heavy skillet or wok, heat oil over medium heat. Add onion and ginger; stir-fry 1 minute. Add broccoli, peppers and more oil if needed; stir-fry 2-3 minutes. Add chicken stock; sprinkle with soy sauce. Serve at once. **Yield:** 8 servings.

CURRIED CHICKEN BALLS

Judy Sloter, Alpharetta, Georgia

- 2 packages (3 ounces *each*) cream cheese, softened
- 2 tablespoons orange marmalade
- 2 teaspoons curry powder
- 3/4 teaspoon salt
- 1/4 teaspoon pepper
- 3 cups finely minced cooked chicken
- 3 tablespoons minced green onion
- 3 tablespoons minced celery
- 1 cup finely chopped almonds, toasted

In a mixing bowl, combine cream cheese, marmalade, curry powder, salt and pepper. Beat until smooth. Stir in chicken, onion and celery. Shape into 1-in. balls; roll in almonds. Cover and chill until firm (can refrigerate up to 2 days). **Yield:** about 5 dozen appetizers.

BLUEBERRY CHEESECAKE

Janet Southwell, Mahone Bay, Nova Scotia

(PICTURED ON PAGE 60)

CRUST:
- 1 cup graham cracker crumbs
- 3 tablespoons sugar
- 3 tablespoons melted butter

CHEESECAKE:
- 2 packages (8 ounces) cream cheese
- 3/4 cup sugar
- 1/4 cup flour
- 2 eggs
- 1 cup evaporated milk
- 1-1/2 teaspoons vanilla

BLUEBERRY TOPPING:
- 3 cups fresh blueberries
- 1/4 cup water
- 1/4 teaspoon nutmeg
- 1 cup sugar
- 2 teaspoons butter
- 2 tablespoons cornstarch
- 2 tablespoons lemon juice

Make crust by mixing ingredients together until blended. Press into bottom of 9-in. spring-form pan; bake at 325° for 10 minutes. Meanwhile, prepare filling by creaming cheese with electric mixer. Add sugar, flour and eggs (one at a time). Beat until smooth; add evaporated milk and vanilla. Mix until blended. Pour slowly over crust; bake at 325° for 40 minutes. Remove to cooling rack. Prepare topping by combining blueberries, sugar, water and nutmeg; cook until blueberries are tender. Add butter and cornstarch dissolved in lemon juice. Cook until mixture thickens, about 2-3 minutes. Cool; spread over cheesecake. Refrigerate until time to serve. **Yield:** 12-16 servings.

BLUEBERRY ALMOND CRUNCH

Loretta Coverdell, Amanda, Ohio

(PICTURED ON PAGE 60)

- 1-1/4 cups all-purpose flour
- 1 cup quick rolled oats
- 3/4 cup brown sugar
- 1/4 teaspoon baking soda
- 1/4 teaspoon baking powder
- 1/4 teaspoon salt
- 1/4 teaspoon cinnamon
- 1/3 cup butter
- 1/4 cup chopped walnuts
- 1 can (21 ounces) blueberry pie filling
- 1/2 teaspoon almond extract

In medium bowl, combine flour, oats, brown sugar, soda, baking powder, salt and cinnamon. Cut in butter with pastry blender until mixture is crumbly. Stir in chopped walnuts. Press 1/2 of mixture in 8-in. x 8-in. x 2-in. glass baking dish. Stir almond extract into blueberry filling. Pour filling over crumb mixture; spread to edges. Sprinkle with remaining crumb mixture. Microwave on 70% power for 9 minutes. Rotate dish a quarter turn every 3 minutes. *Conventional Method:* Bake at 350° for 30 minutes. Serve warm or cold with ice cream. **Yield:** 9 servings.

BLUEBERRY BRAN MUFFINS

Linda Swanson, Kellerton, Iowa

(PICTURED ON PAGE 60)

 This tasty dish uses less sugar, salt and fat. Recipe includes *Diabetic Exchanges*.

- 1-1/2 cups bran cereal
- 1 cup buttermilk
- 1 egg, beaten
- 1/4 cup melted butter
- 1 cup flour
- 1/3 cup brown sugar
- 2 teaspoons baking powder
- 1/2 teaspoon baking soda
- 1/2 teaspoon salt
- 1 cup blueberries

Combine bran cereal and buttermilk; let stand 3 minutes or until liquid is absorbed. Stir in egg and melted butter; set aside. In another bowl, stir together flour, brown sugar, baking powder, soda and salt. Add bran and milk mixture, all at once, stirring until just moistened. Fold in blueberries. Fill 12 greased muffin cups 2/3 full. Bake at 400° for 20-25 minutes. **Yield:** 1 dozen. **Diabetic Exchanges:** One serving equals 1 bread, 1/2 fruit, 1 fat; also, 140 calories, 337 mg sodium, 33 mg cholesterol, 24 gm carbohydrate, 4 gm protein, 5 gm fat.

BLUEBERRY SCONES

Betty Joe Elswick, Priest River, Idaho

(PICTURED ON PAGE 60)

 This tasty dish uses less sugar, salt and fat. Recipe includes *Diabetic Exchanges*.

- 1 teaspoon cinnamon
- 1 cup blueberries
- 1-3/4 cups plus 2 teaspoons all-purpose flour, *divided*

- 1 tablespoon baking powder
- 1/4 cup sugar
- 1/4 teaspoon salt
- 1/3 cup butter
- 2 large eggs
- 3 to 4 tablespoons heavy cream *or* evaporated milk
- 2 tablespoons milk

Cinnamon sugar

Mix 2 teaspoons flour, cinnamon and blueberries together lightly; set aside. Sift remaining flour, baking powder, sugar and salt together; cut in butter. Break eggs into measuring cup; beat with fork. Add enough cream/evaporated milk to make 2/3 cup liquid. Lightly stir egg mixture and berries into dry ingredients. Handle dough as little as possible. Turn dough out onto floured board; divide in two portions. Place on ungreased baking sheet; pat each dough portion into circle 6 in. across and 3/4 in. thick. Cut into six wedges, but leave in a circle. Brush with milk and cinnamon sugar. Bake at 400° for 15 minutes. **Yield:** 12 servings. **Diabetic Exchanges:** One serving equals 1/2 bread, 1 fruit, 1-1/2 fat; also, 167 calories, 227 mg sodium, 63 mg cholesterol, 23 gm carbohydrate, 4 gm protein, 7 gm fat.

BLUEBERRY ORANGE SALAD

June Herke, Howard, South Dakota

(PICTURED ON PAGE 61)

 This tasty dish uses less sugar, salt and fat. Recipe includes *Diabetic Exchanges*.

- 2 cups orange juice
- 1 package (6 ounces) orange-flavored gelatin dessert
- 1/4 cup sugar
- 1 teaspoon grated lemon rind
- 2 cups buttermilk
- 2 cups fresh blueberries

Curly lettuce leaves

Bring orange juice to boil in saucepan over medium heat. Remove from heat; add gelatin, sugar and lemon rind. Stir until gelatin is dissolved. Chill mixture until it is consistency of unbeaten egg whites. Stir in buttermilk; mix well. Fold in blueberries; pour into oiled 6-cup mold. Refrigerate until set. Unmold on lettuce leaves. **Yield:** 8 servings. **Diabetic Exchanges:** One serving equals 1/4 milk, 2 fruit; also, 179 calories, 148 mg sodium, 2 mg cholesterol, 41 gm carbohydrate, 5 gm protein, .3 gm fat.

COLD CREAM: To prepare perfect whipped cream, chill the bowl and beaters before whipping.

BAKED BLUEBERRY PUDDING CAKE

Anna Labarr, Himrod, New York

(PICTURED ON PAGE 61)

PUDDING:
- 2 cups flour
- 1-1/2 cups sugar
- 2 teaspoons baking powder
- 3/4 teaspoon nutmeg
- 1/2 teaspoon salt
- 1/2 teaspoon grated lemon peel
- 3/4 cup butter, softened
- 2 eggs
- 3/4 cup milk
- 2 cups blueberries

LEMON SAUCE:
- 1/2 cup sugar
- 1 tablespoon cornstarch
- 1/4 teaspoon salt
- 1/4 cup cold water
- 3/4 cup boiling water
- 1 egg yolk
- 3 tablespoons lemon juice
- 1 teaspoon grated lemon peel
- 2 tablespoons butter

Combine flour, sugar, baking powder, nutmeg, salt and peel in large bowl. Cut in butter with pastry blender until size of small peas. Add eggs and milk; mix on low speed of mixer for 3 minutes. Pour into greased and floured 9-in. x 9-in. x 2-in. pan; top with blueberries. Bake at 350° for 1 hour and 10 minutes or until tester inserted in center comes out clean. Make sauce by combining sugar, cornstarch and salt in saucepan. Stir in cold water; mix well. Gradually stir in boiling water; cook and stir over medium heat 10-12 minutes or until clear and quite thick. Blend egg yolk with lemon juice; gradually stir into sauce. Stir in peel and butter. Continue cooking for 2 minutes. Serve warm pudding with sauce. **Yield:** 9 servings.

FRESH BLUEBERRY CREAM PIE

Pamela Brandt, LaPorte City, Iowa

(PICTURED ON PAGE 61)

- 1 cup dairy sour cream
- 2 tablespoons flour
- 3/4 cup sugar
- 1 teaspoon vanilla
- 1/4 teaspoon salt
- 1 egg, beaten
- 2-1/2 cups fresh blueberries
- 1 unbaked 9-inch pastry shell

TOPPING:
- 3 tablespoons flour
- 1-1/2 tablespoons butter
- 3 tablespoons chopped pecans *or* walnuts

Combine sour cream, flour, sugar, vanilla, salt and egg; beat 5 minutes at medium speed of mixer or until smooth. Fold in blueberries. Pour filling into pastry shell; bake at 400° for 25 minutes. Remove from oven. Combine topping ingredients, stirring well. Sprinkle over pie. Bake 10 more minutes. Chill before serving. **Yield:** 8 servings.

BLUEBERRY SAUCE

Nellie Brown, Gravenhurst, Ontario

(PICTURED ON PAGE 61)

- 1/2 cup granulated sugar
- 4 teaspoons cornstarch
- 1/2 to 1 tablespoon fresh gingerroot, grated
- Pinch salt, optional
- 2/3 cup cold water
- 2 cups fresh blueberries
- 1 tablespoon *fresh* lemon juice

In small saucepan, stir together sugar, cornstarch, gingerroot and salt. Gradually stir in water; cook over medium heat, stirring constantly, until mixture thickens and comes to boil. Stir in blueberries and lemon juice; reduce heat and simmer on low for 5 minutes until berries are tender. Serve immediately, or let cool, cover and refrigerate for up to 3 days. Serve hot over crepes, pound cake or waffles or cold over ice cream. **Yield:** 2 cups sauce.

BLUEBERRY/KIWI FLAN

Pollie Malone, Ames, Iowa

(PICTURED ON PAGE 62)

CRUST (makes two):
- 1/2 cup granulated sugar
- 1/2 cup confectioners' sugar
- 1/2 cup butter
- 1/2 cup vegetable oil
- 1 egg
- 2 cups plus 2 tablespoons flour
- 1/2 teaspoon cream of tartar
- 1/2 teaspoon baking soda
- 1/2 teaspoon vanilla

CREAM CHEESE FILLING:
- 1 package (8 ounces) cream cheese
- 1/3 cup sugar
- 1 teaspoon vanilla

FRUIT LAYER:
- 3 cups blueberries, washed and drained
- 2 kiwifruit, peeled and sliced thin

CITRUS GLAZE:
- 1/2 cup water
- 1/2 cup orange juice
- 2 tablespoons lemon juice
- 1/4 cup granulated sugar
- 1 tablespoon cornstarch

Mix crust ingredients together well until blended. (If desired, substitute store-bought refrigerated sugar cookie dough.) Grease two 12-in. pizza pans or tart pans with removable bottoms. Divide dough in pans; flatten with hands, dusting with flour if necessary. Build up a slight rim around edges. Bake at 350° for 10-12 minutes or until crust is golden brown. Cool. Carefully remove one crust to round platter (freeze other crust for later use). Cream together cheese filling ingredients; spread on crust. Arrange blueberries and kiwi on top of cheese layer in decorative pattern (other fruits can be substituted if desired). Refrigerate. Make glaze by combining glaze ingredients in saucepan; bring to boil. Boil 1 minute; cool. Spread over fruit layer; refrigerate until serving time. **Yield:** 16-20 servings.

BLUEBERRY LEMON CREPES

Marilyn Miller, Niantic, Illinois

(PICTURED ON PAGE 62)

CREPES:
- 1/2 cup biscuit mix
- 1 egg
- 6 tablespoons milk

FILLING:
- 1 package (3 ounces) cream cheese, softened
- 1-1/2 cups half-and-half
- 1 tablespoon lemon juice
- 1 package (3-3/4 ounces) lemon instant pudding

TOPPING:
- 1 cup blueberry pie filling

Lightly grease 6- to 7-in. skillet; heat until hot. Beat crepe ingredients together until smooth. For each crepe, pour 2 tablespoons batter into skillet. Quickly rotate skillet until batter covers skillet bottom. Cook each crepe until golden brown; loosen edges with spatula and turn. Cook only until golden brown. Stack crepes with paper towel between them. (Crepes may be made in advance and refrigerated, tightly covered, until needed.) Meanwhile, make filling by beating cheese, half-and-half, lemon juice and dry pudding mix on low speed of mixer until well-blended, about 2 minutes. Refrigerate at least 30 minutes. Spoon about 2 tablespoons of pudding mixture onto each crepe; roll up. Top with remaining pudding mixture; garnish with blueberry pie filling. **Yield:** 6 servings.

BLUEBERRY STREUSEL COFFEE CAKE

Jane Lechlitner, Elkhart, Indiana

(PICTURED ON PAGE 62)

COFFEE CAKE BATTER:
- 2-1/3 cups all-purpose flour
- 1 to 1-1/3 cups sugar
- 1 teaspoon salt
- 3/4 cup butter
- 2 teaspoons baking powder
- 3/4 cup milk
- 2 eggs
- 1 teaspoon vanilla
- 1 cup fresh *or* frozen blueberries

CHEESE FILLING:
- 1 cup ricotta cheese
- 1 egg
- 2 tablespoons sugar
- 1 tablespoon grated lemon peel

STREUSEL TOPPING:
- 1 cup reserved batter crumbs
- 1/2 cup chopped nuts (*finely chopped almonds work well*)
- 1/3 cup brown sugar
- 1 teaspoon cinnamon

To make batter, combine flour, sugar and salt in large bowl; cut in butter as for pie crust. *Reserve 1 cup of mixture.* Add baking powder, milk, eggs and vanilla to larger portion of dry ingredients. Beat on medium speed for 2 minutes, scraping bowl constantly. Pour evenly in greased 13-in. x 9-in. x 2-in baking pan. Sprinkle blueberries evenly over batter. Blend cheese, egg, sugar and lemon peel until smooth; spoon evenly over blueberries. Make topping by mixing *reserved crumbs*, nuts, brown sugar and cinnamon. Sprinkle over cheese layer. Bake at 350° for 45-60 minutes or until wooden pick inserted in center comes out clean. Cool slightly before cutting. **Yield:** 20 servings.

BLUEBERRY PEACH TRIFLE

Mary Troyer, Fredericksburg, Ohio

(PICTURED ON PAGE 62)

- 1 can (14 ounces) sweetened condensed milk
- 1-1/2 cups cold water
- 2 teaspoons grated lemon rind
- 1 package (3-1/2 ounces) *instant* vanilla pudding
- 2 cups whipping cream, *whipped*
- 4 cups pound cake, cut in 3/4-inch cubes (*family-size frozen purchased cake is perfect*)
- 2-1/2 cups fresh peeled and chopped peaches (could substitute nectarines)
- 2 cups fresh *or* dry-pack frozen blueberries, thawed, rinsed and well-drained
- Pretty glass bowl, 4-quart size

Combine condensed milk, water and lemon rind in large bowl; mix well. Add pudding mix; beat until well-blended. Chill 5 minutes. Fold in whipped cream. Spoon 2 cups pudding mixture into glass serving bowl; top with 1/2 of cake cubes, all the peaches, 1/2 of remaining pudding mixture, remaining cake cubes, then blueberries and the rest of the pudding mixture, spread to within 1 in. of edge of bowl. (You want the blueberries to show around the edge of bowl.) Chill at least 4 hours. Garnish, if desired, with a sprig of fresh mint. **Yield:** 20 servings.

CRANBERRY CHUTNEY

Mary Eckel, Richardson, Texas

- 2 cans (20-1/2 ounces) pineapple chunks
- 2 cups sugar
- 1 pound fresh cranberries
- 1 cup white raisins
- 1/2 teaspoon cinnamon
- 1/2 teaspoon ginger
- 1/4 teaspoon allspice
- 1/4 teaspoon salt
- 1 cup walnuts, broken

Drain pineapple, reserving juice and fruit. Set fruit aside. Combine pineapple juice, sugar, cranberries, raisins, spices and salt. Cook to boiling; lower heat and simmer for 25 minutes. Add pineapple and nuts. Remove from heat. Store in refrigerator. **Yield:** about 3 cups.

BARBECUE BERRY SHORT RIBS

Marietta Peters, Eldridge, Iowa

- 4 pounds beef chuck short ribs, well-trimmed
- 2 tablespoons vegetable oil
- 2 pounds small white onions
- 2 medium garlic cloves
- 1 can (8-ounce) whole-berry cranberry sauce
- 4 large celery stalks, cut in 2-inch pieces
- 1 cup water
- 3/4 cup catsup
- 1 tablespoon prepared horseradish
- 1-1/4 teaspoons salt
- 1/4 teaspoon pepper

Heat ribs in oil (few at a time) in 5-qt. Dutch oven over medium heat until well-browned on all sides. Set ribs aside. Reduce heat to medium; add onions and garlic to drippings in Dutch oven and cook until lightly browned, stirring occasionally. Spoon off fat. Return ribs to Dutch oven; stir in cranberry sauce, celery, water, catsup, horseradish, salt and pepper. Cover Dutch oven and bake at 350° for 2-1/2 hours, stirring occasionally. Skim fat off sauce. **Yield:** 8 servings.

RUTHE'S FAVORITE FROSTING

Ruthe Stevenson, Minneapolis, Minnesota

- 3 heaping tablespoons creamy peanut butter
- 3 heaping tablespoons butter, softened
- 1 teaspoon vanilla
- 2 cups confectioners' sugar
- 3 heaping tablespoons cocoa
- 1/8 teaspoon salt
- 2 to 4 tablespoons milk plus additional as needed

Mix together peanut butter, butter and vanilla. Stir in confectioners' sugar, cocoa and salt. Add milk, stirring until you reach desired spreading consistency. **Yield:** about 1 cup.

GOING THROUGH A STAGE: If you don't have a candy thermometer handy, use these quick tests to determine the temperature of sugar syrup mixtures:

Thread Stage (230°-233°)—syrup runs from a spoon into a 2-in. fine thread.

Soft-Ball Stage (234°-240°)—a small amount of syrup dropped into cold water forms a ball that, when removed from water, flattens immediately and runs between your fingers.

Firm-Ball Stage (244°-248°)—a small amount of syrup dropped into cold water forms a ball that holds its shape but flattens quickly at room temperature.

Hard-Ball Stage (250°-266°)—a small amount of syrup dropped into cold water forms a ball that can be deformed by pressure but will not flatten.

Soft-Crack (270°-290°)—a small amount of syrup dropped into cold water will separate into hard but pliable threads.

Hard-Crack Stage (295°-310°)—a small amount of syrup dropped into cold water will separate into hard, brittle threads that snap easily.

BEST COOK

Cathy Ireland
Flint, Michigan

Garden-fresh ingredients all year long are part of what makes Cathy Ireland of Flint, Michigan, the "Best Cook in the Country", according to her mother, Alice Robinson of Otisville.

"Cathy cooks the most delicious, nutritious meals!" Alice wrote. "She grows a beautiful garden every summer, canning and freezing enough vegetables to last through the year—and gives many to friends, too.

"She has three daughters, but she's mother to every child she meets, including those who ride her school bus. Cathy decorates her bus for holidays, and hands out homemade treats to the children. She's a Girl Scout leader, and teaches her troop to cook interesting, tasty dishes and make new crafts as well. As Summer Day Camp Director in our county, she's loved by all the young people she comes in contact with—they enjoy camp because she has so much love to give.

"Cathy's one of the busiest people I know, yet finds time to be involved with her daughters' many activities," Alice continued. "And it's a treat to be invited to her house for dinner, because I know that the meal will be outstanding. I am very proud of her!"

Treat yourself and your family to some of Cathy's country cooking by trying the recipes below.

QUICK TACO PIE

- 1 pound ground beef
- 1/2 cup chopped onion
- 1 package (1-1/4 ounces) taco seasoning mix
- 3/4 cup biscuit mix
- 1-1/4 cups milk
- 3 eggs
- 1 cup shredded cheddar cheese
- 1/4 head iceberg lettuce, shredded
- 1 tomato, diced
- 1/3 cup sliced ripe olives

Sour cream, optional

Cook and stir ground beef and onion in skillet until beef is brown; drain. Stir in seasoning mix; spoon into greased 8-in. square dish. Set aside. Beat biscuit mix, milk and eggs with wire whisk or hand beater until almost smooth, about 1 minute. Pour over meat. Bake at 400° for 25-30 minutes or until center is set. Sprinkle with cheese; bake 2 minutes more or until cheese is melted. Cool for 5 minutes; garnish with lettuce, tomatoes, olives and, if desired, sour cream. **Yield:** 6-8 servings.

FRIED GRITS AND SAUSAGE (MUSH)

- 1 pound bulk pork sausage
- 4 cups water
- 1 teaspoon salt
- 1 cup quick-cooking grits
- 1/2 cup cornmeal

Pepper to taste

- 4 tablespoons butter *or* margarine

Cook sausage until brown; drain well. Set aside. Bring water and salt to boil; stir in grits. Return to boiling; reduce heat. Cook 3 minutes, stirring occasionally. Remove from heat. Add sausage, cornmeal and pepper. Stir well; spread in 9-in. x 5-in. bread pan. Refrigerate overnight. Slice 1/2 in. thick and fry in skillet over medium heat in butter or margarine. Serve with syrup or applesauce, if desired. **Yield:** 8 servings.

LAZY DAY LASAGNA

- 12 ounces lasagne noodles
- 1/2 teaspoon leaf oregano, crumbled
- 2 cans (15-1/2 ounces *each*) spaghetti sauce with meat
- 2 cups cottage cheese
- 12 ounces sliced mozzarella cheese

Cook noodles following package directions; drain. Stir oregano into sauce. Layer *half* of noodles, cottage cheese, mozzarella cheese and sauce in 13-in. x 9-in. x 2-in. baking pan. Repeat layers. Bake at 350° for about 1 hour or until bubbly. **Yield:** 8 servings.

STRAWBERRY SHORTCUT CAKE

- 1 cup miniature marshmallows
- 2 cups (2 packages, 10 ounces each) frozen, sliced strawberries in syrup, *thawed*
- 1 package (3 ounces) strawberry gelatin dessert
- 2-1/4 cups flour, unsifted
- 1-1/2 cups sugar
- 1/2 cup vegetable shortening
- 3 teaspoons baking powder
- 1/2 teaspoon salt
- 1 cup milk
- 1 teaspoon vanilla
- 3 eggs

Grease bottom only of 13-in. x 9-in. x 2-in. baking pan. Sprinkle marshmallows evenly over bottom of pan; set aside. Thoroughly combine thawed strawberries and syrup with gelatin; set aside. In large mixer bowl, combine remaining ingredients. Blend at low speed until moistened; beat 3 minutes at medium speed. Carefully pour batter evenly over marshmallows in pan. Spoon strawberry mixture evenly over batter. Bake at 350° for 45-50 minutes until golden brown and toothpick inserted in center comes out clean. Serve warm or cool with ice cream or whipped cream. **Yield:** 16-20 servings.

SOUR CREAM SECRETS: Always stir in sour cream at the end of cooking.
- Never boil sour cream (unless a recipe specifically calls for it.)
- Heat sour cream only at low temperatures.
- Fold sour cream in gently when adding it to other ingredients.
- One tablespoon of sour cream has only 25 calories...compared with 101 in mayonnaise.

ecipes and relatives form a flavorful mix at a family re-union picnic—and we've gath-ered a porchful of recipes that are sure to please!

Two traditional favorites—baked ham and grilled sirloin—are sauced with subtle new tastes, while the perennial potato salad and calico baked beans taste "just like Grandma used to make years ago."

Marinated salads with oil-and-vinegar dressings stand up well in warm weather and can be served as appetizers or a picnic meal-in-a-bowl. Complete the repast with perfect buttermilk yeast buns that make a marvelous complement to meat and are also great to eat simply buttered.

FAMILY REUNION FEAST: Clockwise from lower left—**Old Fashioned Potato Salad** (Pg. 77); **Raspberry Glazed Ham** (Pg. 77); **Antipasto Salad** (Pg. 77); **Marinated Carrot/Mushroom Salad** (Pg. 78); **Broccoli/Cauliflower Salad** (Pg. 77) **Buttermilk Yeast Buns** (Pg. 78); **Three Bean Casserole** (Pg. 77); **Onion Buttered Grilled Sirloin** (Pg. 77).

Sweet treats make picnics perfect, especially after an impromptu softball game, leisurely round of croquet or an afternoon spent pitching horseshoes.

Not just any sweets are suited, though—the best bets are desserts that debuted in picnics past.

Help yourself to such savory memories as homemade ice cream, rich and tangy pound cake or sweet and portable chocolate treats...desserts that bring back the old-time taste of summer.

SUMMER SWEETS: Clockwise from lower left—**Peanut Butter Candy Cake** (Pg. 78); **Orange/Lemon Pound Cake** (Pg. 78); **Orange/Pineapple Ice Cream** (Pg. 79); **Chewy Chocolate Cookies** (Pg. 78).

When It Hailed, They Ran...
To Make Homemade Ice Cream

Nowadays, store-bought ice cream comes in every flavor under the sun. But I can still remember when plain vanilla tasted best of all—after a summer hailstorm.

Years ago, when dark storm clouds came boiling out of the west, Mama shooed our Plymouth Rock hen and her chicks into the coop while my sisters and I raced to bring in the morning wash.

As we grabbed the still-damp clothes, we children hoped for a *little* hailstorm (not bad enough to damage Daddy's cotton and corn). More often than not, we got our wish—and a yard full of icy crystals.

As soon as the storm blew over, we swung into action. Carroll and Doris, our younger brother and sister, quickly gathered two buckets full of hailstones while sister Mattie and I grabbed a milk pail and ran to the pasture to find Old Betsy. Mattie held the gentle cow steady while I filled the pail with creamy milk.

In the kitchen, Mama wrapped the buckets of hailstones in her oldest quilt to keep them cold. Mattie and I got fresh

Modern ice cream can't compare to the kind made with Mother Nature's help.

By Laura Bishop, as told to Sue Ann Dilworth, Tupelo, Mississippi

eggs from the henhouse and meat-curing salt from the smokehouse.

We combined milk, eggs, sugar and vanilla in a clean molasses bucket and tapped down the lid. Then we placed the molasses bucket in a larger water bucket, and packed some hailstones all around it. We added salt to make the hailstones melt faster.

Everyone took turns holding the molasses bucket by its bail and rocking it back and forth, back and forth, in its icy bed. Gradually, the cream mixture sloshed slower and slower as it got thicker and thicker, until *finally* it was frozen.

Then Mama turned the chickens back into the chicken yard and rehung the wash. Daddy returned from the fields, reporting that it hadn't even hailed out there. So he was all the more surprised by our homemade ice cream treat!

Mama let us use her best "company" bowls, and Doris handed them to me one at a time as I scooped up the golden treat. Mattie served Mama and Daddy first, passing them great mounded clouds of vanilla ice cream in the delicate sky-blue bowls.

No modern-day ice cream has ever tasted better. Perhaps it was our simple ingredients—fresh milk, eggs straight from the nest...and hailstones from a summer storm. What could be more natural?

Blue ribbon food! Won't you sample crisp Country Fried Chicken from Indiana, Stuffed and Scalloped Potatoes from Idaho, spicy grilled beef Fajitas from Texas and colorful fresh Salsa from California?

Be sure to leave room to taste tender brown sugar- and mustard- glazed Ham Balls, Amish corn relish and tangy coleslaw.

These are the recipes that win blue ribbons at state and county fairs—and warm praise at America's tables.

Why not give these tried-and-true classics a try today and enjoy a *real* taste of the country?

PRIZE WINNING RECIPES: Clockwise from lower left—**Country Fried Chicken** (Pg. 80); **Corn Relish** (Pg. 80); **Ham Balls in Mustard Sauce** (Pg. 80); **Idaho Dutch Scalloped Potatoes** (Pg. 81); **Nine-Day Coleslaw** (Pg. 81); **Fresh California Salsa** (Pg. 81); **Shrimp Stuffed Potatoes** (Pg. 80); **Fajitas with Pico De Gallo** (Pg. 80).

Best of show! Delicious dessert dishes showcasing juicy golden peaches, flavorful cooking apples and tart-and-sweet Concord grapes take the blue ribbon here. And a classic pound cake goes perfectly with any fruit.

Taste the very best of Wisconsin's dairyland in the lightly spiced Apple/Cheese bars; the fruit-filled goodness of East Coast vineyards in Harvest Grape Pie; and the ultra-smooth delicacy of juicy Southern peaches in Praline Pie or heaped on the rich, golden Pound Cake.

Sweet treats to savor—these are award-winning recipes from across America's great countryside!

JUDGES' FAVORITES! Clockwise from bottom—**Peach Praline Pie** (Pg. 82); **Harvest Grape Pie** (Pg. 81); **Apple/Cheese Bars** (Pg. 81); **Pound Cake** (Pg. 82).

RASPBERRY GLAZED HAM

Ruby Nelson, Mountain Home, Arkansas

(PICTURED ON COVER AND PAGE 70)

1 (8-10 pounds) boneless, fully cooked ham

GLAZE:
*1/4 cup apple juice or dry white wine
2 tablespoons lemon juice
2 teaspoons cornstarch
1/3 cup seedless raspberry jam, divided
1 tablespoon butter
Watercress, parsley or other greens

Score ham in diamond shapes; place on a rack in shallow roasting pan. Bake at 325° about 2 hours until meat thermometer registers 140°. (Ham may also be done on a gas grill or charcoal barbecue-follow manufacturer's directions.) In a saucepan, blend apple juice/wine and lemon juice into cornstarch. Add about 1/2 of jam. Cook and stir until thickened and bubbly. Stir in remaining jam and butter. Heat and stir until butter is melted. Brush ham with glaze. Bake ham 10 minutes more. Spoon any additional glaze over ham. *You may want to double the glaze recipe and thin it slightly with water to pass with ham. Garnish ham with greens. **Yield:** 24-30 servings.

ANTIPASTO SALAD

Marcy Schewe, Danube, Minnesota

(PICTURED ON PAGE 70)

2 green peppers
3 tomatoes
1/4 pound provolone cheese
1/4 pound hard salami, Genoa preferred, sliced thin, quartered
1/4 pound pepperoni, sliced thin
1 small onion, minced
2 stalks celery, cut in thin, bias cuts
1 can (6 ounces) pitted black olives, drained
1 jar (5 ounces) stuffed green olives, drained
About 1 pound rotini or shell pasta, cooked, drained and cooled

DRESSING:
2/3 cup olive or vegetable oil
1/2 cup red wine vinegar
1 teaspoon leaf oregano, crumbled
1 teaspoon pepper
Salt to taste, if desired

Cut peppers, tomatoes and cheese into bite-size chunks in large mixing bowl.

Add salami, pepperoni, onion, celery, olives and pasta; stir to blend. Combine dressing ingredients; shake well to blend. Pour over salad ingredients; stir to blend. Refrigerate, covered, overnight. **Yield:** 15-20 servings.

OLD FASHIONED POTATO SALAD

Margaret Barrow, North Ogden, Utah

(PICTURED ON PAGE 70)

DRESSING:
3/4 cup salad dressing
3/4 cup mayonnaise
1 teaspoon sugar
2 tablespoons dill pickle juice
1 tablespoon vinegar
1 tablespoon sweet pickle juice
1/4 teaspoon celery salt
Dash onion salt
SALAD:
5 medium cooked potatoes, peeled and slightly warm (about 6 cups diced)
1-1/4 teaspoons salt
1/4 teaspoon pepper
5 green onions, thinly sliced
2 tablespoons diced sweet pickle
6 hard-cooked eggs, peeled and diced
GARNISH:
Hard-cooked eggs, peeled and sliced
Green pepper rings
Paprika

Mix together dressing ingredients. Set aside. Combine diced potatoes, salt and pepper in large bowl. Pour dressing over still-warm potatoes, mixing thoroughly. Let stand in refrigerator for at least 2 hours; overnight is preferred. Add green onions, sweet pickle and diced eggs; mix thoroughly. Garnish with additional eggs, pepper rings and paprika, if desired. Serve chilled. **Yield:** 8 servings.

THREE BEAN CASSEROLE

Ida Mae Frey, Topeka, Indiana

(PICTURED ON PAGE 71)

8 strips bacon
2 large onions, cut into rings
1-1/2 teaspoons garlic powder
1 teaspoon dry mustard
1/2 cup brown sugar
1/4 cup cider vinegar
1 can (16 ounces) dark red kidney beans, drained
1 can (16 ounces) New England baked beans, undrained

1 can (16 ounces) green lima beans, drained

Fry bacon until crisp; drain on paper towels, crumble and set aside. Place onion rings, garlic powder, mustard, brown sugar and vinegar in large skillet. Cover; cook 20 minutes over medium heat. Combine beans in 3-qt. casserole. Stir in bacon and onion mixture, blending ingredients. Bake, covered, at 350° for 45 minutes. **Yield:** 10 servings.

BROCCOLI/ CAULIFLOWER SALAD

Shirley Spade, Nashua, New Hampshire

(PICTURED ON PAGE 71)

1 bunch broccoli, small flowerettes only
1 head cauliflower, broken into small flowerettes
1 can (6 ounces) pitted ripe olives, drained
1 jar (6 ounces) stuffed green olives, drained
8 ounces feta cheese, crumbled
1 pint tiny cherry tomatoes, whole
1 cup Italian salad dressing

Place all ingredients in large bowl, preferably one with seal-on lid. Toss to coat. Marinate in refrigerator at least 8 hours, tossing occasionally to distribute marinade over vegetables. **Yield:** 3-4 quarts.

ONION BUTTERED GRILLED SIRLOIN

Margaret Barrow, North Ogden, Utah

(PICTURED ON PAGE 71)

3 to 4 pounds sirloin steak, 1-1/2 inch-thick cut
STEAK SAUCE:
1/2 cup butter
1/4 cup fresh minced parsley
1/4 cup minced onion
2 teaspoons Worcestershire sauce
1/2 teaspoon dry mustard
1/2 teaspoon black pepper

Combine sauce ingredients in saucepan and heat (or microwave in glass container) until butter melts. Set aside. Slash edges of beef sirloin steak. Broil 3-4 inches from heat for 10-12 minutes on each side (rare) or 14-16 minutes (for medium) brushing frequently with butter mixture. Steak may also be grilled on gas or charcoal barbecue following manufacturer's instructions. **Yield:** 6-8 servings.

BUTTERMILK YEAST BUNS

Edna Krahenbuhl, Barron, Wisconsin

(PICTURED ON PAGE 71)

1/2 cake (1 ounce) compressed yeast *or* 1 package active dry yeast
1/4 cup warm water (110-115°)
3 cups buttermilk, room temperature
1/2 cup sugar
1/2 cup butter, melted
2 eggs, beaten
1 teaspoon baking soda
1 teaspoon salt
About 8 cups all-purpose flour, *divided*

Crumble yeast into warm water in large mixing bowl; stir to dissolve. Add buttermilk and sugar; let mixture stand 15 minutes. Add *warm* butter and eggs; mix. Sift soda and salt with 4 cups flour; add to liquid mixture. Beat until smooth batter forms. Add remaining sifted flour, stirring with spoon until dough is no longer sticky. Knead on floured board; place in large greased mixing bowl. Cover; let rise until double, about 1 hour. Punch dough down; form into buns (squeeze dough into balls the size of egg). Place on greased baking sheet; flatten slightly with hand. Let rise until double, about 30 minutes. Bake at 400° for 15-20 minutes or until light golden brown. Remove to cooling rack; brush tops with melted butter. **Yield:** about 4 dozen buns.

BETTER BREAD: To freshen day-old or slightly dry rolls or bread, wrap bread loosely in paper towel and microwave on defrost/low for several seconds. Use immediately.

MARINATED CARROT/ MUSHROOM SALAD

Pat Habiger, Spearville, Kansas

(PICTURED ON PAGE 71)

DRESSING:
2/3 cup vinegar
2/3 cup vegetable oil
1/4 cup chopped onion
2 cloves garlic, minced
1 teaspoon salt *or* to taste
1/4 teaspoon fresh ground pepper
1 teaspoon sugar
1 teaspoon leaf basil, crumbled
1 teaspoon leaf oregano, crumbled
2 cups sliced carrots, cooked

1 can (14 ounces) artichoke hearts, drained and cut in quarters
8 ounces fresh mushrooms, halved
1 cup pitted ripe olives, halved
1 jar (2 ounces chopped pimento) drained *or* 1/4 cup chopped red pepper

In saucepan, combine dressing ingredients; bring to a boil. Reduce heat; simmer, uncovered, for 10 minutes. Combine carrots, artichoke hearts, mushrooms, olives and pimento/pepper in large bowl. Pour hot dressing over vegetables, stirring to coat. Cover; chill for several hours, stirring occasionally. Drain; serve in lettuce-lined bowl. **Yield:** 2 quarts.

PEANUT BUTTER CANDY CAKE

Geraldine Grisdale, Mt. Pleasant, Michigan

(PICTURED ON PAGE 72)

CAKE:
1-3/4 cups boiling water
1 cup quick-cooking rolled oats
1/2 cup butter *or* margarine
1 cup *light* brown sugar
1 cup white sugar
1 teaspoon vanilla
2 eggs
1-1/2 cups unsifted all-purpose flour
1 teaspoon baking soda
1/2 teaspoon baking powder
1/4 teaspoon cinnamon
1/4 teaspoon salt
5 (.6 ounce size) milk chocolate covered peanut butter cups
FROSTING:
3 tablespoons butter
3 ounces unsweetened chocolate
About 3 cups confectioners' sugar
1/4 teaspoon salt
1/2 cup milk
1 teaspoon vanilla

Combine water and rolled oats; cool to room temperature. Set aside. Cream together butter, brown sugar, sugar and vanilla; beat in eggs. Blend in oatmeal mixture. Combine flour, baking soda, baking powder, cinnamon and salt; add to creamed mixture. Beat 1 minute on medium speed. Pour batter into greased and floured 13-in. x 9-in. x 2-in. pan. Chop peanut butter cups and sprinkle on top of batter. *Do not stir.* Bake at 350° for 40-45 minutes or until cake tests done. For frosting, melt butter in small saucepan. Add chocolate; stir constantly over *very* low heat until

melted. Pour into small mixing bowl. Add remaining ingredients; beat until well blended. Chill to spreading consistency, 10-15 minutes. Frost cake. **Yield:** 16-20 servings.

CHEWY CHOCOLATE COOKIES

Rosemary Smith, Fort Bragg, California

(PICTURED ON PAGE 72)

1-1/4 cups butter *or* margarine, softened
1-3/4 to 2 cups sugar
2 eggs
2 teaspoons vanilla
2 cups all-purpose flour
3/4 cup unsweetened cocoa
1 teaspoon baking soda
Dash salt
1 cup chopped nuts, optional

Cream butter *or* margarine and sugar in large bowl. Add eggs and vanilla; blend well. Combine flour, cocoa, soda and salt; gradually blend into creamed mixture. Stir in nuts, if desired. Drop by teaspoonfuls onto ungreased cookie sheet. Bake at 350° for 8-9 minutes. *Do not overbake.* Cookies will be soft. Cool on sheets until set, about 1 minute. Remove to wire rack to cool completely. Store in airtight container. **Yield:** about 4-1/2 dozen.

ORANGE/LEMON POUND CAKE

Norma Poole, Auburndale, Florida

(PICTURED ON PAGE 72)

POUND CAKE:
1 cup butter, softened
1/4 cup vegetable shortening
2 cups sugar
5 eggs, room temperature
3 cups all-purpose flour
1/2 teaspoon salt
1/2 teaspoon baking soda
1/2 teaspoon baking powder
1 cup buttermilk, room temperature
1 teaspoon vanilla extract
1 teaspoon lemon extract
GLAZE:
2 teaspoons grated orange rind
2 teaspoons grated lemon rind
2 tablespoons orange juice, fresh preferred
2 tablespoons lemon juice, fresh preferred
1 cup confectioners' sugar

Cream together butter, shortening and sugar until light and fluffy. Add eggs, one at a time, beating well after each addition. Combine flour, salt, soda and baking powder to creamed mixture alternately with buttermilk, ending with dry ingredients. Beat well after each addition. Add extracts. Spoon batter into well-greased and floured 10-inch tube or fluted pan. Bake at 325° for 45-60 minutes or until cake tests done when a wooden pick inserted in center comes out dry and clean. Meanwhile, make glaze by combining all ingredients, blending well. Set aside. Cool cake in pan on wire rack for 15 minutes; remove from pan. Place cake on wire rack over plate that is slightly larger. Punch holes in still-warm cake with wooden pick and drizzle glaze over cake repeatedly until absorbed. **Yield:** 12-16 servings.

ORANGE/PINEAPPLE ICE CREAM

Vera Straus, Weidman, Michigan

(PICTURED ON PAGE 72)

- 1 package (6 ounces) orange-pineapple gelatin
- 2 cups boiling water
- 4 eggs
- 1-1/2 cups sugar
- 2 tablespoons flour
- 1/4 teaspoon salt
- 2 cups half-and-half
- 1 can (20 ounces) crushed *chilled* pineapple, undrained
- 1 can (14 ounces) sweetened condensed milk, chilled
- 1 carton (8 ounces) nondairy frozen whipped topping, thawed
- 1 can (12 ounces) frozen orange-pineapple concentrate, thawed, *undiluted*

Dissolve gelatin in boiling water; let cool to room temperature. Set aside. Beat eggs in large bowl on medium speed of electric mixer until frothy. Add sugar, flour, salt and half-and-half, mixing to blend. Place mixture in heavy saucepan over medium heat, stirring constantly until mixture coats back of a spoon (soft custard), about 10 minutes. (Mixture may also be cooked in a microwave.) Cool; stir in gelatin mixture and pineapple, condensed milk, whipped topping and concentrate. Chill ingredients thoroughly (overnight is best). Pour into freezer can of a 1-gallon ice cream maker. Freeze according to manufacturer's directions. Allow ice cream flavors to ripen at least 1 hour before serving. **Yield:** 1 gallon.

ITALIAN CREAM CAKE

Floyce Day, Broxton, Georgia

- 5 eggs, separated
- 1/2 cup (1 stick) butter *or* margarine
- 1/2 cup shortening
- 2 cups sugar
- 2 cups flour
- 1 teaspoon baking soda

Pinch salt

- 1 cup buttermilk
- 1 teaspoon vanilla
- 1 small can flaked coconut
- 1 cup nuts, chopped

FROSTING:
- 1/4 cup butter *or* margarine
- 8 ounces cream cheese
- 1 teaspoon vanilla
- 4 cups confectioners' sugar

Milk to mix

Chopped nuts (sprinkle on frosting between layers on top of cake)

Beat egg whites until stiff; set aside. Cream butter, shortening and sugar. Add egg yolks. Mix well. Sift together flour, soda and salt. Add to creamed mixture alternately with buttermilk. Add vanilla, coconut and nuts. Fold in stiffly beaten egg whites. Pour into four layer pans. Bake at 350° for 20-25 minutes until cake springs back to touch. Beat together all frosting ingredients except nuts. Frost, sprinkling nuts on frosting between layers. **Yield:** 12-16 servings.

FRESH STRAWBERRIES AND CREME

Gayle Wilson, Cedarville, Illinois

CREME:
- 1 package (8 ounces) cream cheese, softened
- 1 cup dairy sour cream
- 1/3 cup confectioners' sugar
- 2 teaspoons orange liqueur *or* 1/4 teaspoon grated orange rind

Miniature chocolate cups *or* mini biscuit cases
- 2 quarts fresh strawberries

Combine creme ingredients in small mixing bowl; beat until smooth. Chill an hour or overnight to blend flavors. To serve, place chocolate cups or mini biscuit cases on pretty plate; fill one-half full with creme mixture. Top with one whole, washed strawberry. To eat, dip berry in creme. **Yield:** 8 servings.

CHOCOLATE PIZZA

Norma Oosting, Holland, Michigan

- 8 ounces white chocolate, *divided*
- 8 ounces semisweet chocolate chips
- 1/2 cup *each* salted peanuts, mini marshmallows, crispy rice cereal, coconut, red and green candied cherries

In a heavy saucepan or top of a double boiler, melt 6 oz. white chocolate and all the chocolate chips. Stir in peanuts, marshmallows and cereal. Pour onto a greased 10-in. pizza pan or a 10-in. circle of cardboard covered with foil. Spread to even out top. Sprinkle with coconut. Top with cherries. Melt the remaining white chocolate; drizzle over pizza. Chill. **Yield:** 16-20 servings.

STRAWBERRY CREAM PUFFS

Sherry Adams, Mt. Ayr, Iowa

- 1 cup water
- 1/2 cup butter *or* margarine
- 1 teaspoon sugar
- 1/4 teaspoon salt
- 1 cup all-purpose flour
- 4 eggs

CREAM FILLING:
- 2 pints fresh strawberries, sliced
- 1/2 cup sugar, *divided*
- 2 cups whipping cream

Confectioners' sugar

Additional sliced strawberries

Mint leaves

In a large saucepan, bring water, butter, sugar and salt to a boil. Add flour all at once and stir until a smooth ball forms. Remove from the heat and beat in eggs, one at a time. Continue beating until mixture is smooth and shiny. Drop by tablespoonfuls 2 in. apart on a large ungreased cookie sheet (make 10). Bake at 400° for about 35 minutes or until golden brown. Cool on a wire rack. For filling, combine berries and 1/4 cup sugar. Chill 30 minutes. Beat cream and remaining sugar until stiff. Just before serving, cut tops off puffs. Combine berries and cream mixture. Fill cream puffs and replace tops. Sprinkle with confectioners' sugar, and garnish with additional berries and mint leaves. **Yield:** 10 cream puffs.

COUNTRY FRIED CHICKEN

Edna Hoffman, Hebron, Indiana

(PICTURED ON PAGE 74)

1 fryer chicken (3 pounds) *or* **equivalent pieces**
3/4 to 1 cup buttermilk
COATING:
1-1/2 to 2 cups flour
1-1/2 teaspoons salt
1/2 teaspoon pepper
1/2 teaspoon garlic powder
1/2 teaspoon onion powder
1 tablespoon paprika
1/4 teaspoon ground sage
1/4 teaspoon ground thyme
1/8 teaspoon baking powder
Sunflower oil for frying

Wash and pat dry chicken pieces with paper towel; place in large flat dish. Pour buttermilk over chicken; cover, and allow to soak at least one hour or overnight in refrigerator. Combine coating ingredients in double strength paper bag and shake chicken pieces, *one at a time,* to coat well. Lay coated pieces on wax paper on counter for 15 minutes to allow coating to dry (will cling better in frying). Meanwhile pour oil to depth of 1/2-inch in electric skillet and heat to 350-360°. Fry chicken, several pieces at a time, for about 3 minutes on each side. Be careful not to over-crowd. Reduce heat to 320°, cook chicken, turning occasionally, for 25-35 minutes or until juices run clear and chicken is tender. Remove to paper towel-lined platter. **Yield:** 4 servings.

CORN RELISH

Lucy Zimmerman, Ephrata, Pennsylvania

(PICTURED ON PAGE 74)

6 pints sweet corn, cut from cobs
4 bell peppers, red and green, seeded and diced
3 onions, diced
1 head celery, diced
2 cups granulated sugar
1 pint vinegar
2 tablespoons salt
1 teaspoon mustard seed
1 pint water

Combine all ingredients in large non-aluminum kettle; bring to a boil. Reduce heat; simmer, uncovered, until vegetables are tender, about 30-40 minutes. Pack into hot, sterilized jars, leaving 1/2-inch headspace. Seal. Cool completely. Store in refrigerator or for long-term stor-

age in the freezer for up to 1 year. **Yield:** 9 pints.

HAM BALLS IN MUSTARD SAUCE

Ardath Murray, Bartlesville, Oklahoma

(PICTURED ON PAGE 74)

1-1/4 pounds ground ham
2/3 pound ground fresh pork
2/3 pound ground beef
2 eggs
1 cup tomato juice
2 tablespoons minced onion
1 cup cracker crumbs
1/2 teaspoon salt
2 tablespoons minced green pepper
SAUCE:
1 cup brown sugar
1/2 cup vinegar
1/2 cup water
2 teaspoons dry mustard

Combine ham, pork and beef; add eggs, juice, cracker crumbs, onion, green pepper and salt. Shape into golf-ball size balls; place in flat baking dish and bake at 350° for 1 hour. Meanwhile make sauce by dissolving brown sugar, vinegar, water and dry mustard in pan. Pour over ham balls after they have baked 1 hour. Bake 30 minutes longer. **Yield:** 8 servings.

FAJITAS WITH PICO DE GALLO

Mrs. Richard Moore, Brownsville, Texas

(PICTURED ON PAGE 75)

2-1/2 pounds trimmed beef skirt, flank steak or beef rib meat (boned)
MARINADE:
1 fresh lime
12 ounces beer
1 cup Italian dressing
Teriyaki Baste and Glaze
12 flour tortillas
PICO DE GALLO:
1 large tomato, chopped
1 large green pepper, chopped
1 onion, chopped

Remove any skin and fat from beef skirt or other cut of beef. Combine juice of 1 lime, beer and dressing. Place beef in flat pan; pour marinade over all. Allow to marinate for 2-3 hours. Drain beef; place on hot grill and cook, turning once, about 5 minutes, depending on thickness. Brush with teriyaki glaze. Slice thin, on a diagonal, and place in warm flour tortillas with several tablespoons of Pico

De Gallo (tomato, green pepper and onion which have been combined). Fold tortillas to enclose meat and vegetables. Serve with Picante sauce, if desired. **Yield:** 6 servings.

SHRIMP-STUFFED POTATOES

Aney Chatterton, Soda Springs, Idaho

(PICTURED ON PAGE 75)

6 medium baking potatoes
1/2 cup butter *or* **margarine**
1 cup grated sharp cheddar cheese
1 teaspoon salt
Dash cayenne pepper
2 tablespoons onion, minced
3/4 cup milk
1 can (4-1/2 ounces) broken or tiny shrimp
Paprika
Fresh parsley

Scrub potatoes well; prick with fork. Bake at 400° for 1 hour or until done. Cut potatoes in half lengthwise; scoop out pulp, leaving enough to keep potatoes' shape. Set skins aside. Combine pulp with butter, cheese, salt, pepper, onion and milk. Whip with electric mixer until smooth and fluffy. Fold in shrimp. Refill potato shells. Sprinkle tops with paprika and parsley. Bake at 375° for 15-20 minutes or microwave at 50% power until hot. **Yield:** 6 servings.

CRANBERRY MEATBALLS

Helen Wiegmink, Tucson, Arizona

1 pound lean ground beef
1 egg, slightly beaten
1/2 cup crushed saltine crackers
1/2 small onion, diced
1 teaspoon salt
1/2 teaspoon pepper
1 can (16 ounces) whole cranberry sauce
1 can (10-3/4 ounces) cream of tomato soup, undiluted
Cooked rice *or* **noodles**

In a mixing bowl, combine first six ingredients. Shape into 1-1/2-in. balls. Place on a rack in a baking pan. Bake at 400° for 20 minutes. Meanwhile, combine cranberry sauce and tomato soup. Heat through. Add meatballs and simmer 10 minutes. Serve with rice or noodles. May also be used as an appetizer. **Yield:** 4 main-dish servings. *If Cooking for Two:* Freeze half the cooked meatballs for another meal.

NANA'S DEVILED EGGS

Carol Mersberger, Lynden, Washington

12 eggs, hard-cooked, cooled
FILLING:
Mashed yolks
   1/4 cup melted butter
   2 teaspoons sweet pickle juice
   2 tablespoons prepared
     mustard
   1 tablespoon Worcestershire
     sauce
   1/4 teaspoon dill weed
   1/4 cup real bacon bits
Salt and pepper to taste
   1/2 cup creamy salad dressing
Paprika

Peel eggs; cut in half. Remove yolk; mash with fork. Add all filling ingredients to yolks; mix until smooth. Refill whites; sprinkle with paprika. **Yield:** 12 servings.

EGG TRIVIA: Hard-cooked eggs spin easily; raw eggs won't.
- Hard-cooked eggs keep up to 10 days in the refrigerator. But don't leave them out. Bacteria can enter through the eggshell.
- Brown- and white-shelled eggs have the same nutritional value.

APPLE/CHEESE BARS

Vicki Raatz, Waterloo, Wisconsin

(PICTURED ON PAGE 76)

CRUST:
   1/2 cup granulated sugar
   1 cup butter, softened
   2 eggs, *separated*
   1 teaspoon baking powder
1/2 teaspoon salt
   2 cups all-purpose flour (can
     use part rolled oats, if desired)
FILLING:
   4 medium size cooking apples
     (about 4 cups), grated
   1 package (8 ounces) finely
     grated cheddar cheese
1/4 cup flour
3/4 cup granulated sugar
   1 teaspoon ground cinnamon
TOPPING:
Reserved egg whites
   1/4 cup cream cheese, softened
1-1/2 cups confectioners' sugar

Make crust by combing sugar, butter, *egg yolks*, baking powder, salt and flour. Blend until mixture is crumbly. Press 1/2 of mixture into bottom of 13-in. x 9-in. baking pan; reserve remaining half. Set aside. Grate apples and cheese together in one bowl (food processor works well for this). Add sugar, flour and cinnamon; mix well. Spread apple/cheese filling over crust. Sprinkle remaining half of crumb mixture over filling. Make topping by whipping egg whites until peaks form. Gradually add confectioners' sugar and cream cheese, beating continuously. Spoon evenly over all layers. Bake at 350° for 30-35 minutes or until light golden brown. **Yield:** 36 bars.

NINE-DAY COLESLAW

Ardath Murray, Bartlesville, Oklahoma

(PICTURED ON PAGE 75)

DRESSING:
   1 cup vinegar
   1/2 cup vegetable oil
   2 teaspoons celery seed
   2 teaspoons granulated sugar
   1/2 teaspoon salt
COLESLAW:
   3 pounds cabbage, shredded
   1 cup onion, finely chopped
   1/2 cup green pepper, finely
     chopped
   1/2 cup red pepper, finely
     chopped
   2 cups granulated sugar

Combine dressing ingredients in saucepan; bring to boil, Cool; set aside. Combine cabbage, onion, peppers and sugar. Let stand until sugar dissolves. Pour cooled dressing over cabbage mixture; refrigerate. This coleslaw keeps well under refrigeration. **Yield:** 2 quarts.

IDAHO DUTCH SCALLOPED POTATOES

Gladys De Boer, Castleford, Idaho

(PICTURED ON PAGE 75)

   2 cups milk
   4 cups (about 2 pounds)
     potatoes, peeled and sliced
     1/4 inch thick
   1/4 teaspoon oregano
   1/4 teaspoon thyme
   1/4 teaspoon rosemary
   2 cloves garlic, minced,
     optional
   1/2 teaspoon salt *or* to taste
   1/8 teaspoon white pepper
   1 cup Gouda cheese, shredded
About 1 cup light cream *or*
   half-and-half

Heat milk in large saucepan; add potatoes and seasonings. Cook about 20 minutes, stirring often. Layer in greased baking dish with shredded cheese. Pour cream over all. Bake at 350° for 30 minutes or until potatoes are tender. **Yield:** 4-6 servings.

FRESH CALIFORNIA SALSA

M. Jessie Gates, Riverside, California

(PICTURED ON PAGE 75)

   1 pint canned tomatoes,
     chopped
   2 medium-size fresh
     tomatoes, diced
   1 can (4-ounces) green chilies
   1 bunch green onions, diced
   1/2 bunch fresh cilantro leaves,
     minced
   2 tablespoons cider vinegar
   1 teaspoon salt

Combine all ingredients; mix well. Refrigerate, covered, a minimum of one hour. Serve with tortilla chips. **Yield:** 2 pints.

HARVEST GRAPE PIE

Jeannette Mack, Rushville, New York

(PICTURED ON PAGE 76)

Pastry for 9-inch, two-crust pie
FILLING:
   5-1/3 cups Concord grapes
   1-1/3 cups granulated sugar
   1/4 cup flour
   1-1/4 teaspoons fresh lemon juice
Dash salt
   1-1/2 tablespoons butter

Remove and save skins from grapes by pinching grapes at end opposite stem (pulp pops out). Put pulp in saucepan without water; bring to rolling boil. While mixture is hot, rub through strainer (or use food mill) to remove seeds. Mix strained pulp with reserved grape skins. Combine sugar and flour; mix lightly through grape mixture. Sprinkle with lemon juice and salt. Pour grape mixture into pastry-lined pie pan. Dot with butter. Cover with top crust *or* use decorative pastry cutouts for top crust. Cut slits in top crust; seal and flute edges. Bake at 425° for 35-45 minutes or until top crust is nicely browned and juice is thickened. Cool before serving. **Yield:** 8-10 servings.

PEACH PRALINE PIE

Elizabeth Hunter, Prosperity, South Carolina

(PICTURED ON PAGE 76)

    4 cups (about 3 pounds)
       peeled, sliced ripe peaches
  1/2 cup granulated sugar
    2 tablespoons quick-cooking
       tapioca
    1 teaspoon lemon juice
    1 9-inch *unbaked* pie shell*
PRALINE LAYER:
  1/2 cup all-purpose flour
  1/4 cup brown sugar, firmly
       packed
  1/2 cup chopped pecans
  1/4 cup butter *or* margarine

Combine peaches, sugar, tapioca and lemon juice in large bowl; let stand 15 minutes. Combine flour, brown sugar and pecans in small bowl; cut in butter with fork or mix with fingertips until mixture is crumbly. (Makes 1-1/3 cups.) Sprinkle 1/3 of praline mixture over bottom of pie shell; cover with peach mixture. Sprinkle remaining praline mixture over peaches, allowing peach layer to show, if desired. Bake at 450° for 10 minutes; reduce heat to 350° and bake for 20 minutes longer or until peaches are tender and topping is golden brown. *(Deep dish frozen pie shell works well for this pie.) **Yield:** 8 servings.

POUND CAKE

Paula Higgenbotham, Lilburn, Georgia

(PICTURED ON PAGE 76)

    1 cup butter *or* margarine,
       softened
    3 cups granulated sugar
    6 eggs, room temperature
    3 cups all-purpose flour
  1/4 teaspoon baking soda
  3/4 teaspoon salt
    1 cup sour cream, room
       temperature
    1 teaspoon vanilla extract
  1/2 to 1 teaspoon almond extract
    2 cups *finely* chopped, peeled
       peaches
Whipped cream

Cream butter and sugar together until light and fluffy. Add eggs one at a time, mixing after each. Combine flour, soda and salt in a separate bowl. Add dry ingredients alternately with sour cream to creamed ingredients. Stir in extracts. Bake at 350° in a greased and floured 10-in. tube or fluted pan for 70-80 minutes *or* in two 9-in. x 5-in. loaf pans for 1

hour. Remove from pans to cooling rack. Dust with confectioners' sugar *or* serve with fresh peaches and whipped cream if desired. **Yield:** 16-20 servings.

ONIONS AND STIR-FRY BEEF

Brenda Masters, Palmyra, Missouri

    1 pound *lean* beef steak (flank,
       sirloin or top round) cut into
       1/4-inch-thick strips
    1 teaspoon salt
    1 egg white
    1 tablespoon cornstarch
About 2 tablespoons vegetable oil,
       more as needed
    3 cups mild onions, sliced
    1 tablespoon dry wine *or* sherry
       or wine vinegar
    1 tablespoon sugar
    4 tablespoons light soy sauce
Broccoli cuts, carrot diagonals,
       optional

Combine beef, salt, egg white and cornstarch. Mix well with hands; set aside. Heat oil to 375° in wok or deep skillet. Stir-fry beef (small amounts at a time) until lightly browned; drain on paper towels. Lower temperature to 350°; add additional oil if necessary and stir-fry onions until soft and well-browned. Remove. Add broccoli and carrots if desired; stir-fry until tender/crisp. Add beef and onions, wine/sherry/vinegar, sugar and soy sauce. Stir-fry 2 minutes at 425° until beef is glazed and brown. Serve on a bed of rice. **Yield:** 4 servings.

ONION BREAD KUCHEN APPETIZER

Margo Varo, Eastman, Wisconsin

 This tasty dish uses less sugar, salt and fat. Recipe includes *Diabetic Exchanges*.

    1 loaf frozen bread dough,
       thawed
    1 pound onions, diced
    4 tablespoons butter
    2 ounces thin-sliced ham, diced
    2 eggs
  1/2 cup sour cream
Salt to taste
Caraway seed

Roll bread dough out on greased cookie sheet, forming slight rim around edges, and set aside. Saute onions in butter in skillet until clear; mix in ham, eggs, sour cream and seasonings. Spread

over dough. Bake at 350° for 15-20 minutes or until dough is golden brown on top. Remove from oven; cut into small squares. **Yield:** 30 appetizers. **Diabetic Exchanges:** One serving equals 1/2 bread, 1/2 vegetable, 1/2 fat; also, 72 calories, 117 mg sodium, 25 mg cholesterol, 8 gm carbohydrate, 3 gm protein, 3 gm fat.

ONION/BACON OATMEAL BUNS

Lila McNamara, Dickinson, North Dakota

This tasty dish uses less sugar, salt and fat. Recipe includes *Diabetic Exchanges*.

    2 cups boiling water
    1 cup quick-cooking oats
    3 tablespoons vegetable oil
    2 packages quick-rise dry yeast
  1/3 cup warm water (110°-115°)
  1/4 cup dark molasses
  2/3 cup brown sugar
    1 egg
    2 teaspoons salt
About 6 cups all-purpose flour,
       more as needed
  3/4 pound bacon, cut in 1/4-inch
       pieces, fried but not too crisp
    2 cups diced onion, sauteed
       until slightly brown in bacon
       drippings

Pour boiling water over oats; cool. Add oil, yeast softened in 1/3 cup water, molasses, brown sugar, egg and salt. Beat in 1/2 flour to make soft dough; add bacon and onion pieces. Add remaining flour; knead until smooth. Cover bowl with foil; let dough rise until doubled in bulk. Punch down; let rise again. Pull off lemon-sized pieces; form into round bun shapes; place on greased baking sheets. Let rise until doubled in bulk. Bake at 375° for 18-20 minutes. Brush with melted butter while still hot. Cool. **Yield:** 30 buns. **Diabetic Exchanges:** One serving equals 2 bread, 1/2 fat; also, 170 calories, 186 mg sodium, 11 mg cholesterol, 29 gm carbohydrate, 5 gm protein, 4 gm fat.

ONION ODORS: You can wash onion odors from your hands with fresh undiluted lemon juice or a weak ammonia rinse.

● Rub each finger vigorously with celery salt before washing, to rid hands of onion odors.

● Wash each hand with cold water and salt, then rub chlorophyll toothpaste over fingers and rinse well.

MEALS IN MINUTES

She is a teacher, farm wife and mother—so Marjorie Carey of Belfry, Montana knows the importance of making minutes count.

Marjorie's busy weekday schedule begins early in the morning with home school classes for her own children. "We stick to a routine, just like any other school," she says.

Her day doesn't end when school's out, though—afternoon hours are filled with trips to the library, helping with homework...and, of course, pitching in with farm chores.

"Before I know it, dinnertime is only 30 minutes away," Marjorie reports.

Marjorie's found an added advantage to the quick, easy-to-prepare meal menu featured here—her children often can help with the preparation. "That's a good way for them to practice some of the things they learn in school, like counting and measuring," she notes.

One of Marjorie's favorite fast meals features a flavorful grilled hamburger with a zesty cheese-and-mushroom sauce, accompanied by a garden-fresh cucumber salad and strawberries for dessert.

Your children can help to mix the hamburger seasoning, make the sauce and—if they're old enough—peel and slice the cucumbers and strawberries. But even without young assistants, this appealing meal can be table-ready in just half an hour.

Try it next time you have to pick up the kitchen pace...or anytime you feel like fixing a simply good supper!

PHILLY BURGER

- 1 pound ground beef
- 2 tablespoons Worcestershire sauce, *divided*
- 4 teaspoons Dijon mustard, *divided*
- 1 can (2.8 ounces) french-fried onions, *divided*
- 1 package (3 ounces) cream cheese, softened
- 1 jar (2.5 ounces) sliced mushrooms, drained
- 1 teaspoon parsley flakes
- 4 Kaiser rolls

Combine ground beef with 1 tablespoon of Worcestershire sauce, 3 teaspoons mustard and half the onions. Form into four patties and broil or grill to desired doneness. Meanwhile, in a small bowl, blend cream cheese, remaining Worcestershire sauce and mustard, mushrooms and parsley. Spread the cheese mixture on cooked patties; top with reserved onions. Broil or grill 30 seconds more or until the onions are golden. Serve on Kaiser rolls. **Yield:** 4 burgers.

CUCUMBER SALAD

- 2 medium cucumbers, peeled and sliced 1/4 inch thick

SOUR CREAM DRESSING:
- 1/2 cup sour cream
- 1 tablespoon vinegar
- 1 tablespoon grated onion

Salt to taste
Freshly ground black pepper
- 1 to 2 tablespoons diced pimiento

Prepare cucumbers; set aside. Combine dressing ingredients in a bowl; stir in cucumbers. **Yield:** 4 servings.

STRAWBERRY SPARKLER

- 1 quart fresh strawberries
- 1/2 cup strawberry-flavored yogurt*
- 2 tablespoons sugar

Rinse, hull and slice berries. Spoon into sherbet dishes. Combine yogurt* (to substitute plain yogurt, swirl in a few teaspoons of your favorite strawberry jam or topping) and sugar. Drizzle over berries. **Yield:** 4 servings.

STRAWBERRY STORAGE: Strawberries will stay fresh for several days if you put fresh, unwashed berries in a container and top with a folded napkin. Cover the container, turn it upside down and store in the refrigerator.

R aspberries! Those wonderful warm-weather treats will burst with fruity flavor in our brimming-with-red recipes.

This regal soft summer fruit is delightful in desserts, of course. So you will find a seasonful of them here. But raspberries are equally delicious *during* a meal. Try the imaginative main courses and savory salads…then dig into desserts that will make summer even sweeter!

SUMMER SUPPER: Clockwise from far left—**Indiana-Style Corn Dogs** (Pg. 97); **Huckleberry Cheese Pie** (Pg. 98); **Rave Review Coconut Cake** (Pg. 97); **Marinated Shrimp in Avocado Halves** (Pg. 97); **Chinese Coleslaw** (Pg. 97); **West Coast Chicken** (Pg. 98); **Sesame Cucumber Salad** (Pg. 98); **Barbecued Lamb Kabobs** (Pg. 97).

D on't let summer slip by without trying some of these mouth-watering dishes. Start with a succulent slab of Barbecued Salmon—a mild marinade makes this tender meat delicious to eat.

Next, pass a dish of easy-to-prepare Green Beans with Mushrooms. For dessert, how about a "berry" delightful slice of Southern-Style Soft Custard or a scrumptious scoopful of Heavenly Cherry Angel Food Trifle? Here's summer eating at its best!

EASY EATING: Clockwise from top—**Heavenly Cherry Angel Food Trifle** (Pg. 99); **Green Beans with Mushrooms** (Pg. 98); **Southern-Style Soft Custard** (Pg. 99); **Barbecued Salmon** (Pg. 98).

BEST COOK

Pat Knapp
Mansfield, Ohio

Pat Knapp's culinary skills are well-known in Mansfield, Ohio, where she's been dazzling folks for years, both in her own home and at the weddings and parties she caters.

Her repertoire includes family favorites, new recipes and even some authentic dishes from France, Italy, Brazil and Mexico. Her baking is tops, too—she's won over 100 first- and second-place ribbons at county fairs!

Pat was nominated for the "Best Cook" honor by JoAnn Fisher, who has obviously enjoyed many a feast at her cousin's home.

"A meal at Pat's is one you'll never forget," JoAnn told us. "It might include Cajun blackened steak, sweet potato pone, spinach salad with buttermilk dressing and fresh rolls hot from the oven (with homemade jam or jelly, of course). Then she may serve you lemon slice pie or homemade cherry cobbler ice cream.

"As you can tell, Pat loves to cook!" Pat won't argue with that!

"I come from a long line of cooks," Pat told us. "My mother and her four sisters were all wonderful cooks, and I learned early from Mom and my aunts that hospitality starts with tasty food."

PAT'S BLACKENED FLANK STEAK

    1 or 2 flank steaks
       (1 to 1-1/4 pounds *each*)
1-1/2 teaspoons salt
1-1/2 tablespoons white pepper
1-1/2 tablespoons whole black
       peppercorns
1-1/2 tablespoons fennel seeds
2-1/2 teaspoons cayenne pepper
2-1/2 teaspoons dry mustard
    2 tablespoons garlic powder
Olive oil

Grind all ingredients except steak and oil in a food processor or blender. Coat both sides of flank steak with the mixture. (If cooking only one steak, use half the mixture and save the rest for future use.) Coat a seasoned cast-iron skillet with olive oil; heat until smoking. (You may want to do this outside on a propane grill, as the smoke could set off a smoke alarm.) Sear steak on both sides; meat will be black. For rare meat, cook 5 more minutes on each side. For medium doneness, cook 7 minutes on each side. Slice diagonally in thin strips. **Yield:** 1 steak serves 3-4 people.

MOO GOO GAI PAN

    3 whole medium chicken
       breasts, skinned and boned
    2 tablespoons cornstarch,
       divided
1/2 teaspoon salt
1/3 cup chicken broth
    1 tablespoon soy sauce
    1 tablespoon dry sherry,
       optional
    3 tablespoons peanut oil,
       divided
    1 garlic clove, minced, optional
1/4 teaspoon ground ginger
    3 green onions, bias-sliced into
       1-inch pieces
1/2 pound fresh mushrooms,
       sliced
    1 package (16 ounces) frozen
       edible pea pods, partially
       thawed
Hot cooked rice

Coat chicken breasts with mixture of 1 tablespoon cornstarch and salt. In bowl, combine broth, remaining cornstarch, soy sauce and if desired, sherry; set aside. In a wok, heat 1 tablespoon oil; add garlic and ginger. Stir-fry for 15 seconds. Add onions and mushrooms; stir-fry about 2 minutes or until onions are crisp-tender. Remove onion mixture from wok. Add remaining oil to hot wok. Add chicken; stir-fry 3 to 5 minutes or until done. Push from center of wok. Stir broth mixture; pour into center of wok. Cook and stir until thickened and bubbly. Return onion mixture to wok; add pea pods. Stir all ingredients together to coat with sauce. Cook and stir 1 minute more. Serve immediately on rice. **Yield:** 6 servings.

SWEET POTATO PONE

    4 large fresh sweet potatoes
1/2 cup butter
    2 eggs, beaten
    1 cup whipping cream
1/2 cup all-purpose flour
    2 tablespoons brown sugar
    1 tablespoon baking powder
    1 teaspoon vanilla extract
    1 teaspoon grated orange rind
    1 teaspoon grated lemon rind
1/2 teaspoon ground cinnamon
1/2 teaspoon ground allspice
1/2 teaspoon ground cloves
TOPPING:
1/4 cup butter, melted
1/2 cup packed brown sugar
1/2 cup chopped pecans

Cook sweet potatoes in boiling salted water until tender. Drain; peel and mash. Melt butter and brown slightly over low heat. Stir browned butter into the mashed potatoes. Put into a buttered 13-in. x 9-in. x 2-in. baking dish. Combine remaining ingredients and stir into potatoes. For topping, combine ingredients and sprinkle on top of potatoes. Bake at 350° for 30 minutes. **Yield:** 14-16 servings.

AUNT CATFISH'S BOATSINKER PIE

2/3 cup butter
1/3 cup light corn syrup
2-1/2 ounces unsweetened
       chocolate
    1 cup sugar
    3 eggs
    1 teaspoon vanilla extract
Pinch salt
    1 unbaked pie shell (9 inches)
Ice cream *or* whipped cream
Grated semisweet chocolate,
       optional

Combine butter, corn syrup and chocolate; melt together. Cool. In a mixer bowl, beat together sugar, eggs, vanilla and salt; mix well. Blend in chocolate mixture. Pour into pie shell. Bake at 325° for 15 minutes. Reduce heat to 275° and bake 40-45 minutes longer until set. Cool. Serve with ice cream or whipped cream, and, if desired, sprinkle top with grated chocolate. **Yield:** 8 servings.

Packing a basket for an impromptu picnic in the country? Need a "dish to pass" at a church potluck? Friends and family will rave over this royal-red glazed strawberry pie, and they'll request second helpings of fresh-from-the-garden vegetable salad.

Bring along some hard rolls with your favorite sandwich makings, a thermos filled with ice-cold lemonade and you've got a meal!

BLANKET BRUNCH: Remembrance Strawberry Pie (Pg. 99); Marinated Vegetable Salad (Pg. 99).

RASPBERRY CRUMBLE COFFEE CAKE

Shirley Boyken, Mesa, Arizona

(PICTURED ON PAGE 84)

FILLING:
- 2/3 cup sugar
- 1/4 cup cornstarch
- 3/4 cup water *or* raspberry juice
- 2 cups fresh *or* frozen whole unsweetened raspberries
- 1 tablespoon lemon juice

CAKE:
- 3 cups all-purpose flour
- 1 cup sugar
- 1 tablespoon baking powder
- 1 teaspoon salt
- 1 teaspoon cinnamon
- 1/4 teaspoon mace
- 1 cup butter *or* margarine, softened
- 2 eggs, slightly beaten
- 1 cup milk
- 1 teaspoon vanilla extract

TOPPING:
- 1/4 cup butter *or* margarine
- 1/2 cup all-purpose flour
- 1/2 cup sugar
- 1/4 cup sliced almonds

For filling, combine sugar, cornstarch, water or juice and berries; cook over medium heat until thickened and clear. Add lemon juice. Set aside to cool. In a bowl, combine flour, sugar, baking powder, salt, cinnamon and mace. Cut in butter to form fine crumbs. Add eggs, milk and vanilla; stir until blended. Divide in half. Spread half of the batter into two buttered 8-in.-round baking pans. Divide filling and spread evenly over batter in each pan. Drop remaining batter by small spoonfuls over filling; spread. For topping, cut butter into flour and sugar; stir in nuts. Spread topping on cakes. Bake at 350° for 40-45 minutes. (If desired, one coffee cake can be baked in 13-in. x 9-in. x 2-in. baking pan for 45-50 minutes.) **Yield:** 16-20 servings.

RASPBERRY CUSTARD MERINGUE

Bette Berry, Alamogordo, New Mexico

(PICTURED ON PAGE 84)

MERINGUE:
- 4 egg whites
- 1/2 teaspoon salt
- 1/4 teaspoon cream of tartar
- 1 cup sugar
- 1 teaspoon vanilla extract
- 1 cup finely chopped walnuts

CUSTARD:
- 1/4 cup butter *or* margarine
- 1/4 cup all-purpose flour
- 3 to 4 egg yolks
- 2 cups milk
- 1-1/2 teaspoons vanilla extract
- 1/8 teaspoon salt
- 3/4 cup sugar

TOPPING:
- 8 ounces whipping cream
- 1/3 cup semisweet chocolate chips
- 3 tablespoons butter *or* margarine
- 1 quart fresh raspberries

For the meringue, beat the egg whites, salt and cream of tartar till soft peaks form. Add sugar, 1 tablespoon at a time, beating until whites are thick and glossy. Add vanilla. Fold in the nuts by hand. To form crust, place meringue mixture on parchment paper; spread in a 14-in.-diameter circle (or in several smaller circles for individual servings). Bake at 275° for 1 hour; turn off heat and leave meringue in oven for at least 1 hour longer. Cool slowly. For custard, melt butter and add flour to make a paste. In a separate bowl, stir eggs with fork; add milk. Whisk milk mixture into flour mixture slowly; add vanilla, salt and sugar. Cook over low heat until thickened and bubbly. Pour into bowl; cover with plastic wrap and cool completely. (Can be made the day before using.) Just before serving, whip cream and sweeten to taste. Melt the chocolate chips with butter in a small saucepan. Spoon custard mixture on meringue; top with whipped cream and fresh berries. Drizzle with chocolate mixture. **Yield:** 12-14 servings.

RASPBERRY ICE

Wilma Scott, Tulsa, Oklahoma

(PICTURED ON PAGE 84)

- 4 cups fresh raspberries
- 1/2 cup sugar
- 1 cup water, *divided*
- 1/4 cup orange juice
- 1 package unflavored gelatin

Fresh mint leaves, optional

In blender container, combine raspberries, sugar, 3/4 cup water and juice. Process until smooth. Pour mixture into a saucepan; cook over low heat for 5 minutes, stirring occasionally. Let cool. Soften gelatin in remaining 1/4 cup water. Stir into raspberry mixture; mix well. Pour into a 4-cup container; freeze 2-3 hours or until mixture is slushy. Remove from freezer; beat with electric mixer until sherbet is a bright pink color. Freeze until firm. Garnish with mint leaves, if desired. **Yield:** about 3-1/2 cups.

CHOCOLATE DESSERT WITH RASPBERRY SAUCE

Marilyn Dick, Centralia, Missouri

(PICTURED ON PAGE 84)

- 16 squares (1 ounce *each*) semisweet chocolate
- 2/3 cup butter
- 5 eggs
- 2 tablespoons sugar
- 2 tablespoons all-purpose flour (amount *is* correct)

SAUCE:
- 2 cups fresh *or* frozen whole unsweetened raspberries
- 1-3/4 cups water
- 1/4 cup sugar
- 4 teaspoons cornstarch
- 1 tablespoon water

Whipped cream

Fresh whole raspberries to garnish

Line bottom of a 9-in. springform pan with parchment paper; set aside. Place chocolate and butter in top of double boiler. Bring water to boil; reduce heat and stir chocolate until melted. In a large mixing bowl, beat eggs for 2 minutes. Slowly add chocolate mixture to eggs, beating at medium speed about 10 minutes. Blend in sugar and flour just until mixed. Pour into prepared pan. Bake at 400° for 15 minutes (cake will *not* be set in the middle). Chill. For the sauce, combine raspberries, 1-3/4 cups water and sugar in a saucepan. Bring to boil. Reduce heat; simmer, uncovered, for 30 minutes. Put through sieve; discard the seeds. Add water if needed to make 2 cups juice. Combine cornstarch and 1 tablespoon water in small bowl; stir until smooth. Add cornstarch mixture to raspberry mixture. Cook over medium heat, stirring constantly, until mixture comes to a boil; cook and stir 1 minute more. Remove from heat; cool. To serve, spoon about 2 tablespoons sauce on each dessert plate; place a thin wedge of chocolate dessert on sauce. Garnish with whipped cream and raspberries. **Yield:** 16-20 servings (2 cups sauce).

RED, WHITE AND BLUE BERRY PIE

Cindy Zarnstorff, Anchorage, Alaska

(PICTURED ON PAGE 84)

1 pie crust (9 inches), baked
BERRY LAYERS:
1-1/2 cups sugar
4-1/2 tablespoons cornstarch
1-1/2 cups water
4-1/2 tablespoons raspberry-flavored gelatin powder
1 pint fresh *or* frozen whole unsweetened blueberries
1 teaspoon fresh lemon juice
1 pint fresh *or* frozen whole unsweetened raspberries
CREAM LAYER:
4 ounces cream cheese, room temperature
1/3 cup confectioners' sugar
4 ounces nondairy frozen topping, thawed

For berry layers, combine sugar, cornstarch and water in medium saucepan, stirring to dissolve. Cook until thick and clear. Add gelatin; stir until dissolved. Divide mixture in half. Stir blueberries and lemon juice into half of the mixture; spread over bottom of pie shell. Refrigerate. Fold raspberries gently into remaining half of mixture; set aside. For cream layer, beat together cheese and sugar until smooth. Mix in the nondairy frozen topping; spread over blueberry layer. Refrigerate until set. Carefully spread raspberry layer over cream layer. Chill at least 4 hours before serving. **Yield:** 8 servings.

RASPBERRY CHEESECAKE

Lori Manthorpe, Ile Bizard, Quebec

(PICTURED ON PAGE 85)

CRUST:
3/4 cup all-purpose flour
3 tablespoons sugar
1 teaspoon finely shredded lemon peel, *divided*
6 tablespoons butter *or* margarine
1 egg yolk, slightly beaten
1/2 teaspoon vanilla extract, *divided*
FILLING:
3 packages (8 ounces *each*) cream cheese, softened
1 cup sugar
2 tablespoons all-purpose flour
1/4 teaspoon salt

2 eggs
1 egg yolk
1/4 cup milk
RASPBERRY SAUCE:
1 package (10 ounces) frozen raspberries, thawed and crushed
1 tablespoon cornstarch
1/2 cup black *or* red currant jelly
TOPPING:
3 cups fresh *or* frozen whole raspberries

For the crust, combine flour, sugar and half of lemon peel. Cut in butter until crumbly. Stir in egg yolk and half of vanilla. Pat 1/3 of dough on bottom of 9-in. springform pan with the side removed. Bake at 400° for 7 minutes or until golden; cool. Attach side of pan to bottom; pat remaining dough onto side of pan to height of 1-3/4 in. Set aside. For filling, beat cheese, remaining lemon peel and vanilla until fluffy. Combine the sugar, flour and salt; beat into the cream cheese mixture, mixing well. Add eggs and yolk, beating at a low speed just until combined. Stir in milk. Pour into crust-lined pan. Place on a shallow baking pan in oven. Bake at 375° for 35-40 minutes or until center appears to be set. Cool for 15 minutes. Loosen sides of cheesecake from pan with spatula. Cool 30 minutes; remove side of pan. Cool for 1-2 hours longer. Chill well. To make sauce, combine ingredients in saucepan; cook and stir over medium heat until thickened and bubbly. Cook and stir 1 minute more. Remove from heat; strain to remove seeds. Cool. Just before serving, top cheesecake with raspberries and sauce. **Yield:** 12 servings.

RASPBERRY CHICKEN

Verna Schrock, Salem, Oregon

(PICTURED ON PAGE 85)

4 medium chicken breasts, split, skinned and boned*
2 tablespoons all-purpose flour
1-1/2 tablespoons butter *or* margarine
1 tablespoon vegetable oil
6 tablespoons raspberry vinegar (see recipe on Pg. 95)
1/2 to 3/4 cup chicken broth
1/2 cup heavy cream
Fresh raspberries to garnish

Coat chicken with flour. Melt butter in large skillet; add oil. Brown chicken, turning once. Add vinegar and broth to skillet; stir over low heat until combined. Simmer, uncovered, until the chicken is

done, about 12-15 minutes. Remove chicken to serving platter and keep warm. Add cream to skillet; boil sauce until slightly thickened, about 10 minutes, stirring occasionally. Pour sauce over chicken; garnish with raspberries (and watercress, if desired). Serve at once. *Pork chops may be substituted for chicken. **Yield:** 8 servings.

RASPBERRY VINEGAR PORK CHOPS

Maurita Merrill, Lac la Hache, British Columbia

(PICTURED ON PAGE 86)

 This tasty dish uses less sugar, salt and fat. Recipe includes *Diabetic Exchanges*.

1 tablespoon butter *or* margarine
1 tablespoon olive oil *or* vegetable oil
3 pounds pork chops *or* pork tenderloin, cut 1 inch thick*
1/2 cup raspberry vinegar, *divided* (see recipe on Pg. 95)
3 garlic cloves, sliced thin
2 tomatoes, seeded and chopped
1 teaspoon dried sage *or* thyme *or* tarragon *or* basil
1 tablespoon fresh *or* dried parsley
1/2 cup chicken stock
Salt and pepper to taste
Fresh raspberries and sage to garnish

Melt butter in a large skillet; add oil. Brown the pork on each side over high heat. Pour off oil; reduce heat to medium-low. Add 2 tablespoons vinegar and garlic. Cover; simmer for 10 minutes. Remove pork to heated container; cover to keep warm. Add remaining vinegar; stir up browned bits from bottom of skillet. Raise heat and boil until the vinegar is reduced to a thick glaze. Add the tomatoes, sage, parsley and chicken stock. Boil until liquid is reduced to half of the original volume. Strain sauce; season with salt and pepper. Spoon over chops. Garnish with fresh raspberries and sage. *Chicken breasts may be substituted for pork. **Yield:** 8 servings. **Diabetic Exchanges:** One serving equals 2 meat, 1 vegetable, 1 fat; also, 216 calories, 115 mg sodium, 60 mg cholesterol, 4 gm carbohydrate, 20 gm protein, 13 gm fat.

BERRY BASICS: Store berries in small, shallow containers so that the weight of the top berries doesn't crush those underneath.

RASPBERRY SPINACH SALAD

Rita Underdahl, Fremont, California

(PICTURED ON PAGE 85)

DRESSING:
- 2 tablespoons raspberry vinegar (recipe on this page)
- 2 tablespoons raspberry jam
- 1/3 cup vegetable oil

SALAD:
- 3/4 pound fresh spinach, rinsed well and drained
- 3/4 cup whole pecans, toasted, *divided*
- 1 cup fresh raspberries, *divided*
- 2 large kiwifruit, peeled and sliced 1/4 inch thick

With a whisk or blender, blend vinegar and jam. Add oil in thin stream while whisking. Set aside. Mix spinach, half of nuts, half of raspberries and all of dressing. Top salad with remaining nuts, berries and kiwifruit. Mix again before serving. **Yield:** 4-6 servings.

ROYAL RASPBERRY CAKE

Genevieve Priewe, Whitewater, Wisconsin

(PICTURED ON PAGE 86)

CAKE:
- 2 cups all-purpose flour
- 1/2 teaspoon salt
- 1 tablespoon baking powder
- 1/3 cup butter *or* margarine, room temperature
- 1 cup sugar
- 1 egg, room temperature
- 1 cup milk, room temperature
- 1 teaspoon vanilla extract
- 3-1/2 cups fresh *or* frozen whole unsweetened raspberries

GLAZE:
- 1-1/2 cups confectioners' sugar
- 2 tablespoons cream *or* milk with melted butter
- 1 teaspoon vanilla extract

Stir together first three ingredients in a bowl with wire whisk; set aside. Cream softened butter with mixer; add sugar gradually, beating well after each addition, until mixture is fluffy and light. Stir in egg; beat 1 minute. Combine milk and vanilla. Add dry ingredients alternately with milk/butter/sugar mixture, beating well after each addition. Spread cake batter in greased, floured 13-in. x 9-in. x 2-in. baking pan. Spread the berries evenly over top of batter. Bake at 350° for 30-35 minutes or until center of cake

springs back when lightly touched. Cool 5 minutes. Combine glaze ingredients; spread over cake, leaving berries exposed. Serve warm, with vanilla ice cream if desired. **Yield:** 16-20 servings.

LETTUCE WITH RASPBERRY DRESSING

Harriet Stichter, Milford, Indiana

(PICTURED ON PAGE 86)

 This tasty dish uses less sugar, salt and fat. Recipe includes *Diabetic Exchanges*.

- 6 cups leaf lettuce, washed, drained and chilled
- 1/2 cup coarsely chopped walnuts, toasted

DRESSING:
- 1/3 cup vegetable oil
- 3 tablespoons sugar
- 2 tablespoons raspberry vinegar (recipe at right)
- 1 tablespoon sour cream
- 1-1/2 teaspoons Dijon mustard
- 1/2 cup fresh raspberries

Whisk together all dressing ingredients except raspberries. Fold in raspberries; refrigerate, covered, for at least 1 hour. Place lettuce in glass bowl; add walnuts. Toss with dressing. Serve immediately. **Yield:** 6 servings (3/4 cup dressing). **Diabetic Exchanges:** One serving equals 1/2 fruit, 1 vegetable, 2 fat; also, 157 calories, 22 mg sodium, .8 mg cholesterol, 11 gm carbohydrate, 2 gm protein, 13 gm fat.

FREEZER RASPBERRY SAUCE

Katie Koziolek, Hartland, Minnesota

(PICTURED ON PAGE 86)

- 3 cups mashed fresh raspberries (mash in layers as for jam)
- 3 cups sugar
- 1 cup light corn syrup
- 1 package (3 ounces) liquid fruit pectin
- 2 tablespoons lemon juice
- 4 cups whole fresh raspberries

Combine the 3 cups berries, sugar and corn syrup; stir until well mixed. Let stand 10 minutes. In small bowl, combine pectin and lemon juice. Stir into fruit mixture; mix for 3 minutes to distribute pectin evenly. Add remaining whole berries, stirring carefully to distribute fruit but leave berries whole. Ladle into 1-pint

freezer containers; seal and let stand at room temperature for 24 hours or until partially set. Store in the refrigerator up to 3 weeks or in the freezer for up to 1 year. Thaw and stir before using. Serve over ice cream, sponge cake, shortcake or waffles, or combined with plain yogurt. **Yield:** 4 pints.

RASPBERRY VINEGAR

Francy Nightingale, Issaquah, Washington

- 3 cups fresh raspberries
- 4 cups white wine vinegar
- 1/2 cup sugar

Rinse the berries and air-dry on paper towels. Place berries in a 6-cup jar; set aside. In medium saucepan, combine vinegar and sugar; bring *almost* to a boil over low heat, stirring constantly, until sugar melts. *Do not boil.* Pour hot vinegar mixture over berries; cover jar tightly and let stand at room temperature 48 hours. Strain through several layers of cheesecloth into a clean bottle or jar. Seal tightly with cork or lid. Store in cool, dark place. **Yield:** 4 cups.

RASPBERRY STREUSEL MUFFINS

Rosemary Smith, Fort Bragg, California

MUFFINS:
- 1-1/2 cups all-purpose flour
- 1/2 cup sugar
- 2 teaspoons baking powder
- 1/2 cup milk
- 1/2 cup butter, melted
- 1 egg, beaten
- 1 cup fresh *or* frozen whole unsweetened raspberries, *divided*

STREUSEL TOPPING:
- 1/4 cup chopped pecans
- 1/4 cup packed brown sugar
- 1/4 cup all-purpose flour
- 2 tablespoons butter, melted

In large bowl, combine flour, sugar and baking powder. In a small bowl, blend milk, butter and egg. Stir milk mixture into flour mixture just until moistened. Spoon about 1 tablespoon batter into each of 12 greased muffin cups. Divide half of the raspberries among cups; top with remaining batter, then remaining raspberries. For topping, combine streusel ingredients until mixture resembles moist crumbs; sprinkle over muffins. Bake at 375° for 20-25 minutes or until golden. Let stand 5 minutes; carefully remove from pans. **Yield:** 12 muffins.

NO-COOK RED RASPBERRY FREEZER JAM

Eileen Sterk, Bellingham, Washington

2 quarts fresh red raspberries
   (3-1/4 cups pulp)
1/4 cup lemon juice
1 package (3 ounces) liquid
   pectin
1 cup light corn syrup
4-1/2 cups sugar

Wash and mash the berries. In a 4-qt. saucepan, measure 3-1/4 cups pulp; add lemon juice. Slowly stir in pectin; mix thoroughly. Set aside for 30 minutes, stirring frequently to allow the pectin to dissolve. Add syrup; mix well. Add sugar gradually, stirring well to dissolve completely. Warm mixture to 100°, using a candy thermometer to confirm temperature. Let set for 10-15 minutes; stir occasionally to keep fruit equally dispersed. Pour into sterilized jars or freezer containers and seal. Store in refrigerator for up to 1 month or in freezer for up to 1 year. **Yield:** 7 jars, 8 ounces each.

BARBECUED RASPBERRY CHICKEN

Lorraine Cloutier, Legal, Alberta

1/4 cup raspberry vinegar (recipe
   on Pg. 95)
2 tablespoons vegetable oil
1 to 2 teaspoons dried
   tarragon *or* 1 tablespoon
   fresh tarragon
4 chicken breast halves,
   skinned and boned
Salt to taste
Fresh ground pepper to taste
Fresh raspberries and fresh
   tarragon for garnish
SAUCE:
1 cup undiluted frozen
   raspberry juice
1 tablespoon cornstarch

In medium-size bowl or sealable plastic bag, combine vinegar, oil and tarragon. Whisk or shake until blended. Marinate chicken in mixture for 30 minutes, then season with salt and pepper. Grease grill lightly with oil; place chicken on grill about 4 in. from hot coals. Turn and baste frequently with marinade until chicken feels springy to touch, about 15-18 minutes. While chicken cooks, whisk together sauce ingredients in a saucepan. Cook over medium-low heat, stirring constantly, until thickened and smooth, for about 5-7 minutes. When chicken is done, place sauce in a pool

on warm platter; place chicken on top of sauce. Garnish with fresh berries and a sprig of fresh tarragon. **Yield:** 4 servings.

MARINATED IOWA BEEF

Shary Geidner, Clear Lake, Iowa

 This tasty dish uses less sugar, salt and fat. Recipe includes *Diabetic Exchanges*.

1 beef chuck roast *or* thick
   sirloin
   (3 to 4 pounds)
Sliced tomatoes
Sliced sweet onion
MARINADE:
1 package (.6 ounces) dry *zesty*
   Italian dressing mix
1/4 cup extra-virgin olive oil
1/3 cup tarragon wine vinegar
1/2 teaspoon meat tenderizer,
   optional

Combine marinade ingredients. Pour small amount (enough to cover bottom) in a 13-in. x 9-in. x 2-in. baking pan. Place beef in pan; top with remaining marinade. Pierce meat generously with sharp fork; turn meat and pierce again. Cover; refrigerate for at least 8 hours or overnight, piercing and turning meat often. Before cooking, let beef come to room temperature. Grill over medium coals about 6 minutes per side for medium rare cuts 1 in. thick; 8 to 9 minutes per side for thicker cuts. Serve with tomato and onion slices. **Yield:** 6-8 servings. **Diabetic Exchanges:** One serving equals 5 lean meat; also, 303 calories, 505 mg sodium, 36 mg cholesterol, 3 gm carbohydrate, 37 gm protein, 15 gm fat.

LUSCIOUS RASPBERRY GELATIN SALAD

Bonnie Barclay, Custer, Michigan

2 packages (3 ounces *each*)
   raspberry-flavored gelatin
1 envelope unflavored gelatin
1 cup boiling water
2 cups cold water
1 can (20 ounces) crushed
   pineapple with juice
2 large ripe bananas, mashed
1 pint fresh *or* frozen whole
   unsweetened raspberries
1 cup (8 ounces) sour cream

In a large mixing bowl, combine gelatins. Add boiling water; stir until dissolved. Add the cold water, then pineapple, bananas and raspberries. Stir. Pour half of gelatin mixture into glass serving bowl or 13-in. x 9-in. x 2-in. baking dish; refrig-

erate until firm. Let remaining half sit at room temperature. When refrigerated gelatin is firm, spread sour cream evenly on top, then carefully pour remaining gelatin mixture over the sour cream. Chill until firm. **Yield:** 16 servings.

CHOCOLATE RASPBERRY CREAM

Sally James, Lockport, New York

1 package (4 ounces) sweet
   cooking chocolate, *divided*
2 cups whipping cream
1 tablespoon rum *or* 2 to 3
   drops rum flavoring, optional
3 cups fresh whole raspberries,
   divided
1/4 cup superfine sugar*

Grate chocolate; reserve 3 tablespoons in refrigerator. Whip cream until soft peaks form. Combine remaining chocolate and whipped cream, blending gently but thoroughly. Stir in rum or flavoring, if desired. Reserve 1/4 cup raspberries in refrigerator; toss remaining berries with sugar. (*For superfine sugar, blend granulated sugar in blender until fine.) Fold sugared berries into chocolate mixture. Spoon gently into stemmed glasses; chill for 1 hour. *Do not overchill.* Before serving, sprinkle reserved chocolate on top and garnish with reserved raspberries. **Yield:** 8 servings.

BLENDER RASPBERRY SHERBET

Mary McCrackin, Hollywood, Alabama

2 cups fresh raspberries,
   pureed and frozen *or* 2 cups
   frozen whole unsweetened
   raspberries
2 tablespoons orange juice
   concentrate
1/8 to 1/4 teaspoon vanilla extract
4 tablespoons sugar *or* more
   to taste
1/2 cup plain nonfat yogurt

Puree frozen raspberries in food processor or blender; add remaining ingredients. Blend until creamy. Serve immediately or store in freezer until serving time. **Yield:** 4 3/4-cup servings.

FROZEN FRUIT: To freeze berries, coat cookie sheet with fine layer of nonstick spray; spread berries in single layer on sheet and freeze solid. Transfer frozen berries to plastic bags.

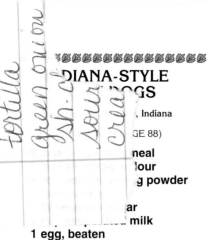

tortilla
green onion
sh. ch
sour
crea

…DIANA-STYLE …GS

…, Indiana

(…GE 88)

…neal
…lour
…g powder
…ar
… milk
1 egg, beaten
1/4 teaspoon paprika
1/2 teaspoon dry mustard
Dash pepper
10 to 16 hot dogs
Wooden skewers
Vegetable oil for deep-frying

In a bowl, mix first 10 ingredients. Pour mixture into a tall glass. Skewer hot dogs with wooden skewers; dip in mixture. Deep-fry at 375° until golden brown (about 2 minutes). Drain on paper towels. **Yield:** 10-16 corn dogs.

BARBECUED LAMB KABOBS

Gloria Jarrett, Loveland, Ohio

(PICTURED ON PAGE 88)

2-1/2 pounds boneless lamb, cut into 1-inch cubes
Skewers

MARINADE:
2 tablespoons parsley flakes
2 tablespoons onion flakes
1 teaspoon salt
1/2 teaspoon black pepper
1/2 cup lemon juice
1/2 cup white wine *or* broth of choice
2 tablespoons soy sauce

DIPPING SAUCE:
1 large onion, chopped
2 garlic cloves, minced
Salt and pepper to taste
1/2 cup vegetable oil
1/2 cup lemon juice
Chopped hot peppers to taste

Combine marinade ingredients in heavy plastic bag; add lamb and refrigerate overnight or at least 5 hours, turning bag occasionally. Put marinated lamb on skewers; broil or grill, turning at intervals until lamb is brown and cooked (about 15 minutes on medium-hot grill). Combine first five dipping sauce ingredients in blender; add peppers last. Serve hot with warm Syrian or French bread. **Yield:** 8-10 servings.

MARINATED SHRIMP IN AVOCADO HALVES

Ruth Larson, Ames, Iowa

(PICTURED ON PAGE 89)

12 ounces fresh *or* frozen shelled medium shrimp
2 tablespoons vinegar
1-1/2 teaspoons lemon juice
1/4 teaspoon salt
1/8 teaspoon dry mustard
Dash freshly ground pepper
1 small onion, thinly sliced, *divided*
1 garlic clove, halved
3 tablespoons cooking oil, *divided*
1 small pickled jalapeno pepper, rinsed, seeded and cut in strips
2 avocados, peeled, halved, pitted and rubbed with lemon juice
Lemon
1 medium tomato, chopped

Thaw shrimp, if frozen; set aside. In bowl, combine vinegar, lemon juice, salt, mustard and pepper; set aside. In medium skillet, cook shrimp, half the onion slices and garlic in 2 tablespoons hot oil over medium-high heat for 4-5 minutes or until shrimp are cooked. Stir occasionally. Remove onion and garlic with slotted spoon; discard. Add shrimp and remaining oil to vinegar mixture, along with jalapeno pepper and remaining onion. Cover; stir occasionally. Chill overnight. To serve, lift shrimp, onion slices and pepper strips from marinade; spoon into avocado halves. Top with tomato; drizzle some of marinade over all. **Yield:** 4 servings.

CHINESE COLESLAW

Marion Stanley, Gilroy, California

(PICTURED ON PAGE 89)

5 cups coarsely chopped Chinese cabbage*
1 cup shredded raw carrots
1/2 cup sliced green onions and tops (cut several times lengthwise, then in 1-inch pieces)
1 can (8 ounces) sliced water chestnuts, drained
2 tablespoons toasted sesame seeds

DRESSING:
1/4 cup vegetable oil
1 teaspoon dark sesame oil
2 tablespoons sugar
1 tablespoon fresh cilantro *or* parsley, minced
1/2 teaspoon salt
1/4 teaspoon black pepper
1/2 teaspoon ground ginger
2 tablespoons wine vinegar
1 tablespoon soy sauce

Toss together vegetables and sesame seeds. Combine dressing ingredients in small bowl; whisk until well blended. Pour dressing over cabbage mixture; toss and cover. Refrigerate 2 hours before serving; toss again before serving. *Chinese cabbage is also sold as Napa cabbage—it is *not* the same as Bok Choy. **Yield:** 12 servings.

RAVE REVIEW COCONUT CAKE

Rena Nabours, Olaton, Kentucky

(PICTURED ON PAGE 89)

CAKE:
1 package (18-1/4 ounces) yellow cake mix
1 package (3-1/2 ounces) instant vanilla pudding mix
1-1/3 cups water
4 eggs, room temperature
1/4 cup vegetable oil
2 cups coconut
1 cup chopped pecans

FROSTING:
4 tablespoons butter, *divided*
2 cups coconut
1 package (8 ounces) cream cheese
2 teaspoons milk
1/2 teaspoon vanilla extract
3-1/2 cups confectioners' sugar

In large bowl, blend cake mix with pudding mix, water, eggs and oil. Beat at medium speed for 3 minutes. Stir in coconut and nuts. Pour into three greased and floured 8-in. cake pans. Bake at 350° for 25-30 minutes or until cake springs back when touched in center. Cool in pans for 10 minutes. Remove to rack to complete cooling. For frosting, melt 2 tablespoons butter in skillet; add coconut and stir constantly over low heat until golden brown. Spread coconut on paper towel to cool. Cream remaining butter with cream cheese, milk and vanilla. Add sugar, beating well to blend; stir in 1-1/2 cups of the toasted coconut. Frost between layers, then top and sides of cake. Sprinkle remaining coconut over cake. **Yield:** 16-20 servings.

SMOKE SIGNAL: When a film of smoke begins rising from hot fat, it's the right temperature for frying doughnuts.

SESAME CUCUMBER SALAD

Craig Towne, Derry, New Hampshire

(PICTURED ON PAGE 88)

✓ This tasty dish uses less sugar, salt and fat. Recipe includes *Diabetic Exchanges*.

- 1 tablespoon sugar
- 1 tablespoon cornstarch
- 1/2 teaspoon salt
- 1 cup rice vinegar
- 2 tablespoons water
- 2 large unpeeled cucumbers (with small seeds), very thinly sliced
- 1 cup diagonally sliced celery
- 1/4 pound cooked small shrimp
- 1/4 pound cooked small scallops
- 1 tablespoon toasted sesame seeds

Combine sugar, cornstarch and salt in small saucepan; stir in vinegar and water. Cook over medium heat, stirring constantly, until mixture comes to a boil and thickens. Cool completely. In large bowl, combine dressing with cucumbers, celery, shrimp, scallops and sesame seeds. Refrigerate 2 hours or overnight. Stir before serving. **Yield: 6 servings. Diabetic Exchanges:** One serving equals 1/2 protein, 2 vegetable; also, 73 calories, 268 mg sodium, 35 mg cholesterol, 10 gm carbohydrate, 8 gm protein, 1 gm fat.

HUCKLEBERRY CHEESE PIE

Pat Kuper, McCall, Idaho

(PICTURED ON PAGE 88)

BUTTER CRUNCH CRUST:
- 1/4 cup packed brown sugar
- 1/2 cup finely chopped nuts
- 1 cup all-purpose flour
- 1/2 cup butter

CHEESE FILLING:
- 1 package (8 ounces) cream cheese, softened
- 3/4 cup confectioners' sugar
- 1 teaspoon vanilla extract
- 1 cup whipped cream *or* frozen nondairy topping, thawed

FRUIT TOPPING:
- 1/2 cup sugar
- 1-1/2 tablespoons cornstarch
- Dash salt
- 1/2 cup water
- 2 cups fresh huckleberries*, *divided*
- 1/2 tablespoon butter

Combine crust ingredients as for pie crust, cutting butter into mixture; mixture will be crumbly. Spread mixture on cookie sheet; bake at 400° for about 20 minutes, stirring occasionally. Remove from oven. While mixture is still hot, press into a 9-in. pie pan, using a smaller-diameter aluminum pie pan to help press crumbs into form. Cool completely. For cheese filling, blend cheese, sugar and vanilla until smooth; gently stir in whipped cream or topping. Pour or spoon filling into cooled crust; refrigerate. For topping, combine sugar, cornstarch and salt in saucepan. Add water, mixing to blend, and 1 cup berries. Cook, stirring, until thickened. Add butter and remaining berries. Cool topping; pour over filling. Top with additional whipped cream, if desired. *Blueberries may be substituted for huckleberries. **Yield:** 8-10 servings.

WEST COAST CHICKEN

Denise Hopper, Logan, Ohio

(PICTURED ON PAGE 89)

✓ This tasty dish uses less sugar, salt and fat. Recipe includes *Diabetic Exchanges*.

- Vegetable oil
- 5 pounds chicken thighs, skinned

SAUCE:
- 2 teaspoons salt
- 1/4 teaspoon black pepper
- 1 cup frozen orange juice concentrate, thawed
- 1/3 cup butter, melted
- 2 teaspoons ground ginger
- 4 teaspoons soy sauce

Grease two 11-in. x 7-in. baking pans well with vegetable oil. Place chicken in single layer in the pans. Combine sauce ingredients and baste chicken well. Cover; refrigerate overnight. Bake, uncovered, at 350° for about 60 minutes, basting with sauce once during baking. **Yield:** 8 (4-ounce) servings. **Diabetic Exchanges:** One serving equals 3 protein, 1 fruit, 1/2 fat; also, 316 calories, 747 mg sodium, 96 mg cholesterol, 20 gm carbohydrate, 22 gm protein, 17 gm fat.

BARBECUED SALMON

Lynda Bridwell, Issaquah, Washington

(PICTURED ON PAGE 90)

- 1/2 cup fresh lemon juice
- 1/2 cup vegetable oil
- 1 teaspoon Worcestershire sauce
- 2 pounds 1-inch-thick salmon steaks *or* fillets
- 1/2 cup wood chips (mesquite, hickory *or* alder)
- 1/2 teaspoon seasoned salt
- 1/2 teaspoon leaf thyme, crumbled
- Cooking oil for grill

In a flat container, mix the lemon juice, vegetable oil and Worcestershire sauce. Place salmon in mixture; marinate 30 minutes. Meanwhile, soak wood chips in enough water to moisten for 15 to 30 minutes. Season salmon with salt and thyme; let stand a few minutes. Preheat charcoal or gas grill to medium-high. Just before cooking, coat grill's grate with cooking oil. Sprinkle wood chips over coals. Cook fish until it loses its translucent appearance and is uniformly colored throughout (about 6 minutes per side for 1-in. cut). *Fillets should be placed skin side down and cooked without turning for total cooking time. Charred skin will peel off easily. **Yield:** 6-8 servings.

GREEN BEANS WITH MUSHROOMS

Judy Miller Hasselkus, Indianapolis, Indiana

(PICTURED ON PAGE 90)

✓ This tasty dish uses less sugar, salt and fat. Recipe includes *Diabetic Exchanges*.

- 2 garlic cloves, minced
- 1/4 pound small fresh mushrooms, trimmed and sliced
- 1 tablespoon butter
- 1 medium red onion, cut in thin strips
- 1 pound fresh green beans, trimmed
- Fresh ground pepper
- 1 teaspoon dill weed
- 2 tablespoons toasted almonds *or* pine nuts

Saute garlic and mushrooms in butter until tender. Stir in onion; set aside. Steam or cook beans in small amount of water until crisp-tender; drain. Combine beans with mushroom mixture; add pepper and dill weed. Garnish with nuts. Serve immediately. **Yield:** 6 servings. **Diabetic Exchanges:** One serving equals 1 vegetable, 1 fat; also, 75 calories, 35 mg sodium, 6 mg cholesterol, 10 gm carbohydrate, 3 gm protein, 4 gm fat.

HEAVENLY CHERRY ANGEL FOOD TRIFLE

Hyacinth Rizzo, Buffalo, New York

(PICTURED ON PAGE 90)

5 cups angel food cake cubes
1/4 cup cherry liqueur, optional
1 cup confectioners' sugar
1 package (3 ounces) cream cheese, softened
8 ounces frozen nondairy whipped topping, thawed, *divided*
1/2 cup toasted chopped pecans
1 can (21 ounces) cherry filling *or* topping

Place cake cubes in large bowl. Sprinkle with liqueur, if desired; let stand 30 minutes. In medium bowl, combine confectioners' sugar and cream cheese; beat until blended. Reserve 2 tablespoons whipped topping; fold remaining topping into cheese mixture, then stir with pecans into cake cubes and mix well. Spoon cake mixture into a pretty glass or crystal bowl. Spread cherry filling evenly over top. (Or, if desired, layer half the cake mixture and cherry filling; repeat layers.) Cover; refrigerate at least 3 hours. Garnish with reserved whipped topping. **Yield:** 8-10 servings.

SOUTHERN-STYLE SOFT CUSTARD

Margaret Wagner Allen, Abingdon, Virginia

(PICTURED ON PAGE 90)

3 egg yolks
4 tablespoons sugar
1/8 teaspoon salt
1 pint milk
1/2 teaspoon vanilla extract
Sliced pound cake
Fresh berries of choice

Beat together egg yolks, sugar and salt. Scald milk (heat to 180°) and pour slowly over egg mixture. Place mixture in top of double boiler and cook over simmering (not boiling) water; stir constantly until mixture coats back of spoon, about 7-10 minutes. (You should be able to run your finger down the center of the spoon and have the pattern stay intact.) Mixture will *not* have the consistency of a firm baked custard. Cool over ice water, stirring occasionally. Add vanilla. If mixture separates, beat with egg beater until smooth. Serve chilled over pound cake and top with berries. **Yield:** 8 servings.

COOK'S HELPER: Next time you need a little more work space for canning or preparing large meals, set up your ironing board in the kitchen! Protect the board by covering it with newspaper and a tablecloth.

BAKED POTATO SKINS

Terry Hill, Hairy Hill, Alberta

8 baking potatoes
1/2 cup butter, melted
1/2 teaspoon salt
1/2 teaspoon paprika
1/2 cup finely chopped green onions
1/2 cup finely chopped cooked bacon
1/2 cup cooked shrimp *or* chopped ham, optional
1/2 cup chopped green pepper
1 cup (4 ounces) shredded cheddar cheese
1 cup (8 ounces) sour cream

Scrub and pierce potatoes; bake at 400° for 1 hour or until tender. Cool slightly; cut in half lengthwise and scoop out pulp, leaving 1/4 in. of pulp attached to skin. (The pulp you remove can be refrigerated for use later.) Cut skins into strips or halves; brush skin sides with melted butter and place on a baking sheet. Sprinkle pulp sides with salt and paprika; cover with green onions, bacon, shrimp or ham, if desired, and green pepper. Top with cheese. Bake at 450° until cheese is melted and skins are crisp, about 10-15 minutes. Garnish each with a dollop of sour cream. Serve immediately. **Yield:** 6-10 servings.

MARINATED VEGETABLE SALAD

Sharon Mensing, Greenfield, Iowa

(PICTURED ON PAGE 92)

1 head fresh broccoli, separated into florets
4 ounces fresh mushrooms, sliced
1 can (5 ounces) sliced water chestnuts, rinsed and drained
1 red onion, sliced and separated into rings
1 bottle (8 ounces) Italian salad dressing
1 to 2 cups cherry tomatoes, halved

Combine broccoli florets, mushrooms, water chestnuts, onion and dressing in a large bowl. Cover; marinate several

---

hours, stirring occasionally. Just before serving, add cherry tomatoes, stirring gently to combine. **Yield:** 6 servings.

REMEMBRANCE STRAWBERRY PIE

Anna Bargfrede, Sweet Springs, Missouri

(PICTURED ON PAGE 92)

1 cup sugar
3 tablespoons cornstarch
1 cup water
3 tablespoons strawberry-flavored gelatin powder
2 pints strawberries, stemmed and halved
1 pie shell (9 inches), baked
Whipped cream *or* nondairy whipped topping

Mix the sugar, cornstarch and water in saucepan; stir constantly, cooking until thickened. Remove from heat; stir in gelatin until dissolved. Pour over strawberry halves; mix well. Pour into pie shell; refrigerate until set. Top with whipped cream or topping. **Yield:** 6-8 servings.

CHOCOLATE MALT CHEESECAKE

Anita Moffett, Rewey, Wisconsin

CRUST:
1/3 cup unsalted butter, melted
1 cup graham cracker crumbs
1/4 cup sugar
FILLING:
3 packages (8 ounces *each*) cream cheese, softened
1 can (14 ounces) sweetened condensed milk
1 cup semisweet chocolate chips, melted
3/4 cup chocolate malt powder
4 eggs
1 teaspoon vanilla extract
GARNISH:
Confectioners' sugar and chocolate curls, optional

Combine crust ingredients. Pat firmly in bottom and 1/2 in. up the side of a 9-in. springform pan; chill. For filling, beat cream cheese until fluffy; add remaining ingredients and blend thoroughly. Pour into prepared crust. Bake at 300° for about 65 minutes or until filling shakes only slightly near center when moved. Cool; chill thoroughly. Garnish with confectioners' sugar and chocolate curls, if desired. **Yield:** 16-20 servings.

99

Taste-tempting tomatoes—summer would not be the same without them! America's No. 1 home garden crop can be served up simply sliced or cleverly cooked in appealing appetizers, marvelous marinated salads and savory soups and sauces such as those pictured below.

TANTALIZING TOMATOES! Clockwise from bottom—**Marinated Herbed Tomato Salad; Appetizer Tomato Cheese Bread; Fresh Tomato Soup; Stuffed Cherry Tomatoes.** (All recipes can be found on Pg. 106).

BEST COOK

Dolores Deegan
Pottstown, Pennsylvania

Special occasions are great reasons for special meals. But this "Best Cook" turns holiday meals into thematic banquets!

Her personal approach to cooking makes Dolores Deegan of Pottstown, Pennsylvania a "Best Cook in the Country" winner, thanks to an enthusiastic nomination from her daughter Diane.

"*Every* holiday is an event at our house," Diane told us. "Bread is Mom's specialty, and on holidays she makes 'theme' loaves—heart-shaped bread for Valentine's Day, shamrock-shaped biscuits for St. Patrick's Day and bunny-shaped rolls at Easter."

We phoned Dolores—known as "Mom" to family *and* friends—to learn more about her personalized cooking.

"Birthdays are my favorite," Dolores chuckled. "On their birthday, each of our five children selects their favorite dinner menu and cake ingredients. Whatever their choice, I aim to please!"

And please she does! For her husband, who loves *The Wizard of Oz*, Dolores topped a green tablecloth with a yellow strip of fabric to depict the Yellow Brick Road…then topped his birthday cake with tiny "ruby slippers"!

"I like things to look pretty as well as taste good," Dolores told us. "And I think a good cook can make a tasty meal without it costing a lot of money."

CHOLESTEROL-FREE OMELET

    4 egg whites
    1 tablespoon skim milk
    3 drops yellow food coloring
    1 tablespoon diced onion
Salt and pepper to taste
    1/2 cup cooked rice *or* leftover mashed potatoes
    3 slices cholesterol-free cheese, cubed
    1 green pepper and 1 sweet red pepper, chopped, optional
    1 tomato, chopped, optional

In a mixing bowl, combine egg whites, milk, food coloring, onion, salt and pepper with a fork. Coat a 9-in. baking dish with no-stick cooking spray. In center of dish, place rice or potatoes in a mound and flatten. Pour egg mixture over all and top with cheese. Add chopped green and red pepper and tomato, if desired. Bake at 350° for about 15 minutes. **Yield:** 1-2 servings.

CHOCOLATE-TOPPED PEANUT BUTTER SPRITZ

    1 cup margarine
    1 cup peanut butter
    1 cup sugar
    1 cup packed brown sugar
    2 eggs
    2 cups all-purpose flour
    1 teaspoon baking soda
    1/2 teaspoon salt
CHOCOLATE TOPPING:
    1-1/2 cups semisweet chocolate chips
    1 tablespoon shortening
Chopped peanuts

In a mixer bowl, cream together margarine, peanut butter and sugars. Beat in eggs until fluffy. Stir together flour, soda and salt; add to creamed mixture; blend well. Chill 15 minutes. Use a cookie press with a zigzag end plate to make 2-1/2-in. strips. Bake at 350° on ungreased sheet for 8-10 minutes. (Watch carefully—cookies brown quickly.) For topping, melt chips with shortening. Using a cake-decorating bag or a heavy plastic bag with corner tip removed, run a strip of chocolate down center of each cookie and top with chopped peanuts. **Yield:** about 16 dozen cookies.

FRIED TOMATOES

    4 to 5 medium tomatoes
    1/2 cup evaporated milk
    1-1/8 cups all-purpose flour, *divided*
    1 cup bread crumbs
    1/2 pound bacon
    2 cups milk
Salt to taste

Slice each tomato into 3 thick slices. Pour evaporated milk in small bowl and place 1 cup flour and the bread crumbs in separate piles on waxed paper. Dip tomatoes in flour, then milk, then crumbs, coating well. Place in refrigerator to dry, about 1 hour. Fry bacon in large skillet until crisp; remove and set aside. In bacon drippings, saute tomato slices until brown. Place tomatoes on a large platter. Pour off all but about 2 tablespoons of drippings. Add remaining flour; cook and stir until bubbly. Add milk and bring to a boil, stirring constantly. Cook and stir for 2 minutes more. Season to taste. To serve, place tomato slice on plate, pour sauce over and top with a bacon slice. **Yield:** 8 servings.

GRINDER REMINDER: To quickly clean a food grinder after chopping nuts, raisins, etc., run half a peeled apple or half a cup of dry cereal through the grinder to pick up the remaining bits of goodies. Then add this to your batter.

● After grinding meats, run a few crackers through the grinder. They can be added to meat loaf or meatballs.

EGGS-CELLENT IDEA: To easily peel hard-cooked eggs, pour off all of the water from the container in which the eggs were cooked. Cover the container and knock the eggs around in it to loosen the shells. Add cold water, and the shells will fall off!

WHIP UP SOME BUTTER! To make your own whipped butter, soften a stick of butter and beat with electric mixer until creamy. Slowly add 2 tablespoons milk to the butter, beating until light and fluffy. Store the butter, covered, in the refrigerator.

Bring a table service, rolls and a dish to pass. That's how the notice reads, and it's your invitation to some classic country eating—at an old-fashioned potluck dinner in the church basement or town hall.

Community cooks bring their best to buffets: Tried-and-true recipes calculated to serve (and satisfy!) a crowd. Hungry neighbors line up at the serving table, eyeing the bounteous offerings and helping themselves to a smorgasbord of delicious dishes, all the while hoping their favorite (always at the far end!) will last till they reach it.

The serving's starting, so take your plate, find a spot in line and enjoy these potluck recipes!

BLESSED BOUNTY: Clockwise on our buffet table from lower left—**Debbie's Deviled Eggs** (Pg. 107); **Company Potatoes** (Pg. 106); **Adreana's Greek Pasta Salad** (Pg. 106); **Spiced Chicken Wings** (Pg. 107); **Zesty Carrots** (Pg. 107); **Bibb Lettuce Salad** (Pg. 107); **Delaware Chicken Divan** (Pg. 107); **Cheeseburger Onion Pie** (Pg. 108).

No potluck would be complete without a fancy, fruit-flavored gelatin dessert such as the Red, White and Blue Salad below right.

And church-basement buffets are bound to boast great baked goods from pie makers and cake bakers who are proud to share their best. Treat your taste buds to their sweet favorites—old-time Chocolate Fudge Cake, taste-tempting Buttermilk Coconut Pie and uniquely delicious Sour Cream Pear Pie. Come on, help yourself!

SWEETS TO SAVOR: Clockwise from bottom—**Sour Cream Pear Pie** (Pg. 108); **Buttermilk Coconut Pie** (Pg. 108); **Chocolate Fudge Cake** (Pg. 108); **Red, White and Blue Salad** (Pg. 108).

MEALS IN MINUTES

SOME DAYS, chores on her family's cattle ranch near Huson, Montana can keep Helen Meadows out of the kitchen right up until almost mealtime.

What does this busy mom and 4-H foods leader do when half an hour or less is left to fix supper for her hungry clan? "Because we raise cattle, I serve beef often—even when I'm in a hurry," she writes.

Bringing beef to the table needn't take time, she adds. "I like this menu because it's quick and nutritious."

Helen's main course is a hearty beef stir-fry salad that's easily prepared. Corn on the cob takes on a lively new flavor with lime juice added to the butter. The corn is cut in 1-inch chunks for easy eating from a fork.

French bread is fast when it's split lengthwise and topped with a cheese-and-seasoned butter that's broiled to a golden brown.

Helen likes to round out her meal with a pretty platter of fresh fruit. If time permits, she mashes 2 cups of fresh raspberries with 1/2 cup sugar and serves the sauce over bananas and grapes. "If you're really rushed, simply sprinkle the fresh berries on top of the other fruit," she suggests.

Either way, your family's sure to enjoy this quick, beefy meal!

BEEF STIR-FRY SALAD

- 4 romaine lettuce leaves, washed
- 1 beef flank steak (1 to 1-1/4 pounds) *or* tender beef steak of choice
- 1 tablespoon vegetable oil
- 1 teaspoon leaf basil, crumbled
- 1/2 teaspoon minced garlic
- 1/2 teaspoon black pepper
- 3 medium tomatoes, cut in small wedges
- 1/4 cup chopped green pepper
- 6 green onions, sliced thin
- 1/2 cup sour cream *or* plain yogurt
- 1/4 cup chopped parsley
- 1 avocado, peeled and sliced

Arrange a lettuce leaf on each dinner plate. Cut steak in half lengthwise, then cut across the grain into 1/8-in. slices. In a heavy skillet, heat oil over medium-high. Add beef, basil, garlic and pepper. Stir-fry just until meat loses pink color, about 2 minutes. Remove from heat. Add tomatoes, green pepper and onions; toss lightly. Transfer beef and vegetables to dinner plates; top with sour cream and parsley. Garnish with avocado slices. **Yield:** 4 servings.

CORN WHEELS WITH LIME BUTTER

- 4 medium ears of corn
- 2 tablespoons butter *or* margarine
- 2 tablespoons fresh lime juice
- 1/2 teaspoon pepper, optional

Using a cleaver or large knife, cut corn into 1-in. lengths. In a large pot, bring water to boil over high heat. Add corn wheels; cover and boil 2 minutes. Melt butter; mix with the lime juice. Transfer corn to serving platter and drizzle with lime-butter. Sprinkle with pepper, if desired. **Yield:** 4 servings.

CHEESE/GARLIC BREAD

- 4 tablespoons butter *or* margarine
- 1 teaspoon minced garlic *or* 1/4 teaspoon garlic powder
- 1 to 2 teaspoons leaf oregano, crumbled
- 1 loaf French bread
- 1/2 cup shredded sharp cheddar cheese
- 1 teaspoon paprika

Melt butter in saucepan; add garlic and oregano. Cut bread in half lengthwise; drizzle butter evenly over cut surfaces. Sprinkle with cheese and paprika. Broil 1-2 minutes until cheese is melted and bread is golden brown. Cut into slices and serve. **Yield:** 12-15 servings.

FIESTA FRUIT PLATTER

Green grape clusters, washed and drained
Bananas, cut in 1/2-inch chunks
Fresh raspberries, rinsed gently and drained

Arrange clusters of grapes on platter with banana chunks. Garnish with a sprinkling of fresh raspberries.

MARINATED HERBED TOMATO SALAD

Frieda Meding, Trochu, Alberta

(PICTURED ON PAGE 100)

6 ripe tomatoes, cut in wedges
3 sweet peppers (combination green, red and yellow), sliced *or* chunked
1 sweet Spanish onion (white *or* red), sliced
1 cup pitted black olives

DRESSING:
2/3 cup vegetable oil
1/4 cup vinegar
1/4 cup fresh parsley, snipped
1/4 cup green onions with tops, snipped
1 teaspoon salt
1/4 teaspoon pepper
1 teaspoon sugar
1/2 teaspoon dried basil (use fresh if available)
1/2 teaspoon dried marjoram (use fresh if available)

Slice vegetables into glass serving bowl; add olives. Set aside. Combine dressing ingredients in screw-top jar; shake well. Pour over vegetables. Cover and refrigerate for 3-4 hours. **Yield:** 6 servings.

FRESH TOMATO SOUP

Rosemarie Johnson, Norridge, Illinois

(PICTURED ON PAGE 100)

 This tasty dish uses less sugar, salt and fat. Recipe includes *Diabetic Exchanges*.

1 cup (2 stalks) chopped celery
1 small onion, chopped
1 carrot, grated
1/2 green pepper, chopped
1/4 cup butter
4-1/2 cups chicken broth, *divided*
1 quart fresh tomatoes, peeled and chopped
1/2 teaspoon curry powder
1/2 teaspoon salt
1/4 teaspoon pepper
4 teaspoons sugar
1/4 cup flour

Saute celery, onion, carrot and green pepper in butter in large heavy pan. Add 4 cups broth, tomatoes, curry powder, salt, pepper and sugar; heat to boiling. Reduce heat; simmer for 20 minutes. Blend flour with remaining 1/2 cup broth. Stir gradually into soup. Cook until slightly thickened, stirring frequently. Serve hot. **Yield:** 2 quarts. **Diabetic Exchanges:** One cup serving equals 1/2 bread, 1/2 fat; also, 57 calories,

368 mg sodium, 9 mg cholesterol, 7 gm carbohydrate, 1 gm protein, 3 gm fat.

APPETIZER TOMATO CHEESE BREAD

Penney Kester, Springville, New York

(PICTURED ON PAGE 100)

1 medium onion, minced
2 tablespoons butter
1/2 cup dairy sour cream
1/4 cup mayonnaise
4 ounces shredded cheddar cheese (about 1 cup)
3/4 teaspoon salt
1/4 teaspoon pepper
1/4 teaspoon leaf oregano
Pinch of sage
2/3 cup milk
2 cups biscuit mix
3 medium tomatoes, peeled, seeded and sliced 1/4 inch thick
Paprika

Saute onion in butter until tender. Blend with next 7 ingredients; set aside. Stir milk into biscuit mix to make a soft dough. Turn dough onto a well-floured board; knead lightly for 10 to 12 strokes. Pat dough over bottom of buttered 13-in. x 9-in. x 2-in. baking pan, pushing dough up sides of dish to form a shallow rim. Arrange tomato slices over dough. Spoon on sour cream/cheese mixture; sprinkle with paprika. Bake at 400° for 25 minutes. Let stand 10 minutes before cutting. **Yield:** 12 servings.

STUFFED CHERRY TOMATOES

Donna Smith, Grey Cliff, Montana

(PICTURED ON PAGE 100)

1 pint small cherry tomatoes
FILLING:
1 package (3 ounces) cream cheese, softened
1/4 cup prepared ranch-style dressing
2 tablespoons thinly sliced green onion
2 tablespoons finely chopped water chestnuts
2 tablespoons finely chopped walnuts

Slice off tops of tomatoes. Scoop out pulp with small melon ball cutter, reserving pulp to use as necessary to thin filling. Drain tomatoes, upside-down, on paper towel. Combine filling ingredients

in small bowl. Stuff tomatoes with filling. Keep refrigerated until serving time. **Yield:** about 24 appetizer tomatoes.

ADREANA'S GREEK PASTA SALAD

Lee Souleles, Northridge, California

(PICTURED ON PAGE 102)

1 pound rotini noodles
1 pound boneless chicken breasts
1 bay leaf
3 stalks celery, chopped
1 sweet red pepper, chopped
1 can (2-1/4 ounces) sliced black olives
1 package (4 ounces) feta cheese, drained and crumbled
3 green onions, finely sliced
1 bottle (16 ounces) Italian salad dressing

Cook noodles according to package directions. Cook chicken breasts in water to cover with 1 bay leaf, 30 minutes or until juices run clear. Remove bay leaf. Cool chicken; remove skin. Cut chicken in bite-size pieces. Combine noodles, chicken, celery, pepper, olives, cheese, onions and salad dressing. Serve warm or cold. **Yield:** 16 servings.

COMPANY POTATOES

Mrs. James Grisdale, Mt. Pleasant, Michigan

(PICTURED ON PAGE 102)

1/2 cup chopped onions
1/4 cup butter
1 can (10-3/4 ounces) cream of chicken soup, undiluted
2 pounds frozen hash brown potatoes
1 pint dairy sour cream
TOPPING:
2 cups shredded cheddar cheese
1 cup corn flake crumbs

Saute onions in butter until transparent. Add soup, potatoes and sour cream. Spoon into a greased 13-in. x 9-in. x 2-in. baking pan. Combine cheese and corn flakes; spread over top. Bake at 350° for 45 minutes. **Yield:** 12 servings.

DEBBIE'S DEVILED EGGS

Debbie Lampert, Milton, Wisconsin

(PICTURED ON PAGE 102)

6 large eggs
1/16 teaspoon ground white pepper
1-1/2 teaspoons prepared Dijon
    mustard
1/4 cup creamy salad dressing
1 teaspoon dill pickle juice,
    optional (reduce salad
    dressing amount if used)
Paprika *or* dill weed *or* pimiento

Before cooking eggs, use a tack to pierce a hole in the broad end of the egg—this centers the yolk. Cook eggs by placing, single layer, in heavy saucepan. Add cold water to cover eggs by at least 1 inch. Bring to boil; cover, shut off heat and let stand on burner for 20 minutes. Pour off hot water; replace with cold. Change water several times until eggs are cold. Push eggs against each other in water to crack shells (loosens the membrane and allows easy peeling). Peel eggs under running water; drain and slice in half, lengthwise, beginning at narrow end. Remove yolks; mash yolks with fork. Combine yolk with pepper, mustard and dressing. Add pickle juice, if desired. Fill cavities using pastry tube. Nest on a bed of alfalfa sprouts; sprinkle with paprika or dill weed or decorate with strip of pimiento. **Yield:** 12 deviled egg halves.

BIBB LETTUCE SALAD

Marcella Swigert, Monroe City, Missouri

(PICTURED ON PAGE 103)

1 head Bibb lettuce
1 head iceberg lettuce
1 bunch fresh spinach
1 bunch escarole
1 bunch endive
1 head Boston lettuce
DRESSING:
1 cup corn oil
6 tablespoons sugar
1 teaspoon dry mustard
1 to 4 tablespoons onion,
    chopped
1/2 cup apple cider vinegar
1 teaspoon celery seed
GARNISHES:
3 ounces blue cheese, crumbled
8 ounces bacon, fried and
    crumbled

Rinse greens; drain well. Tear greens into bite-size pieces; mix thoroughly in large salad bowl. Chill. Combine dressing ingredients in blender; blend well. Sprinkle garnishes over greens; pour on dressing; toss gently. **Yield:** 20 servings.

SPICED CHICKEN WINGS

Marion Stanley, Gilroy, California

(PICTURED ON PAGE 102)

12 whole chicken wings
SAUCE:
3/4 cup soy sauce
1 clove garlic, pressed
1/2 teaspoon dark roasted
    sesame oil
1/2 teaspoon powdered ginger
Pinch of Chinese 5-Spice powder

Remove tips from chicken wings. Cut each wing in half at joint; set aside. Combine sauce ingredients in bowl or heavy-duty plastic bag; add wing pieces and marinate, refrigerated, 1 hour or more. Remove wing pieces from sauce and place, thick-skin side down, in a lightly greased shallow baking pan. Pour sauce over wings. Bake at 375° for 20 minutes. Remove from oven and pour off juices and sauce, reserving liquid. Turn wings. Return to oven; bake 20 minutes more until browned. Serve hot or cold. (Reserved liquid can be heated and used as a dipping sauce.) **Yield:** 4-6 servings.

DELAWARE CHICKEN DIVAN

Joan Rae Mills, Greenwood, Delaware

(PICTURED ON PAGE 103)

2 packages (10 ounces *each*)
    frozen broccoli *or* 1-1/2 pounds
    fresh broccoli, washed, cut in
    spears and lightly steamed
1-1/2 cups cooked chicken (white
    meat), cut in bite-size pieces
SAUCE:
1 can (10-3/4 ounces) cream of
    chicken soup, undiluted
1/2 cup mayonnaise
2 tablespoons fresh lemon
    juice
2 tablespoons sherry *or*
    chicken broth
1/4 cup Parmesan cheese

Arrange broccoli spears on bottom of 1-1/2-qt. buttered casserole; sprinkle chicken pieces over broccoli. Combine sauce ingredients; spoon over top of broccoli/chicken. Bake uncovered at 350° for 30 minutes. **Yield:** 4 servings.

ZESTY CARROTS

James McMonagle, Bethel Park, Pennsylvania

(PICTURED ON PAGE 103)

1-1/2 pounds carrots, washed
    and peeled
1/4 cup water, reserved from
    cooking carrots
2 tablespoons grated onion
    with juice
1 tablespoon prepared
    horseradish
1/2 cup mayonnaise
1/4 cup grated cheddar cheese
1/2 teaspoon salt
1/4 teaspoon pepper
TOPPING:
1 cup fresh bread crumbs
1/4 cup butter, melted
1 teaspoon paprika

Slice carrots 1/4 in. thick; cook in small amount of water for 5 minutes. Drain; reserve 1/4 cup of water for sauce. Combine water, onion/juice, horseradish, mayonnaise, cheese, salt and pepper. Add carrots and spoon into buttered 2-qt. casserole. Combine topping ingredients; sprinkle over carrot mixture. Bake at 350° for 20 minutes. **Yield:** 8 servings.

POTATO NACHOS

Deb Helmer, Winfield, Kansas

1 large baking potato
1/8 teaspoon salt
1 jar (8 ounces) taco sauce
1/2 cup sliced green onions
1/2 cup chopped green chilies
1/2 cup shredded cheddar *or*
    Monterey Jack cheese
1/2 cup sliced ripe olives

Scrub the potato and cut it into 1/4-in. slices. Arrange the slices in a single layer on a greased broiler pan; sprinkle lightly with salt. Broil 4 in. from heat until golden brown. Turn and broil other side until brown and tender when tested with a fork. Top with taco sauce, green onions, chilies, cheese and olives. Broil until the cheese melts. *Microwave Method:* Arrange the slices in a single layer on a microwave-safe pie plate or baking dish; sprinkle lightly with salt. Drizzle with taco sauce. Cover pie plate with plain paper towel. Cook on high for 4-5 minutes or until tender, rotating dish once. Add more taco sauce, top with green onions, chilies, cheese and olives. Cover again and cook 30-60 seconds or until the cheese melts. **Yield:** 2 snack servings.

CHEESEBURGER ONION PIE

Sharon Jakovac, Salmon, Idaho

(PICTURED ON PAGE 103)

1 tablespoon vegetable oil
1 pound mild white onions,
  sliced and quartered to make
  3 cups
1 pound ground beef
1/3 cup catsup
2 teaspoons prepared mustard
1/4 teaspoon salt
1/8 teaspoon ground pepper
2 cans (8 ounces *each*)
  refrigerated crescent dinner
  rolls
1 cup shredded cheddar cheese
2 eggs, beaten

GLAZE:
1 egg yolk, beaten
1 tablespoon water

Heat oil in skillet over medium heat. Add onions; cook, covered, for 10 minutes, stirring occasionally. Remove onions; set aside. Brown ground beef; remove from heat and drain off fat. Stir in catsup, mustard, salt and pepper; set aside. On floured surface, unroll dough from 1 can of rolls. Press together perforations and roll dough to 12-in. square. Place dough in a 9-in. quiche dish, tart pan or pie plate; trim to 1 in. beyond edge of dish. Spoon meat mixture into dish. Sprinkle with cheese; top with onions. Pour two beaten eggs over onion layer. Unroll remaining roll dough; press together perforations and roll out to an 11-in. square. Place on top of onion layer; trim and pinch together with bottom dough layer. Combine glaze ingredients; brush over surface. Bake at 350° for 40 minutes or until browned. Let stand 10 minutes before serving. Serve with chili sauce, if desired. **Yield:** 8 servings.

SOUR CREAM PEAR PIE

Susan Mason, Twin Falls, Idaho

(PICTURED ON PAGE 104)

2 cups peeled, diced ripe pears
1/2 cup sugar
1 egg, beaten
1 tablespoon all-purpose flour
1 cup dairy sour cream
1 teaspoon vanilla
Dash salt
1 unbaked 9-inch pastry shell

CRUMB TOPPING:
1/2 cup sugar
1/3 cup flour
1/4 cup butter, softened

Combine pears, sugar, egg, flour, sour cream, vanilla and salt; blend gently. Spoon into unbaked pie shell. Bake at 350° for 25 minutes. Combine all of the topping ingredients until well-mixed. Sprinkle on top of pie; return to oven for 30 minutes more. **Yield:** 8 servings.

CHOCOLATE FUDGE CAKE

Pat Schaffer, Bark River, Michigan

(PICTURED ON PAGE 104)

1/2 cup butter, softened
1-1/2 cups sugar
2 large eggs
1 teaspoon vanilla
1/2 cup plus 1 tablespoon hot
  water
2/3 cup unsweetened cocoa
1-3/4 cups unsifted all-purpose flour
1 teaspoon baking soda
1 teaspoon baking powder
1/2 teaspoon salt
1 cup sour milk (1 tablespoon
  white vinegar plus milk to
  make 1 cup)

FROSTING:
3 squares (3 ounces)
  unsweetened chocolate
1/4 cup butter
2 cups confectioners' sugar
1/2 cup dairy sour cream
2 teaspoons vanilla

To make cake, combine softened butter and sugar until fluffy. Add eggs, one at a time, beating well after each addition. Mix in vanilla. Stir hot water into cocoa to form a smooth paste; add gradually to creamed mixture. Set aside. Combine flour, baking soda, powder and salt; add to creamed mixture alternately with sour milk. Pour batter into 2 greased-and-floured 9-in. layer pans. Bake at 350° for 30-35 minutes or until wooden pick inserted in center comes out clean. Cool cake 10 minutes in pans; remove from pans to wire racks to complete cooling. Chill before frosting. To make frosting, combine chocolate and butter in small saucepan and melt over low heat, stirring to blend. Pour chocolate/butter mixture into small mixing bowl. Add remaining ingredients; beat until smooth and creamy. **Yield:** 16 servings.

RED, WHITE AND BLUE SALAD

Lanette Wiedner Larson, Washington, D.C.

(PICTURED ON PAGE 104)

1 package (3 ounces) strawberry
  gelatin dessert
1 envelope unflavored gelatin
1 cup sugar
1 cup whipping cream
2 cups dairy sour cream
1 teaspoon vanilla
1 package (3 ounces) raspberry
  or black cherry gelatin dessert
1 can (15 ounces) canned
  blueberries, packed in syrup
  or water

Note: This salad takes time to prepare, since each layer must set until firm before the next layer is added. Dissolve strawberry gelatin in 2 cups boiling water; pour into 3-qt. glass bowl. Refrigerate until firm. Dissolve 1 envelope of unflavored gelatin in 1/2 cup cold water; set aside. Over low heat, dissolve sugar in whipping cream; heat, stirring constantly, until mixture *nearly* boils. Remove from heat; add unflavored gelatin mixture. Cool. Blend in sour cream and vanilla; pour over first layer. Refrigerate until firm. Dissolve 1 package of raspberry/black cherry gelatin in 1 cup boiling water; cool. Add 1 can blueberries, including liquid. Pour over second layer; refrigerate until firm. **Yield:** 10 servings.

BUTTERMILK COCONUT PIE

Marie Brown, Carthage, Mississippi

(PICTURED ON PAGE 104)

1-1/4 cups sugar
2 tablespoons all-purpose flour
1/2 cup butter, melted
3 eggs, beaten
1/2 cup cultured buttermilk
1 teaspoon vanilla extract
1 can (3-1/2 ounces) flaked
  coconut, *divided*
1 unbaked 9-inch pastry shell

Combine the sugar and flour in a large bowl. Add melted butter, eggs, buttermilk, vanilla and two-thirds of the coconut. Mix well. Pour mixture into shell. Sprinkle with remaining coconut. Bake at 325° for 1 hour and 5 minutes or until set. **Yield:** 8 servings.

COLOR IT PRETTY: Add 1/4 teaspoon flavored gelatin powder to vanilla frosting for a colorful cake!

SQUASH-APPLE BAKE

Judith Hawes, Chelmsford, Massachusetts

- 1 medium (about 1-1/4 pounds) buttercup *or* butternut squash, peeled, cut into 3/4-inch slices
- 2 apples, peeled, cored and cut in wedges
- 1/2 cup packed brown sugar
- 1 tablespoon all-purpose flour
- 1/4 cup butter, melted
- 1/2 teaspoon salt
- 1/2 teaspoon mace

Arrange squash in a greased 12-in. x 8-in. baking pan. Top with apple wedges. Combine remaining ingredients; spoon over apples. Bake at 350° for 50-60 minutes or until tender. **Yield:** 4-6 servings.

CHICKEN CASSEROLE

Bonnie Ziegler, Rincon, Georgia

- 2 cups cooked chopped chicken
- 1/2 cup chopped pecans
- 2 teaspoons instant minced onion
- 2 cups sliced celery
- 1 cup mayonnaise
- 2 teaspoons lemon juice
- 1 cup potato chips, broken in small pieces
- 1/2 cup mild grated cheddar cheese

Mix all ingredients together except cheese and chips. Put into a 1-1/2-qt. casserole pan or dish. Mix chips and cheese. Sprinkle on top. Bake, uncovered, at 375° about 30 minutes or until heated through. **Yield:** 6 servings.

MAIN DISH TUNA SALAD

Twyla Richett, North Hampton, New Hampshire

- 7 ounces pasta shells *or* spirals
- 1 can (7 ounces) chunk tuna, drained
- 1/2 cup chopped celery
- 1/2 cup chopped carrots
- 1/2 cup finely chopped green onions
- 1/2 cup chopped sweet pickle
- 3 hard-cooked eggs, chopped

DRESSING:
- 1/2 cup mayonnaise
- 1 to 2 tablespoons sweet pickle juice (to taste)
- 1 tablespoon prepared mustard
- 1/2 teaspoon salt

Freshly ground pepper

Cook pasta according to package directions. Drain; cool. Combine tuna, celery, carrots, green onions, pickle and eggs in a large bowl; add pasta. Blend dressing ingredients. Pour over all; stir to mix. Chill thoroughly. Must be kept chilled. **Yield:** 6-8 servings.

ARTICHOKE GREEN CHILI BAKE

Sylvia Teague, Eureka Springs, Arkansas

- 3 jars (6 ounces *each*) marinated artichokes
- 1 medium onion, chopped, (about 1/2 cup)
- 1 clove garlic, minced
- 10 eggs, beaten
- 1/2 cup fine bread crumbs
- 4 cups shredded Monterey Jack cheese
- 1/2 teaspoon salt
- 1/2 teaspoon dried leaf basil
- 1/2 teaspoon dried leaf oregano
- 1/4 teaspoon pepper
- 1 can (4 ounces) chopped green chilies

Drain artichokes, reserving 2 tablespoons marinade. Coarsely chop artichokes; set aside. Saute onion and garlic in reserved marinade. Mix with eggs, bread crumbs, cheese, salt, basil, oregano, pepper and chilies. Pour into 2 8-in. square baking dishes. Bake at 325° for 35-40 minutes or until set. Cut into squares to serve as appetizers. **Yield:** about 50 appetizer squares.

PLATZ

(Traditional Mennonite Fruit Dessert)
Edith Quapp, Yarrow, British Columbia

CAKE:
- 2 cups all-purpose flour
- 2 teaspoons baking powder
- 1 cup sugar
- 1/8 teaspoon salt
- 1/2 cup butter
- 1 cup milk
- 2 eggs, beaten
- 2 teaspoons vanilla

FRUIT LAYER:
Fresh *or* frozen unsweetened fruit of choice—apples, cherries, blueberries, plums, blackberries, apricots, peaches *or* nectarines

TOPPING:
- 1/4 cup melted butter
- 3/4 cup all-purpose flour
- 3/4 cup sugar

Blend flour, baking powder, sugar, salt and butter in a large bowl. Stir in milk, beaten eggs and vanilla. Spread batter on well-greased 17-in. x 11-1/2-in. x 1-in. baking sheet or jelly roll pan. Cover with fruit of choice. Combine topping ingredients and mix by hand until crumbly; sprinkle over fruit. Bake at 375° for 30-35 minutes. **Yield:** about 40 bars.

HARVEST POTATO CASSEROLE

Cheryl Farmon, Lawrence, Nebraska

- 6 cups frozen shredded hash brown potatoes, thawed
- 1/3 cup chopped onion
- 2 cups dairy sour cream
- 1/2 teaspoon salt
- 1/4 teaspoon ground pepper
- 1 pound pre-cooked little smoked sausage links
- 1 cup shredded cheddar cheese

Combine all ingredients except sausage and cheese. Put in 13-in. x 9-in. x 2-in. greased baking pan. Arrange sausage links on top of potato mixture. Cover; bake at 350° for 35 minutes or until bubbly. Sprinkle the shredded cheese over top; bake, uncovered, 5 minutes more. **Yield:** 6 servings.

BAKED STUFFED TOMATOES

Edna Jackson, Kokomo, Indiana

- 6 medium tomatoes

STUFFING:
- 1 cup garlic/cheese croutons, crushed
- 2 tablespoons grated Parmesan cheese
- 2 tablespoons shredded American *or* cheddar cheese
- 4 tablespoons butter, melted
- 1/2 teaspoon salt *or* to taste
- 1/4 teaspoon freshly ground pepper

Chopped fresh parsley

Hollow out a funnel-shaped hole in each tomato to make room for stuffing. Mix stuffing ingredients except parsley, which is sprinkled on top. Spoon in tomatoes. Place tomatoes in baking dish; cover with aluminum foil to prevent over-browning of stuffing. Bake at 350° for 30 minutes. **Yield:** 6 servings.

SURPRISE POTATOES

Ruth Montgomery, Tullahoma, Tennessee

6 medium white potatoes, peeled
1 cup whipping cream
Salt and pepper to taste

Shred the potatoes and rinse in cold water. Drain thoroughly. Place in a greased 9-in. x 9-in. baking pan; pour cream over all and sprinkle with salt and pepper. Cover with foil and bake at 325° for 1-1/2 hours. Uncover and bake 30 minutes longer or until lightly browned on top. **Yield:** 6 servings.

CASHEW PORK STIR-FRY

Betty Ruenholl, Syracuse, Nebraska

1 pound pork tenderloin
2 tablespoons vegetable oil, *divided*
2 large carrots, peeled and cut diagonally
2 celery stalks, sliced diagonally
1/2 cup cashews
Cooked rice, optional

SAUCE:
1 tablespoon grated orange rind
3/4 cup orange juice
1 tablespoon cornstarch
3 tablespoons soy sauce
1/3 cup corn syrup
1/4 teaspoon ground ginger

Cut tenderloin into thin strips and set aside. Combine sauce ingredients, stirring well. Heat 1 tablespoon oil in large skillet over medium. Add carrots and celery; stir-fry for about 3 minutes. Remove vegetables; set aside. Heat remaining oil in skillet. Add pork; stir-fry for about 3 minutes. Return vegetables to pan; add sauce and cashews. Cook, stirring constantly, over medium-high heat, until thickened. Serve over rice, if desired. **Yield:** 4 servings.

FLAVOR BOOSTER: For savory pork, season with rosemary, thyme, sage, basil, chives or sweet marjoram.

MICROWAVE CHEESY CRUMB TOMATOES

Violet Knoll, Lodi, California

4 tomatoes
1/3 cup dry bread crumbs
2 tablespoons butter
2 tablespoons grated Parmesan cheese
1/2 teaspoon salt
Dash pepper

Cut the tomatoes in half crosswise; arrange cut side up on microwavable plate. Set aside. In small bowl, combine bread crumbs and butter; microwave on high, uncovered, stirring frequently for 3-4 minutes or until golden brown. Stir in cheese and seasonings. Sprinkle crumb mixture over each tomato half. Microwave on high, uncovered, for 3-4 minutes or until hot. **Yield:** 4 servings.

HOT CHICKEN, WILD RICE AND TOMATO SALAD

Jeanette Strobel, Brainerd, Minnesota

4 tablespoons butter
1/2 cup chopped onion
1/2 cup diced celery
2 cups cooked, cubed chicken
2 cups cooked wild rice *or* white rice
1 cup cooked fresh *or* frozen peas
2 tablespoons snipped parsley
1 teaspoon *instant* chicken bouillon
1/2 cup boiling water
Salt to taste
Pepper to taste
1/4 to 1/2 teaspoon leaf basil, crumbled
1 cup pecans, toasted
4 medium ripe tomatoes, cubed

Melt butter in 10-in. skillet or wok. Add onion and celery; saute until tender. Add chicken, wild rice/rice, peas and parsley to skillet. Cook, tossing lightly until all ingredients are hot. Dissolve bouillon in water; add salt, pepper and basil. Sprinkle over ingredients in skillet. Remove from heat. Add pecans and tomatoes, tossing to blend ingredients. Serve immediately while warm. **Yield:** 6 servings.

SWEET TOMATO PIE

Rita Futral, Ocean Springs, Mississippi

SPAGHETTI CRUST:
1 package (7 ounces) spaghetti, cooked and drained
2 tablespoons butter, melted
1/2 cup fresh Parmesan cheese, grated
1 egg, beaten
FILLING:
1 pound sweet Italian sausage
1 clove garlic, minced
1 small zucchini, peeled and chopped
1/2 cup (8 medium) green onions, chopped with tops
1/2 cup (4 large) fresh mushrooms, chopped
2 tablespoons chopped fresh parsley, no stems
5 medium fresh tomatoes, peeled and finely chopped
1/2 teaspoon salt
1/4 teaspoon ground pepper
1/2 to 1 teaspoon Italian seasoning
1 cup mozzarella cheese, grated *or* cubed

Mix together well spaghetti, butter, Parmesan cheese and egg. Spread evenly in well-greased 9-in. or 10-in. pie pan. Remove sausage from casings; crumble into a large skillet. Add the garlic, zucchini, onions, mushrooms and parsley; cook until sausage is no longer pink. Add tomatoes, salt, pepper and Italian seasoning. Mix well. Simmer for 5 minutes, stirring occasionally. Add mozzarella cheese; mix well. Spread meat mixture evenly over spaghetti. Bake at 350° for 25 minutes. Cut in wedges. **Yield:** 6 servings.

CORN AND TOMATO CASSEROLE

Edna Hoffman, Hebron, Indiana

3 strips lean bacon
1/3 cup minced onion
3 tablespoons green pepper, diced
3 large ears sweet corn (about 3 cups) *or* 1 package (16 ounces) frozen sweet corn
2 tablespoons brown sugar, optional
1 teaspoon salt
1/8 teaspoon pepper
1 teaspoon sweet basil
2-1/2 cups canned tomatoes, drained and chopped
TOPPING:
2/3 cup herb-flavored stuffing mix
2/3 cup shredded cheddar cheese

In a large skillet, fry bacon until crisp. Drain on paper towel, reserving the drippings in skillet. Crumble bacon into bottom of a greased 1-1/2-qt. casserole. Add onions and green pepper to bacon drippings; cook over medium heat until tender. Cut corn off cob; add to onion mixture along with brown sugar, salt, pepper, basil and tomatoes. Cook 10-15 minutes. Pour over bacon in casserole. Top with stuffing mix and cheese. Bake at 350° for 30 minutes. **Yield:** 6 servings.

GREEN TOMATO CHOCOLATE CAKE

Dorothy Kubota, Sacramento, California

2/3 cup butter
1-3/4 cups sugar
3 eggs, room temperature
2 teaspoons vanilla
2 teaspoons grated orange rind
1/2 cup unsweetened cocoa
2-1/2 cups all-purpose flour
2 teaspoons baking powder
2 teaspoons baking soda
1 teaspoon salt
1 teaspoon cinnamon
1 cup cultured buttermilk
1 cup pureed, seeded green
  tomatoes (about 3 medium)
1 cup broken pecans
GLAZE:
2 cups confectioners' sugar
3 tablespoons orange juice
Grated rind from 1 orange

In medium bowl, cream together butter and sugar until light and fluffy. Add eggs, one at a time, beating well after each addition. Stir in vanilla and orange peel; set aside. Combine cocoa, flour, baking powder, soda, salt and cinnamon. Alternately stir flour mixture, buttermilk and tomatoes into egg mixture. Fold in pecans. Turn into a greased and lightly floured fluted or tube pan. Bake at 350° for 1 hour or until cake tests done when wooden pick is inserted in center. Invert onto rack to cool completely. Meanwhile, make glaze by combining confectioners' sugar, juice and rind in small bowl. Mix well. Drizzle over cooled cake. **Yield:** 12 servings.

CLEVER CAKE TIPS: When baking chocolate cake, dust pans with unsweetened cocoa instead of flour to avoid a white "floury" look.
● For a moister cake, place a small oven-proof bowl of water in the oven while the cake is baking.

TOMATO CHEESE PIE

Mavis Diment, Marcus, Iowa

4 cups seasoned croutons
2 medium tomatoes, sliced
1/4 cup diced green pepper
2 eggs
1-1/2 cups milk
1 teaspoon salt
1/2 teaspoon white pepper
1/2 teaspoon paprika
1/2 teaspoon basil
1/2 teaspoon dry mustard
2 cups shredded Swiss cheese

Put croutons into a 9-in. pie pan. Slice tomatoes lengthwise and layer on top of the croutons. Mix green pepper, eggs, milk, salt, pepper, paprika, basil and mustard together and pour over tomatoes. Sprinkle on cheese. Bake at 350° for 40 minutes or until brown and puffy. **Yield:** 6 servings.

ICY-HOT TOMATO SALAD

Darlene Smith, Rockford, Illinois

6 large ripe tomatoes
1 large green pepper
1 onion
DRESSING:
3/4 cup cider vinegar
1/4 cup cold water
2 tablespoons sugar
2 teaspoons celery salt
1/8 teaspoon cayenne
1/4 teaspoon black pepper
2 teaspoons dill weed
1 cucumber, sliced, optional

Peel and quarter tomatoes. Slice green pepper into strips. Cut onion into rings. Place all in a 2-qt. covered container. Combine dressing ingredients in small saucepan; bring to boil while stirring. Boil for 1 minute. Pour over vegetables. Sprinkle dill weed on top. Cover and refrigerate. Before serving, place cucumber slices on top of salad if desired. (Salad will keep several days in refrigerator.) **Yield:** 10-12 servings.

SEAFOOD IN TOMATO SAUCE

Jeffrey MacCord, New Castle, Delaware

3 tablespoons cooking oil,
  divided
1/4 pound fresh mushrooms,
  sliced
1 garlic clove, minced
1 can (16 ounces) whole
  tomatoes, diced
1 teaspoon dried thyme
1-1/2 teaspoons dried oregano
1 teaspoon sugar
Salt and pepper to taste
1/2 pound uncooked bay scallops
1/2 pound uncooked small
  shrimp, peeled and deveined
1 cup cooked rice
1/2 pound cooked real *or*
  imitation crabmeat chunks
3/4 cup grated *or* shredded
  Parmesan cheese

In a large saucepan, heat 1 tablespoon oil. Saute mushrooms and garlic 3-4 minutes. Add tomatoes, herbs, sugar, salt and pepper. Cover and bring to a boil. Reduce heat to simmer; cook for 30 minutes. Uncover and cook 10 additional minutes. Meanwhile, heat remaining oil in a skillet over medium. Cook scallops and shrimp until pink, about 3-4 minutes. Divide rice over the bottoms of four individual ovenproof casseroles. Top with shrimp and scallops Stir crabmeat into tomato mixture and spoon into the casseroles. Sprinkle each with Parmesan cheese. Broil until the cheese melts. Serve immediately. **Yield:** 4 servings.

TOMATOES PROVENCALE

Leatrice Simpkins, Cambridge City, Indiana

 This tasty dish uses less sugar, salt and fat. Recipe includes *Diabetic Exchanges*.

4 slices bacon, diced
1 clove garlic, minced
1 medium onion, thinly sliced
1/4 pound fresh mushrooms,
  sliced
1 tablespoon all-purpose flour
1/2 teaspoon seasoned salt
5 medium tomatoes
6 tablespoons grated Parmesan
  cheese, *divided*
1 tablespoon butter

Fry bacon until crisp. Drain on paper towel; reserve drippings in skillet. Set aside. Saute garlic, onion and mushrooms in skillet until tender. Stir in reserved bacon, flour and seasoned salt. Set aside. Cut tomatoes into 1/2-in. slices. Place half of the slices in a lightly greased 8-in square baking dish. Spoon half of bacon/onion mixture over tomatoes. Sprinkle with 3 tablespoons Parmesan cheese. Repeat layers. Dot with butter. Bake at 350° for 25 minutes. **Yield:** 6 servings. **Diabetic Exchanges:** One serving equals 1/2 protein, 1/2 bread, 1 vegetable, 1/2 fat; also, 124 calories, 308 mg sodium, 13 mg cholesterol, 11 gm carbohydrate, 6 gm protein, 6 gm fat.

TOMATO TIPS: To can 1 pint of tomatoes, plan to use 1-1/4 to 1-3/4 lbs. of fresh tomatoes. For 1 pint of juice, allow 1-1/2 to 2 lbs. of tomatoes.
● For best flavor, store tomatoes at room temperature.
● Tomatoes can be ripened and kept for weeks by wrapping individually in newspaper.
● Place unripened tomatoes with other fruit, especially pears, to speed up ripening.

It's time to move meals outdoors again—no matter where you're heading. Whether your summertime fare's being served right off the tailgate of a pickup or at a more leisurely pace from a picnic table in the park, you'll find two hidden ingredients in these recipes that you'll be glad to discover. All these outdoor-oriented recipes emphasize easy eating and quick cleanup, so the cook can get out and enjoy the season, too!

HEARTY HOT-WEATHER HELPINGS: Clockwise from lower left—**Summer Sauerkraut Salad** (Pg. 119); **Perfect Picnic Basket** (Pg. 119); **Spicy Sandwich Loaf** (Pg. 119); **Old-Fashioned Lemonade** (Pg. 120); **Marinated Tomatoes** (Pg. 119); **Sour Cream Chocolate Sheet Cake** (Pg. 120); **Banana Cake with Peanut Butter Icing** (Pg. 119); **Oriental Chicken Cabbage Salad** (Pg. 120).

Pack a picnic basket with these 'stick-to-your-ribs' dishes… and what you have is a movable feast made for the outdoors!

Start with Spicy Picnic Pasties, a tangier version of an ethnic favorite. Add Hearty Baked Potato Salad, a standout side dish you can serve hot or at "field temperature".

And what picnic's complete without baked beans? This Six-Bean Casserole adds the hearty, spicy taste of Italian sausage as well. For dessert, Soft Molasses Cookies are an old-fashioned favorite.

Take your meal to the field…or the park…or the beach to satisfy those fresh-air-whetted appetites!

EATING OUT—AT ITS BEST: Top to bottom—**Soft Molasses Cookies** (Pg. 120); **Hearty Baked Potato Salad** (Pg. 120); **Six-Bean Casserole** (Pg. 121); **Spicy Picnic Pasties** (Pg. 120).

MEALS IN MINUTES

HOMEMAKING, hobbies and the hearty appetites of her farm family keep Sheila Wyum of Rutland, North Dakota on the go.

Luckily, Sheila knows where to go to find man-pleasing meals that still leave her time for church and school projects, Garden Club and work on a state centennial cookbook. She heads for her "Meals in Minutes" menus!

"My husband and two sons, 6 and 13, all prefer straightforward food," she says. "I look for good country-style recipes that are quick and easy to prepare."

This time, Sheila shares her own prompt pork chop recipe, which, along with vegetable and salad, can be prepared and served in *30 minutes or less*.

She begins her meal preparation by mixing seasonal fresh fruit with a tangy dressing made from frozen limeade concentrate. "Add as much or as little of the limeade as you think your family will enjoy," she says.

While the fruit salad chills, Sheila stirs together the glaze ingredients and begins broiling or grilling the pork chops. Garden vegetables such as fresh peas are cooked in a bit of chicken bouillon, with slices of water chestnuts added for extra crunch.

For her meat-and-potatoes men, Sheila keeps frozen Southern-style hash brown potatoes handy. Quickly cooked according to package directions, they complete a satisfying and speedy summer supper.

Serve Sheila's quick recipes the next time you're on the go!

ORANGE GLAZED PORK CHOPS

   1/4 cup grated onion
     1 tablespoon butter
     2 tablespoons brown sugar
1-1/2 teaspoons cornstarch
   1/2 teaspoon ground ginger
     1 cup orange juice
     1 tablespoon bottled
       steak sauce
     6 pork chops, 1-inch-thick cuts

Combine first 7 ingredients to make glaze and cook in microwave or on stovetop until thick. Broil or grill pork chops 5-7 minutes per side (or until the juices run clear), basting with glaze as meat cooks. **Yield:** 6 servings.

PEAS WITH WATER CHESTNUTS

     1 package (10 ounces) frozen
       peas *or* 2 cups fresh
       garden peas
     4 ounces sliced water chestnuts
     1 can (10-3/4 ounces) chicken
       broth *or* 1 teaspoon instant
       chicken bouillon granules
       dissolved in 1 cup water
     1 tablespoon butter
Pinch of salt and sugar, optional

Simmer peas and water chestnuts in chicken broth about 5 minutes or until peas are done. Add butter and seasonings, if desired. **Yield:** 4 servings.

FRESH FRUIT SALAD WITH LIMEADE DRESSING

     2 bananas, sliced
     1 cup green seedless grapes
     1 cup whole strawberries
Watermelon *or* cantaloupe chunks
     2 tablespoons frozen limeade
       concentrate, thawed (add
       additional to taste)

Place fruit in bowl. Pour on undiluted limeade, stir gently. **Yield:** 4 servings.

GRILLING HINTS: A spray bottle filled with water will quickly douse flare-ups in the charcoal grill.

● Remember to pack a basting brush for marinades and sauces, tongs for turning and serving grilled foods, paper toweling for wiping spills, reclosable plastic bags for leftovers and/or dirty utensils and a garbage bag for trash.

If you thought the only way to serve broccoli was steamed or boiled, maybe with a little cheese sauce, you're in for a pleasant surprise! Check out this bounty of broccoli and you'll find plenty of delicious ways to serve this tasty vitamin-filled vegetable.

Here's broccoli at its best! Try some of these intriguing, change-of-pace ways to prepare this nutritious vegetable —you won't see noses turned up at these delicious dishes.

Crunchy florets blend with juicy orange sections in the Fresh Broccoli/Mandarin Salad. Broccoli joins forces with spicy pork in Szechuan Pork and Broccoli—a stir-fry with a difference.

Bits of broccoli give color to creamy Golden Cheese/Broccoli Chowder. And broccoli mingles with other vegetables and tangy cheese for a delightfully different pasta topping in Broccoli Primavera with Cheese Sauce. Broccoli a family favorite? You bet!

BRING ON THE BROCCOLI! Top to bottom—**Fresh Broccoli/Mandarin Salad; Szechuan Pork and Broccoli; Broccoli Primavera with Cheese Sauce; Golden Cheese/Broccoli Chowder.** (All recipes can be found on page 123).

PERFECT PICNIC BASKET

Maralynn Lindstrom, Spring, Texas

(PICTURED ON PAGE 112)

1/2 cup all-purpose flour
1-1/2 tablespoons sesame seeds
1 teaspoon dried thyme
1/2 teaspoon dried tarragon
1/2 teaspoon poppy seeds
1 teaspoon salt
1/2 teaspoon pepper
3-1/2 pounds fryer chicken pieces, washed and drained
2 egg whites, lightly beaten
3 tablespoons butter
2 tablespoons margarine *or* vegetable oil

HERB SAUCE:
4 tablespoons butter, melted
3 tablespoons sesame seeds
1/2 teaspoon dried thyme
1/2 teaspoon dried tarragon
1/2 teaspoon garlic powder
1/2 teaspoon poppy seeds
Large, round loaf of bread

To make coating for chicken, combine first 7 ingredients in a large plastic bag. Dip chicken pieces in egg whites and shake, a few at a time, in coating mixture. Heat butter and margarine/oil in large skillet; brown chicken over medium heat. Remove chicken to casserole dish; cover. Bake at 350° for 30 minutes. Combine the herb sauce ingredients. Set aside. Slice top off bread and hollow out loaf with fork, leaving a 1/2-in.-thick shell. (Save the removed bread for croutons or crumbs.) Brush inside of hollowed loaf and top with herb sauce; place the loaf on baking sheet. Put baked chicken pieces inside hollowed loaf. Bake at 350° for 20 minutes. Remove; put lid on loaf. Serve warm. (To transport, wrap in foil and several layers of newspaper.) **Yield:** 4 servings.

BANANA CAKE WITH PEANUT BUTTER ICING

Carolina Hofeldt, Lloyd, Montana

(PICTURED ON PAGE 112)

CAKE:
2-1/4 cups all-purpose flour
1-1/4 teaspoons baking powder
1 teaspoon baking soda
1 teaspoon salt
1 cup mashed very ripe bananas (2 large)
1 cup buttermilk, room temperature
2/3 cup shortening

1-1/2 cups sugar
2 eggs, room temperature
1 teaspoon vanilla extract
ICING:
1 package (8 ounces) cream cheese, softened
1/2 cup light corn syrup
1/2 cup creamy peanut butter
Chopped unsalted peanuts (about 1 cup)

In a medium bowl, combine flour, baking powder, baking soda and salt; set aside. In a separate bowl, combine bananas and the buttermilk; set aside. Cream together shortening and sugar in large mixer bowl, beating until light and fluffy. Add eggs, one at a time, beating well after each addition. Beat in vanilla. Alternately add flour mixture and banana mixture, beginning and ending with flour. Beat until well blended. Spread evenly in a greased and floured 13-in. x 9-in. x 2-in. baking pan. Bake at 350° for 30 to 35 minutes or until wooden pick inserted in center comes out clean. Cool cake completely in pan on wire rack. To make icing, mix together cream cheese and corn syrup in small mixer bowl until smooth. Add peanut butter; beat until well-blended. Spread on cooled cake. Garnish with chopped peanuts. Refrigerate cake until serving time. **Yield:** 20 servings.

MARINATED TOMATOES

Katie Dreibelbis, Santa Clara, California

(PICTURED ON PAGE 113)

 This tasty dish uses less sugar, salt and fat. Recipe includes *Diabetic Exchanges*.

6 large ripe red tomatoes
MARINADE:
1/4 cup green onions, sliced thinly
1/2 teaspoon dried thyme *or* 2 tablespoons fresh
1 clove garlic, minced fine
1/4 cup minced parsley
1 teaspoon salt
1/4 teaspoon freshly cracked black pepper
1/4 cup red *or* white vinegar
1/3 cup vegetable oil

Peel tomatoes and cut in 1/2-in. thick slices; place in shallow dish. In separate bowl, combine the green onions, thyme, garlic, parsley, salt and pepper. Sprinkle mixture over tomatoes. Combine oil and vinegar in shaker; blend well. Pour over tomatoes. Cover; refrigerate at least 2 hours. Spoon marinade over tomatoes from time to time. **Yield:** 10 servings. **Diabetic Exchanges:** One serving equals

1 vegetable, 1-1/2 fats; also, 93 calories, 218 mg sodium, 0 cholesterol, 6 gm carbohydrate, 2 gm protein, 8 gm fat.

SUMMER SAUERKRAUT SALAD

Karen Ann Bland, Gove, Kansas

(PICTURED ON PAGE 112)

✓ This tasty dish uses less sugar, salt and fat. Recipe includes *Diabetic Exchanges*.

1 can (16 ounces) sauerkraut, drained and rinsed
1/2 cup red *or* green pepper, chopped fine
2 cups celery, chopped fine
1 small onion, chopped fine
1/2 cup sugar
1/4 teaspoon salt
1/8 teaspoon pepper

Combine all ingredients. Refrigerate until serving time. **Yield:** 10 servings. **Diabetic Exchanges:** One serving equals 2 vegetables; also, 54 calories, 424 mg sodium, 0 cholesterol, 14 gm carbohydrate, 1 gm protein, 0 fat.

SPICY SANDWICH LOAF

Judy Smith, Winthrop, Maine

(PICTURED ON PAGE 113)

1 tablespoon butter
1 cup sliced mushrooms
1/2 cup chopped green pepper
1 pound frozen bread dough, thawed
1/4 pound thinly sliced ham
1/4 pound thinly sliced salami, casing removed
1/4 pound thinly sliced mozzarella *or* provolone cheese
1-1/2 ounces thinly sliced pepperoni

Melt butter in a large skillet. Add mushrooms and green pepper; cook, stirring often, until tender. Set aside. On a large baking sheet lined with aluminum foil, press dough into a 10-in. x 13-in. rectangle. Layer ham, salami, cheese and pepperoni down center of dough; top with mushrooms and pepper. Fold sides of dough over filling, lapping the edges. Turn seam side down; pinch ends together and tuck under to seal. Cover and let rise in warm place for 1 to 1-1/2 hours, until doubled in bulk. Brush with egg glaze, if desired. Bake at 350° for 45 minutes until golden brown. Let stand for 10 minutes before slicing. **Yield:** 8-10 servings.

ORIENTAL CHICKEN CABBAGE SALAD

Lonnie Heimer, Fort Collins, Colorado

(PICTURED ON PAGE 113)

1 whole chicken breast,
    cooked, cut and slivered *or* 2
    cans (5 ounces each) canned
    white chicken meat
2 tablespoons toasted sesame
    seeds
2 ounces slivered toasted
    almonds
1/2 head cabbage, shredded fine
2 green onions, chopped fine
1 package (3 ounces) chicken-
    flavored Ramen noodles,
    uncooked

SALAD DRESSING:
1/2 package Ramen noodle
    seasoning mix
3 tablespoons sugar
1/2 cup vegetable oil
3 tablespoons rice *or* wine
    vinegar
1 teaspoon salt
1/2 teaspoon pepper

Combine the chicken with sesame seeds, almonds, cabbage, onion and *uncooked* noodles which have been broken apart. Add the dressing; toss to blend. Cover; refrigerate until serving time. Serve cold. **Yield:** 6 servings.

SOUR CREAM CHOCOLATE SHEET CAKE

Janet Tigchelaar, Jerseyville, Ontario

(PICTURED ON PAGE 113)

CAKE:
2 cups all-purpose flour
1 teaspoon baking soda
1/2 cup dairy sour cream
1 teaspoon salt
2 cups white sugar
3 eggs, beaten
1 cup butter
1 cup water
2 squares (2 ounces)
    unsweetened chocolate

ICING:
1/2 cup butter
1/3 cup milk
1 cup brown sugar
2 squares (2 ounces)
    unsweetened chocolate
1 cup chopped nuts (walnuts
    are excellent)
1 cup confectioners' sugar
1 teaspoon vanilla

To make cake, combine flour, soda, sour cream, salt, sugar and beaten eggs in a large bowl. Mix until smooth; set aside. In a small saucepan, combine butter, water and chocolate; bring to a boil. Add chocolate mixture to batter; mix together very well. Batter will be thin. Pour batter into greased 17-in. x 11-1/2-in. x 1-in. jelly roll pan. Bake at 350° for 25 minutes. Cool in pan on wire rack. To make icing, combine butter, milk, brown sugar and chocolate in heavy saucepan. Bring to boil; *do not stir.* Boil for 3 minutes. Remove from heat; immediately stir in the nuts, confectioners' sugar and vanilla. Pour hot icing onto center of cake; spread gently to outer edges. Cool and cut into squares. **Yield:** 40 squares, 2 inches each.

PICNIC PICKUPS: Pack cut-up chunks of watermelon, rind removed, in a chilled container for a naturally sweet and refreshing snack.

● When there won't be a grill handy, fill a large-mouth thermos with boiling water and drop in a few hot dogs. They'll heat in transit—kids think they're great!

OLD FASHIONED LEMONADE

Laura Helmuth, Nappanee, Indiana

(PICTURED ON PAGE 113)

6 lemons
1-1/2 cups sugar
2-1/2 quarts ice water

Wash lemons; slice thin. Place in a stainless or enamel container. Add sugar. Pound with wooden spoon or mallet to squeeze juice from lemon rings; stir to make syrup. Let stand 20 minutes. Add ice water and 10 to 12 ice cubes; stir well. Serve within 6 hours for best flavor. **Yield:** 3 quarts.

HEARTY BAKED POTATO SALAD

Mary Bengtson-Almquist, Petersburg, Illinois

(PICTURED ON PAGE 114)

8 red salad potatoes
1/2 cup onion, chopped
2 tablespoons parsley, chopped
1 can (11 ounces) cheddar
    cheese soup
1/2 cup mayonnaise
1/2 cup plain yogurt
4 ounces bacon, cooked,
    drained and crumbled
Paprika for garnish

Peel potatoes; boil until soft. Cut in 1-1/2-in. chunks. Spread potatoes evenly over bottom of 13-in. x 9-in. x 2-in. baking pan. Combine onions, parsley, soup, mayonnaise and yogurt; pour over potatoes. Sprinkle cooked bacon on top; garnish with paprika. Cover with aluminum foil and bake at 350° for 1 hour, uncovering during the last 30 minutes. **Yield:** 10-12 servings.

SPICY PICNIC PASTIES

Virginia Doyle, Pinedale, Wyoming

(PICTURED ON PAGE 114)

PASTRY:
2 cups all-purpose flour
1/2 cup butter
1/2 teaspoon salt
6 to 7 tablespoons milk *or* as
    much as needed to make
    dough

FILLING:
3/4 pound ground beef
2 tablespoons chopped onion
1 tablespoon chopped bell
    pepper
1 to 2 tablespoons chopped
    celery
1/4 teaspoon ground cumin
1/4 to 1/2 teaspoon chili powder
1/2 teaspoon salt
2 tablespoons barbecue sauce
Catsup, barbecue sauce *or* chili
    sauce, optional

Combine pastry ingredients as for pie crust; divide dough into four parts. Roll each part thin and cut into a 6-in.-diameter circle, using a small plate as a guide. (If you prefer, substitute store-bought refrigerated pastry.) Combine filling ingredients. Place a fourth of filling in center of each dough circle; pat filling down lightly. Moisten edges of dough with water; fold circle in half to make a turnover. Seal edges well with a fork. Prick to to allow the steam to escape; place on an ungreased cookie sheet. Bake at 375° for about 40 minutes. Serve—hot or cold—dipped in catsup, barbecue or chili sauce, if desired. **Yield:** 4 large servings.

SOFT MOLASSES COOKIES

LaVonne Hegland, St. Michael, Minnesota

(PICTURED ON PAGE 114)

1/2 cup butter, softened
1/2 cup solid vegetable
    shortening (not margarine)

1-1/2 cups sugar
1/2 cup molasses
2 eggs, lightly beaten
4 cups all-purpose flour
1/2 teaspoon salt
2-1/4 teaspoons baking soda
2-1/4 teaspoons ground ginger
1-1/2 teaspoons ground cloves
1-1/2 teaspoons ground cinnamon

In a large mixing bowl, cream together butter, shortening and sugar until light-colored and fluffy. Beat in molasses and eggs; set mixture aside. In another large bowl, combine flour (no need to sift), salt, baking soda, ginger, cloves and cinnamon. Blend thoroughly with wire whisk. Gradually mix flour mixture into creamed ingredients until dough is blended and smooth. Roll dough into 1-1/2-in. balls. Dip tops in granulated sugar; place 2-1/2-in. apart on greased cookie sheet. Bake at 350° for 11 minutes. *Do not overbake.* Cool on wire rack. Store in tightly covered container to maintain softness. **Yield:** about 3 dozen cookies.

SIX-BEAN CASSEROLE

Marsha Ransom, South Haven, Michigan

(PICTURED ON PAGE 114)

1/2 pound bulk sweet Italian sausage
1/4 pound pepperoni, sliced thin
1/2 pound smoked kielbasa, sliced
1/2 cup spicy barbecue sauce
1 can (16 ounces) pork and beans, undrained
1 can (16 ounces) red kidney beans, undrained
1 can (16 ounces) hot chili beans, undrained
1 can (16 ounces) white kidney beans (Canellini), drained
1 can (16 ounces) butter beans, drained
1 can (16 ounces) lima beans, drained
1 can (10-3/4 ounces) tomato soup, undiluted
3 ounces tomato paste
1/2 cup brown sugar *or* to taste
6 slices bacon

Form the Italian sausage into 1-in. balls. Brown in skillet; drain. Combine with remaining ingredients, except bacon, in 5-qt. casserole or in small roasting pan. Partially cook bacon in microwave or on stovetop; arrange over casserole. Bake, uncovered, at 325° for 1-1/2 hours. Serve hot or cold. **Yield:** 16 generous servings.

BROCCOLI CORN BREAD

Carolynn Girtman, Bartow, Florida

(PICTURED ON PAGE 116)

1/2 cup butter, melted
1/3 cup chopped onion
1 teaspoon salt
3/4 cup cottage cheese
1 package (10 ounces) frozen chopped broccoli, thawed and drained
4 eggs, slightly beaten
1 package (8-1/2 ounces) quick corn muffin mix

In mixing bowl combine melted butter, onion, salt, cheese, broccoli and beaten eggs; blend. Stir in muffin mix. Pour into greased 13-in. x 9-in. x 2-in. baking pan. Bake at 400° for 20-25 minutes. Cut into serving-size squares. **Yield:** 12 servings.

BROCCOLI CASSEROLE ELEGANT

Dena Fischer, Manchester, Iowa

(PICTURED ON PAGE 116)

1-1/2 cups hot water
1/4 cup butter
1 package (6 ounces) stuffing mix
2 packages (10 ounces *each*) frozen broccoli spears *or* 1-1/2 pounds fresh broccoli spears*
2 tablespoons water
2 tablespoons butter
2 tablespoons all-purpose flour
1 teaspoon chicken-flavored bouillon granules
3/4 cup milk
1 package (3 ounces) cream cheese, softened
1/4 teaspoon salt, optional
1 cup (4 ounces) shredded cheddar cheese

Place hot water and butter in medium bowl; microwave on high until butter melts. Add seasoning packet from stuffing mix; stir. Microwave on high for 5 minutes. Add stuffing crumbs; stir to moisten. Cover; set aside. Place frozen broccoli in large bowl; add 2 tablespoons water. Cover; microwave on high for 6-8 minutes. Stir; microwave on high 2 minutes or until tender/crisp. Let stand, unstirred, for 2 minutes more. *If using fresh broccoli, place in bowl and add water; microwave on high 3-5 minutes. Spoon stuffing mixture around outside of lightly greased 2-qt. rectangular baking dish, leaving a well in cen-

ter. Place cooked broccoli in well; set aside. Using medium bowl, microwave butter for 30 seconds on medium until melted. Add flour and bouillon granules; stir in milk until smooth. Microwave on high for 1-1/2 minutes. Stir; repeat for 30 seconds until smooth and thickened. Blend in softened cream cheese and salt. Spoon sauce over broccoli; sprinkle with cheddar cheese. Microwave until cheese melts, about 4 minutes. *Conventional Method:* Melt butter and add water to saucepan; add seasoning packet and cook for 5 minutes. Add stuffing mix; cover and set aside. Cook broccoli in 2 tablespoons water until tender/crisp. Proceed with recipe, making sauce on top of stove as for white sauce, adding cheese and salt. Spoon sauce over broccoli; sprinkle with cheese. Place under oven broiler until cheese melts. **Yield:** 10 servings.

BROCCOLI/ MUSHROOM CHOWDER

Lorrie Arthur, Columbus, Ohio

(PICTURED ON PAGE 116)

2 pounds fresh broccoli
8 ounces fresh mushrooms
1 cup butter
1 cup all-purpose flour
4 cups chicken broth
4 cups half-and-half
1 teaspoon salt, optional
1/4 teaspoon white pepper
1/4 teaspoon tarragon leaves, crushed

Clean and cut the broccoli into 1/2-in. pieces. Steam in 1/2 cup of water until tender/crisp; do not drain. Set aside. Clean and slice mushrooms. In a large pan over medium heat, melt butter; add flour to make a roux. Cook, stirring constantly, for 2-4 minutes; do not let brown. Stir in chicken broth; bring just to a boil. Turn heat to low; add broccoli, mushrooms, half-and-half and seasonings. Heat through, but *do not boil.* **Yield:** 8 servings.

OUTDOOR EATING: Put "portable" food in airtight plastic containers with see-through lids to make it easy to tell what's inside.
● Three- or four-section plastic plates are sturdier than paper plates and much less messy.
● Freeze single-serving juice cartons for an hour. They'll help chill food in coolers and thaw to a thirst-quenching slush by the time you get to the picnic or field.

CHINESE BROCCOLI AND BEEF SALAD

Karen Armstrong, Battle Ground, Washington

(PICTURED ON PAGE 116)

3 to 4 pounds fresh broccoli
1/2 to 3/4 cup peanut oil *or* vegetable oil
2 sweet red peppers, cut in narrow strips
4 cups sliced fresh mushrooms
1/2 cup white vinegar
1/4 cup soy sauce
1 to 2 teaspoons salt
2-1/2 dried hot red peppers, crushed *or* 1 teaspoon red pepper flakes
2 pounds rare roast beef, julienne cuts
1 can (8 ounces) water chestnuts, drained and sliced
1 can (8 ounces) bamboo shoots, drained

Wash broccoli. Cut off florets; reserve tender parts of stalks. Cut stalks into 3/8-in.-thick slices. In wok or large skillet, heat oil. Add broccoli stalk pieces; stir-fry for about 1 minute. Add broccoli florets; stir-fry for 3 minutes or until tender/crisp. Transfer broccoli to large bowl. Stir-fry red pepper strips for 1 to 2 minutes; add to broccoli. Stir-fry mushrooms until tender/crisp; add to broccoli. Combine vinegar, soy sauce, salt and crushed hot red pepper. Pour over broccoli mixture; toss well. Add the beef, water chestnuts and bamboo shoots. Toss; cover. Chill 2-3 hours. **Yield:** 12 servings.

FRENCH CHICKEN/ BROCCOLI CASSEROLE

Gigi Adam, Santa Maria, California

(PICTURED ON PAGE 117)

1 pound fresh broccoli, sliced in spears and steamed 2 minutes *or* 3 packages (10 ounces *each*) frozen broccoli spears, thawed
3 to 4 cups cooked chicken, skinned, boned, torn in large pieces
SAUCE:
1/3 cup butter, melted
1/4 cup cornstarch, dissolved in 1/2 cup water
1/3 cup chicken broth *or* white wine
1/4 teaspoon salt
1/4 teaspoon pepper
2 cups milk

1 jar (2 ounces) diced pimientos
1 package (8 ounces) Old English cheese, cubed *or* 8 ounces shredded sharp cheddar cheese

In greased 13-in. x 9-in. x 2-in. baking dish, layer the broccoli spears and chicken pieces alternately. Set aside. In a saucepan over medium heat, combine melted butter, dissolved cornstarch, broth, seasonings, milk and pimientos. Cook until thickened. Add cheese; stir until melted. Pour warm sauce over top of chicken and broccoli layers. Bake at 350° for about 35 minutes or until bubbly. **Yield:** 6 servings.

MEDITERRANEAN CHICKEN 'N' BROCCOLI SALAD

Loralee Hanes, Troy, Ontario

(PICTURED ON PAGE 117)

4 tablespoons butter, unsalted
8 chicken breast halves, skinned and boned
1/2 cup chicken broth *or* dry white wine
2 garlic cloves, minced
1-1/2 pounds fresh broccoli
1/2 cup mayonnaise
1 tablespoon fresh lemon juice
1/2 teaspoon leaf thyme
1/4 teaspoon leaf basil
1/4 teaspoon leaf oregano
1/2 teaspoon salt
1/2 teaspoon pepper *or* to taste
1 medium red onion, quartered and thinly sliced
Fresh tomatoes
Slivered, toasted almonds for garnish

In a large skillet, melt butter over low heat. Add chicken breasts in a single layer; pour in broth. Cook, tightly covered, 8-10 minutes or until chicken is springy to the touch. Remove chicken. Add garlic to broth; cook over low heat for 1 minute. Strain, reserving garlic and liquid; cool. Trim broccoli stems in 1/8-in.-thick slices and florets in 1-in. pieces; blanch in boiling, salted water for 1 minute. Plunge broccoli in ice water. Drain well; set aside. In small bowl, combine the mayonnaise, lemon juice, thyme, basil and oregano; blend well. Whisk in reserved garlic, cooking liquid, salt and pepper. In a large serving bowl, cut chicken into 1/2-in. pieces; add broccoli and onion. Pour on dressing; toss well. Cover; refrigerate for at least 2 hours or overnight. For individual servings, spoon salad in center of a large tomato cut into wedges. For buffet serv-

ing, ring a platter or serving plate with sliced tomatoes; spoon salad into center. Sprinkle with toasted almonds. **Yield:** 8-10 servings.

STIR-FRIED BROCCOLI WITH MUSHROOMS AND CASHEWS

Judi Weidmark, Uxbridge, Ontario

(PICTURED ON PAGE 117)

 This tasty dish uses less sugar, salt and fat. Recipe includes *Diabetic Exchanges*.

2 tablespoons salad oil
1 pound fresh broccoli, cut in florets
1 teaspoon sugar
1/2 teaspoon salt
1/2 pound fresh mushrooms, cut in 1/4-inch slices
2 green onions, finely chopped
1/4 teaspoon ground nutmeg
Dry-roasted cashews

Heat 1 tablespoon oil in wok or large skillet. Add broccoli, sugar and salt; stir-fry for 3 minutes or until broccoli is tender/crisp. Add remaining oil, mushrooms, onions and nutmeg; stir-fry until added vegetables are tender/crisp, about 1-2 minutes. Sprinkle on cashews; serve hot. **Yield:** 6 servings. **Diabetic Exchanges:** One serving equals 2 vegetables, 1-1/2 fats; also, 125 calories, 196 mg sodium, 0 cholesterol, 10 gm carbohydrate, 5 gm protein, 9 gm fat.

BROCCOLI ALMONDINE

Connie Orsua, San Jose, California

(PICTURED ON PAGE 117)

1/2 cup slivered almonds (2 ounces)
1 tablespoon butter
2 packages (10 ounces *each*) frozen broccoli spears *or* 1-1/2 pounds fresh broccoli, washed and cut into spears
2 packages (3 ounces *each*) cream cheese
1/3 cup milk
1 teaspoon grated lemon peel
1 tablespoon lemon juice
1/2 teaspoon ground ginger
1/4 teaspoon salt

In small glass bowl, combine almonds and butter. Microwave on medium/high for 3 minutes. Stir; microwave at medium/high 2 to 3 minutes or until almonds are light brown. Set aside. Place broccoli in 2-qt. glass casserole. Cover; microwave on high for 8-10 minutes (3-5 minutes for fresh). Let stand, covered. Place cream cheese in 2-cup glass measure; microwave on low 2-4 minutes or until softened. Blend in milk, peel, juice, ginger and salt. Microwave on medium/high for 3-4 minutes or until hot. Place broccoli spears on warm serving platter; pour sauce over top. Sprinkle with almonds. *Conventional Method:* Toast almonds and butter in small saucepan until almonds are light brown. Cook broccoli on stove until tender/crisp. Blend softened cream cheese, milk, peel, juice, ginger and salt. Cook until hot. Proceed with recipe. **Yield:** 6-8 servings.

SZECHUAN PORK AND BROCCOLI

Marian Stallknecht, Lawrenceville, Georgia

(PICTURED ON PAGE 118)

 This tasty dish uses less sugar, salt and fat. Recipe includes *Diabetic Exchanges*.

      1 pound fresh lean pork
        (tenderloin *or* roast)
   6 to 8 green onions
      1 green *or* red sweet pepper
  1-1/2 cups fresh broccoli
      1 large onion
     12 edible-pod peas
      3 tablespoons peanut oil *or*
        vegetable oil
SAUCE:
      2 cloves garlic, sliced
      2 slices fresh ginger, chopped
   1/4 teaspoon crushed red pepper
        flakes
      2 tablespoons hot water
      2 teaspoons sugar
      6 tablespoons catsup*
      4 tablespoons soy sauce*

Cut pork into narrow 1-in. strips, 1/4 in. thick; set aside. (Partially freeze pork first for easier cutting.) Cut green onions, peppers, broccoli and onion into 1-in. pieces; set aside. Combine garlic, ginger, pepper flakes, hot water, sugar, catsup and soy sauce (*can substitute 8 tablespoons prepared hoisin sauce for the catsup and soy sauce); set aside. In wok or large skillet, heat peanut or vegetable oil over high heat. Stir-fry the pork in oil until browned; remove from wok and keep warm. Add more oil if necessary and stir-fry all vegetables ten-

der/crisp. Add pork and sauce to mixture; cook until thickened. Serve with boiled rice. **Yield:** 8 servings. **Diabetic Exchanges:** One serving equals 1 meat, 2 vegetables, 2 fats; also, 228 calories, 666 mg sodium, 50 mg cholesterol, 11 gm carbohydrate, 10 gm protein, 17 gm fat.

BROCCOLI PRIMAVERA WITH CHEESE SAUCE

Sherry Krenz, Woodworth, North Dakota

(PICTURED ON PAGE 118)

      4 tablespoons olive oil *or*
        vegetable oil
      1 garlic clove, sliced
      1 medium head of broccoli, cut
        into 2-inch x 1-inch pieces
      1 small red pepper, diced
   3/4 cup green onions, sliced
      1 cup fresh sliced mushrooms
        or 1 can (4 ounces) canned
        mushrooms, drained
   1/2 cup celery, diced
      1 cup milk
      5 ounces process cheese
        spread, cubed
   1/4 cup Parmesan cheese
   1/2 teaspoon leaf oregano
   1/2 pound ground beef *or* bulk
        Italian sausage, cooked and
        crumbled, optional
Cooked spaghetti

In large skillet, heat oil. Cook garlic until browned; discard garlic. Add broccoli, red pepper, onion, mushrooms and celery; cook, stirring constantly, until tender/crisp. Add the milk, cubed cheese, Parmesan cheese and oregano, cooking and stirring until cheese melts. Add meat if desired. Serve over hot, cooked pasta. **Yield:** 8 servings.

GOLDEN CHEESE/ BROCCOLI CHOWDER

Nancy Schmidt, Delhi, California

(PICTURED ON PAGE 118)

      2 cups water
      1 cup celery, chopped
      1 cup carrots, chopped
   1/2 cup onion, chopped
      1 pound fresh broccoli,
        washed and chopped
CHEESE SAUCE:
   1/2 cup butter
   1/2 cup all-purpose flour
      2 teaspoons salt *or* to taste
   1/4 teaspoon white pepper
      4 cups milk

Hot pepper sauce, as desired
      1 pound process cheese
        spread, cut in 1/2-inch cubes
        or 4 cups shredded cheddar
        cheese
      2 cups ham, cut in 1/2-inch
        cubes

In large saucepan, combine water, celery, carrots and onion. Bring to boil; reduce heat. Simmer, covered, for about 5 minutes or until tender/crisp. Add broccoli; cook until broccoli is tender/crisp, about 4-5 minutes. (To keep broccoli bright green, leave the cover slightly ajar.) *Do not drain vegetables.* To make sauce, melt butter in large saucepan; blend in flour, salt and pepper. Cook, stirring, for 1 minute. Stir in milk; cook until mixture thickens. Add several drops of hot pepper sauce if desired. Stir in the cheese and cook until melted; add the ham cubes. Combine cheese mixture with undrained vegetables; stir to blend. **Yield:** 12 servings.

FRESH BROCCOLI/ MANDARIN SALAD

Connie Blommers, Pella, Iowa

(PICTURED ON PAGE 118)

CUSTARD DRESSING:
      1 egg plus 1 egg yolk, lightly
        beaten
   1/2 cup sugar
  1-1/2 teaspoons cornstarch
      1 teaspoon dry mustard
   1/4 cup vinegar
   1/4 cup water
      3 tablespoons butter, softened
   1/2 cup mayonnaise
SALAD:
      4 cups fresh broccoli florets,
        1-inch cuts
   1/2 cup golden raisins
      6 slices bacon, cooked and
        crumbled
      2 cups sliced fresh mushrooms
   1/2 cup slivered almonds,
        toasted
      1 can (11 ounces) mandarin
        oranges, drained
   1/2 medium red onion, sliced in
        1/8-inch-thick rings

In top of double boiler, whisk together egg, egg yolk, sugar, cornstarch and mustard. Combine vinegar and water; slowly whisk into egg mixture. Place over hot water and cook, stirring constantly, until mixture thickens. Remove from heat; stir in butter and mayonnaise. Chill. Toss dressing with remaining ingredients in serving bowl. Refrigerate until serving. **Yield:** 10-12 servings.

PICNIC HERO SANDWICH

Anne Frederick, New Hartford, New York

1/3 cup bottled chili sauce
3 tablespoons mayonnaise
1/4 teaspoon Worcestershire sauce
1 pound loaf French or Italian bread
8 lettuce leaves
1-1/2 cups prepared coleslaw
4 roasted or grilled chicken breast halves, sliced thin
1 jar (11 ounces) sweet roasted red peppers or sliced fresh tomatoes

Combine chili sauce, mayonnaise and Worcestershire sauce in a small bowl and set aside. Using a long, serrated knife, slice bread lengthwise to form *three layers*. Spread each cut surface with chili sauce mixture. Top each layer with lettuce, coleslaw, sliced chicken and peppers/tomatoes. Reassemble the loaf and cut into thick slices for serving. **Yield:** 6 large servings.

SALMON/BROCCOLI CASSEROLE

Leta Tobin, Mabton, Washington

1 can (7-1/2 ounces) canned salmon
1 package (10 ounces) frozen chopped broccoli
1/3 cup chopped onion
1 tablespoon butter
1 can (10-3/4 ounces) cream of celery soup, undiluted
2 tablespoons lemon juice
1 egg, beaten
1/4 cup grated Parmesan cheese
1/2 teaspoon dried dill weed
1/8 teaspoon pepper
1-1/2 cups seasoned croutons or 1 cup dried bread crumbs
1 can (8 ounces) mushrooms, undrained
Lemon slices

Drain salmon, reserving liquid. Remove skin and bones. Break into chunks; set aside. Cook broccoli according to package directions; drain. Saute onion in butter. Add soup; heat thoroughly. Stir in lemon juice, egg, cheese, dill weed, pepper, mushrooms and reserved salmon liquid. Blend in salmon, broccoli and croutons/bread crumbs; place in buttered shallow baking dish. Bake at 325° 20 minutes. Garnish with lemon slices. **Yield:** 4-6 servings.

WARM WEATHER TIPS: Keep summer salads and all chilled foods in coolers or insulated containers, covered and out of direct sunlight. Mayonnaise-based salads, hot dogs, lunch meats, cooked beef or chicken, deviled eggs and custard or cream pies will stay fresh (and safe) for hours if kept cold.

CINNAMON CHEWS

Paula Johnson, Eaton, Colorado

1 package (16 ounces) marshmallows
1 package (9 ounces) red-hot cinnamon candies
3 tablespoons butter
1/2 teaspoon salt
2-1/2 cups crisp rice cereal
Confectioners' sugar

Combine all ingredients except cereal and sugar; melt in top of double boiler. Add cereal, mixing quickly. Spread in buttered 8-in.-square pan. Chill; cut in 1-in. squares. Dust with confectioners' sugar. **Yield:** 64 candies.

MAMA'S STRAWBERRY CAKE

Diane O'Neal, Concord, California

CAKE:
1 package (18-1/4 ounces) white cake mix
3 tablespoons all-purpose flour
1 package frozen strawberries, *divided*
4 eggs
1/2 cup vegetable oil
3/4 cup water
1 package (3 ounces) strawberry gelatin dessert
ICING:
Half of frozen strawberries, reserved from cake
3-1/2 to 4 cups confectioner's sugar
1/2 cup butter

Combine cake ingredients in a large mixing bowl and beat 4 minutes on medium speed. Pour batter into two greased and floured 9-in. layer cake pans or into a 13-in. x 9-in. x 2-in. pan. Bake at 350° for 30-35 minutes or until cake tests done. Cool in pans for 10 minutes; remove cake to wire rack and cool completely. Combine icing ingredients and mix until smooth and fluffy. Frost cool cake with the icing. Serve and store chilled. **Yield:** 16 servings.

BROCCOLI/ONION DELUXE

Leigh Moore, Heffley Creek, British Columbia

1 pound fresh or frozen broccoli
3 medium sweet onions, quartered
SAUCE:
4 tablespoons butter, *divided*
2 tablespoons all-purpose flour
1/4 teaspoon salt
Ground pepper to taste
1 cup milk
1 package (3 ounces) cream cheese
1/2 cup (2 ounces) shredded sharp cheddar cheese
1 cup soft bread crumbs

Cut broccoli into 1-in. pieces. Cook or steam until tender; drain. Cook onions until tender; drain and set aside. In small saucepan, melt 2 tablespoons butter. Blend in flour, salt and pepper. Add milk; cook and stir until thick and bubbly. Reduce heat; blend in cream cheese. Place vegetables in a 1-1/2-qt. casserole. Pour sauce over; mix lightly. Top with the cheddar cheese. Melt remaining butter and toss with crumbs; sprinkle over casserole. Bake at 350° for 30 minutes. **Yield:** 4 servings.

ALMOND ASPARAGUS

Helen Manhart, Neola, Iowa

3 tablespoons butter or margarine, *divided*
3 tablespoons bread crumbs
1 garlic clove, minced
1/2 teaspoon dill weed
1/2 cup sliced almonds
1/4 cup grated Parmesan cheese
1 pound fresh asparagus, trimmed and cut into 1-inch pieces
1 tablespoon lemon juice

In a skillet, melt 2 tablespoons butter over medium heat. Stir in bread crumbs, garlic and dill; saute until crumbs are golden brown. Remove from heat; stir in the almonds and cheese. Set aside. Cook asparagus in a small amount of water until crisp-tender. Drain; heat with remaining butter. Sprinkle with lemon juice. Spoon asparagus into a serving dish and top with the reserved crumb mixture. **Yield:** 4-6 servings.

HANDS-ON HELP: Rub each finger vigorously with celery salt before washing, to rid hands of onion odors.

BEST COOK

**Donna Patterson
Davenport, Iowa**

Donna Patterson of Davenport, Iowa does all her cooking on a grand scale, whether she's working as head baker at an area hospital or treating dozens of friends to a barbecue!

"During the week, Donna cooks for the patients and hospital cafeteria at Franciscan Hospital in Rock Island, Illinois," says Kay Moneysmith, who nominated her friend. "And when we hold our yearly harvest dinner at church for some 300 people, you'll find Donna cooking there, too!"

But Donna doesn't stop there.

"She and her husband, Wayne, annually host an outdoor party for 75 to 100 friends from church to celebrate their wedding anniversary," Kay says. "Donna prepares *all* the food, and it's a real feast—barbecued ribs, fried chicken, at least a dozen different salads, pies, cakes, cookies...you name it, she serves it!"

According to Donna, "The barbecue is our way of showing friends how much we love and appreciate them. It started out very simply, but as our circle of friends grew, so did the size of our barbecue!"

Donna learned how to cook as a teenager. "My mother turned over all the household cooking chores to me for one summer," she says with a grin. "It was sink or swim. Believe me, I learned a lot, although my father and brother suffered for a while!"

Her first dishes were simple—meat, potatoes, and vegetables from the garden. That was acceptable for the hardworking family.

"After I left home, my interests began to widen," she says. "I learned how to make some more unusual dishes, and I grew to love baking and making salads. For a while I worked in the bakery department at Drake University in Des Moines, baking for about 1,700 students. That gave me *lots* of new ideas!"

Help yourself to Donna's Lasagna (shown at left) and to a couple more of her delicious recipes.

DONNA'S LASAGNA

   1 **pound lean ground beef**
   8 **ounces mild** *or* **hot Italian sausage**
   1 **can (14-1/2 ounces) tomatoes, pureed**
   2 **cans (6 ounces** *each***) tomato paste**
   2 **tablespoons sugar**
   3 **tablespoons dried parsley,** *divided*
   1 **tablespoon dried basil**
   1 **garlic clove, minced**
1-1/2 **teaspoons salt,** *divided*
   9 **lasagna noodles (about 8 ounces)**
   3 **cups (24 ounces) cream-style cottage cheese**
   2 **eggs, beaten**
 1/2 **teaspoon pepper**
 1/2 **cup grated Parmesan cheese**
 16 **ounces mozzarella cheese, thinly sliced**

In a Dutch oven, brown ground beef and sausage; drain excess fat. Add pureed tomatoes, tomato paste, sugar, 1 tablespoon parsley, basil, garlic and 1 teaspoon salt; simmer, uncovered, 30 minutes. Meanwhile, cook lasagna noodles in boiling water. Drain; rinse in cold water. In a bowl, combine cottage cheese, eggs, pepper, Parmesan cheese, and remaining parsley and salt. In a 13-in. x 9-in. x 2-in. pan, layer one-third of noodles, one-third of the cheese mixture, one-third of mozzarella cheese and one-third of meat sauce. Repeat layers 2 more times.

Bake at 350° for 1 hour or until heated through. Let stand 15 minutes before cutting. **Yield:** 12 servings.

PORK ORIENTAL

   1 **tablespoon cooking oil**
1-1/2 **pounds lean boneless pork, cut into bite-size pieces**
 1/4 **cup water**
 1/4 **cup packed brown sugar**
   2 **tablespoons cornstarch**
   1 **can (20 ounces) pineapple chunks, juice drained and reserved**
 1/4 **cup vinegar**
   1 **tablespoon soy sauce**
 1/2 **teaspoon salt**
 3/4 **cup green pepper strips**
 1/4 **cup thinly sliced onion**
Chow mein noodles *or* **cooked rice**

In a skillet, heat oil on medium-high. Brown pork slowly. Add water; cover and simmer until pork is tender, about 1 hour (add more water if necessary). Meanwhile, in a large saucepan, combine brown sugar and cornstarch. Add pineapple juice, vinegar, soy sauce and salt. Cook over low heat, stirring constantly, until thick. Drain pork; add to saucepan along with pineapple, green pepper and onions. Cook for 4-5 minutes or until vegetables are crisp-tender. Serve over chow mein noodles or rice. **Yield:** 6 servings.

PEANUT BUTTER PIE

 2/3 **cup sugar**
2-1/2 **tablespoons cornstarch**
   1 **tablespoon all-purpose flour**
 1/2 **teaspoon salt**
   3 **cups milk**
   3 **egg yolks, beaten**
 1/2 **cup creamy peanut butter**
   1 **pastry shell (9 inches), baked**
Whipped cream *or* **topping**

In a saucepan, stir together sugar, cornstarch, flour and salt. Gradually add milk. Cook and stir over medium-high heat until thickened and bubbly. Reduce heat; cook and stir 2 minutes longer. Remove from the heat. Stir about 1 cup of mixture into egg yolks; return all to saucepan. Return to heat and bring to a gentle boil, stirring constantly. Cook and stir 2 minutes more. Remove from heat; stir in peanut butter until smooth. Pour into the pastry shell; cool. Cover and store in the refrigerator. Garnish with whipped cream or topping. **Yield:** 8 servings.

HARVEST SPECIALTIES: Clockwise from lower left—**Spaghetti Sauce** (Pg. 133); **Dixie Henhouse Eggplant** (Pg. 133); **Beer Beef Stew** (Pg. 133); **Potato Chowder** (Pg. 133); **Potato Kugel** (Pg. 134); **Sweet Onion Casserole** (Pg. 134); **Zucchini Soup** (Pg. 134); **Pennsylvania Corn Soup** (Pg. 133).

Homegrown goodness is our goal as we fill the harvest table with the flavors of late summer. You can turn your backyard bounty into delicious dishes with these garden-fresh recipes, reflecting the regional tastes of rural America.

Savor a variety of vegetables in a trio of homemade soups, starring tasty blends of corn and peppers, potatoes and carrots or zucchini, onions and herbs. Change the pace with surprising side dishes such as sweet onions with rice, eggplant spiced with sausage or a cheese-topped potato kugel.

Spice up spaghetti with a home-made tomato sauce, or serve up a rich beef vegetable stew...whatever the occasion, these harvest-time helpings are sure to satisfy!

P ick a peach, pear or apple from your orchard or a roadside stand and enjoy the juicy flavors of summer ripening into fall.

And when the fruit ripens fast, fill a pie dish or a picnic tested favorites. You'll find it hard to pick a favorite from a fruit-filled Pear Cake, an easy Frozen Peach Cream Pie, an old-fashioned Autumn Apple Tart or a Hidden Gold Carrot Cake.

FRUIT-FILLED FAVORITES: From top to bottom—**Pear Cake** (Pg. 134); **Autumn Apple Tart** (Pg. 135); **Frozen Peach Cream Pie** (Pg. 134); **Hidden Gold Carrot Cake** (Pg. 134).

MEALS IN MINUTES

Some working mothers resort to frozen dinners or fast-food restaurants for weekday meals. Anita Foster of Fairmount, Georgia counts on another kind of convenience instead.

"On the weekends," says this busy mother of two young sons, "my life's at a slower pace. During the week, though, there's often little time for anything else *but* 'Meals in Minutes'!"

Anita developed her own 30-minute meal after enjoying a beef and peppers dish at a local restaurant. Back at home, she perfected the recipe. Adding glazed carrots and a tasty fruit salad dessert produced a fast, hearty feast.

"The boys especially love the fruit salad dessert," she notes. "I start out by tossing the fruit with the whipped topping and mayonnaise in a big bowl. Then I chill it until just before serving." At mealtime, she adds, the dessert can be turned out onto a platter like a molded salad.

Next comes the main course. "If, like mine, your husband is a hunter, you can substitute venison for the beef," Anita points out. "Do cook the venison a little longer than beef, though."

Lastly, while the beef and peppers simmer, Anita prepares the glazed carrots, using some fresh or canned carrots from her own garden.

"The garden is a family affair," she smiles. "The boys like shelling peas and shucking corn, and I enjoy 'putting up' the fruits of our labor."

We know you'll enjoy the convenience of Anita's quick, delicious dinner menu at busy times or anytime!

BEEF AND PEPPERS

2 tablespoons cooking oil
1-1/4 pounds beef round *or* sirloin steak, cut into 1-inch cubes
1 garlic clove, minced
1 medium onion, cut into wedges
1 medium sweet red pepper, seeded and cut into strips
1 medium green pepper, seeded and cut into strips
1 can (10-1/2 ounces) beef broth
1/4 cup water
3 tablespoons cornstarch
Salt and pepper to taste
Hot cooked rice

Heat oil in a skillet; brown beef cubes on all sides. Add the garlic and continue to cook for 2 minutes. Add onion, peppers and broth; cover and simmer 20 minutes. Combine the water and cornstarch; stir into broth. Cook and stir until gravy is thick and shiny. Add salt and pepper. Serve on rice. **Yield:** 4 servings.

GLAZED BABY CARROTS

1 pound fresh, frozen *or* canned whole baby carrots
2 tablespoons butter *or* margarine
1/4 cup packed brown sugar

Cook carrots in a small amount of water until tender. Drain. In a saucepan, combine butter and brown sugar; heat until sugar dissolves. Add carrots and toss to coat. Heat through. **Yield:** 4 servings.

AUTUMN FRUIT SALAD

2 bananas, sliced
1 apple, cored and cut into chunks
2 tablespoons orange juice
1 can (11 ounces) mandarin oranges, drained
1/2 cup raisins
1/4 cup chopped walnuts
4 tablespoons frozen whipped topping
2 tablespoons mayonnaise

Toss banana and apple pieces with the orange juice to prevent discoloration. Drain any excess juice. Toss gently with all remaining ingredients. Refrigerate until ready to serve. **Yield:** 6 servings.

HOMEMADE HERB VINEGAR: In a clear jar, put one cup of fresh, coarsely chopped herbs (thyme, basil, marjoram, tarragon, rosemary, fennel, dill or mint) and 2 or 3 cups of white or cider vinegar. Cap jar. Set on a sunny windowsill for about 2 weeks to let the flavors mellow. Then strain into a clean jar. Identify it by inserting a fresh herb stalk.

Versatile zucchini is easily the "most compatible" vegetable in any backyard garden—it finds its way into a surprising variety of palate-pleasing dishes!

Good eating begins and ends with zucchini—from crisp zucchini strip appetizers...to sliced zucchini rounds in a cheese soup ...to grated zucchini, beef and herbs in a delightful meat loaf.

And zucchini-laden cakes, cookies and breads are guaranteed to satisfy your family's sweet cravings, too!

ADAPTABLE ZUCCHINI: Clockwise from bottom left—**Zucchini Meat Loaf** (Pg. 135); **Cheese Zucchini Crisps** (Pg. 135); **Cheese Zucchini Soup** (Pg. 135); **Quick Zucchini Cake** (Pg. 135); **Zucchini Fudge Cake** (Pg. 136); **Zucchini Lemon Butter** (Pg. 136); **Zucchini/ Granola Cookies** (Pg. 135); **Zucchini Parmesan Bread** (Pg. 136).

A mazing, abundant zucchini —you just have to admire a vegetable that tries so very hard to please!

What other vegetable can dress up a stir-fry...crunch up a salad... moisten a fudge cake...or nestle comfortably in a casserole—and do it all so tastefully?

If you're among those who like the fresh, light taste of zucchini in simply prepared dishes, you'll enjoy Zucchini in Dill Cream Sauce.

If you prefer your zucchini "in disguise", try Zucchini Lemon Butter or Zucchini Parmesan Bread. Whichever way, with these recipes, there's a lot to like about zucchini.

ZESTY ZUCCHINI! From top to bottom —**Italian Sausage and Zucchini Stir-Fry** (Pg. 136); **Zucchini Casserole** (Pg. 136); **Zucchini in Dill Cream Sauce** (Pg. 137); **Italian Zucchini Salad** (Pg. 136).

DIXIE HENHOUSE EGGPLANT

Lt./Col. Henry Delaney, Beaumont, Texas

(PICTURED ON PAGE 126)

3 large eggplants
1/2 pound spicy bulk sausage
3 green onions, chopped
1 cup onions, chopped
1 cup celery, chopped
1 package (6-1/4 ounces) cornbread stuffing mix
1/2 teaspoon black pepper flakes
1/2 teaspoon salt
2 cups grated cheddar cheese

Peel and dice eggplant; cook in salted water until tender. Drain well and set aside. Saute sausage in skillet until well done; remove to paper towels and set aside. Saute green onions, onions and celery in skillet until transparent; set aside. Prepare stuffing mix according to package instructions. Combine eggplant, sausage, onion/celery mixture, salt and pepper with prepared stuffing. Transfer to shallow baking dish. Top with cheese; broil until cheese is melted. Serve hot. **Yield:** 12 servings.

SPAGHETTI SAUCE

Nan Banks, Cumberland, Wisconsin

(PICTURED ON PAGE 126)

75 plum tomatoes or 50 medium-sized regular tomatoes
1/4 cup brown sugar
2 tablespoons salt
1/2 teaspoon pepper
3 large onions, chopped
6 cloves garlic
3/4 cup fresh parsley or 1/4 cup dried parsley flakes
1 tablespoon dried basil leaves or 3 tablespoons fresh
1 tablespoon dried oregano leaves or 3 tablespoons fresh
1 tablespoon dried thyme or 3 tablespoons fresh
3 bay leaves

Wash, core and halve tomatoes. (If using regular tomatoes, drain in colander after quartering and squeeze gently to remove seeds and excess juice before cooking.) In 12-qt. kettle, combine tomatoes, brown sugar, salt, pepper. Bring to boil, stirring occasionally. Reduce heat and boil gently, uncovered, for 1 hour. Add remaining ingredients; boil gently, stirring occasionally for 1 hour more or until the sauce reaches the desired consistency. Puree through food mill. Pour hot sauce into sterilized hot pint jars, leaving 1-in. head space. Adjust lids. Process in pressure canner at 10 pounds for 35 minutes. (One tablespoon cornstarch, diluted in water, added to 1 qt. of sauce before reheating will thicken sauce perfectly.)

BEER BEEF STEW

Marge Reiman, Carroll, Iowa

(PICTURED ON PAGE 127)

1 pound boneless chuck roast, cut in 1-inch cubes
1 can (10-3/4 ounces) sodium-reduced cream of mushroom soup
1 package dry onion soup mix
1 soup can beer
1 cup canned tomatoes, drained or 3 fresh tomatoes, peeled and quartered
6 small whole onions or 1 small can pearl onions, drained
4 to 6 medium potatoes, peeled and quartered
2 to 3 ribs celery, sliced in 2-inch chunks
2 to 3 carrots, sliced in 2-inch chunks
1 teaspoon Worcestershire sauce

Combine meat, soup, onion soup mix and beer in oven-proof casserole or Dutch oven with tight-fitting lid. Cover; bake at 300° for 3 hours. Add tomatoes, onions, potatoes, celery, carrots and Worcestershire sauce; return to oven for 1 hour or longer. **Yield:** 6-8 servings.

PENNSYLVANIA CORN SOUP

Mildred Sherrer, Bay City, Texas

(PICTURED ON PAGE 127)

1 cup sweet red pepper, finely chopped
1 cup finely chopped onion
4 teaspoons corn oil
2 teaspoons butter
4 teaspoons whole wheat flour
2 cups milk
3 cups fresh or 1 package (16 ounces) frozen corn, *divided*
1 cup light cream or half-and-half
4 teaspoons tamari*
Dash nutmeg
Parsley for garnish

*Tamari is available at health food stores or Oriental markets. In large saucepan, cook the pepper and onion in oil and butter until tender. Stir in the flour and continue stirring over low heat for 2-3 minutes. Add milk slowly, stirring after each addition to prevent lumping. Set aside. Place 1 cup corn, cream and tamari in blender. Process on medium speed until fairly smooth. Add corn/cream mixture and remaining corn to the milk mixture. Heat thoroughly and serve topped with a dash of nutmeg. Garnish with parsley. **Yield:** 4 servings.

POTATO CHOWDER

Jane Barta, St. Thomas, North Dakota

(PICTURED ON PAGE 127)

4 cups peeled, diced potatoes
1/2 cup finely chopped onion
1 cup grated carrot
1 teaspoon salt
1/4 teaspoon pepper
1 tablespoon dried parsley flakes
4 chicken bouillon cubes
6 cups scalded milk
4 tablespoons butter
1/2 cup all-purpose flour

In a large Dutch oven or kettle, combine potatoes, onion, carrot, salt, pepper, parsley flakes and bouillon cubes. Add enough water to just cover vegetables; cook until vegetables are tender, about 15-20 minutes. *Do not drain.* Scald milk by heating to 180° or until tiny bubbles form around edges of pan. Remove 1-1/2 cups milk and add butter and flour to hot milk, stirring with wire whisk. Add remaining 4-1/2 cups hot milk to undrained vegetables, then stir in thickened hot milk mixture. Stir until blended. Simmer for 15 minutes on low heat. **Yield:** 8-10 servings.

HOMEMADE PICKLING SPICE

Olivia Miller, Memphis, Tennessee

2 tablespoons mustard seed
1 tablespoon whole allspice
2 teaspoons coriander seeds
2 whole cloves
1 teaspoon ground ginger
1 teaspoon dried red pepper flakes
1 bay leaf, crumbled
1 cinnamon stick (2 inches)

Combine all ingredients and store in an airtight jar or container. Use in favorite pickle recipes. **Yield:** 1/3 cup.

SWEET ONION CASSEROLE

Marge Smith, Brawley, California

(PICTURED ON PAGE 127)

1/2 cup long grain rice, uncooked
7 to 8 cups Imperial sweet onions, chopped coarsely
1/4 cup melted butter
1 cup grated Swiss cheese
2/3 cup half-and-half
1 teaspoon salt

Cook rice in 5 cups boiling water for 5 minutes. Drain; set aside. Cook onions in butter in large skillet until limp but not browned. Combine all ingredients, mix well and pour into greased 2-qt. casserole. Bake at 350° for 1 hour. **Yield:** 8-10 servings.

FROZEN PEACH CREAM PIE

Joann Snyder, Fresno, California

(PICTURED ON PAGE 128)

1 can (14 ounces) sweetened condensed milk
Juice of 2 large lemons (about 1/2 cup)
1 cup heavy cream, whipped
2 cups fresh ripe peaches, sliced and cut into small pieces
1 9-inch graham cracker crust*

Mix milk with lemon juice (mixture will thicken). Fold thickened mixture into whipped cream and peaches. Pour into chilled crust. Freeze until firm. Serve frozen. (Can also use raspberries, boysenberries, strawberries or fresh apricots in place of peaches.) *May make in springform pan, as shown. **Yield:** 8 servings.

ZUCCHINI SOUP

Charlotte Janeczko, Davenport, Iowa

(PICTURED ON PAGE 127)

3 slices lean bacon, cut in small pieces
1 medium onion, chopped
1 clove garlic, minced
8 medium zucchinis, cut in 1/2-inch slices (about 8 cups)
1 can (10-1/2 ounces) beef consomme
2-1/2 cups water
1 teaspoon salt
4 tablespoons fresh parsley
1 teaspoon dried basil leaves (can use fresh)
1/8 teaspoon pepper
Freshly grated Parmesan cheese
Bacon bits for garnish, optional

Brown bacon pieces in large skillet; drain off all but 1 tablespoon bacon fat. Stir onion and garlic in fat until onion is tender. Add remaining ingredients except cheese. Bring to a boil, then simmer, uncovered, until zucchini is tender, about 20 minutes. Pour soup into blender, about 2 cups at a time. Cover; blend on low speed until liquified, then blend on high until smooth. Serve hot or cold with Parmesan cheese and additional bacon bits. **Yield:** 8 one-cup servings.

HIDDEN GOLD CARROT CAKE

Lucille Drake, Tecumseh, Michigan

(PICTURED ON PAGE 128)

2 cups sugar
2 cups all-purpose flour
2 teaspoons baking soda
1 teaspoon salt
1 cup vegetable oil
4 eggs, room temperature
3 cups finely grated raw carrots, packed (about 1 pound)
Confectioners' sugar
Lemon frosting or filling*

Mix first four ingredients. Add oil; mix well. Add eggs, one at a time, beating well after each addition. Stir in carrots. Pour batter into greased and paper-lined 13-in. x 9-in. x 1-in. jelly roll pan or 3 greased and floured 8-in. layer cake pans. Bake at 350° for 20 minutes for jelly roll or 35 minutes (or until cake tests done) for layers. (Do not open oven door for first 20 to 30 minutes of baking time.) Loosen edges of cake in jelly roll pan as soon as it is removed from oven. Reverse pan onto a clean towel that has been dusted with confectioners' sugar. Roll up in towel and place on rack to cool. When thoroughly cool, unroll cake to fill and top with favorite lemon frosting or filling. Let layer cake cool in pans for 10 minutes; remove to cake rack. *We used a cooled lemon meringue pie filling combined with chilled whipped cream as a filling. **Yield:** 8 servings.

POTATO KUGEL

Marsha Jordan, Harshaw, Wisconsin

(PICTURED ON PAGE 127)

6 medium-sized russet potatoes, peeled
2 to 3 carrots, peeled
1 onion
1 clove garlic, minced
2 beaten eggs
3 tablespoons vegetable oil
2 teaspoons salt
1/4 cup whole-grain bread crumbs
3/4 cup powdered non-fat milk

TOPPING:
1 cup cheddar cheese, grated
1 cup plain yogurt or sour cream
Fresh chives for garnish, optional

Grate vegetables; drain off liquid. Stir in remaining ingredients except topping, adding powdered milk gradually to avoid any lumps. Spread into greased 7-in. x 11-in. baking pan. (Can also use 9-in. square pan with additional baking time.) Bake at 350° for 40-60 minutes. When kugel is nearly done it will test dry like a cake and the edges will be brown. Add grated cheese and return to oven for 5 more minutes until cheese melts. Remove from oven; cut into 2-in. squares. Top each square with about 2 tablespoons yogurt or sour cream. Garnish with fresh chives, if desired. **Yield:** 6-8 servings.

PEAR CAKE

Hazyl Lindley, Abilene, Texas

(PICTURED ON PAGE 128)

2 cups sugar
1-1/2 cups vegetable oil
3 eggs
3 cups all-purpose flour
1 teaspoon cinnamon
1 teaspoon salt
1 teaspoon baking soda
2 teaspoons vanilla
2 cups flaked coconut, about 1 (7 ounce) package
1 cup chopped dates
3 cups raw or canned pears, drained and chopped
1 cup pecans, chopped, about 1 (4 ounce) package

Cream together sugar and oil. Add eggs, one at a time, mixing well after each addition. Set aside. Sift flour with cinnamon, salt and soda 3 times, then add to creamed mixture. Add vanilla; mix. Add coconut, dates, pears and pecans, stirring by hand (batter will be thick). Pour into greased and floured fluted pan. Bake at 325° for 1-1/2 to 2 hours or until cake tests done with a wooden pick inserted in center. Cool on rack until cake shrinks from sides of pan; remove from pan to complete cooling. **Yield:**

AUTUMN APPLE TART

Grace Howaniec, Waukesha, Wisconsin

(PICTURED ON PAGE 128)

6 medium baking apples,
   peeled, cored and sliced 1/4
   inch thick (use Granny Smith
   or Jonathan, if possible)
CRUST:
1-1/4 cup all-purpose flour
   1 teaspoon baking powder
   1/2 teaspoon salt
   1 tablespoon sugar
   1/2 cup butter *or* margarine
   1 egg, beaten
   2 tablespoons milk
TOPPING:
   1/3 to 1/2 cup sugar
   2 tablespoons butter *or*
      margarine
   1/2 teaspoon ground cinnamon
   1/2 teaspoon ground nutmeg
1-1/2 tablespoons all-purpose flour

Make crust by combining flour, baking powder, salt and sugar in medium-sized bowl. Cut in butter/margarine with pastry blender until mixture resembles fine crumbs. Combine egg and milk; add to flour/butter mixture. Stir to blend. With lightly floured hands, press dough into a 12-in. diameter tart pan (with removable bottom). Press dough up sides to form a 1-in. rim. (May use a 13-in. x 9-in. x 2-in. baking pan instead of tart pan.) Fill tart shell with overlapping apple slices, beginning at outer edge. See diagram on page 128. Combine topping ingredients; sprinkle evenly over apples. Bake at 350° for 50-60 minutes until apples are fork-tender. Cut in wedges; serve warm or cool. **Yield:** 12 servings.

CHEESE ZUCCHINI CRISPS

Julie Ifft, Fairbury, Illinois

(PICTURED ON PAGE 130)

 This tasty dish uses less sugar, salt and fat. Recipe includes *Diabetic Exchanges.*

1/3 cup cornflake crumbs
   2 tablespoons grated
      Parmesan cheese
   1/2 teaspoon seasoned salt
Dash garlic powder
   4 small unpeeled zucchini, cut
      in 1/2-inch strips
   1/4 cup melted butter

Combine cornflake crumbs, cheese, salt and garlic powder; place in plastic bag. Dip zucchini strips in butter then shake in bag of crumbs to coat. Place on baking sheet; bake at 375° for about 10 minutes

or until crisp. **Yield:** 4 servings. **Diabetic Exchanges:** One serving equals 1 bread, 1 vegetable, 2 fats; also, 209 calories, 546 mg sodium, 37 mg cholesterol, 21 gm carbohydrate, 4 gm protein, 12 gm fat.

CHEESE ZUCCHINI SOUP

Jean Thomas, Loysville, Pennsylvania

(PICTURED ON PAGE 130)

   4 slices bacon
   1/2 cup onion, finely chopped
2-1/2 cups zucchini, cut in
      1/4-inch slices
   1 cup water
   1/2 teaspoon salt
SOUP BASE:
   1/4 cup butter
   1/4 cup all-purpose flour
   1 teaspoon salt
   1/4 teaspoon pepper
2-1/2 cups milk
   1/2 teaspoon Worcestershire
      sauce
   1 cup (4 ounces) shredded
      mild cheese

Cook bacon until crisp; set aside for garnish. Saute onion in bacon fat until tender. Add zucchini, water and salt. Cover; bring to boil. Reduce heat; simmer for 5 minutes until zucchini is tender. Set aside. Prepare soup base by melting butter in 3-qt. saucepan. Blend in flour, salt and pepper. Remove from heat; stir in milk and Worcestershire sauce. Heat to boiling, stirring constantly. Boil for 1 minute, stirring constantly. Remove from heat; stir in cheese. Add vegetables *with liquid* to soup base. Heat to serving temperature. Garnish with crumbled bacon. **Yield:** about 6 cups.

ZUCCHINI MEAT LOAF

Nancy Sheets, Delaware, Ohio

(PICTURED ON PAGE 130)

   2 pounds ground beef
   2 cups coarsely grated,
      unpeeled zucchini
   1 cup dry Italian-seasoned
      bread crumbs *or* regular
      bread crumbs plus 1
      teaspoon Italian seasoning
   1/2 cup grated Parmesan cheese
   1 tablespoon chopped parsley
   1 small onion, finely chopped
   2 teaspoons instant beef
      bouillon *or* 2 cubes crushed
      and dissolved in 1 tablespoon
      water
   1/4 teaspoon salt
   1 cup milk
   1 large egg, beaten

Zucchini slices, optional
Paprika

Combine all ingredients in large bowl; mix thoroughly. Pack into 9-in. x 5-in. x 3-in. loaf pan. Bake at 350° for 1-1/4 hours. If desired, garnish with zucchini slices sprinkled with paprika during last 10 minutes of baking. (Leftover loaf, sliced thinly, makes delicious sandwiches.) **Yield:** 6-8 servings.

QUICK ZUCCHINI CAKE

Ann Dudlack, Chicago, Illinois

(PICTURED ON PAGE 131)

   1 box (18-1/4 ounces) yellow
      cake mix
   4 eggs
   1/2 cup vegetable oil
   1 teaspoon cinnamon
   1 tablespoon vanilla
   2 cups unpeeled,
      grated zucchini
   1/2 cup raisins
   1/2 cup chopped nuts
Confectioners' sugar, optional

Beat cake mix, eggs, oil, cinnamon and vanilla together in large bowl for 6-7 minutes. Fold in zucchini, raisins and nuts. Grease and flour a 10-in. tube or fluted pan, spoon in batter and bake at 350° for 40-50 minutes. Test with wooden pick at 40 minutes for doneness; retest at 5-minute intervals. Remove cake from pan; let cool on wire rack. Sprinkle with confectioners' sugar, if desired. **Yield:** 16-20 servings.

ZUCCHINI/GRANOLA COOKIES

Dorothy Dahlin, Minden, Nebraska

(PICTURED ON PAGE 131)

   3/4 cup butter, softened
1-1/2 cups brown sugar
   1 egg
   1 teaspoon vanilla
Grated rind of 1 orange
   3 cups grated, unpeeled
      zucchini
   3 to 3-1/2 cups all-purpose flour
   1 teaspoon baking soda
   1 teaspoon salt
   3 cups granola cereal
   1 cup butterscotch *or*
      chocolate chips

Cream butter and sugar in large bowl; add egg, vanilla, orange rind and zucchini. Stir in flour, soda and salt. Add granola; mix. Stir in chips. (Dough will be sticky.) Drop by spoonfuls on greased cookie sheet. Bake at 350° for 12-15 minutes. Cool on rack. **Yield:** about 100 cookies.

ZUCCHINI FUDGE CAKE

Gloria Kleman, Columbus Grove, Ohio

(PICTURED ON PAGE 131)

CAKE:
- 4 eggs
- 2-1/4 cups sugar
- 2 teaspoons vanilla
- 3/4 cup butter, softened
- 3 cups all-purpose flour
- 1/2 cup unsweetened cocoa
- 2 teaspoons baking powder
- 1 teaspoon baking soda
- 3/4 teaspoon salt
- 1 cup buttermilk
- 3 cups coarsely shredded unpeeled zucchini
- 1 cup chopped walnuts

CHOCOLATE FROSTING:
- 1 cup butter, softened
- 2 pounds confectioners' sugar
- 1/2 cup unsweetened cocoa
- 1 tablespoon vanilla
- 1/2 cup milk

In a large bowl, beat eggs until fluffy. Add sugar gradually; beating until mixture is thick and lemon-colored. Beat in vanilla and butter. Combine flour, cocoa, baking powder, soda and salt; stir 1/2 of dry ingredients into egg mixture. Add buttermilk; mix. Add remaining flour mixture; beat until smooth. Fold in zucchini and nuts. Divide batter into four 8-in. or 9-in. round, greased and floured pans. Bake at 350° for 25-30 minutes or until top springs back when gently pressed. Cool in pans 10 minutes; remove to wire racks and cool completely. Make frosting by combining all ingredients in large bowl; beat until creamy. Frost with chocolate frosting. **Yield:** 20 large servings.

ZUCCHINI PARMESAN BREAD

Mary Webb, Kinsman, Ohio

(PICTURED ON PAGE 131)

- 3 cups all-purpose flour
- 1 cup peeled, shredded zucchini (drain on paper towel)
- 1/3 cup sugar
- 3 tablespoons grated Parmesan cheese
- 1/2 teaspoon baking soda
- 1 teaspoon baking powder
- 1 to 1-1/2 teaspoons salt
- 1/3 cup butter
- 1 cup buttermilk
- 2 eggs
- 1 tablespoon grated onion

Mix flour, zucchini, sugar, cheese, soda,

baking powder and salt together; set aside. Melt butter; stir into buttermilk. Beat eggs in medium bowl; add butter/buttermilk mixture and onion; stir into flour mixture. (Batter will be thick.) Spread in greased and floured 9-in. x 5-in. x 3-in. loaf pan. Bake at 350° for 1 hour. (Use wooden pick inserted at center to test for doneness.) **Yield:** 1 loaf.

ZUCCHINI LEMON BUTTER

Lena McConnell, Tisdale, Saskatchewan

(PICTURED ON PAGE 131)

- 2 pounds zucchini (large size works well)
- Water
- 1/2 cup butter
- 3 cups sugar
- 3 medium lemons *or* 2 large lemons (juice and rind)
  Juice = 1 cup; rind = 3 tablespoons
- 1 package Certo

Peel, slice and boil zucchini until tender in enough water to cover. Strain; cool. Mash or puree until smooth. Place in large saucepan; add butter, sugar, lemon juice and rind. Bring to full boil, stirring frequently. Add Certo; boil hard for 2 minutes. Skim off any foam; pack in hot sterilized jars. Seal. Store in refrigerator for short periods of time; in freezer for long-term storage. **Yield:** 6 cups.

TASTY TARTAR SAUCE: Combine 1/2 cup zucchini relish, 1 cup salad dressing and 2 (or more) tablespoons lemon juice.

ITALIAN SAUSAGE AND ZUCCHINI STIR-FRY

Mary Ballard, La Crescent, Minnesota

(PICTURED ON PAGE 132)

- 1 pound Italian sausage
- 1/2 cup chopped onions
- 2 cups chopped tomatoes, seeds removed
- 4 cups unpared zucchini, julienne cuts (matchstick) *or* coarsely shredded
- 1 teaspoon lemon juice
- 1/4 teaspoon salt
- 1/4 teaspoon hot pepper sauce
- 1/4 teaspoon oregano
- Parmesan cheese

Slice sausage in 1/4-in. slices; brown in wok or large skillet. Add onions when sausage is nearly done. Drain. Add tomatoes, zucchini, lemon juice, salt, hot pepper sauce and oregano. Cook, uncovered, for about 5 minutes, stirring frequently. Remove to serving plate; sprinkle with cheese. Serve with crusty Italian bread. **Yield:** 4 servings.

ZUCCHINI CASSEROLE

Linda Pottinger, Winter Haven, Florida

(PICTURED ON PAGE 132)

- 6 cups diced, unpeeled zucchini
- 1 cup onion, diced
- 1 cup shredded carrots
- 1 can (10-1/2 ounces) cream of chicken soup, undiluted
- 1 container (8 ounces) sour cream
- 1/8 teaspoon garlic powder
- 3 whole chicken breasts, cooked, chopped in 3/4-inch chunks *or* 4 cups chopped leftover chicken *or* turkey
- 1/2 cup butter
- 1 package chicken-flavor stuffing mix
- 1 cup cheddar cheese, grated, optional

Combine zucchini and onion in medium saucepan, add water to cover and bring to boil. Boil for 5 minutes; drain and cool. Combine carrots, soup, sour cream and garlic powder in large bowl. Add zucchini/onion and chicken; mix. Spread in buttered 13-in. x 9-in. baking dish. To prepare topping, melt butter in skillet, add stuffing mix and seasoning packet and toss well. Sprinkle stuffing over casserole. Top with cheese, if desired. Bake at 350° for 1 hour or until golden brown. **Yield:** 6-8 servings.

ITALIAN ZUCCHINI SALAD

Ida Wester, Shelbina, Missouri

(PICTURED ON PAGE 132)

☑ This tasty dish uses less sugar, salt and fat. Recipe includes *Diabetic Exchanges*.

- 2 pounds zucchini
- 1/2 cup water
- 2 teaspoons seasoned salt
- 12 large ripe pitted olives
- 2/3 cup olive oil
- 1/2 cup wine vinegar
- 1 teaspoon salt
- 1/2 teaspoon paprika
- 1/2 teaspoon pepper

1/2 teaspoon sugar
1/4 teaspoon basil leaves
1 clove garlic
1 avocado
Pimiento *or* **red pepper strips**

Wash zucchini; cut off ends. Cut into 3/4-in. slices. Combine water and seasoned salt; pour over zucchini in saucepan. Cook until tender-crisp. Drain; set aside. Cut olives in quarters; add to zucchini mixture. Combine oil, vinegar, salt, paprika, pepper, sugar and basil. Spear garlic on toothpick; add to dressing. Pour over zucchini mixture in bowl; stir gently. Chill overnight. Remove garlic. Several hours before serving, peel avocado; cut into slices. Add to salad; stir. Garnish with pimiento or red pepper. **Yield:** 12 servings. **Diabetic Exchanges:** One serving equals 1 vegetable, 3 fats; also, 167 calories, 469 mg sodium, 0 cholesterol, 5 gm carbohydrate, 1 gm protein, 17 gm fat.

ZUCCHINI IN DILL CREAM SAUCE

Josephine Vanden Heuvel, Hart, Michigan

(PICTURED ON PAGE 132)

 This tasty dish uses less sugar, salt and fat. Recipe includes *Diabetic Exchanges*.

7 cups unpeeled zucchini, cut
   in 1-1/2 x 1/4-inch strips
1/4 cup onion, finely chopped
1/2 cup water
1 teaspoon salt
1 teaspoon *or* 1 cube instant
   chicken bouillon
1/2 teaspoon dried dill weed
2 tablespoons butter, melted
2 teaspoons sugar
1 teaspoon lemon juice
2 tablespoons all-purpose flour
1/4 cup sour cream

In medium saucepan, combine zucchini, onion, water, salt, bouillon and dill weed; bring to boil. Add butter, sugar and lemon juice; mix. Remove from heat; *do not drain*. Combine flour and sour cream; stir 1/2 of mixture into hot zucchini. Return to heat; add remaining cream mixture and cook until thickened. **Yield:** 8 servings. **Diabetic Exchanges:** One serving equals 1 vegetable, 1 fat; also, 73 calories, 419 mg sodium, 11 mg cholesterol, 8 gm carbohydrate, 2 gm protein, 4 gm fat.

POTATOES AND ZUCCHINI AU GRATIN

Nancy Sheets, Delaware, Ohio

3 cups zucchini, cut in
   1/2-inch slices
2 tablespoons water
3 tablespoons butter
3 tablespoons all-purpose flour
1 tablespoon *or* 3 cubes instant
   chicken bouillon
1-1/2 cups milk
1 cup shredded mild cheddar
   cheese
2 tablespoons chopped
   pimiento
1/2 teaspoon thyme leaves
3 cups cooked, peeled and
   sliced potatoes
Canned French fried onions

In medium saucepan, cook zucchini in water 5 minutes or until tender. Drain; set aside. In medium saucepan, melt butter; stir in flour and bouillon. Gradually stir in milk. Cook and stir until bouillon dissolves and sauce thickens. Remove from heat; add cheese, pimiento and thyme. Stir until cheese melts. In 1-1/2-qt. baking dish, layer 1/2 of potatoes, zucchini and sauce. Repeat layers. Bake at 350°, uncovered, 25 minutes or until bubbly. Top with onions; bake 2 minutes longer. **Yield:** 6 servings.

BEST ZUCCHINI BARS

Marilyn Stroud, Larsen, Wisconsin

BARS:
2 cups sugar
1 cup oil
3 eggs
2 cups all-purpose flour
1 teaspoon cinnamon
1 teaspoon salt
2 teaspoons baking soda
1/4 teaspoon baking powder
1 teaspoon vanilla
2 cups shredded, ungrated
   zucchini
1 small carrot, shredded
3/4 cup rolled oats
1 cup chopped hickory nuts
   or walnuts
FROSTING:
1/2 cup soft butter
1/4 teaspoon almond extract
2 teaspoons vanilla
2-1/2 cups confectioners' sugar
1 package (3 ounces) creamed
   cheese, softened

Beat together sugar, oil and eggs in large bowl or in food processor. Beat in flour, cinnamon, salt, soda, baking powder and vanilla. Beat 1-2 minutes until well mixed. Fold in zucchini, carrot, oats and nuts; mix well. Pour into 15-in. x 10-in. x 1-in. pan (jelly roll pan or cookie sheet with sides). Bake at 350° for 15-20 minutes. Make frosting by beating all ingredients together until smooth. Set aside. Cool bars; frost. Cut into bars. **Yield:** 3 dozen.

SANTA FE ENCHILADAS

Barbara Beichley, Gladbrook, Iowa

1-1/2 pounds ground beef *or* pork
1 can (12 ounces) tomato paste
1 cup water
1/2 cup chopped onion
1 package taco seasoning mix,
   optional
Salt, if desired
12 flour tortillas
1 jar (8 ounces) process cheese
1 can (4 ounces) chopped
   green chili peppers, drained

Crumble meat in large mixing bowl; microwave on high 6-8 minutes or until meat loses pink color. Drain. Add paste, water, onion, taco seasoning (if desired) and salt to meat; microwave on high 3 minutes. Set aside. Wrap tortillas in dampened paper towels and microwave on high 1-2 minutes until soft. Spoon 2 tablespoons meat mixture on each tortilla; roll up tightly. Place in lightly greased 9-in. x 13-in. baking dish. Combine process cheese and green chilies; microwave on high for 1-2 minutes until heated through. Pour over tortillas. Top with remaining meat mixture. Microwave on high 5 minutes; rotate dish. Cover with plain paper towel; microwave on high 5 minutes more. Let stand, covered, 5 minutes. **Yield:** 10-12 servings.

> **ZUCCHINI TIPS:** For quick grated zucchini, place unpeeled zucchini chunks in blender; cover with water and blend at "chop" for a few seconds or until processed. Drain off water; pat zucchini with paper towels and use.
>
> • For dried zucchini, wash, peel and grate zucchini; press between layers of paper toweling to remove excess moisture. Spread on dehydrator trays; dry for 8-10 hours. Store in air-tight glass containers or heavy plastic bags.
>
> • For frozen zucchini, shred unpeeled zucchini; drain and pat dry on layers of paper towels. Place 2 cups zucchini in freezer bags; seal tightly. Freeze. Can be used in any recipe calling for shredded zucchini.

MELT-IN-YOUR-MOUTH SAUSAGES

Ilean Schulteiss, Cohocton, New York

**2 pounds Italian sausage
(sweet, mild *or* hot)
48 ounces spaghetti sauce
1 can (6 ounces) tomato paste
1 large green pepper, sliced
thin
1 large onion, sliced thin
1 tablespoon grated Parmesan
cheese
1 teaspoon parsley flakes *or* 1
tablespoon fresh parsley
1 cup water**

Place sausage in skillet; cover with water. Simmer 10 minutes; drain. Meanwhile, place remaining ingredients in slow cooker; add drained sausage (cut in hot-dog lengths if using sweet sausage—it's shaped in large coil). Cover; cook on low 4 hours. Increase temperature to high; cook 1 hour more. Serve in buns or cut sausage into bite-size slices and serve over spaghetti. **Yield:** 8 servings.

CARROT SALAD

Janice Swanson, Galesburg, Illinois

**2 pounds carrots, cut into 1/3-
inch-thick rounds
1 large onion, diced
1 large green pepper, diced
1 can (10-3/4 ounces) tomato
soup
1 cup sugar
3/4 cup vinegar
1 cup vegetable oil
1 teaspoon salt
1/2 teaspoon ground pepper
1 teaspoon dry mustard**

Bring carrots to boil in salted water; boil 5 minutes. Drain; cool. Add onion and pepper. Combine soup, sugar, vinegar, oil, salt, pepper and mustard. Pour over carrots. Refrigerate 24 hours. **Yield:** 12 servings.

QUICK TOFFEE BARS

Jeannette Wubbena, Standish, Michigan

**12 whole graham crackers,
broken into quarters
1 cup butter
1/2 cup sugar
1 cup chopped nuts
1 to 2 cups semisweet
chocolate chips**

Line a 15-in. x 10-in. x 1-in. jelly pan with buttered wax paper. Put graham cracker sections on paper. Combine butter and sugar in saucepan. Melt over medium heat; let boil gently 3 minutes. Spoon over graham crackers; spread evenly. Sprinkle nuts on top. Bake at 325° for 10 minutes; cool. Melt chocolate chips and spread over all. After chocolate sets, peel off paper. Cookies can be frozen. **Yield:** 48 toffee bars.

GOURMET POTATOES

Eula Riggins, Odon, Indiana

**6 medium-sized potatoes
1/4 cup plus 2 tablespoons
butter, *divided*
2 cups shredded cheddar
cheese
1/2 cup cultured sour cream
1 tablespoon minced onion
1 teaspoon salt
1/4 teaspoon ground pepper
Paprika**

Cook unpeeled potatoes until tender. Cool, peel and shred coarsely. Heat 1/4 cup butter in saucepan; remove from heat. Add cheese, stirring until partially melted. Blend in sour cream, onion, salt and pepper; fold in potatoes. Place in greased 2-qt. casserole dish; dot with 2 tablespoons butter. Sprinkle with paprika. Bake, uncovered, at 350° for 30 minutes or until nicely browned. *Note:* Casserole may be assembled day before; if you do, cover and refrigerate, and lengthen cooking time. **Yield:** 8-10 servings.

CHEESE-SCALLOPED POTATOES/CARROTS

Josephine Wilkins, Pleasantville, Ohio

**2 cups boiling water
2 teaspoons salt, optional
2 pounds potatoes (5 cups)
pared and thinly sliced 1/4
inch thick
1-1/2 cups sliced onions
5 medium carrots (2 cups)
pared, diagonally sliced 1/4
inch thick
CHEESE SAUCE:
3 tablespoons butter
2 tablespoons all-purpose flour
1 teaspoon salt
1/8 teaspoon pepper
Dash cayenne
1-1/2 cups milk
1-1/2 cups grated sharp cheddar
cheese, *divided***

Place boiling water and if desired, salt, in large pan and cook potatoes, onions and carrots, covered, for about 5 minutes or until partially tender. Drain. Make cheese sauce by melting butter in small saucepan. Stir in flour, salt, pepper and cayenne, stirring constantly, about 1 minute. Remove from heat; stir in milk and blend well. Bring mixture to boil over medium heat, stirring until thick and smooth. Add 1 cup cheese; stir until melted. Layer half of vegetables in greased 2-1/2-qt. casserole; top with half of cheese sauce. Repeat layers of vegetables and sauce. Top with remaining cheese. Bake, covered with foil, at 375° for 30 minutes. Foil may be removed for last 10 minutes to brown top. **Yield:** 6 servings.

HERB-BUTTERED PASTA

Lizabeth Marris, Neenah, Wisconsin

**1 package (7 ounces) linguine
SAUCE:
1/4 cup butter
1/3 cup chopped fresh parsley
1/2 teaspoon garlic powder
1/2 teaspoon oregano leaves
1 tablespoon lemon juice
Parmesan cheese**

Cook linguine in 3-qt. saucepan according to package instructions. Drain. Melt butter in same saucepan. Stir in linguine and remaining ingredients. Cook over medium heat, stirring constantly, until heated, about 2 minutes. Sprinkle with cheese. **Yield:** 4 servings.

MOM'S BROWN STEW

Barbara Pricer, Meadow Valley, California

**2 pounds beef chuck *or* flank
(cut into 1-1/2-inch cubes
and trimmed of fat—*reserve*
1 tablespoon beef fat for
browning)
1 quart boiling water
1 teaspoon lemon juice
1 teaspoon Worcestershire
sauce
1 clove garlic, minced
1 onion sliced
2 bay leaves
1 tablespoon salt
1/2 teaspoon paprika
Dash ground allspice *or* cloves
1 teaspoon sugar
6 carrots
2 large potatoes**

1 pound small white onions
3 tablespoons all-purpose flour
1/2 cup cold water

Brown meat in melted fat in heavy Dutch oven. Brown meat until all sides are very dark brown but *not burned*. Add boiling water, lemon juice, Worcestershire sauce, garlic, onion, bay leaves, salt, paprika, spice and sugar. Cover; simmer for 2 hours, adding more water if necessary. Cut potatoes into 2-in chunks and carrots into 1-in. diagonal slices; peel onions. Add onions; cook 10 minutes. Add carrots, cook 10 minutes then add potatoes. Cook until potatoes are tender. Remove meat and vegetables to heat-proof casserole; keep hot in oven while thickening stew liquid with flour and water mixture. Bring to boil. Pour hot gravy over meat and vegetables. **Yield:** 8 servings.

REUBEN CASSEROLE

Kitty Monke, Regent, North Dakota

1 can (16 ounces) sauerkraut, undrained
12 ounces corned beef, canned or sliced, crumbled or torn into small pieces
2 cups Swiss cheese, shredded
1/2 cup light mayonnaise
1/4 cup Thousand Island dressing
2 fresh tomatoes, sliced
2 tablespoons melted butter
1/4 cup pumpernickel *or* rye bread crumbs

Place sauerkraut in 1-1/2-qt. baking dish. Top with a layer of beef, then cheese. Combine mayonnaise and dressing; spread over cheese. Top with tomato slices; set aside. Combine butter and bread crumbs in small bowl; sprinkle over tomato slices. Microwave at 70% power for 12-14 minutes or bake at 350° for 45 minutes. Let stand 5 minutes before serving. **Yield:** 6-8 servings.

MEXICAN EGGS

Laura Rothlisberger, Green, Kansas

2 tablespoons butter
1/2 cup chopped onion
1/2 cup chopped green pepper
8 eggs
1/4 cup milk
1 teaspoon seasoned salt
1/2 teaspoon crushed basil
1/4 teaspoon pepper
1 package (3 ounces) cream cheese, cubed
1 medium tomato, chopped
2 to 4 slices bacon, cooked crisp, crumbled

Melt butter in large skillet over medium heat; add onion and green pepper. Cook until tender; set aside. Beat eggs, milk and seasonings. Pour over onion/pepper mixture. Add cream cheese and tomato. Return skillet to heat. Gently push pancake turner completely across bottom and sides of skillet, forming large soft curds. Cook until eggs are thickened throughout, but still moist. Sprinkle with bacon. **Yield:** 4 servings.

BANANA SPLIT DESSERT

Mrs. Elmer Thorsheim, Radcliffe, Iowa

5 cups graham cracker crumbs
2/3 cup butter, melted
2 to 3 bananas
1/2 gallon Neapolitan ice cream
1 cup chopped walnuts
1 cup chocolate chips
1/2 cup butter
2 cups confectioners' sugar
1-1/2 cups evaporated milk
1 teaspoon vanilla
1 pint whipping cream

Prepare crust with crumbs and 2/3 cup butter; reserve 1 cup crumb mixture. Press remaining crumb mixture into bottom of 11-in. x 15-in. baking pan. Slice bananas crosswise and layer over crust. Cut ice cream in 1/2-in.-thick slices; place over bananas. Sprinkle ice cream

with chopped walnuts. Freeze until firm. Melt chocolate chips and 1/2 cup butter; add confectioners' sugar and evaporated milk. Cook mixture until thick and smooth, stirring constantly. Remove from heat; add vanilla. Cool chocolate mixture; pour over ice cream. Freeze until firm. Whip cream until stiff; spread over chocolate layer; top with reserved crumbs. Store in freezer; remove about 10 minutes before serving. (Will keep for several weeks.) **Yield:** 25 servings.

BARBARA'S FARM COFFEE CAKE

Doreen Gerrish, Pawcatuck, Connecticut

2 packages active dry yeast
1/2 cup water (110°-115°)
1-1/2 cups milk, scalded
1/2 cup butter
1/2 cup honey
2 teaspoons salt
2 eggs
7 to 7-1/2 cups all-purpose flour
WALNUT FILLING:
1 cup brown sugar, packed
1/2 cup chopped walnuts
2 teaspoons ground cinnamon
1/2 cup raisins

Dissolve yeast in warm water. In separate large mixing bowl, combine milk, butter, honey and salt. When yeast mixture has cooled to lukewarm, combine it with eggs, 3 cups of flour and milk mixture. Beat until smooth using electric mixer. Stir in enough remaining flour to make soft dough. Knead on floured surface until smooth and elastic, about 10 minutes. Place in greased bowl. Cover; let rise in warm place until doubled, about 1-1/4 hours. Punch down dough. Divide into six pieces. Roll out each to 26-in. x 4-in. rectangle and sprinkle with 1/6 of filling. Roll up like jelly roll, starting from long edge. Repeat with remaining dough. To form each coffee cake (recipe makes two), coil together (like braided rug) three rolls on greased baking sheet. Cut slits in top of coil every 2 in. with scissors. Let rise until doubled, about 1 hour. Bake at 375° for 20 minutes or until golden. Cool partially on rack; drizzle with a thin confectioners' sugar glaze, if desired. **Yield:** 2 cakes.

> **BUTTER UP!** To make raspberry-flavored butter that's delicious on muffins, toast, bagels or pancakes, blend 1 cup softened butter, 2 cups confectioners' sugar and 1 package (10 ounces) frozen, *thawed* raspberries. Store in refrigerator.

Autumn

Fall flavors fill our hearty harvest table with a bounty of family-pleasing recipes for foods from field, forest and garden.

For a delicious change of taste, try game dishes like Pheasant with Creamy Yogurt Sauce. As accompaniments, savor the season's abundant vegetables in flavorful new ways with Oven Fried Potatoes, Wild Rice Soup, Herb Scalloped Tomatoes or any of these fine fall dishes!

FALL FEAST: Clockwise from lower left —**Pheasant with Creamy Yogurt Sauce** (Pg. 147); **Cranberry Plus Relish** (Pg. 147); **Herb Scalloped Tomatoes** (Pg. 147); **Potato Bread** (Pg. 147); **Wild Rice Soup** (Pg. 148); **Smothered Green Cabbage** (Pg. 148); **Oven-Fried Potatoes** (Pg. 148); **Rabbit Dijon** (Pg. 147).

Seasonal desserts make a delicious finish to color-filled days. Taste the flavors of fall in creamy, spicy Pumpkin Cake Roll or extra-rich Southern Pecan Cheesecake...or pucker up to tart/sweet Cranberry Streusel Pie or warm Apple Fritters. These autumn delights capture the savory, spicy tastes of the waning year. Enjoy!

SWEET HARVEST: Clockwise from the lower left—**Apple Fritters** (Pg. 149); **Pumpkin Cake Roll** (Pg. 148); **Southern Pecan Cheesecake** (Pg. 148); **Cranberry Streusel Pie** (Pg. 148).

MEALS IN MINUTES

Farm wife Mary Ellen Agnew of Dundalk, Ontario knows that minutes matter at mealtime with a husband who works two jobs (both "on" and "off" the farm), plus a son working hard to improve his various sports skills after school.

"I could use a different 'Meals in Minutes' menu almost every day!" she says with a laugh.

Mary Ellen's own formula for fast fare uses seasonal foods and can be served up in *30 minutes or less.*

She begins her speedy supper by preparing the lightly seasoned chicken dish (you may want to add some ground white pepper). Cortland apples are great with the chicken, but McIntosh works too, depending on availability.

While the chicken simmers, Mary Ellen heats water for noodles, cleans the green beans and scalds and peels the peaches for dessert.

"To save time with the dessert, I use my own raspberry freezer jam, or frozen or fresh raspberries, dusted with sugar," she notes.

CREAMY CHICKEN AND APPLES

- 1 tablespoon vegetable oil
- 4 chicken breast halves, flattened to 1/2-inch thickness
- 1 medium cooking onion, peeled and sliced
- 1/2 cup chicken broth
- 1/4 cup dry white wine *or* apple juice *or* water
- 1/4 teaspoon leaf thyme
- 1/4 teaspoon salt
- 4 medium red cooking apples, cored and cut in 1/8-inch slices
- 1 tablespoon all-purpose flour
- 3/4 cup light cream *or* evaporated milk
- Cooked egg noodles

Heat oil in frying pan; saute chicken with onion until golden brown on both sides. Reduce heat; add chicken broth, wine/juice/water, thyme and salt. Cover; simmer for 10 minutes. Remove chicken from pan; keep warm. Add apples to pan; cover and simmer for 3-5 minutes until apples are fork-tender, stirring occasionally. Dissolve the flour in cream/milk; stir into pan, cook and stir until slightly thickened. Spoon the sauce over chicken. Serve with egg noodles cooked according to package directions. **Yield:** 4 servings.

GARDEN GREEN BEANS

- 1 pound fresh green beans, washed and stemmed
- Water
- Salt
- Butter

Cook beans in medium saucepan in enough boiling salted water until tender/crisp, about 6 minutes. Drain; dot with butter. **Yield:** 4 servings.

QUICK PEACH MELBA

- 4 fresh ripe peaches, peeled and halved
- 1 pint French vanilla ice cream
- 1/2 cup raspberry freezer jam *or* sugared frozen *or* fresh raspberries
- Sugar cookies, optional

Place a peach half in the bottom of a sherbet dish; top with a scoop of ice cream. Drizzle 2 tablespoons (or more if desired) of jam over top of ice cream. Serve with a sugar cookie, if desired. **Yield:** 4 servings.

Here's another chicken dish that's tasty and quick!

CHICKEN PARMESAN

Vonda Miller, Osgood, Indiana

✓ This tasty dish uses less sugar, salt and fat. Recipe includes *Diabetic Exchanges*.

- 6 chicken breast *halves**, boned, skinned (1-1/2 pounds)
- 1/4 cup butter
- 1/2 cup Parmesan cheese
- 1/2 cup bread crumbs
- 1 tablespoon paprika
- 1/4 to 1/2 teaspoon garlic powder
- 1-1/2 teaspoons Italian seasoning *or* 1/2 teaspoon *each* of rosemary, oregano and basil

*Chicken parts may be substituted for chicken breasts—allow 7 minutes per pound of chicken for cooking. Melt butter in 8-in. x 12-in. glass pan. Dip both sides of chicken in butter. Combine remaining ingredients on paper plate; roll chicken in mixture. Place chicken in dish, with thicker edges toward outside. Cover loosely with waxed paper. Microwave on high for 12 minutes, rotating dish once. **Yield:** 6 servings. *Conventional Method:* Omit waxed paper. Bake at 350° for 35-45 minutes. **Diabetic Exchanges:** One serving equals 3 protein, 1/2 bread, 1 fat; also, 283 calories, 284 mg sodium, 114 mg cholesterol, 7 gm carbohydrate.

P ack up the pickup (or station wagon) and head for the football field or out to the neighborhood woods...it's time for a tailgate party!

Fill the picnic basket and coolers with these good eats—they'll make it easy to satisfy hearty appetites whetted by autumn's crisp air and cooler temperatures.

Start with a thermos filled with hot mulled cider. Tuck in a spicy popcorn snack. Add some substan-

tial main dishes, including meats that have the taste of outdoor grilling without the fuss, and pasties, the perfect, portable meal-in-one. Round out your tailgate party with crunchy vegetable salads and chewy, tasty cornmeal rolls.

Enjoy the company of friends and family...and the satisfaction of preparing these flavorful country classics.

TAILGATE TREATS: Clockwise from lower left—**Barbecued Chinese-Style Spareribs** (Pg. 149); **Cornmeal Rolls** (Pg. 149); **Harvest Popcorn** (Pg. 149); **Broccoli/Bacon/Raisin Salad** (Pg. 149); **Crunchy Cabbage Salad** (Pg. 150); **Appetizer Meatballs** (Pg. 150); **Finnish Pasties** (Pg. 150); **Hot Mulled Cider** (Pg. 149).

Pour the coffee...and pass the dessert! Every good tailgate party or picnic needs a supply of great-tasting portable treats—and the four cookie recipes featured here certainly fit the bill!

Baked to fill a large hand, the Mississippi Oatmeal Cookies and Mother's Oatmeal Cookies both bring country kitchens and Grandma's cookie jar to mind.

Bar cookies are synonymous with pot-lucks and picnics, and these easy, cake-mix-based Pumpkin Cake Bars and Caramel Turtle Brownies are two of the best-tasting take-alongs we've seen. Try them and find out for yourself!

SWEET SUSTENANCE: Clockwise from lower left—**Pumpkin Cake Bars** (Pg. 151); **Mississippi Oatmeal Cookies** (Pg. 150); **Mother's Old-Fashioned Oatmeal Cookies** (Pg. 150); **Caramel Turtle Brownies** (Pg. 151).

HERB SCALLOPED TOMATOES

Lorrie Martin, Phoenix, Arizona

(PICTURED ON PAGE 140)

4 cups canned tomatoes, cut up
2-1/2 cups herb stuffing mix, *divided*
1 small onion, chopped
2 tablespoons sugar
1/2 teaspoon salt
1/2 teaspoon nutmeg
1/2 teaspoon leaf oregano, crumbled
1/4 teaspoon leaf rosemary, crumbled
1/4 teaspoon black pepper
1/4 cup butter

In a buttered 2-qt. casserole, mix together tomatoes and *2 cups* of stuffing mix. Stir in onion, sugar and seasonings. Dot with butter; sprinkle remaining stuffing mix on top. Bake at 375° for 45 minutes. **Yield:** 8 servings.

PHEASANT WITH CREAMY YOGURT SAUCE

Pat Breidenbach, Mitchell, South Dakota

(PICTURED ON PAGE 140)

1 cup fine, dry bread *or* cracker crumbs
1/4 cup grated Parmesan cheese
1 to 2 tablespoons dried minced onion
1/2 teaspoon garlic powder
1 teaspoon seasoned salt
1/4 teaspoon dried leaf oregano, crumbled
1/4 teaspoon dried leaf thyme, crumbled
Dash pepper
4 whole pheasant *or* chicken breasts, skinned, boned and halved lengthwise
1 cup mayonnaise *or* plain yogurt
1/4 cup margarine *or* butter, melted
2 teaspoons sesame seeds
CREAMY YOGURT SAUCE:
1 can (10-3/4 ounces) cream of chicken soup, undiluted
1 carton (8 ounces) plain yogurt
1/2 cup chicken broth
1 teaspoon lemon juice
1/2 teaspoon Worcestershire sauce
Dash garlic powder
Dash seasoned salt

In shallow dish, combine bread/cracker crumbs, cheese, onion, garlic powder, seasoned salt, oregano, thyme and pepper. Rinse pheasant/chicken and pat dry; coat with mayonnaise/yogurt and roll in crumb mixture. Place pheasant in a lightly greased 13-in. x 9-in. x 2-in. baking dish. Drizzle margarine/butter on top. Sprinkle with sesame seeds. Bake, uncovered, at 375° for 40-45 minutes until tender. Make sauce by combining all ingredients in medium saucepan and cooking over a low heat until heated through, stirring occasionally. **Yield:** 8 servings with 2-1/2 cups sauce.

CRANBERRY PLUS RELISH

Marion Reeder, Medford, New Jersey

(PICTURED ON PAGE 140)

4 cups (1 pound) fresh *or* frozen cranberries
4 oranges, peeled, sectioned and seeded
2 cups sugar (add less for tart taste)
1 apple, unpeeled, cut up
1/2 teaspoon almond flavoring
1 can (8-1/2 ounces) undrained crushed pineapple

Chop cranberries in a food processor, then add oranges and chop. Add remaining ingredients; pulse for several seconds to blend. Chill several hours before serving. **Yield:** 7-1/2 cups.

POTATO BREAD

Lynn Clarke, Bellevue, Idaho

(PICTURED ON PAGE 140)

 This tasty dish uses less sugar, salt and fat. Recipe includes *Diabetic Exchanges.*

1 pound potatoes, about 2 cups mashed
1-1/2 cups milk
1/3 cup butter
2 tablespoons honey
2 teaspoons salt
2 packages active dry yeast
1/2 cup warm water (110°)
2 eggs
About 8 cups all-purpose flour

Peel potatoes and boil until tender; drain and mash. Slowly stir in milk, butter, honey and salt. If necessary, heat to 110°. Meanwhile, in large bowl, mix yeast with water; let stand 5 minutes. Combine potato mixture, eggs and 3 cups flour. Gradually mix in 3-1/2 cups more flour. Turn out on floured board; knead until smooth and elastic, about 10 minutes, adding additional flour as needed. Place dough in greased bowl; turn to grease top. Cover; let rise in warm place until doubled, about 1-1/2 to 2 hours. Punch dough down; divide in thirds. Shape each portion into a smooth loaf; place in three well greased 9-in. x 5-in. bread pans. Cover; let rise in warm place until almost double, about 30-40 minutes. Bake at 350° for 35-40 minutes or until loaves are browned and sound hollow when tapped. Turn out of pans; cool on racks. Brush with butter, if desired. **Yield:** 3 loaves (20 slices each). **Diabetic Exchanges:** One serving equals 1 bread; also, 76 calories, 89 mg sodium, 12 mg cholesterol, 13 gm carbohydrate, 2 gm protein, 2 gm fat.

RABBIT DIJON

Kathryn Wolter, Sturgeon Bay, Wisconsin

(PICTURED ON PAGE 140)

2 rabbits *or* chickens, cut in serving pieces
Salt
Pepper
1 cup all-purpose flour
8 tablespoons butter, *divided*
1/4 cup brandy *or* chicken broth
1 cup chopped green onion
1/2 cup chopped parsley
1 pound fresh mushrooms, sliced
2 tablespoons Dijon mustard
1 pint sour cream
Parsley for garnish

Sprinkle rabbit/chicken pieces with salt and pepper; roll in flour. Melt 4 tablespoons butter in large skillet; brown meat pieces and remove to roaster. Add the brandy/broth to pan juices. Scrape browned bits from bottom and sides of skillet; pour over meat. Saute onion, parsley and mushrooms in remaining butter. Pour vegetable mixture over meat; cover and bake at 350° for 1 hour. Remove meat pieces to warm platter; stir mustard and sour cream into liquid in roaster and heat. Pour sauce over meat on platter. (Mustard and sour cream may also be stirred into onion, parsley, mushroom and liquid and baked as above.) **Yield:** 8 servings.

OVEN-FRIED POTATOES

Mary Arnold, Long Prairie, Minnesota

(PICTURED ON PAGE 141)

4 large baking potatoes,
  unpeeled
1/4 cup vegetable oil
1 to 2 tablespoons Parmesan
  cheese
1/2 teaspoon salt
1/4 teaspoon garlic powder
1/4 teaspoon paprika
1/8 teaspoon pepper

Wash unpeeled potatoes and cut lengthwise into 4 wedges. Place skin side down in 13-in. x 9-in. x 2-in. baking dish or pan. Combine remaining ingredients; brush over potatoes. Bake at 375° for 1 hour, brushing with oil/cheese mixture at 15-minute intervals. Turn potatoes over for last 15 minutes. (These are wonderful with any roasted meat or great as a snack.) **Yield:** 4 servings.

SMOTHERED GREEN CABBAGE

Joan Knox, Chicago, Illinois

(PICTURED ON PAGE 141)

1/4 cup butter *or* margarine
2 tablespoons bacon drippings*
1 medium head of cabbage,
  coarsely chopped, core
  removed
1/4 teaspoon dry minced garlic
1 teaspoon caraway seeds
Salt, pepper to taste
1 can (10-3/4 ounces) cream of
  mushroom soup, undiluted

Melt butter and bacon drippings in large saucepan or Dutch oven. Add cabbage; cook and stir over medium heat until cabbage is tender/crisp, about 10 minutes. Add garlic, caraway seeds, salt and pepper. Stir in soup; heat through and serve. **Yield:** 8 servings. (*Keep bacon drippings in small blocks in freezer to preserve fresh flavor.)

WILD RICE SOUP

Elmeda Johnson, East Grand Forks, Minnesota

(PICTURED ON PAGE 141)

1 cup uncooked wild rice
3 cups boiling water
2 strips smoked bacon
1/4 cup chopped onion
3/4 cup sliced celery
1/2 cup sliced carrots
1 can (14-1/2 ounces) chicken
  broth
2 cans (10-3/4 ounces *each*)
  cream of mushroom soup
2 soup cans milk
1 can (4 ounces) mushrooms,
  plus liquid
1 teaspoon seasoned salt
Pepper to taste

Combine rice and boiling water in large saucepan; simmer, covered, 50-60 minutes. Drain off excess liquid; set rice aside. Fry bacon till crisp; remove bacon and saute onion, celery and carrots in small amount of bacon fat. Combine broth, soups, milk, mushrooms, salt and pepper, reserved crumbled bacon, sauteed vegetables and wild rice. Simmer, covered, 1 hour. **Yield:** 8 servings.

CRANBERRY STREUSEL PIE

Mary Ellen Kiesner, Menomonee Falls, Wisconsin

(PICTURED ON PAGE 142)

1/3 cup butter, softened
3/4 cup sugar
1/4 cup brown sugar, packed
1 egg
1/2 teaspoon vanilla
1 cup all-purpose flour
1/2 teaspoon baking soda
1/4 teaspoon salt
2 cups fresh *or* thawed frozen
  cranberries*
1/2 cup chopped walnuts
1 unbaked pie shell (9 inches)
STREUSEL TOPPING:
2 tablespoons all-purpose flour
1/2 cup brown sugar, packed
1/4 teaspoon nutmeg
1/2 teaspoon cinnamon
2 tablespoons butter
1/2 cup chopped walnuts

Cream together butter and sugars. Beat in egg and vanilla. Sift together flour, baking soda and salt; stir into sugar mixture. (Dough is very thick.) Fold in cranberries *(thaw frozen cranberries in refrigerator) and walnuts. Spread carefully into pie shell. Bake at 350° for about 50 minutes or until pie test done with a wooden pick. While pie bakes, blend topping ingredients until crumbly. Sprinkle topping over pie as soon as it's removed from oven; place an inverted bowl over pie and let steam 20 minutes. Serve warm or cool. (You may omit topping and serve pie with whipped cream or ice cream, if desired.) **Yield:** 8 servings.

PUMPKIN CAKE ROLL

Sally Weaver, New Baden, Illinois

(PICTURED ON PAGE 142)

CAKE:
3 eggs
1 cup sugar
2/3 cup cooked pumpkin
1 teaspoon lemon juice
3/4 cup all-purpose flour
1 teaspoon baking powder
2 teaspoons cinnamon
1 teaspoon ginger
1/2 teaspoon nutmeg
1/2 teaspoon salt
FILLING:
1 cup confectioners' sugar
2 packages (3 ounces *each*)
  cream cheese
4 tablespoons butter
1/2 teaspoon vanilla

To make cake, beat eggs in mixing bowl at high speed for 5 minutes; beat in sugar until blended. Stir in pumpkin and lemon juice. Combine flour, baking powder, spices and salt; fold into pumpkin mixture. Spread in greased and floured 15-in. x 10-in. x 1-in. jelly roll pan. Bake at 375° for 15 minutes. Remove cake from oven; turn out on clean linen towel liberally dusted with confectioners' sugar. Starting at narrow end, roll towel and cake together; cool. Make filling by combining ingredients and mixing until smooth. Unroll cooled cake; spread with filling to within 1 in. of edges. Roll back up; chill. Dust with additional confectioners' sugar before serving. **Yield:** 10-12 servings.

SOUTHERN PECAN CHEESECAKE

Katherine Brown, Minot, North Dakota

(PICTURED ON PAGE 142)

CRUST:
1-1/2 cups quick oats
1/2 cup finely chopped pecans
1/2 cup brown sugar
1/3 cup melted butter
FILLING:
5 packages (8 ounces *each*)
  cream cheese, softened
1-2/3 cups light brown sugar
5 eggs
1 teaspoon vanilla
2 cups chopped pecans,
  divided
Whipped cream, optional

To make crust, place oats in food processor or blender; process to consistency of flour. Combine oats with remaining crust ingredients; press into bottom of 10-in. springform pan. Chill. To make filling, beat cream cheese with mixer until fluffy; slowly add brown sugar and mix well. Add eggs, one at a time, mixing after each addition. Stir in vanilla and *half of nuts*. Mix and pour over crust. Bake at 350° for 1 hour; turn oven off but leave cake in oven for 30 minutes more. To reduce chance of cracks on top surface, run a knife around edge of cheesecake as soon as you remove it from the oven. Let cool to room temperature; chill 8 hours. Remove sides of pan. Press additional chopped pecans around sides and pipe top with whipped cream, if desired. **Yield:** 20-24 servings.

APPLE FRITTERS

Ruby Nelson, Mountain Home, Arkansas

(PICTURED ON PAGE 142)

1 beaten egg
1 cup milk
1 cup finely chopped *or* grated
   unpeeled cored apple
1/4 cup sugar
1/4 teaspoon salt
1 teaspoon grated orange peel
3 tablespoons orange juice
2 teaspoons vanilla
2 cups all-purpose flour
1 tablespoon baking powder
Vegetable oil for frying
Sifted confectioners' sugar

In mixing bowl, combine beaten egg, milk, chopped apple, sugar, salt, orange peel, juice and vanilla. Stir together flour and baking powder; fold into egg/apple mixture, stirring just until all flour is moistened. Drop batter by rounded teaspoon into hot oil (350°). Fry until deep golden brown, about 3-4 minutes, turning once. Drain fritters thoroughly on paper towels. Roll in sugar or sift sugar over tops. **Yield:** about 40 fritters.

HOT MULLED CIDER

Maxine Zook, Middlebury, Indiana

(PICTURED ON PAGE 145)

2 quarts fresh apple cider
1 teaspoon grated orange rind,
   (no white membrane)
1/2 teaspoon whole allspice
1/4 teaspoon mace
1/8 teaspoon salt, optional
1/2 teaspoon ground coriander
1 teaspoon whole cloves
1 tablespoon cinnamon candy
   (red hots)
Orange slices *or* whole cinnamon
   sticks

Bring all ingredients, except orange slices/cinnamon sticks, to boil in large kettle; reduce heat and simmer for 30 minutes. Serve hot with orange slices or whole cinnamon sticks. **Yield:** 8 one-cup servings.

BROCCOLI/BACON/ RAISIN SALAD

Kammy Hilby, Manchester, Iowa

(PICTURED ON PAGE 145)

1 bunch fresh broccoli,
   washed, drained and broken
   into flowerettes
1/2 cup chopped red onion
1 cup celery, chopped
1 pound bacon, fried crisp,
   drained and crumbled
1/2 cup hulled sunflower seeds
1/2 cup raisins
DRESSING:
3/4 cup mayonnaise
1/4 cup sugar
2 tablespoons vinegar

Combine salad ingredients together in large mixing bowl. Set aside. Combine dressing ingredients together thoroughly. Pour dressing over salad ingredients; stir to blend. Serve chilled. Refrigerate leftovers. **Yield:** 12 servings.

BARBECUED CHINESE- STYLE SPARERIBS

Mildred Danenhirsch, Bayville, New York

(PICTURED ON PAGE 144)

2 pounds pork spareribs
MARINADE:
2 cloves garlic, minced
3 tablespoons soy sauce
1 tablespoon cooking sherry
3 to 5 tablespoons hoisin
   sauce*
1 tablespoon honey
1 tablespoon chicken broth
1 tablespoon vegetable oil

Have butcher cut between each rib, halfway down, for easier eating of ribs. Trim off excess fat. Mix all marinade ingredients together. *Hoisin sauce, a reddish/brown, spicy, sweet sauce is available in the Oriental section of most supermarkets. Place ribs in a large container and pour marinade mixture over ribs. Marinate, in refrigerator, about 3 hours, turning ribs each hour. Roast ribs on a foil-covered rack in large pan at 400° for 45 minutes. Baste occasionally with any leftover marinade. **Yield:** 4 servings.

HARVEST POPCORN

Deanna House, Portage, Michigan

(PICTURED ON PAGE 144)

2 quarts freshly popped
   popcorn, *unsalted*
2 cans (1-3/4 ounces *each*)
   shoestring potatoes
1 cup salted mixed nuts
1/4 cup butter *or* margarine,
   melted
1 teaspoon dried dill weed
1 teaspoon Worcestershire
   sauce
1/2 teaspoon lemon/pepper
   seasoning
1/4 teaspoon garlic powder
1/4 teaspoon onion powder

In large roasting pan or aluminum foil turkey roasting pan, combine popcorn, shoestring potatoes and nuts. Set aside. In small bowl, combine melted butter, dill weed, Worcestershire sauce, lemon/pepper seasoning, garlic powder and onion powder. Pour over popcorn mixture, stirring until evenly coated. Bake in preheated 325° oven, 8-10 minutes, stirring mixture once. Cool. Store in airtight containers. **Yield:** 2-1/2 quarts.

CORNMEAL ROLLS

Marcella Swigert, Monroe City, Missouri

(PICTURED ON PAGE 144)

1/3 cup cornmeal (stone ground
   preferred)
1/2 cup sugar
2 teaspoons salt
1/2 cup shortening
2 cups milk
1 package active dry yeast
1/4 cup warm water (110-115°)
2 beaten eggs
4 cups flour *or* more as needed
Melted butter
Cornmeal

Cook cornmeal, sugar, salt, shortening and milk in medium saucepan until thick (like cooked cereal). Cool to lukewarm. Add yeast which has been dissolved in lukewarm water, then eggs. Beat thoroughly. Add flour to form soft dough. Knead well on lightly floured surface. Place in bowl; cover; let rise. Punch down. Roll out to 1-in. thickness; cut with 2-1/2-in. biscuit cutter. Brush with melted butter; dust with cornmeal. Place on greased cookie sheet; cover; let rise. Bake at 375° for 15 minutes. (Dough will keep in refrigerator for several days.) **Yield:** 18 rolls.

APPETIZER MEATBALLS

Nona Yohe, Rich Hill, Missouri

(PICTURED ON PAGE 145)

      2 pounds lean ground beef
      1 pound bulk pork sausage
      1 can (5 ounces) evaporated
        milk
      2 cups old-fashioned oats
    1/2 teaspoon ground pepper
      2 teaspoons chili powder
    1/2 teaspoon garlic powder
      2 to 3 teaspoons salt
      2 eggs
    1/2 cup chopped onions
*SAUCE:
      2 cups catsup
  1-1/2 cups brown sugar
      1 teaspoon liquid smoke
    1/2 teaspoon garlic powder
    1/2 cup chopped onions

Mix all meatball ingredients together; shape into small 1-in. diameter balls. Place in baking pan in single layer. Combine sauce ingredients and pour over meatballs. Bake at 350° for 1 hour. *(If you like sauce, you may want to double sauce recipe.) **Yield:** 9 dozen meatballs.

FINNISH PASTIES

Ruth Myers, Manchester, Michigan

(PICTURED ON PAGE 145)

CRUST:
      3 cups all-purpose flour
      1 teaspoon salt
      1 cup lard
      1 egg, beaten
      1 teaspoon vinegar
      5 tablespoons cold water
FILLING:
      2 cups potatoes, peeled and
        diced
    3/4 to 1 cup carrots, peeled and
        diced
    3/4 pound ground beef (can use
        part pork sausage)
    1/4 cup onions, diced 1/2 inch thick
  1-1/4 cups rutabaga, peeled and
        diced
      2 tablespoons Worcestershire
        sauce
Salt
Pepper
    1/4 teaspoon poultry seasoning
Butter
Egg glaze

Cut together flour, salt and lard in mixing bowl. Blend in beaten egg, vinegar and water. Chill dough while mixing filling. Combine filling ingredients (except butter and egg glaze.) Roll out pie crust into six to seven 6-in. rounds. Place approximately 1/2 cup of filling on one-half of pie crust. Put a pat of butter on filling; fold other half of pie crust over filling and pinch edges together. Repeat with other pasties. Brush with egg glaze made of beaten whole egg and 1 tablespoon of water. Make steam vents with fork in decorative starburst pattern. Bake at 375° for 15 minutes; reduce heat to 350° and bake for 60 minutes more. **Yield:** 6-7 pasties.

CRUNCHY CABBAGE SALAD

Elaine Kremenak, Grants Pass, Oregon

(PICTURED ON PAGE 145)

      1 head green cabbage
      4 green onions, sliced thinly
      1 package Oriental chicken-
        flavored noodle mix (reserve
        chicken flavor packet for
        dressing)
DRESSING:
    1/2 cup vegetable oil
      1 tablespoon sugar
    1/2 teaspoon black pepper
      1 package chicken flavoring
        from noodle mix
      2 tablespoons sesame seeds,
        toasted
    1/2 cup sliced almonds, toasted

Shred or finely chop cabbage. Add onions and noodles (crushed with your hands). Mix well; cover; set in refrigerator for 1 hour, no longer. Mix dressing ingredients thoroughly. Refrigerate until serving time. Toast seeds and almonds in oven at 350° for about 7 minutes. Toss dressing with cabbage mixture; add toasted seeds and almonds. **Yield:** 10 servings.

MOTHER'S OLD-FASHIONED OATMEAL COOKIES

Arlene Larges, Hacienda Heights, California

(PICTURED ON PAGE 146)

      1 cup margarine, softened
      1 cup light brown sugar
      1 cup granulated sugar
      2 unbeaten eggs, room
        temperature
      2 teaspoons vanilla extract
  1-1/4 cups sifted all-purpose flour
      1 teaspoon salt
      1 teaspoon baking soda
      1 teaspoon cinnamon
    1/2 teaspoon cloves
    1/2 teaspoon allspice
      3 cups old-fashioned oats
    3/4 cup chopped pecans
Confectioner's sugar

In large bowl, blend margarine, sugars, eggs and vanilla; beat until fluffy. Combine flour, salt, baking soda, cinnamon, cloves and allspice. Add to creamed mixture; mix to blend. Stir in oats and pecans. Drop by teaspoonsful onto cookie sheet lined with parchment paper. Flatten with floured fork to 2-in. diameter (will spread to 4 in. when baked). Bake at 350° for 12-15 minutes. Cool on cookie sheet; remove to cooling rack. Sift confectioners' sugar over tops. **Yield:** 3 dozen large cookies.

MISSISSIPPI OATMEAL COOKIES

Elizabeth McNeely, La Grange, Illinois

(PICTURED ON PAGE 146)

      1 egg, beaten
  1-3/4 cups sugar
    3/4 cup shortening (one-half
        butter; one-half vegetable
        shortening)
    1/2 cup milk
    1/4 teaspoon ginger
    1/4 teaspoon allspice
    1/4 teaspoon cloves
  2-1/2 cups all-purpose flour
  1-1/2 teaspoons baking soda
  1-1/2 teaspoons salt
      2 cups old-fashioned oats
      1 cup raisins
      1 egg white, beaten
Sugar for tops of cookies

Beat egg in mixing bowl; add sugar, shortening, milk and spices; blend. Stir in flour, baking soda and salt. Add oats and raisins; mix well. Chill dough overnight. Next morning, shape dough into golf-ball size balls. Flatten balls on ungreased cookie sheets to 2-in. diameter with fork dipped in beaten egg white and sprinkle with bit of sugar. Brush each cookie with beaten egg white and bake at 350° until golden brown, about 15 minutes for chewy cookie. Let cookies cool on cookie sheet for a few minutes; remove to wire rack to complete cooling. **Yield:** 2 dozen large cookies.

QUICK 'N' EASY APPETIZERS: Combine catsup and brown sugar to taste; add cocktail sausages or slices of hot dogs. Heat and serve in a slow cooker or a fondue pot.

● Spread 1 8-oz. package of cream cheese on a large plate. Top with cocktail sauce; sprinkle with drained canned or frozen shrimp. Serve with crackers.

CARAMEL TURTLE BROWNIES

Betsi Noser, Bowling Green, Kentucky

(PICTURED ON PAGE 146)

1 bag (14 ounces) caramels
1 can (5 ounces) evaporated milk (2/3 cup), *divided*
1 package (18-1/4 ounces) devil's food chocolate cake mix
6 tablespoons butter *or* margarine, melted
1/2 to 1 cup chopped nuts
1 package (6 ounces) semisweet chocolate chips
Pecan halves for garnish, optional

Unwrap caramels (there are enough for the cook to sneak a few) and place in saucepan with 2 tablespoons evaporated milk. Set aside. In a mixing bowl, combine the remaining evaporated milk, dry cake mix, melted butter/margarine and the nuts. Stir until well-blended. Spread half of this mixture in a greased 13-in. x 9-in. x 2-in. baking pan. (Mixture will form thin layer in pan.) Bake at 350° for 10 minutes only. Meanwhile, melt the caramels over medium to low heat; stir constantly. Be careful not to burn. Remove brownies from oven; sprinkle with chocolate chips and drizzle melted caramels over the top. Cover evenly. Drop remaining cake mixture by teaspoons over all. Return pan to oven for 20 minutes more. *Do not overbake.* Cut while warm but do not remove from pan until completely cooled. They must "set up". Garnish with toasted pecan halves, if desired. **Yield:** 24 brownies.

PUMPKIN CAKE BARS

Martha Sue Stroud, Clarksville, Texas

(PICTURED ON PAGE 146)

4 eggs, well beaten
2 cups cooked pumpkin *or* 1 can (1 pound)
1-1/2 cups sugar
1/4 teaspoon salt
1 teaspoon ginger
1 teaspoon cinnamon
1/2 teaspoon cloves
1 package (18-1/4 ounces) yellow cake mix
1/2 cup butter, melted
1 cup chopped pecans
Whipped cream, optional

Mix eggs, pumpkin, sugar, salt, ginger, cinnamon and cloves together; pour into a 13-in. x 9-in. x 2-in. pan. Sprinkle dry cake mix on top. Drizzle melted butter over mix; spread chopped nuts over all. Bake at 325° for 1 hour and 20 minutes.

(Cover with foil loosely to keep from browning too soon for the first half of cooking time.) Cut into squares; serve topped with whipped cream, if desired. **Yield:** 24 bars.

BARBECUED MUFFIN MEATBALLS

Janet Siciak, Bernardston, Massachusetts

SAUCE:
6 tablespoons brown sugar
1/2 cup catsup
1/4 teaspoon nutmeg
2 teaspoons dry mustard
MEATBALLS:
1 pound ground beef
1 pound ground pork
2 eggs
1-1/2 cups seasoned dry bread crumbs
1 teaspoon salt
1/2 teaspoon black pepper
2 tablespoons finely chopped onion

Combine sauce ingredients in a small bowl; set aside. Combine the meats, eggs, bread crumbs, salt, pepper, onion and *half* of sauce; mix gently until all ingredients are blended. Shape mixture into 12 balls and place in 3-in.-deep muffin pans. Make a small indentation in each ball and fill with remaining sauce. Bake at 400° for 30 minutes. **Yield:** 12 meatballs.

POLYNESIAN MEATBALLS

Marcia Baures, Waukesha, Wisconsin

MEATBALLS:
1-1/2 pounds ground chuck
2-1/2 ounces chopped water chestnuts
3/4 cup quick oatmeal
1/2 teaspoon garlic salt
1/2 teaspoon onion salt
1 egg, beaten
1/2 teaspoon soy sauce
1/2 cup milk
SAUCE:
1 cup brown sugar
1/2 cup beef bouillon
1/2 cup vinegar
2 tablespoons cornstarch
2 teaspoons soy sauce
1/2 cup pineapple juice
1 can (8-1/2 ounces) pineapple tidbits, drained
1/2 cup chopped green pepper

Combine meatball ingredients; shape into balls and brown in oil. Drain and set aside. Combine sauce ingredients *except* pineapple tidbits and green pepper; boil until thick. Stir in pineapple,

green pepper and meatballs. Simmer for 30 minutes. **Yield:** 4 dozen meatballs.

MEXICAN SANDWICHES

Dianne Mutcher, Brighton, Colorado

3 pounds ground beef
1 onion, chopped
1 package (10 to 12 ounces) Longhorn cheese, shredded
1 can (15 ounces) tomato sauce
1 can (4 ounces) chopped ripe olives
1 can (4 ounces) salsa
2 dozen hard rolls

Brown ground beef and onion together; drain. Add remaining ingredients except rolls. Pinch bread out of center of rolls; fill with beef mixture. Wrap each roll in foil. Bake at 350° for 30 minutes. **Yield:** 2 dozen sandwiches.

WESTERN MEAL IN ONE

Fern Wenger, Sabetha, Kansas

1 pound ground beef
1 tablespoon vegetable oil
1 clove garlic
1/2 cup chopped onion
1/2 cup chopped green pepper
1 teaspoon salt
1 teaspoon chili powder
1 can (16 ounces) red beans, drained
2-1/2 cups tomatoes with juice, chopped
3/4 cup uncooked rice
3/4 cup grated cheddar cheese
1/4 cup sliced black olives

Brown beef in vegetable oil with garlic. Add the onion and green pepper; cook until onion is transparent. Drain off fat. In a 2-qt. casserole, combine the meat mixture, salt, chili powder, beans, tomatoes and rice. Bake, covered, at 350° for 30 minutes. Uncover and sprinkle with cheese and olives; bake for 15 minutes more. **Yield:** 6-8 servings.

COOL KITCHEN HINTS: To slice meat into thin strips for stroganoff or stir-fry, keep meat partially frozen, to make cutting easier.
● Save the juices from your spiced fruits and other canned fruits in the refrigerator; then use them to pour over ham slices while baking.
● To freeze meatballs, place them on a cookie sheet until frozen. Place in a plastic bag and they'll stay separated so you can remove as many as you want at a time.

AMISH SOUR CREAM APPLE PIE

Clara Yoder, Millersburg, Ohio

1 cup dairy sour cream
1 egg
3/4 cup sugar
2 tablespoons all-purpose flour
1/4 teaspoon salt
1 teaspoon vanilla
2-1/2 cups diced, peeled apples
1 unbaked 9-inch pie shell
CRUMB TOPPING:
1/2 cup brown sugar
1/3 cup all-purpose flour
1/4 cup butter
1 teaspoon cinnamon

Beat sour cream and egg together; add sugar, flour, salt and vanilla. Mix until smooth. Stir in apples. Bake at 400° for 25 minutes; remove pie from oven. Spread with crumb topping that has been mixed until crumbly. Bake 20 minutes more. **Yield:** 8 servings.

HOMEMADE PEANUT BUTTER CUPS

Collette Frederick, Lisbon, Iowa

1 cup semisweet chocolate chips
1 to 1-1/2 cups peanut butter, *divided*
2 tablespoons butter
Small paper liners (bonbon)

Mix chocolate, 2/3 cup peanut butter and butter together in glass measure and microwave on high for 1-1/2 to 2 minutes. Pour 1/2 of chocolate mixture in bottom of paper liners. Melt remaining peanut butter by microwaving on high for 1 minute. Spoon melted peanut butter on top of chocolate layer in liners and cover with remaining chocolate mixture. Cool; store covered. **Yield:** about 1 dozen.

DEL RIO CHILI CON QUESO

Roselle Coates, Big Spring, Texas

1 medium onion, finely chopped
1 tablespoon butter
1 can (4 ounces) chopped green chilies
1 can (8 ounces) jalapeno relish
1 jar (8 ounces) taco sauce
2 pounds process cheese spread, cubed
3 tablespoons milk

Saute onion in butter in 1-qt. glass measure. Add chilies, relish and taco sauce to onion/butter. Stir. Microwave cheese and milk in large mixing bowl on high until cheese is melted. Stir at 1-minute intervals. Add onion mixture. Serve warm with corn chips. **Yield:** 8-10 servings.

CHEESE PUFFS

Margaret Uhen, Waukesha, Wisconsin

3 green onions, finely chopped
1 cup shredded cheddar cheese
1/2 cup mayonnaise
24 toast rounds

Combine onions with cheese and mayonnaise. Spread on toast rounds. In shallow baking dish, microwave half the rounds for 1-1/2 to 2-1/2 minutes (or until bubbly) at 50-60% power. Turn baking dish once during cooking. Repeat with remaining puffs. Serve hot. **Yield:** 24 appetizers.

SNACK OYSTER CRACKERS

David Harter, Allendale, Michigan

1 box (1 pound) oyster crackers
1 cup vegetable oil
1 package reduced calorie ranch-style dressing mix
1-1/4 teaspoon dill weed
1 teaspoon lemon pepper seasoning

Place crackers in 6-quart bowl; set aside. Combine oil, dressing mix, dill weed and lemon pepper; whip well. Pour over crackers; mix thoroughly. Spread on cookie sheet. Bake at 250° for 1 hour; stirring three times. Store in airtight container. Delicious as snack or great with soups. **Yield:** about 10 servings.

BREADED ASPARAGUS STICKS

Linda Ordorff, Waverly, Minnesota

2 pounds asparagus spears
1-1/2 cups grated Parmesan cheese
1-1/2 cups fresh bread crumbs
2 eggs, beaten
1/2 teaspoon salt
Dash hot pepper sauce
2 tablespoons butter *or* margarine
2 tablespoons olive oil
Grated Parmesan cheese, optional

Cook the asparagus in a small amount of water until crisp-tender. Drain well. Combine 1-1/2 cups cheese and the bread crumbs on a plate. In a shallow bowl, stir together eggs, salt and hot pepper sauce. Dip each asparagus spear in egg mixture and roll in crumbs to coat well. Chill 20 minutes. In a skillet, heat butter and oil on medium-high. Brown the spears in a single layer, turning carefully. Remove and keep warm while browning the remaining spears. Serve with additional Parmesan cheese, if desired. **Yield:** 6 side-dish servings.

SPICY SHRIMP

Roselle Coates, Big Spring, Texas

1 package (10 ounces) frozen medium-size shrimp, defrosted, rinsed
1/4 cup melted butter (may substitute 1/4 cup white wine)
1/2 teaspoon garlic powder
1/2 teaspoon parsley flakes
1/8 teaspoon black pepper
1/8 teaspoon salt
1/8 teaspoon tarragon
1 small bay leaf
Dash red pepper flakes *or* pimiento

Combine all ingredients in 2-qt. casserole. Cover with wax paper. Microwave on high for 3-1/2 to 6 minutes or until shrimp are opaque, stirring every 2 minutes. Let stand 3-5 minutes. Remove bay leaf. Serve hot in chafing dish. **Yield:** 6 appetizer servings.

MICROWAVE MAPLE SYRUP

Kathleen Davison, Braddyville, Iowa

1 cup white sugar
1 cup brown sugar
1 cup white corn syrup
1 cup water
1 teaspoon maple flavoring

Combine all ingredients in 2-qt. glass measure. Microwave on high until mixture boils. Boil 5-7 minutes, stirring twice. Store in sterilized syrup bottle and reheat in microwave (remove metal cap). **Yield:** about 1 quart.

APPETIZER ANGLE: Spread cream cheese combined with dill weed on party rye bread slices. Top each with a cucumber slice; sprinkle lightly with dill weed.

MEALS IN MINUTES

Because her husband works long, unpredictable hours and baby-sitting her grandson leaves her little time for kitchen chores, Nancy Johnson of Laverne, Oklahoma appreciates recipes that can be prepared and served on short notice. That's why she stocks up on convenient foods like canned salmon—a tasty choice for her quick burgers.

Nancy starts her speedy supper by preparing Honey-Celery Seed Dressing in the blender, and refrigerating it until mealtime. This dressing is delicious over a variety of greens—cabbage, lettuce, even spinach.

While pan-frying or oven-broiling the Salmon Burgers, she cuts the salad ingredients and slices and toasts whole-wheat buns. You might want to make macaroni and cheese or another side dish, but potato chips will do in a pinch.

For a flavorful finish to a fast feast, she serves up cups of lemon-flavored frozen yogurt and small ginger snaps.

BROILED SALMON BURGERS

2 cups fine soft bread crumbs
2 large egg whites
1/4 cup chili sauce
1 tablespoon fresh lemon juice
1/4 cup minced green onions
1/2 cup finely shredded cheddar
  cheese
1/8 teaspoon ground black
  pepper
1 can (15-1/2 ounces) salmon,
  skinned, boned and drained
1 tablespoon butter, melted

Combine bread crumbs, egg whites, chili sauce, lemon juice, onions, cheese and pepper in medium-sized bowl and mix well. Flake salmon into bowl and blend gently. Form salmon mixture into five patties. Melt butter in non-stick skillet; pan-fry the patties over medium-low heat about 5 minutes on each side or until golden brown. (Patties may also be brushed with melted butter and oven-broiled, 3-4 in. from heat.) Serve on toasted whole wheat buns with extra chili sauce, if desired. **Yield:** 5 burgers.

CONFETTI COLESLAW

4 cups shredded green
  cabbage
1/2 cup diced red pepper
1/2 cup diced green pepper
**HONEY-CELERY
SEED DRESSING:**
3 tablespoons honey
1 teaspoon dry mustard
1 teaspoon paprika
1/4 teaspoon salt
1 tablespoon lemon juice
1/4 cup vinegar
1/8 teaspoon minced dried onion
1 cup vegetable oil
1 teaspoon celery seed

Combine cabbage and peppers in a glass bowl; refrigerate, covered. Next, combine honey, mustard, paprika, salt, lemon juice, vinegar and onion in blender. Slowly add oil through top opening, continuing to blend until thick. Stir in celery seed. Cover; store in refrigerator. Before serving coleslaw, spoon on dressing and toss to coat evenly. **Yield:** 8 servings; 1-1/2 cups dressing.

Here's another quick and easy vegetable recipe:

MICROWAVE VEGETABLE PLATE

Lois Wilger, Lamar, Colorado

Whole fresh mushrooms, cleaned
Summer squash, washed and diced
Cauliflower, broken into flowerettes
Broccoli, broken into flowerettes
Carrots, sliced in 1/2-inch slices
1 tablespoon butter
1 to 2 tablespoons water
Salt, optional

Arrange vegetables on round, flat dish with mushrooms in center, squash in next circle, followed by rings of cauliflower and broccoli. Place carrots around outer edge. Microwave butter and water on high until butter melts. Sprinkle plate of vegetables with mixture, cover tightly with wax paper. Microwave on high for 6-8 minutes, rotating plate every 2 minutes. Salt may be added after cooking, if desired.

If you feel "good old ground beef" can't go much further in the kitchen than humdrum hamburger, hold on tight—you're in for a delicious surprise!

These different ground beef recipes are sure to cause excitement at your table—and we'll bet plenty of them will become family favorites. See for yourself just how grand ground beef can be!

GROUND BEEF ROUNDUP: Clockwise from lower left—**Black Bean Chili Salad** (Pg. 161); **Chili Relleno Bake** (Pg. 161); **Barbecued Meatballs** (Pg. 161); **Shanghai Noodles with Spicy Beef Sauce** (Pg. 161); **Beef Casserole Italiano** (Pg. 162); **Sunday Supper Soup** (Pg. 162); **Tamale Pie** (Pg. 162); **Taco Tartlets** (Pg. 162).

Bored with burgers? Fed up with meat loaf? Can't face another casserole? Then try these tasty recipes. They'll restore your appetite for good old ground beef!

You'll never call Korean Beef Patties run-of-the-mill fare...not with their oriental flair! And Italian Vegetable Soup is a hearty meal-in-a-pot that's sure to become a favorite.

Colorful Mexican Lasagna features south-of-the-border flavor in an easy-to-make casserole. And who can resist a cheeseburger baked into a flaky crust in Crescent Cheeseburger Pie? Ground beef a bore? Not anymore!

GREAT GROUND BEEF: Top to bottom—**Korean Beef Patties** (Pg. 163); **Italian Vegetable Soup** (Pg. 163); **Mexican Lasagna** (Pg. 163); **Crescent Cheeseburger Pie** (Pg. 162).

BEST COOK

Barbara McDougal
Rachel, West Virginia

Making meals memorable is something Barbara McDougal does every school day, as she cooks and serves food to nearly 100 students, teachers and visitors at Downs Elementary School in Rachel, West Virginia. Her meals are so good that Janet Cunningham, one of the teachers there, nominated her as "Best Cook in the Country"!

"Downs is a small, rural school with 79 students, almost all of whom eat the hot lunch in our cafeteria every day. Barbara does the preparation and serving, turning out good home-cooked meals complete with rolls, desserts and special treats.

"Barbara takes time to get to know the children, smiling and talking to them as they go through the line. On holidays, she wears costumes—a witch for Halloween or Mrs. Santa Claus at Christmas—and that delights the children."

On "School Cook's Day" the students and staff of Downs honored Barbara by presenting her with a corsage and a book, written by the students, titled *Why We Think Our Cook Is Great*. Here are a couple excerpts:

"I like our cook because she is nice and her cooking is terrific. I love her pizza, macaroni and pepperoni rolls. She also gives a lot of whatever she has cooked." —*Shannon Fleeman*

"She's a very nice and sweet cook. She makes things people haven't heard of and tells us to taste it. It turns out good." —*Ashley Hillbury*

DEER JERKY

3 pounds venison
1/2 cup soy sauce
1/2 cup Worcestershire sauce
2 teaspoons monosodium glutamate
2 teaspoons table salt
2/3 teaspoon onion powder
2/3 teaspoon black pepper

Cut venison into 3/4-in. strips. Combine the remaining ingredients; pour over meat and refrigerate, covered, overnight. Drain; hang meat over the racks in your oven and bake at 150° or the lowest setting of your oven for 6 to 8 hours, until meat is dried.

PIZZA SAUCE

2 tablespoons oil
1 can (15 ounces) tomato puree
1 can (4-1/2 ounces) tomato paste
1/4 teaspoon parsley flakes
1/2 teaspoon salt
1/8 teaspoon pepper
1/8 teaspoon garlic powder
1 teaspoon oregano
1/2 cup water

Combine all ingredients; simmer 10 minutes on low heat. Bake pizza crust (see bread dough recipe at right) topped with sauce and pepperoni, if desired, at 350° for about 10 minutes. Add other favorite toppings (chopped green pepper, black olives, mushrooms) and shredded mozzarella cheese and bake another 10 minutes or until desired brownness. **Yield:** 1 pizza, 12 inches.

PEACH COBBLER

1/4 pound margarine
3 cups sliced peaches, including syrup
2 cups all-purpose flour
2 teaspoons baking powder
1 teaspoon salt
2 cups sugar
2 cups milk

Melt margarine in bottom of 13-in x 9-in. x 2-in. pan. Add peaches and syrup to melted butter. Combine remaining ingredients; pour over peaches and margarine. Bake at 350° for 45-50 minutes, or until golden brown. Serve in a bowl with milk and sugar or with ice cream on top, if desired. **Yield:** 12 servings.

BASIC BREAD DOUGH

5 cups very warm water
2 eggs, slightly beaten
1/4 cup instant yeast
1/8 cup salt
1 cup sugar
1 cup oil
5 to 5-1/2 pounds flour

Combine water, eggs, yeast, salt, sugar and oil in the order given. Mix. Add 5 lbs. of flour; mix well. If dough is sticky, add a little more flour. Knead about 5 minutes. Put into well-oiled bowl and cover with plastic wrap. Let rise in warm place until double. Dough may be shaped into rolls, loaves, pepperoni rolls* or pizza crust. **Yield:** 2 loaves or 18 rolls or 24 pepperoni rolls or 2 pizza crusts.

*PEPPERONI ROLLS: Form dough into balls about the size of an egg; flatten with hand and place several slices of pre-sliced pepperoni or two pepperoni sticks about 2 in. long and 1/4 in. wide in the middle. Roll, closing ends, and place rolled side down in a greased pan. You may also roll whole wieners this way for wiener wraps. Bake at 350° for 20-25 minutes. **Yield:** 18-24 rolls.

STRAWBERRY BANANA NUT BREAD

1 stick softened margarine
3 eggs
1 cup sugar
1/2 pint fresh strawberries, chopped
3 medium sliced ripe bananas, mashed
1/2 cup milk
1/2 cup chopped nuts
3 cups all-purpose flour
4 teaspoons baking powder
1/2 teaspoon salt

Beat together margarine, eggs and sugar. Stir in strawberries and bananas (strawberries may remain chunky). Add milk, nuts, flour, baking powder and salt. Divide between three 7-3/8-in. x 3-5/8-in x 2-1/4-in. greased loaf pans and bake at 350° for 35-40 minutes. Let cool 1/2 hour before slicing. Spread with butter or eat plain. **Yield:** 3 loaves.

arm market fresh! Bushels of brightly polished red and green apples...brilliantly colored varieties of late summer and winter squash...gunny sacks bursting with freshly harvested potatoes—all sure signs of autumn along country roads.

Here's to the roadside entrepreneur who peddles produce with pride! Pack home a peck of harvest's best and celebrate the season with a lovely Pumpkin Soup... creamy Cajun Cabbage...colorful Cranberry Orange Bread...rich Sweet Potato Pie or Souffle...savory "Feast" Pork Chops...or zesty Potato Romanoff, an elegant, easy-to-make cousin of popular twice-baked potatoes.

Try these recipes for a delicious taste of autumn's bounty!

AUTUMN'S ABUNDANCE: Clockwise from lower left—**Baked Cajun Cabbage** (Pg. 163); **Potatoes Romanoff** (Pg. 164); **Sweet Potato Souffle** (Pg. 164); **Pumpkin Soup** (Pg. 164); **Cranberry Orange Bread** (Pg. 164); **Sweet Potato Pie** (Pg. 164); **Squash Dressing** (Pg. 164); **"Feast" Pork Chops** (Pg. 164).

A ah-h-h, apples! Is there anything that says "autumn" quite as naturally as sweet, crunchy apples? Gather up an orchard's finest and use them in our bound-to-please Taffy Apple Salad...luscious Apple Cream Tart...easy-to-make Creamy Apple Squares...or old-fashioned, oven-baked Quick Apple Dumpling Rolls.

Fill *your* kitchen with the mouth-watering aroma of cooked apples today!

APPETIZING APPLES! Clockwise from lower left—**Quick Apple Dumpling Rolls** (Pg. 165); **Apple Cream Tart** (Pg. 165); **Taffy Apple Salad** (Pg. 165); **Creamy Apple Squares** (Pg. 165).

CHILI RELLENO BAKE

Jan Seibert, Albion, California

(PICTURED ON PAGE 154)

1/2 pound ground beef
1/2 pound chorizo *or* pork
    sausage
1 cup onion, chopped
2 cloves garlic, minced *or*
    pressed
2 cans (4 ounces *each*) whole
    green chilies, drained and
    seeded, *divided*
2 cups shredded sharp cheddar
    cheese, *divided*
4 eggs
1/4 cup all-purpose flour,
    unsifted
1-1/2 cups milk
1/2 teaspoon salt
Hot pepper sauce to taste

In a large skillet, crumble together the beef and chorizo or sausage. Cook over medium heat, stirring until meat is browned. Add onion and garlic; cook until onion is limp. Drain off fat. Line a 9-in. x 9-in. x 2-in. baking dish with half of the chilies; top with 1-1/2 cups of the cheese. Add the meat mixture and top with remaining chilies; set aside. Beat together eggs and flour until smooth; add milk, salt and hot pepper sauce. Blend well. Pour the egg mixture over casserole. Bake uncovered, at 350° for about 40 minutes or until knife inserted off-center comes out clean. Sprinkle remaining 1/2 cup cheese on top. Let stand 5 minutes before serving. **Yield:** 6 servings.

BARBECUED MEATBALLS

Connie Johnson, Friona, Texas

(PICTURED ON PAGE 154)

MEATBALLS:
3 pounds ground beef
1 can (12 ounces) evaporated
    milk
1 cup oatmeal
1 cup cracker crumbs
2 eggs
1/2 cup chopped onion
1/2 teaspoon garlic powder
2 teaspoons salt
1/2 teaspoon pepper
2 teaspoons chili powder
SAUCE:
2 cups catsup
1 cup brown sugar

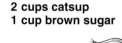

1/2 teaspoon liquid smoke *or* to
    taste
1/2 teaspoon garlic powder
1/4 cup chopped onion

To make meatballs, combine all ingredients (mixture will be soft) and shape into walnut-size balls. Place meatballs in a single layer on wax paper-lined cookie sheets; freeze until solid. Store frozen meatballs in freezer bags until ready to cook. To make sauce, combine all ingredients and stir until sugar is dissolved. Place frozen meatballs in a 13-in. x 9-in. x 2-in. baking pan; pour on the sauce. Bake at 350° for 1 hour. **Yield:** 80 meatballs.

BLACK BEAN CHILI SALAD

Carmen Gratton, New Smyrna Beach, Florida

(PICTURED ON PAGE 154)

1 package (12 ounces) black
    beans
2 cups chopped onion, *divided*
12 cloves chopped garlic, *divided*
2 cans (20 ounces *each*) whole
    tomatoes, chopped,
    undrained
1 pound ground beef
1 green pepper, chopped
1 teaspoon salt
1 teaspoon black pepper
2 tablespoons chili powder
1-1/2 tablespoons ground cumin
1/8 teaspoon crushed red pepper
ACCOMPANIMENTS:
Tortilla chips
1 cup shredded cheddar cheese
1 cup thinly sliced lettuce
1 mashed avocado
1/2 cup sour cream

In large cast-iron pot, cover the black beans with water and bring to a boil. Turn off heat; let the beans soak for at least 4 hours. Turn on heat; add 1-1/2 cups onions and 8 cloves garlic; simmer until beans are tender. Drain liquid from beans. (Beans can be cooked in advance and frozen until needed.) Add tomatoes to beans and cook on low heat. Meanwhile, brown ground beef in skillet with remaining onion, green pepper, 4 cloves garlic, salt, pepper, chili powder, cumin and red pepper. Drain off fat and add meat mixture to beans and tomatoes. Heat through. Serve on individual plates garnished with accompaniments, as desired. **Yield:** 8 servings.

SHANGHAI NOODLES WITH SPICY BEEF SAUCE

Ena Quiggle, Goodhue, Minnesota

(PICTURED ON PAGE 155)

3 tablespoons vegetable *or*
    peanut oil
2 teaspoons minced garlic
1-1/2 teaspoons minced fresh
    gingerroot
1/4 teaspoon crushed red pepper
    or to taste
1-1/2 cups chopped onion
1 pound ground beef
1/2 cup chicken broth, *divided*
1/3 cup hoisin sauce*
1/4 cup soy sauce
1/4 cup dry sherry *or* beef broth
2 tablespoons cornstarch
16 ounces vermicelli noodles,
    cooked and drained
2 tablespoons toasted
    sesame oil
1/2 cup diagonally sliced green
    onions

Heat wok or large skillet until hot; add vegetable/peanut oil, garlic, gingerroot and pepper flakes. Saute about 5 seconds. Add onion; stir-fry until onion is transparent. Crumble in ground beef; stir-fry until the meat is light brown. In a small bowl, combine 1/4 cup chicken broth, *hoisin sauce (can be found in the Oriental section of most supermarkets), soy sauce and sherry/ broth. Stir into meat mixture. Cover, reduce heat and simmer 10 minutes, stirring once or twice. Meanwhile, dissolve cornstarch in remaining chicken broth. Slowly stir into meat mixture; cook and stir until the sauce is thick. In separate bowl, combine the hot vermicelli and sesame oil. Pour sauce over top; toss gently to combine. Serve topped with the green onions. **Yield:** 4-6 servings.

CRAB DELIGHTS

Marie Schomas, Homewood, Illinois

9 slices white bread
1 can (7-1/2 ounces) crabmeat,
    flaked
1 small onion, grated
1 cup grated cheddar cheese
1 cup mayonnaise
1 teaspoon curry powder
1/2 teaspoon salt

Remove crusts from bread; cut each slice into 4 squares, strips or triangles. Mix together remaining ingredients; spread evenly on bread. Place on cookie sheet; broil till golden and bubbly. **Yield:** 36 appetizers.

BEEF CASSEROLE ITALIANO

Susan Longyear, Washington, Virginia

(PICTURED ON PAGE 155)

1 pound ground beef
1/4 cup chopped yellow onion
2 cans (8 ounces *each*) tomato sauce
1 teaspoon parsley flakes
1/2 teaspoon leaf oregano
1 teaspoon leaf basil
1/2 teaspoon salt, *divided*
1/4 teaspoon pepper
2 packages (10 ounces *each*) frozen chopped spinach, thawed and drained well
2 cups ricotta cheese
1 package (8 ounces) mozzarella cheese slices

Brown ground beef and onion; drain off fat. Stir in the tomato sauce, parsley, oregano, basil, 1/4 teaspoon salt and pepper. Simmer, uncovered, for 10 minutes, stirring occasionally. Meanwhile, combine spinach, ricotta cheese and remaining 1/4 teaspoon salt. Spoon spinach mixture around edges of 13-in. x 9-in. x 2-in. baking dish; pour beef mixture into center. Cut each mozzarella slice into three strips and arrange in a lattice pattern over meat. Bake at 375° for 20 minutes. **Yield:** 8 servings.

SUNDAY SUPPER SOUP

Margaret Gage, Roseboom, New York

(PICTURED ON PAGE 155)

MEATBALLS:
1-1/2 pounds ground beef
1 egg, slightly beaten
3 tablespoons water
1/2 cup dry bread crumbs
1/4 teaspoon salt
1 tablespoon chopped parsley
2 tablespoons butter
SOUP:
2 cups water
1 can (10-1/2 ounces) condensed beef broth, undiluted
1 can (1 pound, 12 ounces) tomatoes, undrained, chopped
1 envelope (1-3/8 ounces) dry onion soup mix
1 cup sliced carrots
1/4 cup chopped celery tops
1/4 cup chopped parsley
1/4 teaspoon black pepper
1/4 teaspoon dried oregano leaves
1/4 teaspoon dried basil leaves
1 bay leaf

To make the meatballs, combine beef, egg, water, bread crumbs, salt and parsley. Mix lightly; shape into 24 balls. In 5-qt. Dutch oven, melt butter and brown meatballs, a single layer at a time, on all sides. Drain off fat; remove meatballs and set aside. To make soup, combine ingredients in same Dutch oven. Bring to boiling. Reduce heat; cover and simmer for 20 minutes. Add meatballs; simmer 20 minutes longer. Remove bay leaf. **Yield:** 6-8 servings (about 2 quarts).

TACO TARTLETS

LaVonne Hartel, Williston, North Dakota

(PICTURED ON PAGE 155)

MEAT SHELLS:
1 pound ground beef
2 tablespoons taco seasoning mix
2 tablespoons ice water
FILLING:
1 cup dairy sour cream
2 tablespoons red taco sauce
2 ounces chopped ripe olives
1 cup coarsely crushed tortilla chips, *divided*
1/2 cup shredded cheddar cheese
Additional taco sauce for garnish

To make meat shells, combine ingredients; mix well. Press meat mixture into bottom and sides of tiny tart pans and set aside. Combine sour cream, taco sauce, olives and 3/4 cup tortilla chips. Spoon filling into each shell, mounding slightly. Combine remaining chips and cheese; sprinkle over each tartlet. Bake at 375° for 10 minutes. Garnish with taco sauce. **Yield:** 32 tartlets.

TAMALE PIE

Naomi Giddis, Grawn, Michigan

(PICTURED ON PAGE 155)

FILLING:
1 pound ground beef
1 cup chopped onion
1 green pepper, chopped
1 can (15 ounces) tomato sauce
1 can (28 ounces) tomatoes, cut up
1 can (17 ounces) whole kernel corn, drained
1/2 cup sliced pitted ripe olives
1 clove garlic, minced
1 tablespoon sugar
1/2 teaspoon salt
2 teaspoons chili powder
Dash black pepper
1 cup shredded cheddar cheese

CRUST:
3/4 cup yellow cornmeal
1/2 teaspoon salt
2 cups cold water
1/2 teaspoon chili powder
1 tablespoon butter
Shredded cheese for garnish, optional

To make filling, brown ground beef, onions and green pepper; drain. Add the remaining ingredients except for cheese. Bring to boil; simmer, uncovered for 20 minutes or until thickened. Add the cheese; stir until melted. Set aside. To make crust, combine cornmeal, salt, water and chili powder in saucepan. Cook on medium-high, stirring constantly, until thick. Add butter; mix well. Spread half of crust mixture over bottom of a 12-in. x 8-in. x 2-in. baking dish. (Note: Recipe is pictured in 9-in. square dish.) Add filling; spoon on the remaining crust. Bake at 375° for 45 minutes. Top with shredded cheese, if desired. **Yield:** 6 servings.

CRESCENT CHEESEBURGER PIE

Elinore Dumont, Drumheller, Alberta

(PICTURED ON PAGE 156)

1 pound ground beef
1/2 cup chopped onion
1 can (8 ounces) tomato sauce
1 can (4 ounces) chopped mushrooms, drained
1/4 cup chopped parsley
1/4 teaspoon salt
1/4 teaspoon dried oregano, crushed
1/8 teaspoon pepper
2 packages (8 rolls *each*) refrigerated crescent rolls
3 eggs, *separated*
6 slices (6 ounces) American cheese
1 tablespoon water

Brown the ground beef and onion until onion is transparent; drain off fat. Stir in tomato sauce, mushrooms, parsley, salt, oregano and pepper; set aside. Unroll 1 package of rolls and separate dough into triangles. In lightly greased 9-in. pie plate, arrange triangles with pointed ends to the center and press edges together to form a pie shell. Separate eggs; beat together whites from 3 eggs plus yolks from 2 eggs. Pour *half* of beaten egg mixture over pie shell. Spoon meat mixture into shell; arrange cheese slices on top. Spread with remaining beaten egg mixture. Mix reserved egg yolk with water and set aside. Unroll second package of rolls; place four sections of dough together

162

to form a 12-in. x 6-in. rectangle. Press edges and perforations together; roll dough into a 12-in. square. Brush edges of bottom crust with egg yolk/water mixture; place dough on top of filling. Trim; seal and flute edges. Cut slits in top crust. Brush top with the remaining egg yolk/water mixture. Loosely cover edge with foil strip to prevent over-browning. Bake at 350° for 20 minutes; cover center of pie loosely with foil and bake 20 minutes longer. Let stand 10 minutes before serving. **Yield:** 6 servings.

MEXICAN LASAGNA

Jeanne Bennett, Minden, Louisiana

(PICTURED ON PAGE 156)

1-1/2 pounds ground beef
1-1/2 teaspoons ground cumin
   1 tablespoon chili powder
1/4 teaspoon garlic powder
1/4 teaspoon red pepper
   1 teaspoon salt *or* to taste
   1 teaspoon black pepper *or* to taste
   1 can (16 ounces) tomatoes, chopped
  10 to 12 corn tortillas
   2 cups small curd cottage cheese, drained
   1 cup shredded Monterey Jack cheese with peppers
   1 egg
1/2 cup shredded cheddar cheese
   2 cups shredded lettuce
1/2 cup chopped tomatoes
   3 green onions, chopped
1/4 cup sliced black olives

Brown ground beef; drain thoroughly. Add cumin, chili powder, garlic powder, red pepper, salt, black pepper and tomatoes; heat through. Cover bottom and sides of a 13-in. x 9-in. x 2-in. baking dish with tortillas. Pour beef mixture over tortillas; place a layer of tortillas over meat mixture and set aside. Combine cottage cheese, Monterey Jack cheese and egg; pour over tortillas. Bake at 350° for 30 minutes. Remove from oven; sprinkle cheddar cheese, lettuce, tomatoes, green onions and olives over casserole. **Yield:** 6-8 servings.

KOREAN BEEF PATTIES

Marsha Ransom, South Haven, Michigan

(PICTURED ON PAGE 156)

   1 pound ground beef
   4 tablespoons soy sauce
   2 tablespoons sugar
   1 tablespoon toasted sesame seeds, crushed

   1 tablespoon toasted sesame oil
2-1/2 tablespoons chopped green onion
   1 tablespoon garlic, minced
Black pepper to taste

Combine all ingredients. Form into four balls and flatten into patties. Broil, grill or pan-fry until done. **Yield:** 4 servings.

SALMON/CUCUMBER APPETIZER

Kay Schumacker, Batesville, Indiana

   2 packages (3 ounces *each*) cream cheese
1/2 teaspoon salt
1/2 teaspoon dill weed
   2 medium cucumbers, cut into 1/8-inch slices
   1 can (16 ounces) red salmon, drained and deboned
Pimiento

Combine cream cheese, salt and dill weed; mix until blended. Using a pastry bag with large star tip, pipe a star of cream cheese mixture onto each cucumber slice. Top each star with a small piece of salmon; garnish with a tiny piece of pimiento. Cover with plastic wrap; store in the refrigerator until ready to serve. **Yield:** about 2 dozen appetizers.

ITALIAN VEGETABLE SOUP

Bonnie Vawter, Alton, Missouri

(PICTURED ON PAGE 156)

 This tasty dish uses less sugar, salt and fat. Recipe includes *Diabetic Exchanges*.

   1 pound ground beef
   1 cup diced onion
   1 cup sliced celery
   1 cup sliced carrots
   2 cloves garlic, minced
   1 can (16 ounces) tomatoes
   1 can (15 ounces) tomato sauce
   1 can (15 ounces) red kidney beans, undrained
   2 cups water
   5 teaspoons beef bouillon granules
   1 tablespoon dried parsley flakes
   1 teaspoon salt
1/2 teaspoon oregano
1/2 teaspoon sweet basil
1/4 teaspoon black pepper
   2 cups shredded cabbage
   1 cup frozen *or* fresh green beans, cut in 1-inch pieces, optional

1/2 cup small elbow macaroni
Parmesan cheese

Brown beef in large heavy kettle; drain. Add all the ingredients except cabbage, green beans, macaroni and Parmesan cheese. Bring to boil. Lower heat; cover and simmer 20 minutes. Add cabbage, green beans and macaroni; bring to boil and simmer until vegetables are tender. If you prefer a thinner soup, add additional water or broth. Sprinkle with Parmesan cheese before serving. **Yield:** 12 servings. **Diabetic Exchanges:** One serving equals 1 protein, 1 bread; also 152 calories, 776 mg sodium, 34 mg cholesterol, 17 gm carbohydrate, 12 gm protein, 4 gm fat.

BAKED CAJUN CABBAGE

Rowena Champagne, New Iberia, Louisiana

(PICTURED ON PAGE 158)

   1 large head cabbage
CHEESE SAUCE:
1/2 cup butter
   4 tablespoons all-purpose flour
   1 cup chopped onions
   1 cup chopped celery
   1 cup chopped bell pepper
Salt
Cayenne pepper to taste
1-1/2 cups milk
1/2 pound cheddar cheese, shredded
TOPPING:
   1 cup chopped green onions
1/4 cup seasoned Italian bread crumbs

Remove outer leaves from cabbage. Cut into bite-size sections, removing heart. Boil about 10 minutes, uncovered, until tender/crisp. Drain; set aside. In separate saucepan, combine butter and flour, blending well over medium heat. Add onions, celery, bell pepper, salt and cayenne pepper. Saute for 10 minutes. Add milk, blending well over low heat until creamy. Add cheese; stir until smooth. Place cabbage in 2-qt. casserole; top with cheese sauce. Sprinkle with green onions and bread crumbs. Bake at 350° for about 30 minutes. **Yield:** 6 servings.

TASTY TOPPERS: Crumble leftover biscuits or cornmeal muffins over casserole ingredients. Dot with butter and bake as usual.

● For a crunchy casserole topping, mix 2 cups crushed corn or wheat cereal with 1 tablespoon grated Parmesan cheese and a dash of paprika.

POTATOES ROMANOFF

Jean Giesbrecht, American Falls, Idaho

(PICTURED ON PAGE 158)

6 medium baking potatoes
2 cups dairy sour cream
1 bunch green onions, chopped
  (about 1 cup)
1-1/2 cups shredded cheddar
  cheese
1-1/2 teaspoons salt
1/2 teaspoon pepper
Paprika

Boil unpeeled potatoes until tender, about 20-25 minutes. Cool; peel. Grate into large bowl; add remaining ingredients, except paprika. Mix well. Spoon into 13-in. x 9-in. baking dish. Refrigerate 3-4 hours, covered, or overnight. Bake at 350° for 40-50 minutes. Sprinkle with paprika. **Yield:** 8-10 servings.

SWEET POTATO SOUFFLE

Margaret Allen, Abingdon, Virginia

(PICTURED ON PAGE 158)

3 cups cooked, mashed sweet
  potatoes
3 eggs, *separated*
1/2 to 1 cup sugar
1 teaspoon vanilla
1/4 teaspoon nutmeg
1/4 to 1/2 cup melted butter
2 cups milk
TOPPING:
1/2 cup brown sugar
3 tablespoons melted butter
1/3 cup chopped nuts *or* coconut

Bake pricked sweet potatoes at 400° until tender. Cool; peel and mash. Combine sweet potatoes with beaten egg yolks (reserve whites), sugar, vanilla, nutmeg, butter and milk. Set aside. Beat the egg whites until stiff; carefully fold into sweet potato mixture. Pour into 2-qt. greased baking dish. Combine topping ingredients; sprinkle over top in decorative pattern. Bake at 350° for 30 minutes. **Yield:** 10-12 servings.

"FEAST" PORK CHOPS

Barb Langan, Orland Park, Illinois

(PICTURED ON PAGE 159)

6 loin pork cops, 3/4 to 1 inch
  thick
Seasoned salt to taste
Seasoned pepper to taste
Garlic powder to taste
1 tablespoon butter
SIZZLE SAUCE:
3/4 cup apple juice *or* cider
1/4 cup cider vinegar
2 tablespoons brown sugar
1-1/2 teaspoons molasses
1/2 teaspoon ground cloves
1-1/2 teaspoons dry mustard
1-1/2 teaspoons ginger

Season chops lightly with salt, pepper and garlic powder. Brown chops in butter in skillet on both sides. Combine sauce ingredients and add to skillet. Simmer, covered, for 20 minutes. Remove cover; simmer until sauce thickens. *Do not let burn.* (Chops may also be grilled outdoors over hickory fire and finished off in simmered sauce.) **Yield:** 6 servings.

SQUASH DRESSING

Nila Tower, Baird, Texas

(PICTURED ON PAGE 159)

2 to 3 cups yellow squash,
  cubed (crookneck variety)
1 small onion, diced
2 cups crumbled corn bread
2 tablespoons butter *or*
  margarine, melted
1 can (10-3/4 ounces) cream of
  chicken soup, undiluted
1 teaspoon poultry seasoning
  (marjoram, thyme, sage)
Salt to taste
Pepper to taste

Cook squash and onion in enough water for simmering, about 1-1/2 cups, until tender. Drain, reserving 1 cup liquid. Mix all ingredients lightly; place in 2-qt. buttered casserole. Bake at 350° for 30 minutes or until light golden brown. **Yield:** 6-8 servings.

SWEET POTATO PIE

Evelyn Hill, Crisfield, Maryland

(PICTURED ON PAGE 159)

3 large baked sweet potatoes,
  about 2 cups
1/4 cup butter, melted
3/4 cup sugar
1/2 teaspoon salt
1 teaspoon vanilla extract
1/2 teaspoon lemon extract
2 eggs, *separated*
1 cup half-and-half *or*
  evaporated milk
1 9-inch unbaked pie shell
  (deep dish)

(Bake potatoes at 400° until tender. Cool; remove skins.) Mash or whip potatoes in large mixing bowl. Add butter, sugar, salt and extracts. Set aside. In small bowl, beat egg yolks slightly. Add to potato mixture with cream/milk. Set aside. Whip egg whites until soft peaks form. Fold gently into potato mixture. Pour into pie shell. Bake at 425° for 15 minutes; reduce temperature to 350° and bake 25-30 minutes more until center tests done. **Yield:** 8-10 servings.

CRANBERRY ORANGE BREAD

Elaine Kremenak, Grants Pass, Oregon

(PICTURED ON PAGE 159)

2 cups all-purpose flour,
  unsifted
1-1/2 teaspoons baking powder
1 teaspoon baking soda
1/2 teaspoon salt
1 cup sugar
1 egg, beaten
1/2 cup orange juice
Grated rind of 1 orange
2 tablespoons melted butter
2 tablespoons hot water
1 cup raw whole cranberries
1 cup coarsely chopped
  walnuts

Combine flour, baking powder, soda, salt and sugar in large mixing bowl; set aside. Mix beaten egg with orange juice, rind, butter and hot water. Fold flour mixture into egg mixture until blended. *Do not beat.* Gently fold in cranberries and walnuts. Spoon into greased 9-in. x 6-in. loaf pan or smaller pans of choice. Bake at 325° for 60 minutes; test in center with wooden pick. Cool on rack for 15 minutes before removing from pans. **Yield:** about 10-12 servings.

PUMPKIN SOUP

Shirley Van Garde, Brookings, Oregon

(PICTURED ON PAGE 159)

1/4 cup chopped green pepper
2 tablespoons chopped onion
1 teaspoon parsley flakes *or*
  fresh minced parsley
1/8 teaspoon thyme leaves
1 bay leaf
2 tablespoons butter
1 can (9 ounces) canned
  tomatoes, diced
2 cups mashed cooked
  pumpkin *or* squash

2 cups water
2 chicken bouillon cubes
1 tablespoon all-purpose flour
2 cups milk
1 teaspoon salt
1/8 teaspoon pepper

Saute green pepper, onion, parsley, thyme and bay leaf in butter until tender; do not brown. Add tomatoes, pumpkin/squash, water and bouillon; bring to boil. Reduce heat; simmer 30 minutes, stirring occasionally. In small bowl, combine flour and milk, blend well. Stir into soup mixture; add salt and pepper. Cook over medium heat, stirring frequently until mixture boils. Remove bay leaf. **Yield:** 6-8 servings.

TAFFY APPLE SALAD

Jill Boyce, Zion, Illinois

(PICTURED ON PAGE 160)

1 tablespoon all-purpose flour
1/2 cup sugar
1 egg
2 tablespoons apple cider vinegar
1 can (8 ounces) crushed pineapple, drained (reserve juice)
4 cups (1 pound) red Delicious apples, unpeeled
1 cup salted shelled peanuts
1 carton (8 ounces) nondairy topping
Additional peanuts for garnish, optional

Combine flour and sugar; mix well. Beat egg; add to flour/sugar. Add vinegar and reserved pineapple juice. Cook in small pan on low heat. Stir and cook until thick. Cool. Pour cooled dressing over pineapple, apples and peanuts. Mix in nondairy topping. Sprinkle with additional peanuts over top for garnish, if desired. **Yield:** 10 servings.

APPLE CREAM TART

Gladys Moran, Shohola, Pennsylvania

(PICTURED ON PAGE 160)

CRUST:
1-1/2 cups all-purpose flour
3 tablespoons sugar
1/4 teaspoon salt
6 tablespoons butter
FILLING:
3 peeled, sliced apples to fill 9-inch springform pan
1/2 to 3/4 cup sugar
1 teaspoon cinnamon
1/4 teaspoon nutmeg

TOPPING:
2 egg yolks, beaten
1 cup heavy cream

Combine flour, sugar, salt and cut in butter until mixture resembles cornmeal. Press into bottom and up sides of 9-in. springform pan. Fill crust with sliced apples. Combine sugar, cinnamon and nutmeg; sprinkle over apples. Bake at 400° for 15 minutes. Combine egg yolks and cream; pour over apples. Return to oven. Bake for 30 minutes or until apples are fork-tender. Cool on rack. **Yield:** 10 servings.

CREAMY APPLE SQUARES

Janet Woodburn, Caldwell, Idaho

(PICTURED ON PAGE 160)

1 package (18-1/2 ounces) yellow pudding cake mix
1/2 cup soft butter
3 large red Delicious apples, thinly sliced, unpeeled
1 cup sour cream
1 egg
1/4 cup brown sugar
1/2 teaspoon cinnamon

Combine cake mix and butter; mix until crumbly. Reserve 2/3 cup for topping. Press remaining cake/butter mixture into bottom of ungreased 13-in. x 9-in. pan. Arrange apple slices over base. Blend sour cream and egg together; spread evenly over apples. For topping, mix brown sugar and cinnamon into reserved 2/3-cup cake/butter mixture. Sprinkle topping mixture over all. Bake at 350° for 25-30 minutes or until topping is golden brown and bubbly. Serve warm. Refrigerate leftovers. **Yield:** 12-15 squares.

QUICK APPLE DUMPLING ROLLS

Florence Rasmussen, Amboy, Illinois

(PICTURED ON PAGE 160)

SYRUP:
2 cups water
1-1/2 cups sugar
DOUGH:
3 tablespoons vegetable shortening
2 cups all-purpose flour
4 teaspoons baking powder
Pinch salt
1 egg
1/2 cup milk
FILLING:
2 to 3 cups finely chopped apple

1/4 cup sugar
1/2 to 1 teaspoon cinnamon
1/4 teaspoon nutmeg
Butter

Combine sugar and water in small saucepan; bring to boil. Pour into bottom of 13-in. x 9-in. baking pan. Set aside. Combine shortening, flour, baking powder and salt with mixer (or use food processor). Combine egg and milk; add to creamed mixture. Roll dough out between sheets of wax paper to 1/4-in. thickness. Remove top paper. Spread with filling ingredients which have been combined. Roll up like cinnamon rolls or noodles. Remove bottom paper. Slice into 8-10 rolls with sharp knife. Carefully lay rolls on top of syrup. Dot rolls with butter. Bake at 375° for 20-30 minutes or until golden brown. Serve hot or cold with milk, whipped cream or ice cream. **Yield:** 8-10 servings.

APPLE PUFF PANCAKE

Gloria Shelton, Oakes, North Dakota

 This tasty dish uses less sugar, salt and fat. Recipe includes *Diabetic Exchanges*.

4 tablespoons butter
2 large apples, peeled, cored and sliced thin
3 tablespoons brown sugar
1 teaspoon cinnamon
PANCAKE:
6 eggs, room temperature
1-1/2 cups milk
1 cup all-purpose flour
3 tablespoons sugar
1 teaspoon vanilla
1/2 teaspoon salt
1/2 teaspoon cinnamon

Melt butter in 9-in. x 13-in. baking pan in 375° oven. Arrange apples over butter; return to oven until apples are soft (about 10 minutes). Sprinkle apples with brown sugar and cinnamon. Combine pancake ingredients in blender; pour over apples. Bake for 30-40 minutes. Sprinkle with powdered sugar. **Yield:** 8 servings.
Diabetic Exchanges: One serving equals 1 protein, 1-1/2 breads, 1/2 fruit, 1 fat; also 248 calories, 274 mg sodium, 213 mg cholesterol, 27 gm carbohydrate.

SPECIAL SYRUP: Out of pancake syrup? Make your own! Mix 1-1/2 cups of brown sugar and 1 cup of water in a small saucepan; boil 1 minute. Add 1 tablespoon butter, 1/4 teaspoon vanilla extract and 1/4 teaspoon maple flavoring.

10-MINUTE MEAT LOAF

Carol Pilmer, Alliance, Ohio

1 pound ground beef
1 egg
1/2 cup bread crumbs
1/4 cup milk
2 tablespoons onion soup mix
2 tablespoons catsup
2 tablespoons soy sauce
1/2 cup shredded Swiss cheese

Combine all ingredients and shape into a round oval loaf. Place in microwave-safe dish, cover with wax paper and microwave on high for 10 minutes, turning dish after 5 minutes of cooking. Drain and cover with foil. Let stand 10 minutes before slicing. **Yield:** 4-6 servings.

PIZZA CUPS

Kathy Lutz, Phillipsburg, Ohio

3/4 pound ground beef
1 can (6 ounces) tomato paste
1 tablespoon instant minced onion
1 teaspoon Italian seasoning
1/2 teaspoon salt
1 can (10 ounces) refrigerated biscuits
1/2 to 3/4 cup shredded mozzarella cheese

Brown and drain beef. Stir in tomato paste, onion, Italian seasoning and salt (mixture will be thick). Cook over low heat for 5 minutes, stirring frequently. Place biscuits in a greased muffin tin, pressing to cover bottom and sides. Spoon about 1/4 cup of meat mixture into biscuit-lined cups and sprinkle with cheese. Bake at 400° for 12 minutes or until golden brown. **Yield:** 12 pizza cups.

QUICK BAKED BEANS

Joey Mostowy, Bruin, Pennsylvania

3 to 4 strips bacon
1 clove garlic, minced
1 onion, chopped
1/2 green pepper, chopped
1/2 pound ground beef
Salt to taste
Black pepper to taste
1 can (1 pound) baked beans
2 hot dogs, sliced

Cook the bacon until crisp; set aside. Saute garlic, onion and green pepper in bacon drippings until golden. Add beef. Brown well; drain. Season with salt and pepper, if desired. Stir in beans and hot dogs; cover and simmer over low heat for 10 minutes. Crumble bacon over top and serve. **Yield:** 4-6 servings.

CHILI CON QUESO

Dixie Gaastra, Randolph, Wisconsin

1 pound ground beef
1/2 cup chopped green onion
3/4 cup chopped green pepper
1 can (8 ounces) tomato sauce
1 can (4 ounces) chopped green chilies
1 tablespoon Worcestershire sauce
1 package (1 pound) process cheese spread, cubed
1 teaspoon ground red pepper
Paprika to taste
Unsalted corn chips

Brown beef and drain. In slow cooker, combine beef, onion, green pepper, tomato sauce, chilies and Worcestershire sauce. Cover; cook on low for 2-3 hours. An hour before serving, add cheese, red pepper and paprika. Stir occasionally. *Quick stove-top method:* Brown beef and drain. Add remaining ingredients *except* corn chips. Simmer 1/2 hour, stirring occasionally. Serve with corn chips. **Yield:** 1-1/2 quarts.

MEAT & CHEESE COCKTAIL ROUNDS

Lisa Seaba, Muscatine, Iowa

1 pound lean ground beef
1 pound Italian sausage
1 pound processed American cheese, cubed
Garlic powder to taste
1 package party rye bread rounds
Leaf oregano, crumbled

Brown beef and sausage together in large skillet; drain off fat. Add cheese and garlic powder; simmer until cheese melts, stirring to blend. Spread meat/cheese mixture on rye bread rounds, using 1 teaspoon for each slice. Sprinkle with oregano. Bake at 375° for 15 minutes and serve hot. (You can also cool and freeze flat on cookie sheets until firm; transfer to heavy plastic freezer bags. To reheat, microwave on 70% power for 1 minute.) **Yield:** 68 appetizers.

ROASTED QUAIL WITH WHITE WINE SAUCE

Jordan Hollow Farm Inn, Stanley, Virginia

1 package (6 ounces) long grain and wild rice
1 apple, peeled, cored and cubed
3 small carrots, cubed
12 quail (2 per person)
3 tablespoons soy sauce
1 teaspoon garlic powder, *divided*
1 teaspoon dried tarragon, *divided*
1/8 teaspoon finely ground rosemary, *divided*
1 cup all-purpose flour
1/4 cup grated Parmesan cheese
1/4 cup peanut oil
SAUCE:
1/4 cup white wine (Chablis *or* other dry *or* semi-dry wine)
1 teaspoon chicken stock base
1/8 teaspoon white pepper
2 cups heavy cream

Preheat oven to 400°. Add apple and carrots to rice and cook according to package directions. Season quail inside and out with soy sauce and half each of the garlic powder, tarragon and rosemary. Stuff each bird with the rice mixture, reserving the remaining rice. Mix flour, Parmesan cheese and remaining seasonings and roll each quail lightly in the mixture. Saute in peanut oil until lightly browned. Place in preheated oven and roast for 8 to 15 minutes, until juice runs clear when breast is pierced. Arrange remaining rice on platter, place quail on top, and keep warm. Pour off all but two tablespoons of oil from the saute pan. Add wine, stirring to loosen pan drippings. Add chicken stock base, white pepper and cream; simmer until thickened. Pour over quail, garnish with two tablespoons fresh chopped parsley or other herbs. **Yield:** 6 servings.

CREAM SCONES

Dorothy Child, Malone, New York

 This tasty dish uses less sugar, salt and fat. Recipe includes *Diabetic Exchanges*.

SCONES:
2 cups all-purpose flour
3 teaspoons baking powder
1/2 teaspoon salt
4 tablespoons sugar, *divided*
6 tablespoons butter *or* shortening

2 eggs
1/2 cup light cream
LEMON CURD:
4 tablespoons unsalted butter
1/2 cup sugar
1/2 cup fresh lemon juice
4 egg yolks, slightly beaten
1 tablespoon grated lemon rind,
optional

Make scones by combining flour, baking powder, salt and 2 tablespoons sugar in medium bowl. Cut in butter/shortening until mixture resembles coarse crumbs. Set aside. In small bowl, beat eggs with fork; add cream. Reserve 2 teaspoons of this mixture. Stir remaining egg mixture in flour mixture until just blended. Turn out onto floured board; knead lightly. Shape into 14-in. x 7-in. rectangle. Brush with reserved egg/cream mixture. Sprinkle with reserved sugar. Cut into 16 triangular pieces. Place about 1 in. apart on lightly floured cookie sheet. Bake at 425° for 8-10 minutes. Meanwhile, make lemon curd by combining butter, sugar, lemon juice and egg yolks in heavy saucepan over low heat (may use double boiler). Stir mixture constantly until it thickens enough to coat back of spoon (soft custard consistency). *Do not boil or mixture will curdle.* Stir in lemon rind, if desired. Pour into jar, seal and *refrigerate.* Serve warm scones with lemon curd or jam. **Yield:** 16 scones. **Diabetic Exchanges:** One serving equals 1 bread, 1 fruit, 1-1/2 fat; also, 212 calories, 198 mg sodium, 121 mg cholesterol, 23 gm carbohydrate, 4 gm protein, 8 gm fat.

BUTTERMILK CRANBERRY MUFFINS

Jane Yunker, Rochester, New York

 This tasty dish uses less sugar, salt and fat. Recipe includes *Diabetic Exchanges.*

1 heaping cup of cranberries,
coarsely chopped
3/4 cup sugar, *divided*
3 cups all-purpose flour
3-1/2 teaspoons baking powder
1/2 teaspoon salt
1/4 teaspoon baking soda,
optional
1/2 cup butter
1 egg
1-1/2 cups buttermilk, room
temperature
2 tablespoons frozen orange
juice concentrate, thawed
CRANBERRY BUTTER:
1 cup cranberries

1 cup confectioners' sugar
1/2 cup butter
1 tablespoon lemon juice

Chop the cranberries and combine with 1/4 cup sugar; set aside. Sift together flour, remaining sugar, baking powder, salt, and if desired, baking soda. Cut in butter until mixture resembles coarse meal. Lightly beat together egg, buttermilk and orange juice concentrate. Add the liquid and sweetened cranberries to dry ingredients, stirring only until well-combined. Spoon batter in buttered muffin pans, filling them two-thirds full. Bake at 375° for 25 minutes. To make cranberry butter, puree cranberries in food processor or blender. Add sugar, butter and lemon juice; process until smooth. Refrigerate until ready to use. **Yield:** 18 muffins. **Diabetic Exchanges:** One serving equals 1 bread, 1 fruit, 1 fat; also, 173 calories, 209 mg sodium, 30 mg cholesterol, 27 gm carbohydrate, 3 gm protein, 6 gm fat.

LEMON BREAD

Caryn Wiggins, Columbus, Indiana

BREAD:
1 cup butter
2 cups sugar
4 eggs
1/2 teaspoon salt
1/2 teaspoon baking soda
3 cups all-purpose flour
1 cup buttermilk
Grated rind of 1 lemon *or* 1
tablespoon lemon peel spice
1 cup finely chopped pecans
GLAZE:
Juice from 2 lemons *or* 1/4 cup
lemon juice
1 cup confectioners' sugar

Cream together butter and sugar in bowl on high speed of mixer. Blend in eggs, one at a time, beating after each addition. In another bowl, combine salt, soda and flour; add to creamed mixture alternately with buttermilk. Add lemon rind and nuts, stirring in by hand. Grease and flour one 9-in. x 5-in. loaf pan or two 7-in. x 3-in. pans. Then line bottom with parchment paper or wax paper. Spoon batter into pan(s) and bake at 300° for 1 hour and 20 minutes or until bread tests done with wooden pick. Let bread cool in pans for 10 minutes; remove from pans to cooling racks. Combine glaze ingredients; punch holes in bread with toothpick while still warm. Drizzle glaze slowly over bread. Cool completely before slicing. **Yield:** about 16 servings.

APRICOT BREAD

Bev Bosveld, Waupun, Wisconsin

This tasty dish uses less sugar, salt and fat. Recipe includes *Diabetic Exchanges.*

1 cup dried apricots
3/4 cup hot water
2 tablespoons butter, softened
1 cup sugar
1 egg
2 cups all-purpose flour
1 teaspoon baking powder
1/4 teaspoon baking soda
1 teaspoon salt
1/2 cup orange juice
1/2 cup pecans, chopped
APRICOT SPREAD:
1 package (3 ounces) cream
cheese, softened
2 tablespoons apricots,
chopped and softened

Cut apricots into pieces in small bowl; pour hot water over all. Let soften for 30 minutes. Drain; reserve 1/4 cup apricot water. Set aside apricot pieces. Combine butter, sugar and egg in mixing bowl; cream well. In another bowl, combine flour, baking powder, soda and salt. Add dry ingredients to creamed mixture, alternately with apricot water and orange juice. Stir in apricot pieces and pecans. Spoon into greased and floured 9-in. x 5-in. loaf pan. Bake at 350° for 55-65 minutes or until bread tests done with wooden pick. Make apricot spread by combining ingredients. Refrigerate until serving time. (This bread's flavor improves with age.) **Yield:** 18 slices bread. **Diabetic Exchanges:** One serving equals 1 bread, 1 fruit, 1 fat; also, 179 calories, 183 mg sodium, 23 mg cholesterol, 30 gm carbohydrate, 3 gm protein, 5 gm fat.

"QUICK BREAD" TIPS: Fill pans only about two-thirds full to allow for expansion of batter and give breads pretty, rounded shapes.

● Add a small amount of the recipe flour to raisins, dates and other dried fruits so they don't cling together when added to batter.

● Baking breads at high altitudes? Reduce baking powder or soda in each recipe by one-fourth. Do not decrease baking soda to less than 1/2 teaspoon per cup of sour milk used.

● Most quick breads are best stored overnight before slicing and serving.

● For crusty biscuits, roll dough thinner, cut smaller and place farther apart on cookie sheet. For flaky biscuits, roll dough thicker, cut larger and place close together on cookie sheet.

Pioneer fare, these are hearty foods of the type that sustained our ancestors on their westward journey. They became regional favorites—and are now old standbys found on tables all across the country. You'll probably recognize some dishes from *your* part of the country.

Our buckboard seat displays these flavorful foods—a variety of corn dishes, rich baked beans, distinctive salads and side dishes, dark bread, wild game and highly seasoned-and-sauced meat. Rediscover these time-honored classics …for a real "taste of the country"!

FRONTIER FOOD: Clockwise from lower left—**Hot Bacon Dressing with Spinach** (Pg. 175); **Michigan Bean Bake** (Pg. 175); **Creole Corn Muffins** (Pg. 175); **Big Sky Country Ribs and Sauce** (Pg. 175); **Anadama Bread** (Pg. 176); **Baked Corn** (Pg. 176); **North Woods Wild Fowl and Sauce** (Pg. 175); **Wild Rice Side Dish** (Pg. 175). (Last two dishes shown combined.)

Sunday desserts. These are the kind of fresh-baked goodies that Grandma used to make for Sundays and special occasions.

Made from common ingredients and seasonal orchard bounty, these pies, cakes, kuchens and cookies were the "stuff" of Grandma's kitchen!

Close your eyes...imagine fresh, tart lemon peel...the nutty goodness of hickory trees...the sweet-tart taste of pie cherries...and the sharp, spiced fragrance of molasses spice cookies.

Relive those memories today with our sampling of regional sweet treats. One taste will take you home again!

PASS THE DESSERT! Clockwise from lower left—**Lemon 'N' Apple Chess Pie** (Pg. 176); **Grandma's Hickory Nut Cake** (Pg. 176); **Molasses Crinkle Cookies** (Pg. 177); **Fruit Muerbeteig** (Pg. 176).

MEALS IN MINUTES

Minutes matter to working mothers like Julianne Johnson of Grove City, Minnesota, and she makes the most of them with this simple, satisfying menu.

"I work part-time at a local radio station, and I am also a free-lance writer," this busy mother of two young daughters explains.

"My husband travels a lot with his job, and I never know what time he'll be home for dinner—only that he'll be hungry! Since it's the only meal of the day that we can share as a family, I want our dinner to be both special and nutritious. But, of course, it must be quick and easy to fix, too."

Julianne begins her meal preparation by cooking the rice, using either microwave or range top. Next, she browns the turkey tenderloins or slices and adds the simple sauce ingredients for final simmering.

Her vegetable salad contains ingredients that are usually on hand. She occasionally sprinkles on some Parmesan cheese and croutons to add variety.

While her family clears the dinner dishes, Julianne prepares her quick fruit dessert. For fun, she sometimes quarters the bananas, dusts them in cinnamon sugar and then puts them back in their skins for a sweet surprise.

TURKEY BREAST SUPREME

1 tablespoon butter
1-1/2 pounds turkey breast slices
    or 2 to 4 turkey breast
    tenderloins
1/4 cup chopped green onion
1 can (10-3/4 ounces) cream of
    chicken soup
1/4 cup water
Freshly ground pepper
1 cup (4 ounces) Swiss cheese,
    shredded
Additional green onion, optional

Melt butter in skillet on medium-high heat. Add turkey; brown on both sides. Add onion; saute 1-2 minutes. Stir in soup diluted with water; season with pepper. Reduce heat; cover and simmer 20 minutes. If using tenderloins, turn after 10 minutes. Remove turkey to heated serving dish. Add cheese to sauce remaining in skillet. Stir until melted. Pour cheese sauce over turkey. Serve turkey with cooked white rice or long grain/wild rice mix. Garnish with additional green onion, if desired. **Yield:** 2-4 servings.

MICROWAVE RICE

1 cup long-grain rice
2 cups water
1 teaspoon salt
1 tablespoon vegetable oil

Place all ingredients in a 3-qt. covered casserole. Microwave on high for 8 minutes; stir. Let stand in microwave for 10 minutes; microwave on high for 5 minutes more. Let stand for 5 minutes. **Yield:** 4 servings.

WINTER VEGETABLE SALAD

1 head iceberg lettuce, washed
    and chilled
2 to 3 carrots, peeled and
    sliced *or* chopped
12 to 16 stuffed green olives
Prepared salad dressing of choice
Parmesan cheese, optional
Croutons, optional

Cut lettuce into narrow strips or tear and place on individual salad plates. Add equally divided amounts of carrots and olives to each serving; top with dressing. (A creamy buttermilk salad dressing is especially good on this salad.)

CHERRY/NUT BANANA DESSERT

4 ripe bananas, peeled
Whipped cream (in spray can)
12 walnut halves, chopped
Maraschino cherries

Dice bananas and place in dessert dishes. Immediately before serving, top with whipped cream, nuts and cherries. **Yield:** 4 servings.

> **MICROWAVE TIP:** Wonder what kind of wrap to work with? Use paper towel if you want to absorb moisture and waxed paper to prevent splatters.

It's not just for the holidays anymore! Turkey has taken center stage in plenty of country kitchens, as cooks put scrumptious and surprisingly new twists on turkey these days—serving it up as soups, salads and suppertime stars. Try some of these fresh approaches and enjoy these turkey treats!

TASTY TURKEY: Clockwise from lower left—**Hot Turkey Taco Salad** (Pg. 178); **Barbecued Turkey** (Pg. 178); **Grilled Turkey Steaks** (Pg. 178); **Grilled Turkey Tenderloin Sandwiches** (Pg. 179); **Stir-Fry Turkey with Walnuts** (Pg. 178); **Day-After Turkey Pie** (Pg. 179); **Turkey Scallopini** (Pg. 179); **Turkey Ham Quiche/Hash Brown Crust** (Pg. 178).

Turkey has taken on a whole new role—moving from its place as centerpiece at holiday feasts to a tasty, easy-to-prepare addition to everyday menus.

These four flavorful turkey dishes will be a hit with your family…whether you serve creamy Williamsburg Inn Turkey Soup, spicy Turkey Enchiladas, refreshingly different Tangy Turkey Salad or Turkey Piccata—a new twist on a dinnertime classic. Enjoy the taste of turkey—any day of the year.

TURKEY TREATS: Clockwise from bottom—**Turkey Piccata; Turkey Enchiladas; Tangy Turkey Salad; Williamsburg Inn Turkey Soup.** All recipes found on page 180.

NORTH WOODS WILD FOWL & SAUCE

Mabel Haugen, Tomahawk, Wisconsin

(PICTURED ON PAGE 168)

Pheasant, quail, grouse, guinea hen *or* **other wild fowl**
NORTH WOODS SAUCE:
- 1/4 cup finely chopped onion
- 2 tablespoons vegetable oil
- 1 tablespoon cornstarch
- 1 cup chicken broth (*or* 2 teaspoons chicken bouillon dissolved in 1 cup water)
- 1 teaspoon brown sugar
- 1 teaspoon grated orange peel
- 1/4 cup orange juice
- 1 cup fresh seedless grapes
- 1/4 teaspoon crushed fennel seed
- 2 tablespoons chopped fresh *or* dried parsley

Salt to taste

Roast fowl, covered, in oven at 300° until nearly done or cut fowl in serving pieces and coat with mixture of 1/2 cup finely crushed cornflakes, 1/4 cup flour, salt and pepper. Fry in 2 tablespoons vegetable oil until tender. Set aside. Make sauce by sauteing onion in oil until transparent. Stir in cornstarch, broth, brown sugar and orange peel. Bring mixture to a boil, stirring as it thickens. Add orange juice, grapes, fennel, parsley and if desired, salt. Pour over fried fowl in oven casserole; bake at 350° for 12 minutes. Roasted fowl can be brushed with sauce and returned to oven at 325° to complete cooking. **Yield:** each pheasant serves 2.

WILD RICE SIDE DISH

Gladys Barron, Thief River Falls, Minnesota

(PICTURED ON PAGE 168)

- 1/4 cup butter
- 1/4 cup chopped onion
- 1 cup uncooked wild rice
- 8 ounces fresh mushrooms, cleaned and sliced
- 3 cups chicken broth
- 1 tablespoon soy sauce

Almonds, optional

Melt butter in skillet; add onions. Saute until onions are transparent. Add rice and mushrooms to mixture; stir and cook for about 5 minutes. Set aside. Heat chicken broth and soy sauce to boil. Place rice mixture in 1-1/2- to 2-qt. casserole; pour broth over all. Stir to mix. Cover with lid; bake at 325° for 1-1/2 hours or until all liquid is absorbed.

May add almonds, if desired. **Yield:** 8 servings.

HOT BACON DRESSING WITH SPINACH

Nancy Atherholt, Nazareth, Pennsylvania

(PICTURED ON PAGE 168)

- 4 slices bacon
- 1/2 cup sugar
- 1 tablespoon cornstarch
- 1/2 teaspoon salt, optional
- 1 egg, beaten
- 1/4 cup vinegar
- 1 cup water
Fresh spinach leaves, dandelion greens *or* **endive, washed, drained and chilled**

Fry bacon until crisp. Remove bacon strips to drain on paper towel; reserve bacon drippings. In small saucepan, combine sugar, cornstarch and if desired, salt. Add beaten egg and vinegar; mix well. Add water, crumbled bacon and reserved bacon drippings. Cook to thickness desired. (Extra sugar or vinegar may be added to taste.) Serve over greens. **Yield:** 1-1/2 cups dressing.

OUT OF BROWN SUGAR? Substitute 2 tablespoons molasses and 1/2 cup granulated sugar for every 1/2 cup of brown sugar called for. (Add the molasses to the batter with the other liquid ingredients.)

CREOLE CORN MUFFINS

Alice Mathews, Alexandria, Louisiana

(PICTURED ON PAGE 168)

- 2 eggs, beaten
- 1-1/2 cups milk
- 3/4 cup shortening, melted
- 2-1/2 cups all-purpose flour
- 1 teaspoon salt
- 2 tablespoons baking powder
- 4 tablespoons (heaping) sugar
- 4-1/2 tablespoons (heaping) yellow cornmeal
- 2 tablespoons chopped green pepper
- 2 tablespoons chopped onion
- 2 tablespoons chopped pimiento
- 3/4 cup shredded cheddar cheese

Blend eggs, milk and shortening together. Set aside. Combine flour, salt, baking powder, sugar and cornmeal in mixing bowl. Add green pepper, onion,

pimiento and cheese to cornmeal mixture. Pour milk mixture into cornmeal mixture, stirring just until mixed. Pour batter into *hot* greased muffin pans, 2/3 full. Bake at 400° for 25-30 minutes. **Yield:** 9-12 muffins.

MICHIGAN BEAN BAKE

Sondra Bergy, Lowell, Michigan

(PICTURED ON PAGE 168)

- 1 jar (48 ounces) cooked great northern beans
- 1-1/2 pounds lean 1-inch pork cubes
- 1/2 teaspoon salt
- 1 bottle (14 ounces) catsup
- 3 tablespoons prepared mustard
- 1-1/2 cups brown sugar
- 1/4 large sweet onion, chopped

Combine all ingredients; mix gently but well. Place in beanpot, casserole or crockpot. Bake at 300°, uncovered, for 5 to 6 hours, cover last hour *or* heat on low in crockpot overnight. **Yield:** 10-12 servings.

BIG SKY COUNTRY RIBS & SAUCE

Carolyn Weinberg, Custer, Montana

(PICTURED ON PAGE 169)

- 3 to 4 pounds beef ribs
SAUCE:
- 1 medium onion, minced
- 1 can (10-3/4 ounces) tomato soup
- 1 cup water
- 1/4 cup vinegar
- 1/4 cup Worcestershire sauce
- 1-1/4 cups catsup
- 1/4 teaspoon ground cinnamon
- 1-1/2 teaspoons paprika
- 1/2 teaspoon pepper
- 1-1/2 teaspoons chili powder
- 1/4 teaspoon ground cloves
- 1/8 teaspoon cayenne pepper
- 1 teaspoon steak sauce
- 1-1/4 tablespoons vegetable oil
- 2 tablespoons brown sugar
Salt to taste

Brown ribs in broiler pan of oven at 400° for 30-45 minutes. (May also cook on barbecue grill.) Drain off fat. While ribs are browning, combine all sauce ingredients in saucepan or microwave; simmer for 10 minutes or until flavors are mixed. Cover ribs with sauce. Bake at 300° for 2-3 hours. Baste with sauce as ribs darken. **Yield:** 6-8 servings.

ANADAMA BREAD

Karen Fenley, Greensburg, Indiana

(PICTURED ON PAGE 169)

1-1/2 cups cold *or* warm water
1 teaspoon salt
1/3 cup cornmeal
1-1/2 tablespoons butter
1/3 cup dark molasses
1/4 cup warm water
1 package yeast
1 tablespoon sugar
4 to 4-1/2 cups flour, *divided*
Melted butter
Cornmeal for topping

Combine water, salt and cornmeal in saucepan. Stir over medium heat until mixture bubbles and thickens. Add butter and molasses; remove from heat. Cool. In bowl, combine warm water and yeast; sprinkle on sugar. Stir to mix. Add yeast mixture to cooled cornmeal mixture. Add 2 cups flour; beat well. Add 1 additional cup flour; mix. Put 1/2 cup flour on counter; add additional flour as required to knead. Let dough rest; knead again until smooth. Let rise in warm place; punch down. Form into a loaf; place in greased 9-in. x 5-in. pan. Let rise until dough reaches top of pan. Bake at 375° for 40-45 minutes. Brush top with melted butter; sprinkle with cornmeal. Return bread to oven for 2 minutes. Cool on wire rack before slicing. (Makes great toast.) **Yield:** 1 large loaf.

DEVIL'S FOOD CAKE

Norma Erne, Albuquerque, New Mexico

2 cups packed brown sugar
1/2 cup shortening
2 eggs
1 teaspoon vanilla extract
2-1/2 cups all-purpose flour
1/3 cup baking cocoa
1 teaspoon baking powder
1/2 teaspoon baking soda
1/4 teaspoon salt
1 cup sour milk* *or* whey
FROSTING:
2 egg whites
1-1/2 cups sugar
5 tablespoons water
1-1/2 teaspoons light corn syrup
1 teaspoon vanilla extract

In a large mixing bowl, combine brown sugar, shortening and eggs. Add vanilla; beat well. Sift together flour, cocoa, baking powder, soda and salt. Add alternately with milk or whey to the egg mixture. Pour batter into two greased 9-in.

round cake pans. Bake at 350° for 30 minutes or until cake tests done. Cool 5 minutes before removing to a wire rack. Continue to cool. For frosting, combine first four ingredients in the top of a double boiler; beat with an electric mixer until thoroughly mixed. Place over rapidly boiling water and continue to beat for 7 minutes or until frosting will hold stiff peaks. Remove from boiling water and add vanilla. Continue to beat frosting until thick enough to spread. Frost cake when completely cooled. **Yield:** 12-14 servings. * To sour milk, place 1 tablespoon white vinegar in a measuring cup; add enough milk to equal 1 cup.

BAKED CORN

Jodie McCoy, Tulsa, Oklahoma

(PICTURED ON PAGE 169)

1/2 green pepper, chopped
1/2 onion, chopped
3 tablespoons butter, *divided*
2 tablespoons all-purpose flour
1 teaspoon salt
1/4 teaspoon paprika
1/4 teaspoon dry mustard
1 cup milk
1/2 cup dry bread crumbs
1 beaten egg
2 cups whole kernel corn, canned, frozen *or* fresh

Brown green pepper and onion in 2 tablespoons butter for 5 minutes. Add flour, salt, paprika and mustard; stir until blended. Add milk; stir till thick. Brown bread crumbs in 1 tablespoon butter; add crumbs, egg and corn to mixture. Bake in buttered dish at 400° for 30 minutes. **Yield:** 6 servings.

GRANDMA'S HICKORY NUT CAKE

Evelyn Kennell, Roanoke, Illinois

(PICTURED ON PAGE 170)

CAKE:
2 cups sugar
2/3 cup butter
3 eggs
1/8 teaspoon salt
2 teaspoons baking powder
2-1/2 cups all-purpose flour
1 cup milk
1 teaspoon vanilla
1 cup hickory nuts, chopped (reserve a few halves for garnish)

PENUCHE FROSTING:
1/2 cup butter
1 cup brown sugar
1/4 cup milk *or* cream
2 cups confectioners' sugar
1 teaspoon vanilla
Chopped hickory nuts, optional

Cream together sugar and butter for cake. Add eggs; beat with mixer on medium speed for 2 minutes. Mix dry ingredients together lightly with fork. Add dry ingredients to sugar/egg mixture, alternating with milk. Mix well. Stir in vanilla and nuts. Pour into greased and floured 13-in. x 9-in. pan. Bake at 325° for 45-50 minutes. (Cake may also be baked in 8-in. layer pans.) Cool. Make frosting by melting butter in medium saucepan. Add brown sugar; boil 2 minutes. Add milk/cream; bring to boil. Remove from heat; cool to lukewarm. Beat in sugar and vanilla. (May add 1/2 cup chopped hickory nuts, if desired.) Frost cake. **Yield:** 16 servings.

LEMON 'N' APPLE CHESS PIE

Jodie McCoy, Tulsa, Oklahoma

(PICTURED ON PAGE 170)

1 cup granulated sugar
1/2 teaspoon salt
1/2 teaspoon grated lemon peel
4 eggs, beaten
3 tablespoons lemon juice
1/4 cup butter, melted
1 cup unsweetened applesauce
1 9-inch unbaked pie shell

Make filling by combining sugar, salt and lemon peel; set aside. Combine eggs, lemon juice, butter and applesauce. Add dry ingredients to egg mixture; beat with mixer until well-blended. Pour into unbaked pie shell; bake at 450° for 15 minutes. Reduce heat to 350° and bake 15 minutes longer or until set. (May take total of 40 minutes baking time.) Cool on wire rack. **Yield:** 8 servings.

FRUIT MUERBETEIG (Custard Kuchen)

L. Jonas, Glendive, Montana

(PICTURED ON PAGE 170)

CRUST:
1/2 cup butter

1 tablespoon sugar
1/4 teaspoon salt
1 egg yolk, beaten
1 cup all-purpose flour
FILLING:
3 cups fruit (sour cherries
 or rhubarb)
1-1/4 cups sugar
1/4 cup plus 1-1/2
 tablespoons all-purpose flour
CUSTARD:
1 egg
1/4 cup cream

Blend all crust ingredients together; press onto bottom and sides of 9-in. cake pan. For filling, combine fruit with sugar and flour; spoon over crust. Make custard by beating together egg and cream; pour over filling. Bake at 350° for 45 minutes. **Yield:** 10 servings.

STRAWBERRY CREAM COOKIES

Glenna Aberle, Sabetha, Kansas

1 cup butter
1 cup sugar
1 package (3 ounces) cream
 cheese
1 tablespoon vanilla
1 egg yolk
2-1/2 cups all-purpose flour
Strawberry jam

Note: Have all ingredients at room temperature. Cream together butter, sugar and cream cheese. Add vanilla and egg yolk; mix. Add flour; blend. Chill dough. Shape into 1-in. balls. Using floured thimble, press hole in center of each cookie; fill with 1/4 teaspoon jam. Bake on ungreased cookie sheet at 350° for 10-12 minutes. **Yield:** 5 dozen.

MOLASSES CRINKLE COOKIES

Leta Shankel, Heyworth, Illinois

(PICTURED ON PAGE 170)

1 cup butter
1 cup dark brown sugar,
 well packed
1 egg
1/4 cup dark molasses
1/2 cup nonfat dry milk solids
2 teaspoons baking soda
1/4 teaspoon salt
1/2 teaspoon ground cloves
1 teaspoon ground cinnamon
1 teaspoon ground ginger
1/4 cup wheat germ

2-1/4 cups all-purpose flour
Granulated sugar

Cream butter and brown sugar until smooth and light. Beat in egg until fluffy. Add molasses and dry milk; beat well. Blend in soda, salt, cloves, cinnamon, ginger and wheat germ; beat 1 minute. Stir in flour until blended. Using 1/3 cup dough for each cookie (or a No. 16 ice cream scoop) form dough into round balls. Roll in granulated sugar; place on well-greased cookie sheet. Sprinkle each with few drops of water. Bake at 375° for 14 minutes. Cool on rack. (Cookies freeze beautifully.) **Yield:** 15 large cookies.

CHOCOLATE WHIPPED CREAM CAKE

Ruth Shelliam, Spring Green, Wisconsin

1 box (18-1/4 ounces) chocolate
 cake mix
1 pint whipping cream *or* 1
 container (8 ounces) of
 whipped topping
1/3 cup sugar
1/4 cup cocoa

Mix, bake and cook cake according to package instructions using two 9-in. layer pans. Cool completely. Pour whipping cream into chilled mixing bowl. Beat cream, gradually adding sugar and cocoa. Beat until stiff peaks form. Frost and fill cake with whipped cream/cocoa mixture and refrigerate. Let stand in refrigerator for 24 hours before serving. **Yield:** 16-20 servings.

CARAMEL PUDDING

Mary Ann Smucker, Lykens, Pennsylvania

6 cups milk
3 eggs
1-1/2 cups packed brown sugar
1/2 cup sugar
3/4 cup all-purpose flour
2 teaspoons vanilla extract
2 tablespoons butter *or*
 margarine

In a large saucepan, scald milk. Meanwhile, in a mixing bowl, beat eggs until creamy. Add sugars, flour and 1-1/2 cups of the scalded milk; slowly pour into

saucepan with remaining milk. Cook and stir over medium heat until pudding thickens, about 15-20 minutes. Remove from heat; add vanilla and butter. Stir well. Continue to stir pudding every 10 minutes until cooled. **Yield:** 15 servings.

NEVER-FAIL PECAN PIE

Beverly Materne, Reeves, Louisiana

2 eggs, well beaten
1/2 cup sugar
1 cup dark corn syrup
1 tablespoon all-purpose flour
1/4 teaspoon salt
1 teaspoon vanilla extract
1 cup pecan halves
1 9-inch unbaked pie shell

Combine eggs, sugar, corn syrup, flour, salt and vanilla. Stir in pecans. Pour into pie shell. Cover pastry edges with foil to prevent excess browning. Bake at 350° for 30 minutes. Remove foil and bake another 15 minutes or until golden brown. **Yield:** 6-8 servings.

OLD-FASHIONED BUTTERMILK CAKE

Sibyl Pressly, Valle Crucis, North Carolina

1 cup butter, softened
2 cups sugar
4 eggs
3 cups all-purpose flour
2 teaspoons baking powder
1/2 teaspoon salt
1/2 teaspoon baking soda
1 cup buttermilk
1 teaspoon vanilla extract

In a mixing bowl, cream butter and sugar with mixer on high until fluffy. Add eggs, one at a time, beating well after each. Sift flour, baking powder, salt and soda; add alternately with buttermilk to creamed mixture, beginning and ending with flour. Add vanilla. Pour into three greased and floured 8-in. cake pans. Bake at 375° for 20 minutes or until toothpick inserted in center comes out clean. Cool cakes completely before icing. **Yield:** 3 8-inch layers.

BIRTHDAY CAKE TREAT! Delight your birthday boy or girl with a cake decorated with edible candle holders! Pick up a roll of Life Savers, and you'll find that small candles fit into the centers perfectly.

TURKEY HAM QUICHE/ HASH BROWN CRUST

Dana Tegtmeier, Bern, Kansas

(PICTURED ON PAGE 172)

CRUST:
    3 cups cubed frozen hash
        brown potatoes, defrosted
    1/2 cup onion, chopped, *divided*
    2 tablespoons green pepper,
        finely chopped
    1/8 teaspoon white pepper
    1 egg, beaten
FILLING:
    1-1/2 cups cooked turkey ham,
        diced
    1 cup (4 ounces) Swiss cheese,
        shredded
    1 cup milk (can use skim *or* 2%)
    4 eggs
    2 teaspoons prepared mustard
    1/4 teaspoon white pepper

In medium bowl, combine potatoes, 1/4 cup onion, green pepper and white pepper. Fold in beaten egg. Pat potato mixture evenly into greased 10-in. pie plate to form crust, building up sides to rim. Bake at 400° for 25 minutes or until crust just begins to brown. Remove from oven. (Crust may be prepared to this point, cooled, covered and refrigerated until ready to serve. To reheat, place in cold oven; set temperature to 350°. Heat for 10 minutes.) Sprinkle turkey ham, remaining onion and cheese in layers evenly over crust (crust should be hot when these ingredients are added). Set aside. In a small bowl, combine the milk, eggs, mustard and white pepper; mix well. Pour over crust ingredients. Place in oven; immediately reduce oven temperature to 350°. Bake for 30-35 minutes or until a knife inserted in center comes out clean. Let stand 5 minutes before cutting. **Yield:** 6 servings.

HOT TURKEY TACO SALAD

Jean Bergin, Mishicot, Wisconsin

(PICTURED ON PAGE 172)

    1 tablespoon vegetable oil
    1 pound uncooked ground
        turkey
    1 small green pepper, chopped
    1 package taco seasoning mix,
        mild *or* hot
    1 can (15 to 16 ounces) kidney
        beans, drained
    1 can (6 ounces) ripe pitted
        olives, sliced
    1 fresh tomato, chopped

    1/2 cup taco sauce *or* salsa
    1/4 cup Italian salad dressing
    1/2 medium-size head lettuce,
        shredded
    1 package (8 ounces) nacho-
        flavored tortilla chips
    1/2 to 3/4 cup shredded cheddar
        or Co-Jack cheese
Additional salsa *or* taco sauce

Heat oil in a large skillet; add ground turkey, stirring until turkey browns. Add green pepper and seasoning mix (with amount of water called for on packet instructions). Cook for 10-15 minutes. Add beans, olives and tomato. Combine salsa/taco sauce and dressing; pour into the turkey mixture and heat. Just before serving, place the shredded lettuce and crushed chips on platter, fanning some whole chips around edge of dish. Spoon turkey mixture over chips and lettuce. Serve with the shredded cheese and additional salsa or taco sauce. **Yield:** 6 servings.

BARBECUED TURKEY

Holly Petersen, Hunter, North Dakota

(PICTURED ON PAGE 172)

    1 fresh turkey (12 to 14 pounds)
    1 syringe (12cc) available from
        veterinarian *or* farm supply
        store
INJECTION SAUCE:
    1/2 cup water
    1 tablespoon salt
    1-1/2 teaspoons garlic juice* *or*
        garlic salt
    1-1/2 teaspoons hot pepper sauce
    6 tablespoons lemon juice
BASTING SAUCE:
    1/2 cup butter
    1/2 clove garlic
    2 teaspoons all-purpose flour
    1/3 cup water
    3 tablespoons lemon juice
    1-1/2 teaspoons sugar
    1 teaspoon salt
    1/2 teaspoon pepper
    1/2 teaspoon poultry seasoning
    1/8 teaspoon hot pepper sauce

*Garlic juice can be found in the seasonings section of many supermarkets. Combine injection sauce ingredients; fill syringe and inject into all meaty portions of turkey until skin is tight. (Inject slowly, withdrawing needle gradually to allow maximum juice retention.) Cover turkey loosely; refrigerate for several hours or overnight until time to grill. Place turkey on rotisserie or in shallow drip pan on top of grill. Use indirect heat method if cooking on a covered charcoal grill. Use

low heat setting if cooking on a gas grill. While turkey cooks, prepare the basting sauce by melting butter in saucepan. Add the garlic; cook, stirring for several minutes. Stir in flour; cook until bubbly. Remove from heat; add the remaining ingredients. Return to heat; cook until mixture thickens and boils. Brush on turkey about 15 minutes before removing from grill. Check for doneness after 2 hours by inserting meat thermometer in thickest part of thigh, next to body (not resting on bone). Turkey is done when thermometer registers between 180° and 185°. (Our test turkey, about 11 lbs., was done in 2-1/2 hours. Time will vary with grill.) Let turkey stand for 15 minutes before carving. **Yield:** 20 servings.

GRILLED TURKEY STEAKS

Barbara Wellnitz, Ashby, Minnesota

(PICTURED ON PAGE 172)

    2-1/2 to 3 pounds boneless
        uncooked turkey breast, cut
        into 1-1/2-inch-thick steaks
MARINADE:
    1/4 cup vegetable oil
    2 cloves garlic, minced
    1-1/2 teaspoons oregano
    2 tablespoons lemon juice
    1/2 teaspoon salt
    1/8 teaspoon fresh ground
        pepper
CASHEW BUTTER:
    1/4 cup butter *or* margarine
    2 teaspoons lemon juice
    1/2 cup coarsely chopped
        cashews

Combine marinade ingredients; marinate steaks in refrigerator 2 hours or overnight. Cook on grill over medium heat about 10 minutes per side or until done—*do not overcook*. Heat cashew butter ingredients in microwave or on top of stove. Serve warm with steaks. **Yield:** 6-8 servings.

STIR-FRY TURKEY WITH WALNUTS

Terri Holmgren, Swanville, Minnesota

(PICTURED ON PAGE 173)

SAUCE:
    3 tablespoons low-sodium soy
        sauce
    2 teaspoons cornstarch

2 tablespoons dry sherry wine
or apple juice
1 teaspoon grated fresh ginger
root
1 teaspoon toasted sesame
oil*, optional
1 teaspoon sugar
1/2 teaspoon salt
1/2 teaspoon crushed red pepper
STIR-FRY:
2 tablespoons peanut oil *or*
vegetable oil
2 green *or* red peppers, cut in
3/4-inch pieces
4 green onions, bias-sliced in
1-inch lengths
1 cup walnut halves
1-1/2 pounds uncooked turkey
breast, skinned cut in 1-inch
cubes
Cooked rice

*Toasted sesame oil can be found in the Oriental food section of many supermarkets. In small bowl, blend all sauce ingredients; set aside. Preheat wok over high heat; add oil. Stir-fry green/red peppers and onions in hot oil 2 minutes; remove from wok and set aside. Add walnuts to wok. Stir-fry 1-2 minutes or until golden brown; remove and set aside. Add more oil as needed. Add half of turkey. Stir-fry until done and browned on all sides; remove. Repeat with remaining turkey. Return all turkey to wok; stir in sauce. Stir, cooking until mixture thickens. Stir in the vegetables. Cover; cook for 1 minute. Stir in walnuts. Serve at once with hot cooked rice. **Yield:** 6 servings.

TURKEY SCALLOPINI

JoAnne Hill, Lisbon, Maryland

(PICTURED ON PAGE 173)

1/2 to 3/4 pound uncooked turkey
cutlets (turkey breast slices)
1/2 cup all-purpose flour,
seasoned with salt and pepper
3 tablespoons butter, *divided*
2 tablespoons olive oil
1 small garlic clove, sliced thin
1/4 pound fresh mushrooms,
sliced
1 to 2 tablespoons lemon juice
1/3 cup chicken broth
1/4 cup white wine *or* additional
chicken broth

Pound turkey to 1/8-in. thickness. Flour lightly, shaking off all excess. In skillet, melt 2 tablespoons of butter, adding oil and garlic. Brown meat on both sides until golden brown, about 3 minutes. Place browned meat in ovenproof casserole dish. Add remaining 1 tablespoon of butter and mushrooms to skillet and

saute until mushrooms lose their crispness. Add to casserole. In a skillet, combine the lemon juice, broth and wine; stir and heat until mixture bubbles. Pour over casserole. Bake at 325° for about 30 minutes. (This recipe can be prepared in advance *up to baking*, refrigerated and popped into the oven when guests arrive.) **Yield:** 4 servings.

GRILLED TURKEY TENDERLOIN SANDWICHES

Helen Miller, Teutopolis, Illinois

(PICTURED ON PAGE 173)

1 pound uncooked turkey
tenderloins, 3/4 to 1 inch thick
MARINADE:
1/4 cup low-sodium soy sauce
1/4 cup peanut oil
1/4 cup sherry wine *or* apple
juice
2 tablespoons lemon juice
1/8 teaspoon black pepper
1/8 teaspoon garlic salt
2 tablespoons crushed onion
1/4 teaspoon ground ginger

In a shallow pan, blend all marinade ingredients together. Add turkey, turning to coat both sides. Cover; marinate in refrigerator several hours or overnight, turning occasionally. Grill the tenderloins over hot coals, 8-10 minutes per side, depending on the thickness. Tenderloins are done when there is no pink in center—*do not overcook*. Serve in 1/4-in.-thick slices on toasted buns. **Yield:** 4 servings.

DAY-AFTER TURKEY PIE

Kay Smith, Gooding, Idaho

(PICTURED ON PAGE 173)

CRUST:
1-1/2 cups all-purpose flour
1-1/2 teaspoons baking powder
3/4 teaspoon salt
1/2 cup shortening
6 tablespoons hot water
1 egg, *separated*
2 teaspoons lemon juice
FILLING:
1-1/2 cups cold cooked turkey,
cut up

1 cup turkey dressing,
crumbled
1-1/2 cups turkey gravy (may
extend with undiluted
mushroom soup)
1 cup celery, diced
2 tablespoons butter, optional

For crust, combine flour, baking powder and salt; cut in the shortening. Combine water, beaten egg yolk and lemon juice; stir in until crust mixture forms a ball. Divide into two portions; roll out each to fit 9-in. pie pan or 8-in. square baking dish. Combine all filling ingredients *except butter* and place in a pastry-lined dish. Dot with butter, if desired. Cover with top crust. Cut in steam vents; brush with reserved beaten egg white. Bake at 425° for 30 minutes. **Yield:** 6 servings.

ORANGE BARBECUED TURKEY

Lynn Zukas, Spencer, Massachusetts

4 turkey breast steaks (about
1-1/4 pounds)
1/2 cup orange juice
1 teaspoon grated orange peel
1 tablespoon cooking oil
2 teaspoons Worcestershire
sauce
1 teaspoon dry mustard
1/2 teaspoon ground pepper
1/8 teaspoon garlic powder *or*
1 garlic clove, minced

Place turkey in a shallow glass baking dish. Combine all remaining ingredients and pour over turkey. Cover and refrigerate, turning occasionally, 4-6 hours or overnight. Grill or broil steaks until done, about 3-5 minutes per side. Do not overcook. **Yield:** about 4 servings.

TASTY GROUND TURKEY: Fresh, uncooked ground turkey makes an interesting substitute in dishes that use ground beef. Try it for Stroganoff, "Sloppy Toms", spaghetti sauce, lasagna, tacos, enchiladas, casseroles and as all or part of the meat in meat loaf. Season sparingly, since ground turkey does accept seasoning more readily than do other ground meats.

● When a recipe calls for turkey sausage and none is available, substitute plain ground turkey and add fennel seed, garlic, oregano and basil.

● For a delicious hamburger variation, mix equal parts ground turkey and ground beef.

TURKEY ENCHILADAS

Jo Groth, Plainfield, Iowa

(PICTURED ON PAGE 174)

1/2 cup chopped onion
1 can (4 ounces) green chilies, drained *or* green peppers, *divided*
3 tablespoons butter, *divided*
1/3 cup taco sauce
1 cup dairy sour cream, *divided*
1/8 teaspoon chili powder
2-1/2 cups cooked cubed turkey
2 cups shredded cheddar cheese, *divided*
10 flour tortillas
2 tablespoons all-purpose flour
1 cup chicken *or* turkey broth
1/2 cup chopped fresh tomato

In glass bowl, combine the onions, 2 tablespoons chilies/peppers and 1 tablespoon butter. Microwave on high for 1 minute. Add taco sauce, 1/4 cup sour cream and chili powder. Stir in turkey and 1/2 cup cheese. Divide the mixture among tortillas. Roll tortillas; place seam side down in 13-in. x 9-in. x 2-in. baking dish. Set aside. Microwave remaining 2 tablespoons butter until melted. Blend in flour, then slowly stir in broth. Microwave on high 3-4 minutes until thickened, stirring every minute. Stir in the remaining sour cream and remaining chilies/peppers. Pour over enchiladas. Microwave enchiladas on medium for 6-8 minutes. Sprinkle with remaining cheese and tomato. Microwave at medium until all the cheese is melted. *Conventional Method:* Combine filling ingredients; fill tortillas. Place in greased baking dish and bake 45 minutes at 325°. Sprinkle cheese and tomato over top. Return to oven until cheese is melted. **Yield:** 8-10 servings.

TURKEY PICCATA

Perlene Hoekema, Lynden, Washington

(PICTURED ON PAGE 174)

2 eggs
2 tablespoons milk
3-1/2 cups fresh bread crumbs (about 8 slices processed in food processor *or* blender)
2 packages (14 to 16 ounces *each*) uncooked turkey cutlets *or* half of a 5- to 6-pound frozen turkey breast, thawed and cut in 1/4-inch-thick slices
About 3/4 cup butter *or* margarine
2 large lemons, *divided*
1-1/2 cups water
2 teaspoons chicken-flavor bouillon
1/2 teaspoon salt
Parsley sprigs

Beat eggs with milk in shallow dish until well blended. Place bread crumbs on waxed paper. Dip cutlets in egg mixture then in crumbs, coating both sides. Melt the butter or margarine, as needed, in a 12-in. skillet over a medium-high heat. Brown turkey cutlets, 4 to 6 at a time, on both sides until done. Remove to a plate; keep warm. Reduce heat to low. Squeeze juice of 1 lemon (about 1/4 cup) into pan drippings in skillet; stir in water, bouillon and salt; cover and simmer 15 minutes. Thinly slice remaining lemon. To serve, arrange cutlets on large warm platter and garnish with lemon slices. Pour sauce over cutlets; sprinkle with parsley. **Yield:** 8 servings.

TANGY TURKEY SALAD

Merridy Kienitz, Blue Earth, Minnesota

(PICTURED ON PAGE 174)

 This tasty dish uses less sugar, salt and fat. Recipe includes *Diabetic Exchanges*.

DRESSING:
1/2 cup reduced calorie creamy salad dressing
1/4 cup dairy sour cream
1 tablespoon fresh chives
1 tablespoon sugar
1 teaspoon ground ginger
1/2 teaspoon grated lemon peel
1 tablespoon fresh lemon juice
1/4 teaspoon salt
SALAD:
2 to 3 cups cooked white turkey, cubed
1 cup seedless green grapes, halved if desired
1 cup sliced celery
1 cup drained pineapple chunks, halved if desired
GARNISH:
Curly leaf lettuce
4 cantaloupe rings, peeled and seeded, cut 3/4 inch thick
1/2 cup toasted pecans

Combine all dressing ingredients; mix well. Refrigerate. Prepare salad ingredients and mix lightly with dressing. Cover individual luncheon plates with base of lettuce and cantaloupe; fill center with salad. Garnish with pecans. **Yield:** 4

servings. **Diabetic Exchanges:** One serving equals 3-1/2 protein, 2 fruits, 2 fats; also, 403 calories, 389 mg sodium, 86 mg cholesterol, 29 gm carbohydrate, 34 gm protein, 17 gm fat.

WILLIAMSBURG INN TURKEY SOUP

Muriel Lerdal, Humboldt, Iowa

(PICTURED ON PAGE 174)

1 turkey carcass
4 quarts water
3 large onions, chopped fine
3 stalks celery, chopped fine
2 large carrots, chopped fine
1/4 cup uncooked long grain rice
1 cup butter *or* margarine
1-1/2 cups all-purpose flour
1 pint half-and-half
3 cups diced cooked turkey
1/2 teaspoon poultry seasoning, if desired
Salt, pepper to taste

In large kettle, cook turkey carcass with water to make 3 qts. stock. Remove bones; reserve meat for soup. Strain stock; set aside. In saucepan, combine onions, celery, carrots, rice and 1 qt. of the stock. Cook for 20 minutes; set aside. In a large soup kettle, melt butter/margarine. Blend in flour and heat until bubbly. Add half-and-half and remaining 2 qts. stock to butter/flour mixture; cook and stir until bubbly. Stir in the reserved vegetable mixture, turkey and seasonings to taste. Heat slowly to serving temperature. **Yield:** 4 to 4-1/2 quarts. (This soup freezes well.)

TURKEY TIPS: The best way to roast a turkey is in a shallow pan with a "tent" of heavy aluminum foil over it. Roast at 325° for about 15 to 20 minutes per pound. After roasting, let the turkey stand for 15-20 minutes before carving.

● To remove a large, hot roasted turkey from the pan, slip on a pair of insulated oven mitts and cover them with plastic bags. The bird will lift safely and easily to the cutting board.

● Save the last-minute rush when you're serving turkey and stuffing to a large group! Roast the turkey the day before, carve it, and store the meat and stuffing—separately—in the refrigerator. To reheat, place in wire salad baskets in an improvised steamer. (Place an empty tincan in the bottom of a large kettle and set basket on top of can; add enough water to steam.) Cover; steam for 30 minutes.

TURKEY A LA QUEEN

Martha Kaup, Defiance, Ohio

6 slices white bread, crusts
   trimmed
2 tablespoons melted butter,
   divided
FILLING:
1/4 cup slivered almonds
4 tablespoons butter
2 tablespoons all-purpose flour
Dash black pepper
1 teaspoon salt
1/8 teaspoon paprika
1-1/2 cups half-and-half *or*
   evaporated milk
1 egg yolk, beaten
2 cups diced cooked turkey
1-1/2 cups seedless grapes
Additional almonds for garnish

To make toast cups, brush trimmed bread slices lightly on one side with part of the melted butter. Gently push each slice, buttered side down, into large muffin tins, leaving the corners showing at top. Bake at 375° for 8-10 minutes or until corners are browned. Remove from oven; let cool in muffin tins. To prepare filling, saute almonds in remaining melted butter (about 2 teaspoons) until light golden brown; set aside. In heavy saucepan, melt 4 tablespoons butter. Next add flour, pepper, salt and paprika, stirring until smooth. Slowly add half-and-half/milk. Pour a small amount of sauce over beaten egg yolk, stirring to blend. Return yolk mixture to remaining sauce. Cook and stir until thick. Add turkey and grapes. Heat. Spoon into toast cups. Garnish with almonds. **Yield:** 6 servings.

TURKEY/WILD RICE CASSEROLE

Patty Nelson, Clear Lake, Wisconsin

1 box long grain/wild rice mix,
   prepared according to
   instructions on the package
2 packages (10 ounces *each*)
   frozen broccoli, thawed and
   drained
6 cups leftover cubed turkey
SAUCE:
1/2 cup creamy salad dressing *or*
   mayonnaise
2 cans (10-3/4 ounces *each*)
   cream of chicken soup
4 ounces water chestnuts,
   sliced and drained
1/2 teaspoon lemon juice
1 cup shredded cheddar cheese

Spread cooked wild rice mixture over bottom of greased 13-in. x 9-in. x 2-in. baking pan. Place broccoli spears on top of rice; add cubed turkey. Combine sauce ingredients except cheese; spread over top of casserole. Sprinkle cheese over all. Bake at 350° for 55 minutes or microwave on high for 12 minutes or until casserole is heated through. **Yield:** 8 servings.

GARLIC-ROASTED CHICKEN

Michelle Bouchard, St. Jean-Baptiste, Manitoba

6 medium chicken drumsticks
6 medium chicken thighs
6 medium potatoes, peeled and
   quartered
12 extra-large unpeeled garlic
   cloves
1/4 cup butter *or* margarine,
   melted
1 teaspoon salt
1/4 cup honey

In a large roasting pan, place chicken, potatoes and garlic. Pour butter over all and sprinkle with salt. Bake at 400° for 40 minutes, basting frequently with the pan juices. Heat honey; baste over chicken. Spoon pan juices over potatoes and garlic. Bake 20 minutes longer or until chicken is tender. To serve, arrange chicken, potatoes and garlic on a platter. Skim fat from pan and spoon drippings over chicken. Serve several garlic cloves per person. Each person is to cut through the skin of the garlic and spread the soft roasted pulp over chicken and potatoes. Garlic develops a mild flavor when roasted. **Yield:** 6 servings.

BEST-OF-THE-DINNER SANDWICHES

Freda Holmes, Oklahoma City, Oklahoma

1 English muffin (per person
   served)
Chili sauce
Creamy salad dressing *or*
   mayonnaise
Leftover sliced turkey
Leftover turkey stuffing
Leftover cranberry sauce
Cheddar, American *or* Swiss cheese
   slices
Cooked, crumbled bacon

Lightly toast muffins in 400° oven on ungreased cookie sheet; remove from oven. Combine one part chili sauce with two parts salad dressing/mayonnaise; spread on each of muffin halves. Layer turkey, thin layer of stuffing, thin layer of cranberry sauce and slice of cheese on bottom halves of muffins; reserve tops. Place filled muffin bottoms in oven for 10 minutes or until cheese melts. (May also microwave.) Remove from oven; top with bacon and reserved muffin halves.

FROSTED CHICKEN SALAD

Joyce Carpenter, Darlington Indiana

SALAD:
2 cups diced red apples,
   unpeeled
1 tablespoon lemon juice
4 cups diced cooked chicken
3/4 cup salad dressing
1/2 cup sliced seedless green
   grapes
1/4 teaspoon salt
1/8 teaspoon pepper
1-1/2 cups chopped celery
FROSTING:
1 package (8 ounces) cream
   cheese, softened
1/4 cup salad dressing
Lettuce leaves
Sliced apples and grapes for garnish

Line a 1-1/2-qt. bowl with plastic wrap. Combine all salad ingredients and gently press into the bowl. Cover; chill several hours. Carefully unmold onto a plate lined with a bed of lettuce leaves. Combine the cream cheese and salad dressing; frost salad. Garnish with apples and grapes. Chill for several hours. **Yield:** 6 servings.

SMOKED TURKEY SOUP: The carcass and leftover meat from a 10-lb. to 14-lb. smoked grilled turkey makes a wonderful base for a bean soup. For the broth, cover the carcass with 4 to 6 quarts of water and add 2 cups coarsely chopped onion, 6 cups chopped celery stems (with leaves), 4 peeled and shredded carrots, 4 to 6 cloves chopped garlic, 2 tablespoons of seasoning/herb mixture and salt to taste. Simmer for 2 hours. Remove the bones; reserve meat. Cool stock; skim fat from top. Add about 2 lbs. of soaked navy beans to stock; simmer until the beans are halfway cooked. Add reserved turkey meat; cook until the beans are tender. Enjoy!

resh from backyard branches and nearby orchards, apples are at the heart of many cherished recipes. And here's a bumper crop of guaranteed-to-please apple eating!

There's a quick-to-bake coffee cake...ever-popular apple pie bars ...feathery fruit muffins...creamy bread pudding...cakes of contrasting kinds...a man-pleasing main dish ...and a prize-winning apple pie.

Pick a bag or bushel of apples and put fall at its finest on your table!

AAH...APPLES! Clockwise from far left—**Apple Streusel Coffee Cake** (Pg. 190); **Apple Bread Pudding** (Pg. 190); **Apple Sour Cream Cake** (Pg. 190); **Prize-Winning Apple Pie** (Pg. 191); **Apple Streusel Muffins** (Pg. 191); **Apple/Sausage/Sweet Potato Casserole** (Pg. 190); **Fresh Apple Cake** (Pg. 191); **Apple Pie Bars** (Pg. 190).

Appetizing apples—their crisp-sweet crunch and rose-cheeked cast add color all their own to autumn favorites!

When apples are at their peak, take your pick from among these mouth-watering recipes.

APPLE OF YOUR EYE: Clockwise from bottom—**Apple Sausage Breakfast Ring** (Pg. 192); **Apple/Cranberry Crisp** (Pg. 191); **Fresh Apple Salad** (Pg. 191); **Apple, Raisin, Walnut Cake** (Pg. 192).

BEST COOK

Marietta Saladin
Woodstock, Illinois

Autumn is a special time for this "Best Cook". It's the time when Marietta Saladin of Woodstock, Illinois can get back in her kitchen and do some cooking!

"When it's so hot and humid during the summer, the last place I want to be is in the kitchen," Marietta says. "But when fall rolls around, I really enjoy cooking a hearty meal."

Glazed Apple Cookies (pictured above) are one of her favorite fall treats. She's had the recipe for years, and it's still requested often—year-round!

"I've had that recipe since my first child was little, so I've used it a long time," she says. "It was always one of the kids' favorites, and now it's a favorite of my grandchildren. I like to use Jonathan apples in the recipe, since that's my favorite type of apple."

Learned from Mother

Marietta learned to cook from her mother and picked up many recipes from her.

"I would always watch my mother, who was a good German cook," Marietta explains. "If she was going to be out of town, she'd tell me what to make while she was gone. That was my first cooking experience."

Marietta grew up on a farm near Woodstock, but it wasn't the typical Midwest farm with cows, corn and chickens. Her family operated one of the nation's largest rose farms, providing millions of long-stemmed beauties to the wholesale market in Chicago.

"Our farm was *huge* and oh, so pretty," she remembers. "But when World War II came, my father had to raise tomatoes to help the effort. So we went from red roses to red tomatoes!"

Marietta also picked up cooking skills from her mother-in-law, who operated a boarding house in the Upper Peninsula of Michigan.

"I learned how to make chicken and polenta from her, and it's still a family favorite," Marietta says. "If any member of the family knows I'm making it, they seem to find their way over here just in time to eat."

She was nominated for "Best Cook" by her daughter Gretchen and daughter-in-law Lisa.

"Even now, with all the kids grown and married and with children of their own, Mom's table is a very special place," Gretchen says. "Mom always believed that a healthy, wholesome meal at the end of the day was a must for a happy family."

Marietta enjoys fall cooking best, but the recipes she shares here are delicious anytime of year!

GLAZED APPLE COOKIES

    1/2 cup shortening
1-1/2 cups packed brown sugar
    1 teaspoon baking soda
    1 teaspoon salt
    1 teaspoon ground cinnamon
    1 teaspoon ground cloves
    1/2 teaspoon ground nutmeg
    1 egg, beaten
    1 cup finely chopped peeled
       apples
    1 cup chopped walnuts
    1 cup raisins
    1/4 cup apple juice *or* milk
    2 cups all-purpose flour,
       divided
VANILLA GLAZE:
1-1/2 cups confectioners' sugar
    1 tablespoon butter *or*
       margarine
    1/4 teaspoon vanilla extract
    1/8 teaspoon salt
2-1/2 tablespoons light cream

In a large mixing bowl, combine shortening, sugar, baking soda, salt, spices and egg. Stir in apples, nuts, raisins, juice/milk and half of the flour; mix well. Blend in the remaining flour. Drop by heaping tablespoonfuls onto greased cookie sheets. Bake at 400° for 10-12 minutes. Combine glaze ingredients and frost cookies while warm. **Yield:** about 3 dozen.

BRAISED LAMB SHANKS

    3 tablespoons shortening *or*
       cooking oil
    6 lamb shanks
    1/4 cup prepared mustard
    2 tablespoons horseradish
    2 teaspoons salt
    1/2 teaspoon paprika
    1/2 teaspoon pepper
    1 cup water

In a Dutch oven, heat shortening over medium heat. Brown shanks well. Meanwhile, in a small bowl, combine remaining ingredients. Pour over the shanks; cover and cook over low heat for 2 hours or until meat is tender. If desired, skim off fat from pan juices and make gravy. **Yield:** 6 servings.

CHICKEN AND POLENTA

    1 broiler-fryer chicken (2-1/2 to
       3 pounds), cut up
    2 ounces salt pork *or* bacon,
       diced
    1 garlic clove, minced
    2 tablespoons cooking oil
    1/2 teaspoon dried rosemary,
       crushed
    1 pint whipping cream
POLENTA:
    4 cups water
    1 teaspoon salt
    1 cup cornmeal
Grated Parmesan cheese, optional

In a large ovenproof skillet or Dutch oven, brown chicken pieces, salt pork/bacon and garlic in oil. Sprinkle with rosemary. Cover and bake at 350° for 1 hour. Remove from the oven. Transfer chicken to a warming plate. Drain excess fat from skillet; add cream and simmer until slightly thickened to make gravy. Meanwhile, for polenta, place water and salt in a saucepan. Bring to a boil. Add cornmeal, stirring constantly. Reduce heat to low; cover and cook for 15 minutes or until thick. Spoon polenta onto individual plates and top with chicken and gravy. Sprinkle Parmesan cheese on top if desired. **Yield:** 4-6 servings.

Fruits of Final Harvest
Fill the Heart

For many gardeners, tilling the earth feeds not just the body, but the soul.

By Susan Hauser, Puposky, Minnesota

Photo/Nats

The wildflowers are gone. Only a few lone asters light the roadsides; a handful of staunch pansies grace the gardens. Trees have taken over the job of coloring our lives—maples flame, birches rival the gold of the sun, oaks simmer in rust.

We're glad to be outside for one more day, to work a little longer with our backs to the sky. When we're bent over the ground that way, life seems a little simpler.

Today we'll dig potatoes, the last harvest of the year. The squash already are rescued from the frost, lining the shelves and the sills and the floors around the wood-stove. The heat will harden their shells, and in 2 weeks they'll be ready for the long wintering-over.

Husband Bill and I walk slowly down to the garden, the potato fork and metal baskets rattling in the cart behind us. Unlike the squirrels that raid our bird feeders, we're in no hurry.

Our eyes wander over the marsh that separates our tree line from the one across the way. The sky invites our gaze, too, and our minds drift with the clouds.

The garden brings us back to reality; it's a wreck. The potato plants have shrunk with the cold, and we'll have trouble finding them among the pigweed and nettles that took over while we lost ourselves in other summer plea-sures. But we find the beginning of a row and begin to dig.

Bill thrusts the fork into the ground, steps on the top cross-piece and lets his weight sink the tines deep into the earth. I grasp the base of the plant with both hands.

Bill pushes back on the fork handle. As the earth rises up, I pull on the stalk.

Potatoes tumble up and out of their dark cave. The dirt falls away as we set them in the basket. When the first basket's full, we leave it and start another. When we're done, the garden is dotted with old metal egg crates filled with spuds.

We sit on the edge of the cart and rest a while. This is hard work, and we're not young. In fact, pulling the cart up the hill will use the energy we have left, and some we don't have at all.

For a moment we wonder why we do this. There are only two of us to feed, and we've grown enough pota-toes for a growing family.

Then I rummage in the crate next to the cart and pick out a potato that fits the palm of my hand. I jiggle it, testing its weight. I pick out another, then another, and pull out the front of my shirt, making a basket.

These are the ones I'll use for tonight's soup. The skins are so delicate they'll come off with a light brush-ing. The flesh is so crisp it will crackle when the knife cuts into it.

After simmering in light cream, these potatoes will make today's gardening efforts worthwhile, and body and soul will be nurtured by the gift of this harvest ful-filled. It comes from a labor that has no price, and we'll know again why some of the things we get out of our garden are as much food for the soul as the body.

Maybe somebody ought to switch that old, familiar "meat and potatoes" expression around! When it comes to tasty ways to feed a hungry family anytime of day, there are *plenty* of reasons to put potatoes first.

You'll agree when you see the hearty and filling dishes we've cooked up for you here. So take your pick of potatoes—there's more than enough here for everyone!

PERFECT POTATOES. Clockwise from top—**Berry Mallow Yam Bake** (Pg. 193); **Dublin Potato Salad** (Pg. 193); **Tex-Mex Stuffed Potatoes** (Pg. 194); **Porky Pine Waffles** (Pg. 194).

ass the potatoes, please! That's what you'll hear when you serve your family one or more of these nutritious and delicious potato dishes. Packed with vitamins and minerals, the potato is the world's most widely grown—and perhaps most versatile—vegetable.

Potatoes are tops whether they're baked, boiled, fried or mashed! So try these lip-smacking dishes, and settle once and for all that spuds need not be duds!

TOP TATERS: Clockwise from lower left—**Fat Rascals (Potato Cheese Puffs)** (Pg. 194); **Perfect Potato Pancakes** (Pg. 194); **Sweet Potato Salad** (Pg. 194); **Potato Crust Quiche** (Pg. 194); **Crunchy Swiss and Ham Appetizers** (Pg. 195); **Ranch Potato Casserole** (Pg. 195); **Potato Cheese Soup with Salmon** (Pg. 195); **Potato Onion Supreme** (Pg. 195).

APPLE STREUSEL COFFEE CAKE

Loralee Hames, Troy, Ontario

(PICTURED ON PAGE 182)

2-1/4 cups all-purpose flour
3/4 cup sugar
3/4 cup butter
1/2 teaspoon baking powder
1/2 teaspoon baking soda
1 egg, beaten
3/4 cup buttermilk
1 can (20 ounces) apple pie filling
1/2 teaspoon grated lemon rind or 1/2 teaspoon cinnamon, optional
1/3 cup raisins

Combine flour and sugar in large bowl. Cut in butter until mixture is crumbly; set 1/2 cup of the mixture aside. To remainder, add the baking powder and soda; set aside. Combine egg and buttermilk; add to dry ingredients, stirring just until moistened. Spread two-thirds of batter over bottom and part way up sides of greased 9-in. springform pan. Combine pie filling, flavorings (if desired) and raisins. Spoon over batter. Drop spoonfuls of remaining batter over the filling. Sprinkle with reserved crumb mixture. Bake at 350° for 1 hour. **Yield:** 8-10 servings.

APPLE SOUR CREAM CAKE

Gayle West, Darwin, Minnesota

(PICTURED ON PAGE 182)

1/2 cup chopped walnuts
1 teaspoon cinnamon
1/2 cup sugar
1/2 cup butter
1 cup sugar
2 cups all-purpose flour
1 cup dairy sour cream
2 eggs
1 teaspoon baking powder
1 teaspoon baking soda
1 teaspoon vanilla
1-1/2 cups finely chopped apples, peeled

CINNAMON CARAMEL GLAZE/SAUCE:
3/4 cup brown sugar
2 tablespoons butter
1/2 teaspoon cinnamon
1/3 cup hot evaporated milk

Combine nuts, cinnamon and sugar in small bowl; set aside. In large bowl, cream butter and sugar until light and fluffy. Add flour, sour cream, eggs, baking powder, soda and vanilla; beat 3

minutes. Prepare the apples; set aside. Grease and lightly flour a fluted cake pan. Spread half of the batter in pan; sprinkle with half of the nut mixture, then chopped apples. Sprinkle remaining nut mixture over apples, then spread remaining batter over top. Bake at 350° for 60 minutes or until cake begins to pull away from sides of pan. Make glaze by putting all of ingredients in blender (make sure milk it *hot*), covering and processing on high until sugar is dissolved; set aside. Cool cake slightly on rack; remove from pan. Drizzle glaze/sauce over cake. **Yield:** 12-16 servings.

APPLE PIE BARS

Cindy Cyr, Fowler, Indiana

(PICTURED ON PAGE 182)

CRUST:
2 cups all-purpose flour
1/2 cup sugar, optional
1/2 teaspoon baking powder
1/2 teaspoon salt
1 cup butter
2 egg yolks, beaten
FILLING:
4 cups pared, cored and sliced apples (1/8 inch thick)
1/2 cup sugar
1/4 cup all-purpose flour
1 teaspoon cinnamon
1/4 teaspoon nutmeg
2 egg whites, slightly beaten

To prepare crust, combine flour, sugar, baking powder and salt; cut in butter. Mix in egg yolks (mixture will be crumbly). Press *half* of the mixture in bottom of 15-in. x 10-in. jelly roll pan (may also use 13-in. x 9-in. x 2-in. pan). Set remaining half of the mixture aside. Combine all of filling ingredients *except egg whites*; arrange over bottom crust. Crumble remaining crust mixture over filling. Brush egg whites over all. Bake at 350° for 30 minutes (jelly roll pan) or 40 minutes (13-in. x 9-in. x 2-in. pan). Cool. Drizzle with thin confectioners' sugar glaze, if desired. **Yield:** 3-4 dozen bars.

APPLE ADVICE: To prevent any browning when working with a quantity of peeled apples, slice them into water with 1 tablespoon of fresh lemon juice added.

● Don't forget this fruitful formula: 2 to 3 medium-sized apples usually make about 1 lb.

● For moist and colorful poultry stuffing, add a diced, unpeeled apple to your favorite stuffing mix.

APPLE BREAD PUDDING

Martha Doyle, Kalispell, Montana

(PICTURED ON PAGE 182)

✓ This tasty dish uses less sugar, salt and fat. Recipe includes *Diabetic Exchanges*.

4 cups soft bread crumbs, crusts trimmed
1 cup diced apples, peeled
2 cups scalded milk
2 tablespoons butter, melted
3 eggs
1/3 cup honey *or* 1/2 cup sugar
1 teaspoon vanilla
1 teaspoon cinnamon
1/4 teaspoon nutmeg
1/4 teaspoon cloves
1 teaspoon grated lemon rind
Ice cream *or* whipped cream, optional

Mix bread (white, whole wheat or combination) with apples; set aside. Combine milk, butter, eggs, honey/sugar, vanilla, cinnamon, nutmeg, cloves and rind in blender or with hand mixer. Pour over bread/apple mixture. Spoon into a buttered 2-qt. casserole or individual ramekins, as shown. Set dish in a larger pan of hot water; bake at 350° for 1 hour or until knife inserted in center comes out clean. Serve warm with whipped cream or ice cream, if desired. **Yield:** 6 servings. **Diabetic Exchanges:** One serving equals 1 fruit, 1 bread, 3/4 milk, 2 fats; also 281 calories, 271 mg sodium, 149 mg cholesterol, 38 gm carbohydrate, 9 gm protein, 11 gm fat.

APPLE/SAUSAGE/SWEET POTATO CASSEROLE

Irene Gerdes, Red Wing, Minnesota

(PICTURED ON PAGE 183)

1 pound seasoned lean bulk pork sausage
1/4 cup water
1 can (23 ounces) sweet potatoes, drained
1/4 to 1/2 cup brown sugar
1/4 cup butter, *divided*
3 medium apples, red cooking variety

Form sausage into patties; brown in a skillet. Drain. Place patties in bottom of 2-qt. casserole. Add water. Layer thick slices of sweet potatoes over sausage. Sprinkle with sugar; dot with half of the butter. Top with sliced, unpeeled apple rings, cut 1/2 in. thick. Dot with the remaining butter. Cover; bake 30 minutes at 350°. Uncover; bake for 15 more minutes. **Yield:** 4 servings.

APPLE STREUSEL MUFFINS

June Isaac, Abbotsford, British Columbia

(PICTURED ON PAGE 183)

2 cups all-purpose flour
1 cup sugar
1 tablespoon baking powder
1-1/4 teaspoons cinnamon
1/2 teaspoon salt
1/2 teaspoon baking soda
2 large eggs, beaten
1 cup dairy sour cream
1/4 cup butter, melted
1 cup finely diced apples, unpeeled
STREUSEL TOPPING:
1/4 cup sugar
3 tablespoons all-purpose flour
1/4 teaspoon cinnamon
2 tablespoons butter

In large bowl, stir together flour, sugar, baking powder, cinnamon, salt and baking soda; set aside. In small bowl, beat eggs, sour cream and butter. Add all at once to dry ingredients along with apples. Stir just until moistened. Fill well-greased muffin tins two-thirds full. Combine topping ingredients; sprinkle on top of muffins. Bake at 400° for 20-25 minutes. **Yield:** 18 muffins.

PRIZE-WINNING APPLE PIE

Ruth Unruh, Newton, Kansas

(PICTURED ON PAGE 183)

CRUST:
2 cups all-purpose flour
1 teaspoon salt
1/2 teaspoon baking powder
2/3 cup butter-flavored shortening
1 tablespoon vegetable oil
4 to 5 tablespoons milk
FILLING:
1 cup sugar
4 tablespoons cornstarch
3/8 teaspoon nutmeg
3/8 teaspoon cinnamon
Dash salt
4-1/2 cups thinly sliced, pared tart apples (Jonathans work well)
1 tablespoon water
2 tablespoons butter

Measure flour, salt and baking powder into large bowl; mix well. Cut in shortening until mixture resembles small peas. Sprinkle in oil then milk, 1 tablespoon at a time, tossing with fork after each addition. When it's thoroughly mixed, press dough firmly together with hands as you would a snowball. Divide dough into two balls. Roll out each piece on a lightly floured pastry cloth. Put bottom crust into 9-in. pie pan; set aside. Prepare filling by stirring together the sugar, cornstarch, nutmeg, cinnamon and salt; mix with apples and water. Turn into pastry-lined pan; dot with butter. Cover with top crust; seal and flute. Slit steam vents in top crust. Cover edge with aluminum foil to prevent over-browning. Bake at 425° for 25 minutes. Remove foil last 15 minutes of baking. **Yield:** 8 servings.

FOILED AGAIN! When you're baking a double pie crust, here's a way to keep the outer edges from getting too brown: Cut out the center of a foil pie tin and place the outer ring over the pie. The center crust will get brown, but the outer edges won't burn. It's a lot easier than piecing tin foil around the edges!

FRESH APPLE CAKE

Joan Baskin, Black Creek, British Columbia

(PICTURED ON PAGE 183)

1-3/4 cups coarsely chopped apples, peeled
1 cup sugar
1-1/3 cups all-purpose flour
1 teaspoon baking soda
1/2 teaspoon salt
1 teaspoon cinnamon
1/2 teaspoon nutmeg
1/2 teaspoon allspice
1/2 cup vegetable oil
1 egg
1/2 cup raisins
1/2 cup chopped walnuts
Confectioners' sugar

Combine prepared apples and sugar in large mixing bowl; let stand 10 minutes. Sift flour; add soda, salt, cinnamon, nutmeg and allspice; set aside. Blend oil and egg into apple/sugar mixture. Add dry ingredients, stirring just until blended. Fold in the raisins and walnuts. Spread evenly in a greased 8-in. square pan. Bake at 350° for 50-55 minutes. Cool 10 minutes. Sprinkle with confectioners' sugar. **Yield:** 6-8 servings.

APPLE/CRANBERRY CRISP

Candie Takacs, West Carrollton, Ohio

(PICTURED ON PAGE 184)

3 cups chopped apples, unpeeled
2 cups raw cranberries
3/4 to 1 cup sugar
TOPPING:
1-1/2 cups old-fashioned or quick-cooking oats
1/2 cup brown sugar, packed
1/3 cup all-purpose flour
1/3 cup chopped pecans
1/2 cup butter, melted
Ice cream or whipped cream, optional

Combine apples, cranberries and sugar in 8-in. square baking dish or 2-qt. casserole. Mix thoroughly to blend; set aside. Combine topping ingredients until crumbly; spread evenly over fruit layer. Bake at 350° for 1 hour or until the fruit is fork-tender. Serve warm with ice cream or whipped cream, if desired. **Yield:** 8 servings.

FRESH APPLE SALAD

Becky Druetzler, Indianapolis, Indiana

(PICTURED ON PAGE 184)

 This tasty dish uses less sugar, salt and fat. Recipe includes *Diabetic Exchanges*.

8 cups chopped, tart red apples, unpeeled
1 can (20 ounces) pineapple chunks, juice drained and reserved
2 cups seedless green grapes
1 to 2 teaspoons poppy seeds
1-1/2 cups toasted pecans
DRESSING:
Reserved pineapple juice
1/4 cup butter
1/4 cup sugar
1 tablespoon lemon juice
2 tablespoons cornstarch
2 tablespoons water
1 cup mayonnaise or 1/2 cup reduced-calorie mayonnaise and 1/2 cup plain yogurt

Make dressing first by combining the reserved pineapple juice, butter, sugar and lemon juice in a small saucepan. Heat to boiling. Combine the cornstarch and water to make a smooth paste; add to the hot mixture; cook until thick and smooth. *Chill completely* before stirring in mayonnaise/yogurt. Combine apples, pineapple chunks, grapes and poppy seeds in large glass bowl. Add chilled dressing; refrigerate until time to serve. Stir in pecans right before serving for maximum crunchiness. **Yield:** 16 servings. **Diabetic Exchanges:** One serving equals 1-1/2 fruits, 3 fats; also, 206 calories, 86 mg sodium, 12 mg cholesterol, 22 gm carbohydrate, 2 gm protein, 14 gm fat.

APPLE, RAISIN, WALNUT CAKE

Pollie Malone, Ames, Iowa

(PICTURED ON PAGE 184)

3 eggs
1 cup vegetable oil
2 cups sugar
1 teaspoon vanilla
4 cups grated apples, unpeeled
2 cups sifted all-purpose flour
1 teaspoon baking soda
1/2 teaspoon salt
1 teaspoon cinnamon
1 teaspoon cloves
1/2 cup raisins
3/4 cup chopped walnuts
FROSTING:
1 cup milk
5 tablespoons all-purpose flour
1 cup butter
1 cup confectioners' sugar
1 teaspoon vanilla
1/2 cup broken walnuts

Beat eggs and oil together in a mixing bowl until foamy; add sugar and vanilla and continue to beat. Add apples, beating slightly; set aside. Sift together flour, soda, salt, cinnamon and cloves; add raisins and walnuts to flour mixture. Add flour mixture to egg mixture; beat slightly. Bake at 350° in greased 13-in. x 9-in. x 2-in. pan. Check for doneness after 25 minutes. To make frosting, mix milk and flour in saucepan; heat over medium heat until thick. Chill thoroughly over ice water. Beat in large mixer bowl with butter, sugar and vanilla until mixture is light and fluffy, about 5 minutes (like mashed potatoes). Spread on cooled cake; sprinkle with nuts. **Yield:** 12 servings.

APPLE PITA PIE

Sharon Loh, Trumbull, Connecticut

1 apple, peeled, cored and quartered
1 medium-sized pita (white *or* whole wheat)
1 teaspoon butter
1 teaspoon to 1 tablespoon sugar *or* 1 packet artificial sweetener
Cinnamon to taste
Whipped cream *or* nondairy whipped topping, optional

Stuff pita bread with apple quarters. Add butter, sugar/substitute and cinnamon. Wrap in foil; place on cookie sheet. Bake at 350° for 20 minutes. Remove foil. *Microwave Method:* Wrap in paper towel and microwave on high for 5 minutes. Top with whipped cream, if desired.

FALL APPLE DIP

Loretta Harmon, Utica, Illinois

1 package (8 ounces) cream cheese, room temperature
3/4 cup brown sugar
1 teaspoon vanilla
1 cup salted peanuts, chopped
Golden Delicious apples
Orange juice
Additional peanuts

Blend together all ingredients except last two. Wash and slice apples; dip in orange juice. Drain. Arrange in concentric circles on pretty plate and place the dip in center in a bowl. Sprinkle additional chopped peanuts on top of dip. Refrigerate leftovers. **Yield:** about 6-8 appetizer servings.

FALL APPLE DIP
(Light Version)

1 package (8 ounces) light cream cheese, room temperature
1 carton (8 ounces) vanilla yogurt
1/3 cup brown sugar
1/2 teaspoon vanilla
1 to 2 cups unsalted peanuts, chopped
Granny Smith apples
Orange juice

(Directions same as above.)

> **APPLE SNACK:** Spread crunchy peanut butter on apple wedges for a quick, healthy snack.

APPLE SAUSAGE BREAKFAST RING

Cherie Sechrist, Red Lion, Pennsylvania

(PICTURED ON PAGE 184)

2 pounds lean bulk pork sausage
2 large eggs, slightly beaten
1-1/2 cups crushed butter-flavored crackers
1 cup grated apple, peeled
1/2 cup minced onion
1/4 cup milk
Scrambled eggs

Line a 2-1/2-qt. ring mold with plastic wrap or waxed paper. Combine all ingredients except scrambled eggs; mix well and press firmly into mold. Chill several hours or overnight. Unmold, removing plastic/paper, onto a baking sheet *with raised edges*. Bake at 350° for 1 hour. Transfer onto a serving platter; fill center of ring with scrambled eggs. **Yield:** 8 servings.

SPICED APPLE TWISTS

Amy Kraemer, Glencoe, Minnesota

1/4 cup orange juice (water can be substituted)
1 can crescent rolls
2 large tart, firm apples, peeled and cored
2 tablespoons butter, melted
1/2 teaspoon cinnamon
1/3 cup sugar

Pour orange juice in bottom of buttered 9-in. square baking pan. Unroll crescent roll dough; separate into eight triangles. Cut each lengthwise to make 16 triangles. Cut each apple into eight pieces. Place an apple slice at wide end of each strip; roll up. Arrange in pan. Drizzle butter over tops, then sprinkle with combined cinnamon and sugar mixture. Bake at 400° for 30-35 minutes until golden in color. Serve warm or cold. **Yield:** 16 twists.

APPLE AND BLACK WALNUT CREAM

Teresa Wester, Palmyra, Missouri

1 cup plain yogurt
1 tablespoon lemon juice
1-1/2 tablespoons honey
4 medium-size tart eating apples, peeled and cored
1 cup black walnuts, chopped

Combine the yogurt, lemon juice and honey, mixing well to blend. Shred apples into yogurt mixture, stirring after each addition to prevent discoloration. Stir in nuts and serve immediately. **Yield:** 4-6 servings.

APPLE/RAISIN STUFFING

Grace Howaniec, Waukesha, Wisconsin

3 cups toasted bread cubes
1-1/2 cups chopped apples, unpared

1/2 cup raisins
1/2 cup celery, chopped
1/2 cup onion, chopped
1 teaspoon salt
1/2 teaspoon sage, crumbled
1/4 teaspoon rosemary, crumbled
1/4 teaspoon ground pepper
1 chicken bouillon cube
1/2 cup hot water

Mix together first 9 ingredients. Dissolve bouillon cube in hot water; add to stuffing mixture. Toss lightly to mix. **Yield:** 6 cups stuffing.

BERRY MALLOW YAM BAKE

Connie Bolton, San Antonio, Texas

(PICTURED ON PAGE 187)

1/2 cup all-purpose flour
1/2 cup packed brown sugar
1/2 cup dry oatmeal
1/2 teaspoon cinnamon
1/3 cup butter *or* margarine
2 cups fresh *or* frozen cranberries
2 tablespoons sugar
1 can (17 ounces) cut-up yams, liquid drained and reserved
Miniature marshmallows, optional

In a small bowl, combine flour, brown sugar, oatmeal and cinnamon. Cut in butter as for pastry; blend until crumbly. Set aside. Sprinkle cranberries with sugar. In a 2-qt. casserole, layer half the yams, half the cranberry mixture and half the crumb mixture. Repeat layers, ending with crumbs. Pour reserved yam liquid over all. Bake at 350° for 35 minutes or until heated through. If desired, place several rings of marshmallows around the outer edge of casserole and return to oven just until marshmallows are puffed and lightly browned. **Yield:** 8 servings.

DUBLIN POTATO SALAD

Kathy Scott, Hemingford, Nebraska

(PICTURED ON PAGE 187)

3 large white potatoes (about 1-1/2 pounds)
2 tablespoons white vinegar
2 teaspoons sugar
1 teaspoon celery seed
1 teaspoon mustard seed
3/4 teaspoon salt, *divided*
2 cups finely shredded cabbage
12 ounces cooked *or* canned

corned beef, cubed
1/4 cup chopped dill pickle
1/4 cup sliced green onion
1 cup mayonnaise
1/4 cup milk

Cover potatoes in lightly salted water and boil until tender. Drain, peel and cube. Combine vinegar, sugar, celery seed, mustard seed and 1/2 teaspoon salt; drizzle over still-warm potatoes. Cover and chill. Just before serving, gently fold in cabbage, corned beef, pickle and onion. Combine mayonnaise, milk and remaining salt; pour over salad. Gently toss. Serve in cabbage-lined bowl. **Yield:** 8 servings.

CHICKEN WITH 40 CLOVES OF GARLIC

Mary Swetich, Ely, Nevada

40 small cloves garlic, unpeeled (about 2 or 3 bulbs)
1 fryer chicken, cut into pieces
1/2 cup dry white wine *or* wine vinegar
1/4 cup olive oil
1 teaspoon dried thyme leaves
1/2 teaspoon dried sage leaves
1 tablespoon fresh minced parsley
4 small bay leaves
1 teaspoon salt *or* to taste
1/4 teaspoon pepper
French bread

Scatter garlic cloves over bottom of Dutch oven. Place chicken pieces over garlic, skin side up. Sprinkle wine/vinegar, oil and seasonings over chicken; cover pan tightly with foil and lid. *No steam should escape during baking.* Bake at 375° for 1 hour (remove lid during last 10 minutes of baking to brown slightly, if desired). Discard bay leaves; place chicken on platter. Squeeze garlic from skins onto French bread—it will taste surprisingly mild! **Yield:** 4-5 servings.

GREEN ONION OMELET

Georgia Ebright, Lyons, Kansas

6 slices bacon, crisply fried and crumbled
2 bunches green onions, tops and all, chopped in 1/4-inch pieces
8 eggs
1/2 cup milk
1 teaspoon salt *or* to taste
1/4 to 1/2 teaspoon pepper

Using crumbled bacon and about 1 tablespoon bacon drippings, cook onions over low heat until wilted, stirring frequently. Mix eggs, milk, salt and pepper with fork until blended; pour eggs, all at once, into skillet over bacon/onions. Stir with fork to spread eggs over bottom of skillet. Reduce heat. Lift edges of omelet with spatula allowing uncooked eggs to cook around edges. Cook until eggs are puffy and done; serve immediately. **Yield:** 4-6 servings.

FRENCH ONION CASSEROLE

Shirley Wilson, Elmwood, Illinois

2 large, white sweet onions, peeled and sliced 1/4 inch thick
3 tablespoons butter
1/2 pound Swiss cheese, shredded
1 can (10-3/4 ounces) cream of chicken soup
1/2 cup milk
1 teaspoon light soy sauce
8 slices French bread, cut 1/4 inch thick and buttered

Saute onion in butter until tender; spoon into 11-in. x 7-in. glass dish. Spread cheese over onions. Heat soup, milk and soy sauce together until well-blended; pour over onions and cheese. Mix gently with fork. Place buttered bread slices on top, overlapping if necessary. Bake, uncovered, at 350° for 30 minutes. **Yield:** 6-8 servings.

CHEDDAR SPOON BREAD

Barbara Clouse, Blacksburg, Virginia

2 cups milk, *divided*
1/2 cup yellow cornmeal
1 cup (4 ounces) shredded sharp cheddar cheese
1/3 cup butter
1 tablespoon sugar
1 teaspoon salt
2 eggs, well beaten

Scald 1-1/2 cups milk (heat to 180°). Mix cornmeal with remaining cold milk and add to hot milk. Cook, stirring constantly, over low heat until thickened, approximately 5 minutes. Add cheese, butter, sugar and salt; stir until melted. Remove from heat; stir in eggs. Pour into 1-qt. greased baking dish; bake at 350° for about 35 minutes or until lightly browned and set. Serve immediately. **Yield:** 6 servings.

PORKY-PINE WAFFLES

Ferne Lanou Moe, Northbrook, Illinois

(PICTURED ON PAGE 187)

2 cups leftover mashed
 potatoes
1/2 cup shredded cheddar
 cheese
3 eggs
1/2 cup milk
1 can (8 ounces) pineapple
 tidbits, juice drained and
 reserved
2 tablespoons butter *or*
 margarine, melted
1 cup all-purpose flour
2 teaspoons baking powder
1/2 pound fresh pork sausage
 links
1 cup maple syrup

Combine the potatoes and cheese in a
mixing bowl. Beat eggs with milk,
reserved pineapple juice and butter;
stir into potato mixture and mix well.
Combine flour and baking powder; stir
into potato mixture and mix well. Set
aside. Brown pork sausage. Drain and
cut into bite-size pieces. In a saucepan,
combine sausages, pineapple and
maple syrup; heat through. Bake the
waffles. Serve waffles topped with
sausage-pineapple mixture. **Yield:** 4
servings.

TEX-MEX
STUFFED POTATOES

Karen Johnston, Stouffville, Ontario

(PICTURED ON PAGE 187)

6 large baking potatoes
1/2 pound lean ground beef
1 medium onion, finely
 chopped
1 garlic clove, minced
1 can (16 ounces) refried beans
1 jar (8 ounces) spicy Mexican
 salsa
Dash pepper
1 cup (8 ounces) sour cream
2 tablespoons finely chopped
 green onion
2 tablespoons finely chopped
 tomato
Corn *or* tortilla chips for garnish

Bake potatoes at 400° for 1 hour or
until tender. Meanwhile, in a medium
saucepan, brown beef, onion and garlic.
Drain fat; add beans, salsa and pepper
to taste. Simmer, stirring occasionally,
40 minutes or until thickened. To serve,
cut an "x" in the top of each potato. Fluff
potato pulp with a fork and spoon beef
mixture over each potato. Garnish with
a dollop of sour cream and sprinkle
with green onion and tomato. Serve with
chips, if desired. **Yield:** 6 servings.

POTATO CRUST QUICHE

Nancy Smith, Scottsdale, Arizona

(PICTURED ON PAGE 188)

CRUST:
4 cups coarsely shredded
 potatoes (about 4 large)
1/2 cup diced onion
1 egg, beaten
1 cup all-purpose flour
1/2 teaspoon salt
FILLING:
1-1/2 cups (6 ounces) shredded
 Colby cheese, *divided*
1/2 cup chopped onion
1-1/2 cups diced cooked ham
1-1/2 cups broccoli florets
3 eggs, beaten
1 cup light cream
1/2 teaspoon salt
Dash ground nutmeg
Paprika

Combine crust ingredients and press into
a well-greased 10-in. deep dish pie plate.
Bake at 400° for 20 minutes. Remove
crust from oven; reduce heat to 350°.
Add 1 cup cheese, onion, ham and broccoli to crust. Mix eggs, cream, salt and
nutmeg; pour over all. Sprinkle with
paprika and bake for 35-40 minutes or
until set. Remove from the oven and top
with remaining cheese. Let stand 5 minutes before serving. **Yield:** 8 servings.

FAT RASCALS
(Potato Cheese Puffs)

Naomi Giddis, Grawn, Michigan

(PICTURED ON PAGE 188)

1 cup mashed potatoes
2 eggs, beaten
1/2 cup milk
2 cups (8 ounces) shredded
 American *or* cheddar cheese
1/2 cup all-purpose flour
1/4 teaspoon baking powder
Salt and pepper to taste
Salad oil

Combine all ingredients except oil; mix
well. Pour about 2 in. of salad oil into a
saucepan or frying pan and heat to 375°.
Drop batter by tablespoons, 4 or 5 at a
time, into the hot oil. Fry 3-4 minutes or
until golden brown. Serve immediately.
Yield: about 24 puffs.

PERFECT
POTATO PANCAKES

Mary Peters, Swift Current, Saskatchewan

(PICTURED ON PAGE 188)

4 large potatoes (about 3 pounds)
2 eggs
1/2 cup finely diced onion
1/2 cup all-purpose flour
1 teaspoon salt
1/8 teaspoon pepper
Salad oil
Maple syrup *or* applesauce

Peel and shred potatoes; place in a bowl
of cold water. Line a colander with
cheesecloth or a clean thin dish towel.
Drain potatoes into cloth and squeeze
out as much moisture as possible. Place
potatoes in a mixing bowl. Beat eggs;
add to potatoes along with onion, flour,
salt and pepper. Mix well. Heat about
1/3 cup salad oil in a skillet until hot.
Drop potato mixture 1/4 cup at a time
into hot oil, about 3 in. apart. Flatten with
pancake turner to make a 4-in. pancake.
Cook pancakes until golden brown, turn
and cook other side, about 4 minutes
total. Remove to a cookie sheet lined
with paper towel to drain. Repeat until all
pancakes are cooked. Serve immediately or place in a warm oven until ready
to serve. Top with maple syrup or applesauce. **Yield:** about 16 pancakes.

SWEET POTATO SALAD

Ellen Moore, Springfield, New Hampshire

(PICTURED ON PAGE 188)

4 medium sweet potatoes
1 cup pineapple chunks,
 drained
1 cup pecans, broken
1/4 cup orange juice
1 cup mayonnaise
1 teaspoon vinegar
1 teaspoon curry powder
1 teaspoon grated orange rind
1/4 to 1/2 teaspoon dried
 tarragon
2 tablespoons half-and-half
Lettuce leaves
Prepared chutney

Cook sweet potatoes until tender but
firm. Peel and cut into chunks the size of
the pineapple chunks. Gently toss potatoes, pineapple, nuts and orange juice.
In a small bowl, combine all remaining
ingredients except last two. Pour dressing over potato mixture and gently toss.
Chill for several hours. Serve, the salad
on a bed of greens; pass the chutney.
Yield: 6 servings.

RANCH POTATO CASSEROLE

Lydia Schnitzler, Kingsburg, California

(PICTURED ON PAGE 189)

6 to 8 medium red potatoes (about 2 to 2-1/2 pounds)
1/2 cup sour cream
1/2 cup prepared ranch-style dressing
1/4 cup bacon bits *or* cooked crumbled bacon
2 tablespoons minced fresh parsley
1 cup (4 ounces) shredded cheddar cheese

TOPPING:
1/2 cup shredded cheddar cheese
2 cups slightly crushed corn flakes
1/4 cup butter *or* margarine, melted

Cook the potatoes until tender; quarter (leaving skins on, if desired) and set aside. Combine sour cream, dressing, bacon, parsley and 1 cup cheese. Place potatoes in a greased 13-in. x 9-in. baking dish. Pour sour cream mixture over potatoes and gently toss. Top with 1/2 cup of cheese. Combine corn flakes and butter; sprinkle over casserole. Bake at 350° for 40-45 minutes. **Yield:** 8 servings.

POTATO ONION SUPREME

Claire Stryker, Bloomington, Illinois

(PICTURED ON PAGE 189)

8 medium potatoes (about 2-1/2 pounds)
2 large sweet onions, sliced
1/4 cup water
2 tablespoons chicken bouillon granules
2 cups (8 ounces) shredded sharp cheddar cheese
2 cups (16 ounces) sour cream
3/4 cup bread crumbs
2 tablespoons melted butter *or* margarine

Paprika
Chopped fresh parsley, optional

Cook potatoes; peel and slice 1/4 in. thick. Set aside. Place onions, water and bouillon in a saucepan; bring to a boil, then simmer 5-7 minutes or until onions are tender. Drain and set aside. Combine cheese and sour cream. In a greased 2-1/2-qt. baking dish, layer half the potatoes, onions and cheese mixture. Repeat layers. Combine crumbs

and butter; top potato mixture. Sprinkle with paprika. Bake, uncovered, at 350° for about 20 minutes or until heated through. Garnish with parsley and several onion rings, if desired. **Yield:** 8 servings.

POTATO CHEESE SOUP WITH SALMON

Nancy Horsburgh, Everett, Ontario

(PICTURED ON PAGE 189)

1/4 cup butter *or* margarine
1 large onion, thinly sliced
1-1/4 cups diced celery
3-1/2 cups peeled and sliced potatoes
1 cup chicken broth
3 cups milk, room temperature, *divided*
1 cup half-and-half
2 cups (8 ounces) shredded sharp cheddar cheese
1 teaspoon dried thyme
1 tablespoon Worcestershire sauce
1 can (7-1/2 ounces) red sockeye salmon, well drained with skin and bones removed

Salt and pepper to taste
Chopped fresh parsley

In a 2-qt. saucepan, melt the butter and saute onion and celery until tender but not brown. Add potatoes and chicken broth; cover and cook on low heat until potatoes are tender. Puree potato mixture in a blender with 2 cups milk. Return to saucepan; add remaining milk, half-and-half, cheese, thyme, Worcestershire sauce and salmon. Heat on low, stirring often, until hot. Season with salt and pepper. Garnish with parsley. **Yield:** 6 servings.

CRUNCHY SWISS AND HAM APPETIZERS

Wendy Mitchell, Weyburn, Saskatchewan

(PICTURED ON PAGE 189)

2 cups very stiff mashed potatoes
2 cups finely chopped cooked ham
1 cup (4 ounces) shredded Swiss cheese
1/3 cup mayonnaise
1/4 cup minced onion
1 egg, well beaten
1 teaspoon prepared mustard
1/2 teaspoon salt

1/4 teaspoon pepper
3-1/2 cups corn flakes, crushed

Combine all ingredients except corn flakes; chill. Shape into 1-in. balls and roll in corn flakes. Place on greased cookie sheet and bake at 350° for 25-30 minutes. Serve while hot. **Yield:** about 8 dozen.

RAZORBACK CORN BREAD

Louise Ford, Junction City, Arkansas

8 ounces bulk pork sausage
2 cups cornmeal
1/2 cup all-purpose flour
3 teaspoons baking powder
1 teaspoon baking soda
1 teaspoon salt
2 eggs, beaten
3 hot canned peppers, chopped
1 large onion, chopped
1 can (11 ounces) Mexican-style *or* whole-kernel corn, drained
2 cups buttermilk
1/2 cup shredded cheddar cheese

In a deep 10-in. cast-iron skillet, fry sausage until its done. Reserve 2 to 3 tablespoons of the drippings. Crumble sausage. Combine cornmeal, flour, baking powder, baking soda and salt. In separate bowl, combine eggs, peppers, onion, corn, buttermilk and cheese. Add egg mixture to the cornmeal mixture. Stir in sausage and reserved drippings. Pour into the greased skillet and bake at 450° for 20-25 minutes or until done. Serve warm from skillet. **Yield:** 12 servings.

GERMAN POTATOES

Janice Scherman, Sentinel Butte, North Dakota

6 slices bacon, diced
1 small green pepper, diced
3 tablespoons chopped onion
3 large potatoes, peeled, boiled and diced
Salt and pepper to taste
1/2 cup shredded cheddar cheese
6 eggs

In a skillet, fry bacon. Drain all but 3 tablespoons drippings; add green pepper, onion and potatoes. Season with salt and pepper. Cook and stir until golden brown, about 5 minutes. Sprinkle with cheese and stir. Break eggs over potato mixture, one at a time. Cook over low heat until eggs are set and cooked till done. Serve immediately. **Yield:** 6 servings.

FROZEN CRESCENT ROLLS

Linda Wilson, Anderson, Missouri

2 cups milk
2 packages (1/4 ounce *each*)
   active dry yeast
1 cup sugar
1 cup shortening
2 teaspoons salt
6 eggs, beaten
9 cups all-purpose flour, *divided*
1/2 cup butter *or* margarine,
   melted

Heat milk to 110°-115°. Add yeast; stir until dissolved. Set aside. In large mixing bowl, cream sugar, shortening and salt. Add eggs; mix well. Add half the flour; then add milk mixture, mixing until flour is moistened. Add remaining flour by hand. Turn out dough onto floured board. Knead until smooth and elastic, about 6-8 minutes. Place dough in greased bowl; cover and let rise in warm place until doubled, about 1-1/2 hours. Divide dough into 4 parts. Roll each into a circle and brush with melted butter. Cut each circle into 16 pie-wedge pieces. Roll each piece into a crescent, starting at wide end. Place on baking sheet and freeze immediately. When frozen, place in plastic freezer bags and seal. Store in freezer until ready to use. To bake, place on greased baking sheet and cover; let rise until doubled, about 3-4 hours. Bake at 350° for 12-15 minutes. **Yield:** 64 rolls.

RICOTTA-STUFFED FRENCH TOAST

Christopher Sellers, Waterbury, Vermont

1 loaf (1 pound) Italian bread
1 cup ricotta cheese
4 eggs
1/2 cup light cream
1 tablespoon vanilla extract
1/2 teaspoon nutmeg
1/2 teaspoon cinnamon
1 tablespoon butter *or*
   margarine
Confectioners' sugar
Maple syrup, optional

Slice bread into 24 thin slices. Spread 12 slices with ricotta cheese; top with remaining bread slices. Beat eggs, cream, vanilla, nutmeg and cinnamon together. Dip each sandwich into egg mixture. In skillet, melt butter. Grill sandwiches slowly until golden brown; turn and grill other side. Dust with confectioners' sugar. Serve with maple syrup, if desired. **Yield:** 12 servings.

DELICIOUS APPLE TREATS: Top a toasted English muffin with applesauce and shredded sharp cheese or cinnamon.
● Make mini-caramel apples by dipping quartered apples on toothpicks into melted caramel (1 package of caramels melted in a double boiler).

NEW ORLEANS PECAN PIE

Mitzi Adkinson, Albany, Georgia

2 eggs, *separated*
1 cup (8 ounces) sour cream
1 cup sugar
1/4 cup all-purpose flour
1/2 teaspoon vanilla extract
1/4 teaspoon salt
1 pie crust (9 inches), baked
1 cup packed brown sugar
1 cup chopped pecans

In saucepan, combine egg yolks, sour cream, sugar, flour, vanilla and salt. Cook and stir over medium heat until thickened, about 5 minutes. Pour into pie shell; set aside. In large mixing bowl, immediately beat egg whites until soft peaks form. Gradually add brown sugar; continue to beat until stiff. While filling is still warm, spread egg white topping over filling. Sprinkle with chopped pecans. Bake at 375° for 12-15 minutes or until golden. **Yield:** 8 servings.

POPPY SEED POUND CAKE MUFFINS

Shirley McCluskey, Colorado Springs, Colorado

2 cups all-purpose flour
1 tablespoon poppy seeds
1/2 teaspoon salt
1/4 teaspoon baking soda
1 cup sugar
1/2 cup butter *or* margarine
2 eggs
1 cup plain yogurt
1 teaspoon vanilla extract

In small mixing bowl, stir together flour, poppy seeds, salt and baking soda. In a large mixing bowl, cream together sugar and butter. Beat in eggs one at a time. Add yogurt and vanilla; mix well. Stir in flour mixture until dry ingredients are moistened. Spoon batter into greased muffin tins. Bake at 400° for 15-20 minutes or until a wooden pick inserted in center of muffin comes out clean. Cool muffins on wire rack 5 minutes before removing from pan. **Yield:** 12 muffins.

APPLE BREAD

Phyllis Herlocker, Farlington, Kansas

3 cups all-purpose flour
2 teaspoons cinnamon
1 teaspoon baking soda
1/2 teaspoon baking powder
1/2 teaspoon salt
1/2 cup vegetable oil
2 cups sugar
2 eggs, beaten
1/2 teaspoon vanilla extract
2 cups coarsely chopped,
   peeled and cored apples
1 cup broken walnuts

In bowl, combine flour, cinnamon, baking soda, baking powder and salt; set aside. In large mixing bowl, combine oil, sugar, eggs, vanilla and apples. Stir into flour mixture. Add walnuts and mix. Divide mixture between two greased 8-in. x 4-in. bread pans. Bake at 350° for 40-45 minutes or until breads test done. Cool for 10 minutes on wire rack before removing from pans. **Yield:** 2 loaves.

PORK TENDERLOIN WITH RASPBERRY SAUCE SUPREME

Bernice Janowski, Stevens Point, Wisconsin

1 pound pork tenderloin,
   trimmed and cut into 8
   crosswise pieces
1/8 teaspoon cayenne pepper
2 tablespoons butter
RASPBERRY SAUCE:
6 tablespoons red raspberry
   preserves
2 tablespoons red wine vinegar
1 tablespoon catsup
1/2 teaspoon horseradish
1/2 teaspoon soy sauce
1 garlic clove, minced
GARNISH:
2 kiwifruit, peeled and thinly
   sliced crosswise
Fresh raspberries, optional

Press each tenderloin slice to 1-in. thickness; lightly sprinkle both sides of each slice with cayenne pepper. Heat butter in large heavy skillet over medium-high. Add tenderloin slices; cook 3-4 minutes on each side. Meanwhile, combine all sauce ingredients in small saucepan; simmer over low heat about 3 minutes, stirring occasionally. Keep warm. Place cooked tenderloin slices on warm serving plate; spoon on sauce and top each tenderloin with a kiwi slice. Garnish each plate with remaining kiwi slices and fresh raspberries, if desired. **Yield:** 4 servings.

Meals in Minutes

The wife of an on-the-go harvester, Karen Ann Bland of Gove, Kansas, relies on fast menus to feed hungry appetites each fall.

"My husband, Boyd, is not a sandwich man," says Karen. "I need quick, hearty dishes to serve my family as well as all the hired men that work with us each fall. This meal is one I call on often during this busy season, and it always gets appreciative comments."

Karen likes to make the granola-style no-bake cookies first, then chill them while she fixes the rest of the meal. Her salad is an old-time standby that's ideal for children to assemble with just a little guidance while she's cooking.

As the pasta simmers, Karen cuts and cooks the remaining main-dish ingredients, using the last of her summer garden vegetables. And after putting bread on the table, she says there's usually even time left to make a pot of coffee before the half hour's up.

CONFETTI SPAGHETTI

- **1 cup pepperoni slices** *or* **1 package (4 ounces)**
- **1/2 cup chopped onion**
- **1/2 cup green pepper strips**
- **7 ounces spaghetti, cooked and drained**
- **1/2 cup grated Parmesan cheese**
- **1/2 cup (2 ounces) shredded mozzarella cheese**
- **1/2 cup chopped tomato**
- **1/2 teaspoon oregano leaves**

Fry the pepperoni in large skillet until edges curl. Add onion and green pepper; cook until tender. Toss together cooked spaghetti and cheeses, tomato and oregano; add pepperoni, onions and pepper strips. Heat thoroughly. Sprinkle with additional Parmesan cheese, if desired. **Yield:** 4-6 servings.

JUICE TIPS: To defrost frozen orange juice concentrate, remove lid and put cardboard container in oven. Microwave on high for 15-30 seconds.

● To get more juice from lemons and oranges, microwave on high for 30 seconds per fruit before squeezing.

PEAR/LETTUCE SALAD

- **8 canned pear halves, drained**
- **8 large lettuce leaves**
- **Non-dairy whipped topping**
- **4 teaspoons shredded cheddar cheese**

For each salad, first arrange 2 lettuce leaves on plate; top with 2 pear halves, hollow side up. Fill each pear cavity with a spoonful of whipped topping. Sprinkle each salad with 1 teaspoon cheese. Chill until serving time. **Yield:** 4 servings.

NO-BAKE ORANGE PEANUT BUTTER DROPS

- **3/4 cup sugar**
- **1/4 cup frozen orange juice concentrate, thawed**
- **1/4 cup butter**
- **1/4 cup crunchy peanut butter**
- **1-1/2 cups quick-cooking oats**
- **1/2 cup raisins**

Using medium-size saucepan over medium heat, combine sugar, orange juice concentrate and butter, stirring constantly until mixture boils. Remove from heat; stir in peanut butter until blended. Add oats and raisins; stir to blend. Drop by teaspoonsful onto waxed paper. Chill until firm. **Yield:** 30 cookies (1-1/2 inches each).

QUICK BREAD STICKS

 This tasty dish uses less sugar, salt and fat. Recipe includes *Diabetic Exchanges*.

- **12 day-old hot dog buns**
- **1 cup butter, softened**
- **1 teaspoon sweet basil leaves, crushed**
- **1 teaspoon dried dill weed**
- **1/4 teaspoon garlic powder**

Quarter buns (lengthwise). Combine remaining ingredients in small bowl; mix. Spread butter/herb mixture on cut sides of buns. Place on two cookie sheets or jelly roll pans. Bake at 250° for 1 hour to 1-1/2 hours or until crisp. **Yield:** 48 sticks. **Diabetic Exchanges:** One serving equals 1/2 bread, 1 fat; also, 64 calories, 97 mg sodium, 12 mg cholesterol, 5 gm carbohydrate.

Savor the flavors of the Deep South with this tasty selection of "down-home" dishes! These recipes simmer with a Southern accent reminiscent of the lush gardens of Mississippi...the ripe orchards of Georgia...the fertile fields of Louisiana...the henhouses of North Carolina...and the smokehouses of Virginia. They're sure to bring satisfaction to your home—whatever state it's in.

Sample some simple, but flavorful fare, like Grandmother's Chicken 'n' Dumplings and hearty, regional favorites like Black Bean Soup. Serve side dishes such as light, corn-rich Spoon Bread...ten-

der, tasty Turnip Greens...or orange-sauced Praline/Yam Casserole.

Company's coming! Dish up some Southern-style hospitality with succulent Herb-Seasoned Roast Pork, sweet Stuffed Vidalia Onions or Crab and Country Ham Pasta—farm-fresh food that's fancy enough to serve the city cousins!

The South's as close as your kitchen when you cook up these tasty treats. Enjoy 'em all, y'all!

SOUTHERN STARS: Clockwise from lower left—**Southern Turnip Greens** (Pg. 206); **Spoon Bread** (Pg. 205); **Herb-Seasoned Pork Roast** (Pg. 205); **Grandmother's Chicken 'n' Dumplings** (Pg. 205); **Black Bean Soup** (Pg. 206); **Praline/Yam Casserole** (Pg. 206); **Stuffed Vidalia Onions** (Pg. 205); **Crab and Country Ham Pasta** (Pg. 205).

On a blustery day, chase away the chill with a bowl of steaming Potato Corn Chowder or a pan of hot-from-the-oven Honey-Mustard Baked Chicken. Crowd-pleasing Pizza Joes are a great after-school snack and the recipe doubles easily. Cap off a hot meal in cold weather with moist and tangy citrus-glazed Golden Lemon Cake.

AUTUMN EATING: Clockwise from left—**Potato Corn Chowder** (Pg. 206); **Honey-Mustard Baked Chicken** (Pg. 206); **Golden Lemon Cake** (Pg. 207); **Pizza Joes** (Pg. 207).

BEST COOK

Nancy Ann Lassater
San Pedro, California

Meandering with "one foot always in the kitchen" has taken Kathleen Trepp of Huntington Beach, California along some interesting routes.

One of the people she encountered on her way was Nancy Ann Lassater who worked with Kathleen at a bed-and-breakfast in Seal Beach, California, and nominated her as "Best Cook in the Country".

"Her recipes are of her own creation, and have won local and state awards," Nancy wrote. "She uses only the finest ingredients, her food presentation is creative and artistic, and the aroma of her creations is reminiscent of grandma's house.

"Most importantly, she is someone I truly admire. She lets me help her, never criticizing or making fun of me for being the ultimate 'non-cook'."

Food has played a large part in Kathleen's life and in her work as owner of a cooking school and in restaurants and inns.

She's currently working for a friend in San Pedro, California, in a restaurant called The Grand House, and they've just opened a British pub-style restaurant. As she puts it, "For someone who loves people and entertaining, and who loves to cook and decorate, this kind of work is undeniably the answer to a dream!"

For a little gourmet cooking of your own, try Kathleen's recipes below.

ZUCCHINI PANCAKES

        4 **medium zucchini, shredded**
    1/2 **medium onion, chopped**
        1 **clove garlic, minced**
        2 **egg yolks, lightly beaten**
    1/3 **cup crumbled feta cheese**
    1/2 **teaspoon salt**
    1/4 **teaspoon pepper**
        2 **tablespoons all-purpose flour**
        2 **tablespoons olive oil**

Shred the zucchini and either work quickly and fry the pancakes immediately or allow the zucchini to drain in a strainer and wring out in a towel to dry. Combine the zucchini with onion, garlic, egg yolks, cheese, salt, pepper and flour. Heat oil in a large skillet; drop zucchini mixture by 1 tablespoon portions into the hot oil. Fry for a minute; turn and fry other side. (Pancakes may be held at room temperature and warmed before serving or can be frozen.) **Yield:** 6-8 servings.

WHITE GAZPACHO

        3 **peeled cucumbers, cut in chunks**
        2 **cups chicken broth**
        1 **pint sour cream *or* plain yogurt**
        1 **clove garlic**
    1-1/2 **teaspoons salt**
    1-1/2 **tablespoons white wine vinegar**
GARNISHES:
Avocado
Bell pepper
Almonds, toasted
Tomatoes

Combine all ingredients and mix in blender. Let stand overnight. When serving, garnish with avocado, bell pepper, toasted almonds and peeled and seeded tomatoes. **Yield:** 8 cups.

BAKED EGGS GRUYERE IN SHELLS

        4 **slices bacon, cut into 1/2-inch strips**
    3/4 **cup (3 ounces) shredded Gruyere *or* Swiss cheese, *divided***
        4 **large eggs**
        4 **teaspoons whipping cream**
Salt and pepper

In a 6- to 8-in. frying pan, cook bacon over medium heat until crisp; drain on paper towels. Brush four ceramic scallop shells or four 6- to 8-oz. ramekins generously with some of the bacon fat. Sprinkle 1-1/2 tablespoons of cheese over the bottom of each shell; sprinkle on equal portions of bacon. Break one egg into each shell. Pour 1 teaspoon cream over each egg; sprinkle lightly with salt and pepper and equal portions of the remaining cheese. Bake, uncovered, at 350° until eggs are done. (Eggs continue to cook slightly after coming out of oven.) **Yield:** 4 servings.

FRENCH FRUIT PIES

PATE BRISEE:
        3 **cups all-purpose flour**
Salt to taste
        2 **sticks butter**
    1/3 **cup ice water**
FILLING:
About 6 cups fresh sliced fruit—
        plums, peaches, nectarines
        1 **cup heavy whipping cream**
        1 **cup sugar**
        4 **eggs**
Confectioners' sugar

Put flour and salt in large mixing bowl; cut in butter until dough resembles cornmeal. Add ice water; mix lightly until dough begins to form a ball. Form into two balls. *Do not overhandle.* Let dough rest for at least 20 minutes. (Dough can be stored in refrigerator for a week before being used.) Roll out as for pie crust. Line two 10-1/2-in. tart pans (with removable bottoms) with dough. Fill each crust with sliced fruit; add mixture of cream, sugar and eggs, pouring over fruit. Bake at 350° for 30-35 minutes. Remove from oven; dust with confectioners' sugar. **Yield:** 2 pies.

ONION AND GARLIC KNOW-HOW:
Dice more onions than you need, then freeze the leftovers in well-wrapped 1/2 cup portions in muffin tins. Store these handy ready-to-use portions in heavy plastic bags.

● Leftover onions keep much longer in the refrigerator if you use the top first and leave the root uncut.

● Put a toothpick in any whole garlic cloves you add to meats, stews and salad dressings—they'll slip out easily after cooking.

MOUTH-WATERING MAIN DISHES!
Clockwise from lower left—**Chalupa** (Pg. 208); **Shredded Barbecued Beef** (Pg. 208); **One-Dish Meal** (Pg. 208); **Spiced Lentil Soup** (Pg. 208); **Chinese Cashew Chicken** (Pg. 209); **Apples, Sauerkraut and Chops** (Pg. 209); **Three-Alarm Chili** (Pg. 208); **Chicken Parisienne** (Pg. 208).

H ere's to carefree cooking, the kind that tends to its tasty self while you pitch in with outdoor chores.

These simple, slow-cooking main dish meals don't stint on stick-to-your-ribs goodness. Each features a filling blend of well-seasoned meats and vegetables, in flavors to please every palate.

Enjoy hearty bean and sausage dishes…Old World pork and kraut casserole…standby soups and stews. This is eating that appetites applaud!

Turn to these recipes the next time you need a substantial field lunch, a delectable dish to pass or a mainstay meal that cooks while the cook's away. All were family kitchen-tested and won "second helping, please" praise from everyone who tasted them. So don't be slow in trying them at your table!

What could be more delicious than a dinner simmered all day to its savory best? Just imagine the aroma of these slow-cooking favorites greeting you as you come in the door! Add some freshly sliced bread…and get ready to dig in to a hearty meal that satisfies.

SAVORY SLOW COOKERS: Clockwise from top—**Chicken Cacciatore** (Pg. 210); **Gone-All-Day Stew** (Pg. 209); **Big Red Soup** (Pg. 209); **Kapuzta** (Pg. 209).

HERB-SEASONED PORK ROAST

Carole Boyer, Converse, Indiana

(PICTURED ON PAGE 198)

1 teaspoon fennel
1/2 teaspoon oregano
1/2 teaspoon crushed bay leaves
1/8 teaspoon ground nutmeg
1/8 teaspoon ground cloves
2 teaspoons chopped parsley
1 teaspoon minced onion
1 clove garlic, crushed *or* 1/4
    teaspoon garlic powder
2 teaspoons salt
1/4 teaspoon pepper
1 pork shoulder roast
    (6 to 8 pounds)

Combine all spices, herbs, salt and pepper. Make slits 1/2 in. deep at 1-in. intervals in roast and rub spice mixture into slits and over roast surface. Place roast in covered pan in 2 in. of water; insert meat thermometer in center of roast. Bake at 350° for 1-1/2 to 2 hours or until thermometer registers 160°. **Yield:** 10-12 servings.

CRAB AND COUNTRY HAM PASTA

Julia Wilcox, Williamsburg, Virginia

(PICTURED ON PAGE 198)

1 pound fresh pasta (fettucine
    is best)
2 tablespoons butter
2 tablespoons all-purpose flour
3/4 cup milk
3/4 cup light cream *or*
    half-and-half
3 tablespoons Parmesan
    cheese
2 tablespoons dry sherry,
    optional
1/4 teaspoon cayenne pepper or
    to taste
Salt
Pepper
1 tablespoon vegetable oil
1/4 pound cooked country ham,
    cut in julienne strips*
1 bunch green onions, chopped
1/2 pound crab meat, all shells
    removed
1 red pepper, cut in julienne
    strips

*(Use an authentic, salt-cured country ham.) Cook pasta according to package directions; keep warm. Make sauce by melting butter over low heat in skillet; add flour and blend with whisk to form

a roux. Cook over medium heat for 2 minutes. *Do not burn.* Remove from heat; whisk in milk and cream. Return to heat; add cheese, sherry (if desired), cayenne pepper and salt and pepper. If mixture becomes too thick, add more milk and cream. Keep warm. In another skillet, saute ham and onions in vegetable oil for 2 minutes over medium heat. Add crab and pepper strips; saute for 1 minute. Stir crab mixture into sauce. Serve over hot, drained pasta as an appetizer or as a main dish. **Yield:** 4-8 servings.

SPOON BREAD

Lillie Lowery, Kennesaw, Georgia

(PICTURED ON PAGE 198)

1 pint sweet milk
6 tablespoons butter
1 cup cornmeal
1 teaspoon salt
3 eggs (room temperature),
    separated

Scald milk (do not boil); stir in butter, cornmeal and salt. Cook, stirring constantly, until cornmeal comes away from sides of pan and thickens. Set aside to cool to lukewarm. Add beaten egg yolks; mix thoroughly. Fold in stiffly beaten egg whites; mix gently but thoroughly. Pour into greased and floured 2-qt. baking dish and bake at 375° for 1 hour or until top is golden brown. Serve immediately. **Yield:** 6 servings.

GRANDMOTHER'S CHICKEN 'N' DUMPLINGS

Cynthia Carroll, Cary, North Carolina

(PICTURED ON PAGE 199)

1 large chicken (6 pounds)
2 teaspoons salt
4 quarts water
2 tablespoons vinegar
1 large onion, sliced
2 carrots, washed and chopped
2 stalks celery, washed and
    sliced
DUMPLINGS:
2 cups all-purpose flour
1-1/2 teaspoons salt
1 egg
1 cup reserved chicken broth

Place chicken, salt, water, vinegar, onion, carrots and celery in large soup kettle, adding more water, if necessary, to cover chicken. Bring to boil. Cover; reduce heat to simmer. Cook until meat

nearly falls from the bone. Strain off broth and reserve. Remove and discard chicken skin, bones and vegetables. Cut or tear meat into bite-size pieces and reserve. Set aside 1 cup broth; cool to lukewarm. To make dumplings, combine flour and salt. Make a "well" in flour; add egg. Gradually stir 1/4 cup broth into egg, picking up flour as you go. Continue until flour is used up, adding additional broth as needed, and dough is consistency of pie dough. Pour any remaining reserved broth back into soup kettle. Turn the dough onto a floured surface; knead in additional flour to make stiff dough. Allow dough to rest 15 minutes. Roll out dough on floured surface as if for pie crust (circle about 17 in. round). Cut into pieces 1 in. square. Dust with additional flour; lay aside to dry for 30 to 60 minutes. Bring chicken broth to boil (you should have about 4 qts.). Drop squares into boiling broth; reduce heat to slow simmer. Cover; simmer for 10 minutes. Uncover; cook until a dough dumpling tests done, about 30 minutes. Dust with pepper and add reserved chicken meat. **Yield:** 8-10 servings.

STUFFED VIDALIA ONIONS

Suzanne McKinley, Lyons, Georgia

(PICTURED ON PAGE 199)

4 large Vidalia onions, peeled*
1 package (10 ounces) frozen
    green peas
4 ounces fresh mushrooms,
    sliced
1/4 teaspoon thyme leaves,
    crushed
1/8 teaspoon pepper
2 tablespoons butter *or*
    margarine
1/4 cup hot water
1/2 teaspoon instant chicken
    bouillon granules

*(Substitute any large, sweet onions if Vidalias are not available.) Slice tops off onions; hollow out center of each onion, leaving 1/4-in.-thick shell. Place onion shells in 8-in. x 8-in. baking dish with cover. Combine peas, mushrooms, thyme and pepper. Fill each onion with one-fourth of vegetable mixture. Dot each with 1/2 tablespoon butter; set aside. Combine water and bouillon; pour over onions. Put cover on dish and microwave on high 7-10 minutes, or until tender, rotating onions halfway through cooking time. Baste with cooking liquid. Let stand, covered, 3 minutes before serving. **Yield:** 4 servings.

SOUTHERN TURNIP GREENS

Jennie Lee Hyde, Senatobia, Mississippi

(PICTURED ON PAGE 198)

2 cups cooked, chopped turnip
greens *or* 1 pound fresh
greens
Salt
Pepper
1 teaspoon sugar
2 teaspoons vinegar
1 teaspoon horseradish sauce
1/2 cup mayonnaise
5 ounces cream of mushroom
soup (1/2 of 10-3/4-ounce
can), undiluted
2 eggs, beaten
1/2 cup soft bread crumbs
1/2 cup shredded cheddar cheese
Bacon bits, optional

Stem and wash fresh greens; place in water in large kettle. Bring to boil; reduce heat and cook until tender. Grind in food processor and measure 2 cups for recipe. (Substitute cooked, frozen greens, if desired.) Combine greens with salt, pepper, sugar, vinegar, horseradish sauce, mayonnaise, soup and eggs. Mix well; place in 8-in. x 8-in. casserole dish. Sprinkle crumbs, cheese and if desired, bacon bits on top. Bake at 350° for 1 hour. **Yield:** 6-8 servings.

BLACK BEAN SOUP

Mickey and Don Ertel, Barefoot Bay, Florida

(PICTURED ON PAGE 199)

1 pound black beans (Frijoles
Negros)
1-1/2 pounds slab bacon *or* 2
smoked ham hocks (1-1/2 to 2
pounds)
8 cups water
2 teaspoons celery salt
About 2 cups chicken *or* beef broth
1-1/2 tablespoons olive oil
1-1/2 cups finely chopped, seeded,
cored green peppers
1-1/2 cups finely chopped onions
1-1/2 tablespoons finely minced
garlic
1 teaspoon ground cumin
1 can (19 ounces) tomatoes,
peeled, diced, with juice
(about 2-1/2 cups)
1/4 cup red wine vinegar
2 tablespoons finely chopped
fresh coriander, optional
Hard-cooked egg, sieved, optional

Place beans, bacon/ham hocks, water and celery salt in heavy kettle. Bring to

boil; cover and simmer about 2-1/2 hours or until beans are thoroughly tender. Remove bacon/ham hocks; set aside. Drain beans and reserve along with meat and cooking liquid. (There should be about 6 cups of beans and 4 cups of liquid.) Add enough broth to make 6 cups liquid. Combine the beans with liquid in large bowl. Heat oil in heavy kettle; add peppers, onions, garlic and cumin. Cook, stirring, until onions are wilted. Add tomatoes and vinegar. Let simmer about 15 minutes. Meanwhile, remove and discard skin from bacon, or skin and bones from ham hocks. Chop bacon/ham; set aside. Add bean mixture to cooked tomato mixture. Add chopped meat and if desired, coriander. Simmer until thoroughly heated. Serve in soup bowls; garnish with sieved hard-cooked egg, if desired. **Yield:** 8-10 servings.

PRALINE/YAM CASSEROLE

Alice Mathews, Alexandria, Louisiana

(PICTURED ON PAGE 199)

4 medium yams
2 eggs
1/2 cup brown sugar, *divided*
2 tablespoons butter, melted
1/2 teaspoon salt
1/2 cup pecan halves
1/4 cup melted butter
ORANGE SAUCE:
1/3 cup sugar
1 tablespoon cornstarch
1/8 teaspoon salt
1 teaspoon grated orange peel
1 cup orange juice
1 tablespoon lemon juice
2 tablespoons butter

Cook yams in microwave or on top of stove until tender. Peel and mash in large bowl. Beat in eggs, 1/4 cup of brown sugar, butter and salt. Spoon mixture into 1-qt. buttered casserole. Arrange pecan halves over top. Sprinkle with remaining 1/4 cup brown sugar; drizzle with 1/4 cup melted butter. Bake, uncovered, at 375° for 20 minutes. To make sauce, combine sugar, cornstarch, salt, orange peel, orange and lemon juice in saucepan. Bring to boil over medium heat, stirring until sauce is thickened. Remove from heat; stir in butter. Serve warm orange sauce over casserole. **Yield:** 6 servings.

CHICKEN OF CHOICE: For baked chicken with a beautiful golden-brown color, generously sprinkle it with paprika before cooking.

POTATO CORN CHOWDER

Michelle Howell, Greentown, Indiana

(PICTURED ON PAGE 200)

2 ounces thick-sliced bacon,
diced
1 pound white potatoes, peeled
and cubed
1/2 cup chopped onion
2 garlic cloves, minced
1 cup chicken broth
1/2 teaspoon dried red pepper,
optional
4 cups milk, room temperature,
divided
1 tablespoon cornstarch
1 tablespoon salt
3 cups fresh *or* canned corn
1/3 cup diced green pepper
1/3 cup diced sweet red pepper
2 tablespoons diced green
onion
2 tablespoons chopped fresh
parsley

In a 4-qt. microwave-safe bowl, microwave bacon at full power until crisp, about 2-3 minutes. Add potatoes, onion and garlic; stir to coat with bacon drippings. Cover bowl; microwave at full power 5 minutes. Add broth and if desired, dried red pepper. Cover; return to microwave and cook until potatoes are tender, about 8-10 minutes. In separate bowl, stir 2 tablespoons milk into cornstarch; add to potatoes with remaining milk, salt, corn and peppers. Stir well. Cover and microwave, stirring twice, until vegetables are just tender, about 6-8 minutes. Just before serving, stir in green onion and parsley. **Yield:** 8 servings.

HONEY-MUSTARD BAKED CHICKEN

Kate Peterson, Cincinnati, Ohio

(PICTURED ON PAGE 200)

2 whole chickens, cut up
1/2 cup butter *or* margarine
1/2 cup honey
1/4 cup Dijon mustard
1 teaspoon curry powder
1/2 teaspoon salt

Place chicken parts in a large shallow baking pan. In saucepan, melt butter; stir in remaining ingredients and heat through. Brush glaze over chicken. Bake at 350° for 1-1/4 hours or until chicken is golden brown. Baste chicken frequently with sauce while baking. **Yield:** 6-8 servings.

GOLDEN LEMON CAKE

Mary E. Riggin, Martinez, Georgia

(PICTURED ON PAGE 200)

1 package (18-1/4 ounces)
white cake mix
3/4 cup vegetable oil
3/4 cup warm tap water
4 eggs
1 package (3 ounces) lemon-
flavored gelatin
1 teaspoon lemon extract
TANGY CITRUS GLAZE:
2/3 cup orange juice
3 tablespoons sugar
2 tablespoons lemon juice
3/4 cup confectioners' sugar

For cake, combine all ingredients in large mixing bowl. Beat at low speed until moistened, then at medium speed for 2 minutes. Pour batter into greased and floured 12-cup tube pan. Bake at 350° for 40-50 minutes or until wooden pick inserted in center comes out clean. Let cool 10 minutes, then remove cake and place on wire rack. For glaze, combine ingredients in saucepan; bring to a boil and simmer 5 minutes. Let cool at least 10 minutes. Place platter under wire rack. Using toothpick, poke holes in top of cake; pour glaze over top and sides. Allow cake to cool completely before cutting. **Yield:** 8-10 servings.

PIZZA JOES

Barbara Gorden, Hanover, Pennsylvania

(PICTURED ON PAGE 200)

1 pound Italian sausage,
casings removed
1 medium green pepper,
chopped
1 small onion, chopped
1/2 cup fresh chopped
mushrooms
2 teaspoons Italian seasoning
1 garlic clove, minced
1 can (8 ounces) tomato sauce
6 English muffins, split and
toasted
2 cups (8 ounces) shredded
mozzarella cheese

Brown sausage in skillet; drain any excess fat. Add pepper, onion, mushrooms, seasoning and garlic; cook 2 minutes. Stir in tomato sauce and simmer, uncovered, for 10 minutes. Top each muffin half with 2 tablespoons meat sauce; sprinkle with cheese. Broil until cheese melts and filling is hot. Serve immediately. **Yield:** 12 servings.

CALICO-STUFFED PEPPERS

Joann Krebs, Juniata, Nebraska

 This tasty dish uses less sugar, salt and fat. Recipe includes *Diabetic Exchanges.*

3 large green peppers, halved
lengthwise, seeded,
membranes removed
1 pound extra lean ground beef
3/4 cup chopped onion
1 can (8 ounces) whole kernel
corn
3 tablespoons catsup
1/4 teaspoon garlic powder
1-1/2 teaspoons chili powder, *divided*
1 can (8 ounces) tomato sauce
1/2 cup shredded cheddar cheese

Arrange peppers in 4-qt. casserole or on 14-in. round glass tray. Cover with plain paper towel, turning back one corner to vent steam. Microwave on high 4 minutes. Set aside. In 2-qt. casserole, crumble beef and add onion. Microwave on high 5 minutes, stirring once. Drain. Add corn, catsup, garlic powder and 1/2 teaspoon chili powder to beef. Mix; spoon into pepper shells. Combine tomato sauce and 1 teaspoon chili powder; spoon over pepper halves. Cover; microwave on high 5 minutes. Sprinkle with cheese; microwave on high, uncovered, 1 minute. Let stand 2 minutes before serving. **Yield:** 6 servings. **Diabetic Exchanges:** One serving equals 2 protein, 1 bread, 1 vegetable; also, 247 calories, 524 mg sodium, 92 mg cholesterol, 18 gm carbohydrate.

RED RIVER BEEF STROGANOFF

Mary Alice Cox, Clinton, Tennessee

2 pounds sirloin steak, cut into
thin strips
1/4 cup all-purpose flour
1/2 cup butter *or* margarine,
divided
2 large onions, chopped
1 can (10-1/2 ounces) beef
broth
1 teaspoon dried basil
Salt and pepper to taste
1 jar (4-1/2 ounces) sliced
mushrooms, drained
1 tablespoon Worcestershire
sauce
1 cup (8 ounces) sour cream
Cooked rice *or* noodles

Dredge meat in flour. In a skillet, melt 1/4 cup butter over medium heat; saute onions until tender. Remove from pan; set aside. Melt remaining butter and brown meat on all sides. Add broth, basil, salt and pepper, mushrooms, Worcestershire sauce and onions. Cook until mixture thickens, about 5 minutes. Just before serving, stir in sour cream. Heat through, but do not boil. Serve immediately over rice or noodles. **Yield:** 8 servings.

PORK TENDERLOIN WITH PARMESAN CRUST

Ann Castle, Logan, Ohio

1 whole pork tenderloin
(15 ounces)
1/2 cup all-purpose flour
1/2 teaspoon salt
1/2 teaspoon pepper
1/2 cup butter, *divided*
1 shallot
1/2 cup dry white wine
1/4 cup grated Parmesan
cheese
1/4 cup fine bread crumbs

Preheat oven to 375°. Slice tenderloin in 1/4-in. slices; pound thin between sheets of waxed paper. Dip into flour/salt/pepper mixture and saute very quickly in 2 tablespoons of butter. Place in single layer in 11-in. x 9-in. x 2-in. baking dish. Dice shallot, saute; add white wine and deglaze pan. Add to baking dish. Mix Parmesan cheese, bread crumbs and 1/4 cup butter in food processor. Make a log of the mixture, slice and press one slice on top of each slice of pork. Bake for 15-20 minutes. **Yield:** 4 servings.

FUDGE BROWNIES

Becky Albright, Norwalk, Ohio

1-1/3 cups all-purpose flour
2 cups sugar
3/4 cup baking cocoa
1 teaspoon baking powder
1/2 teaspoon salt
1/2 cup chopped nuts
2/3 cup cooking oil
4 eggs, slightly beaten
2 teaspoons vanilla extract

Combine flour, sugar, cocoa, baking powder, salt and nuts. Set aside. Combine oil, eggs and vanilla; add to dry ingredients. Do not overmix. Spread in a 13-in. x 9-in. x 2-in. baking pan. Bake at 350° for 20-25 minutes or until toothpick inserted in center comes out clean. **Yield:** about 2 dozen.

SHREDDED BARBECUED BEEF

Carol Wilson, Shingletown, California

(PICTURED ON PAGE 202)

5 pounds chuck roast
1/2 cup brown sugar
1/4 cup apple cider vinegar
2 cups water
2-3/4 cups catsup
1 tablespoon dry mustard
1 large onion, chopped
1 to 2 cloves garlic, minced
Sesame buns
Sliced red onion
Grated sharp cheddar cheese

Combine the beef, brown sugar, vinegar and water in 6-qt. cast-iron or other heavy oven-proof pot. Bake at 375° for 3 hours. Remove from oven; cool. Remove all fat and any bones. Shred beef; return to pot. Add mixture of catsup, mustard, onion and garlic; stir to blend. Reduce oven temperature to 300° and cook, covered, for up to 4 hours. Stir every half hour, adding more water/catsup to keep well moistened. Serve on buns with the onion and cheese. **Yield:** 12-14 servings.

ONE-DISH MEAL

Ina Hooper, Elizabeth, Louisiana

(PICTURED ON PAGE 202)

1/2 to 1 pound lean ground meat
12 ounces lean bacon, cut in small pieces
1 cup chopped onions
1/2 cup chopped green onions
1/4 cup chopped green pepper
1/2 pound smoked sausage, sliced 1/4 inch thick
1 can (16 ounces) kidney beans, drained
1 can (16 ounces) pork and beans, drained
1 can (16 ounces) lima beans, drained
1 cup cooked soybeans *or* Northern white beans, drained
1 cup catsup *or* chili sauce
1/4 cup honey *or* brown sugar
1 tablespoon liquid smoke, optional
3 tablespoons white vinegar
1 teaspoon salt
1 tablespoon Worcestershire sauce
Dash red and black pepper

Brown ground beef in skillet (or cook in microwave). Drain off fat; place beef in slow cooker. Brown bacon pieces; remove to paper towel. Drain fat from skillet; lightly brown onions and green pepper. Add bacon, onions and pepper to slow cooker; stir in remaining ingredients. Cover; cook on low for 4-6 hours. **Yield:** 12 servings.

CHALUPA

Gail Koehn, Dalhart, Texas

(PICTURED ON PAGE 202)

3 pounds pork roast, cut in bite-size pieces
1 pound pinto beans (soaked in water overnight, if desired)
3 cloves garlic, chopped
3 teaspoons chili powder
1 teaspoon cumin
1 teaspoon oregano
1 can (4 ounces) chopped green chilies
1 jar (12 ounces) mild chunky salsa
Salt to taste
Tortilla *or* corn chips
Shredded cheese
Chopped tomatoes
Shredded lettuce
Taco sauce

Mix first 9 ingredients together; place in slow cooker. Cover with water (reduce water slightly if beans are pre-soaked). Cover cooker; cook on high for 5 hours. Serve in layers of chips, meat mixture, cheese, tomatoes, lettuce and taco sauce. **Yield:** 15 servings.

CHICKEN PARISIENNE

Caryn Wiggins, Columbus, Indiana

(PICTURED ON PAGE 202)

 This tasty dish uses less sugar, salt and fat. Recipe includes *Diabetic Exchanges*.

6 medium chicken breast halves
Salt
Pepper
Paprika
1/2 teaspoon leaf rosemary, optional
1/2 cup dry white wine *or* water
1 can (10-3/4 ounces) cream of mushroom soup, undiluted
1 can (4 ounces) sliced mushrooms, drained
1 cup dairy sour cream
1/4 cup flour

Sprinkle chicken breasts lightly with the salt, pepper, paprika and if desired, rosemary. Place in 3-1/2-qt. slow cooker. Mix wine/water, soup and mushrooms until well blended. (You may add sour cream/flour mixture now if you will be cooking on *low* temperature.) Pour liquid over chicken breasts in slow cooker. Sprinkle with paprika. Cover; cook on low 6-8 hours. (Or cook on high for 2-1/2 to 3 hours, adding sour cream/flour mixture during last 30 minutes.) Serve chicken and sauce over rice or noodles. **Yield:** 6 servings. **Diabetic Exchanges:** One serving equals 1/2 bread, 1 vegetable, 1 fat; also, 308 calories, 495 mg sodium, 87 mg cholesterol, 11 gm carbohydrate, 29 gm protein, 16 gm fat.

THREE-ALARM CHILI

Lorie Pfeifer, Medicine Hat, Alberta

(PICTURED ON PAGE 203)

 This tasty dish uses less sugar, salt and fat. Recipe includes *Diabetic Exchanges*.

4 tablespoons vegetable oil
2 pounds stewing beef, cut into 1/2-inch cubes
3 medium onions, diced
4 cloves garlic, minced
1 can (28 ounces) whole tomatoes
1 can (16 ounces) tomato sauce
1 cup water
3 tablespoons brown sugar
1 teaspoon oregano
3 tablespoons chili powder
2 teaspoons salt
1/4 teaspoon dried, crushed red pepper
2 cans (16 ounces *each*) kidney beans, drained
1 large green pepper, diced
1 large sweet red pepper, diced

Heat oil in Dutch oven; brown beef on all sides, then remove and drain well on paper towels. Cook onions and garlic in oil; return meat to pan. Add the tomatoes, sauce, water, brown sugar, oregano, chili powder, salt and crushed red pepper. Bring to boil over high heat. Reduce heat; simmer 1-1/2 hours. Add remaining three ingredients. Simmer, covered, until meat is tender. **Yield:** 12 servings. **Diabetic Exchanges:** One serving equals 2 protein, 1 bread, 2 vegetable, 1 fat; also, 289 calories, 746 mg sodium, 69 mg cholesterol, 26 gm carbohydrate, 23 gm protein, 11 gm fat.

SPICED LENTIL SOUP

Marty Rummel, Trout Lake, Washington

(PICTURED ON PAGE 203)

1/2 pound Italian sausage, crumbled, casing removed
1/2 cup diced onion

1/3 cup barley
3 cloves garlic
3 quarts chicken stock
1 cup lentils
1 whole chicken breast, uncooked
1/2 cup parsley, chopped
1 can (15 ounces) garbanzo beans and juice
1/2 to 1 pound fresh *or* frozen spinach
1 jar (12 ounces) mild to medium salsa

Brown sausage, onion, barley and garlic together in skillet. Remove and place in bottom of slow cooker or large stock pot. Add the chicken stock, lentils, uncooked chicken breast and parsley. Simmer for as long as you desire or until lentils are tender. Remove chicken breast, discarding bone and cartilage. Shred meat and return to cooker. Add garbanzo beans, spinach and salsa to soup mixture; heat through. Serve with hot biscuits or muffins. **Yield:** 10 servings.

CHINESE CASHEW CHICKEN

Pamela Friesen, Lemon Grove, California

(PICTURED ON PAGE 203)

1 pound bean sprouts
3 tablespoons butter
1/2 cup chopped green onion
1 can (4 ounces) mushroom pieces
1 can (10-3/4 ounces) cream of mushroom soup, undiluted
1 cup cooked chicken pieces (can use leftovers)
1 cup bias-cut celery
1 tablespoon soy sauce
1 cup cashew nuts

Mix all ingredients except cashew nuts together in slow cooker. Cook, covered, on low for 4-9 hours or on high for 2-3 hours. Stir in cashew nuts; serve with rice or noodles. **Yield:** 6 servings.

APPLES, SAUERKRAUT AND CHOPS

Lois Fetting, Nelson, Wisconsin

(PICTURED ON PAGE 203)

4 pork chops, cut 1/2 inch thick, trimmed
Vegetable oil for browning
1 medium onion, sliced, separated into rings
1/8 teaspoon instant garlic flakes

3 cups drained sauerkraut
3/4 cup apple juice
1-1/2 teaspoons caraway seed
1/4 teaspoon salt
1/4 teaspoon thyme
1/4 teaspoon pepper
1 cup apple slices, unpeeled and cored (red cooking variety)

Brown pork chops in nonstick pan; set aside. (Omit this step if in a hurry.) Place in a slow cooker *half* of onion rings, garlic flakes, sauerkraut, apple juice, caraway seed, salt, thyme and pepper. Add pork chops. Place the remaining *half* of ingredients on top of chops; top with apple slices. Cover slow cooker; cook on low for 6-8 hours or on high for 4 hours. **Yield:** 4 generous servings.

KAPUZTA

Liz Krocak, Montgomery, Minnesota

(PICTURED ON PAGE 204)

1-1/2 pounds fresh pork (any type), trimmed, cut in bite-size pieces
1 medium onion, chopped
1-1/2 pounds Polish sausage, sliced in 1/2-inch pieces
1 quart sauerkraut, fresh preferred
1/4 head fresh cabbage, coarsely chopped
1 tablespoon caraway seed
1 can (10-3/4 ounces) cream of mushroom soup
Pepper to taste

Brown pork and onion in hot skillet until pork is cooked through, about 10 minutes. Combine cooked pork and onion with all other ingredients in 5-qt. Dutch oven or slow cooker. Mix lightly; simmer all day. (The longer you cook this, the better it tastes.) **Yield:** 6-8 servings.

BIG RED SOUP

Shelly Korell, Bayard, Nebraska

(PICTURED ON PAGE 204)

2 tablespoons vegetable oil
2 pounds beef stew meat, trimmed
3/4 cup chopped onion
2 cloves garlic, minced
2 cans (14-1/2 ounces *each*) tomatoes
1 can (10-1/2 ounces) beef broth
1 can (10-1/2 ounces) chicken broth
1 can (10-3/4 ounces) tomato soup

1/4 cup water
1 teaspoon ground cumin
1 teaspoon chili powder
1 teaspoon salt
1/2 teaspoon lemon pepper
2 teaspoons Worcestershire sauce
1/3 cup mild picante sauce, unsweetened variety
8 corn tortillas, cut into quarters
4 ounces mild cheddar cheese, shredded

Heat oil in skillet; brown beef stew meat. Place meat in slow cooker; add remaining ingredients except for tortillas and cheese. Cook on low for at least 10 hours. When serving, place enough tortilla quarters in bottom of each bowl to cover. Pour soup over tortilla pieces; sprinkle with the cheese. **Yield:** 10-12 servings.

GONE-ALL-DAY STEW

Patty Kile, Plymouth Meeting, Pennsylvania

(PICTURED ON PAGE 204)

 This tasty dish uses less sugar, salt and fat. Recipe includes *Diabetic Exchanges*.

1 can (10-3/4 ounces) tomato soup, undiluted
1 cup water *or* red wine
1/4 cup all-purpose flour
2 pounds beef chuck, cut in 1-inch to 2-inch cubes, fat trimmed
3 medium carrots, cut in 1-inch diagonal slices
6 white boiling onions *or* yellow onions, quartered
4 medium potatoes, cut in 1-1/2-inch chunks
1/2 cup celery, cut in 1-inch chunks
12 whole large fresh mushrooms
2 beef bouillon cubes
1 tablespoon Italian herb seasoning mix *or* 1 teaspoon *each* leaf oregano, thyme and rosemary
1 bay leaf
3 grinds fresh pepper

Mix together tomato soup, water/wine and flour until smooth; combine with remaining ingredients in covered roasting pan. Bake at 275° for 4-5 hours. When ready to serve, adjust seasoning, if desired. Remove bay leaf before serving. Serve over noodles or with crunchy French bread (to soak up the gravy). **Yield:** 8 servings. **Diabetic Exchanges:** One serving equals 3 protein, 1 bread, 2 vegetable, 1/2 fat; also, 311 calories, 660 mg sodium, 103 mg cholesterol, 26 gm carbohydrate, 29 gm protein, 10 gm fat.

CHICKEN CACCIATORE

Aggie Arnold-Norman, Liberty, Pennsylvania

(PICTURED ON PAGE 204)

 This tasty dish uses less sugar, salt and fat. Recipe includes *Diabetic Exchanges*.

    2 medium onions, thinly sliced
    1 broiler/fryer chicken (2-1/2 to
        3 pounds), skinned and cut in
        pieces
    2 cloves garlic, minced
    1 teaspoon salt
    1/4 teaspoon pepper
    1 to 2 teaspoons crushed
        oregano leaves
    1/2 teaspoon leaf basil
    1 bay leaf
    1 can (16 ounces) tomatoes
    1 can (8 ounces) tomato sauce
    1 can (4 ounces) mushrooms
        or 1 cup fresh mushrooms
    1/4 cup water *or* dry white wine
Cooked spaghetti, linguine *or*
    vermicelli

Place sliced onions in bottom of slow cooker. Add chicken, seasonings, tomatoes, sauce, mushrooms and water/wine. Cover; cook on low for 6-8 hours or on high for 3-4 hours. Serve chicken with sauce over hot buttered spaghetti, linguine or vermicelli. **Yield:** 6 servings. **Diabetic Exchanges:** One serving equals 3 protein, 2 vegetable; also, 180 calories, 745 mg sodium, 177 mg cholesterol, 10 gm carbohydrate, 26 gm protein, 4 gm fat.

SLOW COOKER ITALIAN SAUSAGE

Mildred Rudolph, Hebron, Ohio

    2 to 3 pounds mild Italian link
        sausage
Water
    1 large onion, sliced
    1 large green pepper, sliced
    1 jar (48 ounces) spaghetti sauce

Place sausage in skillet; add water to cover. Bring to boil; cook 10 minutes. Drain. Add sausage to cooker; arrange onion and pepper on top; pour spaghetti sauce over all. Cover; cook on low for 6-8 hours. **Yield:** 4-6 servings.

QUICK COUNTRY CLAM CHOWDER

Jan Wical, Grundy Center, Iowa

    2 cans (10-3/4 ounces *each*)
        cream of potato soup

    1 pint frozen corn, thawed and
        drained
    1 cup sliced carrots
    1 can (6-1/2 ounces) minced
        clams, drained
Milk
Seasoning salt

Combine all ingredients except milk in slow cooker. Add milk to desired consistency. Cook on low for 6-8 hours. **Yield:** 8-10 servings.

CHEESY ASPARAGUS SOUP

Patricia Lockard, Rockford, Michigan

    3 pounds fresh asparagus,
        trimmed
    1 small onion, chopped
    2 cans (10-3/4 ounces *each*)
        cream of asparagus soup,
        undiluted
    2 soup cans milk
    1 jar (4-1/2 ounces) sliced
        mushrooms, drained
    3 cups (12 ounces) shredded
        cheddar cheese

In a large kettle, cook asparagus and onion in a small amount of water until tender. Drain liquid. Add all remaining ingredients; heat over medium until the cheese is melted and the soup is hot. **Yield:** 8-10 servings.

ITALIAN BEEF AU JUS

Jean Moeller, Pipestone, Minnesota

    3 to 5 pounds thawed boneless
        beef roast
SAUCE:
    1 package (10 ounces) Au Jus
        mix
    1 package (.7 ounce) Italian
        salad dressing mix
    1 can (10-1/2 ounces) beef
        broth
    1/2 soup can water

Place beef roast in slow cooker; combine sauce ingredients and pour over beef. Cover; cook on low for 8 hours. Meat may be sliced and served with hard rolls or shredded with two forks and served over noodles or rice, with broth thickened with flour. **Yield:** 8-10 servings.

SLOW COOKER STUFFING

Elmeda Johnson, East Grand Forks, Minnesota

    1 cup butter
    2 cups chopped celery

    1 cup chopped onion
    1 teaspoon poultry seasoning
1-1/2 teaspoons leaf sage,
        crumbled
    1 teaspoon leaf thyme,
        crumbled
1-1/2 teaspoons salt
    1/2 teaspoon pepper
    2 eggs, beaten
    4 cups chicken broth
    12 cups dry bread crumbs

Mix butter, celery, onion, spices, salt, pepper, eggs and broth together. Add bread crumbs; stir to blend. Cook in slow cooker on high for 45 minutes; reduce heat to low for 6 hours. (This recipe comes in handy when you run out of oven space at a large family gathering!) **Yield:** 10-12 servings.

SLOW COOKER BAKED APPLES

Ann Leggett, Jackson, Louisiana

    6 to 8 medium baking apples,
        washed, cored, with top third
        of apple peeled
FILLING:
Raisins
Chopped pecans
Brown sugar
TOPPING:
    1 teaspoon cinnamon
    1/2 teaspoon nutmeg
    2 tablespoons butter
    1/2 cup water

Place apples in slow cooker; fill apples with raisin/pecan/sugar mixture. Sprinkle with topping spices; dot with butter. Add water. Cover; cook on low for 8 hours or overnight. Delicious for breakfast. **Yield:** 6-8 servings.

OPEN-FACED TUNA LOAF

Sara Tatham, Plymouth, New Hampshire

    1 large loaf Italian bread
Butter, softened
    6 to 8 ounces Monterey Jack
        cheese, sliced thin
    2 cans (6-1/2 ounces) tuna,
        drained
    1/3 to 1/2 cup mayonnaise
    1/4 cup chopped parsley (1
        tablespoon reserved for
        garnish)
Dash pepper
    1 tablespoon lemon juice

Slice bread in half lengthwise; butter both halves. Place bread, buttered side up, in 13-in. x 9-in. x 2-in. glass pan. Cover both halves of bread with cheese slices. Mix remaining ingredients together, adjusting mayonnaise to taste. Spread on top of cheese-covered bread. Microwave on high for 6 to 7 minutes, rotating dish after 3 minutes. Sprinkle with reserved parsley. *Conventional Method:* Broil 3 in. from heat for about 10 minutes or until lightly browned. **Yield:** 8 servings.

DELUXE EGG SALAD SANDWICHES

Audrey Ulmer, Pulaski, Wisconsin

- 1 package (3 ounces) cream cheese with chives, softened
- 2 tablespoons butter *or* margarine, softened
- 2 tablespoons finely chopped celery
- 3 tablespoons mayonnaise *or* salad dressing, *divided*
- 1 teaspoon grated onion
- 1 teaspoon sugar
- 1/2 teaspoon horseradish
- 1/2 teaspoon lemon juice
- 1/4 teaspoon salt
- 1/8 teaspoon black pepper
Dash garlic powder
- 6 hard-cooked eggs, peeled and chopped fine
- 8 slices rye bread
Alfalfa sprouts, optional

In medium mixing bowl, combine cream cheese and butter; stir until smooth. Stir in celery, 1 tablespoon mayonnaise, onion, sugar, horseradish, lemon juice, salt, pepper and garlic powder. Fold in eggs. Cover; chill at least 1 hour. Let stand at room temperature about 15 minutes before making sandwiches. If desired, stir in 1 to 2 tablespoons additional mayonnaise. For each sandwich, spread about 1/2 cup egg mixture on 1 slice of rye bread. Top with another bread slice. Garnish with alfalfa sprouts, if desired. **Yield:** 4 sandwiches.

PARMESAN POTATO STICKS

Lee Herrman, Bismarck, North Dakota

- 2 pounds russet potatoes
- 1/2 cup butter, melted
- 1/2 cup fine dry bread crumbs
- 1/2 cup grated Parmesan cheese
- 1/2 teaspoon salt
- 1/8 teaspoon garlic powder
- 1/8 teaspoon black pepper

Scrub and peel potatoes; cut lengthwise into quarters. Cut each quarter into 3 strips. Roll in melted butter, then roll in combined remaining ingredients. Place potato sticks in a single layer on a cookie sheet. Drizzle melted butter over potatoes. Bake at 400° for 30-35 minutes or until potatoes are tender. **Yield:** 6 servings.

PORK CROWN ROAST WITH APRICOT/APPLE STUFFING

Mary Ann Taylor, Rockwell, Iowa

Pork rib crown roast (5-1/2 to 6 pounds, 12-16 ribs)
Salt and pepper to taste
STUFFING:
- 1 tablespoon sugar
- 1 teaspoon chicken bouillon granules
- 3/4 cup hot water
- 1/3 cup chopped dried apricots
- 4 cups cubed dry whole wheat bread (about 6 slices)
- 1 large apple, peeled, cored and chopped
- 1/2 teaspoon finely grated orange peel
- 1/2 teaspoon salt
- 1/2 teaspoon ground sage
- 1/4 teaspoon ground cinnamon
- 1/8 teaspoon black pepper
- 1/2 cup chopped celery
- 1/4 cup chopped onion
- 1/4 cup butter *or* margarine
GLAZE:
- 1/4 cup orange juice
- 1 tablespoon light corn syrup
- 1/2 teaspoon soy sauce
Apricot halves and fresh sage for garnish

Place roast, bone tips up, on rack in shallow roasting pan. Season with salt and pepper. Make a ball of aluminum foil and press into cavity to maintain shape. Wrap bone tips with foil. Insert meat thermometer, making sure the tip does not touch bone. Roast at 325° until thermometer reaches 150°. To prepare stuffing, dissolve sugar and bouillon in hot water; pour over apricots. Let stand 5 minutes. In a large bowl, combine bread, apple, orange peel, salt, sage, cinnamon and pepper. Add softened apricots. Cook celery and onion in butter until tender; add to bread mixture. Remove foil from roast center; pack stuffing lightly into roast. Combine the glaze ingredients; spoon over meat. Return roast to oven until thermometer registers 160° (total cooking time for roast will be about 2-1/2 to 3 hours). Transfer to warm platter; garnish with apricot halves and fresh sage. Slice between the ribs to serve. **Yield:** 12-16 servings.

HAM AND CREAMY POTATO SCALLOPS

Mabel Courtney, Wauseon, Ohio

- 5 pounds white potatoes, partially cooked
- 3 tablespoons butter *or* margarine
- 1/4 cup all-purpose flour
- 1/4 cup chopped onion
- 1/2 cup sliced celery
- 1 pound cooked ham, diced
- 1 can (14-1/2 ounces) chicken broth
- 1/4 cup mayonnaise
- 1 cup process cheese spread
Salt and pepper to taste

Cool and peel potatoes; slice 1/4 in. thick. Spread in greased 2-qt. casserole. In saucepan, melt butter and stir in flour until well blended. Add onion, celery, ham, broth, mayonnaise and cheese spread; cook until thickened. Season with salt and pepper. Pour ham and cheese mixture over potatoes and toss gently. Bake at 275° for 1 hour or until potatoes are tender. **Yield:** 6-8 servings.

HERBED HARVEST VEGETABLE CASSEROLE

Netty Dyck, St. Catharines, Ontario

- 4 new potatoes, cut in 1/4-inch slices
- 1/4 cup butter *or* margarine
- 1 tablespoon finely chopped fresh sage *or* 1 teaspoon dried sage
- 1 tablespoon finely chopped fresh tarragon *or* 1 teaspoon dried tarragon
- 3 sweet red peppers, seeded and diced
- 1 onion, thinly sliced
- 1/2 cup uncooked long-grain rice
- 3 medium zucchini, thinly sliced
- 4 medium tomatoes, sliced
- 1 cup (4 ounces) shredded Swiss cheese

Grease a 2-1/2-qt. casserole dish and arrange half the potato slices in overlapping rows. Dot with half the butter. Sprinkle with half each of the sage, tarragon, peppers, onion, rice and zucchini. Dot with remaining butter and repeat layering. Cover and bake at 350° for 1-1/2 hours or until potatoes are tender. Remove cover and top with tomato slices and cheese. Bake 10 minutes, or until tomatoes are warm and cheese is melted. Remove from oven; cover and allow to stand 10 minutes before serving. **Yield:** 6-8 servings.

Winter

Chase away winter's chills with these hot and hearty homemade dishes—and perhaps cook up a surprise at the same time!

Meat pies were regular, reliable favorites in Grandma's generation.

They still satisfy country appetites today, and some have gone modern—in taste *and* technique.

Traditional cooks will enjoy practicing their pastry skills on the Salmon Pie and Chicken Pot Pie with Celery Seed Crust. Busy cooks will appreciate other picture-perfect pies that offer time-saving crust alternatives such as stuffing mix, refrigerator rolls and potato flakes.

Meat and potato lovers will find their standbys stand out in Swiss Potato Pie and in Meat and Potato Pie...and younger taste buds will be tempted by tantalizing Tostada Grande, tasty Deep-Dish Cheeseburger Pie and Pop-Up Pizza Pie.

No matter which pie you pick, you can prepare these kitchen- and taste-tested treats with confidence!

MOUTH WATERING: Clockwise from left—**Pop-Up Pizza Pie** (Pg. 220); **Salmon Pie** (Pg. 220); **Tostada Grande** (Pg. 220); **Meat and Potato Pie** (Pg. 220); **Spaghetti Pie** (Pg. 221); **Chicken Pot Pie with Celery Seed Crust** (Pg. 221); **Deep-Dish Cheeseburger Pie** (Pg. 221); **Swiss Potato Pie** (Pg. 220).

Tasty and traditional meat pies are a meal in themselves, brimming with the unmistakable country goodness of abundant meats, wholesome vegetables and tasty gravy. Enjoy some tonight!

MARVELOUS MAINSTAYS. Top to bottom—**Quick Crescent Taco Pie** (Pg. 221); **Turkey Turnovers** (Pg. 222); **Tater Crust Tuna Pie** (Pg. 222); **Chicken and Stuffing Pie** (Pg. 222).

Black Beauties

Those old cast-iron stoves did much more than fix mouth-watering meals... they warmed our hearts!

By Montrue Larkin
St. George, Utah

If you're old enough to remember the slogan "Kalamazoo—direct to you", you remember the cast-iron cookstoves that warmed America's kitchens for decades.

These were the stoves that turned out cherry pies with exquisite crusts. The next evening they'd yield mouth-watering rice-and-custard puddings. Their kettles of soup and big pots of beans warmed us on wash-days. And cottage cheese came not from a carton, but from a pan of milk simmering on the stoves' back plates.

As delicious as it is to reminisce about those old family dishes, these "black beauties" served many useful functions beyond cooking.

On cold winter nights, the stove was used to warm a flatiron, a stove lid or even a rock. Later, these would be wrapped in a towel, and when placed beneath the covers those radiant bundles made your bed cozy for hours.

The Saturday night bath (in a No. 3 tub with water from the stove reservoir) was a national ritual. With blinds drawn and doors shut, the room became hot and steamy and smelled of Palmolive soap. Who can ever forget the wonderful feeling of a hot bath, a flannel nightgown and a warm flatiron?

Even an Incubator

A friend of mine relates she was so tiny at birth that her family lined a shoe box with cotton and set her on the oven door. She got along just fine.

Another friend tells of her premature birth and the doctor who said she wouldn't live unless kept constantly warm. The midwife said, "Give her to me." She emptied the water reservoir and then lined it with a blanket. She lovingly tucked the baby in and vigilantly kept the stove warm. It worked, because that baby grew up to tell the story!

A snapping cookstove fire was just the thing to get you going on cold mornings before work or school. You'd grab your clothes and run downstairs to stand near the stove to dress.

Monday was "washday", and a really hot fire and lots of water were needed to get clothes clean. The copper boiler sat on the front two plates to get maximum heat.

When the water was ready, the whites were put in boiling water with homemade brown soap. Later on, the clothes had to be wrung out by hand. It was long, hard, tedious and even dangerous work. But what woman would dare hang out her wash unless it was just as white as the neighbor's?

Heated the Irons, Too

These were the days before wash-and-wear, so ironing was essential. Flatirons were heated on top of the stove. You used one until it cooled, then released the heavy iron from its handle. You exchanged the cool iron for a hot one by clamping the handle onto another iron atop the stove.

Periodically, you had to let the stove cool so you could apply a liberal coat of stove blacking, which gave the old monster a like-new look.

If you were smart, you held off from doing this job if you were planning to be seen in public anytime soon. It took many hours of washing and rewashing to erase the telltale black from your hands.

> *"Stove blacking gave the old monster a like-new look..."*

Then, when you finished with the blacking, you used Bon Ami to polish the chrome trim. You buffed and buffed it with an old rag or some crumpled newspaper to give everything a nice shine.

Cleaning and maintaining those old stoves required an awful lot of work. But it was important work. For, unlike the impersonal self-cleaning ranges and microwaves of today, those old cast-iron stoves warmed a lot more than just food. More than anything, they warmed our hearts.

Remember comfort foods... those old-fashioned favorites Mom served up with ample portions of love and care? These recipes take you back to kitchens filled with feel-good foods that made bad days better and good days great.

Remember homemade doughnuts? The rich, yeasty aroma of those golden-brown beauties, fried in a cast-iron kettle, made for a wonderful welcome home from school.

Recall Mom's savory meat loaf? It was always filling and substantial, topped with a sweet-sour catsup sauce and served with potatoes, gravy and green beans. What a treat!

And how about made-from-scratch macaroni and cheese... soothing chicken soup...raisin-and-spice-studded noodle pudding ...and hearty, homemade bran muffins! For dessert, there was light, custardy bread pudding with lemon sauce.

Remember? If you don't, just try these flavorful comfort food favorites. They'll take you home in memory.

SOOTHING SPECIALTIES: Clockwise from lower left—**Buttermilk Doughnuts** (Pg. 223); **My Favorite Bran Muffins** (Pg. 223); **Swedish Rye Bread** (Pg. 223); **Homemade Chicken Noodle Soup** (Pg. 223); **Noodle Kugel** (Pg. 223); **Macaroni and Cheese** (Pg. 223); **Sweet-and-Sour Meat Loaf** (Pg. 224); **Bread Pudding** (Pg. 224).

In the chips! Mmmm...nothing comforts and cheers like a really good chocolate chip cookie. And here's a variation for every taste! Choose from a classic drop cookie, a dark and decadent fudgy variety, a brown-sugar-meringue-topped bar cookie or a rich, exotic cookie chewy with coconut and macadamia nuts.

COMFORTING COOKIES: Top to bottom—**Classic Chocolate Chip Cookies** (Pg. 224); **Island Treasure Cookies** (Pg. 224); **Chewy Chocolate Chip Bars** (Pg. 224); and **Double Chocolate Chip Cookies** (Pg. 225).

MEALS IN MINUTES

Grandmothers are known for elaborate, patiently prepared meals. Occasionally, though, even a grandma needs to be quick in the kitchen!

Just ask Faye Johnson of Connersville, Indiana. "With two grown children and two grandchildren nearby, plus a variety of activities, I'm almost as busy today as I was when my family was growing up," she assures. "So I still appreciate 'Meals in Minutes'!"

A member of the ladies' auxiliary, an avid gardener, a seamstress and a Sunday school teacher, Faye enjoys full and rewarding days. Even so, she insists on cooking "from scratch" for herself and husband Clair.

"I like to experiment, adding my own little touches," she says. "I usually prepare a new recipe 'as is' just once. After that, it's never the same!"

The first time you prepare Faye's favorite fast menu, which she shares here, you'll appreciate its simplicity and adaptability. The savory vegetable soup uses either beef or chicken leftovers to make a hearty, economical entree in no time at all.

The golden garlic bread is a speedy but zesty accompaniment that takes just minutes to brown in the broiler.

And the caramel dumplings, simmering on the back burner during dinner, will fill the kitchen with such a wonderful fragrance that you can be sure everyone will save room for dessert!

QUICK VEGETABLE SOUP

- 1 quart chicken broth *or* stock
- 1 can (16 ounces) tomatoes
- 1/2 cup chopped onion
- 1/2 cup chopped cabbage
- 1 package (10 ounces) frozen mixed vegetables, thawed
- 1/2 teaspoon dried basil
- 1/8 teaspoon pepper
- Dash sugar
- 1/4 cup uncooked elbow macaroni
- 1 cup leftover cubed cooked chicken *or* beef roast

In a large saucepan or Dutch oven, bring broth, tomatoes, onion, cabbage, vegetables, basil, pepper and sugar to a boil. Add macaroni and simmer 10 minutes or until tender. Add meat and heat through. **Yield:** 6 servings.

TOASTY GARLIC BREAD

- 1 loaf French bread (12 to 15 inches), cut into 1-inch slices
- 1/2 cup butter *or* margarine, softened
- Grated Parmesan cheese
- Parsley flakes
- Garlic powder

Spread both sides of bread with butter. Place, cut side down, on a cookie sheet. Sprinkle top side with cheese, parsley and garlic powder. Broil 4 in. from the heat until light golden brown. Turn slices and repeat with other side. Serve immediately. **Yield:** about 12-15 slices.

CARAMEL DUMPLINGS

- 2 tablespoons butter *or* margarine
- 1-1/2 cups packed brown sugar
- 1-1/2 cups water

DUMPLINGS:
- 1-1/4 cups all-purpose flour
- 1/2 cup sugar
- 2 teaspoons baking powder
- 1/2 teaspoon salt
- 1/2 cup milk
- 2 tablespoons butter *or* margarine, softened
- 2 teaspoons vanilla extract
- 1/2 cup coarsely chopped peeled apple, optional

In a skillet, heat the unsoftened butter, brown sugar and water to boiling. Reduce heat to simmer. Meanwhile, mix together all dumpling ingredients. Drop by tablespoonfuls into the simmering sauce. Cover tightly and simmer 20 minutes. *Do not lift lid.* Serve warm with cream or ice cream, if desired. **Yield:** 6-8 servings.

TIME-SAVING CHICKEN TIPS:
Combine your favorite dry ingredients for breading chicken and store in a plastic bag or airtight container. Next time you prepare chicken, the breading will be ready!

● To coat chicken quickly, drop the piece into a plastic bag along with seasoned flour, twist the bag closed and shake until coated.

● When simmering chicken to be used in a salad, add salt, dried rosemary and onion powder to the water for extra flavor.

SALMON PIE

Edna Hoffman, Hebron, Indiana

(PICTURED ON PAGE 212)

3 medium potatoes (1 pound), peeled and cut into 1/2-inch chunks
2 medium carrots, sliced
1 medium onion, chopped
4 tablespoons butter
1/4 cup all-purpose flour
1 teaspoon salt
1/4 teaspoon pepper
1/4 teaspoon dill weed
2 cups milk
1 can (15-1/2 ounces) salmon, drained, skin removed and separated into bite-size chunks
1 cup fresh or frozen peas
1 single crust pastry

In saucepan over medium heat, cook potatoes, carrots and onion in butter until almost tender, stirring often. Stir in flour, salt, pepper and dill until blended; cook 1 minute. Gradually stir in milk; cook until the mixture is thickened and smooth, stirring constantly. Gently stir in salmon and peas. Spoon mixture into 2-qt. round casserole; set aside. Roll out your favorite pastry, 1-1/2 in. larger than casserole top. Place pastry loosely over salmon mixture. Trim pastry edge; fold overhang under and crimp edges. Cut slits in pastry top or cut out designs to decorate top of pie. Sprinkle crust with more dill weed, if desired. Bake at 375° for 35-40 minutes or until top is golden brown. **Yield:** 6 servings.

SWISS POTATO PIE

Linda Erdy, West Mansfield, Ohio

(PICTURED ON PAGE 212)

6 medium potatoes
6 tablespoons butter, melted
1 teaspoon salt
1/4 teaspoon pepper
1/4 teaspoon ground nutmeg
1 teaspoon chopped parsley
1-1/2 cups (6 ounces) diced Swiss cheese
1 cup cubed, cooked ham
1 medium onion, grated
3 eggs
1/2 cup milk
Paprika

Peel potatoes and cook in saucepan with water until tender; drain. Mash; stir in butter, salt, pepper, nutmeg and parsley. Spoon about two-thirds of potato mixture on sides and bottom of greased 1-1/2-qt. to 2-qt. baking dish. Set aside. In medium bowl, combine cheese, ham and onion; spoon this mixture into the potato-lined dish. Beat together eggs and milk; pour over ham/cheese. Spoon (or pipe with a pastry tube) remaining potato mixture over top. Sprinkle with paprika. Bake at 400° for 30-35 minutes or until puffed and golden brown. Let stand 10 minutes; cut into serving portions. **Yield:** 4-6 servings.

MEAT AND POTATO PIE

Darlis Anderson, Badger, Iowa

(PICTURED ON PAGE 212)

3 tablespoons vegetable oil
3 cups shredded frozen hash browns
1 cup grated Swiss or cheddar cheese
3/4 cup cooked diced ham, sausage or chopped chicken
1/4 cup chopped onion
1 cup evaporated or whole milk
2 eggs
1/2 teaspoon salt
1/8 teaspoon pepper
Chopped parsley

Mix together vegetable oil and potatoes in 9-in. pie plate. Press into pie crust shape. Bake at 425° for 15 minutes or until crust begins to brown. Remove from oven. Layer on cheese, meat and onion; set aside. Combine milk, eggs, salt and pepper in bowl; beat all until blended. Pour egg mixture over layered ingredients. Sprinkle with parsley. Return to oven (same temperature); bake for 30 minutes or until lightly browned. Allow to cool 5 minutes before cutting into wedges. **Yield:** 4-6 servings.

POP-UP PIZZA PIE

Catherine Beach, Redfield, Iowa

(PICTURED ON PAGE 212)

FILLING:
1-1/2 pounds lean ground beef
1 cup chopped onion
1 cup chopped green pepper
1 clove garlic, minced
1/2 teaspoon oregano
1/2 cup water
1/8 teaspoon hot pepper sauce
1 can (15 ounces) tomato sauce
1 envelope (1.5 ounces) spaghetti sauce mix
POPOVER BATTER:
1 cup milk
1 tablespoon vegetable oil
2 eggs
1 cup all-purpose flour
1/2 teaspoon salt
6 to 8 ounces sliced mozzarella or Monterey Jack cheese
1/2 cup grated Parmesan cheese

In large skillet, brown the ground beef. Drain well. Stir in onion, green pepper, garlic, oregano, water, hot pepper sauce, tomato sauce and spaghetti sauce mix; simmer 10 minutes, stirring occasionally. Set aside. In small bowl, combine milk, oil and eggs; beat 1 minute at medium speed. Lightly stir and spoon flour into measuring cup; level off. Add flour and salt to milk/egg mixture; beat 2 minutes at medium speed of mixer or until smooth. Pour hot meat mixture into ungreased 13-in. x 9-in. pan (or pan of choice). Top with sliced cheese. Pour batter over cheese, covering filling completely; sprinkle with Parmesan cheese. Bake at 400° for 25 to 30 minutes or until puffed and deep golden brown. Serve immediately. **Yield:** 10 servings.

TURKEY/CHEESE PIE

Ann Davis, Dillsburg, Pennsylvania

1 pound ground turkey
1-1/2 cups chopped onion
1-1/2 cups milk
3/4 cup baking mix
3 eggs
1/2 teaspoon seasoned salt
1/4 teaspoon pepper
2 tomatoes, sliced
1 cup shredded cheddar cheese

Cook turkey and onion in skillet over medium heat until turkey is browned; drain. Spread in a greased 10-in. pie plate; set aside. Beat milk, baking mix, eggs, salt and pepper in blender or with hand mixer till smooth. Pour into turkey/onion-lined pie plate. Bake 25 minutes at 400°. Top with tomatoes; sprinkle with cheese. Bake until knife inserted in center comes out clean, about 5-8 minutes more. Cool 5 minutes. **Yield:** 6-8 servings.

TOSTADA GRANDE

Jenny Nichols, Conroe, Texas

(PICTURED ON PAGE 213)

1 pound lean ground beef
2 tablespoons (1/2 package) taco or chili seasoning mix
1 can (8 ounces) tomato sauce
1 can (4 ounces) diced green chilies, drained
3 to 4 drops hot pepper sauce

1 can (8 ounces) crescent dinner rolls *or* 1 can (7.5 ounces) refrigerated biscuits
1 cup refried beans
4 ounces shredded cheese (cheddar and mozzarella mixture preferred)
1/2 head lettuce, shredded
1 large tomato, chopped
1 small onion, chopped

In large skillet, brown ground beef; drain well. Stir in seasoning, tomato sauce, chilies and hot pepper sauce; heat until hot and bubbly. Simmer, uncovered, for 15 minutes or until mixture thickens. Lightly grease 9-in. or 10-in. pie plate. Separate rolls or biscuits; arrange in pan. Press over bottom and up sides to form crust. Spread beans over dough; top with meat mixture. Bake at 375° for 18 to 22 minutes or until crust is golden brown. Sprinkle immediately with cheese. Garnish with lettuce, tomato and onion. **Yield:** 4-6 servings.

DEEP-DISH CHEESEBURGER PIE

Margery Bryan, Royal City, Washington

(PICTURED ON PAGE 213)

DOUGH:
1 cup baking mix
1/4 cup cold water
FILLING:
1/2 cup chopped onion
1/2 cup chopped green pepper
2 tablespoons butter
1/2 cup lean ground beef
1/2 teaspoon salt
1/4 teaspoon pepper
2 tablespoons baking mix
1 tablespoon Worcestershire sauce
2 eggs
1 cup small curd creamed cottage cheese (drain excess liquid)
TOPPING:
2 medium tomatoes, sliced paper thin
1 cup (about 4 ounces) shredded cheddar cheese

In bowl, mix 1 cup baking mix with water until soft dough forms; beat vigorously 20 strokes. Gently smooth dough into a ball on a floured, cloth-covered board. Knead five times. Roll dough 2 in. larger than inverted 9-in. deep dish pie plate. Ease into plate; flute edge if desired. Saute chopped onion and green pepper in butter until tender. Do not brown. Remove onion and green pepper; set aside. Brown ground beef; drain. Remove from heat; stir in reserved onion and green pepper, salt, pepper,

2 tablespoons baking mix and Worcestershire sauce. Spoon into pie crust; set aside. Mix eggs and cottage cheese in bowl; pour over beef mixture. Arrange tomato slices in circle on top; sprinkle with cheese. Bake at 375° about 30 minutes, until set. **Yield:** 6-8 servings.

SPAGHETTI PIE

Ellen Vandyne, Sistersville, West Virginia

(PICTURED ON PAGE 213)

1 package (7 ounces) spaghetti
2 tablespoons butter
1/3 cup Parmesan cheese
2 eggs, well-beaten
1 cup cottage cheese
1 pound lean ground beef
1/2 cup chopped onion
1/4 cup chopped green pepper
1 jar (15-1/2 ounces) spaghetti sauce
1/2 cup shredded mozzarella cheese

Cook spaghetti according to package directions; drain. Add butter, Parmesan cheese and eggs to hot spaghetti. Form mixture into a "crust" in 10-in. pie plate. Microwave on high 2 minutes. Spread cottage cheese over spaghetti crust. Set aside. Crumble ground beef in microwaveable colander and microwave on high for 5 minutes; drain all fat. Add onion and green pepper to ground beef in bowl; microwave on high for 2-3 minutes. Stir in spaghetti sauce; microwave, covered, on high for 5-7 minutes. Stir; add this mixture to spaghetti crust covered with cottage cheese. Microwave 6-8 minutes, turning once. Sprinkle mozzarella cheese on top. Microwave on high for 1 minute or until cheese melts. *Conventional Method:* Follow procedure above, using skillet to cook meat on stove, but do not pre-bake spaghetti "crust". Layer ingredients according to instructions. Bake, uncovered, at 350° for 20 minutes. Sprinkle cheese on top; return to oven for 5 minutes more. **Yield:** 6 servings.

CHICKEN POT PIE WITH CELERY SEED CRUST

Ruth Landis, Manheim, Pennsylvania

(PICTURED ON PAGE 213)

FILLING:
1/3 cup butter
1/3 cup all-purpose flour
1/3 cup chopped onion
1/2 teaspoon salt
1/4 teaspoon pepper

1-3/4 cups chicken broth
2/3 cup milk
2 cups cut-up cooked chicken
1 package (10 ounces) frozen peas and carrots
PASTRY:
2 cups all-purpose flour
2 teaspoons celery seed
1 teaspoon salt
2/3 cup plus 2 tablespoons shortening
4 to 5 tablespoons ice water

In saucepan, melt butter over low heat. Blend in flour, onion, salt and pepper. Cook, stirring, until mixture is bubbly. Remove from heat and stir in chicken broth and milk. Heat to boiling, stirring constantly. Boil; stir 1 minute. Gently stir in chicken and frozen vegetables; set aside. Prepare pastry by measuring flour, celery seed and salt in bowl. Cut in shortening. Sprinkle in water 1 tablespoon at a time, mixing until all flour is moistened and dough almost cleans sides of bowl. Gather dough into ball. On lightly floured board, roll two-thirds of the dough into a 13-in. square. Ease pastry into 9-in. x 9-in. square pan. Pour filling into pan. Roll remaining dough into square; place over filling. Cut slits in center to allow steam to escape. Bake at 425° for 30-35 minutes. **Yield:** 4-6 servings.

QUICK CRESCENT TACO PIE

Jean Moeller, Pipestone, Minnesota

(PICTURED ON PAGE 214)

1-1/4 pounds lean ground beef
1 package taco seasoning mix
1/2 cup water
1/2 cup chunky salsa
1 can (8 ounces) crescent dinner rolls
1-1/2 cups crushed corn chips, *divided*
1 carton (8 ounces) dairy sour cream
6 slices American cheese
Shredded lettuce
Sliced black olives
Diced tomatoes

Brown meat in large skillet; drain. Add seasoning mix, water and salsa; simmer for 5 minutes. Spread the crescent roll dough in 10-in. pie plate to form crust; press edges together at seams. Sprinkle 1 cup corn chips on crust bottom, reserving remaining 1/2 cup. Spoon on meat mixture. Spread sour cream over meat. Cover with cheese slices; sprinkle on remaining 1/2 cup of corn chips. Bake at 375° for 20 minutes, until crust is golden brown. Serve with lettuce, olives and tomatoes. **Yield:** 6 servings.

TATER CRUST TUNA PIE

Cynthia Kolberg, Syracuse, Indiana

(PICTURED ON PAGE 214)

CRUST:
     1 cup all-purpose flour
     1/2 cup mashed potato flakes
     1/2 cup butter
     3 to 4 tablespoons ice water
     1 can (2.8 ounces) french-fried
         onions, *divided*
FILLING:
     3/4 cup mashed potato flakes
     2 tablespoons chopped stuffed
         green olives
     1 can (6-1/2 ounces) tuna,
         drained
     1 can (10-3/4 ounces)
         condensed cream of
         mushroom soup, reduced
         sodium preferred
     1 egg
     1 cup shredded cheddar
         cheese, *divided*

In medium bowl, combine the flour and potato flakes; cut in butter until crumbly. Add water, 1 tablespoon at a time, until dough is just moist enough to hold together. Press pastry over bottom and up sides of ungreased 9-in. or 10-in. pie plate. Flute edge. Reserve 1/2 cup onions; set aside. Sprinkle remaining onions into pastry shell. In medium bowl, combine all filling ingredients except 1/2 cup of cheese. Spoon tuna filling into pastry crust. Bake at 350° for 25-30 minutes or until crust is golden. Sprinkle with reserved cheese and onions; bake for an additional 5-10 minutes or until cheese is melted. Let stand 5 minutes before serving. **Yield:** 6-8 servings.

CHICKEN AND STUFFING PIE

Ina Schmillen, Elkhorn, Nebraska

(PICTURED ON PAGE 214)

CRUST:
     1 package (8 ounces) herb
         seasoning stuffing mix
     3/4 cup chicken broth
     1/2 cup butter, melted
     1 egg, beaten
FILLING:
     1 can (4 ounces) mushrooms,
         drained, liquid reserved
     2 tablespoons all-purpose flour
     1/2 cup chopped onion
     1 tablespoon butter
     1 can (10 ounces) *or* 1 jar (12
         ounces) chicken gravy

     1 teaspoon Worcestershire
         sauce
     1/2 teaspoon thyme
     3 cups cubed, cooked chicken
     1 cup fresh *or* frozen peas
     2 tablespoons diced pimiento
     1 tablespoon parsley flakes
     4 ounces sliced Colby *or*
         American cheese

Mix crust ingredients in medium bowl; press into 10-in. greased pie plate. Set aside. Combine mushroom liquid with flour in small bowl; set aside. In saucepan on top of stove, saute mushrooms and onion in butter. Stir in all remaining ingredients except cheese. Heat thoroughly; turn into stuffing crust. Bake at 375° for 20 minutes. Cut each cheese slice into strips; place in lattice design on pie. Bake 5 minutes more. **Yield:** 6-8 servings.

TURKEY TURNOVERS

Avonel Waller, Lakeland, Florida

(PICTURED ON PAGE 214)

FILLING:
     1 cup chopped celery
     1/4 cup chopped onion
     1/4 cup butter
     1/3 cup all-purpose flour
     1 to 2 teaspoons salt
     1/4 teaspoon pepper
     1-1/4 cups milk
     4 cups cooked, cubed turkey
     1/4 cup chopped parsley
DOUGH:
     4 cups all-purpose flour
     1 teaspoon salt
     1-1/2 cups butter
     2 cups (8 ounces) shredded
         sharp cheddar cheese
     2 cups dairy sour cream

In large skillet on top of stove, cook celery and onion in butter until tender. Blend in flour, salt and pepper. Gradually add milk; cook, stirring constantly, until thickened. Add turkey and parsley. Set aside. In large bowl, combine flour and salt; cut in butter until mixture resembles coarse crumbs. Stir in the cheese. Add sour cream, mixing until dough forms a ball. Divide dough in half. Roll out half of dough into 18-in. x 12-in. rectangle. Cut into six 6-in. squares. Repeat with second half of dough. Place 1/3 cup turkey filling on each square. Fold diagonally to form a triangle; seal edges by pressing down with fork tines. Cut slits in top of turnovers. Place on cookie sheet. Bake at 450° for 10 minutes; reduce heat to 400°. Bake 5-8 minutes more until the crust is golden brown. **Yield:** 12 turnovers.

HAMBURGER UPSIDE DOWN PIE

Dianna Eperthener, Grove City, Pennsylvania

FILLING:
     1 pound lean ground beef
     2 tablespoons vegetable oil
     1 cup chopped celery
     1/4 cup minced onion
     3/4 cup chopped green pepper
     1 teaspoon salt
     1/4 teaspoon pepper
     1/2 clove garlic, minced
     1 can (10-1/2 ounces) tomato
         soup
PARSLEY BISCUIT TOPPING:
     1/2 cup shortening
     2 cups all-purpose flour
     3 teaspoons baking powder
     1 teaspoon salt
     1/4 cup minced parsley
     1 cup milk

Brown ground beef in oil in 10-in. oven-proof skillet. Add remaining filling ingredients; simmer 10 minutes. Meanwhile, make biscuits by cutting shortening into sifted dry ingredients in medium bowl. Stir in milk only until flour is moistened. Drop biscuit topping by spoonful over hot mixture in skillet. Bake at 425° for 20 minutes. (You may serve this from the skillet or turn out on platter.) Serve immediately. **Yield:** 6 servings.

CHICKEN AND WILD RICE CASSEROLE

Crystal Clodfelter, Calhoun, Illinois

     1 package (6 ounces) long-
         grain and wild rice mix
     3 tablespoons plus 1 teaspoon
         cornstarch
     1 teaspoon salt
Dash black pepper
     1 can (12 ounces) evaporated
         skim milk
     12 ounces chicken broth
     2 tablespoons butter
     1/4 cup chopped onion
     5 cups cubed cooked chicken
     1/4 cup chopped pimiento
     1/4 cup chopped parsley

Cook the rice according to package directions, *omitting butter*. Set aside. In a saucepan, mix the cornstarch, salt and pepper; gradually stir in milk and broth until smooth. Add butter and onion. Bring to a boil over medium heat, stirring constantly; cook 1 minute or until mixture thickens. In 2-qt. casserole, combine the sauce, chicken, pimiento, parsley and cooked rice. Bake, uncovered, at 375° for 30 minutes. **Yield:** 6-8 servings.

MY FAVORITE BRAN MUFFINS

Rosemary Smith, Fort Bragg, California

(PICTURED ON PAGE 216)

1-1/4 cups unprocessed bran
1 cup toasted wheat germ
1 cup brown sugar
2-1/2 cups whole wheat flour
2-1/2 teaspoons baking soda
1/2 teaspoon salt
1 tablespoon grated orange peel
2 eggs, slightly beaten
1/2 cup honey
1/4 cup molasses
1/2 cup vegetable oil
2 cups buttermilk
1 cup boiling water

In large bowl, combine bran, wheat germ, sugar, flour, baking soda, salt and orange peel; set aside. Combine eggs, honey, molasses, oil, buttermilk and boiling water; mix well with dry ingredients. Spoon batter into greased muffin tins, filling 2/3 full. Bake at 350° for 20-25 minutes. Batter may be made ahead and stored in refrigerator for up to 1 month to be used as needed. **Yield:** 2 dozen muffins.

SWEDISH RYE BREAD

Marilyn Young, Marquette, Kansas

(PICTURED ON PAGE 216)

2 packages active dry yeast
1/2 cup warm water (110-115°)
1 teaspoon sugar
1-1/2 cups rye flour
1/2 cup sugar
3 teaspoons salt
3 cups hot water
1/2 cup melted vegetable shortening
1/2 cup molasses
9-1/4 cups all-purpose flour

Dissolve yeast in warm water; stir in 1 teaspoon sugar. Set aside. In large mixing bowl, mix rye flour with 1/2 cup sugar and salt. Add hot water gradually, mixing to a smooth paste. Gradually add melted shortening and molasses; beat well. Add yeast mixture and enough all-purpose flour to make a stiff dough. When dough becomes too stiff to work with spoon, knead in any remaining all-purpose flour until dough is smooth and elastic. Place in warm area until doubled in bulk. Divide into three loaves and place in greased 9-in. x 5-in. x 3-in. pans. Let rise until double. Bake at 325° for 40 minutes. Remove from pans; rub tops and sides of bread with melted shortening. **Yield:** 3 loaves.

YEAST TIP: Use a candy thermometer to get correct water temperature for recipes that use yeast. No more failures!

BUTTERMILK DOUGHNUTS

Judy Jungwirth, Athol, South Dakota

(PICTURED ON PAGE 216)

1 package active dry yeast
1/4 cup warm water (110-115°)
3/4 cup scalded buttermilk
1/4 cup sugar
1 teaspoon salt
1/4 cup shortening
1/2 cup fresh mashed potatoes
1 egg, beaten
1 teaspoon nutmeg
3-1/2 to 4 cups all-purpose flour
Confectioners' *or* granulated sugar, optional

Dissolve yeast in water; set aside. Combine remaining ingredients; stir in yeast. Knead 5 minutes until smooth. Let rise until double. Roll out on floured board to 1/2-in. thickness. Cut doughnuts with cutter. Let rise 30-35 minutes. Fry in hot oil until brown on both sides. Drain on paper towels. Dust with sugar, if desired. **Yield:** about 24 doughnuts.

NOODLE KUGEL

Sally Stapleton, Milwaukee, Wisconsin

(PICTURED ON PAGE 217)

12 ounces flat egg noodles
3 eggs
1/4 cup sugar
2/3 cup hoop *or* farmer's cheese, crumbled
1/2 teaspoon salt
1/2 teaspoon cinnamon
1/4 teaspoon nutmeg
1/2 cup dairy sour cream
1/2 cup golden raisins
1/4 cup butter, *divided*

Preheat oven to 350°. Cook noodles in boiling salted water for 8 to 10 minutes or until tender but not soft. Drain; set aside. Beat together eggs, sugar, cheese, salt, cinnamon, nutmeg, sour cream and raisins; set aside. Cut *one-half* of butter into small bits. Stir together noodles, egg/cheese mixture and cut-up butter. Put 1 teaspoon butter in 3-qt. casserole; heat in oven until butter melts. Tilt casserole to coat sides with butter. Spoon in kugel mixture. Sprinkle with additional cinnamon; dot with the remaining butter. Bake at 350° for 25-30 minutes or until golden brown. **Yield:** 6-8 servings.

MACARONI AND CHEESE

Betty Mantz, Philipsburg, Pennsylvania

(PICTURED ON PAGE 217)

1 cup dry macaroni
1 cup cottage cheese
1 cup dairy sour cream
1 cup process cheese spread, cubed
1 cup sharp cheddar cheese, shredded
2 eggs, beaten

Cook macaroni according to package directions; drain. Combine cottage cheese, sour cream, process cheese spread, cheddar cheese and eggs in buttered 2-1/2-qt. casserole. Add cooked macaroni; fold in thoroughly. Bake at 350° for 45 minutes. **Yield:** 6-8 servings.

HOMEMADE CHICKEN NOODLE SOUP

Rita Eipperle, Omaha, Nebraska

(PICTURED ON PAGE 217)

1 fryer chicken (3 to 4 pounds)
1 large onion, chopped into bite-size pieces
1 cup celery, chopped into bite-size pieces
1 cup carrots, chopped into bite-size pieces
2 tablespoons chicken bouillon granules
1/2 teaspoon fresh ground pepper
Approximately 2 quarts water
2 tablespoons freshly snipped parsley
1/2 teaspoon dried lemon thyme, optional
1 cup dry noodles, precooked according to package directions
Salt, pepper to taste

Wash and drain chicken; place in large soup kettle with onion, celery, carrots, bouillon and pepper. Add enough cold water to just cover chicken. Simmer 1 hour or until chicken is tender. Remove chicken from broth; discard skin, fat, bones and cartilage. Reserve all meat; cut or shred as you prefer. Return meat to broth; add parsley, lemon thyme, pre-cooked noodles of choice and salt, pepper to taste. Reheat broth to desired temperature. **Yield:** 3 quarts.

SWEET-AND-SOUR MEAT LOAF

Debbie Haneke, Stafford, Kansas

(PICTURED ON PAGE 217)

1-1/2 pounds ground beef
1 cup dry bread crumbs
1 teaspoon salt
1/4 teaspoon pepper
2 eggs
1 teaspoon instant minced onion
1 can (15 ounces) tomato sauce, *divided*
TOPPING:
Reserved tomato sauce
2 tablespoons brown sugar
2 tablespoons vinegar
1/2 cup sugar
2 teaspoons prepared mustard

Mix together beef, bread crumbs, salt, pepper and eggs. Add onions and one-half of tomato sauce. Form into loaf in 9-in. x 5-in. x 3-in. pan. Bake at 350° for 50 minutes. In saucepan, combine topping ingredients; bring to boil. Pour over meat loaf; bake 10 minutes more. **Yield:** 6 servings.

🐝🐝🐝🐝🐝🐝🐝🐝🐝🐝🐝🐝🐝🐝🐝
BREAD PUDDING

Bernice Harder, Moline, Illinois

(PICTURED ON PAGE 217)

2 cups day-old bread cubes, crusts removed, cut 1/4- to 1/2-inch
2 cups milk
1/4 cup sugar
3 tablespoons butter
2 eggs
Dash salt
1/2 teaspoon vanilla
LEMON SAUCE:
3/4 to 1 cup sugar
2 tablespoons cornstarch
1/8 teaspoon salt
2 cups water
1 tablespoon grated lemon peel
1/4 cup butter
2 tablespoons fresh lemon juice

Place bread cubes in buttered 1-1/2-qt. baking dish (or individual ramekins, as shown); set aside. In small saucepan, mix and heat milk, sugar and butter just enough to dissolve sugar and melt butter. Beat eggs slightly, adding salt to mixture. Stir eggs into warm milk and add vanilla. Pour liquid mixture over bread cubes and set baking dishes in a pan of hot water. Bake at 350° for 1 hour or until a knife inserted in center comes out clean. While pudding bakes, prepare lemon sauce by combining sugar, cornstarch and salt in saucepan. Stir in water and lemon peel; boil for 1 minute. Remove from heat and stir in butter and lemon juice. Serve pudding hot with lemon sauce. **Yield:** 6 servings.

🐝🐝🐝🐝🐝🐝🐝🐝🐝🐝🐝🐝🐝🐝🐝
CLASSIC CHOCOLATE CHIP COOKIES

Lois Miller, Fredericksburg, Pennsylvania

(PICTURED ON PAGE 218)

2-1/4 cups all-purpose flour
1 teaspoon baking soda
1 cup butter *or* margarine, softened
1/4 cup granulated sugar
3/4 cup brown sugar
1 teaspoon vanilla
1 package (3-1/2 ounces) vanilla flavor instant pudding
2 eggs
1 package (12 ounces) semi-sweet chocolate chips
1 cup chopped walnuts, optional

Combine flour and baking soda; set aside. Combine butter, sugars, vanilla and pudding mix in large mixer bowl; beat until smooth and creamy. Beat in eggs; gradually add flour mixture. Stir in chocolate chips and nuts (batter will be stiff). Drop by heaping teaspoonfuls, about 2 in. apart, onto ungreased cookie sheets. Bake at 375° for 9 to 9-1/2 minutes or until browned. **Yield:** 4-1/2 dozen cookies, 2-1/2-inches in diameter.

🐝🐝🐝🐝🐝🐝🐝🐝🐝🐝🐝🐝🐝🐝🐝
CHEWY CHOCOLATE CHIP BARS

Gloria Secor, Kenosha, Wisconsin

(PICTURED ON PAGE 218)

1 cup butter, room temperature
1/2 cup granulated sugar
1 cup brown sugar, *divided*
1 tablespoon water
1 teaspoon vanilla
2 eggs, *separated*
2 cups all-purpose flour
1/2 teaspoon salt
1/2 teaspoon baking soda
1 teaspoon baking powder
3/4 cup semisweet chocolate chips
3/4 cup finely chopped walnuts

Cream together butter, granulated sugar and 1/2 cup brown sugar until light and fluffy. Add water, vanilla and egg yolks (reserve whites in separate bowl); beat for 2-3 minutes. Beat in flour, salt, baking soda and powder. Spread batter onto lightly greased 13-in. x 9-in. x 2-in. baking pan or jelly roll pan. Sprinkle on chocolate chips. Beat egg whites until they form soft peaks, then add reserved brown sugar, blending well. Spread over chips; sprinkle with chopped nuts. Bake at 350° for 35 minutes or until meringue is light brown. Cut while still hot. **Yield:** 3 dozen bars.

🐝🐝🐝🐝🐝🐝🐝🐝🐝🐝🐝🐝🐝🐝🐝
ISLAND TREASURE COOKIES

Dorothy Schafer, Nazareth, Pennsylvania

(PICTURED ON PAGE 218)

1-2/3 cups all-purpose flour
3/4 teaspoon baking powder
3/4 teaspoon salt
1/2 teaspoon baking soda
3/4 cup plus 2 tablespoons butter, softened
3/4 cup brown sugar
1/3 cup granulated sugar
3/4 teaspoon vanilla
1 egg
3/4 cup (2 ounces) toasted coconut
3/4 cup (3-1/2 ounces) chopped macadamia nuts
1 package (11-1/2 ounces) milk chocolate chips

Combine flour, baking powder, salt and baking soda; set aside. In medium mixing bowl, beat butter, sugars and vanilla until creamy. Add egg; mix well. Gradually add flour mixture. Stir in coconut, macadamia nuts and milk chocolate chips. Drop by heaping tablespoonfuls, 3 in. apart, onto ungreased cookie sheets. Bake at 375° for 12 minutes or until lightly browned. Allow to stand for 2 minutes before removing from cookie sheets. **Yield:** 32 cookies, 3-1/2 inches in diameter.

🐝🐝🐝🐝🐝🐝🐝🐝🐝🐝🐝🐝🐝🐝🐝
CANDY BAR PIE

Rosalind Hamilton, Iowa, Louisiana

6 chocolate bars with almonds (1.45 ounces *each*)
1 container (8 ounces) frozen whipped topping, thawed
1 tablespoon vanilla extract
1 prepared graham cracker crust (8 *or* 9 inches)
Shaved chocolate, optional

In a double boiler or microwave oven, melt chocolate bars. Quickly fold into the whipped topping. Stir in vanilla. Spoon into pie crust. Garnish with shaved chocolate, if desired. Chill until ready to serve. **Yield:** 6-8 servings.

DOUBLE CHOCOLATE CHIP COOKIES

Glenna Tooman, Boise, Idaho

(PICTURED ON PAGE 218)

    8 squares (1 ounce *each*)
      semisweet chocolate
    3 squares (1 ounce *each*)
      unsweetened chocolate
    6 tablespoons butter *or*
      margarine
  1/3 cup all-purpose flour
  1/4 teaspoon baking powder
  1/4 teaspoon salt
    3 eggs
    1 cup sugar
    2 teaspoons vanilla
1-1/2 cups semisweet chocolate
      chips
    1 cup chopped pecans
    1 cup chopped walnuts

Melt semisweet and unsweetened chocolates together with butter/margarine over low heat, stirring until smooth. Cool. Sift together flour, baking powder and salt; set aside. Beat eggs, sugar and vanilla until slightly thickened. Add the melted chocolate, mixing well. Add flour mixture, mixing well. Stir in chocolate chips, pecans and walnuts. (If batter is thin, allow to stand for 10 minutes.) Drop by heaping tablespoonfuls onto lightly greased cookie sheets, spacing cookies 3 in. apart. Bake at 350° for 8-10 minutes. Remove to rack to cool. *Do not overbake.* **Yield:** 3 dozen cookies.

WHOLE WHEAT FRENCH BREAD

Roseann Loker, Colon, Michigan

    5 to 5-1/4 cups all-purpose
      flour
    2 cups stone-ground whole
      wheat flour
    2 packages (1/4 ounce *each*)
      active dry yeast
2-1/2 cups water
    1 tablespoon sugar
    1 tablespoon salt
    1 tablespoon butter *or*
      margarine
  Yellow cornmeal
    1 egg white, beaten
    1 tablespoon water

Combine flours. In a large mixing bowl, combine 3 cups flour mixture and the yeast. Set aside. Heat water, sugar, salt and butter to 115°-120°. Add to flour and yeast. Beat with an electric mixer on low for 30 seconds; increase speed to medi-

um and beat 3 additional minutes. Stir in by hand enough remaining flour to make a soft dough. Knead on a lightly floured board until smooth and elastic, about 6-8 minutes. Place dough in a greased bowl; cover and allow to rise in a warm place until doubled, about 1 hour. Punch dough down; divide in half and let rest 10 minutes. Roll each half into a 15-in. x 12-in. rectangle. Roll up jelly-roll style, starting with the long side. Pinch to seal and turn ends under to form a smooth loaf. Sprinkle two baking sheets with cornmeal and place each loaf, seam side down, on the baking sheets. Make slashes every 2-1/2 in. in the top of each loaf. Beat egg white and water; brush some over loaves. Cover and let rise until doubled, about 1 hour. Bake at 375° for 20 minutes. Brush again with egg white mixture and bake 20 minutes more. **Yield:** 2 loaves.

APPETIZER CHICKEN KABOBS

Gail Ponak, Viscount, Saskatchewan

  3/4 cup soy sauce
  1/4 cup sugar
    1 tablespoon vegetable oil
  1/4 teaspoon garlic powder
  1/2 teaspoon ground ginger
    2 boneless skinless chicken
      breasts, cut into 1-inch chunks
    6 to 8 green onions, cut into
      1-inch lengths
    8 ounces medium-size fresh
      mushrooms, stems removed

In a mixing bowl, combine first five ingredients. Stir in chicken and onion; allow to marinate for 30 minutes. Soak wooden skewers in water. On each skewer, thread a piece of chicken, onion, mushroom and another chicken piece. Place on a broiler rack. Broil 5 in. from the heat, turning and basting with marinade after 3 minutes. Continue broiling for another 3 minutes or until chicken is done. Serve immediately. **Yield:** 20-24 appetizers.

HOOSIER CHILI

Jeanne Boberg, Muncie, Indiana

 This tasty dish uses less sugar, salt and fat. Recipe includes *Diabetic Exchanges*.

    2 pounds extra-lean ground beef
    2 cups chopped onion
  3/4 cup chopped celery
  1/2 cup chopped green pepper

    3 garlic cloves, minced
    1 teaspoon salt, optional
  1/4 teaspoon pepper
    1 tablespoon brown sugar
    3 tablespoons chili powder
    2 cans (16 ounces *each*)
      stewed tomatoes
    1 can (46 ounces) tomato juice
    1 can (10-1/2 ounces) beef broth
  1/2 cup uncooked elbow
      macaroni
    1 can (15 ounces) kidney
      beans, rinsed and drained

In a large Dutch oven or soup kettle, brown beef until no longer pink. Add onion, celery, green pepper and garlic. Continue cooking until vegetables are tender. Add all remaining ingredients except last two; bring to a boil. Reduce heat; cover and simmer for 1-1/2 hours, adding macaroni during last half hour of cooking time. Stir in the beans and heat through. **Yield:** 12 servings (about 4-1/2 quarts). **Diabetic Exchanges:** One serving (without additional salt and using sodium-free tomatoes, tomato juice and broth) equals 2 meat, 1 starch, 1-1/2 vegetable; also, 255 calories, 68 mg sodium, 45 mg cholesterol, 23 gm carbohydrate, 18 gm protein, 13 gm fat.

SPICY CITRUS SALAD

Susan Seymour, Valatie, New York

 This tasty dish uses less sugar, salt and fat. Recipe includes *Diabetic Exchanges*.

  1/2 teaspoon cayenne pepper
    1 teaspoon paprika
  1/2 teaspoon garlic powder
    3 tablespoons olive oil
    1 tablespoon wine vinegar
    3 large seedless oranges,
      peeled and sectioned
  1/3 cup chopped fresh parsley
   18 pitted ripe olives, cut in half
      lengthwise
1-1/2 quarts torn mixed greens

In a bowl, whisk together first five ingredients. Stir in the oranges, parsley and olives; allow to marinate 1 hour. Toss with greens and serve immediately. **Yield:** 6 servings. **Diabetic Exchanges:** One serving equals 1 fruit, 1 fat, 1/2 vegetable; also, 112 calories, 114 mg sodium, 0 mg cholesterol, 15 gm carbohydrate, 2 gm protein, 6 gm fat.

EASY FRUIT SYRUP: Combine 1/2 cup water, 2 tablespoons sugar and 1/2 teaspoon lemon juice; heat until sugar dissolves. Cool. Add 1/2 cup jam or preserves. Add more lemon juice to taste.

All-American pies—they're our favorite dessert...and anytime treat. In a fast-food world, pies say "made with love and patience". No wonder we treat pies (and pie makers) with such respect!

Inside every pie—in each circle of delicate dough, spoonful of filling, dab of butter, touch of cream or sprinkle of sugar—is the unmistakable mark of a skilled cook.

Our grandmothers were known by their pie-making skills. The reputation of many a modern cook has also been based on her baking skills.

"You should *see* her pies," admirers whisper in reverential tones of blue-ribbon bakers. "Her crusts are so light, you'd think they would float away!"

Portable, sweet and satisfying, pies have always been the "stuff" of festive family dinners and the crowd-pleasers at potluck suppers.

But it doesn't take a crowd to appreciate a pie...the most loving words anyone with an appetite can hear may be: "I baked your favorite pie —want a slice?" So, why not try baking one of these delicious pies today!

COUNTRY PIES: From lower left, clock-wise—**Banana Cream Chiffon Pie** (Pg. 233); **Buttermilk Pie** (Pg. 233); **Rhu-barb-Orange Cream Pie** (Pg. 233); **Pear Crumb Pie** (Pg. 234); **Pineapple Sour Cream Pie** (Pg. 233); **French Apple and Walnut Tarts** (Pg. 234); **Peanut Butter Crunch Pie** (Pg. 234); **My Mom's Chocolate Pie** (Pg. 233).

As the cream of the crop, these outstanding cream pies are destined to take their place as family favorites in your home.

The Sour Cream Lemon Pie combines farm-fresh dairy products with the tang of lemon while the Chocolate Almond Cream Pie is a rich treat with its luscious chocolate filling and slivered almonds. The Apple Raisin Cream Pie adds a new twist to an old standby and the Cream Cheese/Pineapple Pie offers an unusual combination of creaminess contrasting with a sweet and tart pineapple layer.

PICTURE PERFECT PIES: Clockwise from foreground—**Sour Cream Lemon Pie** (Pg. 234); **Chocolate Almond Cream Pie** (Pg. 235); **Apple Raisin Cream Pie** (Pg. 235); **Cream Cheese/ Pineapple Pie** (Pg. 234).

BEST COOK

**Elsie Pritschau
Ravenna, Nebraska**

Elsie Pritschau of Ravenna, Nebraska does everything the old-fashioned way—right down to cooking delectable homemade dishes with a vintage Home Comfort stove!

Elsie also grinds her own flour—wheat for bread, milo for pancakes and cornmeal for corn bread—and grows her own produce for her delicious pies and vegetable dishes. "I love sharing food with others and seeing that my guests eat a hearty meal," Elsie told us.

Elsie learned to cook by helping her mother bake bread, kolaches, crescent rolls, pies and cakes. Her mom also taught her three daughters how to make such delights as homemade noodles, sauerkraut and dumplings.

"All of us loved cooking, and we especially enjoyed having Sunday dinner guests. We even liked cooking for a hungry threshing crew!" Elsie said.

"I still like inviting guests over for dinner, and I always try to have something special on hand for my husband, Bud, when he comes in from his woodworking shop for a coffee break."

Lawrence Burman, a friend of the Pritschaus', is a fan of Elsie's baked goods, too. "There's nothing like sitting in the warmth of Elsie's Home Comfort stove and sharing a cup of coffee and one of her rolls, or a slice of her fresh bread with homemade jelly," he wrote us. "It makes our friendship that much more rewarding."

SAUSAGE/WILD RICE CASSEROLE

        1 package (6 ounces) long-grain and wild rice mix
        1 pound bulk pork sausage
        1 can (10-3/4 ounces) cream of mushroom soup, undiluted
        1 cup sliced fresh mushrooms
    1/2 cup chopped onion
    1/2 cup chopped green pepper
    1/2 cup shredded sharp cheddar cheese
    1/2 cup chicken broth
    1/4 cup minced celery
        1 teaspoon parsley flakes
    1/2 teaspoon pepper

Cook rice according to package directions. Meanwhile, brown sausage in a skillet; drain excess fat. Combine rice, sausage and remaining ingredients in a greased 2-qt. casserole. Bake at 350° for 1 hour. **Yield:** 6-8 servings.

CZECH KOLACHES

        2 packages (1/4 ounce *each*) active dry yeast
    1/2 cup sugar, *divided*
    1/2 cup warm water (110°-115°)
    1/2 cup butter *or* shortening
        2 eggs, beaten
        2 cups warm milk (110°-115°)
        2 teaspoons salt
        5 to 6 cups all-purpose flour
Fruit, poppy seed *or* cheese filling
TOPPING:
    1/2 cup butter *or* margarine, softened
    1/2 cup sugar
    1/2 cup all-purpose flour
Confectioners' sugar icing, optional

Dissolve yeast and 1 teaspoon sugar in water. Meanwhile, mix butter, remaining sugar and eggs until smooth. Add the milk, salt, yeast mixture and enough flour to form a soft dough. Place dough in a greased bowl, cover and allow to rise in a warm place until doubled, about 1-1/2 hours. Punch dough down and allow to rise again. Punch dough down and divide in half. On a lightly floured board, roll half of the dough to 1/2 in. thick. Using a 3-in. cookie cutter or glass, cut dough and place on a cookie sheet. Repeat with remaining dough.

Cover cookie sheets and allow to rise 1 hour. Make a depression in the center of each dough circle with a glass; fill with a heaping tablespoon of filling. For topping, combine butter, sugar and flour to make a coarse meal. Sprinkle over filling. Let rise 10 minutes. Bake at 375° for 10-12 minutes or until lightly browned. Drizzle with a confectioners' sugar icing, if desired. **Yield:** 4-5 dozen.

MY FAVORITE CHOCOLATE CAKE

    1/2 cup baking cocoa
        1 cup boiling water
    1/2 cup butter *or* margarine
    1-1/2 cups sugar
        3 eggs, *separated*
    2-1/2 cups all-purpose flour
        1 teaspoon baking soda
    3/4 teaspoon salt
        1 cup buttermilk

In a large mixing bowl, dissolve cocoa in boiling water. Cool. Mix in butter, sugar, egg yolks, flour, soda, salt and buttermilk until smooth. In a separate bowl, beat egg whites until stiff peaks form. Carefully fold into batter. Spread into two greased 9-in. round cake pans or a greased 13-in. x 9-in. x 2-in. baking pan. Bake at 350° for 25-35 minutes or until a toothpick inserted in center of cake comes out clean. **Yield:** 12 servings.

ANGEL BISCUITS

        1 package active dry yeast
    1/4 cup warm water (110°-115°)
    3-1/2 to 3-3/4 cups all-purpose flour, *divided*
    1/2 teaspoon baking soda
        2 teaspoons baking powder
    1/2 teaspoon salt
    1/4 cup sugar
    1/2 cup shortening
        1 cup buttermilk
        1 egg, beaten

Dissolve the yeast in warm water; set aside. In a medium mixing bowl, mix 3-1/2 cups flour with other dry ingredients; cut in shortening. Stir in buttermilk, yeast mixture and egg; blend thoroughly. Turn out onto a lightly floured surface; knead slightly, adding remaining flour if needed. Roll out dough to 1/2-in. thickness. Cut with a 2-in. biscuit cutter, dipping cutter into flour as needed. Place on a lightly greased baking sheet; let dough rise slightly. Bake at 400° for 12-15 minutes or until lightly browned. **Yield:** about 24 biscuits.

icture this: You've just spent a few hours in the brisk outdoors...you're chilled and hungry...and you head for the house. You open the door, and the delicious aroma of hearty, home-style soup wafts your way.

The kettle you put on the stove earlier is simmering, and—if it's filled with one of the soups shown below—you and your family are in for a real treat.

These aren't just light broths that you serve before a meal...these

soups *are* a meal! Served with some steaming muffins or with thick slices of homemade bread, these soups are filling enough to satisfy a woodcutter.

So, serve up one or more of these country classics—they're guaranteed to bring satisfying smiles *every* time!

HEARTY, HOME-STYLE SOUPS: Clockwise from lower left—**Cream of Broccoli and Cheese Soup** (Pg. 236); **Fish and Cheese Chowder** (Pg. 237); **Wintery Day Bean Soup** (Pg. 236); **Cheddar Chowder** (Pg. 237); **Czechoslovakian Cabbage Soup** (Pg. 237); **Cheese and Potato Wild Rice Soup** (Pg. 237); **Grandma's Chicken and Dumpling Soup** (Pg. 236); **Upstate Minestrone Soup** (Pg. 236).

Everyone loves muffins! And why not? They're so easy to make…they add a fresh-baked touch to any meal…and somehow remind us of marvelous meals from kitchens past.

With no pun intended, muffins are "hot" these days. Everyone's baking them! No longer humdrum little hand-warmers with ho-hum ingredients, muffins have spiffed up their act and gone a bit glamorous.

Break open today's muffins and you're apt to find shreds of carrot, a hint of maple, chunks of apple or crunchy poppy seed…all mingled together with old-fashioned oats, wheat flour and bran.

So bake a batch and discover why these muffins are not only better tasting…they're better for you.

MARVELOUS MUFFINS! Clockwise from bottom—**Maple Bran Muffins; Carrot Bran Muffins; Poppy Seed Muffins; Oatmeal Apple Raisin Muffins.** All recipes on page 238.

BANANA CREAM CHIFFON PIE

Anne Wrolstad, Molalla, Oregon

(PICTURED ON PAGE 226)

GRAHAM CRACKER CRUST:
1-1/2 cups graham cracker crumbs
1/3 cup butter, melted
3 tablespoons sugar
FILLING:
1 cup top milk (use whole milk with 3 tablespoons cream)
3 egg yolks
1/2 cup sugar, *divided*
1/4 teaspoon salt
1 tablespoon unflavored gelatin
1/4 cup cold water
1-1/2 teaspoons vanilla
3 egg whites
3 bananas
TOPPING:
1/2 cup whipping cream, whipped

For crust, combine crumbs, butter and sugar in bowl; blend well with fork. Spoon crumb mixture into 9-in. pie pan; set 8-in. pie pan on top and press to make even crumb layer. Remove 8-in. pan. Bake crust at 375° for 8 minutes if desired, or use as is. To make filling, scald milk in top of double boiler. In small bowl, beat egg yolks, 1/4 cup sugar and salt. Stir into hot milk; continue cooking until mixture coats spoon (soft custard). Meanwhile, soften gelatin in cold water; let stand 5 minutes. Add to custard along with vanilla; cool mixture over ice water until it thickens. Beat egg whites until foamy; add remaining 1/4 cup sugar gradually, beating until stiff. Fold into cooled custard. Set aside. Slice 1 banana over bottom crust. Pour custard over banana slices. Slice 1 banana on top of custard. Beat whipping cream and pile on top of pie. Slice last banana in circles around top. Refrigerate. **Yield:** 8 servings.

MY MOM'S CHOCOLATE PIE

Suzanne Light, Cassville, New York

(PICTURED ON PAGE 226)

1 9-inch baked pie shell
CHOCOLATE FILLING:
2 to 3 squares (2 to 3 ounces) unsweetened chocolate
2/3 to 1 cup sugar blended with 1/2 cup all-purpose flour
2-2/3 cup milk
1/4 teaspoon salt
1 tablespoon butter
4 egg yolks, beaten

1 teaspoon vanilla
WHIPPED CREAM TOPPING:
1 cup whipping cream, chilled
1/4 cup confectioners' sugar
1 teaspoon vanilla
Chocolate curls *or* leaves to garnish

Melt chocolate in top of double boiler. Add sugar blended with flour, milk, salt and butter to melted chocolate; stir with whisk over hot water until thick. Cook, uncovered, 10 minutes longer. Add 1 cup of chocolate mixture to beaten egg yolks, beating both together. Add chocolate/egg yolk mixture to rest of chocolate filling; cook 5 minutes longer. Remove from heat; add vanilla, stirring to blend. Cool slightly; pour into baked shell. Refrigerate. Make whipped cream topping by placing all ingredients in mixing bowl and beating together until stiff. Pipe onto pie or frost. Top with chocolate curls or leaves, if desired. Store in refrigerator. **Yield:** 8 servings.

RHUBARB-ORANGE CREAM PIE

Wanda Rosseland, Circle, Montana

(PICTURED ON PAGE 226)

1 9-inch baked pie shell
FILLING:
1-1/2 cups sugar
2 tablespoons cornstarch
3 cups fresh rhubarb, cut in 1/2-inch pieces (can use frozen)
1/2 cup cream, half and half *or* milk
1/4 cup orange juice
5 drops red food coloring, optional
3 egg yolks, slightly beaten
MERINGUE:
3 egg whites
1/4 teaspoon cream of tartar
3 tablespoons sugar
1/2 teaspoon vanilla

Combine sugar, cornstarch, rhubarb, cream/milk, orange juice and food coloring in medium saucepan. Cook over medium heat stirring frequently until rhubarb is tender and mixture has thickened. Pour 1 cup hot rhubarb mixture into egg yolks, stirring constantly. Add to rest of hot rhubarb mixture; bring to boil. Cool slightly; pour filling into pie shell. Make meringue by beating egg whites and cream of tartar until soft peaks form. Slowly add sugar and vanilla, beating until stiff peaks form. Spread over filling, sealing edges. Bake at 350° for 12 minutes or until golden brown. Store in refrigerator. **Yield:** 8 servings.

PINEAPPLE SOUR CREAM PIE

Ella Gipman, Choiceland, Saskatchewan

(PICTURED ON PAGE 227)

1 9-inch graham cracker crust*
FILLING:
1/3 to 1/2 cup sugar
1/4 cup all-purpose flour
1/2 teaspoon salt
2-1/2 cups crushed pineapple, undrained
1 cup cultured sour cream
1 tablespoon lemon juice
2 egg yolks, slightly beaten
MERINGUE:
2 egg whites
1/4 teaspoon cream of tartar
1/4 cup sugar

*Use crust recipe from Banana Cream Chiffon Pie recipe. Combine sugar, flour and salt in medium saucepan. Stir in pineapple, sour cream and lemon juice; cook over medium heat, stirring, until mixture comes to boil. Cook 2 minutes. Stir 1/2 cup of cooked mixture into beaten egg yolks; return filling/egg yolk mixture to remaining filling. Cook for 2 minutes more, stirring constantly. Cool slightly. Spoon filling into crust. Make meringue by beating egg whites with cream of tartar until soft peaks form. Add sugar gradually, beating until stiff peaks form. Spread over pie filling; seal edges. Bake at 350° for 12-15 minutes or until golden brown. Store in refrigerator. **Yield:** 8 servings.

BUTTERMILK PIE

Carol Bown, Currie, Minnesota

(PICTURED ON PAGE 226)

4 eggs
1-1/2 to 2 cups sugar
6 tablespoons butter, melted
2 tablespoons all-purpose flour
1 teaspoon vanilla
1/2 teaspoon salt
3/4 cup buttermilk
1 9-inch unbaked pie shell
1/3 cup walnuts, chopped

Beat eggs in medium bowl with electric mixer. Add sugar, butter, flour, vanilla and salt. Reduce mixer speed; slowly add buttermilk and blend well. Pour filling into pie shell. Sprinkle walnuts on top. Bake at 350° for 40-45 minutes or until knife comes out clean and top is golden. Keep refrigerated. **Yield:** 8 servings.

PEAR CRUMB PIE

Edna Hoffman, Hebron, Indiana

(PICTURED ON PAGE 227)

1 9-inch unbaked pie shell with high fluted edge, chilled

PEAR FILLING:
2-1/2 pounds fresh, ripe pears (Bosc, Anjou or Bartlett)
1 tablespoon lemon juice
2/3 cup sugar
1 teaspoon cinnamon
1/4 teaspoon mace
1 to 2 tablespoons all-purpose flour

TOPPING:
1 cup all-purpose flour
1/3 cup light brown sugar
1/3 cup butter, softened

Peel, core and slice pears in large bowl; sprinkle with lemon juice. Combine sugar, spices and flour in small bowl; sprinkle over pears and toss lightly to mix. Spoon filling into prepared pie shell. Combine topping ingredients; sprinkle over filling. Bake at 375° for 40-45 minutes or until juice bubbles up and top lightly browns. (Cover top loosely with piece of foil if it browns too quickly.) Cool. **Yield:** 8 servings.

PEANUT BUTTER CRUNCH PIE

Joey Ann Mostowy, Bruin, Pennsylvania

(PICTURED ON PAGE 227)

1 10-inch baked pie shell
1/2 cup crunchy peanut butter
2/3 cup confectioners' sugar

CREAM FILLING:
2/3 cup sugar
3 tablespoons cornstarch
1 tablespoon all-purpose flour
1/2 teaspoon salt
3 egg yolks
3 cups milk
2 tablespoons butter
1 teaspoon vanilla

MERINGUE:
3 egg whites
1/4 cup sugar
1/4 teaspoon cream of tartar
1 teaspoon cornstarch

Combine peanut butter and sugar until crumbly; spread over bottom of pie shell (reserving 2 tablespoons for garnish.) Make filling by combing sugar, cornstarch, flour, salt, egg yolks, milk and butter in medium saucepan; bring to boil, stirring constantly. Cook for 2 minutes. Remove from heat; add vanilla. Pour cream filling over peanut butter crunch layer. Make meringue by beating egg whites until foamy; add remaining ingredients gradually, beating until whites are smooth and stiff. Spread over cream filling, sealing edges. Top with remaining peanut butter/sugar mixture. Bake at 350° for about 10 minutes or until meringue is lightly browned. **Yield:** 8-10 servings.

MAGNIFICENT MERINGUE: When making meringues, have eggs at room temperature for best volume.

● Use a glass or metal bowl (not plastic) with a tapered bottom and wide top. Egg whites expand six times when beaten, so be sure the bowl is large enough to accommodate.

● Egg whites must have no trace of yolk. To prevent yolks from mixing with the whites, separate eggs in small bowls before adding to your large mixing bowl.

● Don't use super-fresh eggs straight from the henhouse—older eggs whip much better.

● Prevent shrinking meringues by carefully sealing to pastry edges on top of hot pie filling.

● Cool meringue pies to room temperature before refrigerating. Cooling too quickly may cause shrinkage or sticky, beaded meringues.

● To cut meringue without tearing, dip your knife in cold water first.

FRENCH APPLE AND WALNUT TARTS

Rosemary Neeb, Crediton, Ontario

(PICTURED ON PAGE 227)

TARTS:
1/2 cup soft butter
1/2 cup sugar
2 large eggs
3/4 cup all-purpose flour blended with 1/2 teaspoon baking powder
2 tablespoons milk
1/2 cup walnuts, coarsely chopped

FILLING:
4 to 5 apples
2 to 3 tablespoons butter, melted
Confectioners' sugar

In medium mixing bowl, beat butter until light and fluffy; gradually beat in sugar. Add eggs, one at a time, beating until smooth. Fold in flour blended with baking powder. Stir in milk and chopped walnuts. Set aside. Butter 6-8 individual tart tins or Texas-size muffin tins; divide batter mixture evenly between them. Peel, quarter and core apples. Cut each quarter into thin, even slices. Stand apple slices in batter (rounded side up), pressing down lightly so they are all level. Brush with butter. Bake (on cookie sheet, if individual tarts) at 375° for 25 minutes or until golden brown. Cool for 3-5 minutes. *Gently* lift from pans. Just before serving, dust with confectioners' sugar. **Yield:** 6-8 tarts.

CREAM CHEESE/ PINEAPPLE PIE

Elizabeth Brown, Clayton, Delaware

(PICTURED ON PAGE 228)

PINEAPPLE LAYER:
1/3 cup sugar
1 tablespoon cornstarch
1 can (8 ounces) crushed pineapple with juice

CREAM CHEESE LAYER:
1 package (8 ounces) cream cheese, softened to room temperature
1/2 cup sugar
1 teaspoon salt
2 eggs
1/2 cup milk
1/2 teaspoon vanilla
1 9-inch unbaked pie shell
1/4 cup chopped pecans

Combine sugar, cornstarch and pineapple plus juice in a small saucepan. Cook over medium heat, stirring constantly until mixture is thick and clear. Cool; set aside. Blend together cream cheese, sugar and salt in mixer bowl. Add 2 eggs, one at a time, beating after each addition. Blend in milk and vanilla. (If mixture looks slightly curdled, don't worry—it bakes out.) Spread cooled pineapple layer over bottom of pie shell. Pour cream cheese mixture over pineapple; sprinkle with pecans. Bake at 400° for 10 minutes; reduce heat to 325° and bake for 50 minutes more. Cool. Store in refrigerator. **Yield:** 8 servings.

SOUR CREAM LEMON PIE

Martha Sorenson, Fallon, Nevada

(PICTURED ON PAGE 228)

1 cup sugar
3-1/2 tablespoons cornstarch
1 tablespoon lemon peel, grated
1/2 cup fresh lemon juice
3 egg yolks, slightly beaten
1 cup milk
1/4 cup butter
1 cup cultured sour cream

1 baked 9-inch pie shell
1 cup heavy whipping cream, whipped
Lemon twists for garnish

Combine sugar, cornstarch, lemon peel, juice, egg yolks and milk in heavy saucepan; cook over medium heat until thick. Stir in butter and cool mixture to room temperature. Stir in sour cream and pour filling into pie shell. Cover with whipped cream and garnish with lemon twists. Store in refrigerator. **Yield:** 8 servings.

CHOCOLATE ALMOND CREAM PIE

Denise Simeth, Greendale, Wisconsin

(PICTURED ON PAGE 228)

1 package (4 ounces) German sweet chocolate
1/3 cup milk, *divided*
1 package (3 ounces) cream cheese, softened
1/4 to 1/2 teaspoon almond extract
1 carton (8 ounces) extra-creamy whipped topping, thawed
1 prepared graham cracker crust (8 *or* 9 inches)
Sweetened whipped cream
Toasted sliced almonds

In a heavy saucepan, cook chocolate and 2 tablespoons milk over low heat, stirring constantly until chocolate is melted. Set aside. Beat cream cheese until fluffy; add remaining milk, almond extract and chocolate mixture. Beat until smooth. Fold chocolate mixture into whipped topping; blend until smooth. Spoon filling into prepared crust. Freeze 4-5 hours, or until firm. Garnish with whipped cream and sliced almonds. **Yield:** 6-8 servings.

GRANDMA'S SOUR CREAM RAISIN PIE

Beverly Medalen, Willow City, North Dakota

1 9-inch baked pie shell
1 cup raisins (plus enough water to cover)
2/3 cup sugar
3 tablespoons cornstarch
1/8 teaspoon salt
1/8 teaspoon ground cloves
1/2 teaspoon ground cinnamon
1 cup sour cream
3 egg yolks
1/2 cup milk

1/2 cup water (drained off plumped raisins)
1/2 cup nuts, chopped, optional
MERINGUE:
3 egg whites
1/4 teaspoon salt
5 tablespoons sugar

Place raisins in small saucepan. Add water to cover; bring to boil. Turn off heat. Let stand while preparing filling. In heavy saucepan, mix together sugar, cornstarch, salt, cloves and cinnamon. Add sour cream; stir well. Beat in egg yolks. Stir in milk and cook on medium heat, stirring until pudding comes to boil and is pudding consistency (mixture will be thick). Remove from heat. Drain raisins, reserving 1/2 cup liquid. Stir liquid into filling; add raisins and nuts (if desired) and pour into pie shell. Prepare meringue by beating egg whites with salt until foamy. Gradually add sugar while continuing to beat on high. Beat until stiff and glossy. Spread over pie, making sure meringue covers all of pie filling. Bake at 350° for 10-15 minutes or until light golden brown. Serve warm or cold. Refrigerate leftovers. **Yield:** 8 servings.

GOLDEN COCONUT PEACH PIE

4 to 4-1/2 cups sliced, fresh peaches
1 to 1-1/4 cups sugar, *divided*
3 tablespoons all-purpose flour
1/4 teaspoon nutmeg
1/8 teaspoon salt
1/4 cup orange juice
1 9-inch unbaked pie shell
2 tablespoons butter
2 cups flaked coconut
1/2 cup evaporated milk
1 egg, beaten
1/4 teaspoon almond extract

Mix together peaches, 1/2 cup sugar, flour, nutmeg, salt and orange juice in medium bowl. Pour mixture into pie shell. Dot with butter; bake at 450° for 15 minutes. Meanwhile, combine coconut, milk, egg, remaining 1/4 to 1/2 cup sugar and almond extract. Pour over hot peach mixture. Reduce heat to 350° and bake until coconut is toasted, about 30 minutes. Chill pie unless eaten at once. **Yield:** 8 servings.

APPLE RAISIN CREAM PIE

Carolina Hofeldt, Lloyd, Montana

(PICTURED ON PAGE 228)

Pastry for 2-crust, 10-inch pie
FILLING:
7 to 8 cups tart apple slices, 1/8 inch thick
1 cup sugar
1/2 cup all-purpose flour
1/2 teaspoon nutmeg
1 teaspoon cinnamon
3/4 cup raisins
Dash salt, optional
1 to 2 teaspoons grated lemon peel
1 rounded tablespoon butter
3/4 cup heavy cream

Make favorite pastry; line bottom of pie tin with one crust and set aside. Combine apple slices, sugar, flour, spices, raisins, salt and lemon peel; mix together well. Spoon filling into pastry-lined pan; dot with butter. Cover with top crust decorated with steam vents; seal edges. Cut a 1-in. circle from dough in center of top crust. Bake at 400° for 40-45 minutes. Remove pie from oven; slowly pour cream into center hole of top crust. Return to oven; bake 5-10 minutes longer. Let stand 5 minutes before cutting. Refrigerate leftovers. **Yield:** 8-10 servings.

PERFECT PIE TIPS: Store flour in the freezer and use chilled flour in pie dough. This eliminates chilling dough and gives tender, flaky crusts.

• To prevent overbrowning and oven spillovers, make a *pie skirt* by cutting a 2-in. strip of foil 2 in. longer than the circumference of pie tin. Wrap around pie; lap edges. Push foil against pie pan sides below the edge; let top edge stand up.

• To eliminate soggy crusts on custard pies, brush slightly beaten egg around pie crust to seal it. Use egg later in custard filling.

• For a golden brown crust, brush pie top (not edges) with cream or milk before baking. Sprinkle with sugar if desired.

• For flaky pastry, handle dough as *little* as possible. Overhandling toughens dough.

• Roll pastry from center out to edges—never roll back over dough toward center. This keeps dough even in size and thickness.

• Making a lattice crust? Use a pizza cutter to trim dough into perfect strips.

CHRISTMAS MORNING CRANBERRY MUFFINS

Keren Fuller, St. Mary's, Ontario

1 cup fresh cranberries
1/2 cup sugar, *divided*
1-1/2 cups all-purpose flour
2 teaspoons baking powder
1 teaspoon salt
1/2 teaspoon cinnamon
1/4 teaspoon ground allspice
1 egg, beaten
1/4 teaspoon grated orange peel
3/4 cup orange juice
1/3 cup butter, melted
1/4 cup chopped walnuts

Coarsely chop cranberries. Sprinkle with 1/4 cup sugar and set aside. In bowl, stir together flour, remaining sugar, baking powder, salt, cinnamon and allspice. Make a well in center of dry ingredients. Combine egg, peel, juice and butter. Add all at once to flour mixture; stir to moisten. Fold in cranberry mixture and nuts. Fill greased muffin cups; bake at 375° for 15-20 minutes or until golden. **Yield:** 12 large muffins.

UPSTATE MINESTRONE SOUP

Yvonne Krantz, Mt. Upton, New York

(PICTURED ON PAGE 230)

1 pound Italian sweet sausage
1 tablespoon olive *or* vegetable oil
1 cup diced onion
1 clove garlic, finely minced
1 cup sliced carrots
1 teaspoon crumbled basil
2 small zucchini, sliced
1 can (1 pound) Italian pear tomatoes, chopped, undrained
2 cans (10-3/4 ounces *each*) beef bouillon *or* 3 beef bouillon cubes plus 1-1/2 cups hot water
2 cups finely shredded cabbage
1 teaspoon salt
1/4 teaspoon pepper
1 can (1 pound) great northern beans, undrained
Chopped fresh parsley

Slice sausage crosswise about 1/2 in. thick; brown in oil in deep saucepan or Dutch oven. Add onion, garlic, carrots and basil; cook for 5 minutes. Add zucchini, tomatoes with liquid, bouillon, cabbage, salt and pepper. Bring soup to boil; reduce heat and simmer, covered, for 1 hour. Add beans with liquid; cook another 20 minutes. Garnish with parsley. (Soup is even better the second day!) **Yield:** 8 servings.

WINTERY DAY BEAN SOUP

Frances Kissel, New Palestine, Indiana

(PICTURED ON PAGE 230)

2 cups mixed dried beans*
2 quarts water
2 tablespoons salt
2 cups diced ham *or* sliced smoked sausage
1 large onion, chopped
1 clove garlic, minced
1 teaspoon chili powder
1 can (28 ounces) tomatoes, chopped
1 to 2 tablespoons lemon juice

*(Use at least seven varieties of beans—great northern, navy, black, garbanzo, green split peas, pinto and red beans.) Rinse beans; place in large kettle. Cover with water, add salt and soak overnight. Drain; add 2 qts. water and ham/sausage. Simmer for 2-1/2 to 3 hours. Add onion, garlic, chili powder, tomatoes and lemon juice. Simmer 45 minutes more. Add salt and pepper, if desired. **Yield:** 2 quarts.

CREAM OF BROCCOLI AND CHEESE SOUP

Helen Guida, Tyler, Minnesota

(PICTURED ON PAGE 230)

2 cups chopped celery
1 cup finely chopped onion
1 package (10 ounces) chopped broccoli
1 cup cottage cheese
2 cups whole milk
1 can (10-3/4 ounces) cream of chicken soup, undiluted
1/8 teaspoon white pepper
1/2 teaspoon salt, optional

Cook celery, onion and broccoli in 2-1/2-qt. covered casserole in microwave on high for 6 minutes, stirring after 3 minutes. Set aside. Blend cottage cheese in blender or food processor until very

smooth; slowly add milk while continuing to blend. Add chicken soup to cottage cheese/milk mixture; blend; add mixture to cooked, undrained vegetables. Microwave on high until heated through (about 3 minutes) *without boiling*. Add pepper and if desired, salt. **Yield:** 6 servings.

GRANDMA'S CHICKEN AND DUMPLING SOUP

Peggy Bremer, Fairmont, Minnesota

(PICTURED ON PAGE 231)

1 fryer (2-1/2 to 3 pounds) chicken, cut up
6 cups cold water
3 chicken bouillon cubes
6 peppercorns
3 whole cloves
1 can (10-3/4 ounces) chicken broth
1 can (10-3/4 ounces) cream of chicken soup, undiluted
1 can (10-3/4 ounces) cream of mushroom soup, undiluted
1 cup chopped celery
1-1/2 cups chopped carrots
1/4 cup chopped onion
1 cup chopped potatoes
1 small bay leaf
1 cup fresh *or* frozen peas
1 teaspoon seasoned salt
FEATHER DUMPLINGS:
2 cups all-purpose flour
1 teaspoon salt
4 teaspoons baking powder
1/4 teaspoon white *or* black pepper
1 egg, well beaten
2 tablespoons melted butter
2/3 cup milk

Place fryer, water, bouillon, peppercorns and cloves in kettle and bring to boil. Reduce heat; simmer until chicken is tender (about 1-1/2 hours). Cool chicken just slightly; cut into bite-size pieces and set aside. Strain and skim chicken broth. Put the reserved chicken and broth in large kettle; add cans of broth, chicken and mushroom soups, celery, carrots, onion, potatoes, bay leaf, peas and seasoned salt. Put cover on kettle; simmer soup on low heat for 2-3 hours. Remove bay leaf. About 30 minutes before serving, mix up feather dumplings by sifting dry ingredients together. Add egg, melted butter and enough milk to make moist, stiff batter. Drop by teaspoon into boiling liquid. Cook, covered and without "peeking", for 18-20 minutes or until the dumplings are done. **Yield:** 10-12 servings.

FISH AND CHEESE CHOWDER

Pat Paulovich, Manning, Alberta

(PICTURED ON PAGE 230)

- 1 pound fish fillets, fresh *or* frozen
- 2 tablespoons butter
- 6 tablespoons chopped onion
- 1 cup chopped carrots
- 6 tablespoons chopped celery
- 1/4 cup all-purpose flour
- Dash paprika
- 1/2 teaspoon salt, optional
- 2 cans (10 ounces *each*) chicken broth, undiluted
- 3 cups milk
- 1 cup shredded process cheese spread

Thaw frozen fish fillets enough to allow cutting, about 30 minutes. Cut fish in 1-inch cubes. Set aside. Melt butter in large saucepan; add onion, carrots and celery. Cook until onion is transparent. Blend in flour, paprika and if desired, salt. Cook 1 minute, stirring constantly. Gradually add chicken broth and milk. Cook, stirring constantly, until thickened. Add fish; simmer until fish flakes easily (5 minutes for fresh; 10 minutes for frozen). Add cheese; stir until melted. Serve hot. **Yield:** 2-1/2 quarts.

CZECHOSLOVAKIAN CABBAGE SOUP

Patricia Rutherford, Winchester, Illinois

(PICTURED ON PAGE 231)

- 2 pounds beef soup bones
- 1 cup chopped onion
- 3 carrots, pared and coarsely chopped
- 2 cloves garlic, chopped
- 1 bay leaf
- 2 pounds beef short ribs
- 1 teaspoon dried leaf thyme
- 1/2 teaspoon paprika
- 8 cups water
- 8 cups coarsely chopped cabbage (1 head)
- 2 cans (1 pound *each*) tomatoes
- 2 teaspoons salt
- 1/2 to 3/4 teaspoon hot pepper sauce
- 1/4 cup chopped parsley
- 3 tablespoons lemon juice
- 3 tablespoons sugar
- 1 can (1 pound) sauerkraut

Place beef bones, onion, carrots, garlic and bay leaf in roasting pan. Top with short ribs; sprinkle with thyme and paprika. Roast, uncovered, in 450° oven for 20-30 minutes or until meat is brown. Transfer meat and vegetables into large kettle. Using a small amount of water, scrape browned meat bits from roasting pan into kettle. Add water, cabbage, tomatoes, salt and hot pepper sauce. Bring to boil. Cover; simmer 1-1/2 hours. Skim off fat. Add parsley, lemon juice, sugar and sauerkraut. Cook, uncovered, for 1 hour. Remove bones and short ribs from kettle. Cool slightly; remove meat from bones. Cut meat into cubes; return to kettle. Cook 5 minutes longer. Remove bay leaf. **Yield:** 12 servings.

CHEDDAR CHOWDER

Laura Rothlisberger, Green, Kansas

(PICTURED ON PAGE 231)

- 2 cups water
- 2 cups diced potatoes
- 1/2 cup diced carrots
- 1/2 cup diced celery
- 1/4 cup chopped onion
- 1 teaspoon salt
- 1/4 teaspoon pepper
- **WHITE SAUCE:**
- 1/4 cup butter
- 1/4 cup all-purpose flour
- 2 cups milk
- 2 cups cheddar cheese, shredded
- 1 cup cooked cubed ham

Combine water, potatoes, carrots, celery, onion, salt and pepper in large kettle. Boil 10-12 minutes. Meanwhile, in small saucepan, make white sauce by melting the butter. Add flour and stir until smooth (about 1 minute). Slowly add milk; cook until thickened. Add shredded cheese to white sauce; stir until melted. Add white sauce and cubed ham to vegetables that *have not been drained*. Heat through. **Yield:** 6 servings.

CHICKEN WILD RICE SOUP

Amy Kraemer, Glencoe, Minnesota

- 1 3-pound chicken, cut up and rinsed
- 3 quarts water
- 1 teaspoon salt
- Celery leaves (handful)
- 2 cups chopped onion, *divided*
- 1 carrot, chopped
- 2 tablespoons butter
- 3 cups sliced celery
- 2 cups wild rice, rinsed
- 1/4 teaspoon pepper
- 1 to 2 teaspoons salt
- 2 cans (10-3/4 ounces *each*) cream of mushroom soup, undiluted
- 1/4 teaspoon nutmeg
- 1/4 teaspoon garlic powder
- 1 teaspoon instant chicken bouillon

Arrange cut-up chicken in 6-qt. soup kettle. Add water, salt, celery leaves, 1/2 cup onion and carrot. Cook over low heat for 1-1/2 hours or until meat is tender. Strain stock, reserving broth and chicken. Cool chicken; chop into 3/4-in. chunks. Melt butter in skillet; add sliced celery and remaining onion and saute 3 minutes. Place reserved chicken broth (12 cups) back in kettle; add sauteed vegetables, wild rice, pepper and salt. Cook over low heat until rice is tender/crunchy, about 45 minutes. When rice is done, add chopped chicken, mushroom soup, nutmeg, garlic powder and chicken bouillon. Mix gently and heat through, being careful not to scorch (soup is thick). If too thick, add more broth. **Yield:** 5 quarts.

CHEESE AND POTATO WILD RICE SOUP

Gladys Barron, Thief River Falls, Minnesota

(PICTURED ON PAGE 231)

- 1/2 cup wild rice, uncooked
- 1-1/2 cups water
- 1/2 pound bacon, cut in pieces
- 1/4 cup chopped onion
- 2 cans (10-3/4 ounces *each*) cream of potato soup (dilute with 1 can liquid—1/2 milk; 1/2 water)
- 1 quart milk
- 2-1/2 cups shredded American cheese
- Carrot curls, optional

Combine wild rice and water in saucepan and cook over low heat for 45 minutes. Drain. Set aside. Fry bacon pieces and onion in skillet until bacon is crisp. Drain bacon and onion on paper towel. Place soup in large saucepan; dilute as directed above. Stir in 1 qt. milk, bacon, onion, cheese and cooked rice. Stir until cheese is melted. Garnish with carrot, if desired. **Yield:** 8-10 servings.

SOUP'S ON! For rich-seasoned chicken stock, freeze wing tips, necks, any skin or juice/broth. Add to these 1 large chopped onion, 1 to 2 cups celery leaves, 2 chicken bouillon cubes, 1 chopped carrot and 1 teaspoon salt. Simmer 1 hour; strain and use for broth.

● To prevent curdling in cream soups, have all ingredients at room temperature and use low temperatures when cooking.

OATMEAL APPLE RAISIN MUFFINS

Priscilla Weaver, Hagerstown, Maryland

(PICTURED ON PAGE 232)

1 egg
3/4 cup milk
1 cup raisins
1 apple, chopped
1/2 cup oil
1 cup all-purpose flour
1 cup quick oats
1/3 cup sugar
3 teaspoons baking powder
1 teaspoon salt
1 teaspoon nutmeg
2 teaspoons cinnamon

Beat egg; stir in remaining ingredients, mixing just to moisten. Pour into 12 greased muffin cups until 3/4 full. Bake at 400° for 15 to 20 minutes. Serve cool or piping hot with butter. **Yield:** 12 muffins.

POPPY SEED MUFFINS

Germaine Stank, Pound, Wisconsin

(PICTURED ON PAGE 232)

3/4 cup sugar
1/4 cup softened butter
1/2 teaspoon grated orange peel
2 eggs
2 cups all-purpose flour
2-1/2 teaspoons baking powder
1/2 teaspoon salt
1/4 teaspoon ground nutmeg
1 cup milk
1/2 cup golden raisins
1/2 cup chopped pecans
5 tablespoons poppy seeds

Cream sugar, butter and orange peel. Add eggs, one at a time, beating well after each. Combine flour, baking powder, salt and nutmeg. Add to creamed mixture alternately with milk, beating well after each addition. Fold in raisins, nuts and poppy seeds. Spoon batter into greased muffin tins until about 3/4 full. Bake at 400° about 20 minutes. **Yield:** about 16 large muffins.

MAPLE BRAN MUFFINS

Donna Klein-Gebbinck, Elmvale, Ontario

(PICTURED ON PAGE 232)

3/4 cup natural wheat bran
1/2 cup milk
1/2 cup maple syrup
1 egg, slightly beaten
1/4 cup oil
1-1/4 cups whole wheat flour
3 teaspoons baking powder
1/2 teaspoon salt
1/3 cup chopped walnuts
GLAZE:
1 tablespoon butter
1/2 cup confectioners' sugar
1 tablespoon maple syrup

Combine bran, milk and maple syrup. Mix in egg and oil. Set aside. Combine remaining muffin ingredients. Add bran mixture, stirring until just moistened. Divide batter into 12 greased muffin tins. Bake at 400° for 18-20 minutes. To make glaze, combine ingredients, stirring to blend, and spread over warm muffins. **Yield:** 12 muffins.

CARROT BRAN MUFFINS

Lorna Jacobsen, Arrowwood, Alberta

(PICTURED ON PAGE 232)

 This tasty dish uses less sugar, salt and fat. Recipe includes *Diabetic Exchanges*.

3 cups all-purpose flour
1 teaspoon baking soda
1-1/2 teaspoons baking powder
1 tablespoon cinnamon
1/2 teaspoon salt, optional
2 cups bran
4 eggs
1-1/2 cups vegetable oil
1-1/4 cups dark brown sugar
1/4 cup molasses
3 cups finely grated carrots
1 cup raisins *or* currants

Sift together flour, soda, baking powder, cinnamon and if desired, salt. Add bran; set aside. Beat eggs; add oil, sugar and molasses. Add carrots, flour mixture and raisins. Fill 24 greased muffin tins 3/4 full. Bake at 350° for 25 minutes. **Yield:** 24 large muffins. **Diabetic Exchanges:** One muffin equals 1 bread, 1 vegetable, 3 fat; also 264 calories, 239 mg sodium with salt (195 mg sodium without salt), 42 mg cholesterol, 31 gm carbohydrates.

WHOLE WHEAT ENGLISH MUFFINS

Mildred Decker, Sandy, Oregon

1 package (1/4 ounce) active dry yeast
3 tablespoons sugar, *divided*
1/4 cup warm water (110°-115°)
1 cup milk, scalded
3 tablespoons butter *or* margarine
3/4 teaspoon salt
1 cup whole wheat flour
3 cups all-purpose flour, *divided*
1 egg, beaten
Cornmeal

Dissolve yeast and 1 tablespoon sugar in water. Set aside. In a mixing bowl, combine remaining sugar, milk, butter, salt, whole wheat flour and 1 cup all-purpose flour. Beat well with an electric mixer. Add egg and yeast mixture; beat until smooth. By hand, stir in enough remaining all-purpose flour to make a soft dough. Knead on a lightly floured surface until smooth and elastic, about 6-8 minutes. Place in a greased bowl; cover and let rise in a warm place until doubled, about 1 hour. Punch dough down. Place on floured surface. Roll to 1/2-in. thickness. Cut into 4-in. circles. Allow to rise until doubled. Lightly sprinkle an electric frying pan or griddle with cornmeal. Bake over low heat for 10 minutes until nicely browned. Turn and bake 10 minutes longer. Cool. Store in the refrigerator. To serve, split with a fork and toast. **Yield:** about 10 muffins.

ORANGE TEA MUFFINS

Linda Clapp, Stow, Ohio

2 cups sugar, *divided*
1/2 cup fresh orange juice
1/2 cup butter *or* margarine, softened
3/4 cup sour cream
2 cups all-purpose flour
1 teaspoon baking soda
1 teaspoon salt
1 teaspoon grated orange peel
1/2 cup raisins
1/2 cup chopped nuts

Combine 1 cup sugar and the orange juice; set aside. Cream butter and remaining sugar; blend in sour cream. Combine dry ingredients and add to creamed mixture. Beat at low just until ingredients are combined. Stir in orange peel, raisins and nuts. The batter will be stiff. Spoon batter into greased 1-3/4-in. muffin cups, filling each cup completely full. Bake at 375° for about 12 minutes or until done. While still warm, dip each muffin in reserved sugar/orange juice mixture. Cool on wire rack. **Yield:** 36 small muffins.

TASTY TEA: For Apple-Mint Tea, combine 4 cups apple juice with 1-1/2 cups of chopped fresh spearmint. Microwave or cook on stovetop until mixture boils. Let steep 30 minutes; strain. Enjoy!

BEST COOK

Jim Johnson
Atchison, Kansas

Creating and re-creating recipes is a big part of what makes Jim Johnson of Atchison, Kansas the "Best Cook in the Country", according to his wife, Linda, who nominated him for the honor.

"Jim loves to go into the kitchen and experiment, taking my 'good ol' recipes' and adding a bit-of-this and a shake-of-that to see what happens. I'm sometimes skeptical, but often he improves the recipe!

"He loves to come home and re-create something we've tried in a restaurant, too. It may take several tries, but in the end Jim figures out the recipe—sometimes it's better than the original," Linda wrote.

"When we got married, Jim didn't know how to cook, but it didn't take him long to learn—and now he loves it. He often takes a recipe from a magazine or newspaper and disappears into the kitchen 'just to try it'.

"Jim also has great patience when it comes to teaching our girls how to cook (more than I do). One of my greatest joys is to listen to them in the kitchen 'creating'. I'm sure the girls will have happy memories of cooking with their dad.

"Another quality that makes Jim a good cook is that he cleans up the kitchen when he is done creating. When we're both cooking, he will even clean up *my* messes. How can you beat that?"

NEW ENGLAND VEGETABLES

1 package (10 ounces) frozen, chopped broccoli
1/2 cup butter
1 tablespoon cornstarch
1 can (12 ounces) Mexican-style corn, drained
1 can (16 ounces) French-cut green beans, drained
1/4 teaspoon garlic salt
1 tablespoon Parmesan cheese

Cook broccoli according to package directions, drain and set aside. In 2 qt. glass casserole, melt butter in microwave on high 30-60 seconds. Stir in cornstarch; microwave on high an additional 1-2 minutes, stirring every 30 seconds until butter is slightly thickened. Add vegetables, including cooked broccoli, garlic salt and Parmesan cheese. Heat on high in microwave 5 minutes, stirring twice or until vegetables are hot. **Yield:** 8 servings.

HOT SPICED CIDER

1 quart apple cider
1 cup orange juice
1/2 cup pineapple juice
1/2 cup lemon juice
1/2 cup sugar
2 cinnamon sticks (each 2 inches in length)
1 teaspoon whole cloves

Combine all ingredients in 2-qt microwave safe pitcher. Microwave on high 10 minutes; let cider stand 5 minutes. Microwave on high an additional 3-4 minutes. **Yield:** 6-8 servings.

MARDI GRAS RICE

2/3 cup long grain rice, uncooked
1/2 teaspoon salt
12 ounces bacon
1/2 cup green onions, sliced
1 pint canned tomatoes, chopped and drained
1/4 teaspoon leaf thyme
1-1/2 cups shredded cheddar cheese

Cook rice in heavy saucepan in 1-2/3 cups water and 1/2 teaspoon salt. Drain; set aside. Fry bacon; crumble and set aside, reserving 2 tablespoons bacon drippings. Saute onions in bacon drippings until onions are soft. In 1-1/2 qt. casserole, combine the cooked rice, bacon, onions, tomatoes, thyme and cheese; mix well. Cover; bake at 350° for 25 minutes. **Yield:** 6 servings.

HUSHPUPPIES

1-3/4 cups biscuit mix
3/4 cup yellow cornmeal
1/2 teaspoon salt
1 teaspoon baking powder
1/4 cup dried onion flakes
1 tablespoon sugar
1 cup milk
Oil for deep fat frying

Combine all dry ingredients in bowl; add milk, stirring until mixed. Drop by spoonfuls into hot oil. (Form by shaping into walnut-sized balls, but be advised that equal amounts of biscuit mix and cornmeal may have to be added to reduce stickiness of batter.) Deep fry until golden brown, turning once. **Yield:** about 40 hushpuppies.

CHAMPION CHOCOLATE: Don't overcook chocolate. Remove it from the heat before it's completely melted.

● When you melt chocolate by itself, the container and utensil must be *absolutely* dry. If not the chocolate may "stiffen" (harden) and turn grainy.

● If chocolate should stiffen while melting, you can salvage it by adding solid shortening—1 teaspoon for each ounce of chocolate.

● Cocoa may be used in place of baking chocolate. Three tablespoons of cocoa plus 1 tablespoon of shortening or oil equals 1 square (1 ounce) of baking chocolate.

● When melting chocolate chips for recipes, place them in a glass bowl and microwave on low for 1 minute. Stir and microwave 1-2 minutes longer or until chips are melted.

● An electric salad slicer/shredder works beautifully for grating chocolate garnish directly onto cakes or cookies. A manual vegetable grater also works well.

● To make it easier to grate a chocolate square, first place it in the freezer for about 30 minutes.

Stir up some mealtime excitement in your kitchen with these savory skillet dinners and stir-frys that stick-to-your-ribs!

The eight enticing entrees shown here offer a delectable variety of good eating—beef and pork are only the beginning. From Skillet Pizza and Picadillo in Pita Bread to Sweet and Sour Pork, every recipe goes from start to finish in one dish!

SKILLETS SUPREME: Clockwise from lower left— **Skillet Pizza** (Pg. 245); **Fantastic Beef Fajitas** (Pg. 245); **Meaty Spanish Rice** (Pg. 245); **Picadillo in Pita Bread** (Pg. 245); **German Pizza** (Pg. 246); **Spicy Beef with Peppers** (Pg. 246); **Bacon Jardin** (Pg. 246); **Sweet and Sour Pork** (Pg. 245).

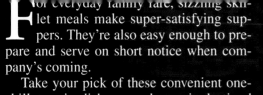

For everyday family fare, sizzling skillet meals make super-satisfying suppers. They're also easy enough to prepare and serve on short notice when company's coming.

Take your pick of these convenient one-skillet main dishes...each one is destined to become a fast—and regular—favorite!

SENSATIONAL SUPPERS. Top to bottom: **Fruited Chops** (Pg. 246); **Chicken Mushroom Stir-Fry** (Pg. 247); **Steak Lo Mein** (Pg. 247); **Chili Skillet** (Pg. 246).

MEALS IN MINUTES

Fishing for new ideas for fast food? Amy Kraemer of Hutchinson, Minnesota shares a speedy seafare menu that's tasty and nutritious—and can be prepared in 30 minutes!

"My husband, Fred, and I are retired now. But when we farmed, I didn't always have much time in the kitchen, especially during planting and harvesting," Amy says. "So I've always liked good, wholesome food that can be quickly prepared."

Amy's tasty main dish boasts a nice healthy bonus, since the fish is oven-fried rather than pan-fried. Any kind of firm white fish (fresh or frozen) works well, she adds. The equally prompt potato side dish she shares can be cooked at the same time.

Her colorful salad features both ordinary and unusual ingredients, including crunchy jicamas. This crisp vegetable is available year-round and is as tasty boiled, fried or steamed as it is raw in salads. If you're really rushed, use a purchased Italian oil and vinegar dressing instead of homemade.

For a sweet finish, the chocolate wafer dessert can be made in a jiffy!

OVEN-FRIED FISH

- 1/4 cup butter, melted
- 1-1/2 tablespoons lemon juice
- 1/2 teaspoon sugar
- 1/4 teaspoon pepper
- 1/4 teaspoon paprika
- 1/4 teaspoon basil
- 1/8 teaspoon garlic powder
- 1/2 teaspoon salt
- 1 pound firm fish fillets (cod *or* haddock), cut in serving pieces
- 1/3 cup dry bread crumbs
- Vegetable oil

Combine butter, lemon juice, sugar and spices. Dip fish in butter/spice mixture; roll in the bread crumbs. Spread enough oil to lightly coat shallow glass baking dish; arrange fish in single layer. Spoon the remaining butter/spice mixture over fish. Bake, uncovered, at 450° for 15 minutes, or until fish flakes easily with fork. **Yield:** 3-4 servings.

IDAHO OVEN FRIES

- 5 medium baking potatoes, scrubbed, unpeeled
- 4 tablespoons melted butter *or* vegetable oil
- Salt, pepper to taste

Slice potatoes into 1/8-in. to 1/16-in. thickness and place in ice water. Drain; pat dry with paper towels. Pour melted butter or oil on large baking sheet. Add potato slices to pan, turning to coat with the butter/oil. Season, if desired. Bake at 450° for 15 minutes or until potatoes are tender. **Yield:** 4 servings.

ORANGE/JICAMA SALAD

DRESSING:
- 4 tablespoons white vinegar
- 4 tablespoons oil
- 1/4 teaspoon paprika
- 1/4 teaspoon salt
- 1/4 teaspoon white pepper
- 1 clove garlic, minced
- 2 teaspoons sugar

SALAD:
- 4 seedless oranges, peeled and cut in small chunks
- 1 medium sweet green pepper, seeded
- 1 small jicama *or* 4 to 6 water chestnuts, peeled and sliced

Make dressing; shake well in covered container. Set aside. Cut pepper into 2-in. x 1/4-in. pieces. Layer oranges, peppers and jicama/chestnuts in bowl; pour dressing over all before serving. **Yield:** 4 servings.

CHOCOLATE WAFER DESSERT

- 1 pint chocolate ice cream
- 6 ice cream wafers

Put scoops of ice cream in glass bowls. Stick wafers at angles in ice cream. **Yield:** 4 servings.

SPEEDY POTATOES: Potatoes soaked in salt water for 20 minutes before baking will bake more rapidly.

e sure to leave plenty of room for dessert—especially when the sideboard boasts these almost-too-pretty-to-eat treats!

Winter gatherings and special occasions call for creative, classic desserts—and that's what you're tasting when you sink your fork into a rich and smooth cheesecake …or a light, chocolate and almond-studded torte with a whipped cream filling. Spoon up some buttery-fresh cranberry topping or a cool, coffee-flavored ice cream pie.

DESSERT DELIGHTS. Clockwise from lower left—**Mississippi Mud Pie; Ultimate Cheesecake; Chocolate Torte; Cranberry Topping.** All recipes on page 248.

SKILLET PIZZA

Darlene Markel, Roseburg, Oregon

(PICTURED ON PAGE 240)

- 1 package (6-1/2 ounces) pizza crust mix
- 1 can (8 ounces) tomato sauce
- 1 teaspoon Italian seasoning
- 1/2 teaspoon oregano
- 1/2 cup pepperoni slices
- 1/4 cup chopped onion
- 1/4 cup chopped green pepper
- 1/4 cup sliced black olives
- 2 cups (8 ounces) shredded mozzarella cheese

Grease a 12-inch electric or stove-top skillet. Prepare pizza crust according to package directions. Line bottom and 1/2 in. up the sides of the skillet with dough. Combine tomato sauce, Italian seasoning and oregano; spread over dough. Layer pepperoni, onion, green pepper and black olives over sauce; sprinkle with cheese. Cover and cook over medium heat (set electric skillet to 375°) for 15 minutes or until crust is brown on bottom and cheese is melted. Slide out onto a cutting board and cut into wedges or squares. Serve immediately. **Yield:** 1 pizza (12 inches).

FANTASTIC BEEF FAJITAS

Marla Brenneman, Goshen, Indiana

(PICTURED ON PAGE 240)

- 1 pound sirloin *or* flank steak, trimmed and cut across the grain into 1/4-inch strips

MARINADE:
- 3 tablespoons cooking oil
- 2 tablespoons lemon juice
- 1 teaspoon dried oregano
- 1 garlic clove, minced
- 1/4 teaspoon salt
- 1/4 teaspoon pepper

FAJITAS:
- 2 tablespoons cooking oil, *divided*
- 1/2 medium onion, sliced
- 1 medium sweet red pepper, sliced into thin strips
- 8 flour tortillas, warmed
- 2 avocados, peeled and sliced

Salsa
Sour cream

In a small bowl, combine all marinade ingredients; toss with beef. Cover and refrigerate 3-6 hours or overnight, stirring several times. Drain meat before cooking. In a skillet, heat 1 tablespoon oil. Saute onion and pepper until crisp-tender; remove from pan. Add remaining oil and saute meat until no longer pink, about 4 minutes. Add vegetables to pan and heat through. To serve, place a spoonful of meat/vegetable mixture on a warmed tortilla and top with avocado, salsa and sour cream. Roll tortilla around filling. **Yield:** 4-6 servings.

MEATY SPANISH RICE

Margaret Shauers, Great Bend, Kansas

(PICTURED ON PAGE 240)

 This tasty dish uses less sugar, salt and fat. Recipe includes *Diabetic Exchanges.*

- 2 tablespoons butter *or* margarine
- 1/2 pound ground turkey
- 1 medium onion, chopped
- 1 medium green pepper, chopped
- 2 cups water
- 1 can (8 ounces) tomato sauce
- 1 cup uncooked long-grain rice
- 2 tablespoons Worcestershire sauce
- 1/2 teaspoon chili powder
- 1/2 teaspoon dried thyme
- 1/4 teaspoon hot pepper sauce
- 1/8 teaspoon cayenne pepper, optional

Black pepper to taste

In a skillet, melt butter over medium heat. Add the ground turkey, onion and green pepper; cook until meat is brown and vegetables are tender. Add all of remaining ingredients and bring to a boil. Reduce heat; cover and simmer until rice is tender, about 30 minutes. **Yield:** 4 servings. **Diabetic Exchanges:** One serving (using margarine) equals 2 meat, 1-3/4 starch, 1 fat; also, 300 calories, 379 mg sodium, 52 mg cholesterol, 27 gm carbohydrate, 17 gm protein, 14 gm fat.

SWEET AND SOUR PORK

Sally Pelszynski, Princeton, Illinois

(PICTURED ON PAGE 240)

- 1 tablespoon cooking oil
- 1 pound pork loin, cut into 1-inch cubes
- 1 teaspoon paprika
- 1/3 cup water
- 3 tablespoons brown sugar
- 2 tablespoons cornstarch
- 1/2 teaspoon salt
- 1 can (20 ounces) pineapple chunks, juice drained and reserved

- 1/3 cup vinegar
- 1 tablespoon soy sauce
- 1 teaspoon Worcestershire sauce
- 1 green pepper, sliced
- 1 small onion, sliced
- 1 can (8 ounces) sliced water chestnuts, drained

Cooked rice

In a wok or skillet, heat oil over medium-high. Add pork; sprinkle with paprika. Brown pork on all sides. Reduce heat. Add water; cover and simmer until meat is tender, about 20-25 minutes. Meanwhile, in a medium bowl, combine brown sugar, cornstarch and salt. Gradually add reserved pineapple juice, vinegar, soy sauce and Worcestershire sauce; blend until smooth. Increase temperature to medium. Stir cornstarch mixture into pork; cook, stirring constantly, until thick and bubbly. Cook and stir 2 minutes more. Stir in pineapple, green pepper, onion and water chestnuts; cover and simmer 5 minutes more or until vegetables are crisp-tender. Serve immediately over hot cooked rice. **Yield:** 4-6 servings.

PICADILLO IN PITA BREAD

Shirley Smith, Orange, California

(PICTURED ON PAGE 241)

- 1 pound ground beef
- 1 garlic clove, minced
- 1/2 medium onion, chopped
- 1 small apple, peeled, cored and chopped
- 1/4 cup beef broth
- 1 tablespoon vinegar
- 1 can (8 ounces) tomato sauce *or* 1 can (7-3/4 ounces) Mexican-style hot tomato sauce
- 1 teaspoon salt
- 1/2 teaspoon ground cinnamon
- 1/2 teaspoon ground cumin
- 1/4 cup raisins
- 1/3 cup sliced almonds
- 3 pita breads, halved
- 1 avocado, sliced
- 1/2 cup sour cream

In a large skillet over medium heat, cook beef, garlic and onion until beef is brown and onion is soft. Drain fat. Stir in apple, broth, vinegar, tomato sauce, salt, cinnamon and cumin; simmer, stirring occasionally, until the liquid is absorbed, about 15 minutes. Stir in raisins and almonds. Adjust seasoning if necessary. To serve, fill each pita half with beef mixture and top with an avocado slice and a dollop of sour cream. **Yield:** 6 servings.

GERMAN PIZZA

Audrey Nolt, Versailles, Missouri

(PICTURED ON PAGE 241)

- 1 pound ground beef
- 1/2 medium onion, chopped
- 1/2 green pepper, diced
- 1-1/2 teaspoons salt, *divided*
- 1/2 teaspoon pepper
- 2 tablespoons butter *or* margarine
- 6 medium potatoes (about 2-1/4 pounds), peeled and finely shredded
- 3 eggs, beaten
- 1/3 cup milk
- 2 cups (8 ounces) shredded cheddar *or* mozzarella cheese

In a 12-in. stove-top or electric skillet over medium heat, brown beef with onion, green pepper, 1/2 teaspoon salt and pepper. Remove meat mixture from skillet and drain fat. Reduce heat to low. Melt butter; spread potatoes over butter and sprinkle with remaining salt. Top with beef mixture. Combine eggs and milk; pour over all. Cook, covered, until potatoes are tender, about 30 minutes. Top with cheese; cover and heat until cheese is melted, about 5 minutes. Cut into wedges or squares to serve. **Yield:** 4-6 servings.

SPICY BEEF WITH PEPPERS

Patricia Ann Fredell, Orion, Illinois

(PICTURED ON PAGE 241)

- 2 tablespoons cornstarch, *divided*
- 4 tablespoons dry sherry *or* beef broth, *divided*
- 4 tablespoons soy sauce, *divided*
- 1 garlic clove, minced
- 1/2 to 1 teaspoon crushed dried red pepper
- 1 pound top sirloin, thinly sliced diagonally
- 1/2 cup water
- 3 tablespoons cooking oil, *divided*
- 1 green pepper, seeded and cut into strips
- 1 sweet red pepper, seeded and cut into strips

Cooked rice *or* chow mein noodles

In a medium bowl, combine 1 tablespoon of the cornstarch with 2 tablespoons of sherry or broth, 2 tablespoons soy sauce, garlic and dried red pepper. Add beef and toss to coat. Set aside. In a small bowl, combine water with remaining cornstarch, sherry and soy sauce. Set aside. In a wok or skillet, heat 1 tablespoon oil on medium-high. Add green and red peppers; stir-fry 1 minute. Remove peppers to a platter. Add remaining oil and half the beef; stir-fry until beef is no longer pink. Remove and stir-fry remaining beef. Return peppers and beef to pan. Stir cornstarch mixture and add to pan; bring to a boil, stirring constantly. Cook 1 minute. Serve immediately with rice or chow mein noodles. **Yield:** 4-6 servings.

BACON JARDIN

Sue Dragon, Orlando, Florida

(PICTURED ON PAGE 241)

- 1/2 pound sliced bacon, cut into 1-inch pieces
- 3/4 cup instant rice, uncooked
- 3/4 cup boiling water
- 1 small zucchini, sliced
- 1/4 teaspoon oregano
- 1 tomato, sliced
- 1 small onion, sliced
- 1 small green pepper, sliced

Pepper to taste

- 4 slices American cheese

In a skillet over medium-high heat, fry bacon until crisp. Pour off fat. Add rice, water and zucchini; sprinkle with the oregano. Arrange tomato, onion and green pepper over the bacon mixture; sprinkle with pepper. Cover and simmer for 10 minutes or until vegetables are crisp-tender. Top with cheese and heat only until melted. **Yield:** 4 servings.

CHILI SKILLET

Katherine Brown, Fredericktown, Ohio

(PICTURED ON PAGE 242)

- 1 pound ground beef
- 1 cup chopped onion
- 1/2 cup chopped green pepper
- 1 garlic clove, minced
- 1 cup tomato juice
- 1 can (8 ounces) red kidney beans, undrained
- 4 teaspoons chili powder
- 1 teaspoon dried oregano
- 1 teaspoon salt
- 1/2 cup uncooked long-grain rice
- 1 cup canned *or* frozen corn
- 1/2 cup sliced black olives
- 1 cup (4 ounces) shredded cheddar *or* Monterey Jack cheese

In a large skillet over medium heat, cook beef, onion, pepper and garlic until meat is brown and vegetables are tender. Drain fat. Add the tomato juice, kidney beans, chili powder, oregano, salt and rice; cover and simmer about 25 minutes or until rice is tender. Stir in corn and olives; cover and cook 5 minutes more. Sprinkle with cheese, cover and cook only until cheese melts, about 5 minutes. **Yield:** 4 servings.

FRUITED CHOPS

Teresa Lillycrop, Puslinch, Ontario

(PICTURED ON PAGE 242)

- 1 tablespoon cooking oil
- 4 pork chops, about 1 inch thick
- 1 can (10-3/4 ounces) condensed chicken broth
- 2 tablespoons soy sauce
- 1 tablespoon vinegar
- 1/2 cup apple juice
- 2 tablespoons brown sugar
- 2 tablespoons cornstarch
- 1 teaspoon ground ginger
- 1 large apple, cored and coarsely chopped

Cooked rice

Sliced green onions

In a 10-in. skillet, heat oil over medium-high. Brown chops on both sides. Stir in chicken broth, soy sauce and vinegar; bring to a boil. Reduce heat, cover and simmer 20 minutes or until chops are tender. Meanwhile, in a small bowl, combine apple juice, brown sugar, cornstarch and ginger; stir until smooth. Remove chops from skillet and keep warm. Increase heat to medium. Stir cornstarch mixture into skillet; cook and stir until thickened. Add chopped apple and heat through. On a platter, arrange chops over rice. Spoon sauce over chops and top with green onions. **Yield:** 4 servings.

SAVVY STIR-FRYING: To prevent uneven cooking when stir-frying in a wok or large skillet, keep the foods in constant motion.

- Make additional sauce in a separate pan to serve at the table. It tastes great over rice or noodles!
- When using leftover cooked chicken (or any other cooked meat) in stir-fry recipes, add it last and cook just long enough to heat.
- If fresh gingerroot is available only occasionally in your area, mince it and freeze in measured portions to fit your recipes. Wrap well to avoid freezer burn.

STEAK LO MEIN

Jo Groth, Plainfield, Iowa

(PICTURED ON PAGE 242)

✓ This tasty dish uses less sugar, salt and fat. Recipe includes *Diabetic Exchanges*.

    1 pound round steak, trimmed
    1 teaspoon beef bouillon
      granules
  3/4 cup water
  1/4 cup soy sauce
    2 tablespoons cornstarch
    2 tablespoons cooking oil
    1 garlic clove, minced
    2 cups shredded cabbage
    1 cup diagonally sliced carrots,
      partially cooked
    1 medium onion, sliced into
      rings
  1/2 cup sliced fresh mushrooms
  1/2 cup diagonally sliced celery
  1/3 cup sliced green onions
   15 fresh snow pea pods,
      trimmed
    1 can (8 ounces) sliced water
      chestnuts, drained
    4 ounces thin spaghetti,
      cooked and drained

Freeze steak just until firm; slice diagonally across grain into 1/4-in. strips. Combine bouillon, water, soy sauce and cornstarch. Set aside. In a wok or large skillet, heat oil on medium-high. Add meat and garlic; stir-fry until the meat is no longer pink, about 5 minutes. Remove meat to a platter. Add cabbage, carrots, onion, mushrooms, celery and green onions; stir-fry for about 3 minutes. Add pea pods and water chestnuts; stir-fry 2 minutes. Add meat. Stir bouillon mixture and pour into skillet; cook and stir until thickened. Gently toss in spaghetti and heat through for 1 minute. **Yield:** 6 servings. **Diabetic Exchanges:** One serving equals 2 lean meat, 1-3/4 starch, 1 vegetable; also, 329 calories, 834 mg sodium, 52 mg cholesterol, 34 gm carbohydrate, 29 gm protein, 8 gm fat.

CHICKEN MUSHROOM STIR-FRY

Christina Thompson, Howell, Michigan

(PICTURED ON PAGE 242)

✓ This tasty dish uses less sugar, salt and fat. Recipe includes *Diabetic Exchanges*.

    1 tablespoon soy sauce
    1 egg white
    1 teaspoon sesame oil
  1/2 teaspoon brown sugar
    1 teaspoon cornstarch
  1/8 teaspoon white pepper
    1 pound boneless chicken
      breasts, cut into 1/2-inch
      cubes
  1/2 cup chicken broth
    2 tablespoons cornstarch
    2 tablespoons cold water
  1/4 cup oyster sauce
    4 tablespoons cooking oil,
      divided
1-1/2 teaspoons minced fresh
      gingerroot
    2 garlic cloves, minced
    2 green onions, sliced
    4 medium carrots, cubed
    1 pound fresh mushrooms,
      quartered
  1/4 pound fresh snow pea pods,
      trimmed and cut in half

Combine first six ingredients; toss with chicken. Refrigerate 30 minutes. In a small bowl, combine chicken broth, cornstarch, water and oyster sauce. Set aside. In a wok or large skillet, heat 2 tablespoons oil over medium-high. Add gingerroot, garlic and onions; stir-fry 1 minute. Add chicken and continue to stir-fry until the chicken is white. Remove chicken and vegetables from pan. Add remaining oil; stir-fry carrots 3 minutes or until crisp-tender. Add mushrooms and pea pods; stir-fry 1 minute. Return chicken and vegetables to pan. Stir broth mixture and pour into skillet; cook and stir until the sauce is thickened. Serve immediately. **Yield:** 6 servings. **Diabetic Exchanges:** One serving equals 3 lean meat, 3/4 starch, 1 vegetable, 1 fat; also, 299 calories, 431 mg sodium, 68 mg cholesterol, 15 gm carbohydrate, 30 gm protein, 14 gm fat.

MEATBALL GARDEN STEW

Bev Hurst, Sweet Home, Oregon

    1 pound lean ground beef
    4 tablespoons all-purpose flour,
      divided
    1 teaspoon salt
Dash pepper
    1 egg
  1/4 cup milk
  1/4 cup chopped onion
    1 tablespoon butter *or*
      margarine
    1 garlic clove, minced
    1 can (14-1/2 ounces) beef broth
  2/3 cup water
  1/2 teaspoon dried thyme
    6 medium potatoes, peeled and
      quartered
    6 medium carrots, halved
      lengthwise and crosswise
    6 green onions, chopped
    1 package (10 ounces) frozen
      peas, defrosted

In a medium bowl, combine beef, 2 tablespoons flour, salt, pepper, egg, milk and onion. Form into 1-in. balls. Melt butter in a large skillet or Dutch oven. Saute garlic for 1 minute. Brown meatballs on all sides. Push the meatballs to the side. Blend remaining flour into the drippings. Add the broth, water and thyme. Cook, stirring constantly, until thickened. Add potatoes, carrots and green onions and stir with meatballs and sauce. Cover and simmer until vegetables are tender, about 30-35 minutes. Add peas and continue to cook 10 minutes. Adjust seasonings, if desired. **Yield:** 6 servings.

NO-KNEAD HONEY OATMEAL BREAD

Janice Dancer, Williamstown, Vermont

✓ This tasty dish uses less sugar, salt and fat. Recipe includes *Diabetic Exchanges*.

    2 cups water, *divided*
    1 cup rolled oats
  1/3 cup butter *or* margarine,
      softened
  1/3 cup honey
    1 tablespoon salt
    2 packages (1/4 ounce *each*)
      active dry yeast
    1 egg
    4 to 5 cups all-purpose flour,
      divided
Melted butter *or* margarine, optional

In a saucepan, heat 1 cup water to boiling. Stir in oats, butter, honey and salt. Cool to lukewarm. Heat remaining water to 110°-115° and dissolve yeast. In a large mixing bowl, combine yeast mixture, egg, 2 cups flour and the oats mixture. Beat until the ingredients are combined and the batter is smooth. By hand, add enough remaining flour to make a stiff batter. Spread batter evenly into two greased 8-1/2-in. x 4-1/2-in. x 2-1/2-in. loaf pans. Smooth tops of loaves. Cover and let rise in a warm place until doubled, about 35-40 minutes. Bake at 375° for 40-45 minutes. Remove from pans and brush with melted butter, if desired. **Yield:** 2 loaves. **Diabetic Exchanges:** One slice equals 1 starch; also, 81 calories, 175 mg sodium, 6 mg cholesterol, 14 gm carbohydrate, 2 gm protein, 2 gm fat.

CRANBERRY TOPPING

Kristi Twohig, Fond du Lac, Wisconsin

(PICTURED ON PAGE 244)

1/2 cup butter
1 cup white *or* brown sugar
1 package (12 ounces) whole cranberries, washed and sorted
1/2 cup orange liqueur *or* orange juice concentrate
1/2 cup whipping cream, optional

Combine butter, sugar, cranberries and orange liqueur/concentrate. Bring to boil over medium heat, stirring constantly. Reduce heat; simmer until berries pop. Remove from heat; stir in cream, if desired. Serve warm or at room temperature over pound cake, cheesecake or ice cream. Refrigerate leftovers. Makes a nice gift—be sure to include instructions to store under refrigeration. **Yield:** 4 cups.

CRAZY FOR CRANBERRIES! For extra-rich-tasting homemade cranberry sauce, add vanilla extract (a teaspoon or more) after cooking.

● Fresh cranberries are easier to grind in a food processor or a food grinder if you freeze them first. Allow ground berries to drain well before using.

THE ULTIMATE CHEESECAKE

Cathy Burke, Oneida, Tennessee

(PICTURED ON PAGE 244)

CRUST:
1 cup all-purpose flour
1/4 cup sugar
1 teaspoon grated lemon peel
1/2 teaspoon vanilla
1 egg yolk
1/4 cup butter, softened
FILLING:
5 packages (8 ounces *each*) cream cheese, softened
1-1/4 cups sugar
3 tablespoons all-purpose flour
1/4 teaspoon vanilla
5 eggs
2 egg yolks
1/4 cup whipping cream
2 teaspoons grated lemon peel
1-1/2 teaspoons grated orange peel
GLAZE:
2 tablespoons sugar
4 teaspoons cornstarch
2 cans (8 ounces *each*) crushed pineapple, undrained
2 teaspoons lemon juice
1 perfect strawberry for garnish, optional

Make crust by mixing all crust ingredients until blended. Pat half of the crust mixture on bottom of greased 9-in. springform pan (sides of pan should be well-greased as well). Bake at 400° until golden brown, about 6-8 minutes; cool. Press the rest of dough to sides of pan; set aside. Make filling by mixing cream cheese, sugar, flour and vanilla at high speed. Add eggs and the egg yolks one at a time, beating well after each addition. Beat in the cream; stir in the grated peels. Pour into assembled springform pan; bake at 500° for 10 minutes. Lower oven temperature to 250°; bake for 1 hour. Remove to rack to cool for at least 2 hours. Refrigerate cheesecake. Make glaze by mixing the sugar and cornstarch together; add pineapple and lemon juice. Bring to boil over medium heat. Cook for 1 minute until thick. Cool; top the cooled cheesecake with glaze. Chill for at least 3 hours (overnight is best). Remove sides of pan; top cheesecake with single strawberry, if desired. **Yield:** 12-16 servings.

CHOCOLATE TORTE

Rose M. Johnson, Virginia Minnesota

(PICTURED ON PAGE 244)

TORTE:
8 eggs, *separated*
1-1/4 cups sugar
3/4 cup all-purpose flour
1/4 cup fine dry bread crumbs
1/4 teaspoon salt
2 ounces (2 squares) semisweet chocolate, grated
1-1/2 teaspoons vanilla extract
CREAM FILLING:
1/2 cup whipping cream
1/4 cup ground almonds
3 tablespoons sugar
FROSTING:
4 ounces (4 squares) unsweetened chocolate
3 tablespoons butter
1 tablespoon brandy *or* 1 teaspoon vanilla
2 to 2-1/2 cups confectioners' sugar
2 to 3 tablespoons milk
Chopped almonds for garnish

Beat the egg yolks until thick and lemon-colored. Gradually beat in the sugar; set aside. Combine flour, bread crumbs and salt. Add chocolate and mix thoroughly, but lightly. Add flour mixture to egg yolk mixture in 4 portions, folding until well-mixed after each addition. Set aside. With clean beaters, beat egg whites with vanilla extract until stiff, but not dry, peaks are formed. Stir 1 cup of beaten egg whites into yolk batter (makes batter less stiff for folding). Gently fold in remaining beaten egg whites. Turn into a well-greased and parchment-lined 9- or 10-in. springform pan or deep round layer cake pan. Bake at 325° for 50-60 minutes. Remove from pan; cool completely. Split cake in half. Set aside. Make filling by whipping cream; fold in almonds and sugar. Spread filling on bottom half of cake. Replace top. Make frosting by melting chocolate and butter together in saucepan; remove from heat. Stir in brandy or vanilla; add sugar and milk, mixing until frosting is of spreading consistency. (Work quickly as frosting sets up fast.) Frost sides and top of cake. Press the chopped almonds around sides of cake. Refrigerate for 4 hours or longer to let the flavors mellow. *Note:* Torte in photo was baked in 8-in. pan. **Yield:** 20 servings.

MISSISSIPPI MUD PIE

Sara W. Carley, Temple, New Hampshire

(PICTURED ON PAGE 244)

CRUST:
24 chocolate wafers, mashed fine, about 1-1/3 cups crumbs, *divided*
3 tablespoons soft butter *or* margarine
FILLING:
1/2 gallon coffee ice cream, slightly softened
HOT FUDGE SAUCE:
2 squares unsweetened chocolate
1/2 cup water
1-1/2 cups light corn syrup
1/8 teaspoon salt
1 teaspoon vanilla extract
WHIPPED CREAM TOPPING:
1 cup whipping cream
1 tablespoon sugar
1 teaspoon vanilla extract

Make the crust by combining crumbs and butter/margarine. Set aside 3 tablespoons of mixture for pie garnish. Press remaining into bottom and sides of 9-in. pie plate. Bake at 375° for 8 minutes; cool. Pack softened ice cream into cooled crust. Freeze until firm. Make fudge sauce by melting chocolate with water in saucepan over low heat until blended. Remove from heat; gradually add corn syrup and salt. Bring to boil; reduce heat and simmer for 10 minutes, stirring often. Add vanilla. Set aside. For topping, whip cream; add sugar and vanilla. To serve, cut pie into wedges, place on dessert plates, pour fudge sauce over all, top with whipped cream and if desired, sprinkle with the reserved crumbs. **Yield:** 8 servings.

GREEK ROASTED CHICKEN AND POTATOES

Pella Visnick, Dallas, Texas

1 whole roasting chicken
   (about 6 pounds)
Salt and pepper to taste
   2 to 3 teaspoons dried oregano,
      divided
   4 to 6 baking potatoes, peeled
      and quartered
1/4 cup butter *or* margarine,
      melted
   3 tablespoons fresh lemon
      juice
3/4 cup chicken broth

Place chicken on a rack in a roasting pan. Sprinkle with salt and pepper and half the oregano. Arrange potatoes around the chicken; sprinkle with salt and pepper and remaining oregano. Pour butter and lemon juice over the chicken and potatoes. Add chicken broth to pan bottom. Bake at 350° for 2 to 2-1/2 hours or until chicken is browned and tender. Baste frequently with pan juices during roasting. **Yield:** about 8-10 servings.

BARBECUED BANANAS

Iris Bates, Midhurst, Ontario

 This tasty dish uses less sugar, salt and fat. Recipe includes *Diabetic Exchanges*.

   6 bananas
1/4 cup fresh lemon juice
   2 tablespoons brown sugar
1/4 teaspoon cinnamon
1/4 teaspoon nutmeg
1/8 teaspoon mace
   3 tablespoons butter

Peel bananas; place on double thickness of heavy-duty foil. Brush with lemon juice; sprinkle with sugar and spices. Dot with butter. Wrap, sealing tightly. Barbecue on grill for 9-10 minutes; unwrap carefully. Eat with a spoon. **Yield:** 6 servings. **Diabetic Exchanges:** One serving equals 3 fruits, 1 fat; also 166 calories, 72 mg sodium, 18 mg cholesterol, 30 gm carbohydrate.

CHICKEN RICE PIE

Trudy Selberg, Rogers, Arkansas

CRUST:
   2 cups cooked parboiled long
      grain rice
1/2 cup cooked chopped spinach,

well drained
   1 cup shredded Swiss cheese
FILLING:
   1 can (10-3/4 ounces) cream of
      mushroom soup, undiluted
1/2 cup milk
   2 cups cooked, cubed chicken
   1 cup shredded mild cheddar
      cheese
1/2 cup Parmesan cheese
   2 ounces green olives, sliced
1/4 cup onion, finely chopped
1/2 cup fresh mushrooms, sliced

Combine crust ingredients; spray 10-in. pie pan with vegetable spray. Press crust onto bottom and sides of pan. Bake at 375° for 25 minutes. Set aside. Combine soup and milk; mixing well. Add remaining filling ingredients; mix gently. Spread mixture over cooked crust. Bake, uncovered, at 350° for 20-25 minutes. Remove from oven; let stand 10 minutes before serving. **Yield:** 6-8 servings.

PRUNE CAKE

Lucille Drake, Tecumseh, Michigan

   1 cup vegetable oil
1-1/2 cups sugar
   3 eggs
   2 cups all-purpose flour
   1 teaspoon cinnamon
   1 teaspoon nutmeg
   1 teaspoon allspice
   1 teaspoon baking soda
   1 cup buttermilk
   1 teaspoon vanilla
   2 cups prunes, cooked, seeded
      and chopped
   1 cup nuts

Beat oil and sugar until well blended; add eggs, one at a time, beating after each addition. Combine dry ingredients; add alternately with buttermilk and vanilla to oil/sugar/egg mixture; beating until smooth. Stir in prunes and nuts. Pour into a greased 13-in. x 9-in. x 2-in. baking pan. Bake at 300° for 45 minutes. Cool. Dust with confectioners' sugar or frost with favorite cream cheese icing, if desired. **Yield:** 16-20 servings.

CHEESY ONION CASSEROLE

Beth Perry, Jacksonville, Florida

   2 tablespoons butter *or*
      margarine
   3 large sweet white onions,
      sliced

   2 cups (8 ounces) shredded
      Swiss cheese, *divided*
Pepper to taste
   1 can (10-3/4 ounces) cream of
      chicken soup, undiluted
2/3 cup milk
   1 teaspoon soy sauce
   8 slices French bread, buttered
      on both sides

In a skillet, melt butter. Saute onions until clear and slightly brown. Layer onions, two-thirds of the cheese and the pepper in a 2-qt. casserole. In a saucepan, heat soup, milk and soy sauce; stir to blend. Pour soup mixture into casserole and stir gently. Top with bread slices. Bake at 350° for 15 minutes. Push bread slices down under sauce; sprinkle with remaining cheese. Bake 15 minutes more. This is good served as a side dish with beef or pork roast. **Yield:** 8 servings.

CORNMEAL MUFFINS

Amelia Moody, Pasadena, Texas

 This tasty dish uses less sugar, salt and fat. Recipe includes *Diabetic Exchanges*.

   1 cup all-purpose flour
   1 cup yellow cornmeal
1/3 cup sugar
   1 tablespoon baking powder
   1 teaspoon salt
   2 tablespoons finely chopped
      onion
   1 cup cream-style corn
1/2 cup mayonnaise
   3 tablespoons vegetable oil
   1 egg

In a large mixing bowl, combine dry ingredients. Make a well in the center and add all remaining ingredients. Stir just until mixed. Spoon into 12 greased muffin tins. Bake at 400° for 20 minutes. **Yield:** 12 muffins. **Diabetic Exchanges:** One muffin (prepared with light mayonnaise and egg substitute) equals 1-1/2 starch, 1-1/2 fat; also, 189 calories, 434 mg sodium, 2 mg cholesterol, 29 gm carbohydrate, 3 gm protein, 7 gm fat.

PERFECT PIZZA DIP: Make a pretty pizza dip for a party or snack by spreading 1 8-oz. package of cream cheese on a plate and topping it with pizza sauce. Then add any or all of the following: chopped onion, green or black olives, peppers, tomatoes or shrimp. Top with mozzarella cheese. Serve with a variety of crackers or melba rounds.

249

Holidays

Want to get oohs and aahs from your family during the Christmas season? Set out a cheery Christmas Braid, serve Cream-Filled Coffee Cake for breakfast, pass the Pop-Up Bread with dinner, or bake any of the other festive breads featured here.

Whether you're baking for family or friends...nothing quite compares to home-baked breads from your country kitchen.

BREAD WINNERS: Clockwise from lower left—**Country Swirl Bread** (Pg. 259); **Whole Wheat Butterhorns** (Pg. 259); **Cream-Filled Coffee Cake** (Pg. 259); **Christmas Braid** (Pg. 260); **Pop-Up Bread** (Pg. 260); **Cheesy Onion Burger Buns** (Pg. 260); **Reuben Loaf** (Pg. 261); **Creamy Chive Ring** (Pg. 260).

ome-baked bread and the holidays—what a warm and perfectly wonderful match they make throughout the season!

The family favorites featured here include breads for breakfast and brunch, lunch and dinner, snacking and supper. But don't confine them to Christmas. They'll bring you compliments year 'round!

BEST BREADS: Clockwise from top—**Poppy Seed Roll** (Pg. 261); **Italian Parmesan Bread** (Pg. 261); **Candy Cane Coffee Cake** (Pg. 262); **Oatmeal Rolls** (Pg. 261).

MEALS IN MINUTES

H er family loves turkey, and that can leave Linnea Rein of Topeka, Kansas with lots of leftovers. So this busy country cook's come up with a quick solution—she turns today's time-consuming turkey into tomorrow's speedy meal!

"I make a lot of cold turkey salads in summer," Linnea says. "But in the cold months, I like serving something hot and hearty. That's how I ended up with my turkey salad burritos."

Creating the side dish was a snap for Linnea, who likes the taste and convenience of quick-cooking rice. In her own timely take-off of traditional Spanish rice, she uses tomato juice instead of water or broth for cooking. "If you want a 'snappy' taste," she adds, "stir some picante sauce into the cooked rice."

Stirring up some other leftovers—cranberry sauce and yogurt—resulted in a favorite fast dessert. Linnea layers the sauce and yogurt together in clear glass dishes for a pretty look, and tops it with granola for crunch. (This combination also makes for a quick, nutritious on-the-go breakfast!)

When there's time, savory roast turkey with all the trimmings *is* hard to top. But when your kitchen fare has to be fast, do like Linnea does—turn that turkey into a tasty time-saver!

TURKEY SALAD BURRITOS

2 cups chopped cooked turkey
3/4 cup finely chopped celery
1/2 cup finely chopped onion
1/4 to 1/2 cup sliced black olives
1 cup shredded cheddar cheese
1/2 cup salad dressing *or* mayonnaise
1/2 cup picante sauce
1/2 teaspoon salt
6 soft flour tortillas (7 to 8 inches diameter)
Picante sauce
Black olives for garnish

In medium mixing bowl, combine turkey, celery, onion, black olives and cheese. In another bowl, whisk together salad dressing, picante sauce and salt. Pour sauce over turkey mixture; blend well. Spoon filling onto tortillas; wrap burrito-style. Heat in 13-in. x 9-in. x 2-in. baking pan at 350° for 20 minutes or until thoroughly warmed, or microwave each burrito 2 to 2-1/2 minutes on high. Serve with additional picante sauce; garnish with black olives. **Yield:** 4 servings.

CONFETTI RICE

2 cups tomato juice
1 cup frozen mixed vegetables, broken apart
1-1/2 cups instant rice
1/8 teaspoon pepper

Combine tomato juice and mixed vegetables in medium saucepan; bring to a boil. Stir in rice and pepper. Cover, turn off heat and allow to stand 6 minutes. Fluff with fork. **Yield:** 4 servings.

CRANBERRY/YOGURT PARFAITS

3/4 cup whole berry cranberry sauce
2 cups plain yogurt
1/2 cup granola, homemade *or* purchased

Place about 2 tablespoons cranberry sauce in bottom of 4 parfait glasses. Layer yogurt, remaining cranberry sauce and granola on top. **Yield:** 4 servings.

Have this dressing on hand when you'd like a tossed salad to accompany your burritos:

FRESH BASIL AND GARLIC DRESSING

Annie Unrein, Gustavus, Alaska

1 ripe, medium-size tomato, cut in wedges
1/2 cup olive oil
1/3 cup red wine vinegar
1/4 cup crushed basil
1/4 cup chopped chives
2 cloves fresh garlic
1/2 teaspoon salt
1/2 teaspoon white pepper

Combine all ingredients in blender; process until smooth. Refrigerate for several hours to blend flavors before serving. **Yield:** 1-1/4 cups.

W hen your family asks you for a sweet treat, chances are chocolate's the most-hoped-for choice. After all, what better way to fill your holiday table than with decadent desserts like these.

Now, you can truly treat those you love to the scrumptious taste of chocolate in a variety of recipes. You'll find rich family favorites, including a few surprises—like Chocolate *Shortbread*—to satisfy sweet tooths for many mouth-watering months to come!

CELEBRATED CHOCOLATE: Clockwise from lower left— **Chocolate Shortbread** (Pg. 262); **Chocolate Pound Cake** (Pg. 262); **Chocolate Angel Food Cake** (Pg. 262); **Milky Way Ice Cream** (Pg. 262); **Chocolate Cinnamon Doughnuts** (Pg. 263); **White Chocolate Fudge** (Pg. 262); **Homemade Fudge Sauce** (Pg. 263); **Old-Fashioned Chocolate Pudding** (Pg. 263).

Sweet surprises mean so much when they're handmade in your own country kitchen. Whether you're concocting candies to give as Christmas gifts or for treating friends, these four confections are sure to be festive favorites whenever you serve them.

They're made with only the best ingredients, such as sweet butter, nuts, coconut, caramels and dark and milk chocolate. Chances are, there's a candy here to suit the tastes of your holiday guests.

Mmmm...homemade candy— how sweet it is!

COUNTRY CONFECTIONS: Clockwise from top jar—**Aunt Rose's Fantastic Butter Toffee** (Pg. 263); **Macadamia Nut Fudge** (Pg. 264); **Mounds Balls** (Pg. 264); **Easy Microwave Caramels** (Pg. 263).

BEST COOK

Shirley Pewtress
Kaysville, Utah

Christmas is always a special time at the Kaysville, Utah home of Shirley Pewtress—as you can see from the photo above!

Shirley loves cooking and teaching others how to cook—but her favorite dishes are her Christmas treats, like the Christmas Tree Bread she's holding.

"I make steamed puddings, fruitcakes and all kinds of chocolates, candies and baked goods. With six children and 12 grandchildren, our Christmas mornings are hectic, and a piece of warm bread with hot chocolate or cider stops the hunger pangs!"

Shirley's relatives aren't the only ones to benefit from her cooking. She's known for her holiday bread-making demonstrations. She also teaches cooking and nutrition classes for low-income young homemakers, and for families at nearby Hill Air Force Base.

"She's adored by the students in her classes," says friend Jo Ann Mathis, who nominated Shirley. "She believes in down-to-earth cooking, and she's a natural at teaching people how to stretch their food budgets."

Shirley says she's happy for the opportunity to share what she's learned.

"I love teaching adults new cooking tricks and new recipes," she says. "My favorite saying is, 'When it comes to cooking, you're only limited by your imagination.'"

CHRISTMAS TREE BREAD

BASIC SWEET DOUGH:
- 1 package (1/4 ounce) active dry yeast
- 1/2 cup warm water (110°-115°)
- 1/2 cup sugar
- 5 tablespoons butter *or* margarine, softened
- 2 cups warm milk (110°-115°)
- 1 teaspoon salt
- 1 teaspoon mace
- 3 eggs, beaten
- 8 to 8-1/2 cups all-purpose flour, *divided*
- 1 teaspoon vanilla extract
- 1/2 teaspoon lemon juice

PECAN CREAM FILLING:
- 1/4 cup butter *or* margarine
- 1-1/4 cups confectioners' sugar
- 1 tablespoon all-purpose flour
- 1 egg yolk
- 1/4 cup finely chopped pecans

GLAZE:
- 2 cups confectioners' sugar
- 4 tablespoons milk
- 1-1/2 teaspoons butter, melted
- 1/4 teaspoon vanilla extract
- Red and green candied cherries

Dissolve the yeast in warm water; set aside. In a large mixing bowl, combine sugar, butter, milk, salt and mace; mix well. Add eggs and yeast mixture; mix well. Add 4 cups flour; beat well. Stir in vanilla, lemon juice and enough remaining flour to form a soft dough. Turn out onto floured surface; knead until smooth and elastic. Add more flour if necessary. Shape into ball; place in a greased bowl. Cover; let rise in warm place until doubled, about 1-1/2 hours.

For filling, cream butter, sugar and flour. Beat in egg yolk. Add pecans. Cover; set aside.

When dough has risen, punch down. Roll one-third of dough into 15-in. x 13-in. rectangle. (Using sharp knife and ruler, trim to make triangle 15 in. tall and 13 in. wide at base.) From trimmings, cut two 3-in.-high tree trunks. Place large triangle on lightly greased 17-in. x 14-in. baking sheet with no sides. Dough will shrink, so form on pan with fingers back to original shape. Center one tree trunk at base of triangle; pinch together where trunk joins tree. Fold top 2 in. of triangle under. Gently spread filling on triangle and trunk to within 1 in. of edges.

Place second trunk over filling on trunk already attached to tree; pinch outside edges to seal. Roll remaining dough into a 15-in. square. With star-shaped cookie cutter, cut one star. With doughnut cutter, cut 25 rounds. Arrange 6 dough rounds, overlapping slightly, across the tree base. Use 5 rounds to make second row. Make third row of 5 rounds, fourth of 4, fifth of 3 and top row of 2. Place star on top. Cover; let rise until doubled, about 45-60 minutes. Bake at 375° for 20-30 minutes or until golden brown. Cool on wire rack. Combine glaze ingredients; spread over tree. Top dough rounds with candied cherries. **Yield:** about 24 servings.

Note: This recipe also can be used to make wreaths or two smaller trees.

EASY CASSEROLE

- 1-1/2 pounds ground beef
- 1 large onion, chopped
- 1 medium green pepper, chopped
- 2 celery stalks, sliced
- 1 quart tomato juice
- 1-1/2 cups catsup
- 1-1/4 cups uncooked macaroni
- 1 teaspoon chili powder *or* to taste
- 1/4 teaspoon garlic powder
- Salt and pepper to taste

In a Dutch oven, brown beef over medium-high heat. Add onion, green pepper and celery. Continue to cook until vegetables are crisp-tender. Drain excess fat. Add all remaining ingredients. Cover and simmer 2 hours or until the macaroni is tender and the liquid is absorbed. **Yield:** 8 servings.

POTATO POINTERS: Let raw potatoes stand in cold water for at least 30 minutes before frying to improve the crispness of French fries.

● A few drops of lemon juice in the water will whiten boiled potatoes.

● If you're making a cream-style soup, add a cubed potato to the mixture as it cooks. When you puree the mixture, you'll love the extra body it gives the soup.

SOUP KIT MAKES TASTY GIFT!
Looking for a practical homemade gift that's also full of fun? Try this:

Prepare a mix of dried beans and peas and place in a canning jar. Take a perky red ribbon; use it to attach the recipe card and a bundle of dried herbs wrapped in cheesecloth. It's a present bound to be appreciated.

Festive desserts and sweets are a delicious way to celebrate the holiday season—especially with the tempting treats featured here.

Top off a holiday dinner with a slice of German Chocolate Cake... or a generous serving of the creamy Swedish Rice Ring with juicy strawberries. For a treat with your evening coffee, pass a plate of rich pe-can Tassies or fruity Apricot Bars.

But don't reserve these recipes just for the holidays. These dressed-up desserts are perfect for special occasions any time of year!

DELECTABLE DESSERTS: Clockwise from top—**German Chocolate Cake** (Pg. 264); **Swedish Rice Ring** (Pg. 264); **Apricot Bars** (Pg. 264); **Tassies** (Pg. 265).

WHOLE WHEAT BUTTERHORNS

Mary June Mullins, Livonia, Missouri

(PICTURED ON PAGE 250)

2-3/4 cups all-purpose flour, *divided*
2 packages (1/4 ounce *each*) active dry yeast
1-3/4 cups water
1/3 cup packed brown sugar
1/2 cup butter *or* margarine, *divided*
2 tablespoons honey
2 teaspoons salt
2 cups whole wheat flour

In a large mixing bowl, combine 1-1/2 cups all-purpose flour and yeast. Heat the water, brown sugar, 3 tablespoons butter, honey and salt to 120°-130°; add to flour mixture. Beat on low for 30 seconds with electric mixer; increase speed to high and continue beating 3 minutes. Stir in whole wheat flour and enough remaining all-purpose flour to form a soft dough. Turn onto a lightly floured surface and knead until smooth and elastic, about 6-8 minutes. Place in a greased bowl, cover and allow to rise in a warm place until doubled, about 1-1/2 hours. Punch dough down and divide into thirds. Shape each into a ball, cover and let rest 10 minutes. On a lightly floured surface, roll the balls into three 12-in. circles. Cut each circle into 6 to 8 wedges. Roll wedges into crescent shapes, starting at the wide end. Place on greased baking sheets. Cover and let rise in a warm place until doubled, about 1 hour. Melt remaining butter and brush some on each crescent. Bake at 400° for 10-15 minutes or until golden brown. Brush again with butter while hot. **Yield:** 18-24 rolls.

COUNTRY SWIRL BREAD

Frieda Miller, Benton Harbor, Michigan

(PICTURED ON PAGE 250)

DARK DOUGH:
1 tablespoon sugar
1-1/2 teaspoons salt
2 packages (1/4 ounce *each*) active dry yeast
1-3/4 cups all-purpose flour, *divided*
3/4 cup water
1/4 cup dark molasses
1 tablespoon instant coffee
1 tablespoon butter *or* margarine
1-1/4 cups pumpernickel-rye flour, *divided*

LIGHT DOUGH:
1-1/2 teaspoons salt
1 package (1/4 ounce) active dry yeast
1-1/4 cups whole wheat flour, *divided*
1-3/4 cups all-purpose flour, *divided*
1 cup water
1/4 cup honey
2 tablespoons butter *or* margarine
1/2 cup uncooked oats

Dark dough: In a mixing bowl, mix the sugar, salt, yeast and 1 cup all-purpose flour. Heat water, molasses, coffee and butter to 120°-130°; add to flour mixture. Beat with an electric mixer at medium. Add 3/4 cup rye flour and beat 2 minutes. Stir in 1/2 cup all-purpose flour and remaining rye flour. Knead for 6-8 minutes, working in the remaining all-purpose flour. Place dough in a greased bowl. Cover and let rise until doubled, about 2 hours.

Light dough: In mixing bowl, combine salt, yeast, 1 cup whole wheat flour and 1/2 cup all-purpose flour. Set aside. Heat water, honey and butter to 120°-130°; add to flour mixture. Beat 2 minutes at medium, adding remaining whole wheat flour. Mix well. Stir in 1 cup all-purpose flour and oats. Knead, working in remaining all-purpose flour if necessary. Place dough in a greased bowl and let rise until doubled, about 1 hour.

Punch doughs down; let rest 15 minutes. Roll *light dough* into a 16-in. x 9-in. rectangle. Roll *dark dough* into a 16-in. x 8-in. rectangle and place on top of *light dough*. Roll jelly-roll style, beginning with long side. Pinch to seal. Place seam side down on greased baking sheet. Cover; let rise till doubled, 45-60 minutes. Bake 40 minutes at 350°. Cool on wire rack. **Yield:** 1 loaf.

CREAM-FILLED COFFEE CAKE

Betty Mezera, Eau Claire, Wisconsin

(PICTURED ON PAGE 250)

1-1/4 cups milk
1/4 cup butter *or* margarine
1/3 cup plus 1 teaspoon sugar, *divided*
1 tablespoon salt
1 package (1/4 ounce) active dry yeast
1/4 cup warm water (110°-115°)
5-1/2 to 6 cups all-purpose flour, *divided*
3 eggs, well beaten
STREUSEL TOPPING:
1/4 cup sugar
1/4 cup packed brown sugar
2 tablespoons all-purpose flour
2 teaspoons cinnamon
1/4 cup butter *or* margarine
CREAM FILLING:
1/4 cup all-purpose flour
3/4 cup milk
3/4 cup butter *or* margarine
3/4 cup sugar
3/4 teaspoon vanilla extract
3 tablespoons confectioners' sugar

Heat milk, butter, 1/3 cup sugar and salt; stir until the sugar dissolves. Set aside. Mix yeast, warm water and 1 teaspoon sugar; let stand 10 minutes. In a large mixing bowl, combine 3 cups flour, milk mixture, yeast mixture and eggs; beat until smooth. Add enough of the remaining flour to form a soft dough. Turn out onto a lightly floured surface and knead until smooth, about 6-8 minutes. Place dough in a greased bowl, turning once to grease top. Cover and let rise until doubled, about 1 to 1-1/2 hours. Meanwhile, prepare topping. Combine sugars, flour and cinnamon in a bowl. Cut in butter; set aside. Punch dough down; divide in half. Pat or roll each half to fit a greased 9-in. cake pan. With a fork, pierce entire cake top. Divide topping and sprinkle over each cake. Cover and let rise in a warm place until doubled, about 1 hour. Bake at 350° for 20-25 minutes. Remove from pans and cool on wire racks. For filling, combine flour and milk in a saucepan; cook, stirring constantly, until mixture thickens. Cool. In a mixing bowl, cream remaining ingredients until well mixed. Add flour mixture and beat until fluffy. Cut each cake in half horizontally; spread the bottom halves with half the filling, then replace top halves. Refrigerate until ready to serve. **Yield:** 2 cakes.

DATE NUT BALLS

Myrtle McSwan, Indio, California

1 cup pitted dates
1 cup raisins
1/2 cup dried apricots
1/2 cup pitted prunes *or* figs
Unsweetened orange juice to moisten
Flaked coconut *or* chopped walnuts

In food grinder, grind together dates, raisins, apricots, prunes/figs. Combine with orange juice in 2-qt. mixing bowl. Roll into bite-size balls. Roll in coconut or in nuts. Refrigerate, covered, until time to serve. **Yield:** about 2 dozen.

CHRISTMAS BRAID

Wendy Tschetter, Swift Current, Saskatchewan

(PICTURED ON PAGE 251)

5 to 5-1/2 cups all-purpose
flour, *divided*
1 package (1/4 ounce) active
dry yeast
2 cups milk
1/2 cup sugar
6 tablespoons butter *or*
margarine
1 teaspoon salt
1 egg
1 cup raisins
1 cup finely chopped mixed
candied fruit
1/2 cup chopped nuts
1 egg yolk
1 tablespoon water

In a large mixing bowl, combine 3 cups flour and yeast. In a saucepan, heat milk, sugar, butter and salt to 120°-130°; add to flour mixture. Add egg. Beat on low speed with electric mixer for 30 seconds; increase speed to medium and continue beating for 3 minutes. Stir in raisins, candied fruit, nuts and enough remaining flour to form a stiff dough. Turn out onto a floured surface and knead until smooth and elastic, about 8-10 minutes. Place in a greased bowl, turning once to grease top. Cover and let rise in a warm place until doubled, about 1-1/2 hours. Divide dough in thirds, then divide each into thirds again. Roll each piece into a 15-in. rope. Place 3 ropes 1 in. apart on greased baking sheet. Begin braiding loosely in the middle and work toward the ends. Pinch ends together and tuck under. Repeat with remaining ropes. Cover and let rise until doubled, about 30-40 minutes. Combine egg yolk and water; brush over braids. Bake at 350° for 20-25 minutes or until browned. Cool on wire racks. **Yield:** 3 breads.

POP-UP BREAD

Bea Aubry, Dubuque, Iowa

(PICTURED ON PAGE 251)

 This tasty dish uses less sugar, salt and fat. Recipe includes *Diabetic Exchanges.*

3 to 3-1/2 cups all-purpose
flour, *divided*
1 package (1/4 ounce) active
dry yeast
1/2 cup milk
1/2 cup water
1/2 cup vegetable oil
1/4 cup sugar
1 teaspoon salt
2 eggs, beaten
1 cup (4 ounces) shredded
cheddar cheese

Combine 1-1/2 cups flour with yeast. Heat milk, water, oil, sugar and salt until warm (120°-130°), stirring to blend; add to flour mixture along with eggs and cheese. Beat with an electric mixer or by hand until batter is smooth. Using a spoon, mix in the remaining flour (batter will be stiff). Divide batter and spoon into two well-greased 1-lb. coffee cans. Cover with plastic lids. Let rise in a warm place until batter is about 1/4 to 1/2 in. below plastic lids, about 45-60 minutes. Remove lids and bake at 375° for 30-35 minutes. Cool for 15 minutes in cans before removing. Cool on wire rack. **Yield:** 2 breads. **Diabetic Exchanges:** One serving (1 slice) equals 1 starch, 1 fat; also, 111 calories, 98 mg sodium, 23 mg cholesterol, 13 gm carbohydrate, 3 gm protein, 5 gm fat.

CHEESY ONION BURGER BUNS

Dolores Skrout, Summerhill, Pennsylvania

(PICTURED ON PAGE 251)

5-3/4 to 6-3/4 cups all-purpose
flour, *divided*
3 tablespoons sugar
1-1/2 teaspoons salt
2 packages (1/4 ounce *each*)
active dry yeast
2 tablespoons butter *or*
margarine, softened
2 cups hot water (120°-130°)
1-1/2 cups (6 ounces) shredded
cheddar cheese
1/4 cup minced onion

In a large mixing bowl, combine 2 cups flour, sugar, salt, yeast and butter. Gradually add hot water. With electric mixer, beat 2 minutes at medium speed. Add 1 cup flour and mix on high speed 2 minutes. Stir in cheese, onion and enough of the remaining flour to form a soft dough. Turn out onto a floured surface; knead until smooth and elastic, about 6-8 minutes. Place dough in a greased bowl, turning once to grease top. Cover and let rise in a warm place until doubled, about 1 hour. Punch dough down and turn out onto a lightly floured surface. Divide dough into 20 equal pieces; shape into smooth balls and place on greased baking sheets. Cover and let rise in a warm place until doubled, about 45 minutes. Bake at 400° for 15-20 minutes. Remove from the pans and cool on wire racks. **Yield:** 20 hamburger buns.

CREAMY CHIVE RING

Pamela Schlickbernd, West Point, Nebraska

(PICTURED ON PAGE 251)

1 package (1/4 ounce) active
dry yeast
1/4 cup warm water (110°-115°)
1 cup milk
1/2 cup butter *or* margarine,
divided
1/4 cup instant potato flakes
1/3 cup sugar
1-1/4 teaspoons salt
1 egg, beaten
3-3/4 to 4-1/4 cups all-purpose
flour, *divided*
Sesame *or* poppy seeds
FILLING:
1 egg, beaten
3/4 cup whipping cream
1/3 cup chopped fresh *or* dried
chives
1/2 teaspoon salt

In a small bowl, mix yeast and warm water; set aside. In a saucepan, heat milk, 1/3 cup butter, potato flakes, sugar and salt to 110°-115°. Cool. Stir in yeast mixture and egg. Gradually add enough flour to form a stiff dough. Turn out onto a floured surface. Knead until smooth and elastic, about 6-8 minutes, adding additional flour if necessary. Place dough in greased bowl, turning once to grease top. Cover and let rise in a warm place until doubled, about 1 hour. Meanwhile, place all filling ingredients in the top of a double boiler; cook and stir until thickened. Cool. Punch dough down; divide in half. On a floured surface, roll each half into a 16-in. x 12-in. rectangle. Spread half the filling mixture on the dough. Roll up, jelly-roll style, starting at the narrow end. Seal edges. Place on a greased cookie sheet, seam side down. Shape into a ring and cut 1-in. slices almost through the roll. Lay slices flat. Melt remaining butter and brush ring. Sprinkle with sesame or poppy seeds. Repeat with remaining dough and filling. Cover rings and let rise in a warm place until doubled, about 1 hour. Bake at 350° for 20-25 minutes or until lightly browned. Cool on wire rack. (Rings freeze well.) **Yield:** 2 rings.

NUTTY NEWS: Toasting nuts brings out their flavor and aroma. Spread whole or chopped nuts on a cookie sheet in a single layer and bake at 350° until lightly browned, about 5 minutes. Watch carefully. Remove from oven and use in favorite recipes or as garnish.

REUBEN LOAF

Elizabeth Eissler, Osage City, Kansas

(PICTURED ON PAGE 251)

3-1/4 to 3-3/4 cups all-purpose
    flour, *divided*
1 package (1/4 ounce)
    quick-rise yeast
1 tablespoon sugar
1 tablespoon butter *or*
    margarine, softened
1 teaspoon salt
1 cup warm water (120°-130°)
1/4 cup Thousand Island salad
    dressing
6 ounces thinly sliced corned
    beef
4 ounces sliced Swiss cheese
1 can (8 ounces) sauerkraut,
    drained
1 egg white, beaten
Caraway seeds

In a mixing bowl, combine 2-1/4 cups flour, yeast, sugar, butter and salt. Stir in warm water; mix until a soft dough forms. Add remaining flour if necessary. Turn out onto a lightly floured surface; knead until smooth, about 4 minutes. On a lightly greased baking sheet, roll dough to a 14-in. x 10-in. rectangle. Spread dressing down center 1/3 of dough. Top with layers of beef, cheese and sauerkraut. Make cuts from filling to edges of dough 1 in. apart on both sides of the filling. Alternating sides, fold the strips at an angle across filling. Cover dough and let rise in a warm place for 15 minutes. Brush with egg white and sprinkle with caraway seeds. Bake at 400° for 25 minutes or until lightly browned. Serve immediately; refrigerate leftovers. **Yield:** 6-8 servings.

POPPY SEED ROLL

Eileen Eck, Edna, Kansas

(PICTURED ON PAGE 252)

3/4 cup milk
1/3 cup butter *or* margarine
1/2 cup sugar
3/4 teaspoon salt
3 eggs, *divided*
1/2 teaspoon vanilla extract
1 package (1/4 ounce) active
    dry yeast
1/2 cup warm water (110°-115°)
5 to 6 cups all-purpose flour,
    divided
1 can (12 ounces) poppy seed
    filling
1-1/3 cups chopped walnuts,
    divided
1 teaspoon water
Icing

In a saucepan, heat milk, butter, sugar and salt. Cool to lukewarm. Add 2 beaten eggs and the vanilla extract. Dissolve yeast in warm water. In a large mixing bowl, combine milk mixture, yeast mixture and enough flour to form a soft dough. Turn out onto a floured surface and knead until smooth and elastic, about 6-8 minutes. Place dough in a greased bowl, turning once to grease top. Cover and let rise in a warm place until doubled, about 1 hour. Punch dough down and let rest 5 minutes. Roll dough into a 12-in. x 18-in. rectangle. Spread with poppy seed filling and 1 cup nuts. Starting with the long side, roll up dough and pinch the edges to seal. Place on a large greased baking sheet, seam side down. Curve slightly to form a crescent shape. Cover and let rise in a warm place until doubled, about 30 minutes. Beat remaining egg with 1 teaspoon water; brush over top. Bake at 350° for about 30 minutes. Cool on wire rack. Glaze with confectioners' sugar icing and top with remaining nuts. **Yield:** 1 bread.

ITALIAN PARMESAN BREAD

Frances Poste, Wall, South Dakota

(PICTURED ON PAGE 252)

 This tasty dish uses less sugar, salt and fat. Recipe includes *Diabetic Exchanges*.

1 package (1/4 ounce) active
    dry yeast
1 cup warm water (110°-115°)
3 cups all-purpose flour,
    divided
1/4 cup butter *or* margarine,
    softened
1 egg, beaten
2 tablespoons sugar
1 teaspoon salt
1-1/2 teaspoons dehydrated
    minced onion
1/2 teaspoon Italian seasoning
1/2 teaspoon garlic salt
1/2 cup grated Parmesan cheese,
    divided
Melted butter *or* margarine

In a large mixing bowl, dissolve yeast in warm water. Add 2 cups flour, 1/4 cup butter, egg, sugar, salt and seasonings. Beat at low speed until mixed, about 30 seconds; increase speed to medium and continue beating for 2 minutes. Stir in remaining flour and 1/3 cup cheese; beat until smooth. Cover bowl and let rise in a warm place until doubled, approximately 1 hour. Stir batter 25 strokes. Spread batter into a greased 1-1/2-qt. casserole; brush with melted butter and sprinkle with the remaining cheese. Cover and let rise until doubled, about 30 minutes. Bake at 350° about 35 minutes or until golden brown. Cool on wire rack 10 minutes before removing from the casserole. **Yield:** 1 loaf. **Diabetic Exchanges:** One serving (1 slice) equals 1 starch, 1/2 fat; also, 97 calories, 216 mg sodium, 21 mg cholesterol, 13 gm carbohydrate, 3 gm protein, 3 gm fat.

OATMEAL ROLLS

Jeanette Fuehring, Concordia, Missouri

(PICTURED ON PAGE 252)

2-1/3 cups water, *divided*
1 cup dry oatmeal
3 tablespoons butter *or*
    margarine
2 packages (1/4 ounce *each*)
    active dry yeast
2/3 cup packed brown sugar
1 tablespoon sugar
1-1/2 teaspoons salt
5 to 5-3/4 cups all-purpose
    flour, *divided*

In a saucepan, bring 2 cups water to a boil. Add oatmeal and butter; simmer 1 minute. Remove to a large mixing bowl and let cool to 120°-130°. Heat the remaining water to 120°-130°; add yeast. To the oatmeal mixture, add brown and white sugars, salt, yeast mixture and half of the flour. Mix well. Add enough remaining flour to make a soft dough. Turn out onto a floured board; knead 6-8 minutes or until smooth and elastic. Add additional flour if necessary. Place dough in a greased bowl, turning once to grease top. Cover and let rise until doubled, about 1 hour. Punch dough down; divide in half and shape each half into 12 balls. Place 1 in. apart on two greased 13-in. x 9-in. baking pans. Cover and let rise until doubled, about 45-60 minutes. Bake at 350° for 20-30 minutes. **Yield:** 24 rolls.

CHILLING BEVERAGES: To chill soda and other beverages for a large party, put bottles and cans in your washing machine, then cover with ice and cold water. When the party's over, spin out the water…no mess to clean!

• When making extra ice cubes, put them in a heavy paper bag. The paper is a better insulator than plastic, so cubes won't stick together in the freezer.

🌿🌿🌿🌿🌿🌿🌿🌿🌿🌿🌿🌿🌿🌿🌿🌿

CANDY CANE COFFEE CAKE

Kelley Winship, West Rutland, Vermont

(PICTURED ON PAGE 252)

- 2 cups (16 ounces) sour cream
- 2 packages (1/4 ounce *each*) active dry yeast
- 1/2 cup warm water (110°-115°)
- 1/4 cup butter *or* margarine, softened
- 1/3 cup sugar
- 2 teaspoons salt
- 2 eggs, beaten
- 5-1/4 to 6 cups all-purpose flour, *divided*
- 1-1/2 cups (12 ounces) finely chopped dried apricots
- 1-1/2 cups finely chopped maraschino cherries

Melted butter

ICING:
- 2 cups confectioners' sugar
- 2 to 3 tablespoons water

In a saucepan, heat sour cream until lukewarm. Set aside. Dissolve yeast in warm water. In a large mixing bowl, add yeast mixture, sour cream, butter, sugar, salt, eggs and 2 cups flour. With an electric mixer, beat until smooth. Stir in just enough of the remaining flour to form a soft dough. Turn out onto a floured surface and knead until smooth and elastic. Place in a greased bowl, turning once to grease top. Cover and let rise in a warm place until doubled, about 1 hour. Punch dough down; divide into 3 equal parts. On a lightly floured board, roll each part into a 15-in. x 6-in. rectangle. Place on greased baking sheets. With scissors, make 2-in. cuts at 1/2-in. intervals on the long sides of rectangle. Combine apricots and cherries; spread 1/3 of the mixture down the center of each rectangle. Crisscross strips over filling. Stretch dough to 22 in. Curve to form cane. Let rise until doubled, about 45 minutes. Bake at 375° for 15-20 minutes. While warm, brush canes with butter. Combine icing ingredients and drizzle over cakes. **Yield:** 3 coffee cakes.

🌿🌿🌿🌿🌿🌿🌿🌿🌿🌿🌿🌿🌿🌿🌿🌿

CHOCOLATE ANGEL FOOD CAKE

Mary Ann Iverson, Woodville, Wisconsin

(PICTURED ON PAGE 254)

- 3/4 cup sifted cake flour
- 1-1/2 cups plus 2 tablespoons sugar, *divided*
- 1/4 cup unsweetened cocoa
- 1-1/2 cups egg whites, room temperature
- 1-1/2 teaspoons cream of tartar
- 1/4 teaspoon salt
- 1-1/2 teaspoons vanilla extract

CHOCOLATE FLUFF FROSTING:
- 2 cups whipping cream
- 1 cup sifted confectioners' sugar
- 1/2 cup unsweetened cocoa

Dash salt

Sift together flour, 3/4 cup plus 2 tablespoons sugar and cocoa three times. Set aside. In a large mixing bowl, beat egg whites, cream of tartar, salt and vanilla until foamy. Add remaining sugar, 2 tablespoons at a time, beating about 10 seconds after each addition. Continue beating until mixture holds stiff peaks. With a rubber scraper, fold in flour mixture, 3 tablespoons at a time. Mixture will be thick. Spread into a 10-in. angel food pan. Cut through batter with a knife to remove air pockets. Bake at 350° for 40-45 minutes or until the top of cake springs when lightly touched. Immediately invert cake in pan; cool. Run a knife around sides of cake and remove. For frosting, combine all ingredients in a chilled bowl. Beat until thick enough to spread. Frost entire cake. Chill until ready to serve. **Yield:** 12 servings.

🌿🌿🌿🌿🌿🌿🌿🌿🌿🌿🌿🌿🌿🌿🌿🌿

CHOCOLATE SHORTBREAD

Katherine Both,
Rocky Mountain House, Alberta

(PICTURED ON PAGE 254)

- 1 cup butter *or* margarine
- 1/3 cup unsweetened cocoa
- 2/3 cup confectioners' sugar

Dash salt
- 1-1/2 cups all-purpose flour

In a large mixing bowl, cream butter until light and fluffy. Blend in remaining ingredients. Chill 1 hour. Drop by rounded teaspoonfuls 2 in. apart on greased cookie sheets. Bake at 300° for about 20 minutes or until the cookies are set. **Yield:** about 4 dozen.

🌿🌿🌿🌿🌿🌿🌿🌿🌿🌿🌿🌿🌿🌿🌿🌿

CHOCOLATE POUND CAKE

Ann Perry, Sierra Vista, Arizona

(PICTURED ON PAGE 254)

- 8 milk chocolate bars without nuts (1.55 ounces *each*)
- 2 tablespoons water
- 1/2 cup butter *or* margarine
- 2 cups sugar
- 4 eggs
- 2 teaspoons vanilla extract
- 2-1/2 cups sifted cake flour
- 1/2 teaspoon salt
- 1/4 teaspoon baking soda
- 1 cup buttermilk
- 1/2 cup chopped pecans, optional

Confectioners' sugar, optional

In a saucepan, melt chocolate with water over low heat. Mixture will begin to harden. Cream butter and sugar. Add eggs, one at a time, beating well after each addition. Blend in the vanilla and chocolate mixture. Stir together flour, salt and soda; add alternately with buttermilk to batter. Fold in nuts, if desired. Pour into a greased and floured 10-in. tube pan or fluted tube pan. Bake at 325° for about 1-1/2 hours or until cake tests done when a wooden pick inserted in the center comes out clean. Allow cake to stand 10 minutes before removing from pan. Cool on wire rack. Sprinkle with confectioners' sugar, if desired. **Yield:** 12 servings.

🌿🌿🌿🌿🌿🌿🌿🌿🌿🌿🌿🌿🌿🌿🌿🌿

WHITE CHOCOLATE FUDGE

Jan Lutz, Stevens Point, Wisconsin

(PICTURED ON PAGE 255)

- 1 package (8 ounces) cream cheese, softened
- 4 cups confectioners' sugar
- 1-1/2 teaspoons vanilla extract
- 12 ounces white chocolate
- 3/4 cup chopped pecans

In a mixing bowl, beat cream cheese, sugar and vanilla until smooth. In a double boiler, melt chocolate. Fold into cream cheese mixture with pecans. Spread into a greased 8-in. baking pan. Chill until ready to serve. Cut into squares. **Yield:** about 48 pieces.

🌿🌿🌿🌿🌿🌿🌿🌿🌿🌿🌿🌿🌿🌿🌿🌿

MILKY WAY ICE CREAM

Jo Groth, Plainfield, Iowa

(PICTURED ON PAGE 255)

- 16 ounces Milky Way candy bars
- 1 quart whipping cream, *divided*
- 4 eggs
- 1-1/2 quarts milk
- 1 package (3.4 ounces) instant vanilla pudding mix

1 package (3.9 ounces) instant chocolate fudge pudding mix

In a double boiler, melt candy bars with half the cream. Beat eggs in remaining cream. Whisk into melted chocolate. Cook and stir for 5 minutes. Cool. Beat milk and pudding mixes. Fold into chocolate mixture. Chill several hours or overnight. Freeze in an ice cream freezer according to manufacturer's instructions. **Yield:** about 3 quarts.

🍫🍫🍫🍫🍫🍫🍫🍫🍫🍫🍫🍫🍫🍫🍫

CHOCOLATE CINNAMON DOUGHNUTS

Judi Eaker, Chaffee, Missouri

(PICTURED ON PAGE 255)

2 eggs, beaten
1-1/4 cups sugar
1/4 cup vegetable oil
1 teaspoon vanilla extract
4 cups all-purpose flour
1/3 cup unsweetened cocoa
4 teaspoons baking powder
1 teaspoon ground cinnamon
3/4 teaspoon salt
1/4 teaspoon baking soda
3/4 cup buttermilk
Oil *or* shortening for deep-fat frying
GLAZE:
4 cups sifted confectioners' sugar
1 teaspoon vanilla extract
1/2 teaspoon ground cinnamon
6 tablespoons milk

In a mixing bowl, beat eggs. Add sugar and beat until mixture is thick and lemon-colored. Stir in oil and vanilla. In another bowl, combine flour, cocoa, baking powder, cinnamon, salt and soda. Stir into egg mixture alternately with buttermilk. Chill. Divide dough in half and put half in the refrigerator. On a lightly floured board, roll to 1/2-in. thickness. Cut with a 2-1/2-in. floured doughnut cutter. Repeat with remaining dough. Deep-fry in fat heated to 375° for 3 minutes, turning once. Place on paper towels. Combine glaze ingredients and dip tops of warm doughnuts. **Yield:** 2 dozen.

🍫🍫🍫🍫🍫🍫🍫🍫🍫🍫🍫🍫🍫🍫🍫

OLD-FASHIONED CHOCOLATE PUDDING

Amber Sampson, Somonauk, Illinois

(PICTURED ON PAGE 255)

2 cups milk
2 tablespoons butter *or* margarine

2 squares (1 ounce *each*) unsweetened chocolate
2/3 cup sugar
1/3 cup all-purpose flour
1/4 teaspoon salt
2 egg yolks, beaten
1/2 teaspoon vanilla extract
Whipped cream, optional

In the top of a double boiler, heat milk, butter and chocolate until the chocolate melts. Chocolate may appear curdled. Combine sugar, flour and salt. Sprinkle over chocolate mixture. *Do not stir.* Cover the mixture and cook on medium-low for 20 minutes. With a spoon, beat mixture until smooth. Quickly add egg yolks; beat well. Cook 2 additional minutes. Remove from the heat and stir in vanilla. Pour into dessert glasses. Serve with whipped cream, if desired. **Yield:** 4 servings.

🍫🍫🍫🍫🍫🍫🍫🍫🍫🍫🍫🍫🍫🍫🍫

HOMEMADE FUDGE SAUCE

Trudy DeFelice, Columbia, South Carolina

(PICTURED ON PAGE 255)

1-1/4 cups sugar
1 cup unsweetened cocoa
1/2 teaspoon ground cinnamon
1 cup whipping cream
1/2 cup milk
1/2 cup unsalted butter, cut into 8 pieces
2 teaspoons vanilla extract

In a heavy saucepan, stir together sugar, cocoa and cinnamon. Add cream and milk; mix well. Over medium heat, bring to a boil, stirring constantly. Cook 2 minutes. Remove from the heat; cool 15 minutes. Add butter and stir until melted. Stir in vanilla. Cool to room temperature. Store, covered, in the refrigerator. Stir before serving. **Yield:** 3 cups.

🍫🍫🍫🍫🍫🍫🍫🍫🍫🍫🍫🍫🍫🍫🍫

EASY MICROWAVE CARAMELS

Darleen Worm, Fond du Lac, Wisconsin

(PICTURED ON PAGE 256)

1 cup sweet butter
2-1/3 cups (1 pound) brown sugar, firmly packed
1 cup light corn syrup
1 can (14 ounces) sweetened condensed milk
1/8 teaspoon salt
1 teaspoon vanilla
1/2 cup chopped walnuts, optional

In 2-qt. microwave-safe pitcher, combine butter, sugar, corn syrup, milk and salt. Microwave on high (100% power) 3 to 4 minutes, stirring once after about 2 minutes. When butter is melted, stir well. Attach *microwave* candy thermometer. Microwave on high about 14 minutes or until mixture reaches 245° (firm-ball stage). No stirring is needed. Remove from microwave; stir in vanilla and if desired, walnuts. Allow to stand for 10 minutes, stirring well several times. Pour into buttered 13-in. x 9-in. x 2-in. pan (smaller 11-in. x 7-in. x 1-1/2-in. pan yields thicker candy as shown in photo). Refrigerate until cool. Invert pan. Carefully tap out whole block of candy; cut in squares. Wrap in waxed paper and store in refrigerator. (Can also freeze.) **Yield:** about 2-3/4 pounds.

🍫🍫🍫🍫🍫🍫🍫🍫🍫🍫🍫🍫🍫🍫🍫

AUNT ROSE'S FANTASTIC BUTTER TOFFEE

Rosie Kimberlin, Los Angeles, California

(PICTURED ON PAGE 256)

2 cups whole unblanched almonds (about 10 ounces), *divided*
11 ounces milk chocolate, *divided*
2 sticks sweet butter
1 cup sugar
3 tablespoons cold water

Spread almonds in a pan and toast in 350° oven for about 10 minutes, shaking pan occasionally. Cool nuts. Grind milk chocolate fine in food processor—*do not overprocess.* Set aside. Chop nuts coarse in food processor. Sprinkle *1 cup* nuts over bottom of greased 15-in. x 10-in. x 1-in. jelly roll pan. Sprinkle *1 cup* ground chocolate over nuts. Set aside. In heavy saucepan, combine butter, sugar and water; cook over medium heat, stirring occasionally until the mixture reaches 290° (soft-crack stage). *Very quickly* pour mixture over nuts and chocolate. Sprinkle remaining chocolate over toffee; top with remaining nuts. Chill and break into pieces. **Yield:** about 2 pounds.

SHORT 'N' SWEET: Decorate shortbread cookies by dipping one end into melted chocolate.

CANDY HINTS: Insert the candy thermometer when mixture boils, not before.
● Don't double candy recipes, as this changes the cooking time.
● Stir and beat with a wooden spoon for safety and comfort.

MOUNDS BALLS

Kathy Dorman Snover, Michigan

(PICTURED ON PAGE 256)

1/2 pound sweet butter
1 pound confectioners' sugar
1 pound flaked coconut
1/2 can (7 ounces) sweetened
   condensed milk or 1/2 cup
1 cup chopped walnuts
1 teaspoon vanilla
CHOCOLATE COATING:
   1 package (12 ounces)
      semisweet chocolate chips
   4 ounces unsweetened
      chocolate squares
2-inch x 1-inch x 1/2-inch piece
   paraffin wax
Round wood toothpicks
Styrofoam sheets

In mixing bowl, cream together butter and sugar. Add coconut, milk, walnuts and vanilla; stir until blended. Chill until slightly firm; roll into walnut-size balls. Insert a toothpick in each ball. Place balls on cookie sheets; freeze. In double boiler over simmering water, melt chocolate chips, chocolate squares and paraffin wax. Keep warm over hot water. Using toothpicks as handles, dip frozen balls into chocolate mixture; stick toothpicks upright into waxed paper-covered Styrofoam sheet. Chill until firm. Remove toothpicks and package candy in individual paper liners. (May also be frozen.) **Yield:** about 7 dozen candies.

MACADAMIA NUT FUDGE

Vicki Fioranelli, Cleveland, Mississippi

(PICTURED ON PAGE 256)

3 cups crushed macadamia
   nuts or toasted pecans,
   divided
4-1/2 cups sugar
1/2 cup sweet butter
   1 can (12 or 13 ounces)
      evaporated milk
   1 box (12 ounces) German
      sweet chocolate squares,
      chopped
   1 package (12 ounces)
      semisweet chocolate chips
   1 jar (7 ounces) marshmallow
      creme
   1 teaspoon salt (omit if using
      salted nuts)
   2 teaspoons vanilla

Crush macadamia nuts/pecans by placing in a plastic bag and pounding with mallet. Set aside. Grease two 9-in.-square pans or line with waxed paper.

Combine sugar, butter and milk in heavy pan; bring to a gentle boil. Cook for 5 minutes, stirring constantly. Remove from heat; add remaining ingredients *except* 1 cup nuts. Pour fudge into prepared pans; sprinkle remaining nuts over top and press in lightly. Chill until firm; cut in squares. **Yield:** about 5 pounds.

SWEDISH RICE RING

Lori Jeane Schlecht, Wimbledon, North Dakota

(PICTURED ON PAGE 258)

2 envelopes unflavored gelatin
1/4 cup cold water
1/2 cup uncooked long-grain rice
3 cups milk
1/2 cup sugar
1/2 teaspoon salt
   1 cup whipping cream
Fresh or frozen sweetened
   strawberries

Soften gelatin in water; set aside. In heavy 2-qt. saucepan, bring rice, milk, sugar and salt to a boil, stirring occasionally. Reduce heat and cover; cook over low heat until rice is tender, about 15-20 minutes. Remove from heat; add gelatin, stirring until dissolved. Cover; chill until partially set. In chilled bowl, whip cream until stiff; fold into chilled rice mixture. Spoon into 6-cup decorative or ring mold. Cover and chill until set, about 3 hours. To unmold, loosen edges with spatula and invert on serving platter. Serve with sweetened strawberries. **Yield:** 10-12 servings.

GERMAN CHOCOLATE CAKE

Joyce Platfoot, Botkins, Ohio

(PICTURED ON PAGE 258)

1/2 cup water
   1 bar (4 ounces) sweet cooking
      chocolate
   2 cups sugar
   1 cup butter or margarine,
      softened
   4 eggs, separated
   1 teaspoon vanilla extract
2-1/2 cups cake flour
   1 teaspoon baking soda
1/2 teaspoon salt
   1 cup buttermilk
FROSTING:
   1 cup sugar
   1 cup evaporated milk
1/2 cup butter or margarine
   3 egg yolks, beaten
1-1/3 cups flaked coconut

1 cup chopped pecans
1 teaspoon vanilla extract
ICING:
   1/2 teaspoon shortening
   1 square (1 ounce) semisweet
      chocolate

For cake, heat the water and chocolate in heavy saucepan until melted; cool. In large mixing bowl, beat sugar and butter until light and fluffy. Beat in 4 egg yolks one at a time. Blend in melted chocolate and vanilla. Combine flour, baking soda and salt. Add alternately with buttermilk to butter/chocolate mixture. Beat until batter is smooth. In separate bowl, whip 4 egg whites until stiff; fold into batter. Pour batter into three 9-in. cake pans lined with waxed paper. Bake at 350° for 30 minutes or until the cake springs back when pressed lightly in center. Cool 15 minutes. Remove cake from pans; cool on wire racks. For frosting, mix sugar, milk, butter and egg yolks in 1-qt. saucepan. Heat, stirring constantly, until thickened. Remove from heat. Stir in coconut, pecans and vanilla. Cool until thick enough to spread. Spread frosting over tops of each cake layer. For icing, melt in saucepan the shortening and chocolate. While warm, drizzle icing down sides of cake. **Yield:** 10-12 servings.

APRICOT BARS

Jill Moritz, Irvine, California

(PICTURED ON PAGE 258)

3/4 cup butter or margarine
1 cup sugar
1 egg
2 cups all-purpose flour
1/4 teaspoon baking powder
1-1/3 cups shredded coconut
1/2 cup chopped walnuts
1/2 teaspoon vanilla extract
1 jar (12 ounces) apricot
   preserves

In a large mixing bowl, cream butter and sugar. Add egg; mix well. In separate bowl, combine flour and baking powder. Gradually add to butter/sugar mixture. Add coconut, walnuts and vanilla; mix thoroughly. Press two-thirds of dough into a greased 13-in. x 9-in. x 2-in. baking pan. Spread with preserves; crumble remaining dough over preserves. Bake at 350° for 30-35 minutes or until golden brown. Cool in pan on wire rack. Cut into squares. **Yield:** 36 bars.

CHOCOLATE FIX: Keep some cocoa powder and chocolate-flavored sprinkles or syrup on hand for garnishes.

TASSIES

Joy Corie, Ruston, Louisiana

(PICTURED ON PAGE 258)

PASTRY:
- 1 package (3 ounces) cream cheese, softened
- 1/2 cup butter *or* margarine
- 1 cup all-purpose flour

FILLING:
- 3/4 cup packed brown sugar
- 1 tablespoon butter *or* margarine, softened
- 1 egg
- 1 teaspoon vanilla extract

Dash salt
- 2/3 cup finely chopped pecans, *divided*

Maraschino cherries, optional

For pastry, blend cream cheese and butter until smooth; stir in flour. Chill about 1 hour. Shape into 24 1-in. balls. Place in ungreased miniature muffin tins or small cookie tarts; press the dough against bottom and sides to form a shell. Set aside. In bowl, beat brown sugar, butter and egg until combined. Add vanilla, salt and half the pecans; spoon into pastry. Top with remaining pecans. Bake at 375° for 20 minutes, or until filling is set and pastry is light golden brown. Cool and remove from pans. Decorate with maraschino cherry halves, if desired. **Yield:** 24 tarts.

CHOCOLATE MALT SHOPPE PIE

Beth Wanek, Little Chute, Wisconsin

- 1-1/2 cups chocolate cookie crumbs
- 1/4 cup butter *or* margarine, melted
- 1 pint vanilla ice cream, softened
- 1/2 cup crushed malted milk balls
- 2 tablespoons milk, *divided*
- 3 tablespoons instant chocolate malted milk powder
- 3 tablespoons marshmallow creme topping
- 1 cup whipping cream

Additional whipped cream
Additional malted milk balls

Combine crumbs and butter. Press into a 9-in. pie pan. Freeze while preparing filling. In a mixing bowl, blend the ice cream, crushed malted milk balls and 1 tablespoon milk. Spoon into crust. Freeze for 1 hour. Meanwhile, blend malted milk powder, marshmallow creme and the remaining milk. Stir in whipping cream; whip until soft peaks form. Spread over ice cream layer. Freeze several hours or overnight. Before serving, garnish with whipped cream and malted milk balls. **Yield:** 6-8 servings.

WHITE CHOCOLATE COOKIES

Shana Bounds, Magee, Mississippi

- 1/2 cup butter *or* margarine
- 1/2 cup shortening
- 3/4 cup sugar
- 1/2 cup packed brown sugar
- 1 egg
- 1-3/4 cups all-purpose flour
- 1 teaspoon baking soda
- 1/2 teaspoon salt
- 2 teaspoons vanilla extract
- 10 ounces white chocolate, coarsely chopped
- 1/2 cup coarsely chopped macadamia nuts, lightly toasted

In a large mixing bowl, cream butter and shortening. Gradually add sugars, beating until light and fluffy. Add egg; mix well. Combine flour, soda and salt; add to creamed mixture. Blend in vanilla. Stir in chocolate and nuts. Cover and chill dough for 1 hour. Drop by heaping tablespoonfuls about 3 in. apart on ungreased cookie sheets. Bake at 350° for 12-14 minutes or until lightly browned. Let stand a few minutes before removing cookies to a wire rack to cool. **Yield:** about 2-1/2 dozen.

MICROWAVE LECHE QUEMADA

Mildred Kneupper, New Braunfels, Texas

- 2 cups pecans (small *or* broken pieces)
- 1/2 cup sweet butter
- 2/3 cup brown sugar, firmly packed
- 1 can (14 ounces) sweetened condensed milk
- 1 teaspoon vanilla

Place pecans on large glass plate and microwave on high (100% power) for 8 minutes, stirring at 2-minute intervals. Set aside. In 8-cup measure, microwave butter on high for 1 minute. Stir in brown sugar and milk until blended. Microwave on high for 7 minutes, stirring at 2-minute intervals. Beat with wooden spoon until stiff, about 5 minutes. Stir in vanilla and roasted pecans. Spread in lightly buttered 8-in.-square glass dish; chill until firm. Cut into squares. **Yield:** 1-1/2 pounds.

CANDIED CITRUS PEELS

Mary Malinowski, Lee Center, New York

- 2 cups fresh orange, grapefruit *or* lemon peels (about 4 oranges)

Cold water

SYRUP:
- 1 cup sugar
- 1/2 cup water

Confectioners' sugar

CHOCOLATE COATING:
- 8 ounces semisweet chocolate chips
- 4 ounces unsweetened chocolate

2-inch x 1-inch x 1/2-inch piece of paraffin wax

Using a metal zester or similar tool, cut peels from fruits in 1/4-in.-wide strips 3 in. long. Place peels in heavy saucepan; cover with cold water. Bring slowly to boiling; reduce heat and simmer 10 minutes. Drain; repeat boiling process 3-5 times, draining well each time. (This cooks the peels and eliminates bitterness of membrane.) In separate saucepan, combine sugar (not confectioners' sugar) and water; cook till clear. Add peels; boil gently until all syrup is absorbed and peels are transparent. Roll peels in confectioners' sugar; place on cooling rack to dry. Combine chocolate coating ingredients in top of double boiler; melt together over simmering water until smooth. Dip half of each peel in chocolate; cool on rack sprayed with non-stick vegetable spray. Store, covered, in refrigerator. **Yield:** about 3 cups.

QUICK TURTLES

Fern Lockwood, Daytona Beach, Florida

- 1-1/2 cups pecan halves
- 1 package (14 ounces) vanilla caramels
- 5 bars milk chocolate (1-1/2 ounces *each*), broken into squares

Arrange pecans in clusters of 3 or 4 halves 2 in. apart on a greased baking sheet. Top each cluster with one caramel, slightly flattened. Bake at 300° for 7 minutes or until caramels soften. Remove to waxed paper. Flatten caramels with spatula; top each candy with 1 milk chocolate bar square while still warm. Spread chocolate when melted. Refrigerate a few minutes until chocolate hardens. **Yield:** 4 dozen turtles.

BUTTER RINGS

Florence McBride, Harvard, Illinois

1 package (1/4 ounce) active
   dry yeast
3 tablespoons sugar, *divided*
1/4 cup warm milk (110°-115°)
4 cups all-purpose flour
1 teaspoon salt
1/2 cup butter *or* margarine
3 egg yolks
1 cup light cream, heated to
   lukewarm
Chopped nuts for garnish
ICING:
1 cup confectioners' sugar
1 tablespoon milk
1/4 teaspoon vanilla extract

Dissolve yeast and 2 teaspoons sugar in milk; set aside. Combine flour, salt and remaining sugar. Cut in butter as for pie crust. Beat the egg yolks into the cream; add to the flour mixture along with the yeast mixture. Blend well and form into a ball. Place dough in a greased bowl; cover and refrigerate overnight. Punch dough down; place on a lightly floured board and divide into six balls. Using hands, roll each ball into a 24-in. rope. On a greased cookie sheet, twist two ropes together, then shape into a 6- to 8-in. ring. Pinch ends together and sprinkle with nuts. Repeat with remaining two rings. Cover and allow to rise until almost doubled, about 30-45 minutes. Bake at 350° for about 25 minutes or until golden brown. Place on wire racks. Combine icing ingredients; drizzle over warm rings. **Yield:** 3 coffee cakes.

GERMAN MEATBALLS

Evelyn Kay, Banning, California

1 pound lean ground beef
1 egg, beaten
3/4 cup soft bread crumbs
1-3/4 cups water, *divided*
1/4 cup chopped onion
1/2 teaspoon salt
Dash pepper
2 beef bouillon cubes
1/3 cup packed brown sugar
1/4 cup raisins
2-1/2 teaspoons lemon juice
1/2 cup coarsely ground
   gingersnaps
Cooked noodles

Combine beef, egg, bread crumbs, 1/4 cup water, onion, salt and pepper. Shape into 1-1/2-in. balls. Set aside. In a large skillet, bring remaining water to a boil. Add bouillon, sugar, raisins, lemon juice and gingersnaps. Stir until thoroughly combined. Add meatballs to skillet. Simmer, uncovered, about 20 minutes or until meat is no longer pink. Stir occasionally. Serve with noodles. **Yield:** 4 servings. *If Cooking for Two:* Freeze half the recipe to enjoy another time.

BEST BEETS

Lucille Terry, Frankfort, Kentucky

3/4 cup sugar
2 teaspoons cornstarch
1/3 cup vinegar
1/3 cup water *or* beet liquid
1 teaspoon dry mustard
1 teaspoon onion powder
4 cups cooked sliced beets
3 tablespoons butter *or*
   margarine
1/4 teaspoon salt
Dash white pepper

In saucepan, combine the sugar and cornstarch. Add vinegar and water/beet juice; bring to a boil. Add all remaining ingredients; reduce heat to simmer. Heat through. **Yield:** 6-8 servings.

CRUNCHY-TOP HAM & POTATO CASSEROLE

Nancy Schmidt, Delhi, California

CASSEROLE:
2 pounds Southern-style
   frozen hash brown potatoes,
   thawed
1 can (10-3/4 ounces) cream
   of chicken soup, undiluted
1/2 cup butter, melted
2 cups (16 ounces) sour cream
2 cups cubed cooked ham
1/2 teaspoon ground pepper
1/3 cup chopped green onion
1-1/2 cups (6 ounces) shredded
   cheddar cheese
TOPPING:
2 cups crushed cornflakes
1/4 cup butter, melted

Combine all casserole ingredients and mix well. Place in 13-in. x 9-in. x 2-in. baking dish. Combine topping ingredients; sprinkle on casserole. Bake at 350° for 1 hour. **Yield:** 10 servings.

NEW ENGLAND APPLESAUCE

Marilyn Tarr, Palos Heights, Illinois

4 pounds Rome Beauty *or*
   McIntosh apples
1 cup honey
1 cup water
1/2 cup lemon juice
1 teaspoon grated lemon peel
1/4 teaspoon cinnamon
2 tablespoons grenadine,
   optional

Peel, core and cut apples in wedges. In a large kettle, combine all ingredients except grenadine; bring to a boil. Reduce heat and simmer 20-25 minutes or until apples are fork-tender. Mash apples to a chunky texture or process with food mill for smooth sauce. Stir in grenadine, if desired. **Yield:** 2 quarts.

MICROWAVE PEANUT BRITTLE

Sue Moore, Hartwell, Georgia

1 cup raw peanuts
1 cup sugar
1/2 cup white corn syrup
1/8 teaspoon salt
1 teaspoon butter
1 teaspoon vanilla
1 teaspoon baking soda

In a 1-1/2-qt. casserole, stir together peanuts, sugar, corn syrup and salt. Microwave on high (100% power) for 4 minutes; stir well and microwave for 4 minutes more. Stir in the butter and vanilla. Microwave 2 minutes longer. Add baking soda and quickly stir until light and foamy. *Immediately* pour onto lightly greased cookie sheet, spreading out thin. Cool; break into small pieces. Store in airtight container. **Yield:** about 1 pound.

GIFT GIVING: Empty Christmas card boxes make nice personal-size candy containers. For make-ahead gifts, cover the boxes in foil, fill with chunks of candy like Rocky Road or peanut brittle, then stack boxes in a heavy plastic bag and freeze. Later, thaw and add a festive red bow.

• Shop rummage sales throughout the year for pretty dishes and cute tins or trays for candy-giving. At holidays or special occasions, fill with homemade goodies, cover with plastic wrap and say, "Keep the dish!"

MEALS IN MINUTES

Time flies for Terry Fulchen, a travel agent in Marco Island, Florida. Booking flights 5 days a week keeps Terry too busy for complicated cooking. That's why she really appreciates tasty, nutritious—but speedy—meals which can be prepared in 30 minutes or less.

"I'm cooking more with turkey lately," Terry relates. "With just my husband and me at home, I don't often buy a whole bird. But these days there are so many different cuts of turkey that can be prepared in so many ways! Turkey's economical, too—there's no waste."

Terry begins her fast menu by mixing her quick-to-bake cranberry cake, made from a prepared biscuit mix. "It bakes while we eat the main course."

Next, Terry prepares the turkey meatballs. "I get all the other ingredients for the stir-fry organized at this point. That makes everything go quickly once I begin cooking."

While she browns the meatballs, Terry heats water to cook the pasta. "My husband likes almost any kind of pasta, so I vary it from time to time," she notes.

A quick, colorful salad rounds out the meal. "I keep all my salad greens washed and crisped in my refrigerator to speed up the process of salad making."

🍂🍂🍂🍂🍂🍂🍂🍂🍂🍂🍂
TURKEY MEATBALLS TETRAZZINI

- 1 slice whole wheat bread
- 3/4 pound uncooked ground turkey
- 1 clove garlic, pressed
- 1/2 teaspoon dried basil leaves
- 1/2 teaspoon salt
- Pepper to taste
- 1 teaspoon butter
- 1 onion, peeled and sliced
- 1/4 pound fresh mushrooms, cleaned and quartered
- 2 tablespoons all-purpose flour
- 1-1/2 cups milk
- 1/4 cup Parmesan cheese
- Angel hair pasta *or* other favorite pasta (cooked according to package directions)
- Chopped fresh parsley
- Additional Parmesan cheese, optional

Crumble the bread into a medium bowl. Blend in ground turkey, garlic, basil, salt and pepper. Form turkey mixture into 1-in. meatballs. Melt butter in large skillet. Saute meatballs on all sides, loosening them carefully before turning. Stir in onion and mushrooms; saute until golden. Whisk flour into milk, whipping until smooth; add to skillet. Cook, stirring constantly, until thickened. Fold in the cheese. Place cooked, drained pasta on serving plate. Spoon tetrazzini into center. Sprinkle with parsley and if desired, additional cheese. **Yield:** 4 servings.

🍂🍂🍂🍂🍂🍂🍂🍂🍂🍂🍂
CAULIFLOWER/PEPPER SALAD

- 1 head Boston lettuce, washed and crisped
- 1 small head cauliflower
- 1 green *or* red pepper
- 1/3 cup commercial oil and vinegar dressing

Line a salad bowl with lettuce. Wash cauliflower and green/red pepper. Cut cauliflower into 1/4-in. slices. Remove seeds from pepper and cut into slices. Place cauliflower and pepper in center of lettuce. Pour 1/3 cup dressing over entire salad. Serve immediately. **Yield:** 4 servings.

🍂🍂🍂🍂🍂🍂🍂🍂🍂🍂🍂🍂
FRESH CRANBERRY CAKE

- 1 cup fresh cranberries
- 1-1/2 cups biscuit mix
- 1/4 cup plus 2 tablespoons sugar, *divided*
- 1 egg, slightly beaten
- 1/3 cup milk
- Vanilla ice cream, optional

Wash and drain cranberries; remove any stems. Set aside. In medium bowl, combine biscuit mix, 1/4 cup sugar, egg and milk until just blended. Spoon into a greased and floured 8-in. round or star-shaped pan. Toss cranberries with 2 tablespoons sugar; spoon evenly over cake batter. Bake at 375° for 20-30 minutes or until golden brown and firm when gently pressed. Cool cake on rack. Remove from pan and cut into wedges. Serve with a scoop of vanilla ice cream, if desired. **Yield:** 6-8 servings.

Here's fancy, festive food that's fit for a season of entertainment and feasting! Press your prettiest tablecloth, polish your silver and celebrate in style with the taste treats pictured here.

Choose from an array of appetizers and desserts, some "fussy" to fix, others fast and easy. No matter which recipe you choose, there's one thing you'll find—every one is delicious!

FANCY FARE! Clockwise from lower left—**Hot Cheddar Stuffed Mushrooms** (Pg. 275); **Pineapple Fruit Plate with Dip** (Pg. 275); **Shrimp Appetizer Platter** (Pg. 275); **Southwest Cheesecake** (Pg. 276); **Mother Ertelt's Meatballs** (Pg. 275); **Stuffed Phyllo Pastries** (Pg. 276); **Salmon Pate** (Pg. 276); **Fudge Swirl Toffee Pie** (Pg. 275).

Enjoy entertaining your friends with party foods from A to D —from appealing appetizers to delicious desserts, that is!

These favorites set a fancy, festive mood from the moment guests set eyes on them. The appealing swirl of the Tortilla Pinwheels... the medley of colors in the Bread Pot Fondue...the smooth white shape of the Russian Creme and the rich look of the Chocolate/Whipping Cream Torte make any holiday buffet table look extra special.

Try one or more at your next get-together...and savor the season!

FESTIVE FAVORITES! Clockwise from top—**Chocolate/Whipping Cream Torte** (Pg. 276); **Appetizer Tortilla Pinwheels** (Pg. 277); **Russian Creme** (Pg. 277); **Bread Pot Fondue** (Pg. 277).

BEST COOK

Fancheon Resler
Goshen, Indiana

Prize-winning baked goods are a delicious specialty of Fancheon Resler, a high school English teacher from Goshen, Indiana.

Outside of school, she's found time to enter—and win—many competitions, including the Indiana Archway Cookie Contest at the State Fair. But more than that, her thoughtfulness makes her the "Best Cook in the Country", according to her good friend Patricia Franke of Wolcottville, Indiana.

Patricia writes, "Fancheon is a dynamic, thoughtful woman...well-known for giving away hundreds of food items each year—for birthdays, Christmas, get-well remembrances, funeral meals...and sometimes just to brighten someone else's day."

APRICOT RING-A-LINGS

DOUGH:
- 2 packages active dry yeast
- 1/2 cup warm water
- 1/3 cup sugar
- 1/3 cup softened butter
- 2 teaspoons salt
- 2/3 cup scalded milk
- 2 unbeaten eggs
- 4-1/2 to 5 cups all-purpose flour

FILLING:
- 1 cup confectioners' sugar
- 1/3 cup butter
- 1 cup finely chopped pecans
- Apricot preserves

To make dough, soften yeast in warm water. Combine sugar, butter, salt and milk in large mixing bowl. Cool to lukewarm; stir in eggs and yeast. Add flour to form stiff dough. On lightly floured surface, knead until smooth and satiny. Place in greased bowl; cover. Let rise 1-1/2 hours. To make filling, combine confectioners' sugar, butter and pecans. Roll out one-half of dough to form 12-in. x 12-in. square. Spread one-half of filling over half of dough. Fold uncovered dough over filling and pinch edges together.

Illus. 1

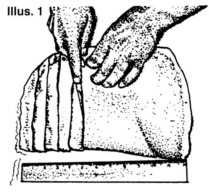

Cut into 1-inch strips (Illustration 1). Twist each strip 4 or 5 times, holding

Illus. 2

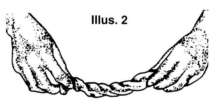

carefully (Illustration 2). Hold down one end on greased baking sheet to form center of roll (Illustration 3). Curl

Illus. 3

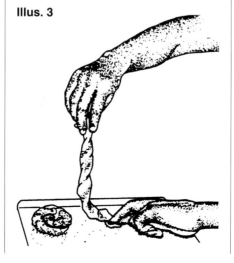

remaining strip around center as for pinwheel; tuck end under. Indent center and fill with 1/2 teaspoon apricot preserves. Repeat with other one-half of dough and filling. Cover; let rise 45 minutes. Bake at 375° for 18 minutes or until lightly browned. Glaze with confectioners' sugar glaze, if desired. **Yield:** 24 pastries.

RHUBARB DREAM BARS

CRUST:
- 2 cups all-purpose flour
- 3/4 cup confectioners' sugar
- 1 cup butter *or* margarine

FILLING:
- 4 eggs
- 2 cups sugar
- 1/2 cup all-purpose flour
- 1/2 teaspoon salt
- 4 cups thinly sliced fresh rhubarb

Mix crust ingredients together; press into 15-in. x 10-in. pan. Bake at 350° for 15 minutes (crust will be very light-colored). Combine eggs, sugar, flour and salt; beat together. Fold in rhubarb. Spread filling mixture on hot crust; return to oven to bake 40 to 45 minutes longer. Cool; cut into bars. **Yield:** 36 bars.

JUST RIGHT CHOCOLATE CHIP COOKIES

- 2/3 cup butter *or* margarine
- 2/3 cup butter-flavored solid shortening
- 3/4 cup white sugar
- 3/4 cup brown sugar, packed
- 2 eggs
- 2 teaspoons vanilla extract
- 3 cups all-purpose flour
- 1 teaspoon baking soda
- 1 teaspoon salt
- 1 package (3-1/2 ounces) instant vanilla pudding mix
- 1 package (12 ounces) semisweet chocolate chips

With mixer, beat shortenings together until fluffy. Add both sugars; beat until well blended. Beat in eggs and vanilla. Set aside. In separate bowl, mix together flour, soda, salt and pudding mix. Gradually add to beaten mixture, stirring well. Stir in chocolate chips. Drop by heaping tablespoonfuls onto ungreased cookie sheet. Bake at 350° for 14-18 minutes. (Longer baking time yields a crunchier cookie; less time a chewy cookie.) **Yield:** 4 dozen.

P ull up a chair and join us—
it's time for holiday feasting
with family and friends! Our
table is decked out with dishes that
provide refreshing new twists on
traditional favorites.

Pique your appetite with spicy, Mississippi-style baked shrimp or the unique flavor of pickled mushrooms. Serve up a crispy, brown roasted duckling, but instead of the usual bread stuffing, try our pleasant brown rice/pecan variation.

Accompany it with acorn squash, baked with an intriguing and flavorful filling of hot Italian sausage and maple syrup. And leave room to savor the taste of a colorful and unusual salad of avocado and pink grapefruit. Round out the feast with apple-studded red cabbage, a cranberry salad liberally laced with pineapple and orange, and flaky, featherweight sourdough rolls.

This sensational meal—enhanced by the mellow glow of candlelight—is perfect for guests or family during the Christmas season or on any occasion that deserves special attention!

Ladle up a generous serving of New England Seafood Chowder, followed by hearty Fireside Beef Stew on a bed of egg noodles with a thick chunk of Colonial Yeast Bread. And for a delicious dessert, savor a slice of California Cranberry Torte.

CANDLELIGHT DINNER: Clockwise from right—**Fireside Beef Stew; New England Seafood Chowder; Colonial Yeast Bread; California Cranberry Torte.** All recipes on page 279.

HOT CHEDDAR STUFFED MUSHROOMS

Joan Ward, Brownsburg, Indiana

(PICTURED ON PAGE 268)

 This tasty dish uses less sugar, salt and fat. Recipe includes *Diabetic Exchanges*.

1 pound large fresh mushrooms (about 16 mushrooms)
6 tablespoons butter
1 cup chopped onions
1 cup soft bread crumbs
1 cup shredded cheddar cheese
1/2 cup chopped walnuts
1/4 cup chopped parsley
1/2 teaspoon salt
1/4 teaspoon black pepper

Rinse mushrooms and pat dry. Remove and chop stems; set aside. In large skillet, melt butter. Brush mushroom caps with melted butter; place on lightly buttered shallow baking pan or broiler pan. To remaining butter in skillet, add onions and reserved mushroom stems. Saute 2 minutes. Add crumbs, cheese, nuts, parsley, salt and pepper; stir lightly. Spoon into mushroom caps, piling high. Bake at 350° until hot, about 20 minutes. Serve hot. **Yield:** 16 stuffed mushrooms. **Diabetic Exchanges:** One mushroom equals 1 vegetable, 2 fat; also, 107 calories, 188 mg sodium, 20 mg cholesterol, 4 gm carbohydrate, 4 gm protein, 9 gm fat.

PINEAPPLE FRUIT PLATE WITH DIP

Virginia Quelch, Las Cruces, New Mexico

(PICTURED ON PAGE 268)

 This tasty dish uses less sugar, salt and fat. Recipe includes *Diabetic Exchanges*.

1 ripe fresh pineapple
1 medium-size watermelon
2 large cantaloupes *or* 1 cantaloupe and 1 honeydew melon
Red seedless grapes
FRUIT DIP:
1/2 cup sugar
4 teaspoons cornstarch
1/2 teaspoon salt
1 cup unsweetened pineapple juice
3 tablespoons lemon juice
2 eggs, beaten
2 packages (3 ounces *each*) cream cheese, softened

Cut pineapple into quarters, starting at top; *do not remove leaves*. Remove hard

center core with sharp knife. Separate remaining pineapple from shell and slice into bite-size pieces. Scoop melon balls from melons; chill. Wash and chill grapes. To make dip, combine sugar, cornstarch and salt in saucepan; blend in fruit juices. Cook, stirring constantly until clear, about 5-8 minutes. Slowly pour cooked mixture into beaten eggs, beating briskly. Return mixture to saucepan; cook over low heat, stirring constantly 3-5 minutes or until mixture thickens slightly. Cool 5 minutes. Beat softened cream cheese in small bowl, then blend into cooled mixture. Chill thoroughly. To serve, place crushed ice on a large glass cake plate with outer lip. Set a pretty glass bowl, about 1-1/2-cup size in center of plate. Tuck down into ice and fill with dip. Place the four pineapple quarters at right angles on plate, with leaves pointing out. Fill spaces between pineapple with melon balls and grapes. Refrigerate leftovers. **Yield:** 32 servings. **Diabetic Exchanges:** One serving equals 2 fruits, 1/2 fat; also, 151 calories, 28 gm sodium, 18 gm cholesterol, 32 gm carbohydrate, 3 gm protein, 3 gm fat.

FUDGE SWIRL TOFFEE PIE

Jan Hill, Sacramento, California

(PICTURED ON PAGE 268)

1/2 cup semisweet chocolate chips
2 tablespoons milk
1 package (8 ounces) cream cheese, softened
1 jar (7 ounces) marshmallow creme
1/2 cup brown sugar
1 cup chopped almonds, toasted
1 container (8 ounces) whipped topping with real cream, thawed, *divided*
1 chocolate wafer crumb crust (9 inches), homemade *or* purchased

Melt chips with milk in small saucepan over a low heat, stirring until smooth. Cool; set aside. Combine cream cheese, marshmallow creme and sugar, mixing at medium speed until well blended. Fold in almonds and 2-1/2 cups whipped topping. Combine the chocolate mixture and *remaining* whipped topping. Spread half of the marshmallow creme mixture over crust; cover with all of chocolate mixture and carefully top with remaining half of marshmallow creme mixture. Cut through layers several times with a knife to swirl. Freeze. **Yield:** 6-8 servings.

SHRIMP APPETIZER PLATTER

Tammy Norberg, Marquette, Manitoba

(PICTURED ON PAGE 269)

1 package (8 ounces) cream cheese, softened
1/2 cup dairy sour cream
1/4 cup mayonnaise
2 cans (4-1/4 ounces *each*) broken shrimp, drained and rinsed
1 cup seafood sauce
2 cups shredded mozzarella cheese
1 green pepper, chopped
3 green onions, chopped
1 large tomato, diced

Combine the cream cheese, sour cream and mayonnaise; spread over 12-in. round platter or pizza pan. Scatter shrimp on cheese layer; cover with seafood sauce. Layer on the mozzarella cheese, green pepper, onion and tomato. Cover and chill until serving time. Serve with assorted crackers. **Yield:** about 25-30 appetizer servings.

MOTHER ERTELT'S MEATBALLS

Earline Ertelt, Woodburn, Oregon

(PICTURED ON PAGE 269)

MEATBALLS:
1-1/2 pounds lean ground beef
1 egg, beaten
1 envelope dry onion soup mix
3 tablespoons water
2 tablespoons Worcestershire sauce
Pitted black olives, green stuffed olives, cocktail onions and pineapple tidbits
SAUCE:
1 bottle (12 ounces) chili sauce
1 jar (18 ounces) grape jelly
1/4 cup lemon juice
3 tablespoons horseradish

Combine all meatball ingredients; mix well. Using about 1 tablespoon of meatball mixture, form balls by covering each olive, cocktail onion and pineapple tidbit. Arrange meatballs in shallow baking dish; bake at 375° for 20 minutes. Combine sauce ingredients; pour over meatballs. Return to oven for 15 minutes or until the sauce thickens slightly. Serve from a chafing dish or slow cooker with wooden picks for easy spearing. **Yield:** about 30 meatballs.

SOUTHWEST CHEESECAKE

Lori Walton, Stuttgart, Arkansas

(PICTURED ON PAGE 269)

16 ounces cream cheese, softened
2 cups shredded sharp cheddar cheese
2 cups dairy sour cream, *divided*
1-1/2 packets taco seasoning
3 eggs, room temperature
1 can (4 ounces) green chilies, chopped and drained
2/3 cup salsa
Tortilla chips

Combine cheeses; beat until fluffy. Stir in *1 cup* of sour cream and taco seasoning. Beat in eggs, one at a time. Fold in chilies. Pour into 9-in. springform pan. Bake at 350° for 35-40 minutes or until center is just firm. Remove from oven; cool 10 minutes. Spoon remaining sour cream over top of cake; return to oven for 5 minutes. Cool completely on wire rack. Refrigerate, covered, overnight. Remove from pan; place on serving plate. Top with salsa. Serve with tortilla chips. **Yield:** 50 appetizer servings.

STUFFED PHYLLO PASTRIES

Anita Moffett, Rewey, Wisconsin

(PICTURED ON PAGE 269)

FILLING:
1 package (10 ounces) frozen chopped spinach, thawed
1 pound feta cheese, crumbled
3 ounces grated Parmesan cheese
2 eggs, beaten
1 teaspoon nutmeg
1/2 teaspoon pepper
1 pound frozen phyllo dough, thawed 24 hours in refrigerator
1 to 1-1/2 cups unsalted butter, melted

To make filling, press spinach in fine strainer to remove all excess moisture; combine with cheeses, eggs, nutmeg and pepper. Set aside. To assemble pastries, have the following ready: melted butter, pastry brush, knife, a clean, slightly damp towel, the filling, baking sheet and large work surface. Open box of dough; carefully unfold sheets. Pull off 2 sheets; place together on work surface and brush lightly with butter. Pull off another sheet. Place directly over others; brush again with butter. Repeat until you have layered 5 sheets. Cover unused dough with damp towel. Cut prepared layers in half vertically, then cut halves into 6 strips vertically. Place 1-1/2 teaspoons of filling at the top of each strip. Fold each strip into triangles (as you would fold a flag), starting at bottom near filling. Repeat with additional layers of phyllo dough until the filling is gone. Place pastries on ungreased cookie sheet; brush with butter. Bake at 400° until golden brown, about 10-15 minutes. (Uncooked pastries can be frozen for later use. Frozen pastries can go directly into oven, but baking time must be increased.) **Yield:** about 60 pastries.

SALMON PATE

Gudrun Braker, Burnett, Wisconsin

(PICTURED ON PAGE 269)

 This tasty dish uses less sugar, salt and fat. Recipe includes *Diabetic Exchanges*.

1 can (15-1/2 ounces) salmon
1 package (3 ounces) cream cheese, room temperature
1 tablespoon fresh lemon juice
1 teaspoon prepared horseradish
1 teaspoon grated onion
1/4 teaspoon salt
1/8 teaspoon pepper
1/8 teaspoon liquid smoke
Garnishes (sliced almonds, stuffed green olive, celery stalk, parsley)

Drain, debone and flake salmon. Mix together with all other ingredients except garnishes. On a pretty platter, mold mixture into a fish shape. Arrange almonds to resemble scales. Use slice of olive for eye, thin strips of celery for the tail. Garnish with parsley. Chill until serving time. Serve with buttery crackers. Refrigerate leftovers. **Yield:** 16 servings (about 2 tablespoons each). **Diabetic Exchanges:** One serving equals 1/2 meat, 1 fat; also, 69 calories, 197 mg sodium, 16 mg cholesterol, .5 gm carbohydrate, 6 gm protein, 5 gm fat.

CHOCOLATE/WHIPPING CREAM TORTE

Rita Futral, Ocean Springs, Mississippi

(PICTURED ON PAGE 270)

CAKE:
1/2 cup butter
3 squares (3 ounces) unsweetened chocolate
1-1/2 cups whipping cream
4 eggs, well beaten
1 teaspoon vanilla
1-1/2 cups sugar
2 cups all-purpose flour
2 teaspoons baking powder
1/2 teaspoon salt
FILLING:
1 cup whipping cream
1 package (8 ounces) cream cheese, softened
1 cup confectioners' sugar, sifted
1 teaspoon vanilla
ICING:
1/4 cup butter
2 squares (2 ounces) unsweetened chocolate
1/2 cup whipping cream
1 teaspoon vanilla
3 cups confectioners' sugar, sifted

To make cake, melt butter with chocolate over low heat. Cool; set aside. Beat whipping cream until soft peaks form. Reduce mixer speed to low; add cooled chocolate mixture, beaten eggs and vanilla to whipped cream until just mixed. Sift together sugar, flour, baking powder and salt. With mixer on low speed, add dry ingredients to creamed mixture until just mixed. Pour into three greased and floured 8- or 9-in. round pans. Bake at 350° for 20-25 minutes or until done. Cool in pans for 5 minutes; turn onto cooling racks. Cool completely; wrap tightly and refrigerate. To make filling, whip cream until soft peaks form. Set aside. Beat the cream cheese until smooth and creamy; add sugar and vanilla, mixing well. Add whipped cream to cream cheese mixture and beat until smooth. Set aside. Split chilled cake layers in half. Divide filling and spread between cake layers. Chill while preparing icing. To make icing, melt butter with chocolate; cool. Add whipping cream and vanilla to chocolate mixture; blend well. Add sugar; beat until of spreading consistency. Frost cake with the icing; refrigerate until serving time. Garnish with fresh strawberries dipped in melted chocolate, if desired. **Yield:** 22 servings.

SESAME ZUCCHINI

Mary Bliss, Canton, Ohio

2 tablespoons cooking oil
4 cups thinly sliced zucchini
Salt and garlic powder to taste
2 tablespoons sesame seeds

Heat oil in a skillet. Saute all remaining ingredients 2-3 minutes. **Yield:** 6 servings.

RUSSIAN CREME

Jeanne Bloedorn, Fond du Lac, Wisconsin

(PICTURED ON PAGE 270)

CREME:
    1 cup sugar
    2 envelopes unflavored gelatin
2-1/4 cups water
1-1/2 cups dairy sour cream
1-1/2 teaspoons vanilla
1-1/2 cups heavy cream, whipped
TOPPING:
    1 package (10 ounces) frozen
        raspberries, juice reserved
    1 package (4-3/4 ounces)
        raspberry-flavored Danish
        Dessert *or* pie glaze

Dissolve sugar and gelatin in water over low heat. Remove from stove; stir in the sour cream and vanilla until smooth. Chill the mix until slightly thickened (like unbeaten egg whites). Fold in whipped cream with wire whisk until well blended. Pour into greased 6-cup ring mold; chill until set. To make topping, drain raspberries, reserving juice. Prepare dessert mix, following package directions for pudding, using raspberry juice as part of liquid. Chill topping; fold in raspberries. To serve, turn molded cream onto glass serving plate (at least 1 in. larger than mold). Put the raspberry topping in small bowl in center of mold. Guests serve themselves by taking a slice of creme pudding and spooning topping over it. **Yield:** 10-12 servings.

BREAD POT FONDUE

Katie Dreibelbis, Santa Clara, California

(PICTURED ON PAGE 270)

    1 firm, round loaf of bread
        (1-1/2 pounds, 8 to 10 inches
        in diameter)
FILLING:
    2 cups (8 ounces) shredded
        sharp cheddar cheese
    2 packages (3 ounces *each*)
        cream cheese, softened
1-1/2 cups dairy sour cream
    1 cup (5 ounces) diced cooked
        ham
1/2 cup chopped green onion
    1 can (4 ounces) whole green
        chilies, drained and chopped
    1 teaspoon Worcestershire
        sauce
    2 tablespoons vegetable oil
    1 tablespoon butter, melted
Assorted raw vegetables for dipping
    (broccoli, pepper strips,
    cauliflower, celery, carrot sticks,
    mushroom caps)

Slice off top of loaf, reserving top. Carefully hollow out inside of loaf with small paring knife, leaving 1/2-in. shell. Cut the removed bread into 1-in. cubes (about 4 cups); reserve. To make filling, combine the cheeses and sour cream in bowl; stir in ham, green onion, chilies and Worcestershire sauce. Spoon filling into hollowed loaf; replace top. Wrap loaf tightly with several layers of heavy-duty aluminum foil; set on cookie sheet. Bake at 350° for 1 hour and 10 minutes or until filling is heated through. Meanwhile, stir together bread cubes, oil and melted butter. Arrange on a separate cookie sheet. Bake at 350°, turning occasionally, for 10 to 15 minutes or until golden brown. Remove filled loaf from oven; unwrap and transfer to platter. Remove top from bread; stir filling and serve with toasted cubes and vegetables as dippers. **Yield:** about 20-24 appetizer servings.

APPETIZER TORTILLA PINWHEELS

Pat Waymire, Yellow Springs, Ohio

(PICTURED ON PAGE 270)

8 ounces dairy sour cream
    1 package (8 ounces) cream
        cheese, softened
    1 can (4 ounces) diced green
        chilies, well drained
    1 can (4 ounces) chopped black
        olives, well drained
    1 cup shredded cheddar cheese
1/2 cup chopped green onion
Garlic powder to taste
Seasoned salt to taste
    5 (10-inch) flour tortillas
Fresh parsley for garnish
Salsa, optional

To make filling, mix first eight ingredients together thoroughly. Divide the filling and spread evenly over the tortillas; roll up tortillas. Cover tightly with plastic wrap, twisting ends; refrigerate for several hours. Unwrap; cut in slices 1/2 in. to 3/4 in. thick. (An electric knife works best.) Discard ends. Lay pinwheels flat on glass serving plate; garnish with parsley. Leave space in center of plate for small bowl of salsa, if desired. **Yield:** about 50 pinwheels.

PICKLED MUSHROOMS

Mavis Diment, Marcus, Iowa

(PICTURED ON PAGE 272)

    2 pounds fresh mushrooms,
        cleaned

DRESSING:
1/2 cup olive oil
1/4 cup lemon juice
1/4 cup water
    1 teaspoon minced garlic
3/4 teaspoon salt
1/2 teaspoon pepper
1/3 cup chopped fresh parsley
1/4 cup diced red bell pepper

Place mushrooms in pretty glass bowl; set aside. Mix oil, lemon juice, water, garlic, salt and pepper in saucepan and bring to a boil. Pour over mushrooms. Cover; refrigerate for at least 2 hours. Add the parsley and red bell pepper, stirring to blend. **Yield:** 10 appetizer servings.

RENAISSANCE RED CABBAGE

Angela Biggin, La Grange Park, Illinois

(PICTURED ON PAGE 272)

    1 head red cabbage (about 5
        pounds)
    1 cup dry red wine, burgundy
        or zinfandel *or* unsweetened
        apple juice
    3 tablespoons white *or* apple
        cider vinegar
1/4 teaspoon salt
1/8 teaspoon ground pepper
1/8 teaspoon ground cloves
    2 teaspoons ground cinnamon
    2 whole bay leaves
    3 tablespoons sugar
    5 tablespoons whole *or* jellied
        cranberry sauce
    2 cooking apples, peeled and
        cubed 1/2-inch
1/2 cup sweetened applesauce

Shred cabbage in food processor or by hand. Combine with wine and vinegar in large kettle. Cover; bring to boil. Reduce heat to low; cook about 5 minutes. Add salt, pepper, cloves, cinnamon, bay leaves, sugar, cranberry sauce and apples. Cook about 20 minutes. Add applesauce. Remove bay leaves before serving. Serve with roast pork or duckling. **Yield:** 16-20 servings.

MAPLE CANDY: For a fun winter treat, place a pint of real maple syrup in a small, heavy saucepan and bring it to a light boil. Using a candy thermometer, reduce the syrup to 270°, the softball stage. Drizzle the syrup into a bowl of finely crushed ice; it will harden immediately into chewy, sweet candy! You can also drizzle the syrup onto a cold cookie sheet taken from the refrigerator. The candy should be eaten within two days.

AVOCADO/GRAPEFRUIT SALAD WITH POPPY SEED DRESSING

Caroline Weiler, Sarasota, Florida

(PICTURED ON PAGE 272)

2 ripe avocados, peeled, pitted
  and sliced lengthwise into
  1/4-inch slices
2 large red grapefruit, peeled
  and sectioned with white
  membranes removed
Boston lettuce leaves, washed and
  chilled
POPPY SEED DRESSING:
1/3 cup sugar
1 teaspoon dry mustard
5 tablespoons vinegar
1 teaspoon salt
1 cup vegetable oil
1-1/2 teaspoons grated onion,
  drained on paper towel
2-1/2 teaspoons poppy seeds

Arrange several slices of avocado and grapefruit on a bed of lettuce, alternating slices for color; chill. Make dressing by mixing sugar, mustard, vinegar and salt. Slowly add oil, beating vigorously between additions (dressing will be very thick). Stir in grated onion and poppy seeds. Spoon on salads and serve immediately. **Yield:** 8 servings.

DUCK WITH BROWN RICE STUFFING

Nancy Brissey, Auburn, Washington

(PICTURED ON PAGE 272)

1 duckling (about 5 pounds)
  rinsed and dried with paper
  towel
STUFFING:
1 cup brown rice
2 cups chicken stock
1 cup green onions, chopped
  into 1/8-inch pieces with tops
1 cup diced celery
1/2 cup butter
5 to 6 ounces (1-1/2 cups)
  sliced fresh mushrooms
1 teaspoon salt
1 cup pecan pieces, 1/4-inch
  pieces

Prepare stuffing by cooking rice in chicken stock in covered heavy saucepan until liquid is absorbed, about 40 minutes. While rice is cooking, saute green onions and celery in skillet in butter until vegetables are tender. Add mushrooms and saute about 5 minutes. Stir in salt, cooked rice and pecan pieces. Stuff duck. Preheat oven to 450°. Place duck on rack in roasting pan; *immediately* lower temperature to 350° and roast, uncovered, until tender, allowing about 25 minutes per pound. Allow to rest for 10 minutes before carving. Serve with stuffing. **Yield:** 4 servings.

BAKED SQUASH WITH SAUSAGE

Donie Kaup, Albion, Nebraska

(PICTURED ON PAGE 272)

2 small acorn squash
4 tablespoons pure maple
  syrup, *divided*
2 tablespoons butter, *divided*
8 ounces bulk hot Italian
  sausage, *divided*

Cut squash in half; clean seeds from cavity. Put a fourth of maple syrup, butter and sausage in each cavity. Place squash on baking sheet. Bake at 350° for 30-40 minutes or until fork tender. **Yield:** 4 servings.

SOURDOUGH BUTTERFLAKE REFRIGERATOR ROLLS

Kalli Deschamps, Missoula, Montana

(PICTURED ON PAGE 272)

SOURDOUGH STARTER RECIPE:
NOTE: Starter must be made 2-3 days in advance.
2 cups all-purpose flour
1 teaspoon salt
3 tablespoons sugar
1 tablespoon dry yeast
2 cups lukewarm water

Stir together flour, salt, sugar and yeast with wooden spoon in large mixing bowl; gradually add lukewarm water. Stir until mixture resembles a smooth paste. Cover with towel or cheesecloth; set in warm (85°) place. Stir mixture several times a day. Ready in 2-3 days. Store in heavy plastic container with air hole for gases to escape.

SOURDOUGH REFRIGERATOR ROLLS:
NOTE: Dough must "rest" overnight.
2 packages dry yeast
1/3 cup warm water (110°)
1 cup sourdough starter
1/2 cup vegetable oil
3 eggs, well beaten
1 cup warm water
1/2 cup sugar
1 teaspoon salt
5-1/2 to 6-1/2 cups all-purpose
  flour, *divided*
1/4 cup melted butter

Soften yeast in 1/3 cup warm water (110°); set aside. In a large mixing bowl, combine the starter, oil, eggs, 1 cup of warm water, sugar, salt and 2 cups flour. Stir vigorously for 1 minute. Stir in softened yeast and enough flour to make dough that pulls away from sides of bowl. Cover with cloth; set in warm, draft-free place to let rise until doubled. Punch down; cover with plastic wrap. Refrigerate overnight. Three hours before baking, roll out dough on lightly floured surface to 1/4-in. to 1/2-in. thick rectangle, about 7-in. x 26-in. Brush with melted butter. Starting with long side, roll up jelly-roll style. Cut into 1-in. slices. Place in greased muffin pans, cut side down. Cover with cloth. Let rise until double, about 2-1/2 hours. Bake at 400° for 12-15 minutes until golden brown. **Yield:** 2-1/2 dozen rolls.

FRESH CRANBERRY SALAD

Cathy Burke, Oneida, Tennessee

(PICTURED ON PAGE 273)

1 package (12 ounces) fresh
  cranberries, washed and
  sorted
1-1/2 cups sugar
3 packages (3 ounces *each*)
  orange gelatin dessert
3 cups boiling water
2 cans (11 ounces *each*)
  mandarin oranges, drained
  and cut in small pieces
1 cup chopped nuts, walnuts *or*
  pecans
1 can (8 ounces) crushed
  pineapple, undrained

Grind cranberries in food grinder or food processor; stir in the sugar to blend. Set aside. Dissolve gelatin dessert in boiling water; cool until mixture begins to thicken. Add to cranberry mixture. Add oranges, nuts and pineapple. Stir well; pour into lightly oiled 8-cup mold. Chill overnight. Unmold and serve on plate of crisp greens. **Yield:** 16 servings.

BILOXI-STYLE APPETIZER SHRIMP

Diane Hixon, Niceville, Florida

(PICTURED ON PAGE 273)

1 bag shrimp and crab boil
2 cans (12 ounces *each*) beer
  or water

1 tablespoon hot pepper sauce
1 tablespoon Worcestershire sauce
1 teaspoon salt
1/2 teaspoon garlic powder
Pepper to taste
3 tablespoons fresh lemon *or* lime juice
5 pounds fresh medium-size shrimp, shelled and deveined
1 cup unsalted butter, melted

Bring spice bag to boil in beer/water in large saucepan. Add the hot pepper sauce and Worcestershire sauce, salt, garlic powder, pepper and lemon/lime juice. Simmer for 10 minutes to blend flavors. Arrange shrimp in an oven-proof casserole. Pour liquid over them. Pour melted butter over all. Bake at 350° for 15 minutes, stirring twice. **Yield:** 20 appetizer servings.

CALIFORNIA CRANBERRY TORTE

Pat Parsons, Bakersfield, California

(PICTURED ON PAGE 274)

6 egg whites
Pinch salt
1/4 teaspoon cream of tartar
1-1/2 cups sugar
1 teaspoon vanilla extract
1 can (16 ounces) jellied cranberry sauce
2 tablespoons raspberry-flavored gelatin powder
1-1/2 cups whipping cream
2 tablespoons confectioners' sugar
Fresh cranberries *or* raspberries for garnish, optional

In a mixing bowl, beat egg whites until foamy. Add salt and cream of tartar; beat until soft peaks form. Gradually add sugar, 2 tablespoons at a time, and continue beating until stiff and glossy. Add vanilla. Place plain brown paper or parchment on cookie sheets. Draw three 8-in. circles on the paper. Spoon the meringue into the circles, spreading with a knife. Bake at 250° for 1 hour. Meringues should sound hollow when tapped. Turn heat off and allow meringues to stay in oven with the door open until cool. Meanwhile, melt cranberry sauce in a saucepan over medium heat. Add gelatin and stir to dissolve. Cool. Whip cream with the confectioners' sugar; fold 1 cup into cranberry mixture. To assemble, place 1 tablespoon whipped cream in the center of serving platter to hold meringue in place. Top with a meringue shell; spread 1/3 of the cranberry mixture on top. Repeat with remaining meringues and cranberry mixture. Frost sides of torte with reserved whipped cream. If desired, a pastry tube can be used to decorate edges of torte. Chill 6 hours or overnight. Garnish with fresh cranberries or raspberries, if desired. **Yield:** 12-16 servings.

NEW ENGLAND SEAFOOD CHOWDER

Jane Chartrand, Orleans, Vermont

(PICTURED ON PAGE 274)

1 pound whitefish, skin and bones removed
1 cup diced celery
1 large onion, chopped
5 medium potatoes, peeled and cubed
3 tablespoons all-purpose flour
1/3 cup cold water
2 cans (6-1/2 ounces *each*) minced clams, liquid reserved
1 can (4 ounces) tiny shrimp, drained
1 can (6 ounces) crabmeat, drained
2 teaspoons salt
1/2 teaspoon pepper
2 tablespoons butter *or* margarine
1 can (12 ounces) evaporated milk
1/2 jar (1 ounce) pimiento, drained
Fresh chopped parsley

In a large Dutch oven, place fish and enough water to cover. Cook over medium heat until fish flakes with a fork, about 10 minutes. With a slotted spoon, remove fish and break into bite-size pieces; set aside. Measure cooking liquid and add enough additional water to equal 4 cups. In the liquid, cook celery, onion and potatoes until tender. Combine the flour and cold water to make a paste; stir into chowder. Cook and stir until mixture boils. Add reserved fish, clams with liquid, shrimp, crabmeat, salt, pepper, butter, milk and pimiento. Heat through, stirring occasionally. Garnish with parsley. **Yield:** 3-1/2 quarts.

COLONIAL YEAST BREAD

Stella Quade, Carthage, Missouri

(PICTURED ON PAGE 274)

1/2 cup cornmeal
1/2 cup packed brown sugar *or* 1/3 cup honey
1 tablespoon salt
2 cups boiling water
1/2 cup vegetable oil
2 packages (1/4 ounce *each*) active dry yeast
1/2 cup warm water (110°-115°)
3/4 cup whole wheat flour
1/2 cup rye flour
4-1/2 to 5-1/2 cups all-purpose flour

In a mixing bowl, combine cornmeal, sugar or honey, salt, boiling water and oil. Let cool to lukewarm. Meanwhile, dissolve yeast in warm water and let stand 5 minutes. Stir into cornmeal mixture. Add whole wheat flour, rye flour and enough all-purpose flour to form a stiff dough. Turn out onto a floured board; knead until smooth and elastic, about 6-8 minutes. Place in a greased bowl; cover and let rise in a warm place until doubled, about 1-1/2 hours. Punch dough down. Divide into two balls. Cover and let rest 10 minutes. Shape into two loaves and place in two greased 8-in. x 4-in. x 3-in. bread pans. Cover and let rise until doubled, about 1-1/2 hours. Bake at 375° for 35-40 minutes. Cover loosely with foil if top browns too quickly. Remove from pans and let cool on a wire rack. **Yield:** 2 loaves.

FIRESIDE BEEF STEW

Donna Nevil, New Glarus, Wisconsin

(PICTURED ON PAGE 274)

 This tasty dish uses less sugar, salt and fat. Recipe includes *Diabetic Exchanges*.

2 pounds lean beef chuck *or* round steak, cut into 1-1/2-inch pieces
1 tablespoon browning sauce
1/4 cup dry cream of rice cereal
4 carrots, cut into 1-1/2-inch chunks
2 cups thinly sliced onion
1 garlic clove, minced
1/2 to 1 teaspoon dried marjoram, crushed
1/2 to 1 teaspoon dried thyme, crushed
1 teaspoon salt
1/4 teaspoon pepper
1 cup dry red wine *or* beef broth
1 jar (4.5 ounces) button mushrooms, undrained
Cooked noodles

In medium Dutch oven or 3-qt. casserole, toss meat with browning sauce. Mix in cereal. Add all remaining ingredients except noodles. Cover and bake at 325° for 2 to 2-1/2 hours or until the meat and vegetables are tender. Serve with noodles. **Yield:** 8 servings. **Diabetic Exchanges:** One serving (prepared with beef broth and no added salt) equals 2 lean meat, 1-1/2 vegetable, 1/2 starch; also, 199 calories, 50 mg sodium, 72 mg cholesterol, 12 gm carbohydrate, 21 gm protein, 6 gm fat.

WISCONSIN POTATO CHEESE SOUP

Darlene Alexander, Nekoosa, Wisconsin

- 2 tablespoons butter *or* margarine
- 1/3 cup chopped celery
- 1/3 cup chopped onion
- 4 cups diced peeled potatoes
- 3 cups chicken broth
- 2 cups milk
- 1-1/2 teaspoons salt
- 1/4 teaspoon pepper
- Dash paprika
- 2 cups (8 ounces) shredded cheddar cheese
- Croutons
- Fresh chopped parsley

In a large saucepan, melt butter over medium-high heat. Saute celery and onion until tender. Add potatoes and broth. Cover and simmer until potatoes are tender, about 12 minutes. In batches, puree potato mixture in a blender or food processor. Return to saucepan. Stir in milk and seasonings. Add the cheese and heat only until melted. Garnish with croutons and parsley. **Yield:** 8 servings.

OSSO BUCO

Karen Jaffe, Short Hills, New Jersey

- 1/3 cup all-purpose flour
- 1 teaspoon salt
- 1/2 teaspoon pepper
- 4 to 6 veal shanks (2 inches thick)
- 5 tablespoons olive oil
- 1 teaspoon Italian seasoning
- 1/2 teaspoon sage
- 1 medium onion, chopped
- 1 garlic clove, minced
- 2 carrots, sliced
- 1 celery stalk, cut in 1/2-inch slices
- 1-1/2 cups dry white wine *or* chicken broth
- 1 can (10-3/4 ounces) condensed chicken broth
- 2 tablespoons tomato paste

GREMOLATA:
- 2 garlic cloves, minced
- 1-1/2 tablespoons chopped parsley
- 1 tablespoon grated lemon peel

Combine flour, salt and pepper; dredge meat. In a large skillet, heat the oil on high. Brown meat on all sides. Lay the shanks flat in a Dutch oven or oblong baking dish and sprinkle with Italian seasoning and sage. Combine onion, garlic, carrots and celery. Sprinkle over meat. In a small bowl, whisk together wine, broth and tomato paste. Pour over vegetables. Cover and bake at 325° for 2

hours or until fork-tender. Just before serving, combine Gremolata ingredients; sprinkle over each shank. Serve immediately. **Yield:** 4-6 servings.

SOUTHWESTERN BEEF BRISKET

Lois McAtee, Oceanside, California

- 1 fresh beef brisket (3 pounds)
- 1 teaspoon salt
- 1/4 teaspoon black pepper
- 2 tablespoons cooking oil
- 1-1/2 cups water
- 1 can (8 ounces) tomato sauce
- 1 small onion, chopped
- 2 tablespoons red wine vinegar
- 1 tablespoon chili powder
- 1 teaspoon dried oregano
- 3/4 teaspoon cumin
- 1/2 teaspoon garlic powder
- 1/4 teaspoon salt
- 1/8 to 1/4 teaspoon ground red pepper
- 1/8 teaspoon black pepper
- 3 medium sweet red peppers, cut into strips
- 1-1/2 cups sliced carrots (1-inch chunks)

Season beef with salt and pepper. In a Dutch oven, heat oil; brown beef on both sides. Meanwhile, combine all remaining ingredients except red pepper strips and carrots. Pour over meat. Cover and bake at 325° for 2 hours. Add red peppers and carrots; bake 1 hour longer or until meat is tender. Remove meat from the pan; allow to stand 15 minutes before cutting. Thicken juices with a little flour or cook over high heat to reduce and thicken. **Yield:** 10-12 servings.

PEASANT BEAN SOUP

Bertha McClung, Summersville, West Virginia

 This tasty dish uses less sugar, salt and fat. Recipe includes *Diabetic Exchanges*.

- 1 pound great northern beans, washed and sorted
- 2-1/2 quarts cold water, *divided*
- 3 carrots, sliced
- 3 celery stalks, sliced
- 2 medium onions, chopped
- 1 garlic clove, minced
- 1 can (16 ounces) stewed tomatoes, cut up
- 1 to 2 bay leaves
- 2 tablespoons olive oil
- Salt and pepper to taste

Soak beans overnight in 2 qts. water. Add remaining water to softened beans and

bring to a boil; reduce heat and simmer 30 minutes. Add all remaining ingredients; simmer 60 minutes or until beans are tender. Remove bay leaves before serving. **Yield:** 8 servings. **Diabetic Exchanges:** One serving equals 2 starch, 2 vegetable, 1/2 meat, 1/2 fat; also, 263 calories, 774 mg sodium, 0 mg cholesterol, 45 gm carbohydrate, 15 gm protein, 5 gm fat.

SUNSHINE CHICKEN

Karen Gardiner, Eutaw, Alabama

 This tasty dish uses less sugar, salt and fat. Recipe includes *Diabetic Exchanges*.

- 2 to 3 teaspoons curry powder
- 1-1/4 teaspoons salt, *divided*
- 1/4 teaspoon pepper
- 6 chicken breast halves, boned and skinned
- 1-1/2 cups orange juice
- 1 cup uncooked long-grain rice
- 3/4 cup water
- 1 tablespoon brown sugar
- 1 teaspoon dry mustard
- Chopped fresh parsley

Combine curry powder, 1/2 teaspoon salt and the pepper; rub over both sides of the chicken. In a skillet, combine orange juice, rice, water, brown sugar, mustard and remaining salt. Mix well. Top rice mixture with chicken pieces; bring to a boil. Cover and simmer 20-25 minutes. Remove from the heat and let stand, covered, until all liquid has absorbed, about 5 minutes. Sprinkle with parsley. **Yield:** 6 servings. **Diabetic Exchanges:** One serving (without salt) equals 2-1/2 lean meat, 2 starch, 1 fruit; also, 304 calories, 66 mg sodium, 73 mg cholesterol, 36 gm carbohydrate, 30 gm protein, 4 gm fat.

SPICED APPLE PORK ROAST

Lydia Robotewskyj, Franklin, Wisconsin

- 1 rolled boneless pork loin roast (4 to 5 pounds)
- 1 garlic clove, cut into lengthwise strips
- 2 tablespoons all-purpose flour
- 1 teaspoon salt
- 1/2 teaspoon sugar
- 1 teaspoon prepared mustard
- 1/8 teaspoon pepper
- 1 cup applesauce
- 1/3 cup packed brown sugar
- 2 teaspoons vinegar
- 1/8 to 1/4 teaspoon ground cloves

Remove and discard all excess fat from roast. Cut slits in top of roast; insert garlic strips. Mix the flour with salt, sugar, mustard and pepper. Rub over the roast. Place the meat, fat side up, on a rack in a roasting pan. Bake at 325° for 30-40 minutes *per pound* or until the internal temperature reaches 160°-170°. Combine applesauce, brown sugar, vinegar and cloves; generously brush over roast during last half hour of baking. **Yield:** 12-15 servings.

CITRUS-BAKED CORNISH HENS

Mary-Lynne Mason, Janesville, Wisconsin

4 Cornish game hens
SAUCE:
  1/4 cup apricot preserves
  2 tablespoons grated onion
  1 tablespoon butter *or* margarine
  1 tablespoon Dijon mustard
  1 garlic clove, minced
Juice and grated peel of 1 lemon
Juice and grated peel of 1 orange

Remove giblets and necks from hens. Tie the legs of the hens together and turn the wing tips under the backs. In a saucepan, combine all sauce ingredients. Simmer 5 minutes. Brush the hens with the sauce and arrange, breast side up, on a rack in a large roasting pan. Bake at 350° for about 1-1/4 hours or until tender. Brush hens occasionally with sauce. **Yield:** 4-8 servings.

WHITE LASAGNA

Gayle Becker, Mt. Clemens, Michigan

9 lasagna noodles
1/4 cup butter *or* margarine
1/3 cup all-purpose flour
  1 tablespoon minced dried onion
1/4 teaspoon garlic powder
1/8 teaspoon pepper
  2 cups chicken *or* turkey broth
  1 cup milk
  1 cup grated Parmesan *or* Romano cheese, *divided*
  1 can (4 ounces) sliced mushrooms, drained
  1 package (10 ounces) frozen cut asparagus *or* 3/4 pound fresh-cut asparagus, cooked and drained
  2 cups cubed cooked chicken *or* turkey
  1 package (6 ounces) sliced *or* shredded mozzarella cheese
  6 ounces thinly sliced cooked ham, chopped

Cook noodles according to package directions. Drain. In a large saucepan, melt butter; blend in flour, onion, garlic powder and pepper. Add broth and milk; cook and stir until bubbly and thickened. Stir in 1/2 cup Parmesan or Romano cheese. Spread 1/2 cup sauce in the bottom of a greased 13-in. x 9-in. x 2-in. baking pan. Stir mushrooms into the remaining sauce. Lay 3 noodles in the pan. Top with asparagus, chicken or turkey, mozzarella cheese and about 1 cup sauce. Top with 3 more noodles, the cooked ham and half of the remaining sauce. Cover with remaining noodles and sauce. Sprinkle with the remaining Parmesan or Romano cheese. Bake, uncovered, at 350° for 35 minutes or until heated through. **Yield:** 8-10 servings.

COUNTRY CHICKEN AND STUFFING

Carolyn Kent, Duncanville, Texas

  2 small packages stuffing mix
  2 cans (10-3/4 ounces *each*) cream of chicken soup, undiluted
  1 cup (8 ounces) sour cream
  3 whole chicken breasts, cooked and cubed

Prepare stuffing mix according to package directions. In greased 13-in. x 9-in. x 2-in. baking dish, combine soup, sour cream and chicken. Top with stuffing. Bake at 350° for 25 minutes. **Yield:** 8-10 servings.

WHITE CHOCOLATE PRETZELS

Jenny Riegsecker, Delta, Ohio

  12 ounces white chocolate, chopped
  2 to 3 dozen twisted pretzels, all whole
  6 ounces semisweet chocolate chips
Finely chopped nuts, optional

Melt white chocolate in microwave or double boiler. With tongs, dip pretzels, one at a time, in chocolate. Let excess chocolate run off back into pan. Place dipped pretzels on waxed paper to cool; chill to harden slightly. Melt the semisweet chocolate; cool several minutes. Using a pastry bag with small round pastry tip (or a plastic bag with the tip snipped off or a large spoon), drizzle dark chocolate squiggles over coated pretzels. Immediately sprinkle with nuts, if desired. Chill. **Yield:** 2-3 dozen.

LEMON SNOWFLAKES

Linda Barry, Dianna, Texas

  1 package (18-1/4 ounces) lemon cake mix with pudding
2-1/4 cups frozen whipped topping, thawed
  1 egg
Confectioners' sugar

In a mixing bowl, combine cake mix, whipped topping and egg. Beat with electric mixer on medium speed until blended. Batter will be very sticky. Drop by teaspoonfuls into confectioners' sugar; roll lightly to coat. Place on ungreased cookie sheets. Bake at 350° for 10-12 minutes or until lightly browned. **Yield:** 5-6 dozen.

CRISP BUTTER COOKIES

Tammy Mackie, Seward, Nebraska

1/2 cup butter *or* margarine, softened
  1 cup sugar
  5 egg yolks
  2 cups all-purpose flour
Colored sugar

In a mixing bowl, cream butter and sugar. Blend in egg yolks. Add flour, 1 cup at a time, beating well after each addition. Dough will be very stiff. On a well-floured board or pastry cloth, roll out dough to a 1/8-in. thickness. Using a pastry wheel or knife, cut into 2-1/2-in. squares, rectangles or diamonds. Place 1/2 in. apart on ungreased cookie sheets. Sprinkle with colored sugar. Bake at 375° for 7-8 minutes or until lightly browned. **Yield:** 6 dozen.

CHOCOLATE CLUSTERS

Sara Ann Fowler, Illinois City, Illinois

  2 pounds white chocolate *or* almond bark
  1 cup creamy *or* chunky peanut butter
  2 cups salted dry roasted peanuts
  3 cups pastel miniature marshmallows
  4 cups crisp rice cereal

Melt white chocolate and peanut butter in microwave or double boiler, stirring often to mix well. Add all remaining ingredients; stir with wooden spoon to coat evenly. Drop by teaspoonfuls onto waxed paper. **Yield:** 11 dozen.

GINGER BISCUITS

Racine Rockwood, So. Weymouth, Massachusetts

2-1/2 cups biscuit mix *or* self-rising
    flour
1/2 cup sugar
1-1/4 to 1-1/2 teaspoons ground
    ginger
1 teaspoon baking soda
Pinch salt
1/2 egg, beaten
1/2 cup corn syrup *or* maple
    syrup
4 tablespoons butter

In a mixing bowl, combine biscuit mix
or flour, sugar, ginger, soda and salt.
Using hands, rub egg into mixture. In a
saucepan, warm syrup and butter; stir
into batter. Let stand for 3-4 minutes,
then knead. Roll heaping teaspoonfuls
into small balls. Place 2 in. apart on
greased cookie sheets. Bake at 325° for
12-15 minutes. Cookies will flatten and
"crackle" when done. **Yield:** 3 dozen.

COFFEE BONBONS

Leitzel Malzahn, Fox Point, Wisconsin

1 cup butter
3/4 cup confectioners' sugar
1/2 teaspoon vanilla extract
1 tablespoon instant coffee
    granules
1-3/4 cups all-purpose flour
CHOCOLATE GLAZE:
1 tablespoon butter
1/2 ounce unsweetened
    chocolate
1 cup confectioners' sugar
2 tablespoons milk

In a mixing bowl, cream butter and sugar
until light and fluffy. Add vanilla. Combine coffee and flour; stir into creamed
mixture and mix well. Chill. Shape into
3/4-in.balls and place on ungreased
cookie sheets. Bake at 350° for 18-20
minutes. Meanwhile, for glaze, melt butter and chocolate together. Add melted
mixture to sugar along with milk; beat
until smooth. Frost cookies while still
warm. **Yield:** 5 dozen.

APPLE PANDOWDY

Doreen Lindquist, Thompson, Manitoba

1 cup packed brown sugar
1-1/4 cups all-purpose flour,
    divided
1/2 teaspoon salt, *divided*
1 cup water

1 teaspoon lemon juice
2 teaspoons baking powder
5 tablespoons butter, *divided*
3/4 cup milk
5 cups sliced pared apples
1/2 teaspoon ground cinnamon
1/2 teaspoon ground nutmeg
1 teaspoon vanilla extract
Cream, optional

In a saucepan, combine brown sugar,
1/4 cup flour and 1/4 teaspoon salt.
Add water and lemon juice; cook over
low heat until thick. Cover and set aside.
In a mixing bowl, combine baking powder and remaining flour and salt. Cut in
3 tablespoons butter. Add the milk and
mix just until moistened (a few lumps will
remain); set aside. Arrange apples in a
9-in. square baking dish; sprinkle with
cinnamon. Add nutmeg, vanilla and
remaining butter to sauce; pour over
apples. Drop dough by spoonfuls over
sauce. Bake at 350° for 55 minutes or
until top is brown and apples are tender.
Serve warm with cream if desired.
Yield: 9 servings.

TWO-MINUTE COOKIES

Kerry Bouchard, Shawmut, Montana

1/2 cup butter *or* margarine
1/2 cup milk
2 cups sugar
3 cups quick-cooking *or* rolled
    oats
5 tablespoons unsweetened
    cocoa
1/2 cup raisins, chopped nuts *or*
    coconut

In a large saucepan, heat butter, milk and
sugar. Bring to a boil, stirring occasionally.
Boil for 1 minute. Remove from the heat.
Stir in oats, cocoa and raisins, nuts or
coconut. Drop by tablespoonfuls onto
waxed paper. Cool. **Yield:** about 3 dozen.

NEVER-FAIL PIE CRUST

Ruth Gritter, Grand Rapids, Michigan

2 cups all-purpose flour
1 teaspoon salt
2/3 cup shortening
1/3 cup milk
1 tablespoon vinegar

Combine flour and salt in a mixing bowl.
Cut in shortening. Add milk and vinegar.
Shape dough into a ball. Chill for 30 min-
utes. Divide dough in half. On a lightly

floured surface, roll out each half to fit a
9-in. pie pan. **Yield:** 2 9-inch crusts.

STEAMED
CRANBERRY PUDDING

Florence Ladwig, Monroe, Wisconsin

1/3 cup hot water
1 tablespoon baking soda
2 cups (8 ounces)
    cranberries, chopped
1/2 cup molasses
1 tablespoon sugar
1/4 teaspoon salt
1-1/2 cups all-purpose flour
BUTTER SAUCE:
1 cup sugar
1/2 cup butter
1/2 cup half-and-half cream

In a mixing bowl, combine water and baking soda. Immediately add all remaining
pudding ingredients; mix well. Pour batter into a well-greased 1-qt. pudding
mold. (If you don't have a pudding mold,
use an ovenproof bowl and cover tightly
with foil.) Put a rack in the bottom of a
large kettle. Place pudding mold or bowl
on rack. Add boiling water to 1-in. depth
in kettle. Cover kettle and boil gently, re-
placing water as needed. Steam 1 hour
or until cake tests done. Cool for 10 minutes; unmold. For sauce, heat all ingredients in a saucepan until butter is melted and sugar is dissolved. Serve pudding
and sauce warm. **Yield:** 8-10 servings.

FRUITCAKE COOKIES

Julia Funkhouser, Carson, Iowa

1 cup butter, softened
3/4 cup packed brown sugar
1 egg
1/2 teaspoon vanilla extract
1-1/2 cups (rounded) all-purpose
    flour
1/2 teaspoon salt
1/2 teaspoon baking soda
4 ounces red candied cherries,
    halved
4 ounces candied pineapple,
    diced
1-1/2 cups dates, finely cut
1/2 cup broken walnuts
1/2 cup broken pecans
1/2 cup whole hazelnuts

In a mixing bowl, cream butter, sugar,
egg and vanilla. Sift together flour, salt
and soda; add to creamed mixture. Stir
in fruits and nuts. Drop by teaspoonfuls
onto greased cookie sheets. Bake at
325° for 15 minutes. Store tightly covered; cookies are best after a few days.
Yield: 3-12 dozen.

MEALS IN MINUTES

H er job making drapes doesn't mean curtains for cooking as far as Lise Thomson of Magrath, Alberta is concerned! Like many busy country women, this rancher's wife and mother of four relies on fast fare that's ready to serve in *30 minutes or less*.

"Between ranch chores, school and church activities, and my outside work, I need 'Meals in Minutes' menus all week long," Lise says. A Thomson family favorite is the speedy south-of-the-border specialty shared below.

Lise begins by mixing up the instant pudding/pie filling and spooning it into a prepared shell, which she then pops in the freezer for fast setting.

With the dessert done, she quickly browns the ground beef, chops the onion and combines the soup ingredients. "As the soup is simmering, I prepare a simple salad of iceberg lettuce with tomato and cucumber slices," Lise goes on. She uses a purchased sour cream dressing or a homemade one that can be prepared ahead and kept in the refrigerator.

With minutes to spare, Lise ladles the soup into bowls and tops it with shredded cheese. She serves tortilla or corn chips in place of crackers.

"The soup is hearty and satisfying," she assures, "like chili—but without the wait!"

TACO SOUP

1-1/2 pounds ground beef
1/2 cup chopped onion
  1 can (28 ounces) whole
    tomatoes with juice
  1 can (14 ounces) kidney beans
    with liquid
  1 can (17 ounces) corn with
    liquid
  1 can (8 ounces) tomato sauce
  1 package taco seasoning
  1 to 2 cups water
Salt and pepper to taste
  1 cup shredded cheddar cheese
Tortilla *or* corn chips

Brown beef in large, heavy kettle; drain and add onions. Cook until onions are tender. Add remaining ingredients except cheese and chips. Simmer for 15 minutes. Ladle into bowls; top with the shredded cheese. Serve with chips. **Yield:** 6 to 8 servings.

GARDEN SALAD

  1 head iceberg lettuce, rinsed
    and chilled
  1 large cucumber, washed
  2 tomatoes, cut in wedges
Store-bought sour cream dressing
Diced green onion

Slice lettuce into 1/2-in.-thick chunks. Score unpeeled cucumber with fork; cut into thin slices. Place the tomato wedges and cucumber slices on the lettuce; top with dressing and green onion. **Yield:** 6 servings.

CHOCOLATE CREAM PIE

  1 baked 9-inch pie crust *or*
    crumb crust
FILLING:
  1 package (4-1/8 ounces)
    instant chocolate fudge
    pudding
  2 cups milk
  1 cup whipping cream, *divided*
  1 chocolate bar, chopped
Mint leaves

Combine the pudding mix and milk according to package directions. Let stand for 5 minutes. Meanwhile, whip cream. Add half of whipped cream to pudding, reserving remaining cream for garnish. Place pie in freezer for 5 minutes; refrigerate until time to eat. Garnish top of pie with remaining whipped cream, chopped chocolate and mint leaves. **Yield:** 6 servings.

SUPER SOUP! To prevent burning when you reheat frozen soup, place it in a kettle. Set kettle in a frying pan containing a small amount of water. Stir occasionally while it's warming.

● A pound of thinly sliced smoked sausage ring can substitute for bulk sausage in most soup recipes.

INDEX